Psychology of the Child

Second Edition

Psychology of the Child

Second Edition

Robert I. Watson

Northwestern University

John Wiley & Sons, Inc.,   New York · London · Sydney

SECOND PRINTING, APRIL, 1966

Library of Congress Catalog Card Number: 65-14262
Printed in the United States of America

Preface

As BOOKS PROGRESS THROUGH EDITIONS, PREFACES BE-
come shorter. Perhaps this indicates that relatively less work is involved; perhaps the author's confidence grows to such an extent that
he seeks criticisms less; perhaps the memories of help given by others
in earlier editions dim. Among these possibilities, I must disclaim
the last. I am keenly aware that critical readings by psychologists
of the original manuscript still remain very helpful.

As always, an author is indebted to those who carried out and reported the research upon which he depends and to those who hold
copyright on these materials. Specific acknowledgments at appropriate points in the book have been made in connection with quotations.
A more general acknowledgment of help must also be given to those
many researchers whose work I have referred to but not quoted directly.

At a more personal level there is the assistance of various undergraduate assistants, especially Miss Rosalyn Gill, who relieved me of many
time-consuming but vital details that go into writing and preparing a
book. As always, Mr. Gordon Ierardi, editor, John Wiley and Sons,
served as a gentle but firm guide. Mr. Arthur W. Hepner of the Wiley
editorial staff read the manuscript and made one word stand where
two stood before. There is also my debt to my wife, a colleague in

. v

preparing several books. Without her help in preparing the manuscript there would probably have been no book at all.   To all of these
goes my thanks.

Robert I. Watson

Evanston, Illinois
January, 1965.

Contents

vii

Part II   Infancy

Part III   Early Childhood

Part IV   Later Childhood

PART I

PRINCIPLES
OF DEVELOPMENT

1

History of the Study of the Child

M ANY PERSONS are interested in the behavior and experience of children. Pre-eminent are parents. Loving their children they watch with interest and affection, blended with a touch of awe, the developing personalities with which they are so intimately bound. But others share this interest.

Scientific and professional men from several disciplines are interested in the child. Although pursuing the common theme of development, each studies the child according to his particular specialization. Among scientists the child psychologist is the most directly concerned with the various aspects of behavior and experience of the child. But characteristically, while studying the child in his own way, he uses the findings of scientific and professional workers from other fields. His use of these findings becomes understandable when we consider the wide scope of the determinants to his activities and experiences.

Some determinants arise from the child's biological heritage; others are aspects of the social situation in which he is immersed. Psychology, including the psychology of the child, relates both to the biological sciences and to the social sciences. Biologists, especially physiologists, anatomists, and embryologists, supply relevant material concerning the determinants of child behavior and experience. Social scientists, especially anthropologists and sociologists, study the child as influenced by society.

The contributions from the biological and social sciences do not exhaust the fields from which child psychology draws. The prevention and treatment of childhood diseases is the concern of the medical

3

practitioners, especially pediatricians and child psychiatrists. Clinical psychologists share with them a professional interest in disturbed children. Although the distinction between the normal and the disturbed child is not as clear-cut as it may first appear, the disturbed child is one who needs special professional help in getting along with himself and with society. Despite the attention here to the normal child, we cannot afford not to be concerned with the development of the disturbed child.

Educators, including educational psychologists, also contribute. They see the child as a growing, plastic creature to be guided in learning those things his society considers worthwhile. Therefore, psychological factors of interest, motivation, learning, and growth are important for them. Here, too, child psychologists profit.

Our study of child psychology shall begin with a consideration of the men and events that have charted its historical course. This takes the form of an examination of the prescientific attitudes taken toward the child before child psychology emerged as a separate field, the nature of the contributions of some of the men who founded the field, the developments in the relatively recent past, the influence other fields have had upon it, and a summary of the current status of modern child psychology.

Prescientific attitudes toward the child

Before the advent in the last century of child psychology as a branch of science, the attitudes held toward the child had one common characteristic. The interest was in what he had been or was to become, not in what he *is*. Interest in the child as such was virtually nonexistent. Whether viewed as a product of original sin, epitome of innocence, reflector of evolution, or future citizen—the child as a child was not of primary concern. Instead he was regarded as if in transition. This does not imply that this view is entirely false, for indeed childhood is a period of transition. But, strictly speaking, childhood is no more exclusively a period of preparation for adulthood than the adult years are preparatory for old age or old age preparatory for death.

Over the centuries many specific instances of the way a child was regarded and treated originated from viewing the child as in transition to becoming an adult. Smaller versions of adult clothes were worn by children, and adult manners and customs were forced upon the child even while he was still a toddler. Early biologists held that in mating the male transmitted to the female a completely formed but minute adult human being. The baby-man or *homunculus*, as it was called, grew in strength, size, and intelligence; when he became a man he was different only quantitatively from the way he had been as a baby.

The obvious differences in physical proportions of children as compared with adults were largely ignored. It was not recognized that the process of growing up involved a readjustment in the relation of the many structures of the mature organism. If the child grew into an adult only by increasing in height and weight, the results would be an enormous head, a long, thick trunk, and very short arms and legs. Physically, a child is definitely not a miniature adult.

With respect to intellectual qualities this attitude was also pervasive. Well into modern times, educational practice rested upon this attitude, as reflected by attempts to teach children in terms of adult interests and aspirations. Textbooks were written to interest adults, not the children for whom they were intended. Education was regarded as an indoctrination into the ways of adult life and a means of getting the child to behave like an adult as quickly as possible.

Hand in hand with failure to appreciate age differences went a general obliviousness to other differences among children. Children were regarded much the same, one as another. They were treated the same, expected to behave in the same fashion, and not allowed to differ in any important way.

To the Greeks, and often later, the child was seen as a future citizen and as a member of a family group. With the coming of Christianity another view appeared. As a result of Adam's fall, all mankind is born in sin. A conception of the child as innately depraved arose, to hold sway for many centuries. The warning, "Spare the rod and spoil the child," exemplifies the attitude that was considered appropriate under these circumstances. Later, a reaction against this view was expressed in the diametrically opposed belief that the child was inherently good. Rousseau and others helped to promulgate the view that the child was unspoiled until corrupted through contact with adults and society. The relation between this view and a present-day emphasis on the necessity of keeping the child free of repressive influences is more than accidental.

In the nineteenth century, the work of Charles Darwin and others on the study of evolution did much to stimulate interest in the study of the child. In testing the hypothesis of man's descent from animals, evidence derived from the study of children was utilized. The baby was regarded as a link between animal and man. Closely allied to this source of interest was the theory that the child relived or successively passed through the different stages of animal life (described by a phrase which a modern advertiser might well be proud to have coined —"ontogeny recapitulates phylogeny"). The crawling of the infant replicated the swimming movements of the fish, creeping, the locomotion of mammals, and running, the stage of man's movement. Survival of specific behaviors from prehuman days was sought, as in the grasp or "Darwinian" reflex, which, according to this theory, came about because the primate infant clung to the mother or tall branch for protection.

Today, the child is not regarded as a stage of evolution in the sense these early biological workers used this phrase. And yet childhood *is* a transitional period. Insofar as growth itself is a manifestation of the evolutionary process, the child is one performer in the evolutionary tableau.

The theory of recapitulation, erroneous though it may be, was rooted in the biology of the day. Hence, in it a *scientific* interest in the child was apparent. This helped to pave the way for the advance of modern child psychology, suggesting concepts which lent themselves to experimental test instead of providing merely a loose philosophical scaffolding.

The beginnings of child psychology

Child psychology came into being from the scientific study of the child through the work of investigators from other fields. Even psychologists who contributed to this beginning were drawn from various specialties other than child psychology. These investigators had the characteristic that they were not primarily identified with child psychology when they did their important work. When it was done, they were the first child psychologists.

Preyer and the Baby Biography

Systematic observation is basic to all scientific investigation as the account in Chapter 2 will attest. Although occasionally attempted before the nineteenth century (for example, Rousseau's *Émile*), relatively systematic observations of children reached a position of importance and significance in the later decades of the past century. The first observational procedure used was the so-called baby biography. The observer, often both parent and scientist, made day-to-day observations of a single "normal" child, starting at or near birth.

The work of Preyer (7), a physiologist, is one of the earliest examples. In his account of his son's mental development during the first four years, he recorded careful and detailed observations, to which he added information contributed by others as well as comparative data from the behavior of animals. He observed the development of reflexes from birth and the influence of experience and learning. *The Mind of the Child* (23), the book resulting from his labors, although justly criticized for not sharply separating fact from inference, is one of the great classics of child psychology. Another pioneer biography was Charles Darwin's diary (6) of his infant son, begun in 1840, but not appearing in print until 1870. In it Darwin revealed another facet of his interest in evolutionary processes.

These biographies served the useful purpose of indicating clearly the value of careful observation and detailed study for the guidance of subsequent psychological workers. At the same time such intrafamily biographies have certain serious weaknesses. One of these is the fact that a naive observer is likely to see merely what he is looking for; especially desirable characteristics are apt to be noted, while such behavior as would blight the family escutcheon might be overlooked. Such biographies differ from observational studies carried out today, which define in advance what is to be included and excluded and make provision for a check on the reliability of observations. (Reliability in this case can be achieved through independent and simultaneous observation by more than one person.)

In the baby biography many of the observations were fortuitous, were perhaps recorded long after the event had occurred, and were thus subject to memory distortion; furthermore, the children selected for study were not typical of children in general. In spite of these weaknesses the baby biographies helped to lay the groundwork for a scientific child psychology by raising problems which could later be answered more adequately by improved methods.

Hall and the Questionnaire

The next major development in the history of child psychology occurred under the leadership of G. Stanley Hall. Hall was stimulated by the theories of biological evolution and recapitulation. He theorized that the normal growth of the mind is to be seen as a series of stages more or less corresponding to those which early man and his ancestors went through in the history of the race. He thus was influenced by the point of view sketched earlier of the child as a stage of evolution. He had teachers question children in the primary grades. By this rather simple technique of asking questions, a great assortment of facts about childhood experiences and problems was assembled. The findings are exemplified by Hall's paper on children's lies published in 1882 and his study of the contents of children's minds published in 1883.

Shortly after the initial studies by Hall an abundance of efforts along similar lines by teachers, parents, and others appeared in the literature. Societies and associations dedicated to the study of the child by this technique were formed both here and abroad. The period of most intense activity of this way of studying children was from about 1890 to 1915.

It should be noted that Hall's own original work in this field was methodologically an improvement over both earlier and later studies using the questionnaire. For example, in his first study (10) he used specially selected teachers, trained them to uniform methods of questioning, and met with them frequently for discussion and critique during data collection. However, he and his students later began the practice of circulating questionnaires on various topics to teachers and parents throughout the country. In this way, a great deal of information could be collected in a relatively short time over wide geographical areas. If the questions were too difficult for the children, their teachers and parents were requested to interpret them to the children.

Still later the scope of the technique was broadened by circulation of questionnaires suitable for adults to record their childhood experiences as they remembered them. Some of the topics (4) Hall studied from questionnaires were appetites, fears, punishments, dreams, memories, toys, early sense of self, prayers, crying and laughing, perceptions of rhythm, and motor abilities.

Only the simplest of statistical devices were used in analyzing the data and no clearly defined or typical samples were gathered. Often the questions were worded to suggest the desired answer. The questionnaire as Hall used it also had certain inherent weaknesses: direct questioning of children, as he attempted it, often produces careless, evasive, imitative answers of a sort the child thinks the adult wishes to hear. His untrained recorders undoubtedly committed many sins both of omission and commission.

In large measure, the child study movement fell of its own weight. Parents and teachers uncritically, enthusiastically, and dogmatically stated the results of their superficial excursions into child development. Hall himself began to lose enthusiasm and turned his energies toward some of his other manifold interests, especially the psychology of religion and of senescence.

Despite its weaknesses, the child study movement of this period made definite contributions to the psychological study of the child. As

Bradbury (4) summarizes, it led to increased recognition of the importance of empirical study of the child, brought forth a realization of the necessity of a critical evaluation of the methods used, and led to a recognition of the importance of childhood *per se*. It might also be added that the questionnaire approach fostered by Hall was the forerunner of modern psychological tests.

Binet and the Intelligence Test

In 1904, the French Minister of Education named a commission to study the measures to be taken to insure that defective Paris school-children receive the best possible educational training. This commission decided that no child suspected of mental retardation should be eliminated from ordinary school classes without first taking a special examination. The task of developing and applying such an examination was taken over by Alfred Binet. The patriarch of all later psychological tests—the Binet-Simon tests—was thus the direct result of an administrative decision in educational practice (3).

The first great advance that Binet made in intelligence testing was to abandon dependence on the artificially simplified laboratory tasks used in mental testing prior to his efforts. Short, discrete, simple tasks, such as tonal memory, estimation of distance, speed of reaction, and rate of tapping are examples of previously used items. Early tests such as these had been found to have little prognostic value in work with children. Whatever they were measuring, it was not intelligence as the term is used today.

Binet, after many years of preliminary work, chose to use the more complex and realistic tasks of everyday life. In his first, or 1905 scale, done in collaboration with Theodore Simon, there were thirty tests (2). Illustrative of the content were the tests requiring verbal knowledge of objects such as parts of the body, naming of common objects, repetition of digits, drawing of a design from memory, finding the right word to complete a sentence, and definitions of abstract terms. These tests were arranged in increasing order of difficulty.

Not until the 1908 and the 1911 revisions of the scales did Binet make his second great contribution to mental testing—the grouping of tests as representative of the age at which they are usually passed. Mental age is the degree of intellectual development of an individual found by comparing his performance with that of other individuals of the same chronological age. Thus, a ten-year mental age is the degree of intellectual development attained by the average child of ten years. Through this procedure was established a frame of reference for interpretation of test results. Of course, crude comparisons using something analogous to this concept had been known before, as exemplified in remarks such as, "He has no more sense than a child." It was Binet's work, however, which firmly established this means of assessing intelligence test results in quantitative form.

In the United States, Lewis M. Terman restandardized and extended the original Binet-Simon Scale for American use and published it in 1916 as the Stanford-Binet Intelligence Scale. This version soon became *the* standard testing instrument for measuring children's intelligence. In fact, it is no exaggeration to say that the principal task of many psychologists working with children was to administer the Stanford-Binet.

The Scale had the great merit of being carefully and objectively standardized. It was constructed with attention to the standards of scientific rigor of its day. As a tool it proved its value in predicting educational status of schoolchildren, in aiding in the diagnosis of mental deficiency in children, and in serving as a means whereby many problems of child psychology became open to investigation. As Goodenough (9) indicates, the rapidity with which Binet testing was adopted in the United States can be traced to a number of conditions which made the times right for its appearance. Compulsory school attendance was beginning to be vigorously enforced and the length of the period of schooling was increased. Backward students in the schools thus became an increasingly important problem. Juvenile delinquency as a social problem was coming into active prominence, and emphasis upon social welfare and prevention of emotional and mental defects was becoming part of the American scene. Such problems called for large-scale assessment by means of a standardized instrument, a commission which was admirably fulfilled by the several revisions of the Binet scales. The revision in current use appeared as recently as 1960 (27).

Watson and the Conditioning Technique

A major pioneer effort is to be found in the work of John B. Watson on emotional responses in infants. Working with animals, particularly the white rat, and human infants, he found it impossible to use the then current major method of psychological investigation—introspection. Earlier investigators who had relied on the method of introspection had almost ruled out children as suitable subjects for psychological investigations because they could not be trusted to report accurately their conscious experiences. In dismissing introspection, Watson made infants and children legitimate subjects for psychological experiments.

He militantly championed an approach to psychology, so-called *be-havorism*, which stressed the behavioral aspects; hence, the name he gave to it. Watson advocated and applied various objective techniques which did not depend on introspection.

One of the techniques he used was that of conditioning. As Pavlov had established, when a dog is making a definite response to a particular stimulus, any frequently accompanying stimulus is likely to be responded to in the same way. Thus, a dog simultaneously presented with food, to which he responds by a flow of saliva, and the sound of a bell will eventually respond by salivating to the sound of the bell alone. Introspection is neither possible nor necessary; the study is performed by presenting the dog with stimuli to which he responds.

Conditioning technique was applied by Watson (*31*) to new-born infants to demonstrate how emotional responses are acquired. His most famous subject, Albert, aged eleven months, was reared in a hospital. When first tested, Albert showed no fear reaction to such stimuli as a white rat or a rabbit, a mask or cotton wool. He reached for practically everything brought near him. Fear, however, was shown by Albert at the sound of a steel bar being struck sharply.

In one of his experiments, Watson presented a rat to Albert. Just as he was reaching for the rat, the bar was struck, producing a loud sound. Albert jumped violently, burying his face in the mattress. When the rat was presented a second time, Albert again reached for it, and again the bar was struck. This time, in addition to jumping violently, Albert began to whimper. A week later the rat was presented without the sound from the bar. Although he eyed the rat there was no tendency to reach for it, and when the rat was placed near him he withdrew his hand. Evidently, the two joint stimulations of the sight of the rat and the sound of the bar had had an effect. Thereafter, joint stimulations of rat and bar were made several times. After five simultaneous presentations the rat was presented alone. The instant Albert saw the rat he began to cry and crawl rapidly away from it. A subsequent check showed that the rabbit and the white mask, formerly eliciting no fear, now were reacted to violently. The fear of the white rat had *generalized* to these other objects.

This and other studies showed that fears might be acquired by conditioning. Watson also demonstrated a lack of specificity—that is, a generalizing of the stimulus—in the S-R relation; a conditioned response to one stimulus was also capable of being elicited by other stimuli having certain common characteristics with it. Conditioned responses were found to persist over periods of time. In general, Watson demonstrated that many fears of infants were acquired.

Through the work of such men as Preyer, Hall, Binet, Terman, and Watson scientific child psychology came into being. Although wrestling with different problems in different countries, these men all shared a common desire for objectivity and the conviction that through quantitative measurement this could be assured. Each pioneer turned his back on philosophical and theological explanations of child behavior and worked toward the goal of new explanatory systems based on scientific research. Each is identified with a technique of study of the child which emphasizes to a greater or lesser degree exactitude and replicability of observations—the true beginnings of the scientific study of the behavior of the child.

Child psychology in the twenties and thirties

Beginning in the last century and extending through the first twenty years of the present one, the pioneers carried on their research. During the twenties and thirties no longer were there only a few isolated giants as in the past, but rather many capable workers collectively making a considerable contribution to knowledge of child psychology.

The type of research was largely determined by advances in methodology made during the pioneering period. Devices for measuring diversified forms of behavior had been developed, and projects were now launched to measure these behaviors. These decades were thus characterized by specialized studies of the different capacities and traits of the child.

These were the years in which specific traits and capacities were being investigated. Emphasis was placed upon the quantitative and the objective. Specialized studies dealing with learning, intelligence, sensory capacity, motor performance, emotion, language, and thinking were carried on. Studies of intelligence and learning loomed the largest. Many workers would turn to a given field when a promising method or challenging theory was advanced, leaving other areas relatively inactive.

With the advent of the First World War the opportunity for large-scale psychological testing of the intelligence of army recruits arose. As a result, tests were developed which could be applied simultaneously to groups of individuals. Based on this experience tests were extensively developed for peacetime uses in the school systems. From the measurement of intelligence the use of tests spread to other areas of ability and personality.

Many of the studies of this period were normative in the sense that they charted measurements of some segment of behavior by age, sex, socioeconomic status, and the like. These studies supplied material to be used as norms with which the performance of other children could be compared. Height and weight charts, intelligence tests, motor-development scales, reading tests, and vocabulary tests are illustrative. Characteristically, in their preoccupation with *tests*, these psychological research workers lost sight of the *child*, who was the object of this measurement.

The investigation of "individual differences" was also typical, superficially appearing to contradict the comment that the individual child was lost to view. These particular studies of individual differences were concerned with variation in only one measure at a time, with the scores on this measure studied to show how the *group* varied. For example, we might administer the Stanford-Binet to 100 children and calculate the average IQ and the spread of scores from low to high. Thus, a given child might be close to the average, another only at the fifth percentile, and still another at the ninety-fifth percentile. Only one psychological measure was obtained from each of these children. All that was available was his score on a test, along with other children's scores on the same test.

At best some investigators administered several tests, and scores on a series of tests might become available for each child. Although a series of separate statements could be made about a child, nothing was known about the relationship of these trait scores to one another. To these investigators the child was merely a series of isolated scores. Norms, useful though they may be, are not explanatory. We must go beyond averages or individual scores to search for the reasons for the child's behavior and experience.

On this issue some doubt was expressed, and still is. "Where in this mass of facts," people asked, "is the child?" The segmented, compartmentalized approach was noted with misgiving by some parents, educators, and others who dealt with children in everyday situations in which the child appeared somehow different from the reactions described in textbooks in child psychology. These critics asked for general principles that would make the child understandable, that would make the isolated facts of his behavior cohere intelligibly. In short, they asked for general principles of personality organization, a theoretical framework into which these facts could fit.

This plea, although justified, was premature. What early critics of this lack of integrative knowledge of the child did not understand was that normative data were essential before a more integrated picture could be assembled. Before developing these theme of personality organization, destined to be a dominant note in the modern period, it is necessary to pause to consider the influence on child psychology of work in other fields.

The influence of other fields upon child psychology

None of the pioneers in child psychology confined his interests to this one area. And just as these workers toiled in other scientific vineyards, researchers outside child psychology made substantial contributions to the cultivation of the new field. From its beginnings child psychology benefited from developments in psychoanalysis, child guidance, clinical psychology, pediatrics, education and educational psychology, and cultural anthropology. Let us consider briefly their various legacies.

Psychoanalysis

A major influence upon modern child psychology has been the work of Sigmund Freud, the founder of psychoanalysis, who was more or less a contemporary of Hall, Binet, and Watson. His influence is to be found not only in the direct utilization of psychoanalytic concepts and findings in child psychology today, but also in the subtle, indirect, and sometimes unnoticed effects upon child-training practices. Bearing the imprint of his thinking are present-day practices concerning the child's experiences in his motivated strivings, parent-child relationships, the effect of unconscious influences, and our understanding of disturbed children.

Psychoanalysis arose as a method of treatment, but almost immediately was seen to be a means of also securing psychological data from patients, which, in turn, not only gave rise to a theory of personality, but also to a psychological system or school. At this juncture something will be said about psychoanalysis as a means of treatment and of securing psychological information. Psychoanalytic theory will receive detailed attention in later chapters.

Toward the end of the last century, while still practicing as a neurologist in Vienna, Freud became interested in the more psychological aspects of the problems of his patients (13). He began a search for a method of treatment to help them with their emotional problems. Ultimately he arrived at what is known as the method of free association in which the patient is asked to say anything that comes to his mind, to relate all of his thoughts as they occur, no matter how trivial, irrelevant, or distasteful they may be. His early patients spontaneously reported their dreams to him and, since they bore considerable resemblance to waking free associations, their interpretation was also incorporated into psychoanalytic procedure.

According to Freud, this "verbal mind wandering," with little or no direction on the part of the psychoanalyst, produced one invariable result—the report of childhood experiences. Gradually Freud was led to the conclusion that adult personality maladjustments were directly traceable to unfortunate experiences in childhood. Moreover, these experiences turned out to be predominantly of a sexual nature—feelings of love and hate toward father and mother, sexual encounters, jealousy of a brother or sister regarded as favored by a parent, and the like.

Freud became convinced that these experiences exerted a profound and heretofore unrecognized influence upon subsequent adult behavior and experience. Although the principles and techniques of psychoanalysis developed from work with adult patients, his findings indicated the crucial role of childhood experiences. Freud thus forcibly called attention to childhood as a critical period of development. Indeed, it was not until Freud emphasized that adult neurotic symptoms were the outcome of childhood experiences that these incidents were studied intensively in order to explain present behavior.

Freud was also struck by his patients' inability to see the significance of their free associations and dreams. Whereas it would be clear to him what the free associations signified, patients would deny, often vigorously, Freud's interpretations when he suggested them. The patients thought and lived on one plane, while on another level, that of the unconscious, many extremely important determinants for their behavior were treated by them as nonexistent. Only after many psychoanalytic sessions did the patients gradually begin to have insight into the unconscious meanings of what they were saying and doing.

Thus, the extreme importance of unconscious determinants of behavior came to the fore. Freud was not the first to point out the significance of unconscious determinants, but he was the first to advance a method—free association—whereby they could be adequately studied. It is to Freud, then, that child psychology owes its interest in and appreciation of the importance of unconscious experiences in childhood.

Some psychoanalysts (8, 13) began to work directly with children. The method of free association is impossible to use with a young child, since it requires a more advanced verbal level than he possesses. The child psychoanalysts emphasized play activities in securing data for analysis and for interpreting their significance. They drew upon the symbolic significance Freud had found to be appropriate with adult patients.

The psychoanalyst is in a favorable position to develop insights into human behavior and to derive principles concerning it. He spends his professional and scientific life examining in minute and exacting detail the behavior and experience of a small number of individuals. Regularities are noted, and any deviation, no matter how trivial, does not escape scrutiny. His training makes him sensitive to the nuances of behavior, the evasions and deceptions so common in our adjustive behavior.

As a method of inquiry, psychoanalysis is essentially a means of reconstructing the individual's past, whether he be adult or child. These hindsights and clinical reconstructions accomplish a great deal. Psychoanalytic findings are more useful, however, as stimuli for research by psychologists than as instances of verified research findings. Their results are not sufficient in themselves, and the further step of scientific verification of clinical findings is necessary.

Child Guidance

The original impetus for the formation of child guidance clinics arose from a desire to combat juvenile delinquency (33). Before the advent of such clinics, the child or adolescent might have had a physical examination by juvenile authorities, but no investigation into why he had performed the delinquent activities was conducted.

The first child guidance clinic was founded in 1909 by William Healy in Chicago. As the child guidance movement spread, the link to delinquency weakened, but not the other major force which led to the clinic's founding—the conviction that delinquency represented aberrant psychological behavior which was amenable to modification. There has been a gradual broadening of scope of these clinics, as it was recognized that substantially the same means of treatment applicable to the delinquent could be applied to the emotionally disturbed non-delinquent child. This broadening came when it was recognized that delinquency and emotional maladjustments were different surface manifestations of what might be highly similar causative pictures.

During the twenties the child guidance clinics were organized in various cities. Maladjustment in school and home, especially that centering upon parent-child relationships, came to the foreground. In many clinics today the influence of psychoanalysis is very evident. Adaptation of psychoanalytic principles and techniques to the setting and personnel of the clinic and to the nature and age of the patients came rapidly. The child, regarded during an earlier period as a passive victim of whatever circumstances were impinged upon him, came to be viewed in the dynamic tradition of psychoanalysis as a very active participant who could be helped by psychotherapy.

The unique characteristic of the child guidance clinic is the use of the so-called team approach, or the coordinated services of the specialists on the staff. Instead of one clinician serving in all phases of work, a flexible division of labor has evolved. In a typical child guidance clinic procedure, the social worker, as intake supervisor, talks to the person requesting clinical services and describes what might be done, provided the facilities of the clinic are appropriate for the child's needs. During the initial contact, a visit of both the parent (generally the mother) and the child is arranged. The child is seen by the psychologist for psychological testing; the child is observed, often in a playroom, by the psychiatrist; and the mother is seen by the social worker who secures a comprehensive family history and an account of the difficulties that the child is exhibiting. Often the psychiatrist also sees the mother.

After sufficient information is collected to make possible some tentative diagnostic appraisal, a case conference is arranged. The psychiatrist, social worker, and psychologist review the information which has been gathered and each discusses his interpretation of the difficulties the child is facing. A general plan of treatment is worked out and psychotherapists are selected for mother and child. In many clinics, the psychotherapist is chosen more for his particular fitness or availability, rather than because he is a representative of one or another of the disciplines. Thus, either a psychiatrist, a psychologist, or a social worker may be the psychotherapist for the child or mother. Later, there are conferences in which the talents of the staff are again pooled in efforts to further the progress of the child and mother.

Clinical Psychology

Some of the influences brought to bear on child psychology helped to shape the history of clinical psychology. The psychological test tradition, the influence of psychiatry and psychoanalysis, and the child guidance movement had their effects upon its development. Clinical psychology, in turn, affected their development. Some of its roots have been traced elsewhere (32).

The opening in 1896 of the Psychological Clinic at the University of Pennsylvania is said by many to mark the advent of clinical psychology (5). Lightner Witmer, the founder and director of the clinic, became interested in helping the educationally retarded and handicapped child. As a consequence, the great majority of the cases seen in the clinic came from the school systems. Cooperation with special teachers of the blind, deaf, and mentally defective was stressed.

This clinic, the first of many organized at universities and teachers colleges, found its particular area of competence in the everyday problems of the child, particularly those relating to academic success, such as reading. Of course, neither emotional nor nonschool problems were ignored; but less stress was placed upon them—perhaps because at that time there was less understanding of them.

This tradition of close cooperation with the schools still has a respected place in the activities of the clinical psychologist. Nevertheless, for good or for ill, clinical psychology as a specialty has outgrown its beginning in a quasieducational setting and found its place in mental hospitals, child guidance clinics, homes for the mentally retarded, and many other settings (32).

Today, the clinical psychologist often carries full diagnostic and therapeutic responsibility not only with the educationally or intellectually handicapped, but also with the emotionally disturbed child or adult. In the next chapter, these two facets of the clinical method of the psychologist, diagnosis and therapy, will be explored as tools of research in furthering our understanding of the child.

Pediatrics

The pediatrician is interested in the behavior and experience of the child, in health as well as illness (26). Pediatrics first emerged as a medical specialty in the middle of the nineteenth century. It was initially a field of teaching rather than practice. Even in diagnosis and treatment of physical disease the child presented his own unique problems.

Interest in the psychological aspects of child medical practice was slow to develop, not reaching any proportions until the end of the first quarter of the present century. Concerning these influences, Senn (26), a pediatrician, has stated that pediatric attention first focused on neurological conditions. This was followed by an interest in the testing of intelligence, which later broadened to an appreciation of the developmental sequence. In the meantime, knowledge of phenomena of conditioning and learning, particularly as stimulated by John B. Watson, led to suggestions on how to rear children.

In later years psychiatric-pediatric collaboration became closer, and child guidance clinics made provision for pediatric service. One expression of appreciation of the importance of psychological aspects was the attempt of some pediatricians to combat the prevalent, rigid, impersonal method of infant feeding by the clock and by the ounce. Pediatrics as a branch of medicine is based on physiology and anatomy, but today it is also concerned with the child as an individual person and as a psychological being.

The fields so far discussed as contributing to child psychology—psychoanalysis, child guidance, clinical psychology, and pediatrics—have in common a desire to understand and to treat the individual child. The intimate, face-to-face situations that practice in each field affords serve to provide its practitioners with excellent opportunities for learning about children. Their professional interests are directed toward variables which when combined offer some chance of seeing each child as a molar unit. Each child who is a patient presents a unique problem, personality, and array of environmental circumstances, and requires a unique form of treatment. Common strands are created by similarities in age, dependent status in a family or institution, and similar cultural backgrounds at a particular time. Each child, nevertheless, presents a different pattern of personality to the clinician and demands understanding in terms of himself.

Education and Educational Psychology

Child psychology and childhood, as education and educational psychology view it, owe much of their development to the same forces. The early attitudes toward the child previously sketched are as much the heritage of education and educational psychology as they are of child psychology. Preyer, Hall, and Binet are part of the history of educational as well as child psychology.

In the more modern period, two individuals stand out as influencing studies of children's learning and of methods of teaching them—John Dewey and Edward L. Thorndike. John Dewey—philosopher, psychologist, and educator—probably had a more profound influence upon education than any other man of this century. His educational philosophy is widely known, though not always put into practice. Through his followers, his work led to the progressive education movement which in essence consists of the application of mental hygiene to education (16).

The studies of Edward L. Thorndike on learning and related topics are part of this heritage. Sharing through his own research in learning the discovery of the child as an individual, he did much to document the newly appreciated fact of individual differences. The existence of individual differences was now established by research instead of being part of the intuitive grasp of the gifted few "born" teachers.

The work of the educational psychologists and that of their colleagues in other disciplines has led to a concern with the growth and development of each child, in spite of the educator's responsibility for large groups of children. Differentiated curricula, the activity program, the advent of elective subjects, concern with each individual student's interest and motivation, the appearance of learning readiness programs, and the presence of psychological services in the schools attest to education's concern with the individual child and his emotional as well as intellectual needs.

Cultural Anthropology

Findings in cultural anthropology have also influenced child psychology. Workers in this field attempt to understand man as a social being. In the main they study the so-called primitive cultures throughout the world, although some anthropologists have begun to interest themselves in contemporary cultures such as our own.

Prior to 1920, cultural anthropology used a descriptive and historical approach relatively uninfluenced by events in other fields (15). E. B. Tylor in his book, *Primitive Culture* (28), published in 1871, laid the foundation of the field. His most celebrated doctrine was that of *animism,* the view that primitive man tended to look upon all things as if they had consciousness or "soul." His point of view influenced the thinking of his contemporaries among evolutionists, especially those who viewed primitive man as essentially childlike. Later, this doctrine came under suspicion as being too sweeping and in need of qualification. True, there are primitive cultures that foster the development of animistic thinking, and, since children in our society think "animistically," an analogy is drawn. But the fact is (20) that there are also primitive societies that discourage animistic thinking in an even more rigorous fashion than our own. Eventually, we have come to the position that there is no such thing as *the primitive;* rather there are *individuals* in many different societies. The pattern of living imposes individuality on members of primitive societies no less stringently than in ours.

Many of the contributions of such distinguished anthropologists as Margaret Mead have been impelled by a desire to test psychiatric-psychological hypotheses in other cultures (15). Often such studies focus attention on younger subjects and are avowedly developmental in character (21). For example, Mead's *Coming of Age in Samoa* (18) and *Growing Up in New Guinea* (19) reveal in their very titles a concern with the developmental sequence.

In her Samoan study, Mead (18) was interested in testing the hypothesis that the so-called storminess of adolescence was a result of particular cultural conditions, instead of being an inevitable manifestation of maturational factors as it was generally assumed to be. Lacking power to construct experimental conditions, she turned to Samoa, a culture far different from our own. Careful and intensive study of fifty adolescent Samoan girls supplied evidence that adolescence was not a period of strain in Samoan society.

This finding is an instance of the corrective principle of "cultural relativity"; psychological assumptions may not be universally applicable. The possibility of cultural relativity must be entertained about given psychological phenomena until evidence becomes available that universal applicability is a reasonable assumption. Adolescence may be a period of stress and strain in American society, but failure to demonstrate its same phenomena in Samoa makes it probable that there are particular social circumstances which account for the difference.

Here the task of the anthropologist is the thankless one of gently but firmly indicating that in such and such a cultural setting a particular generalization does not hold, and hence, the behavior in question is culturally relative. To express the same issue more positively, anthropologists test psychological formulations found to hold in our culture in other cultures to see if they also apply, which they must if they are to have universal validity.

Findings of the anthropologists have forced a recognition that we can never observe human beings who have not been subject to cultural influences. Their findings further indicate that cultural factors are important during the formative phase of personality development; hence, the emergence of the problem of the interrelations between personality and culture.

This brief review could not do justice to the many other influences brought to bear on our knowledge of the behavior and experience of the child. General experimental psychology, most particularly the field of learning, has contributed to child psychology in the modern period. The contribution of sociology, through its study of the family, has not been mentioned; nor have the insights and findings of the linguist, philosopher, artist, or religious leader. These, too, have made contributions to the modern period in child psychology.

The modern period in child psychology

Certain characteristics of the modern period in child psychology help to set the stage for the remainder of this book. Unifying themes running throughout much current activity in the field are identified by certain catch words, namely, "development," "personality," "total situation," "multidiscipline research," "interplay of science and practice," and "behavior theory."

The theme of development can be made central in discussions of child psychology, both as a concept and as a means of presenting the facts and theories concerning the psychological study of the child. Workers in child psychology and related disciplines share the tradition of emphasis on the worth and value of the developing individual. Development is the common interest of workers in all of these varied fields. The developmental emphasis consists in studying the child as he shows change in a time sequence, with attention not only to the progression itself but also to the attempt to predict later phases in terms of earlier ones (22). The developmental concept can be made more specific and meaningful by referring to *personality* development.

The present era is one in which *personality* investigation is paramount in child psychology. On one hand there are certain views of personality long in theory but short on facts; on the other hand, there are various scientific findings short on theory but long on facts. Sometimes an individual child psychologist or a member of another field interested in the child reacts by slavishly accepting a certain theoretical position, say psychoanalysis, and then planning investigations which, provided we accept the major tenets, can be cited as furthering our knowledge of personality theory. Others refuse to see any problem and ignore theory while normatively mapping personality as a separate entity.

There is, as always, a middle ground. With continuing research, a picture will gradually emerge based on scientifically verified facts. As these particular facts emerge into larger structures, a more unified picture combining theory and empirical data can be constructed. In the meantime, unverified but plausible hypotheses can be used to fill in the missing gaps *provided that they are recognized for what they are—as yet unverified assumptions.* In this task of balancing fact and theory, the child psychologist plays an important part.

In this modern period in child psychology the child is seen as an individual in a total situation. He functions as the result of individually determined forces and because of the environmental circumstances pressing upon him. The beginnings of this point of view were apparent in the earlier periods, as in Freud's psychoanalytic view which stressed the effect of adverse circumstances upon personality development. There was definite recognition of external influences in the child guidance movement. William Healy's first major work, *The Individual Delinquent,* showed delinquency as a situational phenomenon, not a characteristic of the child himself. Within child psychology, itself, this stress upon the total social situation gave impetus to social psychology.

This emphasis on all aspects of the child in a total situation has added impetus to another trend of the modern period—the importance of multidiscipline child research institutes. Often psychologists predominate but the personnel of such institutes may also include individuals of different areas of specialty and interest, such as psychiatrists, pediatricians, nutrition experts, and physiologists. Many of their long-term studies have now been going for so lengthy a period that children evaluated in infancy and early childhood have been seen again as adults. Childhood characteristics can now be related to adult counterparts in the same individuals.

The Institute of Child Study of the University of Toronto has been recently described (*1*). In operation for many years it carries on a variety of long-term research programs in close conjunction with many service and training functions. It has its own affiliated nursery, kindergarten, and elementary schools, keeps in close touch with the parents of its students, and trains not only research workers but also teachers and others in the University who desire training in child behavior. Other leading institutes include those at the Universities of California at Berkeley, Iowa, and Minnesota, and the Fels Research Institute in Ohio. Arising from the same recognized need for interdisciplinary collaboration was the organization in 1933 of the Society for Research in Child Development open to all workers on child research (*17*).

The interplay between science and practice is characteristic of the modern period in child psychology. The healthy integrating exchange thus emerging is borne out by many of the facets of history previously outlined. Clinical-child psychologists or, if you prefer, child-clinical psychologists are one manifestation. Still other child psychologists are to be found within education, home economics, pediatrics, parent education, marriage counseling, correctional work, and the gamut of children's agencies. Research stations such as those outlined before are very sensitive to questions of practice.

It is recognized today that science and practice cannot be artificially separated. Nevertheless, there can be a division of labor. The clinical psychologist working with children may on this basis be distinguished from the child psychologist. The former works primarily with disturbed children. The child psychologist, although cognizant of what his brother is doing and sometimes assuming the uneasy role of his brother's keeper, is more concerned with scientific advance and sees the problems of the child in a broader perspective. He sometimes pays for this breadth by less appreciation of individual dynamics.

It is pertinent to report the opinion of others concerning these trends. One authoritative source is in the *Annual Review of Psychology*, in which current research is critically examined by experts in each of the specialties. In the 1955 volume, the Yarrows, who wrote the review of child psychology, had this to say: "Rather slowly, but very perceptibly, a new point of view is emerging in child psychology. It is not a point of view which is an irresponsible, radical departure from the conservative empiricism which has epitomized this discipline, but it is a reformulation of the problems in terms of a more dynamic conception of behavior and development" (*34*, 1).[1]

After examining briefly earlier developments in child psychology in a fashion not too different in spirit from this presentation, they went on to summarize the modern era as follows: "Childhood reemerged as a crucial field of study (the fourth phase) when testable hypotheses based on clinical (mainly psychoanalytic) theories began to be formulated by systematically oriented researchers, when psychological theory and cultural anthropology converged, and when the genius of Kurt Lewin trained the experimental method upon meaningful social psychological questions within a framework of dynamic field theory" (*34*, 2).[1]

That we are not alone in taking this stand concerning the importance of the current dynamic-theoretical phase of child development is also borne out by an analysis of the United States Children's Bureau bulletin which covered the research in progress reported to it for nine months of 1961 (*30*). Omitting a few general, long-term studies, the percentage of studies concerned with physical, motor, perceptual, cognitive intellectual, and learning processes made up only 13 per cent of those reported. Social, familial—cultural behavior—and personality constituted 20 per cent; disturbed children accounted for 24 per cent; while educational, health, and social service studies accounted for the

[1] From Yarrow and Yarrow (*34*). Published by *Annual Reviews, Inc.* and used with permission.

remaining 43 per cent. These percentages lend support to the contention made about the current research scene.

Recommendations concerning research made by the 1960 White House Conference on Children and Youth reflect the emphasis upon research in a social setting, especially that of the family and the school (24). European research in child psychology shows many of the same trends (35).

There are many indications, some of which have been sketched, that psychology as a science is becoming more closely united today than it has been in the past. There is an increasing recognition on the part of psychologists and others of the essential unity of the field. "Schools of psychology" which used to plague the field are almost nonexistent. This does not mean that there are no differences of opinion, but rather that these differences rest upon this or that specific point, not upon some fundamental principle which would tear the fabric of the field into bits.

There is, to be sure, a "latitudinarian" left and a "rigorous" right, but such a distinction is a quantitative, not a qualitative, one. As Hebb puts it, "There appears to be a left wing and a right wing in psychology . . . the Right favors parsimony of explanatory ideas, a simple or mechanical account of behavior, and definiteness even at the cost of being narrow. The Left is prepared to postulate more fully and can better tolerate vagueness and lack of system in its account of behavior" (11, 47–48).[2]

There have been a number of attempts at integration of the areas of psychology—learning, motivation, perception, thinking, and the like—into one unified view. One of the signs of integration in psychology is what is known as behavior theory. Actually, there is a variety of behavior theories, having in common a desire to embrace and unify the various psychological phenomena into one system with emphasis upon learning. Each in its own way accounts for the acquisition and retention of new forms of behavior.

One major stream in behavior theory stems from the work of Clark L. Hull, whose volume, *Principles of Behavior* (12), epitomizes the approach. His efforts at integration are related to the earlier work of John B. Watson in behavioristic study of animals and man and to the work of Edward L. Thorndike on reward and punishment in learning. Hull represents the rigorous right in psychological theory. He was primarily concerned with an analysis of the learning process with par-

[2] From Hebb (11). Copyright 1951 by Duke University Press, and published with permission.

ticular attention to carefully controlled experimental situations. It was part of his strategy to begin the study of human behavior with animal subjects, hoping that their very simplicity would give him access to the fundamentals of learning.

Some of his colleagues and students have extended his theoretical conceptions in an attempt to build a theory of personality development. They thus represent to some degree the latitudinarian left. These efforts have taken them beyond what Sears called "the closely charted regions of rigorous stimulus response theory" (25, 61).[3] In no sense are matters in this extension of learning theory a settled issue. Many areas relevant to their efforts are simply not yet explored; others are only dimly understood and even in the most thoroughly explored areas there is only the most sketchy understanding. Different workers in this tradition have proceeded in different directions. At this point it is enough to say that the works of Dollard and Miller on social learning, Sears on frustration-aggression and patterns of child rearing, and Whiting and Child on socialization are to be emphasized. Each of these men were or are associated with the Institute of Human Relations at Yale University where Hull did his work. Each in his own way has been influenced by his account of learning theory. For present purposes their appeal lies in the fact that each uniquely emphasizes the social aspects of personality.

These related points of view have no commonly agreed-upon name. Following Hull, they might be called behavior theory, but this designation is perhaps best reserved for the more rigorous and narrower Hullian exposition. For convenience and for shortness of statement only, and with the warning that there is no general agreement about the choice of the term, behavior-social learning theory (learning theory, for short) will be used in referring to this point of view in the presentation to follow.

In furthering these themes of modern child psychology in later chapters, the usual format for a text in child psychology will not be followed. Typically in a treatise on child psychology, the topics of psychological growth are divided into areas, such as intelligence, learning, emotion, motor development, social development, and personality. Such a division, although conventional and therefore convenient, would be false to the aim of striving to see the whole child. Any child's behavior at a given moment overlaps these categories. To follow the usual chapter arrangement would also minimize the contribution of the other fields just discussed. Since the disciplines con-

[3] From Sears (25). Copyright 1947 by the University of Pittsburgh Press and published with permission.

tributing to our knowledge of the behavior and experience of the child are all interested, broadly speaking, in personality development in a total situation, the natural sequence would be to follow the child from germination to the end of childhood within a framework of these themes.

As a concession to the impossibility of considering all things at once, the following chapter will be devoted to a discussion of the methods of child study. Immediately thereafter, chapters on basic principles and concepts of development are introduced. This is followed by chapters organized through an artificial, but necessary, separation of development in a framework of the three age periods—infancy, extending through the first two years; early childhood, lasting through the fifth year; and late childhood, continuing until about the thirteenth year.

Two major considerations dictate the choice of infancy and early and late childhood as the periods of division. First, there is popular general acceptance and understanding of this particular division. Infant, preschool child, and school child, for example, are used as synonyms for these ages in educational settings. Often research studies are designed expressly to cover the age span of one of these periods. Second, the tripartite age division corresponds respectively to age stages used by the psychoanalyst, namely, the oral-anal stages, phallic stage, and latency period.

Within each age period a further subdivision is necessary. In one chapter the prenatal life and the birth process and its consequences are considered. Thereafter the infant is examined as relatively independent of the social situation. In subsequent chapters he is viewed as a social being. In still later chapters, early and late childhood are considered in a similar fashion.

Summary

Before the emergence of child psychology as a scientific discipline, there were a variety of points of view or attitudes toward the child. In common they were expressions of points of view about what the child had been or was to become. Only with the advent of scientific study was there much interest in what the child *is*—a study of the child for his own sake.

The beginnings of the science of child psychology are to be found in the work of several pioneers during the period from about 1880 to 1920. Each of these early workers contributed to the founding of the field through the application of some technique of scientific study. Preyer used the baby biography, Hall the questionnaire, Binet the intelligence test, and Watson the conditioning technique. The techniques themselves are less important than what they represent—an attempt by each of these workers to develop objective means of studying the child.

In the twenties and thirties a greatly increased number of workers in child psychology proceeded to place child psychology upon a solid footing. Their research efforts may be characterized as *normative* in that they were concerned with carefully establishing what children at given ages were capable of doing, psychologically speaking. General personality organization and the dynamics whereby a given child might be understood were relatively neglected during this period, as were attempts at explanatory conceptualizations.

It was from other fields that new influences came, helping to shape child psychology into its present form. Psychoanalysis was the most potent of these influences. Its influence was greatest upon the area of motivation, helping us to understand the dynamics of behavior—why a child did what he did. But child guidance, clinical psychology, pediatrics, education and educational psychology, cultural anthropology, and other fields also contributed to the modern period in child psychology.

In the modern period in child psychology, *development* emerges as the unifying theme in the interest of these workers from the various disciplines, including the child psychologists. Even more specifically, interest centers upon *personality* development. In order to hold this interest in focus, the child is seen as he functions in a particular environmental situation. Other unifying attempts that characterize the modern period also make their appearance—the development of multidiscipline research institutes, the interplay of science and practice, and attempts at integration through more comprehensive theories.

For Further Reading

Wayne Dennis has written a brief authoritative account of the beginnings of child psychology. His presentation, "Historical Beginnings of Child Psychology," is to be found in the *Psychological Bulletin*, 1949, 46, 224–235. John E. Anderson gives another interesting account, "Child Development: An Historical Perspective," in *Child Development*, 1956, 27, 181–196. The influence of other fields upon orthopsychiatry and thus upon many aspects of child psychology is sketched by various authorities under the editorship of Lawson Lowrey in the book, *Ortho-psychiatry 1923–1948: Retrospect and Prospect* (New York, American Ortho-psychiatric Association, 1948). This writer prepared "A Brief History of Clinical Psychology," which appeared in the *Psychological Bulletin*, 1953, 50, 321–346. Some conception of the general status of child psychology, year by year, may be gained from the chapter devoted to the subject in the *Annual Review of Psychology* (Stanford, California, Annual Reviews).

References

1. Ainsworth, Mary D. The significance of the five-year research programme of the Institute of Child Study. *Bull. Inst. Child Stud. Univ. Toronto*, 1960, 22, 3–16.
2. Binet, A., and T. Simon. Methodes nouvelles pour le diagnostic du niveau intellectual des anormaux. *Annee psychol.*, 1905, 11, 191–244.
3. Binet, A., and T. Simon. Upon the necessity of establishing a scientific diagnosis of inferior status of intelligence. In W. Dennis (Ed.), *Readings in the history of psychology*. New York: Appleton-Century-Crofts, 1948, 407–411.
4. Bradbury, Dorothy E. The contribution of the child study movement to child psychology. *Psychol. Bull.*, 1937, 34, 21–38.
5. Brotemarkle, R. A. Clinical psychology 1896–1946. *J. Consult. Psychol.*, 1947, 11, 1–4.
6. Darwin, C. A biographical sketch of an infant. *Mind*, 1877, 2, 285–294.
7. Dennis, W. Historical beginnings of child psychology. *Psychol. Bull.*, 1949, 46, 224–235.
8. Freud, Anna. *The psychoanalytical treatment of children*. London: Imago, 1946.
9. Goodenough, Florence L. *Mental testing, its history, principles and applications*. New York: Rinehart, 1949.
10. Hall, G. S. The contents of children's minds on entering school. *Ped. Sem.*, 1891, 1, 139–173.
11. Hebb, D. O. The role of neurological ideas in personality. *J. Pers.*, 1951, 20, 39–55.
12. Hull, C. *Principles of behavior*. New York: Appleton-Century-Crofts, 1943.
13. Jones, E. *The life and work of Sigmund Freud*. (3 vols.). New York: Basic Books, 1953–1957.
14. Klein, Melanie. *Contributions to psychoanalysis, 1921–1945*. London: Hogarth Press, 1948.
15. Kluckhohn, C. The influence of psychiatry on anthropology in America during the past one hundred years. In J. K. Hall (Ed.), *One hundred years of American psychiatry*. New York: Columbia University Press, 1944, 589–617.
16. Krugman, M. Orthopsychiatry and education. In L. G. Lowrey (Ed.), *Orthopsychiatry 1923–1948: retrospect and prospect*. New York: American Orthopsychiatric Association, 1948, 248–262.
17. McLean, Dorothy. Child development: a generation of research. *Child Develpm.*, 1954, 25, 3–8.
18. Mead, Margaret. *Coming of age in Samoa*. New York: Morrow, 1928.
19. Mead, Margaret. *Growing up in New Guinea*. New York: Morrow, 1930.

20. Mead, Margaret.   Investigation of thought of primitive children with special reference to animism.   *J. Roy. Anthrop. Inst.*, 1932, 62, 173–190.
21. Mead, Margaret.   Research on primitive children.   In L. Carmichael (Ed.), *Manual of child psychology.*   (2nd ed.).   New York: Wiley, 1954, 735–780.
22. Olson, W. C.   Developmental psychology.   In C. W. Harris (Ed.), *Encyclopedia of educational research.*   (3rd ed.).   New York: Macmillan, 1960, 370–376.
23. Preyer, W.   *Die Seele des Kindes.*   Leipzig: T. Grieben, 1882.
24. Pringle, Katherine D. (Ed.), *Recommendations: composite report of forum findings 1960 White House Conference on Children and Youth.*   Washington, D.C.: U.S. Government Printing Office, 1960.
25. Sears, R. R.   Child psychology.   In W. Dennis (Ed.), *Current trends in psychology.*   Pittsburgh: University of Pittsburgh Press, 1947, 50–74.
26. Senn, M. J. E.   Pediatrics in orthopsychiatry.   In L. G. Lowrey (Ed.), *Orthopsychiatry 1923–1948: retrospect and prospect.*   New York: American Orthopsychiatric Association, 1948, 300–309.
27. Terman, L. M., and Maud A. Merrill.   *The Stanford-Binet Intelligence Scale.*   Boston: Houghton Mifflin, 1960.
28. Tylor, E. B.   *Primitive culture.*   London: J. Murray, 1871.
29. United States Children's Bureau.   Research relating to children.   *U.S. Dept. Health, Educ. and Welf. Bull.*, 1953, No. 2.
30. United States Children's Bureau.   Research relating to children.   *Clearinghouse for Research in Child Life. Bull.*, 1962, No. 14.
31. Watson, J. B., and Rosalie Raynor.   Conditioned emotional reactions.   *J. Exp. Psychol.*, 1920, 3, 1–14.
32. Watson, R. I.   A brief history of clinical psychology.   *Psychol. Bull.*, 1953, 50, 321–346.
33. Watson, R. I.   Child guidance clinics.   In C. W. Harris (Ed.), *Encyclopedia of educational research.*   (3rd ed.).   New York: Macmillan, 1960, 192–194.
34. Yarrow, Marion R., and L. J. Yarrow.   Child psychology.   *Annu. Rev. Psychol.*, 1955, 6, 1–28.
35. Young, H. B.   European research in child psychology.   *Children*, 1958, 5, 101–104.

2

The Scientific Study of the Child

SCIENCE SHOWS development, just as does a child. Science is a *process*, not a static body of fact. It is an always developing, always changing means of acquiring knowledge. Science arises from observations and experiments which, in turn, lead to other observations and experiments. This particular formulation of science highlights the methods—observation and experiment—by means of which new concepts emerge.

The methods of study

Many different accounts of scientific methodology may be found in the literature; all seem to show that the investigator is offered the opportunity of utilizing either of two major procedures. He may observe differences in nature as they are found to exist, thus using the differential method, or he may intervene with nature and perform an experiment.

The Experimental Method

An experiment is a particular way of carrying out observations, which results in a statement of an antecedent-consequent relation. The experimenter manipulates some form of stimulation, the so-called *independent* variable. For example, the independent variable may be the intensity of sound, the length of exposure time of a visual stimulus, or the like. As he varies the independent variable through prearranged steps, the experimenter observes the effect of this antecedent stimulation upon consequent changes in the *dependent* variable, i.e., that form of behavior which results from the stimulation.

The experimenter, it is important to note, exercises a degree of control over the antecedent. This factor of control, in the sense that the independent variable is altered in a specific and known manner, makes it possible for the original investigator or someone else to repeat the experiment. The need for these "prearranged steps" implies a laboratory situation that is usually the setting in which an experiment is performed. An experimenter causes an event to happen at a certain time and place, and he is thus alerted to make accurate observations by knowing when and where to undertake them.

Not too many years ago it was considered essential for the experimenter to hold constant all variables that might be independent (that is, "affect" the results) except one. Certain factors that might have affected the dependent variable are not allowed to vary during the course of the experiment; that is, they are held constant. Here another meaning of control is introduced (5). If they had not been controlled *in the sense that they were kept constant,* they might have affected the measures under consideration, thus obscuring the effect of the independent variable under study. Of course, in another study they might themselves have been systematically studied. One independent variable studied at a time was at one time considered to be the rule. Certain advances in statistics, particularly analysis of variance, have been made, so that it is possible to handle several independent variables in a particular study at the same time.

When "control" of factors as a restraint of other variables is spoken of, it is important to emphasize that the control is not complete. Indeed, if complete control were possible, only one observation for each degree of change in the independent variable would be necessary. Since we do not always have exact control of variation of the independent variable, various degrees of stimulation are possible. We may vary the intensity, pitch, and timbre of an auditory stimulus through predetermined steps exactly controlled by the experimenter. This is likewise true in other sensory fields and for some other areas of child study. However, for many important problems, we simply do not know enough about the independent variable to vary it through finely graded steps.

After the first experiments on a particular problem establish whether the presence or absence of a certain factor has any effect at all, we can leave for later research the study of gradation of effect.

There are certain experimental procedures which might be identified briefly. Thus, one common research design calls for using the same subjects once under normal conditions and then again with one condition (the independent variable) changed. In this, *the method of difference*, a subject is his own control since he is studied under both conditions.

If practice effects are involved, as in studies of children's learning, it is not practicable to use the same children under both conditions. If doing the task itself makes the child different because he has now learned something new or how to do something better because he went through the first session, he is no longer the same person as he was at the beginning of the session. In order to circumvent this blurring of results, the *control group* technique is used.

In its simplest form, two groups are used. Children of the total sample are assigned to the two groups in such a manner as to make them as alike as possible. For example, suppose that in a study of reading ability one wishes to control (equalize) for the effect on the results of individual differences in intelligence. With scores on an intelligence test available, the top child may be placed in the experimental group, the next highest in the control group, the third highest in the experimental group, and so on, alternating between the groups. Thus, both the average intellectual level and the variability of the two groups are equalized.

The problem of placement becomes more complicated when other matching variables, such as sex, age, socioeconomic status, and so on, must also be considered, but basically the way of equating is the same. In general, the intent is to make the experimental and control groups as similar as possible in the independent variables *not* under consideration, but which may, nonetheless, cause concomitant variation in the dependent variable being studied. The choice of matching the groups on certain variables depends on whether it is known or suspected that there is a concomitant variation with the dependent variable. For instance, as Anderson (3) observes, in studying motor skills with all except very young children, it is not necessary to control intelligence or socioeconomic factors, because concomitant variation with motor ability is known to be very low. On the other hand, in studying language, which is positively related to (concomitantly varies with) these factors, both must be controlled.

Now that this necessity of equation of the groups has been indicated, it is possible to elaborate on the nature of the control group study. Two equated groups of subjects are used, differing only in that one group, the experimental, has the independent variable introduced (or has a greater or lesser magnitude, and so forth), while the second or control group does not.   In the simplest form of this technique, both groups receive a prior test to establish equality; following this, one group undergoes the experimental procedure, while the other does not. Both then take a final test.   The difference in final test results between the two groups is considered the result of the experience undergone by the experimental group which the control group did not undergo, and is the measure of the effect of the experimental (that is, the independent) variable.

In summary then, in an experiment the independent variable is introduced and varied systematically while other variables which might conceivably influence the dependent variable are controlled. Whatever changes occur in the dependent variable are attributed to the changes in the independent variable.   Since science depends upon *verified* knowledge, and verification is relatively more exact when using the experimental than when using the differential method, the former is often the method of choice.   Nevertheless, the differential method is of great value.

The Differential Method

In the experimental method the distinguishing operation is the manipulation by the investigator of some specific stimulating condition, the independent variable.   But there are some problems in which this intervention on the part of the investigator is impossible or even undesirable.   There are certain circumstances in which arrangement of conditions by the experimenter is not feasible, and he must seek a different method of carrying on his research.   Indeed, there are sciences, such as astronomy and geology, in which experiment is impossible so far as major problems are concerned.   The space and time dimensions of these sciences do not permit experimental manipulation.   An astronomer cannot vary the orbit of a star to see its effect; a geologist cannot introduce an ice age in order to observe the resultant changes.

These sciences, as well as certain problem areas in other sciences, depend on the differential method.   This consists of the scientist studying differences found in certain conditions without purposive manipulation—other than selection of phenomena to be studied.   A star already varying in its orbit is studied; evidence of the effect of ice ages is examined in relation to other events occurring at the same time. The differential method is also used in more relevant fields.   The anthropological studies of Mead, mentioned in Chapter 1, in which different cultures were compared and contrasted, the so-called cross-cultural method, is a variant of the differential method.

The scope of children's environments, even within our culture, is extraordinarily wide. Sometimes the environment is such that we can speak of environmental deprivation. Many institutions for children are so understaffed that they cannot provide the usual range and intensity of human contacts that children in a family setting receive. The institutionalized child may lack mothering and receive hardly any personal verbal stimulation. Hence he has less opportunities to learn from these experiences. The psychologist would not deliberately create these situations, but when he finds them already present he utilizes them for study.

Many psychological problems do not encourage experimental manipulation. Sometimes to do so would be too costly in time, money, or effort. Sometimes an attempt to study a problem experimentally would mean ethical or moral violation of the personal rights of others.

An illustration would be the attempt to make the independent variable of an experiment the development of an experimental psychosis in a child; so, too, would be the placement of heretofore emotionally stable children in a family environment designed to produce emotional trauma. Moreover, respect for living things prevents workers in all sciences from inflicting unnecessary pain in the course of their experiments. Child psychologists are further limited in their use of the experimental method because of their desire to avoid interfering in any way with the best development of the child's personality. This precaution is followed even when harmful effects are but remotely suspected.

For instance, a question, which is of considerable relevance for the field of child development and regarding which equivocal data have appeared in the literature, is whether insufficient oxygen (anoxia) at birth causes lasting damage to the child. The surest, most efficient technique of answering this question would be to subject new-born infants to varying degrees of anoxia and to follow their subsequent development. However, so long as there is even the faintest suspicion that such a procedure might cause lasting damage to the children, such a method is not going to be employed. Instead, the differential method, capitalizing upon cases of anoxia that occur, despite the best obstetrical care, must be relied upon to answer the question.

Sometimes the differential method is employed by necessity, but for certain problems it is the method of choice. For some problems, life as it is lived, and thus the differential method, offers greater promise than does an experiment. Studies of normal development, for example, are central to child psychology. Since we are interested in the *normal* changes concomitant with age, we do not attempt to alter the course of development precisely because it is the normal child we are trying to study.

In using the differential method, the investigator finds a situation rather than arranges for it. The children are behaving in ways that are natural to them. The children are already "intelligent," "mentally retarded," or "disturbed" when the differential method is applied.

Independent and dependent variables are still present when applying the differential method. There are independent variables, not in the sense of something that is capable of purposive manipulations, but that is identifiable and often a measurable antecedent condition that can be related to consequent or dependent variables. Subjects are chosen according to a criterion, and the measurements themselves form the variable. Thus, the researcher does not manipulate the independent variable and, consequently, he has less control of it. However, concomitant variation, the use of control groups, and the other characteristics previously described as related to the experimental method are still possible.

The value of a control group in research using the differential method is pertinent. Suppose the problem under investigation is the relation of aggression in children to attitudes of their parents. By a means irrelevant to the issue at hand, 50 already aggressive children are identified. Let us further suppose that in 32 of the homes from which these aggressive children come, it is established that parental rejection of these children takes place. It would be tempting to conclude that parental rejection is associated with aggressiveness. Actually, the results of this study are inconclusive without a control group. We must also isolate a control group of nonaggressive children to find out how often parental rejection is present in homes of this group as well. Only if the two types of homes differ significantly in the number showing parental rejection can we speak with any degree of assurance about the meaning of the results.

Although to some extent it is loose usage, the independent variable can be called the *causal* variable, and the dependent variable the *effect* variable. The nature of the particular problem under investigation defines whether a particular factor is an independent or a dependent variable. What is a cause in one setting may be the effect in another. Intellectual functioning, for example, may be either, depending on the research design in question. When the effect of lack of mothering upon the infant is discussed his intellectual functioning will be used as the dependent variable. That is, if children are deprived of mothering (the independent variable) does this influence their intelligence (the dependent variable)? But when considering the school child, the question will be raised concerning the reasons for superior school work, and intellectual functioning will be explored as an independent variable. That is to say, does school work (the dependent variable) vary as a consequence of intellectual functioning (the independent variable)?

Most, but not all, studies using a correlational technique employ a differential method. Indeed, the term, "correlational technique" is sometimes used as a synonym for the differential method. This is a practice best avoided because confusion with "correlational technique" in its more specific sense of calculating the statistical measure of correlation is thereby obviated.

The techniques of study

Basic to all scientific research, psychological or otherwise, is observation—the noting of events as they occur. Both the experimental and differential method rely on observation. But our senses are faulty and limited, and our wishes as to the outcome can distort our observations. We are set to see certain things, so we see to a certain extent what we expect to see. Thus, one purpose of research techniques and devices is to increase the accuracy of our observations. A handmaiden of accurate observation is immediate and accurate recording, necessitated by faulty and distorted memory to which all of us are subject. Many of the techniques discussed in this and later chapters—chronoscopes, tests, motion pictures, and so on—are means of making observations more correct and their recording less subject to error. Just as eyeglasses are worn to enhance vision, so, too, are the devices and procedures employed in psychological research the means of making more exact and more acute the observational processes of the investigator; and, just as watches are carried to help us establish the time of events, so, too, are other devices used to help to make sure that what is observed is recorded accurately.

In a sense all observation is subjective because it depends on the organism of the observer. We attempt to make it as objective as possible by arranging conditions of observation so that the human element can be minimized, although never eliminated. Devices and procedures increasing objectivity are attempts to reach the goal of minimal dependence on subjective impression. It follows that all such devices have varying degrees of objectivity-subjectivity; they represent quantitative differences along this continuum.

In many research situations, especially in clinical settings, the investigator does not merely passively record observations but also interacts actively with his subject. He becomes, in Sullivan's apt phrase, a "participant observer." This may lend subtlety to the situation, but it also makes it more complex. In effect, the investigator, because he is part of the research situation, becomes a variable in the research thereby affecting the results. It becomes necessary to consider carefully precisely what the investigator is to do, in order to make sure that his participation does not cause him to commit errors in his evaluation of the situation.

There is also a more restricted meaning for the term observation. This is so-called "systematic observation," first carried on in the twenties and thirties (12, 20) and further exploited in the years thereafter (22). Just as a mining engineer takes a sample of ore, the child psychologist takes a sample of behavior through observing children in one of their natural habitats—a schoolyard, a classroom, a doll-play setting, or a party. It was recognized early that the sample could not be everything the children were doing; samples would have to be directed to be relevant to a particular problem. Illustrative problems might be the popularity of children at a party or their attempts at dominating one another on the playground.

A variety of considerations must be dealt with by the investigator in carrying out research using systematic observations. He must decide upon the time sample to be used; he has to select the particular series of short time periods during which observations are to be made in such fashion that they are representative of the whole period being studied. He must also define the area selected for study and develop a recording scheme for the categories of behavior to be observed. And he must make provision for evaluating the reliability of the observations of his observers. Observer reliability, or more precisely, interobserver reliability, is the extent to which two or more observers agree in independently recording the behavior they are seeing.

A measure of maternal care developed by Rheingold (14) will serve as an illustration. A checklist of 30 mothering and 12 infant activities was prepared. The operations of mothers in caring for their infants were then sampled in the setting of homes and an institution. Some of the mothering-caretaking activities were the ones to be expected— patting, diapering, dressing, and so on. Others had to do with the number and location of the caretakers. Infant activities observed included vocalizing, crying, playing with toys, and the like.

The time observation was one in 15 seconds with recording taking place during the remaining 14 seconds. The cycle was then repeated with four observations in each minute for a total of ten minutes. After a break of five minutes, the cycles started again. For each infant this was done for four hours one morning, followed the next day by the same schedule in the afternoon for a total of eight hours of observation. There were three observers in all, but only one observed an infant in a four-hour period. Another observed that same infant the second day. Observer agreement was calculated for each item. For all items it was found to be 90 per cent—thus showing high observer agreement. The instrument in actual use in this research is described on page 216.

The investigator must select the techniques he is going to use on his particular problem. Unless he can demonstrate that a technique measures something relevant to his problem, his findings, even if they are published, would be ignored by those familiar with the necessity of an investigator's taking into consideration the *validity* of his measures. Validity is demonstrated when an investigator shows that what he is doing actually measures what it is supposed to measure.

Sometimes mere description supplies information that is sufficient to establish validity. In learning studies, for example, we arrange for the child to be faced with a new problem, and if after practice trials the child commits fewer errors and takes less time, we can say that learning has taken place. Or an investigator asks a child to tell which of two lights is the brighter, and can then say that he has studied visual brightness discrimination. Or he asks a child to press a key as soon as a light flashes, and can then say that he has measured reaction time to a visual stimulus. In these instances there is some direct, unequivocal connection between what he says he is studying and what he is actually studying.

In a similar manner marks on a weight scale may be used directly to measure weight. But if weight is used *indirectly* as a measure of nutrition, then it is up to the investigator to demonstrate that there is a necessary connection. The relation between the indicator and what it indicates must be determined, not assumed. Only if it measures what it purports to measure is it valid.

As measures increase in complexity, the assumption of validity becomes risky. A measure of "intelligence" before Binet might have been made up of tonal memory, estimation of distance, speed of reaction, and rate of tapping. These did not sum up to "intelligence" simply because the research man said so. As a matter of fact, when such measures were submitted to critical examination, their claims were found to be false.

Binet abandoned this approach and substituted his familiar measures. But this shift, although ultimately proven to allow increased validity, did not, in itself, demonstrate the fact. Evidence had to be accumulated that the Binet Scale measured what it purported to measure. Such findings as the increase of scores with an increase in age, a high degree of relationship with independently made derivations of intelligence, and success in isolating mentally retarded individuals indicate that the Binet is a valid measure.

Reliability of a measure, as distinguished from reliability of observers, must also be established. Often reliability is found by measuring the consistency of the results by repeating the measures on the same subject a second time. A thermometer reading of a normal temperature that measures it as 90.1 on one occasion, and as 99.3 on another would be unreliable. So, too, psychological measures that fluctuate because of imperfections of the instrument are faulty because they are inconsistent, i.e., unreliable. A psychological measure is considered reliable if it yields substantially the same results on the first and second testings when there is no reason to believe the individual has changed in respect to what is being measured.

Now that certain characteristics have been described, we are in a position to examine some of the techniques used in child psychology. We follow Rosenzweig (16) in classifying the numerous techniques available into objective, subjective, and projective.

Objective Techniques

Objective techniques depend on the subject's behavior as noted by the observer-investigator. The child does something spontaneously in a free situation, such as in a playroom, or on request, as when he reads from a book, pushes a button when he sees a light, learns a problem, or lifts a weight. Characteristics of his physiological processes, such as blood pressure, may also be investigated. In objective techniques, then, the observer looks at the subject and reports on his observations.

Infants are studied by objective methods as in the work of Watson on emotional responses. An extensive review of techniques suitable for use with infants was divided into those used for controlling the stimulus situation and those used for recording responses (15).

Techniques used in controlling visual stimuli will serve as illustrations. In the study of color vision, representative methods of controlling stimuli include colored cards, yarns of known saturation, hue, and brightness, and colored light stimuli. For the study of brightness and form, light without color, two and three dimensional forms on paper and spheres, and cubes and cylinders have been used. With respect to the recording of responses, work with infants has included the use of recording drums, timing devices, conditioning apparatuses, galvanometers and, indeed, the gamut of laboratory devices developed over the years for investigating psychological phenomena.

Cinemanalysis was developed and refined by Gesell and his co-workers. This technique refers to an analytic study of a motion picture film either as a sequence or individually, frame by frame. Exactitude of original observation and accurate recording can be no more vividly illustrated than by this type of motion-picture study. What the infant or child did is available on photographic film long after the original moment and thus may be studied and restudied. The work of Gesell on the development of behavior, frequently referred to throughout this book, is based primarily on cinemanalysis. Figure 1 shows a drawing of his cinemaphotographic observation unit. The observer records the entire behavior, later studying any selected portions which meet his particular research needs.

Figure 1. Schematic drawing of the Yale Photographic Observation Unit.

Measuring general activity of the infant is often done through a device called the stabilimeter. The infant is placed on a platform that is so arranged as to be sensitive to the slightest movement. The movements of the platform are recorded by pens writing on a moving tape. To control other unintended sources of stimulation, the apparatus is frequently enclosed in an observation cabinet so that temperature, humidity, sound, and light can be regulated in order to keep them constant.

Objective measures have been devised for a wide variety of behaviors. Often they are the preferred means of study. The majority of the studies of infant and child reported in the chapters to come will be found to depend on objective techniques.

Subjective Techniques

Subjective techniques make use of what the subject has to say about himself to an observer. They consist of an account of his experiences, points of view, traits, aims, needs, or interests. These statements are taken by the investigator for what they are—disclosures by the subject about himself. Thus, the subject looks at himself and reports to the observer. Asking children what is a good boy or girl, what they think of their parents' disciplinary practices, where the "self" is located, or what is meant by a lie are illustrative of matters investigated by subjective techniques.

Subjective techniques are based on what the individual can reveal and what he chooses to reveal about himself. Some things he does not know and other things he does not choose to tell. In other words, in varying degree, subjective techniques are weakened by selection on the part of the person concerned. Often subjective techniques depend on the subject's interpretation of the meaning of the material at hand without his being given much of a guide or source of reference as to how to interpret it. The autobiography, for example, has the disadvantages associated with its adult use—selection, conscious and unconscious, of what the informant should tell—plus the additional disadvantage of language and other developmental limitations of the child. Subjective techniques nevertheless possess value. It is undoubtedly important to know what a person thinks about himself. An unfounded belief, even if only masquerading as a fact, is still a valuable datum for psychology. In addition, there are certain problems for which subjective techniques are particularly appropriate.

With children the questionnaire and the interview (23) are the most widely used of subjective techniques. Research using the questionnaire, initiated by G. Stanley Hall, has gone through many guises and still has value, as research findings given later will attest. The interview will be illustrated from the work of Piaget (13) who has used the interview as a research tool with revealing and inportant results. Illustrative of his approach is a quotation from a phase of one of his studies of the development of moral judgment in children, aged five to seven. (In the quotation that follows "CLAI" is the code name of the subject.)

CLAI (6): Do you know what a lie is?—*It's when you say what isn't true.*—Is '2 + 2 = 5' a lie?—*Yes, it's a lie.*— Why?— *Because it isn't right.* —Did the boy who said '2 + 2 = 5' know that it wasn't right or did he make a mistake?—*He made a mistake.*—Then if he made a mistake, did he tell a lie or not?—*Yes, he told a lie.*—A naughty one?—*Not very.*— You see this gentleman (a student)?—*Yes.*—How old do you think he is?—*Thirty.*—I would say he is 28. (The student says he is 36.)—Have we both told lies?—*Yes, both lies.*—Naughty ones?—*Not so very naughty.* —Which is the naughtiest, yours or mine, or are they both the same?— *Yours is the naughtiest, because the difference is biggest* (Cf. moral realism).—Is it a lie, or did we just make a mistake?—*We made a mistake.*— Is it a lie all the same, or not?—*Yes, it's a lie.* (13, 140) [1]

From these and a wealth of similar findings Piaget concluded that children of this age, while aware of the distinction between an intentional act and an involuntary mistake, did not stress the distinction and, on the contrary, grouped both together as "lies." It is hard to conceive of other than a subjective technique revealing this particular facet of child life.

Questionnaires and interviews are also used with parents. In recent years an extensively used instrument has been the Parent Attitude Research Instrument (PARI) developed by Schaefer and Bell (17). Each of the 23 five-item scales has been established as empirically homogeneous and each measures a specific attitude, such as supression of aggression, strictness, acceleration of development, or fostering of dependency. Satisfactory internal consistency and test-retest reliability have been established.

Projective Techniques

Projective techniques (7) are concerned neither with consciously held opinions of the subject nor with his overt behavior but with imaginative responses aimed to uncover indirectly the characteristics of the child. The subject reveals something about himself to the ob-

[1] From Piaget (13). Copyright 1948 by the Free Press and published with permission.

server by the way he organizes the material presented to him—the way he projects meaning into neutral or ambiguous material. This is tantamount to having both the subject and the observer "look the other way" at some neutral object that is capable of permitting the subject's personality dynamics to be "projected" out where they can be observed (16).

Since idiomatic responses are sought, no external criterion of what is right or what is wrong is used. Since the situation is arranged in such a fashion that the child does not know what precisely is expected of him, he reveals by his spontaneous manner of handling the stimulus materials some of the ways he organizes his view of the world. As he imparts a structure to the relatively unorganized material, the child reveals his principles of structure which are, it is hypothesized, the principles of his personality.

It is evident that the projective approaches put a heavy burden on the interpreter. Since he is dealing with relatively unorganized material, the clinician or researcher must be alert lest he read his own projections into the material. The observer must ever be aware that his own anticipations are not those to be found à la Tom Thumb. This subjective element in interpretation of projective material has justifiably been a source of criticism. Only through the awareness of this danger, the use of norms, the investigation of validity and reliability, and careful cross-checking can this criticism be partially met.

Projective instruments such as the Rorschach Ink Blots, play techniques, drawings, and the spontaneous telling of stories to pictures all have in common the fact that they all are relatively unstructured and yet provide a standardized stimulus situation. They are stimuli which readily enable the child to impose upon them his own meaning and organization, private and idiosyncratic though they may be. The stimuli are to some degree unclear or equivocal, allowing the child to interpret or give structure to them himself. The same principle applies to the instructions given to the child. For all of these techniques in essence the instructions reduce to, "Do with or interpret the material as you want to."

The Rorschach Ink Blot examination. Looked at without any background of expectation and knowledge, the Rorschach Ink Blots are really meaningless blobs of ink on paper on which somehow we can see something. How can anything meaningful and worthwhile come from such unlikely material? Their "meaninglessness" is the crux of the matter. If the same splotch of ink looks like convicts, lizards and tigers, clowns, or rockets hurtling through space to different individuals, the diversity of response to the same physical stimulus must indeed appear provocative. In view of the identity of the stimulus blot, the differences must stem from the way the individuals perceive it, which in turn must be related to differences in their experience.

This lack of structure and idiomatic reactions to blots are shown in Table 1 which contains hypothetical reactions of two children to a short series of ink blots.

TABLE 1

REACTIONS TO A SERIES OF INK BLOTS

	Child 1	Child 2
Blot A	Pretty flowers	Meat, all bloody
Blot B	Butterfly	A hobgoblin mask
Blot C	Ladies	Icicles
Blot D	Picture puzzle	A gorilla

The two children are seeing the blots but "seeing" them differently. We do not have to know the nature of blots to see that there is a difference between the chlidren. Neither does it require clinical skill to recognize that if we had to choose which child was emotionally disturbed, the modicum of evidence we have would point to it being the second child. Of course, we do not have enough evidence to make any such decision.

Until recently, the use of the Rorschach was hampered by lack of adequate norms for use with children. Fortunately, this has now been remedied in part (1, 2). The newer findings also support the clinical impression that the Rorschach yields meaningful material for children even as young as two-and-one-half-years of age.

Thematic Apperception Technique. The Thematic Apperception Technique (TAT) is another widely used projective device. It consists of pictures somewhat similar to illustrations for magazine stories. The child is told that he is to be shown some pictures and that a story is to be made up for each one. In telling his story he is to imagine what led up to the event shown in the picture, to relate what is happening in the picture, and to tell what the outcome will be. Any questions asked by him are answered noncommittally, with the nature of the situation and kind of story left entirely to the child.

The fundamental assumption concerning projection with the TAT is that the child identifies himself with a central figure in the story. The way the figure is described, the problem faced, and how it is handled are considered to be reflections of the child's own feelings and attitudes. There are many nuances to the scoring and interpretation of TAT protocols which need not be discussed, but are presented in the extensive literature which has appeared (21).

Play technique. For the younger child, play is a natural medium through which he "tells" and "lives" in much the same way as does an adult in using words. First utilized as a diagnostic-therapeutic tool, play came to be employed also as a research technique. Its functioning in clinical settings is reserved for later discussion.

Play technique is used projectively when the child is encouraged to play in spontaneous fashion with toys provided him—to do with them as he wishes, in a manner akin to the story telling of the TAT. Used projectively, however, the child may not only be the author, but also the stage director who sets his scene by selecting from the available props supplied to him. The instructions are simple enough for the children to understand. They have the physical abilities to perform the activities and, above all, they are interested in doing what comes naturally (10).

Playing allows the child to dramatize and verbalize experiences so that he may be understood by those who observe him. The precautions of "systematic observation" are adapted to play technique; there are definitions of the behaviors to be noted, units devised to separate the various kinds of behavioral acts, tests for reliability, and classification of the results obtained.

The media for play technique are varied—drawings, paintings, modeling in clay, puppets, sand, water, and toys of all sorts. Doll play is one important variety. A typical arrangement is pictured in Figure 2.

The variables present in projective doll play were studied systematically by Robert Sears and his associates (18, 19). They were interested primarily in carrying out research problems directed to a variety of theoretical issues (described in later chapters), but they recognized that there had to be a preliminary phase "of brush-clearing and hump-leveling" in which the technique itself was assessed.

Pauline Sears (18) gives a description of procedures subsequent to these methodological studies which yielded conclusions on the most useful ways of carrying on doll play. A family of five *easily identified dolls,* father, mother, boy, girl, and baby, *irrespective of the actual family constellation of the particular child,* was used along with *realistically designed furniture* for six rooms, such as beds, table, refrigerator,

Figure 2. Doll play equipment. (Courtesy of Robert R. Sears.)

and a toilet, and the walls of a house and rooms. The house was presented to the child *with the furniture already arranged in an organized fashion*, but none of the pieces were stationary, permitting easy manipulation if the child wanted to do so. Two, *20-minute sessions* of doll play, usually on consecutive days, were given each subject. In keeping with the projective hypothesis, the instructions were general, amounting to nothing more than calling the child's attention to the whole house and the dolls for the house, and saying that he was to play with them as he saw fit.

During the play itself, there was a *high level of interaction, the experimenter encouraging the child* to continue to play with the material and elaborate what he was doing, but not suggesting any particular play action or offering interpretations. The findings from the earlier methodological studies were underlined. For each of these points, a procedure, *not* followed in the earlier work, were compared with it. For example, an unrealistic arrangement, an hour's session, and a low level of interaction, each had been found to be less productive than the procedures adopted. In studies by other investigators, of course, there is a variation, e.g., no house is supplied, or the family of dolls duplicates the child's own family, or only one session is held.

The clinical approach

The clinical approach [2] is an application of scientific findings within a clearly recognized value system—for example, helping individuals with their difficulties. A concrete illustration of the clinical approach in action was given in Chapter 1 in the setting of the child guidance clinic. Using a clinical approach, the disciplines of psychiatry, clinical psychology, and social work developed information useful in understanding and helping children.

A person comes to the clinician because he is troubled. As has been said of the clinician, the extent to which he helps the patient is his criterion of success (9). Those from whom the patient seeks help have in common an aim, the alleviation of his difficulties, and an approach, the clinical. This aim and this approach hold whether psychiatrists, pediatricians, clinical psychologists, or educational remedial specialists are called upon for this help. The clinician views the person as a *patient,* not as a *subject.*

In the course of diagnosis and treatment, the clinician uses knowledge obtained from the experimental and differential methods. He also draws upon his personal social heritage of insight into human nature and upon his personal clinical experience. Since the patient is a patient, he needs help *now.* The clinician cannot pause, as does the scientist, and depend only on scientifically verified knowledge. Therefore, imperfectly validated diagnostic and therapeutic procedures may be used when there are no thoroughly established scientific guideposts. The clinician does not necessarily hold that what he does could not benefit from scientific verification; it is merely that he cannot always wait before proceeding.

All clinicians share an interest in or focus on the individual child. The nature of the professional activity calls for attention to the child as a person in his own right. The clinician is also interested in the general as a guide to the particular. Hence, his interest in diagnosis and classi-

---

[2] "Approach" is used to designate the matter under consideration to avoid using the word "method" in a second and confusing sense. The writer, as well as others, has in the past used the expression "clinical method" to refer to the questions discussed here. No fundamental change in position is implied by this change in terminology.

fication, a reflection of this general interest, is a device to use other clinical experiences with the single case (9). There is no contradiction between placing primacy upon the unique, because in order to know the unique, we need to know the common background—the background from which the individual case stands out as unique.

The clinical setting may be used for this service function and it may be used for research. In fact, research and practice are hard to distinguish; the noting of similarities and differences leads to both individual diagnostic and therapeutic skill and to the adroit formulation of fruitful hypotheses. In the course of ministering to his patients, the clinician may originate many promising ideas for research from what the patients reveal about themselves, from the professional contacts through colleagues, and from his readings in the literature. Though vague and ill-formed at first, his idea will serve to sensitize him to other instances he finds in these same sources pointing in the same direction as his "hunch." The primary source is his contact with individual patients.

A specific illustration is to be found in David Levy's account (11) of how his work in maternal overprotection came about. He relates that in listening to case reports being given at a staff meeting of the Institute of Child Guidance, someone discussed a woman having a child after ten years of sterility. The record also showed that she was very solicitous and indulgent toward this child. These two events were not in any way considered interrelated at this point. They were merely aspects of a voluminous case record. Levy raised the question to himself: Assuming she wanted the child, would not this ten years' wait cause her to be very solicitous toward him? The idea intrigued him and he began to search the case records of the clinic for cases showing maternal overprotectiveness and then to study the case records to see what other attitudes were shown by the same mother. This is the process of hypothesis forming that takes place in scientific investigation in general.

There is always a ragged advance guard of knowledge in that no man's land between pure speculation and scientific verification. As a clinician, the individual finds that certain ways of viewing the patient strike him as true, and this apparent truth is accepted until verification of its truth or falsity can be brought about. Unfortunately, some clinicians hold that no verification is necessary. They would argue that purely clinical procedures are all that are needed. For example, the clinical procedure that Freud followed to formulate hypotheses was to draw upon his experience with patients, and then to test these hypotheses against later cases. If, in these later cases, consistency with the hypothesis was observed, he considered the hypothesis verified. As Boring puts it:

Freud's technic lay somewhere between that of the experimental psychologist, who alters an independent variable and observes the result, and the philosopher-psychologist, who induces generalization about human nature from the reservoir of his experience. Freud made his generalization from a wealth of specialized experience and then tested his hypotheses out against particular cases, increasing his assurance about the validity of each induction as the number of consistent cases grew. He had, however, no control, either in the sense of the rigorous constraint of contributing factors or in the sense of adding the method of difference to the method of agreement. Indeed, he seems to have been restricted to Mill's method of agreement, pure and simple, a method which by itself is clearly unsafe (5, 586).[3]

It has been demonstrated that scientific methodology embraces both experimental and differential methods. This was done in a setting primarily of the *laboratory approach* to child psychology. Now it is seen that there is also a second, the *clinical approach,* through which research may be initiated.

The differential method is often used. Frequently, clinical research is concerned with tracing back into the past for what has made the child (or adult) patient what he is today, and thus depends on the differential method. The effects of psychotherapy is a distinguished, although barely explored, area in which experimentation may be used.

Clinical research is by no means as fully developed as is laboratory research, because the clinician is usually confronted by a complex situation in which variables are more numerous and more uncontrollable than in a laboratory setting. He strenuously objects to attempts to simplify the task prematurely by experimental control of these variables. His objection may be stated in the form of an aphorism, "Research contamination is clinical enrichment." The clinician wants as much information as possible about his patient in reaching a decision. Since he is dealing with a patient in a complex, everyday setting, all sources are used. But allowing all these factors to vary without the control called for by scientific research, in effect, so contaminates the situation that he cannot trace down the precise effect of each variable.

The classic methods of experimental and differential research called for varying systematically a single factor and restraining all other factors that might affect the dependent variable. This way of studying

[3] From Boring (5). Copyright 1954 by the American Psychological Association and published with permission.

children ran counter to the deeply held conviction of clinicians that the *interaction* among the various factors of the personality of the patient was important.

> In clinical practice it is a commonplace that similar symptoms may arise from quite different origins; or even that the same cause can give rise to very different symptoms. This observation is crucial for the clinician. Expressed conceptually, it tells us that the most basic attribute of an inter-acting set of variables is not the component variables themselves but the *interaction* (9, 43).[4]

Now that statistical techniques are available to permit simultaneous study of several variables used by both laboratory and clinical workers, this source of difference is disappearing. Thus, laboratory and clinical work share a common aim.

The use of different means to secure this information has occasionally created a situation wherein those individuals or experimenters in one tradition or the other have denied the value or even the respectability of the other. Arguments from the traditionalists center on what they believe to be the lack of exactitude of the clinician, while those of the clinician seize on what they consider to be the sterile rigor focused upon trivial problems by the more traditional researcher.

It is neither profitable nor relevant to continue this line of discussion, except to state that the position taken here attempts to draw on both approaches for information. In so doing, the validity of the charges of lack of exactitude of one and the incompleteness of knowledge of the other are tentatively accepted with this important reservation—that instead of rejecting one or the other, both are accepted with, it is hoped, some recognition of the merits and deficiencies of each.

It is recognized that the psychology of the child is not a finished body of knowledge, but a vital and rapidly changing structure. All ap-proaches have something cogent to say about the child. It is manda-tory to use both the most accurate and the most meaningful contributions to a given problem. It does not follow, however, that accuracy and meaningfulness always reside to an equal degree in the same finding. Experimental-differential evidence found in the tradi-tional fashion will be chosen when such is available and when it ap-pears to be the appropriate method for a particular problem. There will be no hesitation, however, in using clinical findings when they seem more meaningful and relevant than data obtained from laboratory investigations.

[4] From Klein (9). Copyright 1949 by The American Psychological Association and published with permission.

Summary

The methods of study used by the child psychologist are those he shares with other scientists—experiments in which he controls to some degree the independent variables; and observations in which he has no control over these independent variables, but, instead, depends on their prior differential effect on children. Both the experimental and the differential methods have their place and their particular advantages and disadvantages.

Specific techniques—instruments and procedures by which to secure the relevant data—are applied to the children. These techniques may be used with either the experimental or differential methods. They may be classified into three major categories: objective techniques which involve the noting of the child's behavior by the psychologist; subjective techniques which depend on the child reporting his observations about himself to the psychologist; projective techniques which depend on the child giving his own meaning and organization to the material to which he is exposed, which is noted and then interpreted by the psychologist. Each of the three categories of techniques and the particular instruments included in these three categories have their particular advantages according to the problem being investigated.

The clinical approach is used for helping disturbed individuals, including children. In the clinical approach diagnostic evaluation of the individual is carried out and a course of treatment followed. In addition to its service function, the clinical approach is also used in connection with scientific research.

From clinical settings the psychologist often arrives at fruitful hypotheses which he then proceeds to investigate. For a variety of reasons, but particularly because of lack of appropriate controls for all relevant independent variables, sometimes research done in clinical settings lacks precision and exactitude in contrast to research done in a laboratory setting.

Choice among research efforts for presentation in the chapters to follow will depend not only on their exactitude but also on their relevance to the problem at hand. On this basis of this last criterion there will be no hesitation in using clinical findings when clinical research is judged important and relevant.

For Further Reading

Suggestions for topical reference may be conveniently grouped as discussions of methodology in general and statistics in particular. A major volume has been edited by Paul H. Mussen, *Handbook of Research Methods in Child Development* (New York: Wiley, 1960). Sponsored by the National Academy of Sciences— National Research Council and prepared by child specialists, this book of over 1000 pages is by far the best single source for information on methodology. Authoritative accounts of practically every major topic and subtopic of this chapter are included.

Two excellent statistical texts are the books by Quinn W. McNemar, *Psychological Statistics:* Third Edition (New York: Wiley, 1962); and by Benton J. Underwood, Carl P. Duncan, Janet A. Taylor, John W. Cotton, *Elementary Statistics* (New York: Appleton-Century-Crofts, 1954). Both contain discussions of central tendency, variability, correlation, and tests of significance of differences, and Underwood *et al.,* in addition, is oriented to the use of statistics in an experimental setting.

References

1. Ames, Louise B. Longitudinal survey of child Rorschach responses: younger subjects two to 10 years. *Genet. Psychol. Monogr.,* 1960, 61, 229–289.
2. Ames, Louise B., Janet Learned, Ruth W. Metraux, and R. N. Walker. *Development trends in child Rorschach responses.* New York: Hoeber, 1952.
3. Anderson, J. E. Methods of child psychology. In L. Carmichael (Ed.), *Manual of child psychology* (2nd ed.). New York: Wiley, 1954, 1–59.
4. Bijou, S. W., and D. M. Baer. The laboratory-experimental study of child behavior. In P. H. Mussen (Ed.), *Handbook of research methods in child development.* New York: Wiley, 1960, 140–197.
5. Boring, E. G. The nature and history of experimental control. *Amer J. Psychol.,* 1954, 67, 573–589.
6. Boring, E. G. Review of E. Jones. The life and work of Sigmund Freud: Vol. 1. *Psychol. Bull.,* 1954, 51, 433–437.
7. Henry, W. E. Projective techniques. In P. H. Mussen (Ed.), *Handbook of research methods in child development.* New York: Wiley, 1960, 603–644.
8. Kessen, W. Research design in the study of developmental problems. In P. H. Mussen (Ed.), *Handbook of research methods in child development.* New York: Wiley, 1960, 36–70.
9. Klein, G. S. A clinical perspective for personality research. *J. Abnorm. Soc. Psychol.,* 1949, 44, 42–49.
10. Levin, H., and Elinor Wardwell. The research uses of doll play. *Psychol. Bull.,* 1962, 59, 27–56.
11. Levy, D. M. In J. Kasanin (chm.), Research in orthopsychiatry. *Amer J. Orthopsychiat.,* 1943, 13, 230–232.
12. Olson, W. C. A study of classroom behavior. *J. Educ. Psychol.,* 1931, 22, 449–454.

13. Piaget, J. *The moral judgment of children.* Glencoe, Illinois: Free Press, 1948.
14. Rheingold, Harriet L. The measurement of maternal care. *Child Develpm.,* 1960, 31, 565–575.
15. Richards, T. W., and O. C. Irwin. Experimental methods used in studies of infant reactions since 1900. *Psychol. Bull.,* 1934, 31, 23–46.
16. Rosenzweig, S. Available methods for studying personality. *J. Psychol.,* 1949, 28, 345–368.
17. Schaefer, E. S., and R. Q. Bell. Development of a parental attitude research instrument. *Child Developm.,* 1958, 29, 339–361.
18. Sears, Pauline S. Doll play aggression in normal young children: influence of sex, age, sibling status, father's absence. *Psychol. Monogr.,* 1951, 65, No. 6.
19. Sears, R. R. Influence of methodological factors in doll play. *Child Developm.,* 1947, 18, 190–197.
20. Thomas, D. S., *et al.* Some techniques in studying social behavior. *Child Developm. Monogr.,* 1929, No. 1.
21. Watson, R. I. *The clinical method in psychology.* New York: Harper, 1951.
22. Wright, H. F. Observational child study. In P. H. Mussen (Ed.), *Handbook of research methods in child development.* New York: Wiley, 1960, 71–139.
23. Yarrow, L. J. Interviewing children. In P. H. Mussen (Ed.), *Handbook of research methods in child development.* New York: Wiley, 1960, 561–602.

3

The Process of Development

OBSERVATION of the process of development in young children is a fascinating enterprise and one which never ceases to delight and amaze parents and other participants. The addition of two ounces to the weight chart, the sudden ability of the baby to hold his head in the midplane rather than turned always to one side, the momentous transfer of a rattle from one hand to the other, the solemn embarking on the first solo step, or the articulation of the first distinct word—all provide manifestations of this potential for development. Furthermore, within certain rather broad limits the development is orderly and sequential. Just as a flower proceeds from bulb to stalk to leaf to bud to blossom and never, except under certain artificial conditions, modifies this sequence or short-circuits one or another stage, the development of the child proceeds in a lawful manner according to certain rules established by the fact that he is a living organism and, specifically, a member of the human species.

For example, every parent knows that, in general, a child will sit before he stands, walk before he talks, gain control of his bowel movements before the ability to regulate bladder functioning, and so on. On the other hand, it is unlikely that every parent or interested observer has noted important, if subtler, general trends in the developmental process. One of the purposes of this chapter is to call attention to some of these trends.

Within every living organism, whether composed of one or myriads of cells, there occurs a constant process of change. When this change is orderly and harmonious and enhances the ability of the organism to adjust to its environment, it merits the label of development. When the pattern of change is of such a nature that loss of function and decreasing ability to cope with the environment are signified, the process becomes one either of chaotic growth, as in the production of certain tumors, or of decline, as in old age. Throughout the life span, from conception to death, there is a constant interplay of the forces of development and decline, with the former far more significant and more readily observable during the period with which this book is concerned.

Development is observable in every phase of life. Whether the field of observation is at the level of the cell, the organ, the organism, or the person, it is still safe to generalize that some development is always occurring. Development begins before birth. During the interim between conception and birth much that is of significance has occurred. But, if we are to understand the process in its entirety, even the moment of conception would mark a tardy entrance on the observational stage. The birth of a baby and the changes which will manifest themselves in all its future behavior represent in one sense a condensation of the entire history of life up to the time of the observation. Reflected in every act will be the evolution of the entire biological drama as performed within the confines of a complex physical and social world.

The fact that development is a *process* rather than a thing makes reliable (i.e., repeatable) observation difficult. In other words, development does not sit and wait for precise measurement of any kind to be made; the organism is constantly changing, and prior conditions can never be exactly duplicated. In actuality no one can claim to have observed the process itself, for development refers to a change detectable from observations made at two or more points on a time continuum. No matter how fine or how gross the temporal units, development itself remains an abstraction, an inference from incremental differences detected by the chosen method of observation. We might take sequential pictures of the metamorphosis from caterpillar to butterfly, project them continuously as motion pictures, and thus apparently compress the development in such a way as to make the *process* itself appear to be the unit of observation. But no matter how much, for purposes of more careful study, we either accelerate or retard representations of development, we can do no more than infer the process from more or less discrete observations made at different temporal points.

Major trends in development will first be identified. Manifestations of development through the reciprocal influences of maturation and learning will then be considered. Finally, the significance of age as a developmental indicator will be evaluated.

Trends in development

Development refers to an orderly change, either in the status of the organism or in behavior exhibited by an organism, which occurs during the interval between successive observations. One major aspect of the scientific study of child development may be conceived as a search for the variables of which that change is a function. For example, changes in weight and height may be shown to be in part a function of the child's nutrition; acquisition of new motor skills might be a function of such things as age of the child and opportunities for practice.

A fundamental prerequisite to an understanding of the process is a recognition of the interaction of all developmental phenomena. Although we can observe a great variety of changes which may appear to be unrelated to one another, it is unlikely that this is ever the case. For the only functionally discrete unit of observation *is the whole child reacting to his total environment*. Only with acceptance of the unitary nature of the entire drama of development can we hope to gain understanding of its range. This integrative view does not, however, assert that the forces acting on different organisms are completely identical in their patterning; for, as will be seen, the factors that influence and shape the developmental patterns in each individual child are diverse. Furthermore, these forces do not operate evenly in different individuals.

Consider, for instance, a mentally retarded child whose condition is clearly caused by some organic deficit, such as brain damage, insufficient thyroid during fetal life, or the like. Equal exposure of this child and of another whose nervous structures are conducive to maximum sensitivity to external stimuli will undoubtedly yield different results. Whereas the former may be relatively impervious to such influences, the latter could be significantly affected by heightened responsivity.

Other, less marked instances of individuality due to differential sensitivity will be encountered. For example, normal newborn infants without neurological defects still show wide differences in sensitivity.

In selecting a locus for studying the developmental process, we might choose to observe certain physical properties (for example, the size of a muscle) or attributes which will be exhibited only when the organism is in action (such as strength of grip on a hand dynamometer). This is the traditional distinction between *structure* and *function*. In order to understand the complex process of human growth, we should know something about each of these aspects of the process and at the same time recognize that they are not completely separable from one another. That is, structure can often be best understood in relation to the function or behavior which it makes possible, and function obviously does not magically occur independently of a particular structure or set of structures.

To place the terms in a developmental setting, it can be said that maturity of structure—that is, the size and complexity of organization of component parts at a given time in relation to the corresponding organization when maximum development has been attained—has relevance only with respect to the functions to be served. It is frequently necessary to use functional criteria to define maturity of structure; the sex organs are considered "mature" when the individual is capable of reproduction. The digestive tract of the infant changes in structure as he grows older, permitting digestion of more complex and varied foods. By feeding him different foods, the mother finds out whether they "agree" with him. Structural readiness, or lack of it, is shown by how his digestion fares when he eats these new foods.

From a study of the development of physical structures, we can learn much about behavior, and vice versa. Indeed, the emergence of certain behavior patterns provides tangible evidence that the destiny of certain physical structures has been fulfilled. In ordinary usage the term *morphology* is used to designate the total process of structural development. Gesell (6) reminds us, however, that the term morphology pertains only to form and that behavior as well as physical substance has shape and form. Thus, we would use the term *morphology of behavior* to designate the orderly patterning of behavior which can be observed in the process of child development.

After this declaration of faith in the inseparability of developmental phenomena, it is perhaps safe to mention that the present exposition will highlight the development of function or behavior rather than that of structure. However, this emphasis does not imply that these features are any more important than others for an understanding of the general process of development, and certainly not that they occur independently. It merely reflects the necessity of adopting a point of view for the sake of exposition.

At times a capricious and paradoxical irregularity may appear to be the only predictable feature of development. This impression will most likely arise from a unit of observation too narrow to permit an event to reveal its contribution to the total pattern. But despite the vagaries of chance that may appear to toy with the growing organism and defeat precise prediction, there is apparent in every aspect of development an orderliness which, within broad limits, permits pre-dictability. Some of the patterns that represent the orderliness in development shall be dealt with now.

Developmental Direction

The general direction of growth moves in fairly steady progression from the head region of the organism downward. This directional gradient has been labeled the *cephalocaudal* (literally, head-to-tail) sequence. A correlated type of directionality is the *proximodistal* (near-to-far) pattern, which means that development proceeds from the axis of the body toward the periphery. That growth should so proceed seems determined by the fact that the most rapid embryo-logical development occurs in or near those parts of the cells destined to be nervous structure. There appears to be a heightened sensitivity in these areas that facilitates faster growth.

This directionality is characteristic of both structural and functional change. That is, observation of the human embryo and infant reveals that at any given temporal point, the head is relatively more devel-oped than the legs and feet (see Figure 4 on page 141). At the func-tional or behavioral level, this means that the baby will gain control of his eyes and head before the trunk or legs, and that he can co-ordinate gross arm movements prior to precise and refined finger manipulation. Further exemplification of this trend in development will be found in subsequent chapters.

Differentiation and Integration

The potential for every phenomenon later to be observed must exist in that original cell from which the organism developed. To a large extent, therefore, development must be the creation of differences, or differentiation, and integration, the continuous reorganization into a unitary whole of the differences which thus emerge. Differentiation and integration are facets of the progressive changes in organization of the individual as a functioning system (*21*).

The original cell from which a child develops may be thought of as *totipotent*, that is, as possessing the capacity to become any structure which will later be found in the embryo. But if growth is to occur, the cell must abandon its totipotency for individuality, its versatility for specialization. As cell division continues, a milestone is eventually reached at which point a parent cell gives birth to a particular kind of offspring—nerve, muscle, or gland—and these resulting cells will in turn produce only their own kind and no other. Coincident with the increased differentiation, however, is an integration which enables the organism at any stage of development always to act as a coordinated whole. The integration of the ever increasing specificities increases the organism's ability to adapt by assuring harmony among the interacting parts of the total structure.

A similar process of differentiation and integration can be found at the behavioral level. In some notable experimental and observational work on the development of aquatic locomotion in the salamander, Coghill (3) observed that the first movements were gross flexions of the entire trunk initiated in the head region and progressing toward the tail. The flexions may occur either to the right or to the left, and as the reaction becomes more complex a second contraction in one direction may occur before a contraction in the opposite direction has dissipated itself. When these alternating coils occur rapidly enough, pressure upon the water is exerted and the animal propelled forward.

Walking on land follows a similar pattern, although of course this cannot proceed until anatomical development has progressed to the point at which limbs have emerged. There are at first only mass movements of the trunk succeeded by gradual differentiation or individuation of action of the limbs as they become able to function relatively independently of the movement of the trunk. Some of these activities are depicted in Figure 3. McGraw (14), who has studied intensively the acquisition of prone locomotion in infants, aptly remarks on the close similarity between this description by Coghill and that which occurs in the human infant.

Although generalization from the behavior of lower animals may often be justified, it is never judicious to do so when a direct check at the level of human behavior is possible. Some authorities have challenged the explanation in terms of differentiation, stressing the point that individuation from a generalized response may be too simple an explanation of the development of similar patterns of human behavior. In the human fetus no observations have been reported of trunk movements in the absence of associated arm movements (2). Certain local reflexes—isolated behavior independent of functioning in other parts of the organism—can be observed at a very early stage in the development of the embryo, and more complex patterns of behavior may represent simultaneous individuation from a generalized response and a knitting together of specific local movements. As early as 14 weeks the human fetus has largely abandoned the generalized response, and, instead, acquired a variety of discrete responses which can appear either singly or in combination (9).

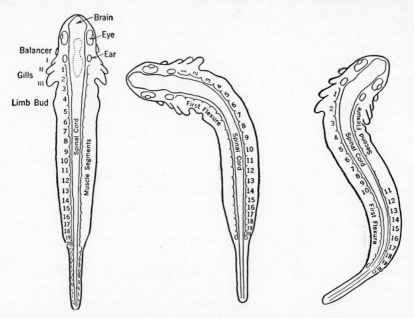

Figure 3. Three diagrams of Amblystoma. (From Coghill (3). Copyright 1929 by Cambridge University Press, and published with permission.)

Another example of this constant interweaving of differentiation and integration can be found in the development of voluntary prehension in young babies. The infant possesses at birth a grasping—sometimes called Darwinian—reflex. Place your finger in a baby's palm and his fingers will close around it with what sometimes appears to be a vise-like grip. This is a clear illustration of a specific response to local stimulation. After about six weeks, however, this reflex begins to disappear or lapses into a relatively static phase during which an object, once grasped, will not be released until the hand makes contact with another surface which relieves the pull on the tendons. When attempts at voluntary prehension begin, this precise gesture is of little or no assistance, and the new skill must be refined gradually by the perfection of ever more precise movements which become differentiated out of gross movements.

Perhaps the most adequate summary of the conflicting points of view would be one which emphasized the simultaneous refinement of a generalized responsivity and a process of integration of isolated reflexes into a total pattern. These in turn split into behavior patterns which enable the organism to adjust to environmental conditions to be encountered later. There would seem to be little doubt that both processes, integration and differentiation, are simultaneously operative in the morphogenesis of behavior. The almost infinite array of behavioral acts of which the human adult is capable apparently cannot be explained completely in terms of a simple process of differentiation from global, generalized performance. Rather there occurs a constant interlacing of differentiation and integration. As soon as a new pattern emerges it will be absorbed into the total, ever-expanding tapestry of development.

Cumulative Influence

Some events predispose the individual to certain kinds of behavior in later life. Behavior at any moment is a function of the life history of an organism and of the stimuli acting upon it. A significant alteration of either the life history or of the stimulating conditions is likely to produce a different type of behavior. The very concept of development makes it necessary to stress the fact that change is one of the essential attributes of all living organisms and thus by implication that the individual is constantly being altered. Although the events or experiences in the life of the child may themselves be ephemeral and transient, the effects may be stable and permanent. A tornado may last only a few seconds, but its brief visit may leave a permanent scar on the geography of a region.

The principle of cumulative influence is a prosaic way of recognizing the wisdom in the poetic reminder that "The child is father of the man." Development is an irreversible process, just as the flow of time itself is irreversible. The importance of early experiences arises not so much because of their immediate impact but because of whatever residual they leave. A traumatic experience or series of experiences in the life of the child—a serious illness, desertion, or rejection by the parents, consistent favoritism shown to another child in the family— should be evaluated in terms of the possible change in the potential for future adjustment as well as the immediate effects. Likewise, favorable early experiences become important not only because they supply immediate need gratification for the child but also because of their contribution to a life history that will be conducive to continuing good adjustment.

Critical Periods

In the Biblical admonition that there is "A time to be born, and a time to die; a time to plant, and a time to pluck up that which is planted," we find a concise statement of much that is implied in the principle of critical periods.   That is, it does provided we interpret it to mean that attempting to plant during the periods when we should be harvesting or vice versa is unwise.

A life history is characterized by a sequence of important formative events sharply etched against a background of seemingly less significant experience.   Furthermore, within any given culture, the critical events will show a high degree of similarity.   For example, for the American child there are such memorable occasions as the first day of school, loss of the first baby teeth, being permitted to walk to school alone, the first date, graduation from high school, and many, many more.   Most of these events will be retained in the memories of the individual; other significant ones, such as the first solo step, the first use of comprehensible speech, and so on, may be remembered only by other family members, but are nonetheless important items on the developmental chart.   Another notable thing about such developmental crises is that an inversion in the time schedule is almost invariably a conversation piece.   The fact that Mary talked before she walked was long a subject of family discussion; that Harold had not had his first date at the time of graduation from high school identified him as deviant from the developmental pattern followed by most of his contemporaries.

The critical period hypothesis suggests that interference with certain developmental phenomena occurring at one point in the life history rather than at another may be of greater significance for establishing future trends.   Evidence for this hypothesis will be sought in a variety of developmental phenomena.

We can find support for the critical period hypothesis at virtually every level of observation.   Some of the developmental changes occur at the cellular level—the transition from an undifferentiated totipotency to a regimentation and constant regrouping of the growing multitude of cells.   During this transition certain critical mileposts appear which demarcate the limits of cellular versatility.   Up to a point the individual cells are apparently susceptible to diverse influences and, as it were, reveal a chameleonic adaptability.   Evidence on this point comes from transplantation experiments on lower animals during the embryonic stage of development.   In such experiments the timing of events is all important.

Suppose some of the cells from the section of the embryo which, if unmolested, would develop into the digestive tract were removed operatively and anchored in the vicinity of the developing heart.   If this were done early enough in the life history of the embryo, the cells would develop into a type associated with circulatory functioning, namely, liver cells.   Their status at maturity would then seem controlled largely by the situation in which they found themselves. Had the same operation been performed only a day or two later, when the cells of the digestive system had made further headway in their initial surroundings, then transplantation would result only in the juxtaposition of heart and intestines.

What is the significance of such a principle when we look at overt behavior? The answer to that question would require first of all some specification as to the type of behavior concerned and also a defense of the position that a timetable is likely to be followed in any dimension of development. With respect to motor behavior there is some experimental data bearing directly on the question.

It has been demonstrated (16) that salamanders kept in an anesthetic solution during the time when aquatic locomotion should be developing can later acquire precise swimming movements after removal from the solution. However, if left in the anesthesia for longer than a certain length of time (about 13 days), the animals are unable to learn to swim normally. This suggests a critical duration beyond which recovery of normal function is impossible. Likewise, in a famous study of motor development, McGraw (13) found that attempts to accelerate the acquisition of certain muscular skills were likely to be ineffectual unless introduced at a propitious time in the child's developmental cycle.

From sources as diverse as the animal laboratory, the classroom, and the psychotherapeutic session have come data relevant to the hypothesis. Although these approaches differ in terminology, in the extent to which hypotheses have been put to experimental test, in the populations to which generalizations can be made, and in the kinds of phenomena selected for observation, all nonetheless show an undercurrent of similarity. That is, they all stress the importance of certain events in relation to the time at which these occur.

A good description of the critical-period hypothesis from the perspective of education is that of Havighurst (7). He uses the term *developmental task* to convey the notion of crises in development with which the growing individual must inevitably cope. A developmental task is defined as "a task which arises at or about a certain period in the life of the individual, successful achievement of which leads to his happiness and to success with later tasks, while failure leads to unhappiness in the individual, disapproval by the society, and difficulty with later tasks" (7, 2).[1] In other words, certain developmental tasks *must* be mastered if the child is to develop normally thereafter. These tasks may arise from physical maturation, from cultural pressures, or

[1] From Havighurst (7). Copyright 1953 by Longmans, Green and Co., and published with permission.

from the emerging personality that must somehow integrate the forces emanating from the other two sources.

Examples of such tasks that must be faced in early childhood are learning to walk, to talk, and to comprehend and manipulate letter and numerical symbols. Inadequate achievement in any one of these tasks handicaps the individual to a certain extent in his efforts to cope with later contingencies. Consider, for example, the handicap of the child who cannot talk when he begins to try to establish rewarding social relationships. These learning tasks represent an approach toward integration of the demands made on the child by his physical organism and by the society in which he must develop. They will obviously differ in various social and cultural groups with respect to the manner in which they will be expressed. At the same time, there should be considerable similarity from culture to culture with respect to the tasks themselves if not to the exact manner in which they are revealed.

The Freudian or psychoanalytic description of character development, in which the meaning of the term "character" is actually closer to that ordinarily ascribed to "personality," could legitimately be labeled a critical-period hypothesis. Psychoanalysts postulate several major developmental stages during which the major focus of biological and psychological energy is to be found in one or another bodily zone of development. For example, during the early weeks and months of life, the major source of gratification and, accordingly, of potential frustration, resides in those activities associated with the intake of nourishment. Calling attention to the importance of these incorporative activities, Freud labeled this the "oral" stage. Later the focus of energy was presumed to shift to the anal and eventually the genital zone, at which time the primary source of gratification or satisfaction of important biological and psychological needs was similarly shifted.

Insufficient gratification at any one of the periods in effect "freezes" a certain amount of mental energy (Freud's term for this was "fixation of libido") and hampers subsequent normal development. That is, the child who does not receive sufficient gratification of his oral needs may be destined to continue to seek substitute (or direct) gratification of such needs and thus be unable to effect smooth transition to the next developmental stage. In line with this theory a child weaned prematurely or too harshly, or, for that matter, indulged too long in sucking activities, might become fixated at the oral level and be unable to move on freely to more mature developmental levels. We shall forego examination of the evidence concerning this contention until later chapters.

In discussing the importance of timing in the developmental process, it is easy to make the hypothetical timetable sound too rigid, with lengthy barren intervals existing between the crisis points. Variability is as likely to be present in the time schedules of different children as it is in the manner in which patterns of overt behavior are expressed. In order to avoid this implication, it must be mentioned here that the critical period for the development of any form of behavior will be to a certain extent unique for each individual and, furthermore, that there is likely to be some overlapping of the periods no matter the conceptual scheme being considered.

Under the rubric of critical periods, several apparently disparate theoretical formulations have been brought together in the foregoing analysis. Considerable space has been devoted to the topic, as it is regarded as a most useful scheme for orienting research data to be presented in subsequent chapters. Also, the hypothesis is congruent with the general approach of this book, in which material has been organized developmentally. In each of the major sections to follow (infancy, the preschool period, the elementary school years), there will be a concentration of attention on those activities regarded as relatively crucial for each period. The present account hardly touches upon the evidence. In later chapters this evidence will be considerably expanded.

Discontinuity and hierarchization. Development is not just an additive or continuous process, such as that taking place in adding to height, weight, or mental age. Other aspects of development show a reorganization in a fashion not predictable from knowledge of the constituents on which it is based. In this way there is a discontinuity of development. Some later forms cannot be reduced to earlier forms; there is an emergence of new ones. Locomotion in the human infant will be found to show four stages—lying prone, crawling, creeping, and walking—and each stage involves movements not present at the earlier stage.

This developmental trend of discontinuity is attacked by some psychologists as being nonparsinonious and, somehow, non-scientific. Properly understood, there is nothing mystical or strange about it. Discontinuity is present in other sciences where it is accepted without question. Water, from two parts of hydrogen and one part of oxygen, has properties not found in either; the tulip bulb contains the potentialities successively of leaves, bud, and blossom, without their being evident in the bulb. The visible spectrum based on quantitative changes of wavelengths shows as certain points an abrupt change, as when passing from violet to indigo, blue, green, yellow, orange, and red.   There is no *a priori* justification for suspicion when the same trend is shown in psychology.   It stands or falls upon the evidence that can be adduced.

The structures and functions show an organization into more inclusive patterns than those exhibited at lower levels.   This particular form of discontinuity is referred to as hierarchization (23).   An illustration may be drawn from the work of Piaget (20).   He conceives the levels or stages of conceptual development as showing a hierarchy of progressive differentiation.   Leaving details for later, each new level of thought, of intelligence, and the like, uses the material of the lower level or levels, but transforms it by greater differentiation and a new coordination so that the new stage draws upon the old, yet becomes a new stage.   Each level is an organized totality which is a new entity understandable in terms of itself.   A new level is fundamentally an innovation, not derivable from the characteristics of the previous levels. How this supposed discontinuity of development may be reconciled with the continuity shown in intelligence tests will be examined later on page 189.

Manifestations of development in maturation and learning

Something is known about the influence of inheritance upon the obviously static, gross factors of the human organism, such as skin pigmentation, sex determination, stature, and eye color.   It is also known that heredity influences some generalized functions—intelligence, aggressiveness, and the like.   In a broad sense, heredity sets the limits of variability.   Complex features of inheritance in which combinations of factors are at work are not yet sufficiently understood to make detailed discussion worthwhile.   Precise specification of the relevant genetic mechanisms and their interrelationships is a task for future research.   Instead of heredity, it becomes plausible to emphasize the maturation-learning relationship.

Generally psychologists characterize the spontaneously appearing and externally instigated forms of behavior development, respectively, as *maturation* and *learning*.   They may be referred to as *manifestations* of development, the ways in which development exhibits itself.

Many definitions have been proposed for both of these concepts.   Of the two, learning has been defined with much less equivocation and with greater community of meaning.   Munn offers the definition "Learning may be said to occur whenever behavior undergoes incremental modification of a more or less permanent nature as a result of activity, special training, or observation" (17, 374).[2] Some of the crucial terms in this definition differentiate learning (a) from fatigue (which would involve a performance decrement rather than an increment), (b) from sensory adaptation (relatively impermanent modification), and (c) from maturation (which should not depend on special activity or training). Changes in function—in ability to do things—are shown by learning. It is not simply a change in physical equipment but in capacity to perform. Details about the learning process are reserved for discussion in a later chapter.

Definitions of maturation have not revealed as much uniformity of thinking. In its original scientific usage the term was used by geneticists to denote the development occurring within the immature germ cell prior to the process of fertilization. Gesell (5) was one of the first writers to use it in a broader sense, applying it to those developmental phenomena that appear to develop in an orderly fashion without the intervention of any known external stimuli. This usage applies the term to *behavior* as well as to changes in the nerves, muscles, and glands which provide the necessary implements for the execution of behavioral activities.

Carmichael (1) avoids the formulation of an explicit definition by proposing three criteria by means of which changes attributable to maturation can be distinguished: (a) the behavior should be demonstrated as developing universally in all or almost all apparently normal organisms of similar physiological endowment; (b) the behavior change must occur in an organism too immature to be able to form stable habit patterns; and (c) the behavior should appear in an organism that has had no opportunity to observe the act in question in another member of the species. Rigid adherence to these criteria, especially the third, would virtually preclude application of the term to any type of human behavior. " 'Maturation' is simply development in which commonly observed differences between individuals are correlated with previous differences in the inner organism rather than in the environment" (10, 29).[3]

The generally unwieldy nature of the concept of maturation and its resistance to precise definition have led some writers to favor abandonment of it altogether and to encourage instead the adoption of what has been called a *convergence* definition in which outer conditions and inner characteristics "converge" (12). As Piaget (19) puts it, or-

[2] From Munn (17). Copyright 1954 by John Wiley and Sons, and published with permission.

[3] From Howells (10). Copyright 1945 by the American Psychological Association, and published with permission.

ganism and environment form an entity. There is an irreducible interdependence that extends over the subject and object. We can never isolate maturation from learning. Maturation, Piaget goes on, is the organism's fundamental tendency to organize experience so that it can be assimilated; learning is the means of introducing new experiences into that organization.

This approach would recognize the inseparability of the maturational and learning processes. Some writers have objected to such attempts on the grounds that fusion of the two concepts makes scientific investigation of the developmental process difficult and shuns precise explanation in favor of global description. Marquis has thus asserted that the two concepts can be separated and proposes as the distinguishing criteria the following: "Both processes, it is true, represent an interaction of organism and environment, but learning is distinguished from maturation by this fact: It represents a modification of the organismic pattern in response to specific stimuli present in the external environment at the time of the modification. Maturation, on the other hand, is a modification of the organismic pattern in response to stimuli present in the inter-cellular and intra-cellular environments which at the given moment are independent of external influence" (15, 347–348).[4]

Although at first glance this definition may appear to emphasize a fundamental distinction, the ambiguity of such concepts as "organismic pattern" and "internal and external environments" soon becomes apparent. Thus we are left with the inevitability of defining both maturation and learning in terms of each other—behavior change not attributable to learning is said to be due to maturation, and vice versa. This is a rather ineffectual way of establishing the independence of either concept. Nevertheless, maturation will be found to be demonstrated primarily through studies in which there is little or no opportunity for learning to take place. Chapter 7, concerned with psychological development in infancy, is replete with illustrations of this way of studying maturation.

Maturation (nature) interacts with learning (nurture) to form development (18). It is important to note that they are not additive (+) but interactive (×). The formula is:

$$\text{Maturation} \times \text{Learning} = \text{Development}.$$

In the absence of experience of a specified sort the equation becomes:

$$\text{Maturation} \times \text{Zero Learning} = \text{Zero Achievement}.$$

Cases in point would be the absence of enuresis in a culture where

[4] From Marquis (15). Copyright 1930 by the American Psychological Association, and published with permission.

there are no bed clothes to soil or the absence of reading in that same primitive group.

Another formula that applies in the absence of maturation is:

Zero Maturation × Learning Opportunity = Zero Achievement.

Illustrative would be the findings of differences between species. In studying this problem the Hayes family (8) reared an infant, female chimpanzee in their own home in as close approximation to care of the human infant as possible. The family endeavored to lavish upon her the affection and to give the instruction that might be given to one's own child. Various motor skills, such as pulling the thumb on the hand, holding the feeding bottle toward her, or later, doing the same to a string to which the bottle was attached, were relatively easily developed. Peek-a-boo, hand clapping, and bead stringing were in her repertoire. In these performances the chimpanzee was not too different from a human infant. But in language there was a marked contrast. Here she was very deficient. She never cried, but gave a chimpanzee bark at five weeks and a bark signifying food at fourteen weeks. Only with great difficulty was she taught to sound approximately a few words. Structural and functional differences from the human did not allow the chimpanzee to show maturation in language development.

It has often been said that progress in any field of scientific inquiry is made less by finding the right answers than by asking the right questions. An integrative approach to the developmental process seems to facilitate phrasing questions in such a way that meaningful answers can be found. Viewed in this way, the proper question becomes one *not* of the priority of maturation or learning. Rather it seems more appropriate to inquire into the extent to which the process of development can be influenced or modified by *intervention*. Is development an inexorable, immutable process which will attain realization regardless of the kind of environmental influences to which the organism might be exposed? Or, if it is modifiable, to what extent is this possible? And, as might be predicted from the discussion of critical periods, are there times when modification is more feasible than others? Likewise, if emerging functions are interfered with, is this likely to have a deleterious effect on the total development? To these questions considerable attention will be devoted in later chapters.

The significance of age

The relating in some lawful way of a child's behavioral manifestation to age indicates that the psychologist is dealing with a developmental characteristic (11). This can be expressed in the formula $R = f(A)$, in which response R is whatever behavior the research man may be interested in studying, while age A represents chronological age or some variant, such as mental age. Many problems can be studied in terms of this formula, answering such questions as what a newborn infant, a child of two, or a child of seven can or cannot do. But this is not enough.

The task of the psychologist is not complete when he demonstrates a relationship between age and a psychological characteristic. To relate a given vocabulary to a given age in children is informative, but it by no means explains the association that has been found. Psychologists want to be able to specify the determinants of this characteristic, to isolate the antecedents that brought about its psychological quality. Something other than sheer age is operative in most of the problems of child psychology.

Size of vocabulary, for example, can be related to age in a reasonably consistent way, but, despite increase with age, there is wide variability at a given age. Other aspects of the child's history must be examined to discover the factors that help to account for its size, rather than saying that his vocabulary is so and so *because* of age. Moreover, knowledge of age alone does not tell how to manipulate the phenomena in question for the best interest of the child and of society. If we wish to deal with variables under manipulatable control, we must isolate characteristics other than age itself, a factor which we cannot prevent changing in a given child.

Summary

The concept of development—orderly and harmonious change that enhances the ability of the organism to adjust—has been examined in its myriad ramifications. Any discussion of trends in development leads to emphasis on the fact that the unit of observation is the whole child reacting to his total environment. There is also the recognition that we must break down this unity for purposes of some of the discussions that follow. This is the case in the distinction made between structure and function. It is also the case in discussing the more prominent trends in development, such as developmental direction, differentiation and integration, cumulative influence, critical periods, and discontinuity and hierarchization.

Manifestations of development have been seen in forms of behavior development called maturation and learning. These two are distinguished hereafter, although they are only aspects of the same fundamental process.

The significance of age as functionally related to developmental characteristics was also noted. Important though the demonstration of these relationships may be, the additional task of isolating and measuring the antecedents accompanying age in relation to their consequents for development is also necessary.

For Further Reading

A valuable book devoted to the process of development has been edited by D. B. Harris, *The Concept of Development: An Issue in the Study of Human Behavior.* (Minneapolis, Minn.: University of Minnesota Press, 1957). Here J. E. Anderson's, "Dynamics of development: system in process," presents a detailed analysis of the factors in the process of development in a different fashion from that followed in the text. In the same volume Viktor Hamburger's, "The concept of 'development' in biology," gives a lucid account of biological development in which he argues for priority of maturation over learning. Aspects of development falling within the scientific method, biology, psychology, education, humanism, history, and the social sciences are the bases of other chapters. Leonard Carmichael in a chapter, "The onset and early development of behavior," in the book edited by him, *Manual of Child Psychology:* Second Edition (New York: Wiley, 1954), gives a detailed account of development written by a psychologist for psychologists. The chapter by Gesell, "The Ontogenesis of Infant Behavior," in the same book gives a characteristic account of his view of development.

References

1. Carmichael, L. Ontogentic development. In S. S. Stevens (Ed.), *Handbook of Experimental Psychology.* New York: Wiley, 1951, 281–303.
2. Carmichael, L. The onset and early development of behavior. In L. Carmichael (Ed.), *Manual of child psychology* (2nd ed.). New York: Wiley, 1954, 60–185.
3. Coghill, G. E. *Anatomy and the problems of behavior.* New York: Macmillan, 1929.
4. Gerard, R. W. *Unresting cells.* New York: Harper, 1940.
5. Gesell, A. Maturation and the patterning of behavior. In C. Murchison (Ed.), *A handbook of child psychology* (2nd ed., rev.). Worcester: Clark University Press, 1933, 209–235.
6. Gesell, A. The autogenesis of infant behavior. In L. Carmichael (Ed.), *Manual of child psychology* (2nd ed.). New York: Wiley, 1954, 335–373.
7. Havighurst, R. J. *Human development and education.* New York: Longmans, Green, 1953.
8. Hayes, C. *The ape in our house.* New York: Harper, 1951.

9. Hooker, D. Reflex activities in the human fetus. In R. G. Barker, J. S. Kounin, and H. F. Wright (Eds.), *Child behavior and development.* New York: Mc-Graw-Hill, 1943, 17–28.

10. Howells, T. H. The obsolete dogmas of heredity. *Psychol. Rev.,* 1945, 52, 23–34.

11. Kessen, W. Research design in the study of developmental problems. In D. B. Harris (Ed.), *The concept of development: an issue in the study of human behavior.* Minneapolis: University of Minnesota Press, 1957, 36–70.

12. Koffka, K. *The growth of the mind: an introduction to child psychology* (2nd ed.). London: Routledge & Kegan, Paul, 1928.

13. McGraw, Myrtle B. *Growth: a study of Johnny and Jimmy.* New York: Appleton-Century-Crofts, 1935.

14. McGraw, Myrtle B. Maturation of behavior. In L. Carmichael (Ed.), *Manual of child psychology.* New York: Wiley, 1946, 332–369.

15. Marquis, D. G. The criterion of innate behavior. *Psychol. Rev.,* 1930, 37, 334–349.

16. Matthews, S. A., and S. R. Detwiler. The reaction of Amblystoma embryos following prolonged treatment with chloretone. *J. Exp. Zool.,* 1926, 45, 279–292.

17. Munn, N. L. Learning in children. In L. Carmichael (Ed.), *Manual of Child Psychology* (2nd ed.). New York: Wiley, 1954, 374–458.

18. Olson, W. C. Developmental theory in education. In D. B. Harris (Ed.), *The concept of development: an issue in the study of human behavior.* Minneapolis: University of Minnesota Press, 1957, 259–274.

19. Piaget, J. *The origins of intelligence in children.* New York: International Universities Press, 1952.

20. Piaget, J. *The psychology of intelligence.* Paterson: Littlefield, Adams, 1960.

21. Schneirla, T. C. The concept of development in comparative psychology. In D. B. Harris (Ed.), *The concept of development: an issue in the study of human behavior.* Minneapolis: University of Minnesota Press, 1957, 78–108.

22. Spemann, H. Some factors of animal development. *Brit. J. Exp. Biol.,* 1925, 2, 493–504.

23. Werner, H. The concept of development from a comparative and organismic point of view. In D. B. Harris (Ed.), *The concept of development: an issue in the study of human behavior.* Minneapolis: University of Minnesota Press, 1957, 125–148.

4

Socialization, Behavior
Tendencies, and Personality

How does the child become a particular person in a particular culture? The answer lies in how his unique characteristics emerge, those which mark him as different from other persons, and in how the characteristics he shares with other persons in his culture come about. Both types of characteristics depend on how his living in a world of other persons influences his development. In short, we must evaluate the process of socialization and its influences on personality formation.

Socialization

Socialization (7, 33, 34, 35) is the process of helping children to become functioning adult members of their society. Through this process an individual becomes a member of a society by achieving ways of experiencing and behaving which conform with that society's values. The child learns the norms of his society—the common forms of behavior expected from him. Within the limits of what is considered customary and acceptable, the infant, and the child he is to become, is encouraged by his parents to perform certain activities; other activities are viewed neutrally, while still others are actively discouraged. For example, parents try to channel sexual behavior, to regulate aggression toward one's fellows, and to help their child find a balance between dependence and independence upon others in ways expected in their culture.

The child is led by the individuals in his social environment to develop an actual behavior repertoire considerably narrower in range

74

than that of which he is capable. A homely example of this process is the difficulty children in an English-speaking culture have with the French "u." In learning to speak French this letter gives English-speaking students great difficulty. It seems to be an unnatural sound that is very hard for us to utter correctly. And yet, as a basic speech sound our infants have had it in their repertoire to the same extent as do infants in French families. It dropped out with us because it does not appear as a sound in English. In a broader view, all cross-cultural studies in the field of cultural anthropology stand witness to differences among groups of individuals due to the influence of this process of socialization. For example, the various studies of Margaret Mead aim at showing the ways socialization varies from one society to another.

We are justified in speaking of socialization without being mystical in any sense. Socialization is always mediated by individuals, but it does rise above them in that you can detach the teaching from the teacher. Illustrative is the comment: "If a random third of the parents of Cambridge, Massachusetts, were to die tomorrow and their children were to be socialized by their surviving relatives and friends in Cambridge, it may safely be predicted that what these children would learn—would be approximately the same taking the group as a statistical whole as if their parents had survived" (23, 15).[1]

Socialization and Learning

Socialization, a means by which conventional patterns of behavior are acquired, is a process of learning. Through socialization a child learns to fit in with the manners and customs of the family, the neighborhood, the community, and the society in which he finds himself. Since we are concerned with learned behavior, it follows that social influences on the child's personality can eventually be understood in terms of learning principles. To be sure, the patterns of socialization in terms reducible to the details of learning theory remains to be worked out, but there is nothing insuperable about this as a task for the psychologists of today and tomorrow.

Socialization and Constitutional Factors

Even biological, constitutional factors are subject to socializing influences. The infant's maturational equipment for eating, defecating,

---

[1] From Kluckhohn and Mowrer (23). Published 1944 by the American Anthropological Association, and used with permission.

and sleeping from birth is faced with a series of social pressures (10). He is expected to eat certain things at certain times in a certain manner, to eliminate waste in a prescribed place and manner, and to sleep at certain times in a prescribed object and even for a prescribed length of time. For each of these functions his particular society prescribes what is right and proper, although differing radically one from the other on what this might be. Eventually his eating is regulated not only by a changing blood sugar level, but also by the family meals, his elimination not only by internal pressures, but also by the aforementioned time and place, and his sleep behavior not only by biological demands, but also family schedules.

One research example will suffice. The experiment of Dorothy Marquis (27) is described on page 163. In the context of the present discussion, what she demonstrates is that variation in feeding schedule during the first ten days of life leads to a learned modification of the restlessness accompanying hunger on the part of the infants she studied. The onset of restlessness in these infants becomes associated with their feeding time established by other persons. Thus, her study illustrates the modification of constitution by socialization practices.

The Agents of Socialization

Elements of the social situation in which a human infant finds himself at birth are universal. Everywhere, when infants are born, they are helpless and dependent on adults. Everywhere infants are suckled, subjected to restrictions for their protection, and provided with care and training.

Children learn from certain individuals and not from others. Insofar as these persons are sources of learning for a particular child we can speak of them as agents of socialization. The mother serves as the major agent through which the infant and younger child learns. She selects those forms of socialization she considers desirable for her child to learn. Even in infancy the father is a secondary source of learning, as are other individuals in the immediate family, such as siblings.

As the child enters early childhood, the agents of socialization with which he comes in contact increase in number. Neighborhood children and preschoolmates enter the picture as do adult supervisors such as nurses, baby sitters, preschool teachers, and the like. It is in late childhood that the peers become very important. In fact, Chapter 17, concerned with later childhood, is devoted to consideration of their significance.

In addition to the parents, other agents of socialization come into prominence with the widening of his social horizon as the child grows older. Thus, his siblings, his peers, his teachers, and in varying degrees, other adults become part of each child's social scene and serve to encourage and to discourage specific activities.

Countless little acts must be done in a "right" or "proper" way and are learned without either agent or child being aware of his role as teacher or learner. Socialization takes place whether we know it or not. Often socialization is imparted implicitly and learned incidentally. We have some difficulty in seeing the process of socialization as separate from ourselves—at a distance as it were. We are so deeply immersed in our own cultural traditions that we find it difficult to visualize any other way of carrying out a given task of child rearing, say toilet training, except as we are doing it (1). Each of us is apt to feel that his particular ways are the only proper ways to think and to behave.

We "know" that, of course, breakfast starts with orange juice and ends with the last sip of coffee. Of course, we have eight (plus or minus one) hours of sleep. Of course, babies use potties. But in other societies, of course, you would not be a man until you have had a vision, and, of course, twenty varieties of ice formation are obviously distinguishable, each with its right name, and no other.

Socialization Practices in Different Societies

Socialization practices differ from society to society. In one a given practice may be condemned, in another not even seen as a "practice" and hence accepted. There is abundant evidence that in the absence of organic bases, a given problem does not develop in children unless the conditions for its formation are present in the environment. To use an obvious example, in a primitive culture there are no schools and hence no truancy. Somewhat less obvious is the absence of stealing in certain cultures. Stealing as a symptom occurs only in cultures where there is a strong emphasis on property rights. Among the Kaingang Indians of Brazil there is no such emphasis and thievery is absent (15). Other behavior problems show this relation as well. Enuresis (bed wetting) is not uncommon in the American culture, but in many primitive groups it is nonexistent. Consider the Pilaga Indians of the Amazon area. From the standpoint of our group, they have no toilet training. They have no beds to soil and are indifferent to urine (16). Why should there be toilet training under these circumstances? It is no wonder that enuresis is not present among the Pilaga, since the conditions for its appearance are not present.

There is present in each society a whole series of attitudes about what is desirable and undesirable. There is a patterned consistency within a given society which allows some accuracy in predicting how people in that society will think and feel. Consequently, socialization attitudes that characterize a society have been subjected to study. One of these is the general attitude that members of these societies hold toward children as such. In some societies, a child is desired and tenderly cared for. In others, he may be considered a nuisance and treated as such. Other societies fall between these extremes of indulgence and severity.

An illustration of socialization in different societies may be drawn from the work of Whiting and Child (35), who studied comparatively the literature available about a large sample of societies including one from middle-class families in our own society. The task they assigned to their judges was for each independently to read the same material about each of the societies and then to arrive at ratings on certain selected variables. Among other categories were a considerable number concerning various aspects of child training. For each society they selected for study, ratings were made on such matters as age at, and severity of, both weaning and toilet training. The ratings with which we are concerned at the moment, though on a variety of topics, have in common the fact that they run from one extreme of indulgence to the other of severity.

One source of variation in child training they investigated was the extent to which each society allowed the child initial indulgence in nursing. They included in this category factors such as the duration of the nursing behavior permitted, the freedom the infant was permitted in the performance of nursing, and the encouragement the mother gave to the infant to nurse. They found that about half of the societies showed typical high oral indulgence, whereas the other half showed gradually decreasing degrees of oral indulgence.

The lowest (most severe) rating on indulgence was given the Marquesans. To illustrate the attitude in this culture (25), Marquesans believe nursing contributes to difficulty in raising since the children will not be properly submissive if given too much breast feeding. Moreover, women take great pride in the shape and firmness of their breasts which are important in sex play. Nursery periods are short and feeding times irregular, dependent on the convenience of the mother rather than the needs of the child. It was on the basis of this and similar evidence that the raters marked this particular society as severe in their attitudes toward nursing.

The sample from our own society was the next most severe after the

Marquesan in the matter of nursing. This rating in the direction of severity was influenced considerably by the short duration of nursing in the American middle-class group and the low degree of indulgence of oral interests permitted these American infants. In the other sources of variation on child training studied, the American group was not necessarily as severe as in the instance just given. Characteristically, however, the American group was on the severe rather than the indulgent side. There is a current widespread impression that the practices of the American middle-class are changing in the direction of greater indulgence; thus the results obtained in the early forties may not adequately represent this group at the present time. Further discussion of this question of the degree of severity in classes in our society is given in the next section.

It is not necessary to turn to primitive societies to find differences from our society in maternal attitudes. A cross-cultural study was conducted in New Haven, Connecticut and Basle, Switzerland (18). The same questions concerning child-rearing practices were asked of 40 mothers from each country of upper-lower and lower-middle class. The questions concerned stuttering, lying, masturbation, bed wetting, and weaning. More than the American mothers, the Swiss mothers had recourse to heredity and poor upbringing as explanations of the causes of childhood disturbances and tended to be stricter in their enforcing a demand that the children "grow up." The Swiss mothers seemed to regard the children as little grown-ups, while the Americans saw them as "kids" to be allowed more time to grow up.

Different Attitudes toward Socialization Practices in our Society

There is no universal American pattern of socialization practice. Some conception of the diversity can be obtained from the findings of Sears, Maccoby, and Levin (32), who report comparative data on three communities. Two of these were small New Mexican villages, just a few miles apart: Homestead, with a population drawn mostly from the dust bowl areas of Texas and Oklahoma, and the other, Rimrock, containing mostly old American stock with Mormon traditions. The third community was from a suburban metropolitan area of New England. Whereas 50 per cent of the Homestead mothers had completed weaning before the child was eight months old, none had in Rimrock. In the New England sample, 37 per cent had completed weaning by this age. In questioning about which parent had the chief responsibility in deciding child-rearing policies, the mother said the father did in 8 per cent of the New England sample, in 22 per cent of the Homestead group, but in 67 per cent of the Rimrock group. These findings indicate some of the diversity to be found.

In our society there has been considerable controversy concerning the proper way to bring up children, this being based on two different conceptions of what is healthful and socially useful in socialization. Escalona, in commenting on child-rearing practices, contends that a remarkable change has taken place recently. The older, disappearing point of view she characterizes as follows:

> Bodily and mental health is based on an orderly, strictly scheduled existence from early childhood onward. Prescribed formulae are superior to breast feeding, chiefly because the ingredients are known and nutrition becomes, therefore, a controlled process. When babies or children cry without recognized legitimate cause it is best to let them cry it out. It is the responsibility of adults to teach children what is "right" and what is "wrong" in regard to meal times, sleeping hours, play interests and most other activities (9, 158).[2]

She comments that this point of view is one which is highly rational, largely based on a combination of adult patterns of living and of knowledge of the scientific facts of physical growth. She could also have added that the prevalence of behavioristic teachings, so ably advanced by John B. Watson (who wrote a popular book on child care), was also influential in stressing the use of impersonal practices of child care.

This point of view about child care is in keeping with the belief in a spirit of stability of our society that was characteristic of the early decades of this century. In recent years, this spirit of certainty and belief in stability has diminished. The atom bomb, and all that goes with it, has forced upon us a reluctant belief that our main source of danger is human nature itself. An appreciation of the irrationality of man has come upon us. The considerable influence of psychoanalysis in shaping newer views about socialization Escalona considers to be a consequence, not a cause, of our loss of a stable value system.

The view that there has been a shift in attitude in recent years is supported by the findings of Radke (30). She found that parents showed significant differences in behavior toward their children as compared with what they had experienced previously from their parents. In the younger generation, there was a less dictatorial quality to discipline, a greater participation on the part of the fathers, and a greater consideration for the child's interests and needs.

What is this newer point of view about socialization? Quoting Escalona's account:

[2] From Escalona (9). Copyright 1949 by the Society for Research in Child Development, and published with permission.

It is now thought that it is up to us as adults to meet the needs of the younger child, rather than to expect early adaptation from him.   To wit, self-demand schedules and all that goes with them. . . .   Among the needs of the young child we recognize the need for affection and for an intimate relationship with the mother as of very great importance, tending to evaluate it as more crucial than the need for good physical care.   We prize self-expression, sincerity of feeling and spontaneous interest above good manners, self-restraint, or intellectual accomplishment (9, 160).[2]

A characteristic procedure arising from this point of view that she mentions is self-demand feeding.   This procedure refers to allowing the infant to express his need for food himself and set his own rhythm of feeding rather than being fed by the clock and by the ounce.

The two general points of view have never been given commonly agreed-upon, identifying names.   For convenience, they will hereafter be referred to as the "regulatory" and "permissive" points of view, respectively.   The quotation marks serve to remind us that these terms are tentative.

The very fact that contrasting child-care practices are held in our society and the further fact that protagonists of both points of view are able to point to supporting evidence drive home the realization that the empirical data at our command must be too scanty to bring about stabilized practice.   It may even be that change from one to the other point of view reflects changing biases in the subcultures in which it takes root, rather than mirroring new, firmly established knowledge.

Research workers in the field of child personality are also parents and citizens.   The contrasting regulatory and permissive views inevitably influence their thinking.   Their attitudes expressed through this influence may serve to some extent as a guide for the research problems they choose to formulate and investigate.   The relation is reciprocal; their research and clinical findings influence attitudes of the general public toward problems of socialization.

By and large, workers of a psychoanalytic orientation hold to a "permissive" point of view—although not to all of the excesses about their views which are attributed to them.   They tend to stress the importance of the relationship of the child to his mother during his early years.   If the relationship is satisfactory, it is believed that there is every likelihood that the child will develop similar satisfactory relationships in later life with other people.   Conversely, if the relationship develops unsatisfactorily, it is considered likely that the child will become disturbed emotionally to a greater or lesser degree and that he may be confronted throughout his life by difficulties in personal relations.

Child specialists subscribing to the regulatory point of view are more heterogeneous. It would seem that those who stress constitutional and biological factors tend to be in this group. In general, members of this group tend to see the infant and child as more capable of self-regulation and more able to stand vicissitudes and come through unscathed than do representatives of the permissive point of view.

At Yale University School of Medicine, a research project has been organized to investigate the rival positions. It is too early for their answers on the major issue to be definitive, but some relevant results have already been published (19, 20, 21). One study (21) adopted the hypothesis that either extreme rigidity (regulatoriness) or permissiveness would be associated with problem child behavior. Case records of 50 mothers and infants were chosen from their files for analysis. The children's behavior was rated in the areas of feeding, sleeping, toilet habits, and socialization in terms of degree of problem behavior shown. Evidences of emotional maladjustment in the child in areas other than these four were also sought from the records. The mother's behavior was defined as to degree of rigidity-permissiveness in her dealings with the child. Either extreme on the scale of maternal behavior was taken to represent deviant handling. Those falling in the middle area of the rating scales were considered as representing optimal and flexible handling.

In their first analysis of results, the investigators found that comparison of the rigid with the overpermissive parents showed there were nonsignificant differences in the problem behavior of their children. Thus, the question of whether regulatory or permissive parental behavior is superior in avoiding problem behavior in children, so far as this study is concerned, is answered that extremes of both are equally pernicious. For final analysis of results they divided the mothers into optimal and deviant (rigid and overpermissive being classed together). To quote their own words on the results:

> The following statistically significant relationships were found: within the first year, deviant maternal practices in sleep were associated with problem behavior in the child, though no relationships were found between practices and behavior in the areas of feeding, toileting, and socialization. In the second and third years, significant relationships were found between deviant maternal practices and problem behavior in the child in all four areas. Deviant adjustment to the maternal role was found to be related to deviant practices in sleep and socialization during all three years. Similarly, children showing other evidences of emotional maladjustment were found to have a significantly higher proportion of sleep and socialization problems (21, 93).[3]

[3] From Klatskin et al. (21). Copyright 1956 by the American Orthopsychiatric Association, and published with permission.

Evidently, optimal practice, as distinguished from either extremes of rigidity or overpermissiveness, makes for less problem behavior in infants and young children. Important though this finding may be, it still leaves unanswered the question as to the relative superiority of the regulatory or of the permissive points of view. The results do suggest that an extreme position of regulation expressed in rigidity and an extreme position of permissiveness expressed in overpermissiveness are both to be avoided in the interest of the child's adjustment.

Social-Class Difference in Socialization Practices

Acceptance of the concept of social class is a recognition that people live, think, work, and play in different ways. One of the forms of distinctions among social classes that has been seen as worthy of investigation is the possibility of class differences in parent-child practices. Presumably differences in socialization may be mediated through the respective child-rearing practices of these social classes.

In contemporary thinking three divisions of social class are generally accepted—upper, middle, and lower—with each of these three subdivided into an upper and lower group, making six groups. The so-called upper-class category is somewhat more tenuous than the others, although there is certainly agreement that numerically it is smaller than the others. Since it is also a group in which little research evidence is available, attention will be directed to the middle and lower classes. The upper-middle class includes professional and technical workers, managers, officials, and proprietors. The lower-middle class would involve clerical and sales workers. The upper-lower class would comprise craftsmen and foremen. In the lower-lower class would fall machine operators, laborers, and service workers. In more detailed classifications of social class the number of years of education and place of residence are combined with occupations.

From the forties to the present time shifts in attitudes toward permissiveness-regulatoriness seem to have taken place. In the forties a research investigation (8) reported class differences between lower- and middle-class groups. One hundred mothers, about equally divided as to social class, were interviewed about their practices concerning weaning, thumb sucking, cleanliness, and environmental exploration, and concerning the sex and age roles they expected their children to play.

Middle-class families were generally found to be more exacting in their expectations. In middle-class families training was begun earlier, more emphasis was placed on responsibility, and closer supervision was observed. In these families, fewer children were breast fed; when breast feeding did occur it was carried on for a shorter time. Three times as many middle-class children as lower-class children were reported by their mothers to be thumb suckers. Bowel and bladder control were begun earlier in the middle-class families, although the children did not achieve control any earlier. This study which indicated more rigid child care practices in middle-class groups was conducted before the permissive point of view became as prevalent as it is today.

In a study conducted in 1951 and 1952, it was reported (26) that middle-class parents were more permissive than lower-class parents, thus disagreeing with the earlier studies. Sears and his associates (32), in a more detailed examination of the data used in the previous study, demonstrated that the middle-class mothers were gentler than the working-class ones. They were more permissive in toilet training, in allowing dependency, in sex training, toward aggressiveness, and seemed to impose fewer restrictions and demands on their children. Only in infant feeding was there no significant difference in the direction of greater permissiveness on the part of the middle-class group.

An analysis (5) of seven unpublished and nine published reports of researches concerned with children as early as 1928 and as late as 1957 indicated certain general conclusions. Not only were mothers at all social-class levels becoming more permissive concerning infant feeding and weaning, but also the middle-class mother as contrasted with the lower-class mother in the past was now more permissive concerning weaning, feeding, and toilet training.

Differences in degree of permissiveness are capable of modification by training. In a New Haven hospital a study (19) was conducted using prospective mothers drawn from various social classes. These mothers participated in an elaborate teaching program which stressed leniency and flexibility. One year after exposure to the program, the participating families were studied as to their practices in regard to feeding, toilet training, strictness of regime, and the degree of the father's participation in the care of the child.

On the whole, there was a shift in the direction of greater leniency in all classes although with different degrees of leniency. When related to social class (upper-middle, lower-middle, and upper-lower) differences in the direction of earlier date of beginning of toilet training and in greater strictness of regime were found in the lower-class families. However, significant differences were not found among the social-class samples in duration of breast feeding, leniency in the feeding practices, or the extent of father's participation. The results indicate that parent-child care practices *are* capable of modification, and also that education may result in a reduction in so-called social-class differences. The findings (5) suggest that changes in infant care are most likely to be instituted in those segments of society having ready access to individuals and institutions that advocate change, such as clinics, counselors, and baby-care literature.

Familial and Individual Differences in Socialization Practices

Emphasis upon class differences should not leave the impression that other sources of distinction do not cut across these lines. Age differences of parents, for example, with some older than others, although from the same social class, would presumably show differences in their practices. Moreover, within a given class, other sources of difference would appear.

For instance, two men may work side by side at lathes in a large industrial plant and still be different in almost all other respects, except for social class. One may be a recent immigrant from a rural region in Poland, married to a girl from a neighboring village, a devout Catholic, from a large family dominated by a grandmother with whom his family lives. The other may be a fourth-generation Negro from a large Southern city, separated from his parents at birth, with neither present religious affiliation nor family ties. Can we expect the views on child rearing of these two men to be so guided by class conditions as to reduce the influence of their different backgrounds to a position of minor importance? It is imperative to consider familial and individual differences in socialization practices.

Whether the baby is satisfying or frustrating depends upon (1) the personality of the parents; and (2) the personality of the child.

(1) To the parent the child may be frustrating or satisfying according to his or her own particular makeup. If the mother receives satisfaction from gratifying needs of the helpless (nurturance), then motherhood serves as a satisfying outlet. If she is a dominating person, her relationship to her child may be rewarding. If she needs to have a feeling of belonging, then the addition of the child to her family may serve to gratify this feeling. On the other hand, if she requires an orderly scheduled environment, or a great number of social contacts, or a freedom from responsibility, then a baby might be seen as a nuisance or as a restriction. Another even more pervasive factor in determining how she views motherhood is her concept of the role and significance of motherhood. A mother may place a high value upon motherhood, feeling that it is a fulfillment of her personality; another

mother may place a low valuation upon it, seeing motherhood as a series of monotonous routines.

(2) The characteristics of the child contribute to determining parental reactions. His physical appearance, whether pleasing or displeasing, is one such characteristic. His development, whether advanced or retarded, may be another. But often the particular characteristic is not, in itself, decisive in how he is received in the family. Any one characteristic may be pleasing or displeasing according to its reception by the parents. To some parents an active child would be a joy; to others, he would be a source of distraction. Similarly, mischievousness or obedience may be reacted to differently, sometimes serving as endearing characteristics, sometimes as repelling ones. In any case, personal characteristics of the infant help to determine the parents' attitudes. Chronologically, the parents' personality comes first and starts the sequence of interactive behavior. But once the infant is perceived by them, no matter the nature of their perception, he becomes a stimulus to them and influences their behavior toward him. The relationship is circular, the cause-effect relation reciprocal.

Parent behavior, moreover, is not rigid and unchanging, even within a specific family. Not only may parents vary in their responses toward different children, they will also vary with respect to their handling of the same child. One study (29), for example, found some mothers who were highly punitive in regard to property destruction, but quite the opposite regarding sibling aggression. Some attention to such variations must be paid in the discussion of socialization. Within this welter of differences—societal, social-class, familial, and individual—we must search for the regularities of personality as they relate to them and interact with them. Since our interest is primarily in the personality of the child which emerges from the process of socialization it is appropriate now to turn more directly to that question.

Socialization and Role

A role is the customary behavior that society expects of a child as a member of a particular group. In a family a boy is a son (2); in a school he is a pupil; in a play group he is a peer. In each role he behaves somewhat differently. To give one illustration for each role in a middle-class culture—as a son, obedience is expected of him; as a pupil, he is expected to learn; as a peer, he is expected to play fairly. Whether the child is a boy or a girl creates a particular role for each, based on adult expectancies. The boy is expected to fight back when attacked; the girl is expected to take an interest in homemaking.

It becomes clear that the process of socialization is again being invoked, since the child's roles are motivated by adult expectancies concerning what is appropriate for him, just as in all socialization these roles and norms are taught through direct instruction and nonplanned exposure. The child is not a passive pawn; he may not accept the roles assigned him; he may rebel or evade them, and, thus, perform differently from expectation.

Culture and personality

Socialization is the mechanism of cultural transmission. These manmade patterns of behavior, culture, are conveyed to the young through socialization. The culture supplies the child with a set of ready-made ways of behaving, including, for example, a language, a set of scientific beliefs, and a religion. In this sense, culture is a precipitate of the history of the group which is kept alive by transmittal to the next generation. In even more abstract terms, culture is a logical construct used by anthropologists and other social scientists to refer to, in the words of Kluckhohn, "a network of abstracted patterns generalized . . . to represent the regularities distinctive of the group in question" (22, 942).[4] It is in this sense that we can speak of a given culture such as the Trobriand, Samoan, or American.

Aspects of the culture become part of the child. One of the figures of speech of Park, the sociologist, is apt. Man is like an oyster; he built a shell which has become a significant part of him. Man, too, builds his culture which is a part of him. According to Kluckhohn (22), this introduces a second meaning to the term culture, namely, culture as norms of behavior internalized by the individual. Since we focus on the individual, our greatest emphasis is upon this latter meaning rather than on culture as the knowledge we transmit to the next generation.

No one individual bears the impress of all aspects of his culture. In socialization he internalizes certain aspects only. Moreover, he is the product of specific situations in which this internalization takes place— relations with particular parents, teachers, and peers. Inevitably he shows individuality in his behavior. At every stage of development the individual selects from the socialization variables available to him. He is not passively molded by the processes and agents of socialization. Instead, he chooses according to his past experience and his constitutional background. What emerges from these interactions is his per-

[4] From Lindzey (22). *Handbook of social psychology*, 1954. Addison-Wesley, Reading, Mass.

sonality—his own unique pattern of tendencies supplied by constitution and culture, but modified by the particular situations and adventitious circumstances of his experience. In this process the personality itself meets the new situation as a dynamic organization which, in turn, modifies his particular way of reacting to that situation.

The definition of personality offered by G. W. Allport is considered to be in the spirit of this point of view. He defines personality as "the dynamic organization within the individual of those psychophysical systems that determine his characteristic behavior and thought" (2, 28).[5] This definition stresses the uniqueness and dynamic character of personality organization previously indicated as imperative.

Behavior tendencies

Allport goes on to indicate that, since personality *does* something, a term is needed for the various systems that constitute personality. He calls them, "determining tendencies," and we shall follow his lead, except that it may be more convenient to draw attention to their behavioral component by referring to *behavior tendencies*. By tendencies are meant traits, habits, dispositions, drives, needs, interests, attitudes, and related psychological phenomena. A behavior tendency implies an inclination, a directive process that results in behavior oriented either toward certain objects or persons or away from certain objects or persons, varying, of course, with the tendency in question, its strength, and the other circumstances of the situation. Psychological science has not yet reached a stage of development that always permits us to give precise meanings to these terms. Much less does it allow us to state unequivocally their relations, one with another.

Some of the socialized behavior tendencies are originally constitutional in nature, aroused from internal conditions. They are sufficiently specific to be referred to as primary needs or drives. Among them are some that seem universal—hunger, thirst, rest, fatigue and sleep, elimination, temperature regulation, and breathing. They are internal in that there is a deprivation, a lack of something—air, food, water— which must be replenished (rewarded, reinforced). Once this deprivation is replenished, the drive diminishes or, to put it technically, it is "reduced."

Pain avoidance, although not a result of deprivation, serves as a primary need because it is potentially ready to act when a painful stimulus

[5] From Allport (2). Copyright © 1961 by Holt, Rinehart, and Winston and published with permission.

is present. Hence, it is episodic, unlike the cyclical primary drives dependent on bodily metabolism.

No one will doubt that hunger and thirst are important needs, but the rest of the list may give one pause. Temperature regulation, to use the most extreme instance, is not always recognized as a need. Only under relatively unusual circumstances are we aware of it as a need. Nevertheless, along with all the others, it is a biological drive whose satisfaction is necessary for sheer survival.

It is quite understandable that these drives are primary in that they take precedence over all others. If one is drowning for lack of oxygen or starving or dying of thirst, all other considerations, including other behavior tendencies, disappear. They also are primary in the sense that some form of their expression is demanded of all members of the human species. Their expression must be satisfied in infants and also in octogenarians.

An important aspect of behavior tendencies is their association with instrumental activities (31). Between the drive stimulation—the hunger or the thirst—and the goal response—the eating or the drinking—there are activities that are instrumental in placing the child in such position as to consummate the drive. For example, the infant's crying and bodily movement before the mother feeds him are the instrumental acts. The instrumental behavior is rewarded (reinforced), which increases the probability that the same behavior will occur on subsequent occasions in the presence of the same stimulating conditions. Consequently, crying and random movements are apt to recur when the infant is again hungry.

Certain other behavior tendencies are referred to as secondary drives because, according to a theory of their origin, they came into existence from their association with primary drives through what had been learned. Consequently, secondary drives involve a relatively large component of learning. Aggression, sex, and dependence-independence were seen earlier as forms of behavior subject to socialization. In present perspective they are important forms of secondary drives. How such drives are learned is taken up in the next chapter.

One important consideration in the selection of the various tendencies for later discussion has been the availability of research evidence. As a means of advancing knowledge research always shows a ragged edge in its advance guard. Certain areas later found to be important may, at any one moment, be relatively neglected. Some important behavior tendencies may be neglected, because this criterion of available research is going to be applied.

So far we have been dealing with motives or needs about which there is little question as to their drive properties. But there are other behavior tendencies whose status as drives are more suspect. For example, curiosity, considered by some psychologists to be a drive, may be a well-established habit and not a drive at all. Curiosity certainly plays a basic part as an instigator to learning. Whether habit or drive, it is certainly a behavior tendency.

Discussion hereafter is of forms of behavior, isolated either in theory or research, or both, that do not possess the widespread acceptance of the tension-reducing motives or needs heretofore considered. It is difficult, if not impossible, to specify their physiological bases and sometimes even the class or classes of objects or persons toward whom they are directed. Through future research some of these tendencies will probably emerge as strong contenders for status on a par with those called primary and secondary drives; others will certainly be found wanting or, at best, seen merely as aspects of some other more inclusive or fundamental drive.

No one doubts that something called affection does exist. The question concerns its exact manifestation. It may be a drive in its own right, or, perhaps, will be found to be related to other drives. This relation may be either of two kinds. Affection may be only an aspect of some more inclusive need, such as sex. Or affection itself may be broken down into two or more components, such as need for contact and ego enhancement. It should be added that these illustrations are hypothetical, being based only on surface plausibility. These relationships have not been established by research.

Some behavior tendencies seem to depend on external arousal rather than on an internal drive state. Consider the following sample of terms used in current psychological research: curiosity, exploratory behavior, mastery of stimuli, mastery motive, seeking tension, self-directed activity, information processing, contact comfort, activity level, spontaneous activity, investigation, manipulation, arousal seeking, activity seeking, play, general activity, need for achievement, competence, ego autonomy, enhancement, ego need, desire for attention, and affection. These behavior tendencies, it will be noted, concern exploratory, externally aroused behaviors in some way adjustive to our particular environment. They tend to emphasize the role of the external stimulus or incentive as distinguished from the internal physiological primary drives. They are not satiated, as such; rather, they produce a new direction, as when a child, tired of playing with a given toy, turns to another and then another.

Exploration, too, has this characteristic of redirection or change while the drive is maintained but with different objects or persons. Above all, these behavior tendencies seem *not* to require a release of tension or drive reduction (*13*). These tendencies, or at least most of them, do not require a conception of motivation as a ceaseless round of meeting basic drives. Moreover, denial that all that motivates a child is a drive to reduce tension is contradicted by even cursory observation. Tension may even be a positive experience. Instead of tension reduction, tension increase may be sought. Homeostasis, as Buhler (*6*) reminds us, is a state of equilibrium, not a state of rest. Homeostasis calls for an optimal, not a zero level of tension. So the child sometimes reduces tension, sometimes increases it. There seems to be a readiness for experience, a positive striving; the child ventures into the untried to explore in order to experience.

What may also characterize these behavior tendencies is their diverse means of satisfaction. There appears to be no generalized need or drive for play. Rather, the child is drawn to certain activities to which he seems to have some sort of affinity. It is not play *per se;* the infant likes to do certain things for the fun of it, in and for itself. He likes them because they are what they are, not because they reduce a play drive. Even rats, deprived of normal movement, will seek to engage in activities for their own sake (*14*). Certainly by three months of age the infant is not only aroused by the environment but also seeks to be aroused by it (*3*).

Monkeys will take apart mechanical equipment with no reward other than the satisfaction of manipulation (*14*). Investigators provided four rhesus monkeys with puzzles which they could manipulate 12 days in succession. Solution did *not* lead to food or water. Control monkeys had the disassembled puzzles in front of their cage for the same period of time. Thereafter both groups were compared on their solution of this kind of puzzle. The ones who had manipulated them were clearly superior to the control monkeys in number of correct solutions and the ratio of correct to incorrect responses. The investigators concluded that positing a manipulation drive best accounted for the results.

As the child develops, he may shift or change the direction from flight to experimentation and later turn to mastery of the stimuli (*6*). This becomes a behavior tendency in itself. Woodworth (*36*) considered mastery to include both curiosity and the desire to master the environment. An infant approaches many of his tasks in this spirit. The drinking from a cup or pulling himself upright seem to be activities from which he obtains satisfaction deriving from an enhanced view of the self because he is learning to manipulate and control the environment.

The self and personality

The personality of the child as an object of external observation is important, but there is an additional facet of interest to child psychology—how his behavior appears to the child himself. He is not an immature adult; he experiences and thinks in a world of his own which is inherently different from that of the adult, including his views of self. It gives, as Koffka puts it, ". . . our richly furnished, multi-colored and finely organized outlook upon the world . . ." (24, 161).[6] The discussion in an earlier chapter of subjective methods used in studying children not only reminded us this was the case but also gave a clue to the reasons for the subordinate status of the self concept in child psychology.

The personality when subjectively viewed is referred to as the *ego* or *self*. These terms will be used interchangeably, except in a setting such as in psychoanalytic theory where one term is preferred or used in a special sense.

The concept of self, as Allport (1) has indicated, although central to the study of personality has been neglected in recent years. This neglect stems mainly from the difficulty of coming to grips experimentally with the phenomena subsumed by this concept. But as Allport says, "The existence of one's own self is the one fact of which every mortal person—every psychologist included—is perfectly convinced" (1, 451).[7] It follows that such an important problem as the beginnings of self in infancy and its development in childhood cannot be ignored merely because of an embarrassing lack of evidence. The task that is being set is the delicate one of dealing with a topic on which there is little or no definitive research. Much of what is written about this topic in the chapters to follow is highly speculative.

The terms self and ego both are used in two distinct senses by different specialists. First, there is the self-as-object, which refers to the person's attitudes and feelings about himself—perception of himself as an individual. In this sense, a self is what a person thinks of himself. This is first expressed in self-awareness. Although awareness is a unitary thing simultaneously involving the "I" and, "not I," it is convenient to distinguish self-awareness from awareness of others, that is, social awareness. Not only are we individuals, we feel ourselves separate

[6] From Koffka (24). Copyright by Routledge & Kegan, Paul and published with permission.

[7] From Allport (1). Copyright 1943 by the American Psychological Association and published with permission.

from others as well. Hence, self and social awareness are but two sides to a shield. Self-awareness and social awareness are a unity which for matters of emphasis we separate. Thus, in addition to personal awareness, there is social awareness—the attitude the individual holds about the world and by which he interprets it. Second, there is the self-as-executor, the self as engaged in thinking, remembering, and perceiving. Here the self is the doer.

Summary

The fact that the infant becomes a person with his own unique characteristics while sharing with other persons certain common characteristics necessitates our examination of socialization and personality.

Socialization is the term applied to the process whereby the children in a given society are encouraged or discouraged from certain activities by their parents (or other agents) because these older members conceive these activities as reflecting or not reflecting that society's values. Socialization, then, is the process by which children by the time they are adults learn to share in varying degrees the values of their society. In shaping this process, constitutional factors, although present, are so poorly understood as to be capable only of illustration. Learning the process is consequently emphasized. Evidence that socialization practices differ from society to society is then adduced, as is evidence concerning differing attitudes toward socialization as well as class differences within our own society and differences within familial settings and among individuals. In extra-, intrasociety, and familial settings the dimension of permissive (indulgent)-regulatory (severe) seems to be one which includes within its scope a considerable portion of the phenomena covered under the heading of socialization practices.

In a different perspective, socialization becomes the mechanism of cultural transmission. The child internalizes aspects of his culture. From the specific situations he faces and from the broader cultural forces that are operative, there emerges the infant's personality—his own unique patterns of behavior tendencies. These traits, habits, drives, needs, interests, and attitudes embrace those dynamic pressures to action which all human beings share, though with wide differences based on cultural expectancies prevailing at that particular time and in that particular place. Although basic needs, such as temperature regulation and oxygen, are not neglected, selected for special emphasis are certain tendencies—hunger, elimination, dependence-independence, aggressive, and sexual tendencies. Also important in evaluating the personality of the child are those amorphous behavior tendencies which seem to have in common arousal by external stimuli and freedom from tension reduction.

Personality has a subjective aspect, the self, which also merits attention. Just as there is an emerging awareness of self as a person, there is a social awareness of other persons. The self is conceived as intimately intertwined with its social aspect. Self-awareness and social awareness are aspects of a unity, which only for heuristic purposes we may separate.

For Further Reading

A description of the child training techniques from about 1750 to the mid-fifties is given by D. R. Miller and G. E. Swanson in *The Changing American Parent,* (New York: Wiley, 1958).

Popular presentations of permissiveness are widely circulated in the United States. Dr. Benjamin Spock's *Pocket Book of Baby and Child Care* (New York: Pocket Book, 1946) contains a wealth of illustrations.

References

1. Allport, G.W.   The ego in contemporary psychology.   *Psychol. Rev.,* 1943, 50, 451–578.
2. Allport, G. W.   *Pattern and growth in personality.*   New York: Holt, Rinehart, & Winston, 1961.
3. Bayley, Nancy.   Current research relating to children at the National Institute of Health.   *Child Developm.,* 1960, 31, 209–214.
4. Bishop, Barbara M.   Mother-child interaction and the social behavior of children.   *Psychol. Monogr.,* 1951, 65, No. 328.
5. Bronfenbrenner, U.   Socialization and social class through time and space.   In Eleanor E. Maccoby, T. M. Newcomb, and E. L. Hartley (Eds.), *Readings in social psychology.*   New York: Holt, Rinehart, & Winston, 1958, 400–425.
6. Buhler, Charlotte.   Maturation and motivation.   *Personality,* 1951, 1, 184–211.
7. Child, I. L.   Socialization.   In G. Lindzey (Ed.), *Handbook of social psychology.*   Cambridge: Addison-Wesley, 1954, 655–692.
8. Ericson, Martha C.   Child-rearing and social status.   *Amer. J. Sociol.,* 1946, 52, 190–192.
9. Escalona, Sibylle.   A commentary upon some recent changes in child-rearing practices.   *Child Developm.,* 1949, 20, 157–162.
10. Frank, L. K.   Culture control and physiological autonomy.   In C. Kluckhohn and H. A. Murray (Eds.), *Personality in nature, society and culture.*   New York: Knopf, 1948, 119–122.

11. Goldfrank, Esther. Socialization, personality, and the structure of pueblo society. In D. G. Haring (Ed.), *Personal character and cultural milieu: a collection of reading*. (Rev. ed.) Syracuse, New York: Syracuse University Press, 1949, 247–269.
12. Harlow, H. F. Mice, monkeys, men, and motives. *Psychol. Rev.*, 1953, 60, 23–32.
13. Harlow, H. F., M. K. Harlow, and D. R. Meyer. Learning motivated by a manipulation drive. *J. Exp. Psychol.*, 1950, 40, 228–234.
14. Henry, J. *Jungle people*. New York: Augustin, 1941.
15. Henry, J. Environment and symptom formation. *Amer. J. Orthopsychiat.*, 1947, 17, 628–632.
16. Hill, W. F. Activity as an autonomous drive. *J. Comp. Physiol. Psychol.*, 1956, 49, 15–19.
17. Hollingshead, A. B., and Redlich, F. C. *Social class and mental illness*. New York: Wiley, 1958.
18. Jarecki, H. G. Maternal attitudes toward child-rearing; a cross-cultural pilot study. *Arch. Gen. Psychiat.*, 1961, 4, 340–356.
19. Klatskin, Ethelyn H. Shifts in child care practices in three social classes under an infant care program of flexible methodology. *Amer. J. Orthopsychiat.*, 1952, 22, 52–61.
20. Klatskin, Ethelyn H., and Edith B. Jackson. Methodology of the Yale rooming-in project on parent-child relationship. *Amer. J. Orthopsychiat.*, 1955, 25, 81–108.
21. Klatskin, Ethelyn H., Edith B. Jackson, and Louise C. Wilkin. The influence of degree of flexibility in maternal child care practices on early child behavior. *Amer. J. Orthopsychiat.*, 1956, 26, 79–93.
22. Kluckhohn, C. Culture and behavior. In G. Lindzey (Ed.), *Handbook of social psychology*. Cambridge: Addison-Wesley, 1954, 921–976.
23. Kluckhohn, C., and O. H. Mowrer. Personality and culture; a conceptual scheme. *Amer. Anthrop.*, 1944, 46, No. 1.
24. Koffka, K. *The growth of the mind*, (2nd ed.), London: Routledge and Kegan Paul, 1928.
25. Linton, R. Marquesan personality. In A. Kardiner, *The individual and his society*. New York: Columbia University Press, 1939.
26. Maccoby, Eleanor E., and Patricia K. Gibbs. Methods of child-rearing in two social classes. In W. E. Martin and Celia B. Stendler (Eds.), *Readings in child development*. New York: Harcourt, Brace, 1954, 380–396.
27. Marquis, Dorothy P. Can conditioned responses be established in the newborn infant? *J. Genet. Psychol.*, 1931, 39, 479–492.
28. Miller, D. R., and G. E. Swanson. *The changing American parent: a study in the Detroit area*. New York: Wiley, 1958.
29. Nowlis, V. The search for significant concepts in a study of parent-child relationships. *Amer. J. Orthopsychiat.*, 1952, 22, 286–299.
30. Radke, Marion J. The relation of parental authority to children's behavior and attitudes. *Univ. Minn. Child Welf. Monogr.*, 1946, No. 22.
31. Sears, R. R. Personality development in the family. In R. F. Winch and R. McGinnis (Eds.), *Selected studies on marriage and the family*, New York: Holt, 1953, 215–240.
32. Sears, R. R., Eleanor E. Maccoby, and H. Levin. *Patterns of child rearing*. Evanston: Row, Peterson, 1957.

33. Whiting, J. W. M.   *Becoming a Kwoma.*   New Haven: Yale University Press, 1941.
34. Whiting, J. W. M.   Socialization process and personality.   In F. K. Hsu (Ed.), *Psychological anthropology.*   Homewood, Ill.: Dorsey, 1961, 355–380.
35. Whiting, J. W. M., and I. L. Child.   *Child training and personality: a cross-cultural study.*   New Haven: Yale University Press, 1953.
36. Woodworth, R. S.   *Adjustment and mastery.*   Baltimore: Williams & Wilkins, 1933.

5

Personality, Behavior Theory, and Psychoanalysis

MEN FROM THE FIELDS of psychology, psychiatry, anthropology, and sociology have attempted to bring together knowledge of their own and related fields in order to give an integrated psychological perspective on personality. An adequate theory of personality gives attention both to the structure and to the development of personality.

The structure has to do with the organization of the personality, how it is put together. It is made up of the relatively stable enduring components of the personality inferred from the consistency of behavior over relatively longer periods of time. The units or patterns used vary from theory to theory, but there are always present certain elements of structure. The second aspect has to do with how the individual develops, the processes by which the infant becomes the man. Thus, the vicissitudes of the individual's journey in time occupy the personality theorist as well as the cross-sectional view of his personality at a given point in time.

Some of the more prominent views of personality are orthodox psychoanalysis, neo-Freudian modifications of psychoanalysis, trait theories, organismic theories, field theories, and type theories. Each of these approaches to personality has its proponents and adherents. Each quite possibly has its modicum of truth and each in some measure is relevant to child psychology. Certain views, however, either have had more profound effect upon child psychology or are considered to be potentially important. Most prominent are psychoanalysis, neo-Freudian derivatives of psychoanalysis, and behavior-social learning theory. This chapter explores the first and last of these three, whereas neo-

Freudian derivatives will be considered later in the book in relation to specific ages and research issues.

Behavior-social learning theory

A theory of learning is an attempt to account for the acquisition and retention of new forms of behavior and the extinction of these or other forms of behavior. In learning there is a tendency for some responses to occur with increasing frequency, strength, or efficiency with repeated experience, while there is a tendency for other responses to drop out.

The point of view most fully developed and most directly capable of being related to socialization of the child is a derivative of Hull's reinforcement theory, referred to as behavior-social learning theory. This particular point of view will be utilized whenever an account of the condition of learning is necessary. Both conditioning, from which Hull derived his point of view, and behavior-social learning theory, as conceived by Dollard and Miller (2, 24), have been described in historical context in Chapter 1. Let us consider a succinct statement of the various facets of learning that are essential aspects of the theory. Fortunately, some prior acquaintance with the psychology of learning may be assumed on the part of readers and only the bare essentials of the theory need to be indicated here. Application to specific problems occurs in later chapters.

Fundamental Factors

Dollard and Miller (2) make four factors fundamental to their presentation of learning. These factors are drive (motivation), responses (act or thought), cue (stimulus), and reinforcement (reward). All of these factors are interrelated, but it will be found that reinforcement is made central to their conceptualization of learning. Consequently, before examining the interrelationships, some preliminary approximation of the meaning of reinforcement is appropriate. Reinforcement is any event following a response that strengthens the tendency for the response to be repeated. Reward is a synonym, although reinforcement is the preferred term.

An experiment by Dorothy Marquis (23) illustrates the four factors. She was interested in whether infants could learn immediately after birth. Eight infants were studied from their first to their tenth day of life. Hunger was used as the *drive*. Ringing of a buzzer was the *cue*. Amount of activity was the *response*. Receiving the bottle was the *reinforcement.* These were interrelated in the following fashion. Each infant at his feeding time was placed in a stabilimeter (an apparatus described on page 42 for measuring amount of bodily activity) and observed for other forms of behavior. After the lapse of a few minutes to establish a base line, the experimenter sounded a buzzer for five seconds. Immediately afterward the bottle was inserted in the infant's mouth. After a period of from three to six days, seven of the eight infants began to show changes of behavior on the sounding of the buzzer. An infant would now show, after the buzzer sounded, an increase in mouth opening, sucking movements, and a decrease in bodily movements. It will be noted that these reactions that accompany food-taking actually occurred *before* food-taking.

To summarize in terms of the four factors, with hunger serving as the *drive,* the *cue* of the buzzer now brought forth *responses* of sucking, mouth opening, and cessation of movement, with the *reinforcement* of food-taking occurring after these responses. That the drive factor is important may be illustrated by what happened to the eighth infant who did *not* show these responses. This infant had the cue of the buzzer and the reinforcement of the bottle, but "he never seemed hungry" (23, 483).[1] In other words, the absence of *drive* accounts for the failure of the responses to occur. The absence of learning when *reinforcement* is not given is shown by Marquis's control group. They received identical treatment to that given the experimental group except they were not fed at the sound of the buzzer. In these infants learning did not take place. If an infant who was deaf had been used, he would not have learned because the *cue* of the buzzer would have been missing. In all three instances the responses were not given, so nothing would have been learned. It is now plausible to examine each of these factors, one by one, as Dollard and Miller (2, 24) conceived them.

Drive. Drives are any strong stimuli that impel action. Certain drives are not dependent for their appearance upon learning and consequently are primary or innate. In Chapter 6 the primary drives or needs of the newborn infant will be classified as hunger and thirst, sleep, elimination, sex, temperature regulation, and need for oxygen. There are, then, strong stimuli that we cannot ignore; they are those to which we must act. The utilization of certain drives and no others, however, is not in any sense fixed or immutable and the theory does not demand that only certain specified primary drives be considered. In

---

[1] From Marquis (23). Copyright 1931 by the Journal Press, and published with permission.

addition to discussing several of the aforementioned drives Dollard and Miller also speak of pain and fatigue as primary drives. Primary drives are those that are unlearned and consequently do not require the presence of reinforcement.

Cue. A drive, by definition, must be responded to. But when and where the individual responds and which particular response he will make are due to the cues to which he is exposed. Just as a cue to an actor is a signal for his lines, a cue is a stimulus that guides the response of the individual. Simple illustrations of cues are the class bell, the stop sign, and the instructions, "Go ahead." Each in its own way helps to determine when and where the individual responds. If cues are obscure or absent, if these "guide posts" are not present, learning becomes more difficult or impossible.

Response. Before a particular response can be linked to a given cue, the response must occur. That is, before a response can be reinforced (rewarded) and learned, it has to occur. The production of appropriate responses becomes a crucial stage in the individual's learning. In any given situation not encountered before, a number of so-called trial and error responses are likely. Owing to innate factors or to past learning in similar situations, certain responses are likelier to occur than others, whereas certain other responses are less likely to occur. Their order of probability of occurrence is called the initial hierarchy of responses. The most likely response to occur, the dominant response, as it is called, is the strongest. If this response, once given, is *not successful,* that is, not reinforced, then the next most dominant occurs, and so on.

If learning is to occur, the correct response must ultimately be made and be followed by reinforcement. This reinforcement makes the response likelier to occur earlier the next trial, until eventually, the correct response is the first one made. Thus, this learning changes the probability of occurrence of the initial hierarchy of responses, yielding what is called the resultant hierarchy of responses. This is because a certain response is reinforced, making it likelier to appear—that is, it shifts its position from that it had in the initial hierarchy of responses. The reinforced response, initially weaker, now occupies the dominant position. Operationally, this is shown by decrease in the number of responses from learning trial to learning trial which do not result in reinforcement. Thus, if 16 errors are committed on the first trial before the reinforced response is made, this position of being the seventeenth response is expressive of the position in the initial hierarchy of the response followed by reinforcement. After, say, ten trials, the reinforced response is given first, showing a shift of this response in the hierarchy of responses to a position of primacy in the resultant hierarchy.

The correct response, it will be noted, occurs *before* it is rewarded. It is made before it is reinforced. What, then, is new in the learning? It is that the response in question occurs when a specific cue is present, whereas its previous occurrence in this situation may have been very infrequent. The product of learning, then, in this context, is a connection between a cue and a response.

As is well known, the effects of learning in one situation transfer to other situations. This is called generalization. An illustration given in the first chapter was Albert's fear of white, furry objects. After fear responses had been conditioned to the white rat, fear could now be elicited by a white piece of fur or white rabbit, despite the fact that the infant had not feared them before, and no reason is known why he should. To state it more precisely in the present theoretical context, reinforcement for making a specific response to a given set of cues strengthens the tendency not only for the response in question, but also for other *similar* patterns of cues to elicit these same responses.

One of the central areas of research efforts concerning generalization is that of the shape of the gradient of generalization. By a gradient of generalization is meant the change in the strength of the response as the test stimulus changes. As we make the stimulus less and less similar to the conditioned stimulus, there is often found to be a weakening of the strength of the response as similarity decreases. The less the stimulus is similar to the original stimulus, the weaker the response. Or to state it again in terms of cues, the less similar the cue, the less the generalization. Thus, in research described in some detail in Chapter 19 it was found that children punished for being aggressive in the home were also inhibited from being aggressive in the school setting, which is very similar to the home. However, the less similar cues of doll play were sufficiently dissimilar for the same children to release aggression.

There are a number of ways in which the responses to be connected to a given cue as a new habit may first be elicited. In other words, there are different ways of producing responses likely to be reinforced. To name some of the ways mentioned by Dollard and Miller, there is conditioning, trial and error, insight, and imitation.

In classical conditioning the presence of the unconditioned stimulus (the food or noxious stimulus) insures that the response to be learned will be made. Learning in this instance consists of "connecting" the old responses to a new stimulus, the conditioned stimulus. The presence of the unconditioned stimulus insures that the subject will be reinforced independent of what he does. In all other ways of producing responses there is no guarantee that the correct one will occur; obtaining a reinforcement is dependent on the occurrence of the correct response.

In trial and error learning the drive elicits one response after another in an order decided by the initial hierarchy of responses. If a response is nonrewarded, it is extinguished and the next response in the hierarchy occurs. When the desired response takes place, it is rewarded and the learning begins to be established. This process is generally a gradual one.

Insight learning in this perspective becomes learning in which a relationship is perceived; whenever this occurs it leads almost immediately to a solution. Instead of there being gradual improvement, there is a solution because the individual holds a verbal hypothesis (or some other cue-producing response) and quick learning thereafter results. Sometimes there is little preliminary fumbling and the correct response is made quickly. But this need not be the case. Fumbling may be long or short. The essential feature is that, instead of gradual improvement, the preinsight period, which may be of any duration, gives little or no indication of progress toward the solution, but is followed by a rapid solution. Thereafter, the correct response tends to be made "full strength," as it were. To put it graphically, insight learning is "step-shaped." If the initial practice before might be compared to the floor, then insight is the riser (or vertical part) of the step, with the new step representing the level of learning thereafter. It would seem that the function of ". . . insight seems to be to produce a response which might otherwise not be made. If this response is rewarded, it will be learned as the response to that situation. If the insight is not rewarded, it will be abandoned" (2, 38).[2] Insight learning differs from trial and error learning in that in an extreme case the correct response is the dominant one in the hierarchy of responses to the unconditioned stimulus. This causes the individual to make the correct response.

Imitation is a way of learning in which similar acts are brought about in two (or more) people and connected to appropriate cues. According to Miller and Dollard (24), imitation appears in two forms—copying and matched dependent behavior. Copying is deliberate in the sense that the copier tries to bring his response to approximate that of a model. Learning to write by copying from the blackboard would be an illustration. In matched-dependent behavior the follower is not directly aware of the cues present in the environment, but is dependent

[2] By permission from *Personality and Psychotherapy* by Dollard and Miller. Copyright 1950. McGraw-Hill Book Company, Inc.

on the leader for signals as to which act is to be performed and where and when it is to occur.   In this way he "matches" his response to that of the leader.   He need not be aware he is imitating, as in a crowd moved by its leader or leaders.   Naturally, both copying and matched-dependent forms of imitation required conditions favorable to learning, that is, the presence of the factors of drive, response, cue, and reinforcement.

These different ways of producing responses have in common that they are likely to be rewarded.   The responses, when they occur, follow the same fundamental laws of learning which result either in rejection or selection on the basis of reinforcement or nonreinforcement.

Reinforcement.   When a response has occurred, what happens thereafter depends on whether or not it is rewarded or reinforced.   It is important to note that repetition does not always strengthen the tendency for a response to recur.   When a "mistake" is made in connection with learning something, say a maze pathway, the tendency to repeat a blind alley entry is weakened.   This weakening of a response is called extinction.   When the action results in a correct response, the tendency to repeat the response is strengthened.   Any event following the response which strengthens the tendency for a response to be repeated is called reinforcement.

The drive is maintained until it is reinforced.   This reinforcement may be expressed through reduction in the strength of a drive.   For example, eating is a reinforcement of hunger which reduces the drive. As Dollard and Miller put it ". . . reduction in the strength of a strong drive stimulus acts as a reinforcement" (2, 40).[3]

An important element in child psychology is the presence of a great variety of needs and motives which are not apparent in the child's initial needs and motives.   For example, the young infant is not aggressive, or in need of self-esteem, or in love in the adult sense; nor is the infant fearful in situations that, later in life, seem to upset him emotionally and from which he strives to escape without apparent cause.   From where do these needs and motives come?

In learning behavior-theory, these derived needs or motives are said to arise from several sources.   In some instances, these learned motivational states are aroused by originally neutral situations which have been consistently experienced in conjunction with a primary need state. For example, a young child who is ill may be taken on a number of occasions to a doctor's office for rather painful medical treatment.

[3] By permission from *Personality and Psychotherapy* by Dollard and Miller, 1950. McGraw-Hill Book Company, Inc.

Pain, of course, is a primary motivational state that the child attempts to reduce by escaping. After a number of such visits, the child begins to cry, shows other evidences of being emotionally upset, and endeavors to get away merely at the sight of the doctor or his office. The capacity of such previously neutral stimuli to arouse needs, after repeated pairings with primary needs, seems to occur most frequently when the primary motive is evoked by some unpleasant kind of stimulation.

Still other secondary needs arise from secondary reinforcement. However, it is first necessary to explain secondary reinforcement before dealing with derived needs based on them. A crying infant who is hungry or wet may cease to cry, at least temporarily, at the sight of his mother. His mother has consistently been associated with a primary reward, for example, being fed or changed, and has as a result taken on the properties of a secondary reinforcement. Thus, derived or secondary reinforcement is the partial reduction in a need occurring upon the presentation of a stimulus previously associated with the specific stimulus that reduces the need more directly. Often children learn to "need" these secondary reinforcers for themselves—and in the absence of any primary rewards. Thus, the child comes to seek out his mother's company, even in the absence of hunger, pain, or the like.

Many needs are said to come into existence in this way: through persistent conjunction with objects that reduce primary needs (primary reinforcers). Thus, previously neutral objects or events themselves take on reinforcing properties. In many instances the child begins to strive for these secondary reinforcers for their own sake and, hence, is said to have learned to have a need for them.

The emphasis so far has been on the conditions of development. In the course of discussing the process of learning we have touched on the dynamics of personality which involves the interplay of drives and the environment.

The Development of Personality

The development of personality is conceived primarily as a process of learning which arises when the infant's innate behavior repertoire is exposed to environmental circumstances. The infant brings into the world a relatively small number of specific reflexes, as well as a number of tendencies for certain responses to appear in particular situations, these being the innate hierarchies of responses. A small number of primary drives that have already been specified are also included in this innate repertoire. As the infant is exposed to environmental influences, the learning process becomes operative and learned responses, including secondary drives, take over.

Conflict and critical training situations.   In keeping with the critical period hypothesis, Dollard and Miller (2) selected four so-called critical training situations which are important because of their pronounced effect in forming the personality of the child.   These critical situations are feeding, cleanliness training, sex training, and training for control of anger.   They are major sources of conflict within the child.   The child wishes to do what comes naturally in connection with each of these critical situations; the parents want him to do something different, more in keeping with grown-up cultural standards.   Conflict in the child becomes inevitable because his desires are incompatible with those of his mother.   He wants something, but what he wants is different from what his mother wants, so he reacts emotionally.   As will be seen, these conflicts may produce long-enduring effects upon the child's personality.

The frustration-aggression hypothesis.   Behavior-social learning theorists frequently utilize the frustration-aggression hypothesis.   Frustration arises when a goal response is thwarted; aggression is the response of attempting injury, all the way from biting remarks to murder, to the person or object considered to be the frustrating source.

Differential responses to frustration may be attributed to differing circumstances.   For example, Whiting (26) found that children of a particular age responded to frustration by younger children with aggression but to frustration by older children with fear or avoidance. Other situational or individual circumstances account for the differential responses to frustration.   We shall treat aggression as a behavior tendency that is evoked by frustration.

Despite the emphasis upon the instigation of aggression by frustration, behavior-social learning theorists will admit that aggression is not an invariable consequence of frustration and that it can occur even in the absence of frustration.   Anticipation of punishment, for example, may inhibit aggression, even those workers who have placed the most emphasis on frustration leading to aggression (1) will concede. Many other reactions to frustration include dependency, fear, guilt, anxiety, lowering of performance level, increased effort, removing oneself from the scene of frustration, or going "out of the field," to use Lewin's (22, 90) [4] phrase.   Nor does aggression always arise because

---

[4] By permission from *A Dynamic Theory of Personality*, by Lewin.   Copyright 1935. McGraw-Hill Book Company, Inc.

the child is frustrated. To use only one illustration, an especially important source of aggressive tendencies not instigated by frustration is the influence of aggressive models, such as exposure to aggressive fathers.

The Structure of Personality

When we turn to the structural elements of the personality, we are referring to the nature of its relatively stable unchanging aspects. These elements are the characteristics that endure, to some extent, with the passage of time. In a sense, when we view the personality structurally a cross-sectional view of the personality is being taken. In behavior-social learning theory, habit is the basic unit in the structure of personality (2). Consequently, we must relate habit to the previous discussion of the process of development. Habit is a stable stimulus-response connection. Much of our behavior is made up of simple automatic habits in which we respond directly to cues and internal drives without taking thought. This is one level of learned behavior habits.

There is another level of learned behavior: in the higher mental processes instead of responding immediately and automatically we take time to think. In other words, instead of being guided by a cue or cue situation, these processes are mediated by internal mechanisms though still based on habits.

In thinking, cue-producing responses are important. The main function of these responses is to lead or mediate for still other responses. Their nature may be made clearer if a distinction is made between cue-producing responses and those that are referred to as instrumental responses. Instrumental responses are those that have some immediate effect on the environment. Responses that have this instrumental character include opening the mouth, closing the door, jumping the puddle, and so on. They change one's relationship to the external environment directly and immediately. They do not serve to produce a cue that is a part of a pattern leading to another response as do cue-producing responses.

Cue-producing responses obviously include language although it may or may not necessarily be spoken language. Cues of this sort allow labeling and other processes of reasoning. In addition to habits and higher mental processes, response hierarchies making one cue response more available than another also contribute to the structure of personality.

We shall return to behavior-social learning theory after discussing psychoanalysis in order that its relation to other principles of child psychology may be made clear.

Psychoanalysis

Freud's work has already been examined as an approach to psychotherapy with patients and somewhat less obviously as a method of research from which to learn about their personalities. At this point interest shifts to the theory of personality that emerged from his labors. From a psychoanalytic point of view, personality is essentially an interplay of reciprocally urging and checking forces (6). Both the nature of these forces and the structure through which their interplay is carried on must be examined. As with behavior-social learning theory, we explore the dynamics and structure of personality.

Dynamics of Personality

Freud specified the dynamics of personality as a theory of instincts, intrinsic maturational factors (25). Taken together, the instincts are the sum total of psychic energy. An instinct has four functional characteristics: (a) *impetus*, the motor element in the amount of force it represents; (b) *aim*, the satisfaction obtained by abolishing the condition of stimulation; (c) *object*, that through which the aim can be achieved; and (d) *source*, the somatic process in a body part from which eventuates a stimulus (7).

The cardinal assumption of psychoanalysis is that sexuality is the basic human motive. The orthodox psychoanalysts state that various manifestations of infant and child behavior are of a sexual nature. Oral (mouth-centered) activity of the infant, for example, is considered as qualitatively continuous with adult sexuality through other intervening stages. These pregenital stages are considered as the forerunners of adult heterosexual behavior (the genital stage), with nearly as much sexual energy employed as later when full psychosexual prowess emerges with the physical changes of adolescence. In sexuality is to be found the biological determinant of personality.

Freud and his followers never attributed adult sexuality to the infant or child. Child sexual behavior is not equated with adult sexuality. Instead, they insisted that there was a direct, continuous connection between the behavior of the child in oral and other pregenital stages and his behavior in the genital (adult heterosexual) stage. Infantile sexuality foreshadows but does not completely define the adult pattern.

If one looks at a tulip bulb, he does not see the shape, color, or size of the ultimate blossom. However, the blossom would not exist were it not for the bulb. Growing out of the bulb first comes the leaves, again an inherent part of the total plant, but still not the blossom. Finally the bud shapes, and ultimately the flower. Infantile sexuality and its vicissitudes of development determine the final successful blossoming or failure of fruition of heterosexuality (21, 38–39).[5]

Just as the ovum contains the adult potentialities, so infantile sexual behavior foreshadows genital behavior. Sexual factors are accepted as the fundamental motivation; nonsexual motivation stems from the sexual.

Psychoanalysis posits as energy for the sexual drives, the libido. Almost any impulse to receive pleasure would be an expression of libido, and, hence, considered sexual. In one sense this energy is nonspecific in that it energizes any activity, but in another sense it is quite specific in that the natural expression is sexual. The libido may be defined as that fixed quantity of sexual energy available to an individual from birth onward. Simple physical needs, such as hunger and thirst, are accepted as having drive energy (3), but these needs are considered relatively uncomplicated and of minor importance.

Freud also postulated a second class of drives, the self-preservative drives. In the development of psychoanalysis in still later years, he spoke of life and death instincts in which the latter was invested with a self-destructive quality, including the direction of destructive tendencies upon other persons as expressed in aggressive acts toward them. Aggression is an independent instinctual disposition (11).

As implied by their acceptance of a relative independence of aggression, psychoanalysts have tended to minimize somewhat in recent years the all-pervasiveness of the sexual motive in accounting for behavior. For the moment, discussion of this point is deferred until we discuss ego autonomy.

Structure of Personality

Freud, early in his work with patients, was struck with the ever-recurring phenomenon of their failing to be aware of certain significant aspects of or events in their lives which, nevertheless, he found had affected them profoundly. Since they behaved as if they were unaware of these determinants of their behavior and aspects of mental life, he referred to them as unconscious. Consequently, in his theoretical

---

[5] From Josselyn (21). Copyright 1948 by Family Service Association of America, and published with permission.

formulation he stressed the unconscious aspects of mental life. Freud likened the mind to an iceberg, only its summit of consciousness being above the surface, while its great mass lay below the surface.

Originally Freud adopted a threefold classification of mental life—conscious, foreconscious (capable of becoming conscious but not attended at the moment), and unconscious (repressed, that is, actively excluded from consciousness or instinctual drives that were never conscious). Later, while preserving these distinctions he preferred, on the grounds of greater dynamic possibilities, to speak of structural divisions of personality—the id, the ego, and the superego.

In his conception of the structural divisions of personality, the deliberately neutral term id (it) was given to the source of unconscious energy. In his earlier formulation Freud had referred to unconsciousness in much the same manner as he now used the term id. Some psychoanalysts continue to use id and unconscious more or less interchangeably. However, it is more exactly considered as one segment of the unconscious because, although all of the id is unconscious, not all unconsciousness is id.

Other characteristics of id are important. Freud said of it, "It contains everything that is inherited, that is present at birth, that is fixed in the constitution" (14, 14).[6] The id's aim is the gratification of its impulses with no sense of morality, logic, or unity of purpose. The major function of the id is to provide free uninhibited discharge of energy. Its activity is in the service of the pleasure principle, that is, the seeking of pleasure and the avoidance of pain with no other considerations entering the picture. This is a kind of animal-like existence with satisfaction only of bodily desires. There is no vestige of "reasonableness" or consideration for the rights of others.

The infant is born with id. The other two structural constituents of personality, his ego and superego, are partially developed from the id in the course of his daily life. The ego and superego derive at least some of their energy from the primary psychic energy reservoir of libido in the id. The libido consequently is not only the basic force for personality dynamics but a major source of organization of the personality structure as well. How the ego and superego came into being is described later. At the moment, the fully formed mature personality is under consideration.

Since the id is unconscious, it has no direct relation with the external world; it can only be known through the ego which does have the characteristic of being conscious (14). Dreams, for example, show

[6] From Freud (14). Copyright 1949 by W. W. Norton and Company, Inc., and published with permission.

the intrusion of id tendencies into consciousness, since the ego is partially relaxed in sleep. Examination of dreams is one way to gain some dim (and frightening) knowledge of id sources. The dreams of even the most straight-laced person are said to contain amoral elements, illustrative of the functioning of the id.

The ego includes the conscious portion of the personality structure. The processes of the ego alone are capable of being conscious (15). Only a small part of the ego is conscious at any time. A great portion of the ego exists outside of awareness but can be called into consciousness when needed (the preconscious).

Still another part of the ego is unconscious. The unconscious portion of the ego results from repression. Materials once conscious, but unacceptable to the ego, are pushed back into the unconscious (14). Because of its origin this portion of the ego is called the repressed, and the action of refusing to allow unwelcome impulses to appear in consciousness is known as the mechanism of repression (10). What is repressed has an "upward driving force," that is, an impulsion or drive to break through into consciousness (12). The ego, under the influence of external reality, controls the entrance into consciousness; therefore, an interplay of reciprocally checking and urging forces is developed in which libido must be expended. To repress requires a continuous expenditure of effort (13).

The self is not identical with the ego. Knowledge of the self is a sense of awareness and therefore conscious. This is not so with repressed aspects of the ego. Although each individual recognizes himself, he has no immediate knowledge of the repressed facet of the ego.

The ego involves both an awareness of self and the carrying on of executive functions. In connection with the latter, as a representative of reality, the ego serves to mediate among the pressures arising from the id (libidinal pressures), the superego (the conscience and "ego-ideal"), and the demands of external reality. Evaluation of an existing situation, which the individual faces, whatever it might be, and anticipation of the future by him are functions of the ego. Obeying the "reality principle," the ego operates through realistic thinking. Plans are formulated for the satisfaction of needs and carried out (reality testing). In evaluating a situation and in anticipating the future the ego must reckon with the demands of reality as they exist. As an approximation, the ego represents reason, whereas the id represents the untamed passions, although, of course, the latter are represented in consciousness through the ego (12).

The ego is in control of voluntary movement and is aware of external events (*14*). It stores up experiences in memory; it adapts; it learns; it avoids. Thus, it has relation both with the id and the external world. In following the reality principle, the ego mediates between the imperative pressures from the id, the structures of the superego, and the demands of external reality.

The ego, operating through the reality principle, is capable of investing energy in an object either inanimate, as in some "favorite" possession, or in some other person. This energy attachment, Freud called *cathexis*. Cathexis is a sum of psychic energy with which an object is invested (*5*). This attachment of energy is analogous to an electric charge (*14*). When libido of the ego is invested in an object, including persons, it becomes object-libido (*16*). This process of investment is one in which ego-libido is transformed into object-libido (*12*). The reverse also takes place; object-libido can return to ego-libido. Moreover, libido is mobile (*14*) in that it can pass from one object to another.

A form of cathexis is operating within the structure *per se* in the process of ego-id interaction (*14*). In its check upon the id, the ego must automatically expend a great amount of energy. This checking force is anticathexis and is the principle that maintains the repression (*9*).

Anxiety serves as a signal to the ego, alerting it to danger, internal or external. Anxiety, strictly speaking, cannot exist except in conscious awareness. It is an affective state experienced by the ego, not by the id or superego. The id cannot show anxiety because it cannot estimate danger, having no knowledge of the external world. In the face of danger or threat of danger, anxiety develops. Although often considered synonymous with fear, Freud preferred the term anxiety, because fear is often interpreted as related to something in the external world. Anxiety refers to perception of internal as well as external dangers. The internal conditions giving rise to this anxiety expressed by the ego have to do with unacceptable id impulses or superego demands.

The so-called ego defense mechanisms need preliminary exposition (*4*). Each child uses his ego to defend himself in characteristic fashion against anxiety. Since a large number of defense mechanisms are present, and each individual has a characteristic pattern for their employment a considerable variety in personality structures is available. Repression is one of the major ego defense mechanisms. By preventing the entry of unpleasant thoughts into consciousness, anxiety of a conscious sort is prevented.

Two other illustrative defense mechanisms are *projection*, or attributing to other persons or objects one's own shortcomings as does the inept workman who blames his tools; and *regression,* or returning to less mature forms of behavior than the individual is capable of, as when a ten-year-old throws a temper tantrum. Just as in repression, these defense mechanisms have the characteristic of demanding the expenditure of libido to keep anxiety from appearing. They maintain the *status quo* but in a manner analogous to a garrison keeping the otherwise restive population in check. At best, they maintain a stale-mate; at worst, they express themselves in neurotic or psychotic symptoms.

Sublimation is an important ego mechanism that does not require this continual expenditure of energy. It is the most successful of the mechanisms, since its discharge of energy brings about a significant cessation of impulses without the continued defensive function of the other mechanisms. Sublimations are the socially approved ways of discharging libido without anxiety; they are desexualized expressions of libido. Sublimation takes on the protean forms with manifestations in law, order, social progress, interaction, and achievement as areas of manifestation.

In the preceding pages qualifications were offered concerning the derivation of the ego from the id. It was spoken of as being "partially" so derived and securing "some" of its energy from that source. In recent years there has been an increasing trend to see the ego as less at the mercy of the id and even to attribute independent status to some aspects. In other words, some ego functions exist at least partially independent of derivation from the id.

The ego arises not from the id alone, but from a more or less un-differentiated substratum from which both id and ego arise. The ego then possesses some autonomy in the sense that it is partially inde-pendent of the influence of the id. The ego, according to Hartmann (18), is a structural aspect of personality to be defined by its functions —control of motility, perception, reality testing, and thinking. There is a factor in the ego that possesses an autonomy and independence of instinct, developing through learning and maturation. This position would make development not entirely an id-instigated matter—there are factors in this undifferentiated phase that are attributable to neither instinct nor reality (18). Consequently, ego development involves not only instinctual drives and outer reality but also inherited ego char-acteristics which have an energy of their own. Some of our life, then, is conflict-free, mature functioning, not a ceaseless struggle against primitive id forces.

The third component of the personality structure is the superego.

In a preliminary, tentative fashion it can be said to resemble the conscience. Leaving aside for the moment details of its development, it is derived from the ego in the course of childhood. At birth, the infant does not have a superego, in the sense of a conscience. The superego is differentially related to the ego according to whether it is in opposition or in harmony. The superego serves, from the first point of view, as a pressure upon the ego. In brief, the superego behaves toward the ego as the parents once did toward the child. The superego makes the child feel guilty just as did the parents. The reproaches of the superego function as did the reproaches of the parents. Instead of parental criticism there is now self-criticism (19). The superego has turned aggression against itself.

The prohibitions of the superego must be reckoned with by the ego in expressing id impulses. In this way the superego serves as the vehicle of conscience (14). However, when the ego and the superego are in harmony, the relationship between the two is felt as pride in accomplishment, and the ego-ideal is manifested. The ego in this case measures itself against the superego and finds that its accomplishment does not fall short of its demands. The requirements of the ego-ideal are being met. The ego-ideal strives after perfection—and occasionally attains it. There are two major aspects, then, of the superego, the moral prohibitions and restrictions, and the ego-ideal. The former is restricting; the latter is satisfying.

The superego serves as an important means of control of those sexual and aggressive impulses, which, if not so controlled, would endanger the very foundation of social life.

The interrelation of the ego, superego, and id with reality may be summarized by a graphic illustration from Josselyn:

> On a dark night one walks down a street passing a jewelry store. No one is around. In the window showcase is a beautiful diamond ring. The id says: "I want that diamond. I want it because I love myself, because it would make me beautiful and would thus make other people love me, because I am angry at others having what I have not, and because I am uncomfortable under the tension of wanting what I do not have." The superego says, arbitrarily, "No, you can't break the window and take it." The ego solves the impasse by advising, "But you shall have it if you will save your money until you can buy it (21, 24).[7]

Neither the earlier discussion nor Josselyn's analogy should be taken to imply that the id, ego, and superego are to be thought of as *dei ex machina* which operate the personality, as a puppeteer would his

[7] From Josselyn (21). Copyright 1948 by Family Service Association of America, and published by permission.

puppets. They are constructs, each operating upon its own systematic principles despite Freud's over picturesque language.

Stages of Psychosexual Development

Psychoanalysis posits several stages in psychosexual development. In brief, its view is that the infant shows the capacity to receive erotic pleasure from stimulation of various erogenous zones which assume successive centrality in sequence through the various stages of psychosexual development. An erogenous zone is an area of the body which is sensitive to stimuli and is capable of being stimulated in such a way as to arouse pleasurable libidinal feelings. The lips and oral cavity form one such erogenous zone, the anal region another, and the genital organs still another. Each of these in turn becomes the center of focus of erotic pleasure in the course of psychosexual development. Table 2, suggested by one elsewhere (20) but considerably enlarged and modified, will expedite understanding of these stages. From birth through to adulthood there occurs the oral, anal, phallic, and genital psychosexual stages with the latter two stages separated by the so-called latency period.

Although the sequence is fixed, these stages are not separated one from the other in any rigid fashion. All stages overlap and pass gradually one into another. For example, while phenomena and problems of the oral stage are still very much in evidence, the anal stage has begun, and, as we shall see, the satisfactions of one stage are not entirely given up when the child has moved on to another stage.

The psychosexual stages through which the child passes are characterized by differing areas of libidinal localization, expressed in differing modes of pleasure finding and differing object relations. At each stage there is a characteristic structural organization of the personality and the emergence of certain characteristic mechanisms of adjustment, which, with the emergence of the ego, become the defense mechanisms. At appropriate places in later chapters these stages are described in detail.

In the light of this table it is possible to state another important contention of the psychoanalyst. This is the insistence on the tremendously important effect of these early years upon later personality structure. It will be noted that Table 2 gives most space to infancy (here taken by the psychoanalyst to be the first five years or so), a small amount to latency, and a still small but somewhat larger amount to adolescence and concluding with only a passing reference to adulthood. Since psychosexual development is crucial to psychoanalysis and its vicissitudes seem to become stabilized in an individual characteristic fashion with adolescence, this underscores the relative unimportance of later years. Actually, events in adult life are given attention in psychoanalysis, but there is no doubt that orthodox psychoanalysis considers a lifelong personality structure to be molded by the experiences of these earlier stages. Indeed, Freud was convinced from his experiences with his patients that personality is rather completely formed by the end of the fifth year and that further development primarily consists of elaborating the basic structure.

Relation of learning theory and psychoanalysis to other principles

Behavior-social learning theory and psychoanalytic contentions both bear important relations to the other principles of child psychology discussed in earlier chapters. This is the case with development, especially stages of development as expressed in critical periods; with socialization; and with the frustration-aggression hypotheses.

The critical-period hypothesis emphasizes the kinds of experiences crucial to healthy individual development at particular stages of growth. Psychoanalysis is the much more explicit of the two approaches in specifying the stages of development. It is primarily a developmental theory in the sense that it explains behavioral manifestations in terms of their genesis. Dollard and Miller's behavior-social learning theory in its stress on four characteristic training situations, each having long-lasting effects on the developing child, is not incompatible with the critical-period hypothesis. However, its adherents do not venture anything resembling a complete account of the factors responsible or of stages through which the child is supposed to develop. Psychoanalysis, on the other hand, in its theory of psychosexual development, provides a blueprint of what its advocates suppose occurs in the critical periods.

Behavior-social learning theory to a greater extent than psychoanalysis places weight upon the conditions of learning. Although acknowledging the importance of the first five or six years of life, behavior-social learning theorists are apt to regard the child (and the adult) as more modifiable at any age. Consequently they place relatively less emphasis upon infancy and early childhood as permanent formative influences while stressing the importance of learning throughout the entire span of childhood.

TABLE 2

THE COURSE OF PERSONALITY DEVELOPMENT ACCORDING TO PSYCHOANALYSIS

Areas of Libidinal Localization	Modes of Pleasure Finding	Object Relations	Structural Organization	Mechanisms
		Infancy Period		
1. Oral stage Early oral phase	Sucking, swallowing (incorporating)	Mother as first object	Id present. Beginnings of ego emerges in awareness, but it is essentially passive.	Fixation Regression Introjection Projection
Late oral phase	Biting (devouring destroying)	Ambivalence		
2. Anal stage Early anal phase	Expelling (rejecting, destroying)	Continued ambivalence	Ego strengthened and more active by mastering of motility and development of judgment. Anxiety appears. Forerunner of superego.	Denial
Late anal phase	Retaining (controlling, possessing)			
3. Phallic stage	Touching, looking at and exhibiting genitals	Oedipus complex	Superego develops out of reaction to Oedipus complex. Ego emerges in full form.	Beginning of mechanisms ego defense Sublimation Repression Reaction formation Undoing Isolation Displacement

		Latency Period		
No new area	All previous modes, but relative general drop in sexual interests	Extension to peers, sublimation of affection toward parents	Consolidation and strengthening ego and superego. Struggle quiescent among ego, id, and external environment.	No new mechanisms, but sublimation and reaction formation are prominent.
		Adolescent Period		
4. Genital stage Prepubertal phase	Revival of infantile modes of pleasure finding	Reactivation of love objects of childhood	Disruption of truce among units of structural organization.	Intellectualization Asceticism
Pubertal phase Heterosexual-genital	Adult modes of pleasure finding	New nonparental object relations	Reorganization of units in adult personality.	

Many psychoanalytic statements, particularly in the classic or ortho-dox formulation, make no clear distinction between maturation and socialization as a matter of learning. Psychoanalysis, although it does not formulate the problem in this fashion, has contributed a con-siderable number of specific hypotheses about how socialization influences personality. But these formulations, in turn, suggested to others, especially the so-called neo-Freudians, related ways of viewing socialization. A reconciliation among and integration of psycho-analytic and socialization and behavioral concepts would appear to be a fruitful approach to the personality of the child.

Psychoanalysis places heavy emphasis on intrinsic maturational factors, as distinguished from learning (25). The sequence of the psychosexual stages unfolds remorselessly, requiring hardly more than environmental triggering. Freud's position emphasizes intrinsic ma-turational factors which are met by experiences in which the indi-vidual learns to use his instinctual equipment.

Socialization has been influenced by and is capable of being recon-ciled with behavior-social learning theory. The same intellectual climate and locus for behavior-social learning theory gave us the contributions of Irvin L. Child and J.W.M. Whiting (27) on the process of socialization. Socialization centers on the question of how the infant and child becomes an adult in his own society. Learning theory provides us with the principles of learning; socialization pro-vides us with an important facet of the conditions of learning.

Miller and Dollard (24) explicitly relate their analysis of learning to the structure of the social environment. They compare the rat in the maze to the human being in his maze, i.e., his social environment. No psychologist would try to predict the rat's behavior in a maze without knowing the nature of the reinforcement and on which arm of the T-maze it is located. So, too, no psychologist would try to predict human behavior without knowing the nature and location of the reinforcement received from the human's culture.

It has been already indicated that socialization is a particular kind of learning. It is not surprising that in behavior-social learning theory, socialization provides a valuable way of understanding the types of responses that have been reinforced. Socialization in terms of rein-forcement requires three steps: (a) The infant is motivated by a *drive*. (b) He is faced with problems of behavior which serve as *cues* for imitation. (c) He acts and secures a reward which is drive reducing and the acquired pattern is *reinforced*.

In psychoanalysis, socialization is seen in a developmental matura-tional framework in which the child's libido shows the characteristic changes that have been described.   The development of the superego is especially vivid as a socialization phenomenon.   From the psychoanalytic standpoint, the child is very much a product of the family in which he is reared.   Nevertheless, as compared with behavior-social learning, psychoanalysis is relatively less well equipped to handle problems of socialization because of its contention that so much of behavior is instinctively determined, leaving less psychological space in which socialization may operate.

Although the frustration-aggression hypothesis was explicitly stated in connection with the behavior-social learning theory, it had been utilized in psychoanalysis before the appearance of the work of Dollard and his associates.   In his later work Freud postulated a death instinct in which external aggression was this instinct turned outward; earlier he had regarded frustration as leading to aggression when pleasure seeking or pain avoiding were blocked (8).

Summary

To supplement the principles of development and socialization discussed in earlier chapters, an additional framework for considering the psychology of the child is provided by two seemingly quite different theoretical orientations—behavior-social learning theory and psychoanalysis.

In an attempt at an integrated view of the structure and development of personality, various approaches have been advanced.   Behavior-social learning theory and psychoanalysis are considered to be fruitful approaches to the personality of the child.

Behavior-social learning as a process of the development of the personality rests on four fundamental factors: drive, responses, cue, and reinforcement.   All are essential for learning to occur, but reinforcement is made central.   The reinforcement is any event following the response which strengthens the tendency for the response to be repeated.   Derived needs are learned on the basis of the pattern of factors operative.   In addition to the development of personality, the structure of personality receives attention.   Habit is the basic unit, but there are other levels of learned behavior in the higher mental processes and in response hierarchies.

Psychoanalysis posits the existence of libidinal and aggressive instincts to serve as the vehicles for the dynamics of personality.   Its structure is to be accounted for by the interplay of id, ego, superego, and the environment. The viscissitudes of the developing personality are to be traced through various developmental stages—the oral, anal, phallic, and genital stages with the last two separated by the latency period.

Behavior-social learning theory and psychoanalysis complement each other. Where one is weak, the other is strong. Behavior-social learning theory supplies relatively few details in the structure of personality; psychoanalysis supplies an almost overwhelming mass of detail. Consequently, specification of the consequences of personality in psychoanalytic terms is more specific and intricate, although not necessarily more accurate. Psychoanalysis centers on motivation, or the dynamics of development; behavior-social learning theory on the process and condition of learning. Attempts to translate psychoanalytic concepts into more general psychological terms is one of the goals of later chapters. In this way child psychology may be more dynamic and psychoanalytic theory more precise.

For Further Reading

In their books *Personality and Psychotherapy* (New York: McGraw-Hill, 1950) and *Social Learning and Imitation* (New Haven, Conn.: Yale University Press, 1941) John Dollard and Neal E. Miller state behavior-social learning theory. For an account of both psychoanalytic and nonpsychoanalytic approaches to personality, the book by Calvin S. Hall and Gardner Lindzey, *Theories of Personality* (New York: Wiley, 1957), is recommended. Gerald S. Blum has written an excellent summarization of psychoanalytic theory in developmental terms, *Psychoanalytic Theories of Personality* (New York: McGraw-Hill, 1953).

References

1. Dollard, J., L. W. Doob, *et al.* *Frustration and aggression.* New Haven: Yale University Press, 1939.
2. Dollard, J., and N. E. Miller, *Personality and psychotherapy: an analysis of learning, thinking, and culture.* New York: McGraw-Hill, 1950.
3. Fenichel, O. *The psychoanalytic theory of neurosis.* New York: Norton, 1945.
4. Freud, Anna. *The ego and mechanisms of defense.* New York: International Universities Press, 1946.
5. Freud, S. *Wit and its relation to the unconscious.* New York: Moffat, 1916.
6. Freud, S. Psychogenic visual disturbances according to psychoanalytic conceptions. In *Collected papers.* Vol. 2. London: Hogarth, 1924.
7. Freud, S. Instincts and their vicissitudes. In *Collected Papers.* Vol. 4. London: Hogarth, 1925.

8. Freud, S. Mourning and melancholia. In *Collected Papers.* Vol. 4. London: Hogarth, 1925.
9. Freud, S. The unconscious. In *Collected Papers.* Vol. 4. London: Hogarth, 1925.
10. Freud, S. Repression. In *Collected Papers.* Vol. 4. London: Hogarth, 1925.
11. Freud, S. *Civilization and its discontents.* London: Liveright, 1930.
12. Freud, S. *New introductory lectures on psychoanalysis.* New York: Norton, 1935.
13. Freud, S. *The problem of anxiety.* New York: Norton, 1936.
14. Freud, S. *An outline of psychoanalysis.* New York: Norton, 1949.
15. Freud, S. *The question of lay analysis.* New York: Norton, 1950.
16. Freud, S. *Three essays in sexuality.* London: Hogarth, 1953.
17. Freud, S. *Group psychology and the analysis of the ego.* London: Hogarth, 1955.
18. Hartmann, H. Comments on the psychoanalytic theory of the ego. *Psychoanal. Stud. Child.,* 1950, 5, 74–95.
19. Hartmann, H., and R. M. Loewenstein. Notes on the superego. *Psychoanal. Stud. Child.,* 1962, 18, 42–81.
20. Healy, W., Augusta F. Bronner, and Anna M. Bowers. *The structure and meaning of psychoanalysis.* New York: Knopf, 1930.
21. Josselyn, Irene M. *Psychological development of children.* New York: Family Service Association, 1948.
22. Lewin, K. *A dynamic theory of personality.* New York: McGraw-Hill, 1935.
23. Marquis, Dorothy. Can conditioned responses be established in the new-born infant? *J. Genet. Psychol.,* 1931, 39, 479–492.
24. Miller, N. E., and J. Dollard. *Social learning and imitation.* New Haven: Yale University Press, 1941.
25. Rapaport, D. Psychoanalysis as a developmental psychology. In B. Kaplan, and S. Wapner (Eds.), *Perspectives in psychological theory: essays in honor of Heinz Werner.* New York: International Universities Press, 1960, 209–255.
26. Whiting, J. W. M. *Becoming a Kwoma.* New Haven: Yale University Press, 1941.
27. Whiting, J. W. M., and I. L. Child. *Child training and personality: a cross-cultural study.* New Haven: Yale University Press, 1953.

PART II

INFANCY

6

Prenatal Development,
Childbirth, and the Neonate

THE PROCESS of development begins, not at birth, but at conception. Here the child starts the long journey in his prenatal development from a fertilized egg cell to an organism and on to that change of environment we call childbirth, thereafter to face the world as a *neonate*. Let us consider this sequence in order, beginning with prenatal development.

From cell to organism

At conception the shuffling and chance combinations that occur during germ cell maturation are completed, and a new zygote is formed. From the moment of conception its genetic history and, to a certain extent, its heritable future are fixed. The genetic pool from which succeeding generations can draw is now created. In the absence of extremes of environmental conditions (such as excessive dosages of X-rays) or of spontaneous modifications (mutations) which can alter the germ plasm, the genetic components available to future generations are established. Reproduction during maturity will provide the opportunity for interaction with new elements from a different genetic population, and the consequent formation of a new genetic pool.

Although the genetic past and potential future of the new organism are now restricted and delimited, its present is far from stabilized. During the ten lunar months between conception and birth the genes are given an environment in which to produce their chemical reactions.

125

This environment will be crucial for determining whether a given complex of genes will be permitted to express itself in observable structure or function, or whether its influence will be suppressed or aborted. This is true for any type of organism. For example, experiments have shown that vestigial wings which result from a hereditary mutation in the fruit fly may fail to appear unless the larvae are kept at low temperatures. Insects with the same genetic history will, if incubated at higher temperatures, fail to develop the abnormal wing structure. This is no different from the practical situation faced by the farmer who knows that he will not get a good crop from the best of seeds unless optimal soil and weather conditions prevail.

The developing organism lives in a sequestered environment—the uterus of the mother—to which, except in cases of multiple birth, he has exclusive property right. During this period, the mother plays the truly unique role for which nature has so admirably equipped her. Although perhaps always of value, at no other time in life will she be completely indispensable to her child. In his *Brave New World*, Aldous Huxley fantasied a process by means of which children would develop in demijohns rather than uteri, would have a blood surrogate pumped mechanically through a synthetic lung, and, after having been exposed to a precisely regulated set of conditions, would eventually be decanted with a minimum of trauma. At our present state of knowledge, however, there appears to be no satisfactory surrogate for the mother during the vital phase of development from cell to organism.

Conditions for Development

In discussing external influences upon embryological development, Hamburger (16) has distinguished between conditions for and modifiers of development. Certain essential agents found in the prenatal environment are conditions for development so long as they remain within the normal range. Should they exceed this range, they become modifiers of development. An example is the amount of available oxygen. Should this deviate too drastically from an optimal level, then the course of development would be drastically modified by death or various kinds and degrees of fetal damage.

Sequence of prenatal development. Almost immediately following fertilization, the zygote begins the process of cell division which will transform it into a highly differentiated multicelled organism. This transformation occurs both by increase in the number of cells and by increase in size and weight of many individual cells. As direct observation of this process *in vitro* is impossible, precise charting of the embryological timetable, especially the first two weeks of intrauterine life, is difficult. During this period, the conceptus retains its egglike state and derives its nourishment from parts of the zygote that will not be used in the subsequent development of the organism. Appropriately, this period is generally called the *ovular* or *germinal* stage.

The period from about the second through the fifth weeks is called the *embryonic* stage. During this time, the important cellular layers are differentiated and the various body parts begin to appear. After the sixth week, the new organism is known as the fetus, and the period is designated as the *fetal* period.

In early divisions, the cells become differentiated into formative and auxiliary components of the ovum. One function of the auxiliaries is to form a covering for the cells from which the embryo proper will develop. Very soon fluid appears, giving the early ovum the appearance of a fluid-filled sphere. At this stage, it is known as a blastula. As this fluid collects, the formative cells are pushed into one side of the blastula and, with other cells of the region, form the embryonic disc, from which the embryo develops. In this clump of cells, a smaller cavity forms, later to be recognized as the amnion. The outer layer of cells, called the trophoblast, forms the means of attaching the embryo to the uterine wall and also prepares for the subsequent interchange of nutritive and waste products.

As the trophoblast cells produce a greater accumulation of fluid, the embryo becomes what is known as a blastocyst and is now ready for implantation. The inner mass of cells in this rapidly proliferating system quickly produces a new layer of cells, the endoderm, which will line the blastocyst and produce another closed space called the yolk sac. This is an extremely important structure in other species than man, as it is the chief source of nutritive materials during early developmental periods. In man, however, its value is transitory and by the end of the fourth week of gestation, it has largely disappeared. Also arising from the endoderm is the allantois, a sausage-shaped tube that extends outward toward the periphery of the embryo. That part that remains in contact with the embryonic disc will ultimately constitute the bladder.

Soon a third layer of cells, the mesoderm, spreads out into the original blast-cyst cavity. These cells become thickened at one end and form the *body stalk*, which will fuse with the allantois to form the *umbilical cord*—the chief avenue over which maternal-fetal interchange will occur. The outer layer of the entire embryo is called the chorion. On the outside of the chorion, little spidery filaments, called villi (singular, villus), appear and secure themselves in the endometrium or lining of the uterus. As soon as blood vessels appear, as they do from the allantois and body stalk, they find their way into the openings of the villi and thence into the uterine walls.

The nutritional demands of the rapidly growing embryo cannot for long be satisfied by materials contained within the ovum, and more permanent arrangements must be made. As soon as the zygote is implanted in the uterine wall, the *placenta* begins to develop. This new and temporary organ will handle the interchange of nutrients and waste products until such time as the new organism can sustain independent existence. The placenta is a truly amazing structure which shows great interspecies variability. Corner (5) has emphasized this fact with the reminder that placentas of such organisms as mouse, elephant, and man differ from one another more than do the brains or noses of these animals. In fact, a good case could be made for classifying mammals according to the type of their placentation.

The Biological Mother-Child Relationship

An adequate discussion of the placenta requires clarification of the biological relationship between mother and child during the prenatal period. Essentially this relationship is that of host and parasite. The mother takes care of all the vital functions, including provision of nutrients and oxygen and the expulsion of carbon dioxide and other waste products. The nutrients provided the fetus are already carefully "screened"; that is, they are those that have already found their way into the mother's blood stream. Consequently, the circulatory systems of the two organisms are of crucial importance for future development. Corner has provided an effective metaphorical description of the placenta-uterus association as follows:

If the reader has difficulty visualizing the relation of the placenta to the uterus, let him imagine a piece of ground (representing the uterine wall) beneath which is a network of terra cotta pipes (the blood vessels). Dig a hole in the ground, breaking off the pipes as you dig, and make it just large enough to receive the dense roots of a tree (the placenta). Pave the ground over the hole and all about it, the paving representing the chorio-amniotic surface of the placenta. . . . The trunk of your tree is the umbilical cord. The roots will be bathed in fluid from the cut ends of the underground pipes; in like manner the root system of the placental villi dips into a sort of pool filled with maternal blood from the opened ends of small arteries and drained by opened veins. This blood is the source of oxygen and nourishment for the infant and the means of disposal of carbon dioxide and organic wastes which filter back into it from the villi-roots of the embryo (5, 46).[1]

Should the placenta fail to develop properly, or should its function be seriously impaired at any time during the pregnancy, then damage to the fetus is virtually inevitable. The placenta is truly the lifeline of the new organism, and, no matter how excellent the seed that was fertilized and that formed the basis for the new life, normal development cannot occur without adequate placental attachment.

Although the placental villi dip into "pools" or sinuses of maternal blood, there is no direct connection between the bloodstream of mother and child. Indeed, during the early weeks of gestation, the infant does not have anything that could technically be called a bloodstream. Rather he has cells that are developing into blood cells and the beginnings of a circulatory system capable of effecting transfer across the placental barrier. Very early in embryonic life the fetal heart begins to pulse and to force its own blood through its own closed vascular system. However, very quickly the outer layer of the embryo begins to form capillaries which terminate close to terminals on the maternal side. Actual exchange of chemical materials is accomplished by diffusion through these capillary walls. Thus, although there is no direct connection between the circulatory systems of the two organisms, there is certainly interaction between them.

It is now appropriate to consider the other major circulating and communicating network—the nervous system. Again, there is no direct connection between mother and child in the sense that the nerve fibers of one organism form an open system and become affiliated with fibers from the other system. In order to help demolish certain persistent stereotypes about the influence of the mother on the fetus, it has become customary in recent years to emphasize the lack of direct connection between the nervous system of the mother and that of the fetus. Montagu, however, cautions that such assertions, unequivocally made, are based on an inadequate conception of the nervous system. He writes:

> A still widely prevalent belief has it that there is no connection between the nervous systems of mother and fetus. This notion is based on a very narrow conception of the nervous system. It is through the neurohumoral system, the system comprising the interrelated nervous and endocrine systems acting through the fluid medium of the blood (and its oxygen and carbon-dioxide contents), that nervous changes in

[1] From Corner (5). Copyright 1944 by the Yale University Press, and published with permission.

the mother may effect the fetus. The common endocrine pool of the mother and fetus forms a neurohumoral bond between them. The endocrine systems of mother and fetus complement each other.

All this is not to say that there is anything in the old wives' tale of "maternal impressions." The mother's "impressions," her "psychological states" as such, cannot possibly be transmitted to the fetus. What are transmitted are the gross chemical changes which occur in the mother and, so far as we know at the present time, nothing more (26, 152).[2]

Perhaps an accurate way of summarizing the relationship is that the two systems, although separate and distinct, nonetheless interact.

Prenatal development is so orderly a process that it is possible to chart its important features in succinct form. In Table 3 a brief summary of some of the more significant events in the prenatal calendar has been assembled. Study of this table will acquaint the reader with a sequence of prenatal growth and will give some idea of the patterning and interlocking of growth during this developmental phase.

TABLE 3

APPROXIMATE TIMETABLE OF PRENATAL DEVELOPMENT *

First Month

Fertilization, descent of ovum from tube to uterus. Early cell division and formation of embryonic disc from which new organism will develop. Early formation of three layers of cells—the *ectoderm*, from which sense organs and nervous system will develop; the *mesoderm*, from which circulatory, skeletal, and muscular systems will develop; and *endoderm*, from which digestive and some glandular systems will develop. Special layer of cells formed in the uterus which will become the *placenta* and through which nutritive substances will be carried to the new organism and waste products carried away. Special layer of cells forms the *amnion* or water-sac, which will surround the developing embryo except at umbilical cord. Heart tube forms and begins to pulsate and force blood to circulate through blood vessels in embryonic disc. Nervous system begins to arise, first in form of neural groove. Development of intestinal tract, lungs, liver, and kidneys begins. By end of one month, the embryo is about one-fourth inch long, curled into a crescent, with small nubbins on sides of body indicating incipient arms and legs.

Second Month

Embryo increases in size to about 1½ inches. Bones and muscle begin to round out contours of body. Face and neck develop and begin to give features a human appearance. Forehead very prominent, reflecting precocious development of brain in comparison to rest of body. Limb buds elongate. Muscles and cartilage develop. Sex organs begin to form.

[2] From Montagu (26). Copyright 1950 by the Josiah Macy, Jr. Foundation, and published with permission.

Third Month

Beginning of fetal period. Sexual differentiation continues, with male sexual organs showing more rapid development and the female remaining more neutral. Buds for all 20 temporary teeth laid down. Vocal cords appear; digestive system shows activity. Stomach cells begin to secrete fluid; liver pours bile into intestine. Kidneys begin functioning, with urine gradually seeping into amniotic fluid. Other waste products passed through placenta into mother's blood. Bones and muscles continue development, and by end of third month spontaneous movements of arms, legs, shoulders, and fingers are possible.

Fourth Month

Lower parts of body show relatively accelerated rate, so that head size decreases from one-half to one-fourth of body size. Back straightens; hands and feet are well-formed. Skin appears dark red, owing to coursing of blood showing through thin skin, and wrinkled, owing to absence of underlying fat. Finger closure is possible. Reflexes become more active as muscular maturation continues. Fetus begins to stir and to thrust out arms and legs in movements readily perceived by the mother.

Fifth Month

Skin structures begin to attain final form. Sweat and sebaceous glands are formed and function. Skin derivatives also appear—hair, nails on fingers and toes. Bony axis becomes quite straight, and much spontaneous activity occurs. Fetus is lean and wrinkled, about one foot long and weighs about one pound. If aborted, it may respire briefly, but will soon die as it seems unable to maintain movements necessary for continued breathing.

Sixth Month

Eyelids, which have been fused shut since third month, reopen; eyes are completely formed. Taste buds appear on tongue and in mouth and are, in fact, more abundant than in the infant or adult. If born, the six-month fetus will perhaps live a few hours or longer if protected in an incubator. During brief extrauterine life, may exhibit "Moro" or startle responses.

Seventh Month

Organism capable of independent life from this time on. Cerebral hemispheres cover almost the entire brain. Seven-month fetus can emit a variety of specialized responses. Generally is about 16 inches long and weighs about three pounds. If born, will be able to cry, breathe, and swallow, but is very sensitive to infections and will need highly sheltered environment for survival.

Eighth and Ninth Month

During this time, finishing touches are being put on the various organs and functional capacities. Fat is formed rapidly over the entire body, smoothing out the wrinkled skin and rounding out body contours. Dull red color of skin fades so that at birth pigmentation of skin is usually very slight in all races. Activity is usually great, and he can change his position within the somewhat crowded uterus. Periods of activity will alternate with periods of quiescence. Fetal organs step up their activity. Fetal heart rate becomes quite rapid. Digestive organs continue to expel more waste products, leading to the formation of a fetal stool, called the *meconium*, which is expelled shortly after birth. Violent uterine contractions begin, though milder ones have been tolerated earlier, and the fetus is eventually expelled from the womb into an independent physiological existence.

* This is adapted largely from *Biography of the Unborn* (10), by M. S. Gilbert. Material from other sources has been added where relevant.

Figure 4 (page 141) pictures changes in prenatal form and proportion. It is not until about the third month that the fetus resembles a human being. The head is still disproportionately large with legs much shorter than they will be later—an exemplification of the principle of cephalo-caudal developmental direction. The entire course of prenatal development illustrates the principle of differentiation and integration. Even as early as the eighth week, differentiation is exhibited. It shows, for example, in the heart beat, and in simple body movements, such as the bending of the neck in a prematurely born fetus when stimulated by stroking the cheek with a hair (17). By about 14 weeks the early predominately generalized responses are less prominent, and less stereotyped forms of activity are being exhibited.

It is clear that there are external and internal environments for the prenatal infant. "Spontaneous" movements are, of course, very much present as any mother can attest. Referring to them as "spontaneous," although carrying a certain air of knowledge, is actually a confession that the stimuli that give rise to them cannot be identified precisely. Evidence of influence from the external environment upon the fetus is also available. Events happening in the external world elicit movements from him. After activity on the part of the mother, fetal activity decreases as compared to such activity when the mother is quiet (34). This decrease in activity after maternal exercise is attributed to the increased oxygen supply available to the fetus.

In the table of prenatal development it was mentioned incidentally that conditioning of the fetus could take place. In one study (37), pairing of noise and vibriotactile stimulation to the mother's abdomen was used as the response measure, while fetal movements were measured by recording tambours taped to her abdomen which recorded on kymograph paper. Between 15 and 20 paired stimulations were required to establish the conditioning to the point where the sound alone produced fetal movement. Thus, learning *in utero* was demonstrated.

Other environmental influences are at work—physical agents, such as X-rays; nutritional effects, such as vitamin deficiencies; drugs; infections; maternal illnesses, such as hypertension where there is no infection; and maternal sensitizations, such as the Rh factor in the blood, in which antibodies are produced resulting in incompatibility of maternal and fetal blood types (26). Mere mention is sufficient to give some conception of their range. Despite the presence of environmental sources of stimulation, the influence of maturation is obviously the more important factor in the developmental process during the prenatal period.

The sheer amount of fetal activity found by objective measurement of movement in the mother's body is related positively to scores of the same infants on the Gesell developmental schedule at 12 months postnatally to judge from a correlation of .62 (32). The finding itself seems well established. Interpretation, however, is difficult.

The investigators themselves suggested several possibilities. They thought the activity might result from facilitation arising from six months of prenatal practice in the function measured. However, they suggested that it might also stem from a tendency of mothers who, in order to have the movement recorded, reported the subjective experience of movement—the same mothers incidentally who tended to transmit genetically greater ability to their offspring. Or it might have been that the mothers with higher fetal activity tended later to surround their children with more stimulating conditions for mental development. It is difficult, if not impossible, to choose among these possibilities. Performance postnatally can be predicted from the amount of fetal activity, but at present the causes are not capable of precise specification.

Pregnancy and the Mother

A moment's consideration will help to show why it is appropriate to examine the question of maternal attitudes as they exist before the birth of the child. Pregnancy is a developmental crisis for the mother (3), "a critical period of adulthood." Inescapably, she must adjust her manner of living to the coming infant. Necessarily this has ramifications in all aspects of her behavior. The mother has some conception of what she would like the infant to be. These attitudes will carry over into her relationships with the child helping to direct her behavior as she strives to guide the infant's behavior.

Before the birth of the child she has developed a pattern of characteristic attitudes. Does she look forward with eager anticipation to

the coming child?   Does she hate the very thought of the new stranger?
Or, as is not unlikely, is her attitude a mixed one?   A mother who was
never irritated with the thought of the coming child would be more (or
less) than human.

Sears, Maccoby, and Levin (35) in the "pattern" study, the procedure
for which is described on page 233, found that in a group of about 400
mothers, 50 per cent were rated as delighted with the coming child,
another 18 per cent as pleased but with no evidence of enthusiasm,
while 25 per cent had either mixed feelings or were displeased.   Those
mothers having only their first child included more who were pleased
than among those reporting on later children as well.   The mothers
with more than one child tended to be more pleased the greater the
distance between their pregnancies, and to be more pleased if their
existing children were girls rather than boys only, or were both boys
and girls.   Consciously at least, few of the mothers carried over their
doubts or displeasure into the period after the child was born.   For
example, although a mother might have "wanted to wait," once the
child was born, her doubts tended to disappear.

To express this question of attitudes in more general terms, a continuum extending from enthusiastic acceptance of the child at one end
to rejection of the child at the other is suggested.   Even a so-called
rejecting mother almost always shows some positive reaching-out, accepting behavior as well.   Mothers reject some trends in their children
and accept and stimulate others.

These attitudes and behaviors of the mother also shift with changes
in the mother, the child, and in the situation.   To speak of rejection
means merely that negative feelings are dominant in a particular
mother at a particular time.   Levy's findings on mothering which
follows can be interpreted as consistent with this dimension—with the
more maternal subjects toward the accepting end of the continuum
and the less maternal subjects toward the rejecting end of the
continuum.

There is a suggestion that there is a biologically determined potentiality for motherliness.   Levy (23) related favorable attitudes toward
mothering to the duration of menstrual flow.   Indications of "mothering," used in making the rating, included playing with dolls in childhood, taking care of babies, "baby carriage peeking," number of
children wanted, and anticipation of care and breast feeding of their
babies.   He found that the longer the duration of menstrual flow, the
greater the amount of mothering behavior.   This was expressed in a
correlation coefficient of 0.58.

For a statistically significant relationship to be found between attitudinal matters and the physiological function of menstrual flow implies either that there is a constitutional basis of maternal attitudes or, conversely, that attitudes are able to bring about actual physiological differences among potential mothers. Irrespective of which relationship ultimately proves correct, a close relationship has been demonstrated between the psychological function of mothering and a physiological factor.

Some psychiatrically oriented pediatricians, child psychiatrists, and psychologists are convinced that a considerable amount of the discomfort experienced by mothers during pregnancy arises because they are anxious and expect to have a difficult time. This is due, in turn, either to not wanting the child or to any one of a number of other reasons.

Zemlick and Watson (39) were interested in learning whether attitudes of acceptance or rejection had an effect on the prospective mother's psychological and physical adjustment during pregnancy. In other words, they wished to know whether a prospective mother who tended to reject her coming child also showed psychological and physical differences from a mother who adopted a positive accepting attitude toward her child-to-be. Mothers expecting their first child were their subjects. Each mother was studied by means of: (1) a selection of Thematic Apperception Test cards (TAT), through which was established her level of anxiety; (2) a psychosomatic inventory (PS), in which she reported her psychological and somatic symptoms; and (3) a Pregnancy Attitude Scale (ZAR), composed of items which supplied information about her attitudes toward pregnancy, such as the degree to which she wanted the child.

Independently of these data, adjustment to pregnancy, in terms of physical and emotional symptoms, was rated by an obstetrician who saw each mother, on the average, ten times. He also rated the mother's behavior during labor and delivery in terms of her adequacy in meeting this crisis (delivery adjustment rank).

Some of the obtained relationships among these measures are reported in Table 4. Both in early and late pregnancy, the physical symptoms found by the obstetrician (the first entry at the top of the table) did not correlate too highly with the predictors of anxieties, symptoms, and attitudes (down the table). Correlations at both early and late pregnancy, significant at the ten per cent level, were found only between the report of the physical symptoms by the obstetrician and the scores on the psychosomatic inventory. Emotional symptoms and delivery adjustment rank (the second and third entries at the top of the table), as judged by the obstetrician, showed substantial positive correlation with the anxiety these mothers displayed, the symptoms they recognized, and the attitudes of rejection they exhibited.

TABLE 4

CORRELATION OF RATINGS OF MOTHER'S ADJUSTMENT DURING PREGNANCY AND HER ANXIETY, SYMPTOMS, AND ATTITUDES OF REJECTION °

		Physical Symptoms	Emotional Symptoms	Delivery Adjustment Rank
Early Pregnancy (2 to 5 months)				
Anxiety	(TAT)	0.17	0.44†	0.54†
Symptoms	(PS)	0.56†	0.74†	0.51†
Attitudes	(ZAR)	0.30	0.64†	0.66†
Late Pregnancy (7½ months)				
Anxiety	(TAT)	0.41	0.52†	0.47†
Symptoms	(PS)	0.51†	0.79†	0.50†
Attitudes	(ZAR)	0.11	0.53†	0.40

° From Zemlick and Watson (39). Copyright 1953 by the American Orthopsychiatric Association, and published with permission.
† Significant at least at 0.10 level.

This positive correlation between attitudes of rejection or acceptance verbalized by the mothers on the attitude scale on the one hand, and emotional symptoms exhibited and delivery adjustment rank on the other, is particularly noteworthy. Mothers with acceptant attitudes tended to have fewer emotional symptoms and higher delivery adjustment, whereas mothers who exhibited rejecting attitudes tended to have more emotional symptoms and lower delivery adjustment. The more the mothers rejected their coming child, the stormier pregnancy they seemed to have.

It is important to note that these mothers were not emotionally disturbed or abnormal individuals. None was neurotic, psychotic, or mentally retarded. And yet, in these more or less normal, well-meaning mothers varying degrees of acceptance and rejection were found, thus disposing of the allegation sometimes made that only abnormal mothers reject their children.

As pregnancy proceeds, the mother is apt to become increasingly concerned with the coming birth process of which she is to be so much a part. Considerable effort in recent years has been directed toward inculcating in her a psychologically healthy receptive point of view toward the coming experience. If approached properly, Grantley Dick Read (30) contends, only a small percentage of births need be traumatic. Perhaps 95 per cent of mothers have no physical abnormalities that would prevent normal childbirth. He maintains that fear is the chief pain-producing agent in what otherwise would be uneventful labor.

Labor is hard work, to be sure, but not intrinsically a fearful experience. The confusion of work with pain is the consequence, he holds, of negative suggestions that lead the mother to view childbirth as a frightening ordeal. The notion that it is the "softness" of modern life that brings on these difficulties is rejected by him as fallacious on the basis of the cogent argument that women's health and longevity are at their greatest in contemporary life. Fear, he says, prevents the balance of effort and relaxation that is an aspect of any hard work. Consequently, teaching the mother correct ways to relax is an important aspect of his methods.

Use of drugs to make the mother less aware of what is happening only on those few occasions when definite medical indications are present allows most mothers to experience to the fullest this important event. Most mothers who follow Read's prescription report that giving birth becomes a profoundly moving, even exhilarating experience. Although Read has produced impressive statistics concerning the value of his method and has won numerous professional supporters and the enthusiastic testimonial of many mothers, it is only fair to add that not all experts accept his methods, especially in their more radically expressed forms.

It is apparent that procedures advocated by Read align themselves with the general trend of opinion described in an earlier chapter as "permissive" rather than "regulatory." Another procedure favored in these circles is "rooming-in." This is a hospital arrangement whereby the mother cares for her newborn baby in her hospital room, rather than having the infant lodged in the nursery, except for his visits to the mother at feeding time. This procedure signifies more than mere rearrangement of physical facilities. It recognizes the importance of mother and child as a physical and psychological unit both before birth and thereafter.

Childbirth

A full-term baby is delivered on the average after 40 weeks, ranging from 37 to 42 weeks (8). If all goes well, the birth process, although work for the mother, and always containing some element of danger for both her and child, is completed in a very large propor-

tion of cases without physical or psychological harm to either.   Nevertheless, something can be learned from study of that small percentage
where something does go wrong.

Influence of Difficult Birth upon the Newborn

For the infant a long and difficult birth may be accompanied by
anoxia, i.e., a reduced oxygen supply; by toxins in the blood supply;
or by direct injury to the brain.   The effect of anoxia and other birth
traumata has received careful study (11, 12, 13).   The investigators
first devised tests differentiating normal newborns, none over seven
days of age, from traumatized infants.   The measures that differentiated babies from the two groups included threshold for pain, ability
to fixate the eyes, maturity, muscular activity, irritability, and muscle
tension.

Subsequently they studied whether indications of impairment were
still present three years after birth.   The anoxic children were significantly poorer on cognitive measures, such as the Stanford-Binet vocabulary size, and a concept test requiring placing blocks according to
color, form, and size.   They also exhibited more neurological signs
and some differences in personality with greater distractibility being
the most prominent.   The damage was seldom severe; few of them
were either palsied or mentally retarded.   Anoxia did not have an all-
or-none effect, but brain damage formed a continuum from a majority
of anoxic children with a minimal amount of impairment to a few at
the extreme of severe impairment.

A careful study (33) was undertaken of the birth records of a large
number of schoolchildren who manifested behavior problems.   About
900 problem children from the Baltimore public schools were each
matched with a nonproblem control child drawn from the same classroom.   The behavior problem sample showed a significantly greater
proportion of premature birth or abnormalities during birth.   Although
by no means all the children exhibited the same symptons, hyperactiv-
ity, confusion, and disorganization were conspicuous among those with
abnormalities of birth.   As the investigators themselves were careful
to point out, many other factors contribute to behavior disorders.

Anxiety in the Newborn and the Birth Process

The differential responses of newborns to various birth processes or
even the general effect of birth on all infants can only be guessed.

Freud suggested that the sudden flooding of excitation that strikes all infants at birth was the prototype of later anxiety. After the calm of uterine existence, with its relatively constant temperature, its lack of sensory stimulation other than kinesthetic and vibratory, the newborn infant might be faced with an overwhelming situation with which he cannot cope. Freud, himself, attached only some slight general significance to it. However, Otto Rank, who worked with him for a time, designated birth trauma the major causative factor for later neurotic manifestations of all kinds. Associated with the view that birth is an upheaval, a thrust into the cruel world, is the proposal that this psychological shock produces a permanent unconscious yearning for the protection and security once afforded by the womb. This return to the womb becomes a goal of those who would escape the world. Aside from this, psychoanalytic thinking is not concerned with the neonatal period as such.

The view that some anxiety arises on the basis of the birth process at least appears possible, even plausible. The difficulty, of course, is to demonstrate this unequivocally. A study (4) presented as suggestive, not conclusive, examined two groups of children, aged between seven and twelve. In one, the experimental group, the birth duration was prolonged; the other, the control group, the birth duration was short. Experimental group mothers described their children as nervous and showing more fears than reported by mothers of the control children. Rorschach indices of anxiety and immaturity were more prevalent among the children whose birth had been prolonged. The results are hard to interpret properly. One complication was that the mothers in the experimental group could hardly have been unaware of the prolonged birth that may well have colored their behavior toward the child over the years.

Maternal Reactions to Childbirth

Physical complications and consequence to childbirth for the mother are outside the scope of this book. However, brief reference should be made to the considerable evidence that emotional disturbances subsequent to childbearing occasionally do occur (27). The figure commonly accepted is in the neighborhood of one in 400 deliveries. It appears that childbirth itself is merely a precipitating feature for the appearance of a personality disturbance rooted farther in the past. In one study (27) of 54 mothers, it was found they tended to come from homes in which the mother was the dominant parent and that they, themselves, were often aggressive, nonfeminine, compulsive persons.

This suggests that a particular personality constellation in the mother predisposes her to develop emotional disturbance on the birth of her child.

The Neonate

During the first month of life an infant is called a *neonate* (28). The neonatal period, then, is a stage preceding the rest of infancy. It will serve as a means against which to sketch the behavoir repertoire of the newborn.

It would be fruitless to try to state the sensitivities and activities of which the infant is capable only at the moment of birth. We shall therefore discuss whatever appears in his behavior during the first month of life, even if it is known that a particular function appears earlier or later during the neonatal period. For example, even within the span of the first four days of life, the threshold for pain sensitivity diminishes (24). Studies of the newborn infant cast in developmental form are not discussed here but in the next chapter concerned with development in infancy. This means that the cumulative influence principle of development does not figure in the discussion that follows. The neonatal period provides the base line of behavior against which to see the later effects of maturation and learning.

Physical Appearance and Bodily Proportions

Even a fond mother may experience a sense of shock at the first sight of the tiny, wizened, red creature that is her offspring. (The "newborn" babies of the advertisements are apparently about two months of age.) The eyes are approximately one-half their adult size, and the body as a whole is only one-twentieth of its adult dimensions. The head is about one-fourth of body length as compared to the adult's one-seventh. As a consequence of these proportions the neonate appears all head and eyes. Figure 4 below shows something of his general appearance. At birth, the average newborn weighs seven or eight pounds and measures about 20 inches. The range, however, is from three to 16 pounds and from 17 to 21 or 22 inches. Boys are generally slightly larger and heavier than girls.

The Neonate as an Organism

We may speak of the neonate as an organism as distinguished from the person he is to become. The human being may be viewed on vari-

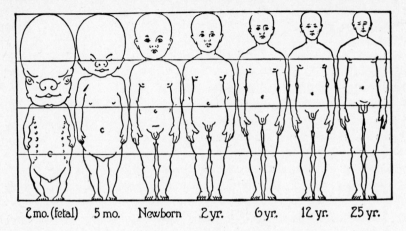

2 mo. (fetal)　5 mo.　Newborn　2 yr.　6 yr.　12 yr.　25 yr.

Figure 4. Changes in body form and proportion during prenatal and postnatal growth. (From C. M. Jackson (Ed.), Human Anatomy, 9th ed. Copyright 1933 by Blakiston Division, McGraw-Hill Book Company, and published with permission.)

ous levels. He may be seen as a molecular aggregation, an organism, a person, as an aspect of a diadic unit of two or more persons, and as an aggregate in a group. In other words, he may be viewed in order of expanding perspective at a physical-chemical level, a biological level, a psychological level, a social psychological level, and a sociological level.

The scientific laws laboriously worked out at one level are not necessarily suitable for application at a different level. In scrutinizing the child at a given level, we view him in a different light and see different phenomena than we would if another level were applied. The physical-chemical level is too far removed for direct concern; the psychological level has not yet come into being.

We shall look at the neonate as a biological organism viewed in cross-sectional perspective. We take our vantage point at the biological level because in the neonate there has occurred a minimum of psychological interaction with others. Psychological laws either of the individual person or of the diadic (social) sort are not relevant in this examination of the neonate's behavior repertoire.

In the light of these principles our organization of the findings on the neonate becomes clear. We must consider reactions to various forms of stimuli and the motor responses of which he is capable.

Sensory Stimulation [3]

There is no question that the neonate can see, hear, smell, and taste. What we need to know are some of the particulars about his prowess with respect to these sensory processes.

Reactions to visual stimuli. The neonate reacts to light, but it is not certain whether he distinguishes color as such. In other words, at birth he may be temporarily color-blind. He does, however, respond to different degrees of brightness. Closing the eyes spontaneously to a flash of light and to objects moving toward the eyes has been noted. Within a day or two after birth the pupillary reflex (widening or narrowing of the pupil in response to light) has been observed. Eye movements of various sorts have also been found. These include: pursuit (following a visual stimulus with movement of the eyes); saccadic (quick jerky fixations as in adult reading); coordinate (eyes moving together); and coordinate compensatory (head quickly moving in one direction, with eye movements in opposite direction).

The eye movement responses just defined are either reflex in character or, at least, of a circumscribed nature. More gross muscular patterns or general mass behavior has also been elicited. Practically any visual stimuli, if sufficiently intense, will release circulatory and respiratory (for example, "catching" the breath) responses in the neonate. The startle response involving coordination of many parts of the body is also elicited by intense visual stimulation. Thus, both reflex and mass activity are reactions to visual stimuli.

Reactions to auditory stimuli. There is some question as to whether the neonate can hear immediately at birth. Certainly neonates vary in sensitivity, with some showing an imperviousness to the influence of sound, despite later normal hearing. Neonatal infants fail to make pitch discriminations, but they do respond differentially to various intensities of sound.

As in visual responses, both specific reflexes, such as blinking the eyes and gross muscular patterns of response, appear. An investigator (38) found that an an infant ten minutes old was able to turn his eyes in the direction of an auditory stimulus. A crude form of auditory localization (coordination of auditory and visual functioning) appears to be possible without learning.

Reactions to other sensory stimuli. Both taste and smell are well developed at birth. The neonate responds to odors even during sleep by squirming, crying, and sucking. As for taste, sugar solutions tend

[3] The present account leans heavily upon that of Pratt (28).

to elicit sucking which is maintained; acid solutions evoke sucking which lasts for a shorter period; salt solutions, after being tried a bit, are not sucked; while bitter solutions, such as quinine, are seldom sucked.   However, wide individual differences among neonates to taste thresholds are found.

The neonate's skin is sensitive to touch, temperature, and pain.   Concerning skin sensitiveness, there is a general principle that with increase in intensity there is a progression from more localized to more general bodily movements.   A light touch may bring about a slight withdrawal of the part touched and no more, a heavy pressure brings out much more violent and widespread activity.

Sensitivity to being moved or changed in position, which stimulates the static receptors, is shown in postural or "balance" responses, by which the neonate rights himself when not too far off-balance.   Reactions to internal (organic) stimuli are present.   Although the respiratory and circulatory system supply some of these, the preponderance of the internal stimuli comes from the digestive and excretory systems. Regurgitation, hiccoughing, urination, and excretion are illustrative of this.

It is apparent, even from this brief summarization, that the neonate exhibits a varied repertoire of reactions to sensory stimuli.   His sensory capacities allow him to be sensitive to his external and internal environment.   Although sensory capacities will increase in sensitivity and scope, a considerable variety is available during the neonatal period.

Motor Responses

The distinction between reactions to sensory stimulation and motor responses, although clear enough in some respects, is nothing more than a matter of emphasis.   In the preceding section, focus was on the sensory modality originating the response.   Nevertheless, sensory stimulation was known to occur through the responses elicited.   We now group responses by the motor areas served.   Naturally, many of the same kinds of responses appear again, but they are now in the setting of such areas as the eye, mouth, and trunk.

Representative motor responses.   A succinct indication of some of the motor responses of the neonate is adapted from a summary by Dennis (6).

1. EYE RESPONSES—opening and closing eyelids, pupillary, pursuit, saccadic, and coordinate compensatory responses (described in reactions to visual stimuli).

2. FACIAL AND MOUTH RESPONSES—opening and closing mouth, lip

movement, sucking, pushing objects from mouth, yawning, and grimacing.

3. THROAT RESPONSES—crying, swallowing, coughing, gagging, vomiting, hiccoughing, cooing, and holding the breath.

4. HEAD MOVEMENTS—upward and downward, side to side, and balancing in response to change of bodily position.

5. ARM RESPONSES—closing hand, arm flexion, rubbing face, grasp reflex, and "random" movements.

6. TRUNK REACTIONS—arching back and twisting.

7. FOOT AND LEG RESPONSES—knee jerk, flexion, extension, kicking (both legs simultaneously), stepping (when neonate held upright with feet touching surface), and toe flexion.

8. COORDINATE RESPONSES OF MANY BODY PARTS—resting and sleeping position (legs flexed, fists closed, upper arms out straight from shoulder with forearms flexed at right angles parallel to the head), springing position (infant held upright and inclined forward, the arms extend forward and legs are brought up), stretching, shivering, trembling, unrest with crying, creeping, bodily jerk, Moro reflex (throwing arms apart, spreading of fingers, extension of legs, and throwing head back).

Despite the list's incompleteness, the neonate's behavior repertoire may still appear surprisingly diversified. Only to the uninitiated eye is the infant a mass of twists and squirms. The neonate starts life with a rather large number of often complicated responses. Potentialities for both differentiation and integration are present. There are both specific movements and mass activity present in his behavior.

Admirable though they may be, the analytic classifications of sensory and motor responses are directed, for the sake of precision of classification, to as simple and reflexive units as can be found. This impression is unintentionally strengthened by the sheer economy of presentation of findings. Sucking has been reported as the focal activity; the variety of associated movements accompanying the focal reflex activity has been ignored.

At the same time as the sucking there is a host of movements in other parts of the body. Even stimuli arousing responses in the neonate may be irrelevant as when sucking movements are set off by stimuli having nothing to do with sucking, such as those (21) of hair pulling or even pinching the big toe! Moreover, the specific response is not invariably produced by the same stimulus. A tap on the left knee with the patellar hammer may bring out the patellar reflex (knee jerk); it may also produce general increased bodily movement. External stimuli, moreover, sometimes reduce the amount of total behavior as when the neonate "quiets down" to look at some object (28).

"General activity" or "mass activity" is also found. The study of these larger patterns of behavior in the newborn has been hampered by the lack of a satisfactory classification of response measures until recently (22). These now include hand-mouth contacting, mouthing, crying, and general movement.

Other Responses

Since most studies of emotion concern somewhat older infants or are so patently developmental in nature, detailed discussion is foregone until the next chapter. There are no clearly defined or distinct emotional responses in the neonatal period, although a disorganized excitement does seem to be present.

Emotional reactions of a global, all-embracing sort are present in the neonate. Crying is the most striking and omnipresent of the emotional responses of waking. Although it is frequently impossible to determine the exact stimulus, there is little doubt that crying means the child finds something painful in the situation, as when in need of food or when environmental press arising from temperature, pressure, or moisture acts on him.

That learning does take place is obvious; a specific instance is the study by Marquis of neonate activity associated with hunger, described on page 98. Ceasing to cry on being picked up, a response often noted by mothers, would seem to be an everyday illustration. It is as though the infant responded to the cue of being picked up as a signal that he would be fed or comforted. Early vocalizations and facial expressions, originally associated with respiration and feeding, also become easily associated with these psychological processes (28).

Since the neonate is essentially noncortical, it is paradoxical to speak of neonatal intelligence. Degree of motor development may nonetheless be related to later intellectual development.

The Needs of the Neonate

Certain coordinated responses present in the neonate are so vital for his survival and so demanding in their need for satisfaction that they may be conceptualized as needs or primary drives as they are called in behavior-social learning theory.

Hunger and thirst. Responses such as sucking, swallowing, and head movements, which are aspects of the feeding and drinking responses, have already been mentioned in connection with representative motor responses. Present concern is with coordinated activities expressive of hunger and thirst needs.

Pratt (28) indicates neonatal feeding involves a series of three activities: (1) head-mouth orientation—contact stimulation of the neonate's cheek evokes head turning toward the source of stimulation, followed by opening of the mouth and snapping movements; (2) lip reflexes coordinated with head-mouth orientation—pursing the lips to contact with the nipple; and (3) sucking and swallowing movements that form a rhythm. Swallowing imparts its rhythm upon sucking; this combined rhythm is in turn imposed upon respiration so that breathing is not interfered with. General activity is reduced when sucking starts, the neonate becoming relatively quiescent.

When viewed in the perspective of the neonate's day-to-day behavior, hunger and thirst are clearly seen not to be automatic reflex activities. Although based on a reflex pattern, sucking is influenced by repeated reinforcement in securing nourishment. If the infant's hunger and thirst are not reduced, and reduced quite quickly, tensions mount and provoke a considerable amount of bodily activity. Consequently, they are important in his learning activities.

These responses, although they form a coordinated series, are not reflexlike in that, once started, the chain is not invariably completed (21). For example, it has been found that sucking of air may occur without swallowing. It is well known that sucking of some substances, instead of being followed by swallowing, results in spitting out or rejection.

Neonates show individual differences in the efficiency with which they carry out these coordinated activities. Although some authorities insist, as did Ribble (31), that a large number of infants show such feeble sucking movements as to require adult help, the weight of evidence appears to indicate that only a small proportion of infants need assistance or prompting. Whatever the proportion may be, there is considerable variability among neonates in this respect as well as in other facets of feeding responses.

A neonate must give his active cooperation if the feeding process is to be carried out smoothly and efficiently. In a modern version of the saying about a horse and water, Escalona comments, "You can put him to the breast, but you can't make him swallow" (7, 14).[4] If he is tired, in pain, drowsy, or not hungry, he simply does not suck. In general, if the situation is a pleasurable one, he will do so. To bring about this state, cooperation and coordination between mother and neonate, is necessary. Discussion of the significance and ramifications of this social relationship is, however, deferred until Chapter 8 which is concerned with psychosocial development.

[4] From Escalona (7). Copyright 1953 by The Josiah Macy, Jr., Foundation, and published with permission.

As prerequisites for arousal of hunger and thirst, the neonate needs to be awake and close in time to a nursing period. The neonate shows his hunger and thirst by crying and restless movements until he is fed. He then tends to quiet down and fall asleep. This cycle of feeding and sleeping is the major cycle of activity that neonates show—restless when hungry, quiescent or asleep when fed (1).

Healthy neonates demand food about every three hours. Gesell and Ilg (9) report that, on the average, newborn babies take seven or eight feedings per day. Nevertheless, there is wide individual variation. Some neonates may reach a peak of maximum activity in as short a time as two-and-a-half hours, while others may go for as long as five hours between peaks. Moreover, neonates who regularly show a given cycle, say, three hours, may have some intervals shorter or longer than the usual interval.

It should come as no surprise by now that individual differences among infants in the number of feedings should vary both between infants and in the same infant from time to time, making relative and tentative these seemingly precise statements. Using as an example (36), one neonate fed on self-demand each day between the second and tenth day of life; it was found that on one of these days he demanded to be fed eleven times but on another day, only six times. But there is apt, nevertheless, to be a sort of consistency as shown by the fact that this same neonate five days out of nine demanded nine feedings. Variability, but still with some degree of consistency, seems to characterize the feeding behavior of the neonate.

Sleep. Sleep is very much a need. Without its nourishing restorative function, the organism would die. As Gesell (9) reminds us, sleep is behavior. It is not the cessation of behavior; it is a kind of behavior in which certain forms of waking behavior are minimized or modified.

Sleep conceived in terms of a gradient of motility seems to fit the situation of the neonate most adequately. We do not have available for use the cultural criteria of adult sleep such as going to bed, closing the eyes, assuming a restful posture, and inability when wakened to give an accurate account of the time intervening. For the neonate the application of these criteria is not possible. What is present is a gradient of motility extending from considerable activity with eyes open to "inactivity," regular breathing and absence of eyelid and mouth movements. It is generally agreed (28) that during sleep, irritability, in its general sense, is decreased and reaction times lengthened. Responses decrease as depth of sleep increases. However, it is difficult, even for trained observers, to agree in some intermediate stages whether the infant is asleep or awake.

Despite these difficulties in measurement it would appear that the neonate sleeps about 20 hours in a 24-hour period (29). Duration of each sleep period is approximately three hours in length. Much of the neonate's time, then, is spent in sleeping. Gesell (9) reports that the neonate averages seven or eight sleep periods in 24 hours. During this period the distinction between the night as the time for sleeping and the day as the time for wakefulness is, of course, nonexistent.

Elimination. Waste products must be eliminated from the body. Three processes are available—sweating, urination, and bowel movements. They are involuntary and automatic in the neonate. Increased pressure in the bladder and in the bowel results in relaxation of muscles and the contents are involuntarily released. The neuromuscular apparatus for voluntary control has not yet developed.

Temperature regulation. In the fetal period, the environment of the mother's womb supplies a constant temperature. After birth, the neonate faces a fluctuating temperature in the environment. He is exposed to these changes and to drafts. Within certain limits his automatic physiological mechanisms maintain body temperature. However, when these limits are exceeded, adjustment through external assistance by the parents is needed. The neonate, of course, is not "aware" in any true sense of his need for temperature regulation. He, like adults, is aware of it only when something goes wrong. But, unlike the adult, he does not know what he needs when pain and discomfort arise.

Oxygen needs. Vital to the preservation of life is an adequate oxygen supply. In the neonate this need is intensified by the fact that although respiration is a reflex activity, it is not necessarily stabilized in rhythm and efficiency at the time of birth. In a few days, however, it reaches a level of efficiency quite adequate for ordinary needs. Its relative instability dramatically calls attention to respiration as serving a need of the organism. As in the case of temperature regulation it becomes noticeable as a need only when not met.

Precursors to sexual needs. It is a matter of some controversy whether we can speak of sexual needs in the neonate. The path of conservatism at this juncture is to speak of forerunners or precursors of sexual needs and leave the matter unsettled until later discussion.

Susceptibility to external genital stimulation in very young infants has been established. Infants are quite responsive to stimulation in the genital area. If an infant is having a crying spell, such stimulation tends to quiet him. Lustman (25), in research described in more detail on page 263, found that newborn infants were quite sensitive to both manual and air pressure stimulation of the genital region, as shown by temperature increase in this area. In another study (14) nine male infants were observed for eight-and-a-half consecutive hours per day for ten days. Tumescence (erection) occurred at least once every day in seven newborn infants, while the other two showed such behavior on nine and eight days, respectively. These responses were primarily to internal stimulation—strong sucking or a full bowel or bladder setting off the reflex response. Great individual differences were noted, with the actual number of instances of tumescence varying from a median of four to a median of 35 per day.

Tumescence was, in general, accompanied by what can be referred to as unpleasantness—restlessness, crying, fretting, and stiff legs—to name the most prominent concomitants. Detumescence, in contrast, was apparently pleasurable—crying, during it, for example, was almost nonexistent.

Homeostasis and neonatal needs. We have examined the neonate as a biological organism. Like all organisms it is found equipped to survive and to develop. Its behavior repertoire demonstrates its ability to relate to its environment. It shows homeostasis, a maintenance of stability in its biological functioning. Given certain assistance from its environment, particularly from the mother, it maintains its organism through meeting its needs, particularly hunger and thirst, sleep, elimination, temperature regulation, oxygen content, and possibly sexual needs. It preserves its equilibrium in the manner and within the limits sketched in the earlier presentation.

Interrelation of Behavior

An important study by Bell (2) dealt with the interrelation of behavior manifestation. Derived from the rating of filmed observation of 32 neonates, each of 37 behavioral measures was correlated with every other measure. A factor analysis of these intercorrelations was then performed. Factor analysis, it should be explained, is a means of statistically manipulating the measures until a clear picture of how some are related to others, either positively or negatively. By this procedure, Bell arrived at several patterns and tried to find names that best suited each of the factors that emerged. A requirement for a factor is that it be relatively independent of the others in the correlation table. In short, factor analysis is a means whereby we can find the smallest number of independent factors from a table of intercorrelations. It is an attempt to capture the essence of the relationships among the measures used.

Bell found "level of arousal" was the first factor to emerge. It included the tests concerned with amount, loudness and pulsation (periodic changes of pitch and intensity) of crying, rate of return to sleep, number of movements while awake, hand-mouth contacts, and a negative loading with amount of time spent in sleeping. In other words, those neonates high in these various forms of activity also spent less time sleeping.

The second factor, "depth of sleep," was shown not only by ease of being awakened, length of time to return to sleep, and other measures taken while asleep, but also by waking sensitively to auditory, tactual, and visual stimuli. The three other factors had to do with "tactile sensitivity," "oral integration," (sucking efficiency), and "fetal position." This last factor was derived from the finding that birth length and weight tended to go with a predisposition for the neonate to assume the leg retracted (knees fixed) position, characteristic of that held by the fetus in the womb.

Bell's results do not support the contention sometimes advanced that there is a single unitary "sensory barrier" common to all infants. The infants do not show a general sensitivity level. High sensitivity, he found, is apt to be confined to one or two sense modalities, not all of them. If there are sensory barriers, they are at the level of specific sense modalities, making for an auditorially sensitive child, a visually sensitive child, and so on. That he found an oral factor tended to give credence to the conception of the importance of orality in young infants. Nevertheless, even here not all oral activities formed an entity, some measures being found in the level of arousal factor. Bell considered level of arousal to account for much neonatal behavior, with some infants easy to arouse, and others not.

These factors are larger groupings of behavior characteristic of the neonate. They help us to understand individuality in the neonate.

Individuality in the Neonate

One of the most obvious sources of individuality among neonates is the degree of maturity at birth. With normal full term being 40 weeks, neonates who are capable of remaining alive vary as widely in birth age as from 26 to 46 weeks (8). Infants before full term are usually referred to as "premature" babies. But infants born after equal periods of gestation may also show considerable degree of developmental prematurity or postmaturity. More or less than full development occurs in children even of the classic term of 40 weeks.

Premature children whether because of being born earlier than usual or because of other factors have in common the fact that they are not as fully equipped for the business of living an "independent" life as infants of normal term. In them the physical characteristics of the newborn are accentuated, their nervous systems are less developed, and instability of vital functions such as breathing are more precarious than they are in normal infants. Hence, it is customary to use incubators to simulate as closely as possible the conditions of the mothers' wombs.

Studies have been conducted of general activity level of infants during periods when no external stimuli have been applied (18, 19). In one of these studies (18) the amount of activity as measured by a stabilimeter between two nursing periods of 73 infants, almost all of neonatal age, was investigated. Variations among infants and for temporal units within the activity period were reported and found to be considerable. In the other study (19) where observation extended over ten days, some infants were five times as active as others.

Summary

At conception the genetic history of the individual is fixed. During the ten lunar months between conception and birth the development that is taking place is that from cell to organism. During this and later prenatal periods, the organism-to-be is given an environment, a sequestered one to be sure, but, nevertheless, an environment. The state of this environment becomes the conditions for and modifiers of development.

The normal sequence of prenatal development is predictable to a high degree. The zygote begins the process of cell division with increase in number, size, and weight of the cells of the so-called ovular or germinal stage. Specialization of function of these cells begins during the embryonic stage. This stage, in turn, gives way to the fetal period which ends with birth.

The biological aspects of the mother-child relationship, essentially that of host and parasite, were considered. The significant internally instigated events occurring during the months of this relationship were sketched. Evidence of the nature of the influence of the external environment on the fetus were considered separately. The attitudes of the mother during her pregnancy were seen to lie somewhere along a continuum of acceptance-rejection of her coming child.

Childbirth is ordinarily a normal, maturing experience. Nevertheless, difficulties in birth and anxiety arising from the birth process as well as more normal natural reactions to the child bring out some of the psychological reactions of the mother.

The neonatal period of the first month of life provides the baseline against which to compare the developments taking place in infancy. Consideration was given to both sensory and motor responses. It was impossible, to do full justice to the multiplicity of responses that the neonate exhibited. Suffice it to say here that the evidence indicated a much broader repertoire both of specific and mass responses than casual observation would make us believe possible.

The coordinated responses of the neonate necessary for his survival, here conceptualized as needs, received the most detailed attention. Hunger and thirst illustrated the coordinated series of activities that are necessary for satisfaction of these needs. Cooperation of the neonate with the mother and vice versa were seen as part of this pattern. Other needs—sleep, elimination, temperature regulation, oxygen, and the forerunners of sexual needs—are also reported as they were observed in infancy.

Other responses, such as emotion and intelligence, were examined. Interrelation of behavior, showing several patterns of behavior in the neonate, was presented. Individuality in terms of sensitivities and levels of activity was also found.

The neonatal period is one in which the infant recovers from the birth process and begins to adjust to the external world, while exhibiting a behavior repertoire that forms a valuable base line for an understanding of his development through infancy and later life.

For Further Reading

An excellent discussion of the prenatal development of behavior in infrahuman as well as human mammals is Davenport Hooker's *The Prenatal Origin of Behavior* (Lawrence, Kan: University of Kansas Press, 1952). The article by K. C. Pratt on the neonate in the *Manual of Child Psychology: Second Edition* (New York: Wiley, 1954) edited by Leonard Carmichael is authoritative.

References

1. Bayley, Nancy. Normal growth and development. In P. H. Hoch and J. Zubins (Eds.), *Psycopathology of childhood*. New York: Grune and Stratton, 1955, 1–14.
2. Bell, R. Q. Relations between behavior manifestations in the human neonate. *Child Developm.*, 1960, 31, 463–477.
3. Bibring, Grete L., T. F. Dwyer, Dorothy S. Huntington, and A. F. Valenstein. A study of the psychological processes in pregnancy and of the earliest mother-

child relationship: II. Methodological considerations. *Psychoanal. Stud. Child,* 1961, 16, 25–72.

4. Bolin, B. J. An investigation of relationship between birth duration and childhood anxieties. *J. Ment. Sci.,* 1959, 195, 1045–1052.

5. Corner, G. W. *Ourselves unborn: an embryologist's essay on man.* New Haven: Yale University Press, 1944.

6. Dennis, W. A description and classification of the responses of the newborn infant. *Psychol. Bull.,* 1934, 31, 5–22.

7. Escalona, Sibylle. Emotional development in the first year of life. In M. J. E. Senn (Ed.), *Problems of infancy and childhood: transactions of the sixth conference.* New York: Macy, 1953, 7–92.

8. Gesell, A., and Catherine S. Amatruda. *Developmental diagnosis: normal and abnormal child development* (2nd ed.). New York: Hoeber, 1947.

9. Gesell, A., and Frances L. Ilg. *Child development: an introduction to the study of human growth.* New York: Harper, 1949.

10. Gilbert, Margaret S. *Biography of the unborn.* Baltimore: Williams and Wilkins, 1938.

11. Graham, Frances K. Behavioral differences between normal and traumatized newborns: I. The test procedures. *Psychol., Monogr.,* 1956, 70, No. 427.

12. Graham, Frances K., Claire B. Ernhart, D. Thurston, and Marguerite Craft. Development three years after perinatal anoxia and other potentially damaging newborn experiences. *Psychol. Monogr.,* 1962, 76, No. 522.

13. Graham Frances K., Ruth G. Matarazzo, and Bettye M. Caldwell. Behavioral differences between normal and traumatized newborns: II, Standardization, reliability, and validity. *Psychol. Monogr.,* 1956, 70, No. 428.

14. Halverson, H. M. Genital and sphincter behavior of the male infant. *J. Genet. Psychol.,* 1940, 56, 95–136.

15. Halverson, H. M. The development of prehension in infants. In R. G. Barker, et al., (Eds.), *Child behavior and development.* New York: McGraw-Hill, 1943, 49–65.

16. Hamburger, V. *A manual of experimental embryology,* Chicago: University of Chicago Press, 1942.

17. Hooker, D. Reflex activities in the human fetus. In R. G. Barker, *et al.,* (Eds.), *Child behavior and development.* New York: McGraw-Hill, 1943, 17–28.

18. Irwin, O. C. The amount and nature of activities of newborn infants under constant external stimulating conditions during the first ten days of life. *Genet. Psychol. Monogr.,* 1930, 8, 1–92.

19. Irwin, O. C. The distribution of the amount of motility in young infants between two nursing periods. *J. Comp. Psychol.,* 1932, 14, 415–428.

20. Irwin, O. C. Research on speech sounds for the first six months of life. *Psychol. Bull.,* 1941, 38, 277–285.

21. Jensen, K. Differential reactions to taste and temperature stimuli in newborn infants. *Genet. Psychol. Monogr.,* 1932, 12, 363–479.

22. Kessen, W., E. Jane Williams, and Joanna P. Williams. Selection and test of response measurement in the study of the human newborn. *Child Developm.,* 1961, 32, 7–24.

23. Levy, D. M. Psychosomatic studies of some aspects of maternal behavior. *Psychosom. Med.,* 1942, 4, 223–227.

24. Lipsitt, L. P. and N. Levy. Electrotactual threshold in the neonate. *Child Developm.,* 1959, 30, 547–554.

25. Lustman, S. L. Rudiments of the ego. In Ruth S. Eissler *et al.* (Eds.), *The psychoanalytic study of the child*, Vol. 11. New York: International Universities Press, 1956, 89–98.
26. Montagu, M. F. A. Constitutional and prenatal factors in infant and child health. In M. J. E. Senn (Ed.), *Symposium on the healthy personality*. New York: Macy, 1950, 148–175.
27. Ostwald, P. F., and P. F. Regan. Psychiatric disorders associated with childbirth. *J. Nerv. Ment. Dis.*, 1957, 125, 153–165.
28. Pratt, K. C. The neonate. In L. Carmichael (Ed.), *Manual of child psychology* (2nd ed.). New York: Wiley, 1954, 215–291.
29. Pratt, K. C., Amalie K. Nelson, and K. H. Sun. *The behavior of the newborn infant*. Columbus: Ohio State University Press, 1930.
30. Read, G. D. *Childbirth without fear* (Rev. ed.). New York: Harper, 1953.
31. Ribble, Margaret A. *The rights of infants*. New York: Columbia University Press, 1943.
32. Richards, T. W., and H. Newberry. Studies in fetal behavior: III. Can performance test items at six months postnatally be predicted on the basis of fetal activity? *Child Developm.*, 1938, 9, 79–86.
33. Rogers, M. E., A. M. Lilienfield, and B. Pasamanick. Prenatal and postnatal factors in the development of childhood behaviour disorders. *Acta Psychol. et Neurol. Scand.*, 1955, Suppl. 102.
34. Schmeidler, Gertrude. The relation of fetal activity to the activity of the mother. *Child Developm.*, 1941, 12, 63–68.
35. Sears, R. R., Eleanor E. Maccoby, and H. Levin. *Patterns of child rearing*. Evanston: Row, Peterson, 1957.
36. Simsarian, F. P., and P. A. McLendon. Feeding behavior of an infant during the first twelve weeks of life on a self-demand schedule. *J. Pediatrics*, 1942, 20, 93–103.
37. Spelt, D. K. The conditioning of human fetus *in utero*. *J. Exp. Psychol.*, 1948, 38, 338–346.
38. Wertheimer, M. Psychomotor coordination of auditory and visual space at birth. *Science*, 1961, 134, 1692.
39. Zemlick, M. R., and R. I. Watson. Maternal attitudes of acceptance and rejection during and after pregnancy. *Amer. J. Orthopsychiat.*, 1953, 23, 570–584.

7

Individual Development

I T IS necessary to think of the child as a developing biological organism. This is an imperative, never to be ignored fact in infancy since development is proceeding so rapidly. A tremendous amount of biological change is compressed into the first two years of life.

Now that the constant internal environment of the fetus has been left behind sources of external stimulation become much more important. This is another way of saying that learning assumes greater importance. From his experiences with the world, the infant is to acquire new ways of behaving. In fact, the scope and intensity of learning during infancy exceeds that of any other period of development. Nevertheless, the influence of maturation remains very evident, most clearly exemplified in physical growth.

Physical growth

Consideration has already been given to the physical appearance and bodily proportions of the newborn infant. Attention is now directed to the physical growth that takes place during infancy (74). It will be remembered that, on the average, the neonate weighs seven or eight pounds and is about 20 inches tall. During the first year of life the infant increases his length by over a third and his weight almost triples. Owing to the greater weight than height gain, the infant at one year appears more thick-set. The "top-heaviness," characteristic at birth, gradually decreases as legs and trunk increase.

Physical development in the second year proceeds rapidly but at a slower rate than in the first year. At age two, the average child is 32 or 33 inches tall and weighs about 27 pounds (74). On the average boys are heavier and taller than girls (57). Height and weight are correlated about .60, showing a relatively high degree of relationship between the two indices of physique.

Changes in form and proportion are illustrated in Figure 4 on page 141, which shows that parts of the body do not grow equally and at the same rate. The principle of developmental direction is operating here in a very obvious fashion. During the prenatal period growth proceeds cephalocaudally and proximodistally (74). Head precedes neck development and this in turn precedes chest growth, and so on; meanwhile, upper arm (or leg) growth precedes lower arm (or leg) growth which in turn precedes hand (or foot) growth. Thereafter until puberty, once these trends are established, the greatest growth takes place at the extremities. Hence, head growth is slow, limb growth is rapid, and trunk growth is intermediate.

Changes in height and weight are taking place as Figure 5 attests. In general, height increases at a rapid rate during infancy and then slows down during childhood and still more later. Weight gain, after an initial spurt in infancy, slows down thereafter. Fairly large varia-

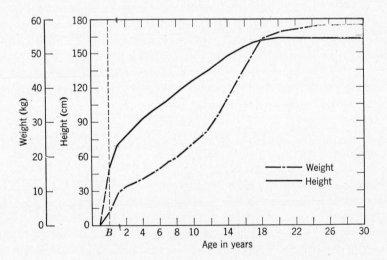

Figure 5. Growth curves for height and weight. (Adapted from Thompson in Carmichael, Manual of Child Psychology (74). E. Boyd, Growth of the Surface Area of the Human Body. Copyright 1935 by the University of Minnesota.)

tions in both height and weight are common and considered to fall within normal limits.

Growth and maturation of parts of the body are basically the products of hereditary biological determinants. Nevertheless, the body cannot increase in size and weight without nutritional supplies from the environment. For example, nutritional intake affects weight and height, with infants from poverty-stricken environments tending to be smaller (3). Neither can there be neuromuscular coordination without opportunity for practice. Both learning and maturation are necessary for physical growth.

Sensorimotor development

Examination of the neonate's behavior has shown that at birth he is capable of many complex sensorimotor responses. Infancy, nevertheless, is a period of considerable sensorimotor development. Reflex activities mature. A rapid growth of the sensorimotor system in conjunction with both training and autogenous (self-initiated) activity allows for increased voluntary control of activities through the brain; there is also considerable physical growth resulting in stronger bones and greater muscular strength. These factors cooperate to bring about an increase in the scope, precision, and specificity of both sensitivity and response capabilities. Neither the sensory nor the motor phase operates in isolation although emphasis will be placed upon the latter.

Learning and Maturation in Sensorimotor Skills

During infancy a considerable repertoire of skills is developed that the infant uses to manipulate and orient himself to his environment (54). Both learning and maturation play a part. Some skills are probably more a function of maturation. These include crawling, walking, and finger-thumb opposition. Although we customarily speak of "learning" to walk, neuromuscular maturation is involved, and it is perhaps the more important of the two conditions of development. If anything, earlier experimenters overstressed the importance of maturation as compared with learning.

A typical illustration is the study of Hopi Indian babies bound to cradleboards, thus experiencing a good deal of movement restraint during their first year of life. They walked independently about as early as did infants who had had much more previous practice (21).

Practice missed by being strapped to the cradleboard did not seem to prevent walking from appearing at the usual age. This finding is interpreted by the particular investigator as indicative of the clear primacy of maturation over learning in the emergence of walking.

Another representative study (33) compared the behavior of 46 week-old twin girls in stair climbing and cube building. The choice of the age of 46 weeks for initial study was dictated by the fact that this was about the age at which infants were at the threshold of stair-climbing and cube-building responses. Twin T (trained) was given a ten-minute practice session each day for *six* weeks. Twin C (control) was given no training until the end of the six-week period at which time she was given *two* weeks of practice. At the end of this practice period, Twin C was performing these activities as well as Twin T who had the four more weeks of practice but at an earlier age. The investigators concluded that the time of appearance of stair climbing and cube building was not influenced by practice but by the ripening of neural structures.

Recently, investigators with this attitude have come under criticism for overemphasizing the influence of maturation (26). The roles of perception and experiences, it is argued, have been ignored. Moreover there is a strong probability that the more complex the skill concerned, the greater are their roles. These critics say that there is a receptive phase to any motor activity—perceiving the cubes in three-dimensional space or learning to coordinate visual movement and tactual experience—which has a large perceptual component and which cannot be alleged to be innate. Moreover, there is apt to be opportunity for experience through autogenous practice. In the stair-climbing study, Twin C was not actually permitted to climb stairs or to play with cubes but the constituent activities nevertheless could have been practiced in his day-to-day living. Learning at a given later age may be more efficient than practice at an earlier age, but this does not mean learning did not take place earlier. Even though Twin T had more "practice" than Twin C, he did *learn* at an earlier age. Again we find that maturation and learning interact and that, perhaps, it is futile to try to differentiate precisely their effect.

Major areas of motor development during early infancy are manipulation and locomotion.

Manipulation

The arm and hand are the vehicles of manipulation. The sequence of development of prehension (grasping) has been intensively studied with infants between 16 weeks and one year of age (36). The seated infant was given an opportunity to grasp a cube. Photographs were studied to arrive at the developmental sequence that had grasping as its culmination. Preceding grasping itself a series of stages of development was found. At 16 weeks the infants generally made no contact at all with the cube; at 20 weeks they made contact, or squeezed it without grasping. From 24 weeks onward, grasping developed. Grasping at first is a clawing type of activity with the thumb inactive, followed later by a nipping pressing kind of closure in which thumb and forefinger dominate, but which is still a form of manipulation that involves much palming.

After one year, however, an entirely new level of skill is likely to have made its debut: with elevated palm and a precise plucking motion the pellet is grasped with no waste motion (and, it should be added parenthetically, almost invariably thrust immediately into the mouth). Historically, we might find roots of the eventual precision in the unfailing appearance of the initial reflex grasp, but observation of the entire sequence reveals that much simultaneous integration and differentiation must be accomplished before such refined movement is possible.

Manipulation exemplifies the general orderliness of sensorimotor development; sequential steps follow one another with each stage forming a new level of maturity.

Locomotion

The neonate has no effective means of movement from place to place. From its supine ("face up") or prone ("face down") position it may shift about a bit, but this movement can hardly be called locomotion in the sense of movement from place to place. Shirley (72) has carefully studied the development in posture and locomotion of a group of 25 infants. Figure 6 shows the steps that she found in the motor sequence. The very fact that we can use the sequence in this figure to represent changes in locomotion shows that again there is a progressive regularity of development despite variability from infant to infant.

The five major stages are very uniform and involve the following order: (1) passive postural control as in sitting with support; (2) active postural control such as sitting alone; (3) active efforts toward locomotion; (4) creeping and walking with support; and, finally, (5) walking alone. The last stage occurred on the average at about 15 months, although some children in the sample walked alone as early as 11½

Figure 6. The motor sequence. (Mary M. Shirley, The First Two Years, Vol. II: "Intellectual Development." Copyright 1933 by University of Minnesota.)

months, while others did not do so until 17 months. Each major stage has within it several steps. Although these steps may vary in sequence from infant to infant, each stage is a prerequisite for the immediately succeeding one. Walking is the climax of a long series of activities that are not directly locomotor in themselves but which proceed in an orderly fashion in each infant.

Although Shirley's general sequence has been verified, other investigators (5) have tended to find reversals of steps. Instead of a regular order of appearance of special abilities there was a more irregular growth in the ability in question. Moreover, the stages seemed to occur at earlier ages. In Bayley's study (5) the average age of onset of walking was found to be 13 instead of 15 months, which is probably more accurate.

The developmental principles of differentiation and integration along with cumulative experience are involved in walking. Not so obvious, perhaps, is the exemplification of the principle of discontinuity and hierarchization in that each stage involves muscular movements not present in earlier stages. Study of Figure 6, picture by picture, will show that different muscle groups are being controlled at different stages. First the eye, head, and neck are involved, then the arms and upper trunk, later the hands and lower trunk, and last the pelvic region and the legs.

Beginning to walk has profound psychological consequences. The infant is more able to bring himself in contact with "people, places, and things." This he does because *he* wants to. Others do not have to come to him. To a much greater degree he now may be independent of adult control. He may walk into areas of which his parents approve, but he may also walk into those of which they emphatically do not. To modify a saying, "Fools, and little children, rush in where angels fear to tread." Thus, beginning at about the age of 15 months and continuing to roughly the age of four, there is a period of great locomotor activity. The period, a strenuous one from the parental point of view, is brought about by the simple fact that the infant is able to walk and run.

Motor Development in Later Infancy

Motor development in locomotion has been discussed up to the advent of walking at about 13 to 15 months, while manipulation has been discussed as it takes place during the first year of life. Some later motor behaviors with characteristic age of appearance are given in Table 5. Both the older infant's versatility and his steady gain in motor skills are exemplified. Other activities such as language and feeding, too, have their motor components which are progressing rapidly.

TABLE 5

MOTOR DEVELOPMENT IN THE SECOND YEAR *

Age in Months	Characteristic Motor Skill
15	Creeps up stairs Makes two-cube tower Helps turn book pages
18	Walks upstairs, one hand held Climbs into adult chair Hurls ball
21	Squats while playing Walks upstairs holding rail Kicks large ball
24	Runs well, no falling Walks up and down stairs alone Makes a six- or seven-cube tower

* Adapted from Gesell and Amatruda (*31*). Copyright 1947 by Paul B. Hoeber, Inc., and published with permission.

Developmental changes in primary needs

Progressive changes in how often and in what manner the infant satisfies his basic needs are especially prominent and important features of his development. These include feeding, sleep, elimination, and sex. We shall consider secondary needs only insofar as they derive directly from the basic needs, deferring further attention to them until the next two chapters where they are examined in a social setting. This is also the case with exploratory, externally aroused behavior tendencies.

Developmental Changes in Feeding

Gesell and Ilg (32) report that neonates require about seven or eight feedings per day. By the time they are four weeks old the number of feedings becomes reduced to five or six, and reduces further to three to five in the following weeks. Beginning at 16 weeks this number of feedings, or a little less, is maintained until toward the end of the first year, by which time the three-meals-a-day regime of our culture is fairly well established, along with one or two snacks.

Supplementation by solid foods goes on from about 20 weeks of age. Cup and spoon feeding takes place during this time and by 40 weeks the infant helps himself in feeding, incidentally making a fine mess of it in the process. Preference for certain foods is well defined at one year, for example, certain vegetables, or hot as compared to cold cereals.

Scheduling and self-demand feeding. Among a large group of mothers, Sears and his associates (70) found the prevalent practice to be neither a self-demand system nor a rigid scheduling but something between. Only 12 per cent of the mothers always fed the infant when he cried and permitted him to eat as much as he wanted, whereas eight per cent fed him by the clock, waking him for feedings. The remainder followed practices that were between these extremes.

It was the pioneer study of Clara M. Davis (18) in 1928 that probably served as the original scientific impetus for changing adult attitudes in the direction of greater permissiveness toward infant feeding and self-regulation in scheduling. In her study 15 infants of about weaning age were presented with a variety of foods from which they could choose kind and amount. In the first few days of free choice there were great individual differences among the infants as to what and how much they ate. Gradually all of the infants selected diets that, according to adult standards, were well balanced and nutritious. Moreover, none of them developed feeding problems. In a later study (19), she permitted infants free choice of different formulas at a single feeding and found that highly variable amounts and kinds were taken at different meals. Davis's studies and those that followed helped to usher in an era of greater trust in the infant's capacity to select how much to eat, at what times, and how often.

Despite this tendency toward variability infants are fully capable of learning to adapt to the feeding schedules introduced by adults. This was neatly demonstrated by Dorothy Marquis (51) who studied the learning of a feeding schedule by infants during the first ten days of life while they were still in the hospital. The experimental group was on a three-hour feeding schedule, except during the day before discharge when these infants were shifted to a four-hour schedule, while the control group was on a four-hour feeding schedule throughout its hospital stay.

She measured the activity patterns (restlessness) of both groups by a mechanical device that supported the bassinets in which the infants lay. Their activity was the criterion of adaptiveness to the schedule. When the interval of feeding was changed from three to four hours in the experimental group on the tenth day, these infants showed a sharp rise in their activity during this extra hour between feedings. At the end of three hours, their heretofore habitual feeding time, body movements increased abruptly and continued throughout the fourth hour. Apparently, the infants had learned to respond to hunger cues at the end of three hours. Failure to receive their accustomed feeding markedly increased restlessness. Control infants fed on a four-hour schedule from birth to what was now their ninth day showed only their usual gradual increase in activity as feeding time approached.

Having learned a particular schedule, the experimental group became increasingly restless when the accustomed feeding time had passed. Marquis suggests that this is an instance of an early form of socialization. It made a difference for these newborn infants to have to wait an extra hour, whereas the control infants, already habituated to their constant four-hour schedule, showed no increased restlessness.

Breast and bottle feeding. In the Sears, Maccoby, Levin study (70) 40 per cent of the infants were breast fed, the majority for only three months. In view of the large number being fed by bottles and the relative shortness of breast feeding by those who did receive it, it is of interest, despite its somewhat digressive character, to examine the reason the mothers gave for not breast feeding. Over 40 per cent claimed they were unable to breast feed for physical reasons, such as not having enough milk or the presence of inverted nipples. Another 16 per cent reported that the doctor advised against breast feeding without specifying any physical difficulty. Thirty-five per cent did not want to breast feed, some for emotional reasons, others because they did not want to be tied down, and still others for unspecified reasons.

The two groups who gave "physical reasons" or "doctor's advice" seem quite large, too large in fact for the reasons given to represent actually the true state of affairs. There is a strong possibility that the objections they offered to breast feeding were rationalizations and that they did not want to for reasons other than the ones given. For example, "inability" may more correctly have been dislike of breast feeding.

Weaning. The sucking movements of the neonate are adapted for taking liquid foods from breast or bottle. With increased maturation at about the third or fourth month, mouth movements begin to change in a direction suitable for eating solid food and biting movements begin to appear. By seven to nine months these movements have become stronger.

Repeated reinforcement of sucking has occurred during these early months and sucking has become a well-established habit in securing nourishment. The process of weaning means these now habitual patterns must be eliminated and new activities learned.

Weaning at first glance may appear to be a simple straightforward practice; in reality, it is a very complicated one. Even the term is used in more than one sense. Sometimes, weaning refers to a shift from breast to bottle feeding. In the sense used here, however, it means the process of giving up sucking for a new mode of food-getting through eating solid foods and drinking (not sucking) of liquids. As Sears, Maccoby, and Levin indicate, weaning involves five tasks:

> The child must learn *not to want* to get his food by sucking. He must learn to *like* to *drink* the same food he formerly got by sucking. He must learn to *want solid foods*. He must learn the *manipulative skills* required for eating them—biting, chewing, and the use of fingers and utensils, as well as drinking from a cup. He must learn to do *without being held* while he is eating (70, 69).[1]

Now each of these tasks may be presented to the child in an endless variety of ways. For example, solid foods can be thrust at him all at once or their presentation can be spaced almost from birth, long before the process of weaning. Frustrations arising from the tasks of weaning will depend on many things, not very precisely summed up as "weaning."

[1] From Sears, Maccoby and Levin (70). Copyright 1957 by Row, Peterson, and published with permission.

In their sample of mothers, Sears *et al.* (70) found that two-thirds had started the weaning process by the time the infant was 11 months old. For the majority, the process of weaning took four months to complete. Nevertheless, at least 12 per cent took a year or more.

Developmental Changes in Sleep

As the infant grows older, his general activities increase while his sleep decreases. By the end of infancy he may be sleeping as little as 11 hours at night with one or two naps during the day. Gesell (32) offers a detailed description of sleep behavior at various ages. At four weeks he reports that typically the infant gradually drops off to sleep toward the end of the nursing period. At this age the infant has four to five sleep periods in 24 hours. By 16 weeks he has established something of a night sleep rhythm, falling asleep after the six P.M. feeding and waking between five and six A.M. He does not fall asleep immediately after each feeding and has about three naps during the day in addition to his sleep periods. At 40 weeks he tends to fall asleep after his six P.M. feeding and and sleeps through to five to seven A.M. There may be one long midmorning nap or as many as four short nap periods.

Although the total number of hours of infant's sleep is decreasing, the periods are increasing in length. Whereas hunger and pain may awaken him at any time, loud sounds and other stimuli are decreased in our culture at night and consequently, during this period he is less disturbed by environmental stimuli.

The infant must learn to sleep in the same way he learns to creep, stand and walk, and grasp a spoon (32). He must also learn to stay awake! Although learning is undoubtedly important, maturation is also important. As he grows older he is not so subcortical (without the service of the highest nerve centers of the brain) as Gesell puts it. Millions of cortical cells, previously nonfunctional because they had not matured sufficiently, are beginning to make connections between eyes, ears, and the muscles of the eyes. Their maturation serves to keep his cortex "awake" and thus make him more receptive to his surroundings. Staying awake for longer periods of time with increasing amounts of time spent in acts other than those associated with feeding is an important part of the process of early development (7). These longer periods of waking afford opportunity for more intensive and varied experiences with the environment.

There are, of course, individual differences in sleep requirements among infants and in the same infant from one time to another. By and large, however, we are not too demanding in our culture and allow the child during infancy to express his individuality in this regard. He generally may be said to sleep as much as he needs. Consequently, sleep is not a vehicle upon which extremes of social pressure are practiced, which accounts for its omission when socialization practices in infancy are discussed later.

Developmental Changes in Elimination

Gesell's normative findings (32) in relation to elimination changes show that at four weeks the infant tends to have three or four bowel movements in a 24-hour period. He may now cry when his diaper is wet, quieting when changed. At 16 weeks there are one or two movements, most commonly after a feeding. By 28 weeks there is apt to be only one movement, usually at nine to ten A.M. Urination is still occurring at frequent intervals. At 40 weeks the infant may be dry after an hour's nap and sometimes an infant may respond to the pot. Changes hereafter will be described in the context of the problem of toilet training which this need engenders.

Social demands in our culture require that the child learn voluntary control of bladder and bowel so as to void at an acceptable time and place. The neonate is cheerily oblivious to these demands. He voids and urinates by the involuntary relaxation of sphincter muscles when pressures have built up to a certain point. Voluntary control of bowel and bladder must be superimposed upon an involuntary activity. Optimally, changes in eliminative processes await the age at which neuromuscular mechanisms have sufficiently matured for them to be voluntarily controlled. As a neonate he cannot do so, even if by some miracle, he "wanted" to do so. Punishment, bribes, and scolding may go on relentlessly, but the learning remains incidental and sporadic until he is maturationally ready for voluntary control.

The importance of maturation in bladder control is shown in a study by McGraw (50) on twin boys. With one of them, bladder training was started at about 50 days by placing him on the toilet every hour. Until about 600 days there was little evidence of learning. After 600 days the curve of success increased sharply, and by 700 days successes were close to 100 per cent. No training whatsoever was started with the other twin until 700 days. His performance was almost immediately as good as that of the twin with the longer period of training. This rather startling difference is not an isolated phenomenon as another record of twins by McGraw shows. Evidently, training started later rather than earlier takes advantage of maturation and is more effective than trying to train earlier.

The results found by McGraw, however, should not be taken as definitive concerning the *date* to begin training or to expect its ending. This is subject to individual variation. Her data are indicative merely of *relative* relationships in these twins and are in no way an index of what happens in sample groups. This normative question is considered in a moment.

Toilet training is a learning situation (22) in which the reward is not in the satisfaction of the basic need. His social eliminative needs are, if we may slip into the vernacular, learned the hard way.

The infant is not repelled by his bodily products. He will play with them when the opportunity arises. Parents vary in their reaction to this situation, but having to face it is inescapable. They may arrange to direct attention elsewhere by diverting the child from this interest, or become angry and repressive, or show any other of a hundred other responses, but deal with it they must. In dealing with the problem they train their infants whether this be formal avowed training or the unacknowledged unintentional facets of their teaching.

The learning of toilet training practices begins without verbal aids because the infant does not have either the active verbal repertoire or the understanding to deal with training in this fashion. As a consequence, training in cleanliness proceeds by a process of trial and error. To quote Dollard and Miller:

> The child must learn to wake up in order to go to the toilet, though sleep seems good. It must learn to stop its play even when social excitement is strong. It must learn to discriminate between the different rooms of the house—all this by crude trial and error. In this case, "trial" means urinating or defecating in an inappropriate place, and "error" means being punished for the act so that anxiety responses are attached to the cues of this place. In the trial-and-error situation this must be repeated for each inappropriate place—bed, living room, dining room, kitchen, "outside." The function of this training is to attach anxiety responses to the defecation drive so that they win out over the immediate evulsion response. These anxiety responses also motivate and cue off the next responses in the series, such as calling to the parents, running to the bathroom, unbuttoning the clothes, and the like (22, 138).[2]

This process naturally arouses strong emotional reactions in the child. Anger, defiance, stubbornness, and fear appear in response to this situation.

We are now in a position to examine the scheduling of toilet training by parents in our culture. Pediatricians generally encourage mothers to postpone training until the second year. In the "pattern

[2] By permission from *Personality and Psychotherapy*, by Dollard and Miller. Copyright 1950, McGraw-Hill Book Company, Inc.

study" of Sears, Maccoby, and Levin (70) the average age for beginning bowel training was about 11 months and for completion about 18 months. For any two-month period the greatest percentage started between nine and 11 months. Almost 75 per cent were trained between ten and 24 months. A few (8 per cent) were trained between five and nine months and 15 per cent took longer than 24 months. Some mothers claimed it took only a few weeks, but others found it took a year-and-a-half to carry out the process of training. Generally speaking, if begun later it took less time. For example, if begun at five months it took ten months; if begun at 20 months it took only five months. This again emphasizes the importance of maturation.

Developmental Changes in Sex

It is paradoxical to consider this topic since we know almost nothing about its developmental changes; there is even some question if we can accurately speak of a "sex need" during infancy. As was done with the neonate, it is perhaps most fitting to speak of precursors of sexual needs.

Activity in the sex organs of infants is certainly present, even during the neonatal period. Observation by Kinsey and his associates (44) showed that in 317 two-to-twelve-month-old male infants nearly one-third had an orgasm—naturally without ejaculation. The orgasm's reward value may be entirely a matter of pleasurable tactile stimulation. Certainly, it has no heterosexual intent.

We also know from the detailed observations of Halverson (37) that there seems to be a close relationship between erection and reflex activities associated with sucking. He was concerned with all activities of sucking behavior including measures of general bodily muscular tenseness. Tumescence when the infant sucked was frequently found. This occurred when sucking was interrupted, particularly on removal of the nipple.

Emotional development

Tension arises in the infant when he is placed in a stress situation such as that described in elimination training. Tension in infants is manifested by such phenomena as heightened muscle tonus, temperature increase, alteration in heart and respiratory rate and rhythm, and gastrointestinal upset. These responses form the physiological basis of emotional states. Tension is the characteristic common to all kinds of emotionality.

In tension states disturbances interrupt smooth functioning. Infants show varying degrees of susceptibility to tension. In the last section of the chapter concerned with individuality, Fries speaks of varying types of activity patterns in infants. Hyperactive infants, as she uses the term, would be particularly vunerable to tension, while hypoactive infants would be at the other extreme. Hyperactive infants show tension to stimulation which for the ordinary infant is not tension producing. If the stress is severe or prolonged, tensional indices of profound disturbance in the form of psychosomatic symptoms may occur.

Frustration and Enhancement of Needs

The tension of emotion is aroused when the needs of the infant are frustrated. The relation of frustration and emotional responses in infancy has already been discussed incidentally in connection with earlier topics—crying and restlessness when hungry or during toilet training.

A clear illustration of the relation of frustration to emotion is contained in a study by Dorothy Marquis (52). Frustration was investigated in seven newborn infants as it occurred during the delay before feeding. This was done by recording the amount of crying, general bodily activity, and mouth activity the infants showed. The amount of formula to be received at a given feeding was divided into fourths and amount of activity shown during each of these fourths was recorded separately. In other words, amount of activity was recorded for the infant's behavior for each fourth as well as for a fixed delay period without feeding which followed each of the feeding "fourths." As amount of milk consumed increased, there was a decreased amount of activity and increased tolerance of the delay period. To put it succinctly, as frustration from hunger decreased, emotional reactions also decreased.

Not only frustration but also that which furthers or facilitates meeting the infant's needs may be provocative of emotion. Delight and affection are emotional responses illustrative of enhancing emotional responses. They are in themselves tension producing. In fact, if this tension is prolonged or intense it may bring about displeasure. Too many toys can bring about an excited delight which readily passes over into displeasure and crying spells (45).

Differentiation

It is hardly likely that the infant is capable of intense emotional experiences as *adults know them*. We may, for example, see a newborn infant squirming, kicking, and crying. We may infer that the infant is experiencing what we would feel if we were in his place. But we are not in his place. In support of the position that there is considerable difference between infantile and adult emotional experience several points can be offered. We know that neural maturation is still incomplete in the infant, particularly in the cerebral cortex. We also know that there is little if any knowledge of self on the infant's part and that personal reference, so characteristic of adult emotional responses, must be lacking with him. Most important perhaps, certain research studies show that we can be fooled by what we read into the situation when observing "emotional experiences" of infants. Thus when such terms as "excitement," "distress," and "delight" are used, they should be viewed as if they carried quotation marks to indicate only a tentative similarity to those that adults experience.

This "adultomorphic" tendency of interpreting the behavior of an infant as if we experienced it is at the root of the methodological confusion that occurred in John B. Watson's classic study of 1920 (78) in which he claimed that he had demonstrated the primary emotions of the newborn to be fear, rage, and love, and no others. Fear in newborn infants, he claimed, was produced by loud sounds and loss of support. Rage was brought about by hampering of movements. Love was released by stroking and petting. All other emotional reactions, he went on to state, were the consequence of conditioning of these three primary emotions.

The validity of Watson's theory rests upon a matter of fact—whether the emotions he described could be identified by others in such a fashion that the three patterns of emotion would be found to be separable and identifiable. Sherman (71), in 1927, demonstrated that this was not the case. The situations he used to bring about emotional responses—delay of feeding beyond the usual time, sudden loss of support, restraint of head movements, and pricking with a needle—were first presented to the observers as preludes to the emotional reactions of the infants.

Under these conditions the observers were generally able to offer "correct" identifications of the emotions with considerable interobserver agreement, though some disagreements existed. Thus, observers who saw the infant lose his support and then the emotional reaction which followed tended to label the emotional reaction "fear." But when they saw motion pictures of the infant's emotional reactions cut so that the stimulation period was eliminated, and hence could not know which particular stimulus was being used, they failed to agree on what emotion was being expressed. Moreover, when the film was so spliced as to give the impression that the stimuli preceding the infant's emotion was the actual one to which the infant was responding, the observers tended to ascribe to the infant the emotion appropriate to that stimulus, and not to the one for which it was actually the response. In general, Sherman could find no characteristic emotional patterns that would allow one emotion to be distinguished from another. Rather, there were uncoordinated, unspecialized, and diversified responses with no particular patterns of differentiation. Situations that at a later age arouse a variety of emotions produced the same general undifferentiated emotional reactions in these infants.

Using a somewhat casual cross-sectional approach, with age as the independent variable, Bridges (12, 13, 14) observed 62 infants from two weeks to two years of age. A convenient summary of her results is to be found in Figure 7. Undifferentiated excitement (or agitation) is found initially, shown by uncoordinated overt and visceral reactions to intense stimulation of any sort, internal or external. The vigorous but ill-coordinated movements of the infant's body show little relation to a particular stimulus. Undifferentiated *mass action* is prominent; the baby cries with his whole body. Bridges' finding concerning initial undifferentiated excitement receives support (12) from the fact that there are no distinctive unique patterns of visceral or physiological responses each corresponding to a different emotion.

Despite the presence of generalized excitement it is also an inescapable fact that in the older infant and child other emotions do emerge. It was to their study that Bridges addressed herself. Her results follow what is expected from the developmental principle of differentiation. Emotional differentiations in the infant she found to begin at about three weeks of age when distress characterized by muscular tension, trembling, crying, and checked breathing can be distinguished from excitement. At about two months of age delight, manifested by smiles and cooing when nursed or petted, emerges with excitement. As Figure 7 brings out, distress and delight are the two emotional patterns first differentiated from excitement. Each become further differentiated as the infant grows older. Fear, anger, and disgust are differentiated from distress before the age of six months. Elation, as differentiated from delight, emerges at about nine months. Subsequently, affection emerges before 12 months, jealousy before the age of 18 months, and joy shortly after that age. Thus, at the age of 18 months a rather extensive repertoire of differentiated emotional reactions seems to be present in the infant. However, neither the ages at which a particular "emotion" emerged, nor the precise sequence she found can be given much credence. Lack of control of an adultomorphic tendency and a lack of adequate provision for checking ob-

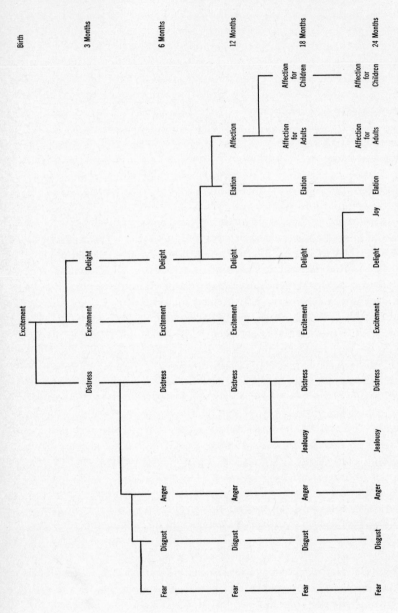

Figure 7. The approximate ages of differentiation of the various emotions during the first two years. (From Bridges (14). Copyright 1932 by the Society for Research in Child Development, and published with permission.)

server reliability are present. These difficulties make her specific results suggestive, not definitive. Emotional differentiation was established; the precise sequence and names of the emotions she gave must be held suspect.

Changes of Mode of Responses and of Sensitivity

In addition to the progressive differentiation of emotions as the infant grows older changes in the mode of responses take place—changes in the way the emotion is expressed. Fear in the 20-month-old, for example, is different from the eight-month-old infant. The former now can move away from the feared stimulus, not merely cry. As the infant grows older, more nuances of an emotional situation are capable of being perceived. As intellectual development proceeds, new situations become capable of eliciting the emotion. Emotional reactions are intimately bound with the intellectual stages of maturation reached. An individual reacts emotionally only to situations in which he is able to discriminate in some fashion between their disturbing or satisfying qualities. To respond emotionally he must "interpret" the situation in some fashion.

A young infant is undisturbed by conditions that will later arouse emotion. At ten weeks confinement in a pen is accepted without any indication of emotion, at twenty weeks he is apprehensive, at thirty weeks he cries vigorously. A bright two-year-old may show fear of a strange room or of a snake that leaves blithely oblivious until he is older a child of the same age who is of average intelligence (39).

The Role of Maturation and Learning

The differentiation of emotions, changes of mode of responses, and of sensitivity in emotions with increasing age relate to maturation and learning. An illustration was just given in the differential responses of fear stimuli of a bright and an average two-year-old. Presumably both maturation and learning were operative. The bright two-year-old in responding to stimuli which his peer did not sense not only was expressing a faster maturation, but also that he had learned to perceive what his age peer had not.

Emotion as a product of maturation is shown in studies in which there is no opportunity for the usual learning to take place. This may be studied either through differential studies where restriction on infants or children had already taken place or through experimental arrangements to restrict their learning. As an example of differential restriction, a child blind and deaf since birth is not in a position to learn facial or general emotional behavior from others. Goodenough (35) studied such a girl when she was ten. Her facial expressions and general behavior under conditions that usually arouse anger, fear, or pleasure in other children were very much like those exhibited by seeing, normal children. Her forms of emotional expression had arisen through maturation without opportunity for imitation through auditory or visual channels.

Goodenough, although considering the primary forms of emotional expression as determined by maturational factors, did admit that a socialization veneer may appear. This was confirmed in a later study by Thompson (75). This study involved a considerably larger number of subjects both blind and seeing, of ages ranging from seven weeks to 13 years. Their varying ages made it possible to study the effect of socialization with increasing age. In addition to confirming Goodenough's general finding concerning maturation, the investigator found also that beyond two or three years of age the blind subjects showed a decrease in facial activity in smiling and laughing. Among seeing children this did not take place. Social reinforcement which was lacking with the blind children was operative with them. The influence of a learning factor was thus apparent.

An experimental study which demonstrates the influence of maturation is that of Dennis (20). He reared two infants from one month of age until the age of seven months in such a way that the adult voices they heard were not associated with other smile-provoking stimuli. Under these conditions the human voice never caused smiling. Nevertheless, smiling upon *seeing* the adult developed to a marked degree, occurring more markedly when the adult bent over to minister to their needs.

The appearance of different emotional responses to stimuli which previously did not elicit them demonstrates the importance of learning (42, 43, 77, 78). The classic pioneer study of the conditioning of infant fear responses was performed by Watson and Raynor (78). It will be remembered from Chapter 1, that Albert, an infant slightly less than a year old, was found originally to have no fear of furry objects but rapidly was conditioned to be afraid of them. Thus a fear response was given to stimuli that formerly did not elicit them.

Cognitive development

Although the terms perception, language, intelligence, and concept formation are used to describe the experience and behavior of infants, they take on greater exactitude in later years. As with sensorimotor and emotional development, something resembling mass perceptual, intellectual, linguistic, and conceptual thinking seems to take place. Only as the child grows older will there be clear individuation. Let us therefore first consider cognitive development, understanding, or thinking in general.

To follow this path is to walk in the spirit of Jean Piaget (58, 59, 60, 61, 62, 63, 64, 65, 66, 67) who has done more to lay bare the thought of the infant and young child than any other psychologist. He regards cognitive processes as also being expressed in thought and intelligence between which he makes no sharp distinction. They are aspects of the same central cognitive process. Moreover, Piaget defines perception to cover a much smaller area of psychological phenomena than is customary, while simultaneously making it subordinate to intelligence as a means of individual adaptation or adjustment to the environment (25). Without doing too much of an injustice to Piaget, his perceptual studies, as such, will not be introduced into this account.

To Piaget thought is a biological function (25) in that intellectual functioning is a matter of adaptative interaction or organism and environment. Adaptation is expressed in two complementary functions— assimilation and accommodation (67). Assimilation takes place when the organism uses some object in the environment in the course of its activity. It occurs when the new is drawn into the old behavior repertoire and becomes part of the infant's inner organization. For example, when something new is perceived that resembles an old, already familiar object, it is used as would be the old object. Accommodation, on the other hand, occurs when the old repertoire is adjusted to account for the new object experienced. Hence, new activities are added to the infant's repertoire and the old activities modified to that extent.

In order to aid the reader to "assimilate" and "accommodate" this discussion, the former includes what in old familiar terms we would call generalization and discrimination, whereas accommodation includes differentiation, or the learning of new responses. This adaptational process, embracing assimilation and accommodation as its functions, remains the same as the child grows in age (25).

Cognitive structures change with age and Piaget's theory of intelligence is primarily a theory of structure. These structures are interposed between the ever-changing contents and the nonchanging functions of intelligence. They are organized through their functioning. To anticipate later discussion, these so-called structures include concepts, such as egocentrism, animism, realism, and artificialism (see pages 312 and 486. These structures are exhibited at certain ages, and, since they follow one another, they can also be called *stages*. Since cultural and other factors may affect the particular age at which a stage appears, each step cannot be too closely tied with age. The sequence *a,b* is invariant; the particular age for *b* to appear after *a* is not. In two children of the same age *b* might appear months apart.

Piagetian Levels of Cognition

Piaget conceives of three developmental periods: (*a*) sensorimotor activity; (*b*) preparation and organization of concrete operations; and (*c*) formal operations (*25*).

It is the first developmental period that merits attention at this point, since the sensorimotor level stretches from birth until roughly 18 to 24 months. At birth the only organization available to the infant is the congenital sensorimotor responses described in the previous chapter as characteristic of the neonate. During this period the infant's actions are not yet internalized in the form of thoughts (*66*). When functioning at this level, the infant assimilates external realities in a fashion corresponding roughly to the problem-solving abilities of the subhuman animals (*64*). He exercises these sensorimotor capacities and gropes about in his environment, for example, in showing sucking responses to almost any stimulation of the lips.

Realities are not yet entities; they are only functional elements— something to be sucked, to be handled, or to be moved. Objects do not yet exist as objects. "Out of sight, out of mind" might be said to characterize the view of the infant. He behaves as if objects that have disappeared from view have ceased to exist. For example, Piaget tells us that an infant of five to eight months of age, already old enough to seize a solid object, will lose interest and turn away if a cloth be thrown over the object before his hand reaches it. At a slightly older age he is capable of seeking an object behind a screen and thus shows the beginnings of the notion of the real exterior permanence of objects. Nevertheless, he is still functioning at the more primitive level.

An infant at the just-mentioned level was given the experience of retrieving an object that he saw placed under the left of two pillows. On the next occasion, he sought the object where he had found it before, despite the fact that the examiner, in full view of the infant, had placed it under the *right* pillow. As Piaget indicates, it is as if his action in reaching under the left pillow was decided by the success of his actions by which he had secured it previously and not by the reality of its external placement under the right pillow on this new occasion. At the sensorimotor level the world to the infant is not that of permanent objects with an autonomy of their own; it is a series of perceptive views which periodically disappear into nonexistence only to be brought back as the function of the proper action on the infant's part.

The infant comes to realize that objects are stable, independent of himself; that they have a shape which remains the same even though as he turns the object its visual appearance varies; that objects retain identity despite varying in apparent size as they approach or recede; and perhaps to him, most surprising of all, that they continue to exist when out of sight. Nor does the infant have as part of his native endowment conceptions of either space or time. Above all, he has to learn about cause and effect. This life-long process begins during the first year (65). His pushing and pulling make them move, rattle, and squeak. At first he does not realize that it is necessary for him to touch them to cause these effects. He tries magic by waving his hands at them from a distance. It is only during his second year that he seems to realize that in order to make an object move he must touch it.

All of these conceptions he must build up in the course of his interaction with the world. Since symbolic manipulations of these concepts are absent until the very end of infancy, let us postpone consideration of them until we turn to early childhood.

Perceptual-conceptual development

As a first approximation of their meaning, perceptions require not only the presence of stimuli as do sensations but also the interpretation of these stimuli based on the previous experiences of the individual. Meanings, of some sort, are given to the stimuli. It is not merely a bright flashing, it is a neon sign; it is not merely a clanging, it is the sound of a church bell. In concept formation he goes a step farther. The infant has already perceived objects as shown by his responses. A concept is attained when he can make the appropriate response to stimuli he has not previously observed.

The development of perception is originally dependent on sensory development. If deprived of one or more senses, to that extent the infant is handicapped in the development of understanding. If severely handicapped in several major sensory areas, as was Helen Keller who was deprived of both hearing and vision shortly after birth, the task of "interpreting" the world becomes a very difficult one. Perforce he must learn to interpret the external world through the remaining senses. If completely deprived of all senses, he would have no way of interacting with the world.

Fortunately, in the first few weeks of life the sensory apparatus of a typical infant is in good working condition. Nevertheless his understanding of what is going on around him is negligible. When something breaks through his hazy awareness, it produces excitement. Otherwise, when he is satisfied—when his stomach is full, digestion is proceeding smoothly, and he is warm and snug—awareness fades out and he drifts into sleep. Gradually, his periods of wakefulness increase. As he grows older, the infant's understandings come from his active sensory exploration of his environment.

Observation suggests that during the first year of life the infant spends a considerable amount of time getting acquainted with his world—reaching, fondling, poking, hefting, mouthing, staring, rubbing, tasting, and smelling the objects and persons that come his way. Externally aroused behavior tendencies, then, are very much operative in his beginning to understand both himself and his environment.

The infant seeks out and discovers the qualities of objects—their particular tastes, contours, warmth, and other qualities. His perception of people and objects, his pleasurable recognition of the familiar and his displeasure at the strange, show that objects and persons are beginning to be perceived. Much of what is written about the emergence of the self and social perception in Chapter 9 shows these beginnings. It must be emphasized that the infant perceives emotional significances as well as intellectual ones. It is even probable that these affective perceptions actually precede and are more important for the young infant than are the nonaffective meanings which he is developing.

It was found through observation of direction and duration of visual fixations that infants between one and 15 weeks of age exhibited consistent preferences for one of a pair of patterns to which they were exposed (27). This led to the conclusion that some degree of form perception was innate. Further development of visual behavior is acknowledged to be a complex of maturation and learning. In a later study (28) involving pattern vision in infants during the first six months, it was confirmed that the infant could see more than vague masses of light and dark since he is able to discriminate various patterns. Independently, another investigator (9) found that infants preferred (fixated more often) those patterns with more rather than less contour.

Some researchers (76) have investigated infantile perception of situations suggesting the possibility of differences in depth. The setting was downward depth, such as that experienced when looking toward the ground from a high building. The apparatus consisted of a center "crawl" way with sheets of glass extending on each side below which a checkerboard pattern was visible. On one side, the checkerboard was directly beneath the glass; on the other side, it was far below the glass giving what, to an adult, appeared to be a drop off, or cliff side. Despite entreaties of the mother to crawl toward her none of the infants would do so on the cliff side but did so readily on the other. Since even the youngest infants were six months of age, the youngest age at which the essentials of the act of creeping appear, they all had had opportunities for previous experiences from which they might have learned some of the cues to depth perception. Nevertheless, the evidence suggests that at least some aspects of depth perception are unlearned.

The developmental principle of differentiation holds in infantile perception. The child learns to make finer and finer distinctions. It has been said that the infant's world is a confused blur, but he still appears able to isolate and perceive certain stimuli; it may be more accurate to speak, not of a confused blur, but of a hazily organized field with lights and shadows that give some structure.

As formulated in behavior-social learning theory, perceptions and conceptualizations serve as cue-producing responses (22). It follows then that they should be modifiable by further learning. This modification of perceptions and conceptualizations is borne out in a general way throughout this and subsequent sections of the chapter. No matter the specific point being made, cue production is implied in the discussion of the growth of understanding. Language is, of course, a series of cue-producing responses. Gellermann's study of the influence of verbalization on form conceptualization, described presently in this context, could be rephrased as a study of the influence of verbal cues on form discrimination. Perceptions and conceptions come about as a result of learning.

Words are cues. As soon as the child discovers that words have meaning (are cues for something else) and that for every object there is a word (cue), he has made a tremendous step forward in understanding. Words also exist for conceptions that are independent of objects. Thus qualities of objects, which may be understood without referring to a particular object, also come to be understood. Roundness, independent of round apples or round balls, is illustrative.

Conceptual discrimination rests on language in the sense that language discrimination improves conceptualization. Nevertheless, conceptualization may appear without language. Ling (46) demonstrated this in an ingenious study in which the infants showed their conceptual discrimination of a correct form by licking it, instead of other forms that were also present. He did this by presenting to six to 15 months' old infants blocks differing in form, including circles, crosses, and triangles. Successful selection of one form was rewarded by a coating of saccharine it had on its surface. Discrimination shown by licking the correct form was found as early as the sixth month of life. Changing the position of the correct form relative to the others or varying its size had only a slight effect upon accuracy.

Another investigator, Long (47), has shown through a manual response setup that somewhat older subjects in the preschool years also can discriminate forms without being able to name them. He was able to demonstrate that very young children formed a given concept, as shown by going through a test series without error, and yet thereafter were quite unable to give anything approaching a verbal formulation of what they were doing. Thus, form concepts precede ability to verbalize these concepts.

It is significant, however, that some, but not all, of Long's older subjects did use such words as "balls" in talking to themselves in the course of their selections.

Language naturally aids a child in concept formation. This may be illustrated by a study of form discrimination by Gellermann (30) in which he compared two-year-old children and chimpanzees in discriminating triangularity. The investigator gave no verbal instructions to the children. Some of them formulated the problem, which he had been careful not to verbalize for them, by gestures and verbal behavior instructions to themselves. He found that the children were definitely superior to the chimpanzees in discriminating triangularity. In part, at least, this seemed to be due to their greater verbal facility. The children's verbalizations did seem to help in arriving at conceptualizations as shown by the higher precentages of correct responses in those using them.

Concepts, such as those just discussed, have their beginning in infancy, but they are so grossly inaccurate and so primitive in nature as hardly to deserve the name concepts. The studies of conceptualization which have been described, with the exception of Ling's, either used infants just barely within the age of infancy as did Gellermann or actually used preschool-aged children as did Long. It is possible that these studies may have given too mature a cast to the concepts of the infant. Rather than space concepts, he has poor orientation in space shown in often reaching for an object in the wrong direction. Rather than inaccurate concepts of weight, it is more parsimonious to speak of his making mistakes in weight, such as his being forced to drop too heavy objects when he attempts to hold them.

Language development

All human societies have languages. In fact, language is perhaps our most peculiarly human characteristic. Out of the vocalization of babes emerges our most powerful vehicles of thought, expression, and communication. Language is a means of learning other aspects of socialization and also a means of expressing already established socializations, particularly as these are expressed in interpersonal relationships.

These accomplishments are the goals of language development. They are not the realities of language at the beginning of infancy, since, actually they are so nonsocial in nature as to be called egocentric by Piaget (58). The infant believes that he *is* the world and has no appreciation of the viewpoints of others of whose very existence he is unaware. He has no need to communicate. Speech is to and for himself, i.e., egocentric. Fortunately for the infant, and for us, the world pierces through to him and speech begins to carry on a communicative function.

Language and thought are intimately related. To put it succinctly, thoughts are manipulations of meanings; words facilitate these manipulations, render them more precise and make them more easily recalled. Functionally speaking, language may be said to embrace three kinds of activities—inner, receptive, and expressive (55). Sometime during the first eight or nine months inner language appears as the infant talks to himself in his private egocentric fashion. Thereafter, until about 12 or 13 months receptive language is in the process of formation. The infant now begins to comprehend others but is not yet able to express himself. Expressive language, the ability to make oneself understood by words, begins toward the end of infancy. Its initial appearance must wait until inner and receptive language have been partially established.

Inner language is a form of play and self-stimulation expressed in babbling just for the fun of it. This activity bears considerable resemblance to the initial egocentricity that Piaget found to exist in infants.

Receptive language begins when the infant learns to tease out from the total mass of impression of sounds to which he is exposed those sounds that are the spoken language of other persons. Actions going hand in hand with language are the language units that are probably learned first. Thus, "pat-a-cake," "bye-bye," and "here's your bottle" are accompanied by appropriate actions on the part of adults. At about 12 months the infant obeys simple commands (34). For example, it is at this age that, on command, he will place a cube in a cup. This is a relatively complex activity. Compared to his command of active language, which reference to Table 6 will show is only about four words at this age, it is illustrative of his relatively greater receptive language comprehension.

In the infant's earliest vocalizations a considerable variety of basic sounds, or phonemes, appear. The delimitation and isolation of the phonemes were arrived at in the course of many investigations by listening to infant vocalizations and recording them phonetically. Some phonemes appear in these vocalizations more often than do others, with vowel sounds predominating (40). Some of these phonemes appear later in English, but many are not elements of any language, let alone English. The infant also uses phonemes destined to be used in languages other than English. Thus, an infant in our culture uses sounds corresponding to the German ü, the Danish ö, the French u, and the guttural r. This "initial hierarchy" of basic sounds is modified as the infant grows older. Consonant sounds increase, non-English phonemes drop out, and the resultant hierarchy of English sounds comes into being.

Lynip (48), after recording the sounds made by an infant, used the Sound Spectrograph to analyze pictorially the samplings. The pictorial representations on this instrument of the infant's vocalizations could then be compared with those for the various letters used in adult speech. His results illustrate very vividly why phoneticians sometimes disagree among themselves in their phonetic translations of what they have heard in the speech of infants. The visible patterns on the Spectrograph of early infant sounds were blurs, unlike the pictorial representations of adult vowel sounds. As the infant grew older, the sounds that he made soon came to resemble adult vowels, so far as hearing them was concerned, but the Spectrograph showed that they were still quite different from adult sounds. These results, however, do not vitiate findings from phonetic transcription (79). After all, psychological interest centers on the linguistic analysis carried on by the human ear. The Sound Spectrograph measures only the physical characteristics of the sound, not the psychological, and the two data series may not be perfectly correlated.

Expressive language development starts, not with the emergence of the first words, but much earlier with the first vocalizations. In a sense, it starts with the birth cry. The presence of overt linguistic activity long before the infant speaks his first word is shown in many ways—calls to attract attention and inflections in his vocalization that show his reaction to a situation quite clearly in scolding, squeaks of delight, and grunts of disgust. Moreover, gesture language such as pointing, looking, and reaching serve as another means of communication.

So far as the differential use of sounds which characterizes language is concerned, it is at about one month of age that Gesell and Thompson (34) have established that infantile cries of discomfort, pain, and hunger are differentiated by the observer. Mothers claim discriminatory ability along those lines at even younger ages. Vocalization in the form of small throaty noises also appear at about four weeks. This and other representative findings of normative age for kinds of vocalizations, as established by Gesell and Amatruda (31), are given in Table 6. Their results will be supplemented by some of the findings of Shirley (73) in her longitudinal study.

TABLE 6

NORMS OF VOCALIZATION *

Age in weeks	Behavior
4	Small throaty noises
8	Single vowel sounds—ah, eh, uh
12	Coos, chuckles
16	Laughs aloud
20	Squeals
24	Grunts, growls
28	Polysyllabic vowel sounds
32	Single syllables—da, ba, ka
36	Dada (or equivalent)
	Imitates sounds
40	Mama, and one other word
52	Four words
78	Ten words, including names
104	Jargon discarded
	Three word sentences
	Uses I, me, you
	Names various objects

* Adapted from Gesell and Amatruda (31). Copyright 1947 by Paul B. Hoeber, Inc., and published with permission.

Gesell and Amatruda, as shown in the table, place the first word at 40 weeks. On the average, Shirley's babies used their first word in her presence at about 65 weeks. In some of these infants the first word appeared as early as eight months, and its appearance in others was delayed to as late as two years of age. The mothers themselves cred-

ited their infants with a vocabulary of two or three words at 52 weeks
which agrees with the findings of Gesell and Amatruda. With due
allowance for individual variation, it would appear that the average
child says his first word before the end of the first year (17). Gifted
children may do so at an even earlier age, whereas other children are
retarded to the point of not using words until after their second year.

That these findings about the first word seem to vary according to
the observer is perhaps because some observers, especially mothers,
have a strongly developed tendency to credit the child with speaking
words based on utterances which actually are quite far removed from
the word in question. It will be remembered that Lynip found that
the sounds of the infant he studied, although interpreted as being adult
vowels, were still a blur on the Spectrograph. Moreover, the word or
words for which they are credited by their mothers may be part of a
private language wherein a certain sound, perhaps having no resemblance to the word (such as "yo-e" for water), functions as a word
in that particular family.

Shirley found that at 66 weeks her infant subjects used seven comprehensible words. There was little improvement until 86 weeks; she
believed that probably this lag was due to the infant's preoccupation
with locomotion during this period. By two years of age the average
number of words used by her infant subjects was 32. Her findings
may be supplemented by returning to those of Gesell and Amatruda
as reported in Table 6. At two years of age, not only has jargon been
discarded but three word sentences have made their appearance as
well as the beginnings of the use of pronouns. Considerable development of expressive language ability during the second year has evidently taken place.

The infant's eagerness to speak and to learn names is a major feature
of the development of speech. Children have a mania for naming
things. Entirely divorced from actual biological needs, this deserves
to be called a hunger for names since their learning of names is quite
the reverse of a mechanical process approached with reluctance. In
a subsequent chapter we shall see that according to psychoanalytic
theory language assumes a magical character during infancy. Moreover, the use of language in a threatening manner can and is communicated to the infant. Hence, language can be anxiety producing. The
presence of anxiety is also hinted at by this hunger for naming. It is
a psychoanalytic contention that having a name for a potentially threatening object gives the child a feeling that he has power to control
that object.

As most mothers know to their embarrassment, an infant able to use the word "daddy" may apply it on occasion to any male he sees. Or having learned to use "kitty" for a cat, he is apt to apply it to a dog, a squirrel, or even when playing with the fur collar of his mother's coat. Generalization is operating here as it was in other situations we have examined; it is characteristic of the infant to assimilate the new aspect of a situation to what is now old and familiar to him. As he grows older, his cues for discriminatory decisions increase in precision. Illustrative of his growing discrimination is the use by a somewhat older child of an expression such as "funny kitty" for a squirrel. No longer is it a "kitty" alone but a "funny" one. Some of the cues for kitty are present but also something else. The new is seen for what it is, assimilated with the old, and the way prepared for cue discrimination. Attaching distinctive cue-producing responses to heretofore similar stimuli tends to increase their distinctiveness.

The infant applies a word to a wide variety of objects or persons that later will be differentiated by different words. "Dog" means many things according to his total reaction conveyed by the tone of voice, gestures, and bodily movements: "I want that dog, I want to pet and hug him," or "there is an interesting object; you should look at it too," or, "I'm scared, hold me, and get me away from here." "Dog" is only one word, to be sure, but with many meanings. The few words the infant does have are made to stand for many objects and actions.

Imitation plays an important role in verbal learning. It will be remembered from Chapter 5 that imitation was defined by Miller and Dollard (53) as a way of learning in which matched (similar) behaviors are not only brought about in two people but also connected by appropriate cues. A way of expressing this is contained in the following quotation:

> When the child accidentally, and later purposefully, reproduces sounds which he himself has made, the adults in the environment usually say a real word which the child's sounds appear to approximate. This tends to give auditory reinforcement to the sounds the child has made, at the same time making for more precise perception and rendition of the approved sound groups. Thus there occurs a progressive elimination of errors and a selection of movements which give the best approximation to the real word heard in the speech of adults. Continued practice thus results in the fixation of the sound groups, which come to be uttered habitually. (49, 518).[3]

The infant and child tend to learn whatever responses are reinforced by reward of the immediate drive reducing variety or by some indirect

[3] From McCarthy (49). Copyright 1954 by John Wiley and Sons, and published with permission.

secondary cue of an eventual reward to come.   The responses rewarded tend to be repeated; those not rewarded tend to drop out.

The mother is the first language teacher and the infant soon begins
to echo back to her in vocal play, in cooing and babbling.   Her smiling,
fondling, and vocalization, as well as that of other adults, increase his
prelinguistic utterances.   This point has received clear-cut experimental confirmation through conditioning the vocalizations of infants (68).
Infants characteristically vocalize on seeing an adult.   Taking advantage of this fact, investigators counted the number of vocalizations
made during nine three-minute periods distributed throughout the day
for each of 21 institutionalized infants of a median age of three months.

The results for the first two days provided a base line.   These were
days when the experimenter merely leaned over the crib with an ex-
pressionless face.   The second two days the experimenter reinforced
vocalizations by smiling, clucking, and touching the infant; the last two
days were again concerned with nonreinforcement (base line behavior).   Conditioning (reinforcement) raised the rate of vocalizing to
a statistically significant extent over the baseline while nonreinforcement lowered it to a level approaching the baseline.   Social vocalizing
in infants, it would appear, may be modified by the kind of responses
adults make to them.

Environmental restriction, such as occurs to many infants and
children living in institutions, presumably has an effect on the learning of language.   Characteristically these children do not receive as
much individual attention as do children living in the normal family
atmosphere.   Babies under six months of age raised in the unstimulating environment of an orphanage have been found to be retarded in
frequency of vocalization and kinds of sounds as compared with children raised at home (15).   Conversely, enrichment will increase the
speech sounds made.   Systematic reading of stories to infants from the
age of 13 months to that of 30 months leads to a significant difference
in the number of vocalizations from this group and another group of
infants matched with them for economic status of the father's occupation (41).   After about four months the infants read to showed
reliably more speech sounds.

Intellectual development

The somewhat amorphous nature of the behavior of the infant is
reflected in referring to intelligence as a form of general ability in
problem-solving capacity.   Only later in life is it necessary to be more

precise about its meaning and to use such terms as abstract or verbal ability. Aspects of thinking—sensorimotor, perceptual, conceptual, and linguistic activity—are all involved in intellectual activity. When they are used for adaptive purposes to solve the problems the infant encounters, they are being used intelligently. The same active strivings described in the development of thinking are to be seen as operating in intellectual activity. Perception of objects outside of himself is a spur to the infant's intellectual functioning. His tasting, smelling, looking, and feeling show intelligence in operation. Without this active exploration, intellectual development would be stunted. The research findings on environmental restriction described in the next chapter testify to what happens to intellectual functioning when the incentive to carry on this active exploration is stunted in an unstimulating environment.

One of the more widely used infant scales will be utilized to demonstrate the changes in performance expected of the younger and older infant. The Cattell Infant Intelligence Scale (16) is a downward extension of the Revised Stanford-Binet Intelligence Tests (see page 499), and is similar to them in that the items are grouped according to age levels. It is suitable for children as young as two months and, for those 30 months of age, it merges with Stanford-Binet tests.

At the youngest levels, the tasks are often perceptual-motor in nature. For example, to receive credit for an item at the two-month level, the child may be expected to show head and eye movements in following a moving stimulus. Beginning at about five months the scale contains a gradually increasing number of manipulatory items. Prior to the age of about 12 months, administration of the items involves neither imitation of the examiner's behavior nor response to verbal requests. Rather, a controlled stimulus is simply presented to the child and his response observed.

For example, does a four-month-old infant become more active at the sight of a toy? When a small one-inch block is placed on the table in front of him, what does he do? Chances are if he is an average three-month-old, he will focus his eyes on it; if he is six months old, he can probably pick it up and even reach for another one. If he is seven months old, he can probably hold two blocks simultaneously. But not before the age of 14 months is he likely to be able to hold three such blocks at one time.

After the age of one year, the items become increasingly dependent upon verbal factors. Either the child himself must demonstrate his emerging ability to use speech (be able to say one word at 11 months, two words at 12 months, combine words at 22 months, and so on) or at least be able to respond to verbal instructions given by the examiner. Despite this gradual increase in the use of spoken or comprehended language, manipulatory items still predominate until approximately the two-year level.

With items similar to those in the Cattell Scale, Bayley (4) found that the mental growth curve was of the sort given in Figure 8. The rapid increase in scores during the first year and a gradual leveling off thereafter seem to characterize the changes over the two-year period. It is evident that infancy is a period of considerable mental growth.

Intelligence is a sequence of developing functions which differ as age increases (6). At the youngest ages the intellectual accomplishments of the infant are of the sort attributed to them by Piaget as presented in the account of cognition. At later ages, adaptive behavior of a more abstract nature will be sampled, but for the young infant this is impossible. Indeed, we cannot be sure he is capable of such behavior until at least later infancy.

Two independently conducted research studies lend support to these contentions. Richards and Nelson (69), using items developed by Gesell for infant testing at six, 12, and 18 months, found by statistical manipulation that two factors accounted for the interrelations they obtained. They called one factor "alertness" and the other "motor ability." The two factors were more closely intertwined than is usually the case with factors found with older subjects. They mention that the motor factor is present practically in all test items. Alertness is con-

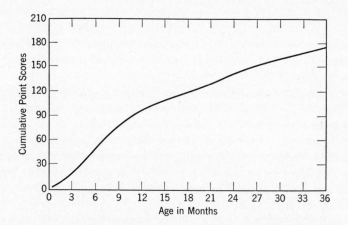

Figure 8. Mental growth curve in terms of cumulative point scores. (From Bayley (4). Copyright 1933 by the Journal Press, and published with permission.)

sidered to be present when in addition to motor activity, there is also either distance reception, as in looking for a fallen object; or playfulness, as in laughing at the sound of music. In another study Hofstaetter (38) found that one factor which he named "sensory motor alertness" predominated in the intelligence of infants. In their general findings, the two studies differ only in that in the former two factors are found, which in the latter are combined into one factor.

An attempt should be made to reconcile the principle of the continuity of development with the discontinuity principle implicit in the preceding paragraph. Piaget recognized that discontinuity of development ran counter to theories of continuity. How are the shifts in intellectual level to be reconciled with intelligence tests, which are arranged as metrical scales increasing by months and years? Piaget acknowledged that with this continuous arrangement of material the tests still served their purpose of providing an accurate, rapid measurement. This is possible because intelligence tests measure what was referred to earlier as *products* and not the operations used by the children in reaching their answers. There may be a steady increase in score with age, but the underlying operation at one stage may be different from those at another stage.

It has been generally found that tests given in infancy are not very predictive of later intellectual prowess as measured in preschool ages or later. Despite the standardization of the Cattell Scale as a downward extension of the Stanford-Binet, it is essentially nonpredictive of later results on the Stanford-Binet. For example, the correlations found between Cattell measures for three, six, and nine months and the Stanford-Binet at 36 months are respectively 0.10, 0.34, and 0.18 (16). For older ages the correlations become progressively greater. Using the same standard of 36 months on the Stanford-Binet, those for 12, 18, 24, and 30 months are, respectively, 0.56, 0.67, 0.71, and 0.83. Predictions of intelligence measures obtained before the age of one year against measures in later years are so low as to be essentially meaningless, but are more adequate thereafter.

The reasons for their relatively poor predictive value generally are not hard to establish. The young infant is not interested in his own performance because he is not even aware of it as a performance. He cannot be guided by verbal instructions to any great degree, and his attention is not easily directed to the tasks selected. His behavior repertoire is much more restricted in breadth than is the older child's. Most important of all is the still unsettled question whether intelligence, as we conceive of it in the adult, can be said to have emerged before symbolic language processes have been established. Since motor performance is stressed in the testing of intelligence of infants, their repertory may well include very little which is directly related to later intelligence. For these reasons, it is hardly surprising that the results obtained with infant tests of intelligence are not as highly correlated with later performance as are tests given at later years.

These limitations should not be interpreted as suggesting that infant tests should be discarded (8). If an infant is below average in the activities that make up infant scales, it is still an indication that something is amiss. Current status is still an important source of information despite limited usefulness for prediction of future status.

Infant intelligence tests are especially useful in clinical settings when markedly deviated individuals are being examined (23). Careful examination, when part of a complete case history, proves of considerable value—for example, in placement for adoption.

Individuality and consistency

The neonate shows only the barest beginnings of individuality; he cannot be said to have a personality in the sense that he has characteristic organized ways of behaving. Rather, he has the potentiality for such behavior expressed in certain forms of individuality already noted in the previous chapter. There is no question that personality in the sense just mentioned makes its appearance during the two years of infancy, even though it is fruitless to try to give it a more precise date.

The unequal rapidity of various forms of development is a major factor in the appearance of individuality of the infant. The development process is not uniform. In some respects an infant may be in advance of what may be expected of him; in other respects he may be behind. True, this happens later as well, but never again will the contrasts be so great. This individuality of development is attributable to inheritance and environmental opportunities to which the particular infant is exposed. With further development these individualities become patterned and a characteristic personality emerges in the infant.

Infants show persistent variabilities in psychological characteristics. Variability in amount of crying among infants is considerable. It was found (1) that within a 24-hour period time sample, infants varied in amount of crying from 48 to 243 minutes. Among the infants studied by Marquis (52) and referred to in connection with the relation of frustration to emotion, one showed five times as much bodily activity in the frustrating situation as did another in the same situation.

Another investigator (29) was concerned with degree of activity. On the basis of many years' observation she would categorize the differences among infants in this regard in terms of activity types. She found five types—the normal range including quiet, moderately active, and active, and two pathological groups, one at each of the extremes, the hypo- and hyperactive. Observing these same children as they grew older, she concluded that markedly active infants were markedly active at later ages and that neonates who were relatively quiet tended to remain relatively inactive individuals in childhood.

Unusual sensitivities among infants to external stimuli have been noted (24). One sleeping infant may be disturbed by sounds through which other infants sleep undisturbed. In sensitive infants, a startle to sound may appear and the infant may seem to "wince" as if stimuli only moderately intense by usual standards are actually painful. Escalona and Bergman consider that these sensitivities may be conceptualized as showing in these infants that there are weak barriers between the stimuli of the external world and the infant. If ordinary stimuli are overwhelming, the sensitive infant may have to withdraw from stimulation to a greater degree than the ordinary infant. Bell's results (9), reported in the previous chapter, would make it appear that the barrier is confined within one sense modality, and not a general sensitivity extending across the modalities.

Not only variability from infant to infant but also consistency within a particular infant has been observed. In a study based on cinema records, speed of creeping and climbing and manipulating was measured at monthly intervals (2). A remarkable constancy of psychomotor tempo of activities was found. The infant who crept fastest manipulated fastest with a similar constancy in other infants.

Shirley (72) who closely studied 25 babies from birth to three years described characteristics distinguishing one infant from another in terms of irritability, tone, and timbre of crying, and motility and tonicity of muscles. This individuality in expression of emotion tends to be maintained within particular gross limits as the infant grows older. For example, she (73) described certain infants in which timorousness and irritability had appeared earlier and persisted throughout the ensuing months of her study. Moreover when "profile charts" were prepared involving a variety of characteristics they differed so much from one infant to another that the examiner could identify the infants from the charts alone.

This particular study assumes even greater importance because 16 years later these same children were restudied (56). Without seeing the personality sketches made by Shirley, the investigator restudied them and prepared adolescent personality sketches. Judges then matched the infant and adolescent personality sketches with success far above chance expectation. Temperamental qualities present in infancy still characterized these individuals when they were adolescents.

Summary

Physical growth and motor development may be conveniently considered together. Changes in size, strength, and agility are very evident in infancy, perhaps showing greater changes during these two years than during any similar span of years. In motor development, the effects of both maturation and learning reveal themselves with clarity and sharpness. Two of the most important aspects of motor development during infancy are hand manipulation and walking.

Developmental changes in primary needs have been examined. Prominent in feeding are the reduction in the number of occasions the infant is fed, the phenomena associated with scheduling and self-demand feeding, and the varying degrees of permissiveness shown by parents. The infants' learning to adapt to feeding schedules was demonstrated. On examination of weaning as a product of both maturation and learning, a quite complicated process was found to exist.

A progressive increase in waking activity, as contrasted with sleep, was found to characterize the changes over the two years of infancy. An increase in sheer length of sleep periods was also noted.

Developmental changes in elimination take place during infancy. Both bladder and bowel control were found to be complicated processes. The neuromuscular maturation essential for adequate control was found to be important for bringing about failures to achieve as early control as some parents would like. Learning of control proceeds without benefit of verbal aids since the infant is so limited in passive and spoken vocabulary. It is hardly surprising that, by and large, toilet training begun later in infancy rather than earlier takes less time to be accomplished.

The infant faces, as do all of us, the stresses of daily living. He reacts by tension which is an invariable characteristic of emotionality. Emotionality arises from the frustration or enhancement of needs.

When considering the phenomena of infant emotionality it was found that young infants lacked differentiated emotional responses. Instead, under emotional stress the young infant reacted with generalized excitement.

By the age of 18 months, the human infant has a rather extensive repertoire of emotional responses. Along with sheer differentiation goes progressive change in the modes of responses—the ways in which the child reacts to emotion-provoking stimuli. Improvement in muscular abilities and learning to appreciate the meaning of situations contribute heavily to these changes. Cumulative influence, differentiation, and integration as trends in development are clearly demonstrated in the emotional responses of infants.

Cognitive development concerns the higher mental processes that aid in dealing with the world—understanding, perception, concept formation, language, and intelligence. It was explored first through consideration of the position taken by Piaget—that it is a biological function showing adaptation, expressed in assimilation and accommodation, with a cognitive structure interposed between these constant functions and the ever-changing contents of experience. The structures in the experience of infancy are expressed in sensorimotor activity.

Perceptual-conceptual development may be examined in terms of the infant's seeking such experiences and in research investigations of depth and form perception. Their examination leads to the tentative conclusion that in infancy perception is not without some organization. The relation between forming concepts and language shows that, although facilitated by language, some concepts may be formed in its absence.

Language in its egocentric aspects and language as expressed functionally in inner receptive and expressive forms were examined. From the phonemes of the infant emerges the language the child learns in his particular culture. Language thus begins with the first vocalizations, not the first words. Development proceeds rapidly. From the small throaty noises at four weeks to the three-word sentences of two years of age is a remarkable development, with tremendous yet predictable strides being taken in the learning of one's language by the infant. Hand in hand with language development goes the development of understanding. If handicapped in sensory development, the infant is handicapped in language and in understanding. An account of how language develops in terms of behavior-social learning, particularly imitation, is a consequence. Special emphasis is placed upon perception and conceptualization serving as cue-producing responses.

Intellectual prowess, too, shows a steady rate of growth during infancy. It is significant that after about one year of age verbal factors are considered more and more responsible for growth in intelligence. Despite predictable changes, however, the instruments developed for the measurement of infant intelligence still lack any great efficiency in predicting intellectual developmental standing at older ages.

In all of these areas of psychological development, individual differences from infant to infant are very obvious. Relating these differences to a scale of activity, ranging from excessive activity to passivity, seems to account for many of these observed differences. But consistency appears within a given infant and patterning of his individual differences takes place. There is even some evidence that characteristics identified in infants may be discerned when they are adolescents.

For Further Reading

A convenient summarization of the norms of development through 36 months is contained in Arnold Gesell and Catherine S. Amatruda, *Developmental Diagnosis: normal and abnormal child development* (New York: Hoeber, 1947). A fuller account by Gesell and Frances Ilg may be found in *Child Development: An Introduction to the Study of Human Growth* (New York: Harper, 1949). For most of the specific topics covered in this chapter, authoritative, encyclopedic statements may be found in the book edited by Leonard Carmichael, *Manual of Child Psychology: Second Edition* (New York: Wiley, 1954). The articles on physical growth by Helen Thompson, and on learning by N. L. Munn are especially recommended.

Piaget's work is given in a bewildering profusion of books and papers, some translated, some not. It is fortunate that we have a convenient and authoritative source readily available in John H. Flavell's, *The Developmental Psychology of Jean Piaget* (Princeton, New Jersey: Van Nostrand, 1963).

References

1. Aldrich, A. A., C. Sung, and C. A. Knop. The crying of newly born babies: II. The individual phase. *J. Pediatrics,* 1945, 27, 89–96.
2. Ames, Louise B. The constancy of psycho-motor tempo in individual infants. *J. Genet. Psychol.,* 1940, 57, 445–450.
3. Bakwin, H., and Ruth Bakwin. Growth of thirty-two external dimensions during the first year of life. *J. Pediatrics,* 1936, 8, 177–183.
4. Bayley, Nancy. Mental growth during the first three years: a developmental study of sixty-one children by repeated tests. *Genet. Psychol. Monogr.,* 1933, 14, No. 1.

5. Bayley, Nancy. The development of motor abilities during the first three years. *Monogr. Soc. Res. Child Develpm.*, 1935, No. 1.
6. Bayley, Nancy. On the growth of intelligence. *Amer. Psychologist*, 1955, 10, 805–818.
7. Bayley, Nancy. Normal growth and development. In P. H. Hoch, and J. Zubin (Eds.), *Psychopathology of childhood*. New York: Grune and Stratton, 1955, 1–14.
8. Bayley, Nancy. Value and limitations of infant testing. *Children*, 1958, 5, 129–133.
9. Bell, R. Q. Relations between behavior manifestations in the human neonate. *Child Develpm.*, 1960, 31, 463–477.
10. Berlyne, D. E. Recent developments in Piaget's work. *Brit. J. Educ. Psychol.*, 1957, 27, 1–12.
11. Berlyne, D. E. The influence of the albedo and complexity of stimuli on visual fixation in the human infant. *Brit. J. Psychol.*, 1958, 49, 315–318.
12. Bridges, Katherine, M. B. A genetic theory of the emotions. *J. Genet. Psychol.*, 1930, 37, 514–527.
13. Bridges, Katherine, M. B. *The social and emotional development of the preschool child*. London: Kegan, Paul, 1931.
14. Bridges, Katherine, M. B. Emotional development in early infancy. *Child Develpm.*, 1932, 3, 324–341.
15. Brodbeck, A. J., and O. C. Irwin. The speech behavior of infants without families. *Child Develpm.*, 1946, 17, 145–156.
16. Cattell, Psyche. *The measurement of intelligence of infants*. New York: Psychological Corporation, 1940.
17. Darley, F. L., and H. Winitz. Age of first word: review of research. *J. Speech Hear. Dis.*, 1961, 26, 272–290.
18. Davis, Clara M. Self-selection of diet by newly-weaned infants. *Amer. J. Dis. Child.*, 1928, 36, 651–679.
19. Davis, Clara M. Choice of formulas by three infants throughout the nursing periods. *Amer. J. Dis. Child.*, 1935, 50, 385–394.
20. Dennis, W. An experimental test of two theories of social smiling in infant. *J. Soc. Psychol.*, 1935, 6, 214–223.
21. Dennis, W., and Marsena G. Dennis. The effect of cradling practices upon the onset of walking in Hopi children. *J. Genet Psychol.*, 1940, 56, 77–86.
22. Dollard, J., and N. E. Miller. *Personality and psychotherapy*. New York: McGraw-Hill, 1950.
23. Escalona, Sibylle. The use of infant tests for predictive purposes. In W. E. Martin and Celia B. Stendler (Eds.), *Readings in child development*. New York: Harcourt, Brace, 1954, 95–103.
24. Escalona, Sibylle, and P. Bergman. Unusual similarities in very young children. *Psychoanal. Stud. Child*, 1949, 3, 333–352.
25. Flavell, J. H. *The developmental psychology of Jean Piaget*. Princeton: Van Nostrand, 1963.
26. Fowler, W. Cognitive learning in infancy and early childhood. *Psychol. Bull.*, 1962, 59, 116–152.
27. Frantz, R. L. The origin of form perception. *Scient. American*, 1961, 204, 66–72.
28. Frantz, R. L., J. M. Ordry, and M. S. Udelf. Maturation of pattern vision in

infants during the first six months. *J. Comp. Physiol. Psychol.*, 1962, 55, 907–917.

29. Fries, Margaret E., and P. J. Woolf. Some hypotheses on the role of the congenital activity type in personality development. *Psychoanal. Stud. Child*, 1953, 8, 48–62.

30. Gellermann, L. W. Form discrimination in chimpanzees and two-year-old children: 1. Form (triangularity) *per se*. *J. Genet. Psychol.*, 1933, 42, 3–27.

31. Gesell, A., and Catherine S. Amatruda. *Developmental diagnosis: normal and abnormal child development*. (2nd ed.). New York: Hoeber, 1947.

32. Gesell, A., and Frances L. Ilg. *Child development: an introduction to the study of human growth*. New York: Harper, 1949.

33. Gesell, A., and Helen Thompson. Learning and growth in identical infant twins. *Genet. Psychol. Monogr.*, 1929, 6, 1–124.

34. Gesell, A., and Helen Thompson. *Infant behavior*. New York: McGraw-Hill, 1934.

35. Goodenough, Florence L. Expressions of the emotions in a blind-deaf child. *J. Abnorm. Soc. Psychol.*, 1932, 27, 328–333.

36. Halverson, H. M. An experimental study of prehension in infants by means of systematic cinema records. *Genet. Psychol. Monogr.*, 1931, 10, 107–286.

37. Halverson, H. M. Infant sucking and tensional behavior. *J. Genet. Psychol.*, 1938, 53, 365–430.

38. Hofstaetter, P. R. The changing composition of "intelligence": a study technique. *J. Genet. Psychol.*, 1954, 85, 159–164.

39. Holmes, Frances B. An experimental study of the fears of young children. In A. T. Jersild and Frances B. Holmes (Eds.), Children's fears. *Child Develpm. Monogr.*, 1935, No. 20, 167–296.

40. Irwin, O. C. Research on speech sounds for the first six months of life. *Psychol. Bull.*, 1941, 38, 277–285.

41. Irwin, O. C. Infant speech: effect of systematic reading of stories. *J. Speech Hear. Res.*, 1960, 3, 187–190.

42. Jones, Mary C. The elimination of children's fears. *J. Exp. Psychol.*, 1924, 7, 382–390.

43. Jones, Mary C. A laboratory study of fear: the case of Peter. *Ped. Sem.*, 1924 31, 308–315.

44. Kinsey, A. C., W. B. Pomeroy, and C. E. Martin. *Sexual behavior in the human male*, Philadelphia: Saunders, 1948.

45. Leitch, Mary, and Sibylle Escalona. The reaction of infants to stress: a report of clinical observation. *Psychoanal. Stud. Child*, 1949, 3, 121–140.

46. Ling, B. C. Form discrimination as a learning cue in infants. *Comp. Psychol. Monogr.*, 1941, 17, No. 2.

47. Long, L. Conceptual relationships in children: the concept of roundness. *J. Genet. Psychol.*, 1940, 57, 289–315.

48. Lynip, A. W. The use of magnetic devices in the collection and analysis of the preverbal utterances of an infant. *Genet. Psychol. Monogr.*, 1951, 44, 221–262.

49. McCarthy, Dorothea. Language development in children. In L. Carmichael (Ed.), *Manual of Child Psychology*, (2nd ed.), New York: Wiley, 1954, 492–630.

50. McGraw, Myrtle B. Neural maturation as exemplified in achievement of bladder control. *J. Pediatrics*, 1940, 16, 580–589.

51. Marquis, Dorothy P. Learning in the neonate: the modification of behavior under three feeding schedules. *J. Exp. Psychol.*, 1941, 29, 263–282.

52. Marquis, Dorothy P. A study of frustration in newborn infants. *J. Exp. Psychol.*, 1943, 32, 123–138.
53. Miller, N. E., and J. Dollard. *Social learning and imitation.* New Haven: Yale University Press, 1941.
54. Munn, N. L. Learning in children. In L. Carmichael (Ed.), *Manual of Child Psychology* (2nd ed.). New York: Wiley, 1954, 374–458.
55. Myklebust, H. R. Language disorders in children. *Except. Child*, 1956, 22, 163–166.
56. Neilon, Patricia. Shirley's babies after fifteen years. *J. Genet. Psychol.*, 1948, 73, 175–186.
57. Norval, Mildred, R. L. J. Kennedy, and J. Berkson. Biometric studies of the growth of children of Rochester, Minnesota. *Hum. Biol.* 1951, 23, 273–301.
58. Piaget, J. *The language and thought of the child.* New York: Humanities Press, 1926.
59. Piaget, J. *Judgment and reasoning in the child.* New York: Harcourt, Brace, 1928.
60. Piaget, J. *The child's conception of the world.* New York: Humanities Press, 1929.
61. Piaget, J. *The child's conception of physical causality.* New York: Harcourt, Brace, 1930.
62. Piaget, J. Children's philosophies. In C. Murchison (Ed.), *A handbook of child psychology* (2nd ed. rev.). Worcester: Clark University Press, 1933, 534–547.
63. Piaget, J. *Factors determining human behavior.* Cambridge: Harvard University Press, 1937.
64. Piaget, J. *The origins of intelligence in children.* New York: International Universities Press, 1952.
65. Piaget, J. *The construction of reality in the child.* New York: Basic Books, 1954.
66. Piaget, J. *Logic and psychology,* New York: Basic Books, 1957.
67. Piaget, J. *The psychology of intelligence.* Paterson: Littlefield, Adams, 1960.
68. Rheingold, Harriet L., J. L. Gewirtz, and Helen W. Nelson. Social conditioning. *J. Comp. Physiol. Psychol.*, 1959, 57, 68–73.
69. Richards, T. W., and Virginia L. Nelson. Abilities of infants during the first eighteen months. *J. Genet. Psychol.*, 1939, 55, 299–318.
70. Sears, R. R., Eleanor E. Maccoby, and H. Levin. *Patterns of child rearing.* Evanston: Row, Peterson, 1957.
71. Sherman, M. The differentiation of emotional responses in infants. I. Judgments of emotional responses from motion-picture views and from actual observations. *J. Comp. Psychol.*, 1927, 7, 265–284.
72. Shirley, Mary M. *The first two years: a study of twenty-five babies,* Vol. 1. *Postural and locomotor development.* Minneapolis: University of Minnesota Press, 1931.
73. Shirley, Mary M. *The first two years: a study of twenty-five babies,* Vol. 3. *Personality manifestations.* Minneapolis: University of Minnesota Press, 1933.
74. Thompson, Helen. Physical growth. In L. Carmichael (Ed.), *Manual of child psychology,* (2nd ed.). New York: Wiley, 1954, 292–334.
75. Thompson, J. Development of facial expression of emotion in blind and seeing children. *Arch. Psychol., N. Y.*, 1941, 37, No. 264.
76. Walk, R. D., and Eleanor J. Gibson. A comparative and analytical study of visual depth perceptions. *Psychol. Monogr.*, 1961, 75, No. 15.

77. Watson, J. B. *Psychology from the standpoint of a behaviorist.* Philadelphia: Lippincott, 1919.
78. Watson, J. B., and Rosalie Raynor. Conditioned emotional reactions. *J. Exp. Psychol.,* 1920, 3, 1–14.
79. Winitz, H. Spectrographic investigation of infant vowels. *J. Genet. Psychol.,* 1960, 96, 171–181.

8

Parental Influences

INFANT RESPONSES to the primary drives of hunger, thirst, elimination, and sleep are socialized in accordance with the demands of society. Feeding schedules as well as time and place to sleep and to evacuate are established to meet the expectations of the adults who care for the infant. In another society different schedules and times would have been thrust upon him. Language development is also influenced by social stimulation. In each society the child learns to conform to what is expected of him or suffers social penalties if he does not. How, then, are the infant's behavior and experience modified, accelerated, and retarded by the persons who serve as the agents of his socialization?

Learning and socialization

Socialization is a particular setting for learning. The infant learns through the reinforcements he receives, especially from the mother. How one investigator summarized the situation follows:

> She can offer rewards, incentives, or punishments; she can facilitate or inhibit certain activities; and she can influence behavior by direct or indirect means. These three general ways of classifying her behavior overlap, and each is subject to further categorization. For example, if the mother wishes to stop a specific act, she may present a direct interference, she may provide the stimulus for an alternative response, she may punish the unwanted activity or reward the substituted behavior, she may arrange environmental conditions to obstruct the behavior, she may offer incentives to change the child's motivation, and so on.

199

The child learns to react in certain ways to these various forms of stimulation. The mother's behavior provides stimulus cues which are generalized from previous situations to the present and thus serve to call forth a similar response. In addition, the types of stimulation which are employed by the mother present the child with a model for his own behavior in controlling individuals. Through the mother's response to these stimulus aspects of his behavior he is also learning which techniques are most successful in goal-attainment.

The child, then, is developing patterns of behavior both as an individual response to the particular behavior which the mother evidences in her relationships with him and as a direct incorporation of certain aspects of her behavior (11, 29–30).[1]

Throughout the chapter examples of these learning principles will appear.

The mother as the agent of socialization

The most obvious thing about the behavior of any newborn infant is his complete helplessness. When a need arises, his only means of tension reduction is random motor discharge. Unable to move about, to keep warm, to feed himself, to avoid danger, the infant is entirely dependent on his mother or some other person who takes her place. Since he is unable to cope with his needs, she ministers to him. The infant is a member of a household or an institution which forms his universe. The infant's universe is mediated to him through the one who fulfills his needs—his mother or his nurse. Other individuals are to be found in his social environment, but they are as a shadowy background to the emerging foreground of the mother figure.

The average infant is in continuous contact with his mother. "Fed," "fondled," "talked to," "changed," and "carried about" express only a few of these forms of contact. This contact is a constant source of stimulation (46). The infant is encouraged to babble, to form words, to move about, and eventually, to sit up, to stand up, and to walk. He is carried about through a house, filled with many interesting objects and persons. In this atmosphere of contact between mother and child, the infant learns to reach out to his environment, to make his wants known, and to become a social creature.

It should be apparent by now that what a mother does in caring for an infant is more than simple carrying out of a series of acts. She is

---

[1] From Bishop (11). Copyright 1951 by the American Psychological Association and published by permission.

also communicating something of herself. Contact between infant and mother is, of course, partly verbal. Sometimes overlooked because of its nonverbal character is the important socializing factor of empathy (77). Sensitivity on the part of both mother and infant to one another's touch, bodily tensions, and (later) expressions are an important source of communication between them.

Escalona (30) distinguishes between communication, a purposive attempt to convey information, and contagion, the process by which a feeling state is transmitted from the mother to the infant. A tense and anxious adult may engender crying in an infant who, if shifted to a relaxed adult, may quiet down. Contagion is not entirely subject to voluntary control. A worried mother trying to convey assurance to her infant may find that he responds to her actual feeling state and not to what she wants him to feel.

A writer who has aroused considerable interest by her plea for the necessity of mothering is Margaret Ribble. In her volume, *The Rights of Infants* (93), she pleads that an infant needs psychological mothering because he has such inadequate and unstable physiological organization of primary bodily functions. Her book, whose sale approached the level of a best seller, has been one of the more popular to advance the plea that the infant needs psychological mothering because of the alleged delicate, precarious balance of his physiological functioning.

Her evidence on the infant's instability and inadequate organization in circulation, oxygen supply, digestive functioning, nervous system, and muscle tonus have been very effectively challenged by Pinneau (84). It would appear from his review that the evidence she advanced is contradicted by an even more impressive array of contrary evidence. Stone, in analyzing Pinneau's critique, indicates that the demolition of Ribble's evidence is "a kind of hydrogen bomb perfection of destructive criticism; not a paragraph is left standing for miles around" (111, 14).[2] It is necessary, then, to reject her evidence as inconclusive.

From this it might appear that discussion of her work is unnecessary. This is not the case. In view of her popularity, the inadequacies of her work as shown by Pinneau and others have been used by some antagonists to throw suspicion on the view that maternal interaction with the infant is of any psychological importance. Such a sweeping conclusion is similar to the well-known cliché about throwing out the baby with the bath water because the water is dirty. What Pinneau conclusively demonstrated is that Ribble's argument that psychological

[2] From Stone (111). Copyright 1954 by the Society for Research in Child Development, and published with permission.

mothering is necessary because of physiological instability is untenable. This is different from demonstrating that other reasons cannot be advanced to support Ribble's contention concerning the importance of interaction with the mother. As, in substance, Kubie (65) puts it, she was right for the wrong reasons.

Maternal Influences upon Socialization

That there is a causal relationship between particular kinds of maternal child-rearing behaviors and the infant's subsequent behavior has appeared to many research workers to be worthy of investigation. Accordingly, some of the research devoted to this relationship will be evaluated. To give some structure to the discussion, three aspects will be taken up in turn: (1) specific maternal practices such as weaning; (2) general maternal attitudes; and (3) patterns of maternal behavior.

Specific Maternal Practices Influencing Socialization

A wealth of studies has appeared concerning breast versus bottle feeding, short versus long breast feeding, gradual versus abrupt weaning, self-demand versus scheduled feeding, gradual versus abrupt toilet training, and the effect of these infantile experiences on subsequent development. In a careful review, Orlansky (82) demonstrated that many of these studies were inadequate in research design, in small number of subjects used, and in control of other variables that might affect the results. Moreover, even the most carefully conducted studies turn out to be contradictory in their findings. For example, several of these studies questioned the duration of breast feeding was related to later adequacy of personal adjustment. In one study children breast fed less than six months or more than ten months showed more behavior problems than did children who had been breast fed between six and ten months. But in another study the most "secure" college students were those either breast fed little, if at all, or breast fed for over a year; these results flatly contradicted the first study.

Subsequent to the Orlansky review, Sewell and Mussen (102) reported the infant training practices that had been used with about 160 five- and six-year-old children. They hypothesized that better adjustment and fewer oral symptoms would be found in (1) children who were breast fed as compared with those bottle fed; (2) children who were fed on a demand schedule as compared with those on a regular schedule; and (3) children who were weaned gradually as compared with those weaned abruptly. Data on infant training practices were obtained from interviews with the mothers. Indices of present adjustment were also obtained from these interviews, along with personality test scores and teachers' ratings of adjustment. In all, there were 26 adjustment or symptom items showing adjustment of these children. No direct relationship was found between any method of feeding gratification and later good or poor adjustment.

The evidence concerning specific practices appears to be contradictory and to lead to no reconcilable results. Perhaps a partial explanation is found in a study (103) that indicates little relationship between the mother's permissiveness in one aspect of socialization, such as feeding, and later aspects, such as toilet training. This finding suggests that we must look beyond specific practices for maternal influences that affect the personality adjustment of infants.

These contradictory results indicate why it is futile to search for practices that will give the one "right" way to raise children. There are many patterns of mother-child interaction. A particular mother, a particular child, a particular set of environmental and hereditary circumstances combine to produce a particular result. A search for simple correlations between characteristics of the mothers and the "consequences" in their children simply does not work.

It appears likely that the specific discipline is not ordinarily of critical significance in and for itself. More plausibly a specific practice may be regarded as part of a larger pattern in which it is imbedded. Practices and consequent personality development may be indirectly related in that, say, self-demand feeding and gradual weaning reflect a warm reaching-out for the infant on the mother's part. It may be that specific practices are but facets of a general attitude toward the infant. Consequently, attention will be given to the relation of maternal attitudes and personality development.

Maternal Attitudes Influencing Socialization

A specific practice of a mother such as breast nursing, self-demand feeding, and gradual weaning may or may not reflect a warmly accepting attitude on her part. A failure to use one or another of these techniques may come about because of reasons quite apart from accepting attitudes. Available data illustrate this point (80).

About 100 mothers in a maternity ward were interviewed immediately after delivery and classified into three groups on the basis of the attitudes they expressed toward breast feeding their infants. In those judged as having positive attitudes, 74 per cent were found later to breast feed their infants successfully. For the mothers originally classified as having doubtful and negative attitudes, respectively, 35 and 26 per cent breast fed successfully.

Let us suppose that these mothers were now studied in the fashion of the "practice" studies described earlier and that they had been divided into breast feeders and nonbreast feeders with no knowledge of their attitudes. In studying later personality adjustment, the breast fed group would have included not only 74 per cent of the positive attitude group but 35 and 26 per cent of the doubtful and negative attitude groups, respectively. Similarly, the nonbreast fed group would have included 26 per cent of those showing positive attitudes. If later study of the personality adjustment of individuals in the two groups had been made without this information, it would not have been known that each group contained individuals judged in terms of *attitudes* who belonged in one or the other group. This analysis does not demonstrate that attitudes are more important than practices. It does, however, illustrate that studies based on specific practices may not take sufficiently into account the attitudes held by the mothers.

To anticipate the research studies discussed in a moment, they suggest very strongly that general maternal attitudes most profoundly influence later personality development. If we ask how these broad general attitudes can be communicated to an infant, we must remember that attitudes are *constructs*. The infant still is stimulated by maternal behavior that manifests the attitude she holds, not the attitudes themselves. The evidence presented in the chapter on prenatal maternal attitudes would seem to bear this out.

The results of the study of Behrens (5) are relevant and important because she studied *both* specific practices and general attitudes in the same group of mothers. Her subjects were 25 Jewish, urban, lower middle-class families who were coming to a mental health clinic. Her small sample and other selective factors make suspect wide generalization of the results she obtained, but the results she found are clear-cut and apparently unequivocal. She investigated infant-rearing practices in feeding, weaning, and toilet training in their relation to adjustment of these children at the age of three. She found no correlation between the three infant-rearing practices and the children's adjustment. So far, this study bears out the previous studies using the same approach in that the findings were negative.

Behrens went another step. She investigated what she called the "total mother person," her term for general maternal attitudes and conduct. This was divided into three components based on what she considered to be the mother's underlying attitudes (character structure), the manner of meeting the maternal role demanded of her (maternal role), and observed conduct toward the child (maternal conduct). This last has reference to consistency, overprotection, and adaptation of her discipline to the child's needs rather than to specific practices.

The results in terms of correlation are reported in Table 7. She now obtained highly significant correlations between child adjustment and maternal attitudes with this same group of children that showed no correlation between child adjustment and specific maternal-rearing practices. She was still concerned with the behavior of the mother, but not specific practices. It would appear that positive and negative attitudes are more predictive of the nature of the child's later adjustment than the nature of the specific practices followed by the mother in the infant's socialization.

TABLE 7

COEFFICIENTS OF RANK CORRELATION BETWEEN TOTAL MOTHER PERSON AND
ITS COMPONENTS AND CHILD ADJUSTMENT *

	Child Adjustment
Total mother person	0.75
Character structure	0.80
Maternal role	0.69
Maternal conduct	0.93

* From Behrens (5). Copyright 1954 by the Society for Research in Child Development, and published with permission.

Maternal rejection and acceptance. One attitude dimension observable in interactions of mother and infant is that of acceptance and rejection. From the investigation of maternal attitudes by Zemlick and Watson (125), there is another phase to be reported. This has to do with how each of the mothers reacted *after* the birth of her child. A new investigator, who had no knowledge of the previously reported findings on prenatal anxiety, symptoms, and attitudes, studied the interaction of mother and the newborn child while they were still in the maternity hospital. She was interested in the mother's evaluation of the baby (approval, solicitude, and contentment, or their opposites), her cooperativeness in meeting the needs of the infant in feeding, and the like. The specific ratings of these factors were summarized in general ratings in a sequence extending from the most solicitous to the least solicitous mother. These general ratings were correlated with the measures of prenatal anxiety, symptom, and attitude (page 135).

Conceivably, the resulting correlation coefficients could have turned out in any one of three ways. There might have been found low, nonsignificant correlations, implying a lack of relationship between prenatal indices and the mother's behavior with her baby. Or positive correlations might have been found, implying that mothers who "accept" their coming children behave in a solicitous fashion toward their children after birth. Neither of these results was found. Instead, *negative* relations were found between indices of care of the child after birth and prenatal anxiety, symptoms, and attitudes of rejection. At first this might seem to imply that mothers who reject their children before birth treat them with greater devotion after birth! Fortunately, this is not the only conclusion open. The investigators summarized their interpretation as follows:

> Mothers who subjectively and objectively display the greatest degree of symptomatology express their rejection through psychosomatic avenues during pregnancy and later exhibit overindulgent, oversolicitous and compulsive behavior (maternal persistence) with respect to the child. In their extreme forms the criteria for the mother-child adjustment used in this study are indicative of maternal overprotection. A qualitative, clinical analysis of the personal data on the subjects shows that two women had been sterility cases, one had had a previous miscarriage, three were obviously ambivalent about the pregnancy, and one had verbally acknowledged she did not want pregnancy. Clinically these factors are to be found in mothers who reject and overprotect their children. In an overwhelming majority of instances these seven mothers achieved the highest, "most accepting," post-partum ranks. An alternative hypothesis, that instead of being "overprotecting" the mothers are showing protection within normal limits, is rejected because it requires the assumption that mothers without a stormy pregnancy are less protecting of their infants. Therefore, fairly convincing qualitative evidence is at hand to support the statement that symptom-oriented mothers who generally are rejecting frequently show their rejection through an overprotecting attitude toward the child (*125*, 582–583).[3]

The mothers, then, who *appeared* most solicitous were really oversolicitous and overprotecting. Maternal overprotection refers to excessive maternal care. Levy (*68*), a pioneer in studies of overprotection, describes the maternal characteristics that are indicative of this excessiveness as prolongation of infantile care, excessive contact, and prevention of independent behavior. Naturally, these newborn infants in the study under consideration were not old enough for the mothers to show these characteristics. Rather, their behavior appeared to be within normal limits because their children were so young. These results strongly suggest, assuming no change in the mothers, that as the child grows older, overprotective attitudes will emerge.

[3] From Zemlick and Watson (*125*). Copyright 1953 by the American Orthopsychiatric Association, and published with permission.

Acceptance within optimal limits, in contrast to overprotection, is something healthy and healthful. Porter (86), in constructing a *Parental Acceptance Scale,* paid particular attention to this point. He defined parental acceptance in terms of unconditional love, recognizing that the child has rights as a person, the right to express feelings, the right to uniqueness, and the right for the child to become an autonomous individual. Infantilization, excessive contact, and prevention of independent behavior or the overprotecting form of the accepting attitude are specifically repudiated. There is no reason to believe that most mothers do not tend to fall somewhere within these optimal limits. Nevertheless, the evidence of Zemlick and Watson does suggest that some mothers do not accept their children in this healthful way even at birth.

Sewell, Mussen, and Harris (103) found no general factor reflected in training practices. In their sample then there was no evidence of a pervasive, underlying attitude. Nevertheless, the first two factors emerging were identified as permissiveness in early feeding and permissiveness in toilet training. After a parent-child interaction factor, there was a nonpunitive treatment factor and then a factor of promotion of independence. Both of the latter two factors, along with the first two, can easily be subsumed under the concept of acceptance; this lends support to the contention that a maternal attitude of acceptance or rejection is of some importance in understanding infantile behavior.

Rejection may lead to what Spitz (109) has called a psychotoxic disorder—a disturbance in which the mother's personality serves as a disease provoking agent, a psychological toxin. In this case where there is massive all-embracing rejection, the infant may react by becoming stuporous; falling into deep sleep with shallow, fast breathing; extreme pallor; and diminished sensitivity. A case history follows:

> The mother was a 16 year old, unmarried, Catholic girl who had been seduced by the son of her employer. The child was undesired and severe guilt feelings were present. Delivery was uneventful, and the attempts to nurse were uneventful although milk could be produced only by manual pressure. During nursing the mother behaved as if the infant was a complete alien; she withdrew from the baby which she held in a rigid and tense way. After five days, the baby was observed in the coma previously described. Energetic methods including tube feeding were necessary to bring the baby out of the condition. Equally vigorous, very directive and authoritarian methods were used with the mother so that nursing thereafter went on relatively successfully.[4]

Relations have also been traced clinically between frustrations

[4] Adapted from Spitz (109). Copyright 1951 by the International Universities Press, and published with permission.

brought about by anxious overpermissiveness and "three month colic"; hostility (appearing to be merely anxiety) leading to rash; and an oscillation between pampering and hostility leading to hyper-mobility, particularly in the form of rocking.

Variations in maternal attitudes. There are variations in maternal attitudes in infancy, the nature of which have not yet been fully understood. The Yale Child Study Center has begun to study some of the variations in early parental attitudes. Only snatches from some findings (21) may be given in the form of characteristic vignettes.

1. A mother who held an initially close relationship with her infant was negatively influenced when he was ten months old by his striving toward lessened dependence although this is normal at this age. Now he was no longer so close, not so much "a part of her." As a consequence she became less accepting, although not to the extent of rejecting the infant. She was merely less "in tune" with him.

2. Originally somewhat negative, because the infant was active, hypertonic, easily startled, and sensitive to external stimuli, another mother lost confidence in herself. She regained her confidence and became more accepting of the infant when she could recognize the social responsiveness of the infant to her, and the infant's obvious need for her.

It will be noted that the characteristics of the child influence the attitudes of the mother. Variations in attitudes were found as the infant changed. Other results (36) give similar indications.

One infant's early-formed quiet pattern, shown by his rarely crying and by his tendency to sleep more than the usual infant, was welcomed by the parents since it did not disturb their work. Another baby who was very active in her motor achievement was approved by her compulsive intellectualizing mother who wanted signs of her child's advanced state and found them in the motor area. Turning to an instance where there was an increasingly poor mother-child relationship, a third very active infant drove her compulsively overconscientious mother to seek treatment because she could not keep up with the child in his "all-day" running in the park.

These illustrations of variations in attitudes show that our earlier account oversimplifies the relation of mother and infant.

Maternal Behavior Patterns Influencing Socialization

Another approach to maternal influences on infant socialization is through studying *patterns* of maternal behavior. For example, a mother's feeding behavior, cleaning, caressing, and moving the infant about may be studied to see if they form a pattern, instead of being examined one at a time as is done in specific practice studies.

Apropos of this point, Escalona indicates that it is appropriate to "think of all the different variables which constitute a given situation as mutually interrelated in such a way as to form a constellation (or pattern, or whole, or Gestalt) which will alter the manner in which each of the single variables is related to the phenomena in question" (29, 159).[5] Breast versus bottle feeding, for example, is never the single factor that will shape the course of the mother-child relationship. She goes on to add that what we need to know is the circumstances under which breast feeding may be (1) a medium for a wholesome relation; (2) a deterrent to such a relation; and (3) an irrelevant feature. The factors entering the situation which determine the responses of a given infant are many and complex. At times certain factors may reinforce one another, at other times they cancel one another, and always they are in a state of dynamic flux. Such studies of infant socialization in terms of patterns of behavior are in their barest beginnings.

Brody (18) has carried on a very detailed study of behavior patterns of mothers whose 32 infants were between four and 28 weeks of age. The setting was an observation room containing a crib and other baby things. Each mother was asked to come to the observation room with her baby for a four-hour period and, while there, carry on with him as she would at home, feeding him, changing his diapers, putting him to sleep, and so on. The mother took care of the infant in any way she saw fit, combining her activities with chatting, reading, needlework, or just sitting. Carefully planned-for notes were taken by three women observers. The observer who functioned as interviewer also served as "hostess," making the situation as natural as possible, but also questioning the mother concerning child-care practice according to a prearranged general plan.

The investigators selected six kinds of overt maternal activities to be observed during the sessions. These activities were (1) feeding— offering, withdrawing, forcing food; (2) cleaning—skin care, wiping saliva, hair combing; (3) moving (of whole body),—hugging, bouncing, standing-up; (4) touching—minor contacts, stroking, kissing, fingering; (5) offering objects (playthings, pacifiers, empty food utensils); and (6) speaking. Scales of maternal response were developed for each kind of activity. These scales were designed to measure the sensitivity with which the mother responded to the needs of the infant. Each scale had a mid-point of smooth, effective re-

[5] From Escalona (29). Copyright 1950 by the American Orthopsychiatric Association, and published with permission.

sponse to the infant. In one direction away from the mid-point it extended to reluctant or perfunctory answering of infant's needs and, in the other direction, to control or domination of the infant.

TABLE 8

GROUPS ISOLATED IN STUDY OF MOTHER-INFANT INTERACTION *

		N
Group A	Sensitive, consistent, attentive	7
B	Less sensitive, less consistent, somewhat overactive	4
C	Insufficiently sensitive, moderately inconsistent, adequately attentive	6
D	Hypersensitive, inconsistent, and hyperactive	11

* Adapted from Brody (18). Copyright 1956 by the International Universities Press, and published with permission.

Each unit of behavior in the protocols obtained from observation of mother-child interaction was evaluated and coded against the scales. The investigators grouped the results separately for each mother and for each of the six kinds of activity. For each mother and each kind of activity three measures were calculated: (1) the frequency—a measure of how often the activity appeared; (2) the mean—the average degree of sensitivity for an activity with a middle value showing of optimal sensitivity; and (3) the standard deviation—the measure of consistency of her behavior since it showed how much she varied from the mean.

The next step in analysis was to inspect the results for each of these mothers and to group together those for whom the means for the six kinds of activity fell at roughly the optimal, middle position. The group of mothers selected in this fashion were also found to have small standard deviations and thus to be consistent. They were found also to be moderate in the frequencies of their activities with the infants and thus to be attentive, or active. In short, the mothers of this group were sensitive, consistent, and attentive. This group, numbering seven mothers, the investigators called group A. By a similar procedure of case selection, each time starting with the measure of degree of sensitivity (the mean), three other groups were isolated, accounting for all but three of the mothers. Their frequencies and standard deviations were then examined and characterized. Table 8 presents a summarization of the groupings that emerged from the total group of mothers.

It would appear that these groupings give us a first approximation of meaningful types of maternal behavior. A summary of the types of maternal behavior is quoted:

> The mothers of group A were conspicuous for their ability to accom-
> modate to the needs of their infants. By virtue of the kind of physical

and emotional support they provided and the steadiness of their interest in and communicativeness toward their infants, they gave them freedom to move about, to vocalize, feed, rest or play with a minimum of interference. More regularly and with more ease than all the other mothers they recognized and tried to relieve passing discomforts in the infants. The mothers themselves were not without tension, but most of the time that tension appeared to heighten their intimacy with the infants.

The mothers of group B were conspicuous for their conscious willingness to accommodate to their infants. At first glance some of their behavior resembled that of the A mothers, but on the whole they were more tense, less communicative and less steadily attentive. At times they tried more actively to stimulate their infants and at other times they were mildly distant or insensitive to the infants' immediate needs. The quality of satisfaction with the infant and of enjoyment of their mothering tasks, outstanding in the A mothers, was much less evident, although B mothers were generally positive toward their infants.

The mothers in group C were conspicuous for their lack of spontaneity and their intentions to be efficient above all else. Physically and socially they were detached from their infants. Some reduced their attention to the carrying out of a minimum of essential details of infant care, and showed a low degree of interest in any activity with the infant of a nonphysical nature.

The mothers of group D were conspicuously active but also erratic in their attentiveness, efficiency and sensitivity. They quite sedulously governed their infants' actions by stimulating, restricting or instructing them, apparently hardly aware of the possible effects of their behavior on the infants' condition (18, 265–266).[6]

Brody objects to giving the groups specific descriptive names on several grounds, but particularly on the basis of the fear that the terms used, for example, permissive, would carry moral connotations. This writer, with apologies to Brody, would suggest that group A might be labeled as permissive, group B as less permissive, group C as restrictive, and group D as inconsistent.

During the same sessions that supplied these behavioral findings the mothers verbally expressed to the observers many opinions and attitudes about child care. Considerable consistency was found between the behavioral group in which a mother fell and the attitudes she expressed. The permissive mothers were confident in their role, planned their training practices in keeping with the infants' behavior, preferred to use verbal forms of discipline, and expressed tolerance of adjustment difficulties. The less permissive showed attitudes and planned practices somewhat less adequately than did those in the permissive group but, just as in patterns of behavior, were rather close in their attitudes to that group. The restrictive group, although confi-

[6] From Brody (18). Copyright 1956 by the International Universities Press, and published with permission.

dent, showed some mothers whose confidence was vulnerable, who were explicitly nonindulgent toward their infant in their attitudes, and a little more inclined to consider resorting to corporal punishment in the future. The inconsistent group was nonpermissive in spirit of conscious attitudes to the contrary, planned to institute weaning and toilet training at earlier ages than the other groups, and more inclined to use corporal punishment. Thus a regularity of attitudes corresponding to regularities of patterns of behavior was found. This adds credence to the belief that both attitudes and patterns of behavior are promising approaches to the study of infancy socialization practices and of the development of personality.

The effects of restriction and stimulation

Because restrictions of stimulation and increased stimulation both bear on the socialization of the infant, researchers have delved into these behaviors in order to understand their effects. The matters to which they have paid attention include material deprivation, specific forms of adult stimulation, discontinuity in the presence of the mother figure, sensory deprivation and stimulation, and imprinting. Let us observe what they have discovered about each of these.

Maternal Deprivation

One dramatic way in which the crucial significance of mothering has been demonstrated arises from the study of infants deprived of maternal care. Maternal deprivation is quite different in atmosphere and in effect from that experienced by the rejected child. In rejection, hostility is directed toward the child by one or both parents. He is made to feel unwanted. There is a severity rather than a lack of stimulation. A rejected child meets adults, and, although they may block him, he is stimulated to meet and solve problems even though his solutions are distorted.

A number of different situations are covered by the term maternal deprivation. It may be that a child is frustrated by being deprived even when living at home with his mother, or he may be looked after by a relative stranger in a foster home, or he may be almost completely deprived, as in many institutions. The differences in degree of maternal deprivation are signalized by distinguishing between partial and total deprivation.

Partial deprivation refers to those children who, after establishing a satisfactory emotional relationship with the mother for the first six months of life, are thereafter frustrated by being separated from her. This is supposed to lead to a condition which Spitz called *anaclitic depression*. A case description derived from Spitz (108) follows:

There is first what is described as a "search" for mother. Such infants cannot be quieted, some cry bitterly, others less vehemently but they cannot be soothed. Nevertheless, at this stage they cling to the available adult.

The picture changes on failure of the mother to return. He becomes quiescent, does not look up when adults enter the room, does not play and does not grasp at objects. Along with passivity and dejection he develops eating difficulties, loses weight and shows sleep disturbances. In general, the level of development does not proceed normally or even drops.

This occurs often enough, according to Spitz, to be considered a disorder of infancy attributable to frustration brought about by partial deprivation.

In total deprivation, the infant does not have, early or late, anything resembling emotional ties with a mother figure. The importance of these maternal contacts for normal development is dramatically illustrated by infants almost completely deprived of these experiences.

In infancy, a condition called *marasmus* is said to develop from the frustrations of total maternal deprivation. The following case adapted from one described by Ribble (93) illustrates not only the conditions but also something of the general situational background from which it is said to come.

The child was full-term and weighed six pounds, three ounces at birth. The two weeks' stay in the hospital was uneventful. On returning home the mother discovered her husband had deserted her. Thereafter her milk did not agree with the baby. Since the infant refused the breast and began to vomit he was hospitalized. The mother did not come to see him at this time or later, thus deserting him.

He was in a crowded ward, and received little attention or handling. He became a finger sucker and a ruminator (regurgitating food). At two months of age, he weighed about five pounds and had an appearance of a seventh month fetus with arms and legs wasted, large head and large protruding abdomen.

He was transferred to a small children's hospital, where a thorough physical examination revealed nothing of an organic nature. Concentrated nursing care was given him, with his being held in the nurse's lap for a feeding of one half hour duration, his position changed frequently and his being carried about whenever possible. After some slow improvement, a volunteer "mother" began to come to the hospital twice daily. Her visits were gradually lengthened until she was spending an hour with him on each visit. She had been told the infant needed loving care and physical contact which she gave him.

The results were such that by five months of age he weighed nine pounds without rumination. He was now alert and vigorous, although some remnants of his difficulties remained, such as retarded motor coordination and finger sucking.

In the first flush of enthusiasm for this field of research, many studies made their appearance. The diversity of studies both here and abroad, which supported the general conclusion of a pernicious effect from maternal deprivation (15, 44, 45, 46, 47, 48, 106, 107, 108, 109) was impressive. Impetus to this view had been furnished by observation of infants in adverse conditions, particularly those in Great Britain who were evacuated to the country during the Second World War and those living in institutions. In general, it had been found (45) that infants living in their own homes suffer from considerably fewer personality difficulties than those living in the impersonal environment of an institution. Almost needless to add is the fact that the extent and quality of the damage vary with the age of the child, the specific kind of deprivation, its severity, the length of time it continues, and other relevant factors. When these infants are older, although still within the range of childhood, they seem to be characterized by superficial relationship with other persons, lack of emotional responses in situations where it would be normal to display them, lack of concern about most matters, and pointless deceit and evasion (15). After examining the literature on maternal deprivation, under the aegis of the World Health Organization, John Bowlby (15) wrote an eloquent defense of the thesis that an essential of mental health was the necessity for the infant to experience warm continuous relationship with a mother or mother surrogate.

Recently there have been sobering second thoughts about these findings. When critically examined, the studies reveal a host of methodological weaknesses which cast doubt on their conclusions.

The criticisms, presented in devastating reviews (81, 85, 124), preclude the use of these and many other studies as evidence. Inadequacies of design, uncontrolled factors, lack of precise measurement, failure to report crucial data, and many other errors render the conclusions suspect. The criticisms include the clinical pictures of anaclitic depression and marasmus derived by Spitz. Other clinical patterns or none at all may appear as a consequence of institutionalization (81).

Despite this negative criticism something included under the rubric of maternal deprivation seems to have been confirmed. The varieties of study, each with specific inadequacies but of a kind varying from study to study, still led the investigators to reach the same general conclusion. It behooves us to take a more cautious, specific, and rigorous approach to this problem by examining more precisely what went wrong in the earlier studies, and then to turn to some studies that seem to help clarify the problem.

So-called maternal deprivation is a jumble of conflicting and confusing ideas which mean many and different things from one study to the next. Often the situational factors have been studied, not the component psychological factors. It is now recognized that maternal deprivation is not a single homogeneous variable. The events presumably illustrating such deprivation must be more precisely defined for their effects to be predicted. The sheer breadth of characteristics shown by deprived children also suggests not some isolated effect on some specific aspect of personality, but a vast complex that may well have a complicated etiology.

The oft repeated finding of a significant relationship between the development of the infant and the nature of his early mothering experiences cannot be denied. Gross neglect or prolonged institutionalization seemingly *does* have pernicious effect. But even here the causative features have not been precisely isolated. We can conclude only that under circumstances as yet not exactly specified, deleterious effects may result from institutional living.

The Effect of Specific Forms of Adult Stimulation

A beginning has been made in quantifying the differences in "caretaking" that institutionally reared and home reared babies receive. Rheingold (92) has supplied a quantified answer through methods described in the first chapter as illustrating systematic observational techniques. Her method measured the actual operations in caring for an infant. She found home infants received four-and-a-half times more care than institution babies. It should be noted that these differences were obtained in an institution not nearly as barren as many of those used in earlier studies.

One study frequently cited as evidence of no ill-effect from early "deprivation" is referred to more neutrally as a study of "minimum social stimulation" (23). This is the study of twins, by Dr. and Mrs. W. Dennis (24). They reared the two babies from one month through six months under conditions of social isolation. Human contacts were kept at a minimum, with the intent of not fondling, playing, or talking to them during their first six months of life. Thereafter, conditions of social isolation were eased for the remainder of the first year.

These babies showed a record of early development very much like that of infants reared in an environment with the usual social contacts and experiences of fondling, play, and talking. They even responded by smiling when an observer attempted to preserve a pronounced stolidity. These infants emerged from their first year as healthy, alert, and happy.

Fortunately, the "lack" of stimulation the twins received is capable of rather precise statement. Stone (111) studied this issue and concluded that the conditions under which the twins were raised represented minimum adequate social stimulation and was at a much higher level than that provided in many institutions. There is some clinically observed evidence suggesting that it is the second six months that is crucial with respect to the damage produced by isolation. The most marked isolation of these infants was during the first six months. Moreover, Dr. and Mrs. Dennis did see a lot of the infants, both from sheer decent human impulses and from the fact that they were interested in them too much as "subjects" to stay away. On the average one or both were in their room for a total of two hours a day. The study, it seems, provides information not about deprivation, but about the lower limits of adequate social stimulation.

Dennis, himself, concluded that (1) practically all the common responses of the first year of life may be developed autogenously, i.e., from self-initiated practice; (2) social responses, as such, prior to the second year are few and unimportant; and (3) if his physical well being is cared for, the infant's behavioral development will proceed along normal lines without intercession from adults.

A well-executed study designed to see the effect of increased "mothering" was carried on by Rheingold (90). Her infant subjects were drawn from an institution where it was evident that considerable effort in giving this care was expended. Volunteers and hospital personnel were encouraged by the Sister in charge of the floor to talk to the babies and to hold them. Her research situation, then, was unlike more impersonal institutional situations, and did not, by any means, represent the extremes of emotional deprivation that may be found. She was using a situation somewhat closer to that normally prevailing in an infant's home. Hence, if she were to find differences in the infants because of the increased "mothering" she introduced, she would be submitting her hypothesis to a more difficult test than if she had used a more impersonal institution for her study.

Sixteen infants between five and seven months of age were her subjects. She cared for the experimental group four at a time for nearly eight hours per day, five days a week for eight weeks. Adapting herself to the individual needs of each infant, during these hours she alone bathed, diapered, held, talked to, and soothed these infants. She repeated the procedure for the second group of four. Two control groups, each time numbering four, were cared for in the usual hospital routine.

Observation by an independent observer showed that Rheingold gave the experimental group much more in the way of care than the control subjects received. For example, for the first experimental group care-taking acts were recorded for 23 per cent of the observations, while in a comparable period of time with the control infants caretaking acts involved only seven per cent of the observations with these acts per-formed by seven different persons.

This established a situation in which one "mother" gave more in-tensive care than did many "mothers." The effect of this differential situation on social responsiveness of the infants was assessed. Among other results the experimental infants to a greater degree than the control subjects (1) were more socially responsive to her; (2) were more responsive to another person (the examiner); and (3) made slightly higher scores on postural tests, cube manipulation, and on the Cattell Infant Intelligence Scale. That "mothering" has a considerable effect upon the infant's social development has been neatly demon-strated by Rheingold.

However, these infants were followed up at 19 months of age when they were in adoptive homes (91). No lasting impact from the special experience given the experimental babies could be established. It is possible that these infants, experimental and control alike, were never as severely deprived as were the children used in those studies that showed effects of deprivation. That this is a plausible interpretation is strengthened by the fact that, unlike many of the other institutional groups studied, there was no significant intellectual loss from the beginning to the end of their institutional stay.

Significant gains by retarded children, when given the intellectual stimulation of an experimental nursery school, are described by Skeels (105). This investigation by Skeels and his colleagues demonstrates how much devoted, interested adults can do to give support to chil-dren so they can be free to explore, be curious, and reach out for the environment. At the start of the study these children, although pre-viously left to shift for themselves, were less able to care for them-selves than children raised in a family. They had to be shown how to use the equipment of the playground; they had short attention spans and were destructive of property. About six months of intensive contact with adults was necessary before these children were able to profit from the nursery school; at this point they began to hold their own or gained in test intelligence quotient. In contrast, the control group with whom they were matched deteriorated.

Discontinuity of the Presence of the Mother Figure

Clinical evidence suggests not only that warmth of relationship between mother and infant is necessary for healthful adjustment but also that it is necessary for it to be carried on as a continuous relationship (15). It is contended that inconsistency or changes from one mother figure to another can have a pernicious effect, quite apart from warmth. The collective Israeli settlements, or *Kibbutzim* are a natural laboratory for investigation of this problem. Here the prevailing social structure calls for care not only from the working mother but also from the caretaker or *metapalet*, who has charge of the infant while the mother works (88).

Comparison with control children from ordinary Israeli villages showed that although there was relative intellectual retardation of the Kibbutz-reared infants, it was not observed among children nine to 11 years of age who had been originally reared in *Kibbutzim*. Instead, there was clear superiority both in intelligence and in social and emotional maturity. The environment of a *Kibbutz* is both warm and stimulating. Despite the discontinuity of her presence, the child is not deprived of his mother who sees him at regular intervals. He does not experience anything resembling the deprivation of the infant in an institution with a large caretaker-infant ratio.

Another form of noncontinuous mothering is created by college courses in home management wherein the class members in rotation share in the care of infants for a few days at a time. Taking advantage of this setting, one study (38) involved three groups of infants 24 months of age: (a) home-management course infants for their first four months who were then adopted; (b) foster home children on a boarding arrangement for the same length of time prior to being adopted; and (c) a control group living with their parents the entire time. In addition to an array of psychological tests given at frequent intervals, each infant was placed in two controlled stress situations; the first consisted of trying to place wooden pegs into circular openings that were actually too small to contain them ("peg-frustration") and the second, occurring immediately thereafter, left him alone in the testing room into which a stranger came a few moments later ("stranger-relationship"). The protocols of their behavior in these situations were supplied for ratings of frustration and stress to judges who did not know into which of the three groups a given infant fell. There was no clear evidence of effects from either stress situations or from the tests which could be associated with early residence in the home management course group, despite the wide differences from infant to infant in all of the groups.

In another study a group of children aged eight to 17 who had lived in a college home-management house during infancy and had subsequently been adopted were located (37). They were paired with children from the same communities and school classes and matched individually on sex, age, and intelligence. On a variety of tests for school achievement, personal adjustment, anxiety level, and responses to frustration, no significant differences between the groups were obtained. Investigators concluded that on none of these characteristics could differences be attributed to discontinuity of mothering in infancy.

Another pattern of discontinuity of mother-infant interaction (20) contrasts families in which mothering is provided by one person, the mother (monomatric), with that by more than one person, such as older sisters, grandmothers, hired caretakers in their own or other homes (polymatric). The investigators collected information by both interview and observation and found only slight differences between the two groups of infants. These differences were consistent with the interpretation that those infants raised by one adult found it easier to relate to other people and were more comfortable in strange surroundings. Developmental data, such as obtained from the Cattell Infant Intelligence Scale, yielded no significant differences. There was no suggestion that infants raised by more than one mother figure were handicapped by this particular experience.

From these various studies it would appear that multiple discontinuous adult care *per se* is not damaging to the infant although personality differences have been found between monomatric and polymatric infants.

Sensory Deprivation and Stimulation

It is probable that in many studies sensory deprivation has entered into so-called maternal deprivation. Consider the situation prevailing in some of the institutions studied by Spitz. The sides of the infants' cribs were covered by blankets and no toys were available so that the only visual experiences came from staring at the blank ceiling; certainly these were conditions making for visual deprivation. In present perspective, infrequent human contact becomes infrequent opportunity for tactile or kinesthetic stimulation. Renaming a phase of the problem "sensory deprivation" permits more precise definition of a relevant variable.

That sensory deprivation in infancy results in deficient adult "in-

tellectual" behavior has been found in studies with dogs (114). Hebb
(57) argues that the need to seek sensory stimulation is present in the
human being and that for the human infant in the first few months of
life learning by trial and error cannot proceed unless there is stimulation external to the infant himself. At this age if there is no external
stimulation, there is relatively little learning. Hebb's contention corresponds with the known relatively undifferentiated anatomical structure
of the brain at this age.

Harlow's rigorous experimental work (54) with monkeys lends support to the belief that tactile contact is sought by infants. His ingenious investigation concerned the surrogate mothering provided to
infant monkeys. The infant rhesus monkey is particularly suitable for
study because it is more mature at birth and develops its motor skills
much more rapidly than does the human infant (55). It can carry out
complicated motor behaviors at an age at which human infants can do
no more than twist and squirm. Despite this, there are close similarities of behavior patterns in monkey and human babies, not only of
affection but also of fear, anger, and even intellectual growth.

Young monkeys separated from their mothers were "mothered" by
the two kinds of surrogate mothers illustrated in Figure 9. One figure
was made of a block of wood covered with rubber and cloaked in
terry cloth. The second figure, made of wire mesh, differed only in

Figure 9. Cloth and wire mother surrogates. (From
Harlow (54). Copyright 1958 by the American Psychological Association, and published with permission.)

being unable to supply "contact comfort," but in one series of trials it supplied the milk for the infant from a bottle's nipple protruding from the figure's front. Light bulbs supplied warmth to both figures. When allowed free access to either mother, the "lactating," wire mesh mother was sought less and less, whereas the terry-cloth mother, who provided no milk, was sought more and more. When frightened or placed in a strange situation, the monkey rushed to the cloth mother, clung to her, and caressed her. When the terry-cloth mother was present, the infant monkey would venture out to explore a fear arousing stimulus; when the wire-mesh mother was present he tended to explore neither the surrounding space nor the strange object. It was found that this seeking of the cloth mother, "affectional contact," was retained for long periods of time.

Harlow concluded that the stimulation obtained from the terry-cloth mother was innately satisfying and led to an emotional attachment to it. Since the wire-mesh mother was entirely adequate to supply nourishment and physical support, contact comfort was the only essential way in which the two differed. Tactile sensory contact, as such, has been demonstrated to be significant in the behavior of infant monkeys, and it is plausible to suppose in human infants as well.

Interpretation

A clarification of many of the confused issues concerning the effects of restriction and stimulation on infantile behavior is provided by Gewirtz (42, 43) in his analysis couched in instrumental learning terms (see page 106). In keeping with a variety of our earlier incidental comments and with our later analysis of exploratory, external behavior tendencies, Gewirtz argues that the infant actively seeks stimulation. In privation the environment fails to provide the functional stimuli necessary for what is usually learned during the infancy period. It is not only a question of whether stimuli are present, it is more whether they are functional or not; that is, does the particular state of development of the infant allow him to respond to these stimuli when they occur?

Gewirtz conceives deprivation, in contradistinction to privation, to be a state of frustration arising when stimuli, once present, are no longer available to the infant. To illustrate this distinction, infants fed by cup from birth may show privation in sucking responses; other infants, first fed by sucking from the breast or bottle, and then put on cup feeding, are exposed to deprivation. Using these distinctions Gewirtz proceeded to formulate a variety of kinds of privation and deprivation:

Under *total privation*, the environment provides few stimuli that might evoke or reinforce behavior. Hence, neither learning nor emotional response habituation would occur, and the infant would develop as unresponsive to stimuli (i.e., passive and asocial), except to those eliciting emotional-startle behaviors. Under *functional privation*, there may be abundant stimuli, but, because they are not discriminable or in proper timing or sequence relationships, they rarely function effectively. Some emotional behaviors may habituate, but little learning would occur. Hence, the child develops as unresponsive to stimuli generally, despite an abundance of access to them. Under the *functional privation of specifically social cue stimuli*, abundant stimuli for effective learning contingencies are provided, but without discriminable social cues. Like the normal child, he can become habituated for most emotional responses and generally responsive to stimuli, but not as such to social conditioned reinforcers and cues available from people (i.e., he would appear 'autistic'). For the *normal* child, there would be available from the beginning evoking, cue, and reinforcing stimuli for behavior, functional for effective learning. These stimuli need not be available in great abundance. In this case, the child's emotional behaviors habituate and he becomes responsive to his environment and oriented toward attaining conditioned social reinforcers. For deprivation, the general case of a major shift in reinforcing-maintaining envirnoment (e.g., from a home to an institutional environment) was illustrated; after which the sub-case of an extreme environmental shift which *separation* from an attached (object) person constitutes was considered.[7]

Whether it be in terms of Gewirtz's formulation or not, there is no question that one of the tasks of future research is to formulate in precise terms the stimulus and response factors involved in privation and deprivation. We shall then be in a position to evaluate more clearly, accurately, and concisely this very active research issue.

Imprinting

In the cross discipline field of ethology, concerned with comparative study of animal behavior, the phenomenon of imprinting has excited considerable research effort that promises to be relevant to the problem of human infantile stimulation and lasting attachments. For some time it has been known that various species of animals, particularly birds, who have their first social contacts with humans rather than with members of their own species, tend as adults to prefer social contacts with humans over those with their own kind. Lorenz (70), a European naturalist, intensively studied this phenomenon in greylag geese. He divided a clutch of eggs laid by a goose into two groups; leaving one group with the mother, but hatching the second group from an in-

[7] From Gewirtz (43). Copyright 1961 by John Wiley and Sons, and published with permission.

cubator. The goslings hatched by the mother immediately followed her; the incubator raised goslings saw Lorenz only, and followed him. When both groups were intermingled, with the mother and Lorenz present, they immediately headed for their respective "parents." He found this preference for humans to be invariable, provided only that they be the first postnatal social contact.

Lorenz and others extended the work to other species, such as guinea pigs, deer, buffalo, and sheep. ("Following like sheep" is now seen as an instance of imprinting.) It has been established that imprinting is a positive approach on the part of newly born animal infants either seeking proximity and or following the first animate object seen. A great variety of information on a variety of species, some of it anecdotal in nature, has made its appearance. Lorenz (71) tells of a human imprinted male bittern in a zoo who would chase his mate from the nest when the zoo director appeared and show by his actions that he expected the director to sit on the nest with him to incubate the eggs!

After this naturalistic phase, more precise work followed. Although imprinting on human adults has its well-known "human interest" value, it is, in itself, of no great scientific concern; for a variety of reasons, principally ease of control of variables, other species and even inanimate objects have been used for its study.

The carefully controlled work of Hess (58, 59) is outstanding. With suitable apparatus controls, a duckling is placed on a circular runway behind a movable model of a male duck wired so as to emit a sound, an arbitrarily chosen human rendition of "gock, gock, gock" occurring all the while the duckling is in the apparatus.

The procedure consists of two parts. First there is imprinting itself, usually taking less than an hour, during which time the newly born duckling is exposed to the moving and sounding male duck model which it tends to follow. At a later time a test series is given during which the duckling is released from a box midway between two duck models placed four feet apart. In one test the stationary male model used for imprinting was paired while emitting his "gock" call with a stationary model bearing female markings and emitting the real mallard female call to her young. Other paired test conditions included both models stationary; a silent, stationary male and a stationary, calling female; and a stationary, silent male and a moving, calling female. If the duckling made positive response to the male model under all conditions, imprinting was considered complete (100 per cent) and correspondingly less if the duckling failed under one or more conditions.

Imprinting in ducklings is most effective about 13 to 16 hours after hatching. There seems to be a critical period for its occurrence, even though its span seems to be widening as further studies are made (121). In other words, if imprinting does not take place within a circumscribed period, differing from species to species and animal to animal, it fails to appear. In the duckling, decrement in imprinting after 16 hours has been attributed by Hess (59) to fear of new objects, a response seen at this age for the first time. Onset of fear seems to signal the end of imprinting, suggesting that in the human species maximum imprinting should occur before five-and-a-half months, since that is the age of onset of fear. He does caution that imprinting in the human infant is certainly more complicated than this suggestion might seem to imply.

Gray (52) interprets "human imprinting" as a disposition directed toward attachment to the parent, shown by smiling. Functional equivalence of smiling in human beings and following in lower animals is postulated and, therefore something resembling imprinting is considered to have taken place. Gewirtz (43), on the other hand, interprets imprinting as an instance of especially rapid, efficient, instrumental learning. Smiling then becomes one, but only one, among the responses that make for attachment. Any responses (reaching, talking, even crying) which enable contact with another individual would be instances of imprinting. All cause the mother figure's behavior to be continued and maintained.

The rapidity with which imprinting takes place and its relative insusceptibility to extinction characterizes the process. Massed trials seem to be more effective than spaced trials, and primacy more effective than recency. It is different from conditioning in these respects where the reverse of these characteristics hold (58). There is no evidence for the immediate formation of attachment a certain number of hours after birth. Nevertheless, imprinting in the future may be shown to play a part, even an important part, in the process of human socialization.

Summary

The infant has now been examined in the setting of a matrix of other persons.

Because the mother serves as the principal agent of socialization, she is the most important of these other persons. The evidence shows that there are varying degrees of causal relationship between the child-rearing procedures of the mother and the behavior of her children. Classification into specific practices, attitudes, and patterns of maternal behavior allows us to see more clearly the degrees of relationship between child rearing and children's behavior. Specific practices in maternal behavior have not been found to show invariant relationships with consequent personality development. Maternal attitudes were found to be much more closely related to behavior in the children. The use of attitudes as a conceptual framework supplied us with a means for understanding of the mother's part in the socialization of the infant. Basically, this was because behavior expressed in terms of attitudes allows us to embrace within one construct many specific behaviors. This same advantage accrues to patterns of maternal behavior. Moreover, maternal attitudes and maternal patterns of behavior were found to be interrelated.

It would appear that maternal attitudes of acceptance or rejection and the maternal pattern of behavior in terms of the amount and the degree and the consistency of sensitivity mothers exhibit are significant and important approaches in the understanding of the effects of infant socialization and personality development.

The confused and confusing problems of maternal deprivation were explored though formulating the problem as the study of the effects of environmental restriction and stimulation through an attempt to be as precise as possible as to the nature of these effects. Operationally speaking, maternal deprivation was found to lack predictive power. When the areas of adult stimulation, continuity or discontinuity of the maternal figure, and sensory deprivation and stimulation are isolated from each other for discussion, their effects became clearer and more precise. In varying degrees some significance for the development of the infant can be attached to them. Much work remains to be done. This is also the case with imprinting.

For Further Reading

For an account of the literature on maternal deprivation, the review by John Bowlby under the auspices of the World Health Organization makes vivid reading, although we must be careful to keep in mind the somewhat dampening available negative evidence. The review by Pinneau (84) although limited to the specific issue of Ribble's contentions, is a masterpiece of critical analysis.

References

Follow Chapter 10.

9

Behavior Tendencies, Self, and Peer Relationships

HAVING SEEN the infant's social behavior in the perspective of parental influences, we now examine it as it is expressed in certain behavior tendencies, self and social awareness, and relationship to peers.

Behavior tendencies

For infancy there is less definitive, experimental evidence on behavior tendencies than for older children. With certain distinguished exceptions, observational and anecdotal material and plausible but unverified appeals to common experience are sources of such evidence.

Dependence and Independence Tendencies

The research of Harlow (54, 55) on infant monkeys serves as an excellent introduction to the problem of dependence tendencies. It will be remembered that when the cloth mother was not present, and infant monkeys were confronted by strange surroundings or objects, they showed pronounced fear. When "she" was present, they fled to her protection and comfort, getting over their fears so quickly that they soon could leave her and explore the feared object.

The human infant during the second year of life also becomes fearful and anxious when the mother leaves him temporarily as found in a study by Arsenian, described in more detail on page 375. Infants and young children placed in a strange room without their mothers showed

226

anxiety; those whose mothers were present played adaptively. The mother's presence produced security; her absence evoked anxiety, thus indicating the infant's dependency upon her. The infant learns to be dependent on the mother and expresses this dependence by showing anxiety when she is not present.

One aspect of dependence is a tendency to rely on the help of others in striving to reach one's goals. Or to put it another way, dependence is the tendency to seek to obtain support from other people. Dependent behavior has its beginning in infancy: each infant must be dependent because of his helplessness. He may be, as the psychoanalysts say, in the period of infantile omnipotence, but he is learning to be dependent, not all-powerful. He is not born with a need for dependency: helplessness thrusts dependence on him.

The mother is the agent for meeting his needs despite his helplessness. His mother satisfies his needs and, in terms of learning theory, becomes the agent of drive reduction. She is the configuration or pattern of stimuli that is consistently associated with the reduction of his needs—she feeds him when he is hungry, changes him when he is wet, and warms him when he is cold. He learns to be dependent on her as the instrument for meeting his needs. This aspect of dependence occurs when the infant learns to seek help from others. He is learning, to use a term of Heathers (56), *instrumental* dependence.

There is another aspect of dependence—*emotional* dependence. This may be illustrated by considering what happens after instrumental dependent tendencies have begun to be learned. After the first few days or weeks it is observed that an infant will cease crying when picked up *before* he is relieved of his hunger or other discomfort. His mother's mere presence has acquired reward value for him. Her comforting presence has become a secondary drive in itself. Receiving from others comfort, love, notice, and praise becomes a secondary drive on his part. Instrumental dependence leads to emotional dependence.

It is in this perspective that the need for mothering is interpreted. The rocking, stroking, cuddling, and being fussed over in countless ways are what is meant by mothering. Instead of the need for mothering being innate as Ribble contended, this need is interpreted here as a secondary drive based on learning emotional dependence in the fashion just described.

The infant learns not only to discriminate among persons, but he also shows differential reactions to them. One facet of his differential behavior toward persons can be referred to as affectionate behavior. (The other facet, hostile behavior, will be described in connection with aggressive tendencies.) He learns to find pleasurable responses in his relations with others, to have affection for various people, and to wish to be near them. What are the antecedents of this affectionate behavior? It may have a sexual component, and probably has a tactile component as we have seen from the study of Harlow, but the greatest stress can be placed on emotional dependence. The mother's presence has acquired reward value. The infant reacts with affection because of emotional dependent tendencies.

One investigator (3) has studied the development of affectionate behavior avowedly and directly. She observed 900 infants who were between four weeks and two years of age. These observations were made incidental to the giving of intelligence tests and, consequently, she reports in an anecdotal, qualitative fashion. Although her results are not gathered in as carefully controlled and specified conditions as one would like, they are reported because of their original nature.

The infant's affectionate behavior is first shown at about four months by outgoing strivings and approach—his smiling gaze fixed on the person's face. He waves his arms and tries to rise from the crib. Without coordination or too much success, he strives to get closer to the attractive person. At about six months, he reaches out to pat the person. This is roughly the same age as when he begins to discriminate between persons. This is also the age when he responds to affectionate cuddling. As memory develops, so, too, does anticipation. Toward the end of the first year he shows anticipation of the mother coming for feeding, and laughs, squirms, and wiggles with delight on her approach. During the second year affection extends by the process of generalization to objects—his toys, clothes, chair, favorite blankets, and the like. These then are manifestations of affection in infancy.

Almost as fast as an infant learns to seek help, he learns to get along without it (99). Independence becomes an end in itself.

Independence like dependence is the result of socialization. Dependent habits over and over again must be interfered with in this new phase of socialization. As Dollard, Doob et al. put it:

> Under normal circumstances each child may also be said to decrease steadily its dependence on its parents. It must learn to walk where it has formerly been carried; and being carried is, of course, a *response* in this situation. It learns not to be picked up when it has experienced some small disaster. It must give up much of the cuddling, holding, and petting which is the prerogative of the smallest darling. Childish approximations of table manners and etiquette must be altered in favor of the customs preferred by adults. The child must learn to wait for its food, to keep its face clean, to submit to having its hair combed, to eat in the regular stages designated by our table techniques. At some time or another all

of these lengthened sequences involve frustrations and elicit protest from the child (26, 64–65).[1]

In his second year, the infant is now able to move about. In doing so, he shows the overwhelming importance of independence. He is enthusiastically everywhere and as much as possible doing so on his own. He walks, climbs, jumps, and trots; he pushes his stroller instead of riding in it; he carries things, wants to put on and take off his own clothes. Most of the time he does what he is told, but he shows his dawning independence in saying, "no," "no," to anything and everything persistently and vehemently. This tendency toward independence is also brought out when we reconsider the evidence about the emergence of self during infancy. The infant has the sense of being a person, a bit fuzzy as to the boundaries to be sure, but a person for all that and *he* wants what *he* wants when *he* wants it. It will be found that one of the factors making for the emergence of the self is the oppositional quality of many of the infant's activities. In emerging as a person, he wants to be independent. In addition to protesting against help, there is the obvious pride he takes in doing something on his very own, which also points to independence tendencies.

But in all of this pushing out into the world, in his seeking of independence, there is vacillation. The infant takes two steps forward and one step backward, sometimes literally. Off on some gallant adventure, but just out of mother's sight, he bursts into tears and flees back.

Frustration and dependency. Intruding then, upon the idyllic scene so far sketched is the fact that there is discomfort and pain in the life of the infant, too. He becomes hungry or experiences a pain of one sort or another. In other words, as Dollard and Miller (27) put it, a goal response is interfered with. In the course of learning to be dependent, the infant is inevitably frustrated. The mother is not always there at the instant he wants help. Frustration results. The process is very well illustrated by Whiting in discussing frustration in a primitive group, the Kwoma. He writes:

> Kwoma infants are cared for almost exclusively by their mothers. For approximately the first three years of his life a Kwoma infant sits in the lap of his mother during the day and lies by her side at night. It is the Kwoma mother's duty to care for all the needs of her child during this period. When, despite this constant care, Kwoma infants suffer frus-

[1] From Dollard, Doob *et al.* (26). Copyright 1939 by the Yale University Press, and published with permission.

tration, crying is the response which becomes most firmly fixed. A Kwoma mother, whenever her infant cries, does her best to comfort him. If he is hungry she feeds him; if he is cold she warms him; if he is sick or in pain she tries to soothe him. Thus by removing the source of frustration or pain the Kwoma mother rewards crying as a response to these conditions. Toward the end of infancy, when the child begins to talk, he responds to frustration or pain by asking for help, and his mother complies with his request whenever it is possible for her to do so. Thus during infancy a frustration-dependence sequence is established (*118*, 138).[2]

This relation of frustration and dependence is continued and strengthened as the child becomes less dependent, when adult care is withdrawn as he becomes older. For example, learning to keep clean, to care for himself, and to take responsibility inevitably brings about frustrating situations.

Determinants of dependence tendencies. A variety of reasons have led psychologists to postulate that a relation would be found between the severity of frustrations in infancy and later magnitude of dependence tendencies infants exhibited. Although the dependence tendencies under consideration are those learned in infancy, their effects are apt to be more evident when the child is somewhat older, that is, when he is of preschool age or older. In other words, to study the antecedents of dependency in an infant we examine what sort of preschool child he has become.

The clearest evidence of infantile antecedents of dependency is to be found in a study of preschool children by Sears and his associates (*67*). Since they were interested in the antecedents of both dependency and aggression in infancy and in early childhood, this study will be referred to on several occasions. For convenience it will be referred to as the "antecedent" study. The children in the antecedent study were rated by their nursery school teacher on a scale of dependency based on instances of seeking help, praise, physical contacts, and nearness. These same categories were used to find (1) dependency toward the teacher; and (2) dependency toward other children. A trained observer also obtained the number of instances of dependent behavior in a time sample with the same children. Through an interview, material concerning infant socialization, particularly about feeding and weaning and toilet training practices, was gathered from the mothers.

Amount of dependent behavior in these children at preschool age

---

[2] From Whiting (*118*). Copyright 1944 by the Royal Anthropological Institute of Great Britain and Ireland, and published with permission.

was found in their sample to be positively correlated with the rigidity of their infantile feeding schedule in girls, but not in boys; and, especially, with the severity of weaning in both boys and girls. Both rigidity of feeding and severity of weaning are frustrating. Their prediction, that "degree of early infant frustration will vary positively with later overt dependency behavior" (100, 187) [3] was borne out. Frustration in infancy expressed through rigidity of scheduling and severity of weaning tended to be related to extent of dependency in early childhood. In other words, the greater the rigidity of scheduling and the severity of weaning there were during infancy, the greater the amount of dependency during early childhood. Infantile frustration leads to later dependent strivings.

Severity of toilet training, another source of frustration in infancy, was found *not* to be related to dependency during the preschool years. It becomes necessary to consider how this finding of a form of frustration not correlated with dependency may be reconciled with the substantial correlation of severity of weaning and subsequent dependency. A clue is obtained from the fact that weaning takes place in the first year; toilet training does not take place until later. If toilet training frustration is unrelated to dependency in nursery school whereas severe weaning frustration is, it suggests that the critical period for the development of dependency is the last part of the first year of life, that is, during weaning but before toilet training. This would imply that for the present findings to make sense, as Sears and the others (100) point out, the dependence drive had to be formed during the first few months, that is, when rigidity and scheduling were operative. They state this and a related point as to why severity of toilet training and dependency are not correlated as follows:

> It may be suggested, then, that the child begins to develop dependency actions and drive from birth. The actions change continuously as new understanding of how to get help occurs, but dependency drive reaches an asymptote early in infancy. Only in cases of severe deprivation of parental nurturance will the dependency drive fail to develop. Once the drive is developed, non-nurturance and other social frustrations will serve not to weaken the dependency drive, but to strengthen the reactions designed to gratify it. Hence, degree of early infant frustration will vary positively with later overt dependency behavior.
>
> Another point worth considering is the lack of correlation between severity of toilet training and dependency. The feeding process involves the mother in a diadic relationship in which her main function is to give the child help. She acts in a supportive manner, giving, providing,

---

[3] From Sears *et al.* (100). Copyright 1953 by The Journal Press, and published with permission.

bringing to him. In toilet training her role is quite different. She does nothing *for* the child, only *to* him. He has no initial desire to use the potty; her putting him on it is not a reward, as is her giving him food. Only gradually does he learn to *want* to have approved toilet habits, and the desire comes at the end of the mother's training activity; it is not there while she is teaching. Thus, toilet training fills no need, satisfies no initial drive; it is nothing but a modifier of behavior, a frustration, mild under the best procedure and dreadful under the worst (100, 187).[3]

Thus, both positive relation between events in early infancy and dependency in the preschool years and the lack of relation of events in later infancy and dependency in the preschool years are satisfactorily accounted for.

According to theoretical expectation and according to our introductory paragraphs in the present account of how dependence is formed, dependency should be positively related to gratification of nurturance. That is, the child who received a great deal of gratification through nurturance should show considerable dependency. In the "antecedent" study, the interview with the mother sought data about the amount of nurturance she gave the child. It had been hoped that information on self-demand feeding would supply the index of nurturance, but this proved disappointing since no clear relation between it and dependency was found. Instead, the other end of the scale of nurturance, that of rigid scheduling, was found to be an index of frustration correlated with dependency as mentioned earlier.

Although admittedly there was difficulty in measurement, the investigators suggest that the lack of relationship between nurturance and dependency is due to all the children in the sample receiving enough reinforcement of dependent behavior so that what became crucial in creating individual differences were the differences in frustration, not nurturance. If the last part of the first year of life be crucial for establishment of dependency then it was the nurturance *offered then* which would be important in the formation of dependency. Measurement of nurturance thereafter would be too late. It had already served its function.

With preschool children subjects about equally divided as to sex, Beller (7) investigated the relationship of dependence or independence behavior tendencies to the history of oral (for example, nail biting and over eating) and anal traits (for example, lack of bowel control and smearing) as observed by nursery school teachers. These teachers reported their observations by means of a rating described elsewhere (page 367). Beller then hypothesized that dependency would be positively correlated with both oral and anal traits, but more highly with the former, and that independence tendencies would be negatively correlated with both, but more highly (negatively) with the anal. Over-all, the relative magnitude of the correlations obtained were consistent with his hypotheses. Among his various results those most comparable to the Sears study were the ones in which his severely disturbed subjects were eliminated.

Although the small size of Beller's sample is regrettable and certain correlations are statistically insignificant, the results are still impressive. Inspection of Table 9 shows that dependency and oral tendencies were correlated, .42 for boys and .60 for girls, with the correlations for anal proclivities respectively .42 and .34. Sears' findings (100) concerning feeding frustration and dependency are verified in this case by a measure other than rigidity of scheduling and weaning, namely the oral symptoms found to be present.

TABLE 9

CORRELATIONS OBTAINED BY BELLER (7) BETWEEN CERTAIN VARIABLES

Variables	Boys N = 15	Girls N = 18
Dependency-independence	.41	−.45
Dependency-orality	.42	.60*
Dependency-anality	.42	.34
Independence-orality	.07	−.45
Independence-anality	−.38	−.23
Orality-anality	.57†	.64*

* p < .01. † p < .05.

A study of Sears, Maccoby, and Levin (99) supplies much valuable data about infants, including some bearing on the present topic. Both as background for their findings concerning dependency in infancy and for the sake of future reference to their findings, a somewhat detailed statement of their procedure and subjects will be given. Hereafter it will be referred to as the "pattern" study.

The mothers studied were chosen from those living in two suburbs of a large metropolitan area in New England. One suburb was primarily residential and the occupants were mostly of middle-class occupational level, whereas the other suburb contained considerable heavy industry with the population mostly working-class people. Eight schools supplied the sample. Standardized interviews were conducted by ten trained women interviewers with nearly 400 mothers of five-year-olds. These interviews were recorded for later analysis. Information about both mother and child was secured. The investigators chose to describe various dimensions which will be referred to as they become relevant in the topics considered here. These were based on interview schedules or rating scales. Analysis of the interviews was made to decide on the ratings to be given and ratings made by ten advanced graduate students. Each interview was rated independently to test the reliability of rating. Final scores were on pooled judgments of the two raters. Dimensions concerning the mother had to do with (1) her disciplinary technique; (2) her permissiveness; (3) her severity in applying techniques; (4) her temperamental qualities; and (5) her positive inculcation of more mature behavior in her child. We are at present concerned with their findings on dependency in infancy.

The Sears "pattern" study (99) did not verify the earlier antecedent study. Either negative or even diametrically opposite results were found. No general connection between severity of weaning and dependency could be elicited. Instead of girls showing a relationship of scheduling and dependency, none was found, but boys fed on self-demand (nonrigid) scheduling were more dependent.

From the conflicting results of the two studies, it would appear that the relation between frustration and dependency is not unequivocal. We may either take the position that the evidence is contradictory and that no clear relationship between infancy training and dependency has been established, or decide on the basis of the merits of the designs of the two studies which should be tentatively accepted as the more valid. The latter course is recommended.

A tentative conclusion may be drawn that the earlier antecedent study focuses more sharply and precisely on the problem at hand. In the later "pattern" study, mothers gave their opinions about infancy practice at least two more years removed from actual weaning experience than was the case for the mothers in the earlier study. This time lapse may have distorted their perception of the situation. Research evidence is available on this point. Mednick and Shaffer (76) found that mothers' reports of child rearing practices some time after the events in question when compared with records actually taken at the time were quite unreliable.

Moreover, it should be noted that in the "pattern" study the mothers themselves were the ones supplying information about dependency. Sears and his associates comment on how the mothers' attitudes, favorable or unfavorable, influence their perception of their children's dependency. In the antecedent study, trained observers sampled dependence reactions, on the spot as it were. Presumably, they were freer from the effects of this distorting factor. Therefore, more credence is placed on the positive results of the earlier study, which showed a relationship between the frustrations of weaning and scheduling and later dependence reactions. Frustration from rejection leads to greater dependency.

Determinants of independence tendencies. Most of our information about independence tendencies concerns preschool children and is reported in a later chapter. Although Beller (7) used children of that age, he did report their oral and anal behaviors in relation to independence tendencies. As shown in Table 9, the correlation between independence and oral behavior in girls is −.45, not enough to achieve statistical significance, and the other correlations are even lower. We must conclude that no relationship between independence and oral or anal behavior has been demonstrated for either boys or girls.

Aggressive Tendencies

It will be remembered that Bridges (17) in exploring the emotional process in infancy found that both undifferentiated and ill-defined positive *and* negative feelings were prominent. As the infant grew older, they gave way to the emergence of focused positive and negative feelings directed toward specific persons.

Important in aggression are anger responses—the vigorous reactions of crying, hitting, screaming, thrashing, and striking out—described in Chapter 7. Constitutional and hereditary factors seem to give us such responses to restraint and to discomfort. Frustration was found to be an antecedent of anger; anger comes about when the infant is frustrated. The frustrating character of weaning and cleanliness training can hardly be doubted.

But this does not relate them to aggression as such. Frustration gives rise to striking out, which in turn results in satisfaction of a need. That is, expression of anger is successful in bringing maternal aid that results in gratification or relief from tension. Thus anger responses, too, are reinforced and acquire reward value. From them emerge aggressive tendencies.

This occurs in what Sears and his associates (100) refer to as instrumental aggression—hurting someone to obtain some goal. Certainly, a newborn infant cannot be charged with being aggressive in this sense; at this stage there is no clear knowledge of the individual as a person, as later discussion of the emergence of self will demonstrate. Anger responses of infants instigated by frustration do not yet have an aggressive character. As the child grows older, angry behavior begins to include the intent to attack, to injure, to destroy. The child, instead of striking out blindly, discovers that he secures his own way by hurting other people. This learned, instrumental aggressive action becomes a drive practiced for its own sake.

It should be noted that this emphasis on injury distinguishes aggression from such assertive behavior as competition or dominance. While aggressive tendencies may easily be an accompaniment or even be the source of assertive tendencies, they should not be confused.

As with dependence, aggressive tendencies are also secondary drives. The secondary drive character of aggression arises from a discovery that the infant secures compliance with his wishes by hurting (100). Success of his aggression reinforces this drive. At first, it is more or less crude striking out, but with age he becomes more skilled and more sophisticated forms of aggression appear. A special form of aggressive activity emerges—fighting. Other nuances, sarcasm, destructiveness, and noncooperation, also appear as means of control. The discovery that he can, if he chooses, not give his cooperation to his mother, not turn his head when she wants a kiss, make his body stiff when clothing is being removed, does not require striking out, but is nevertheless aggressive in character.

Some aggressive responses may appear divorced from anger as when an individual coldly and calmly carries out some act that is intended to injure another person. Partial divorce of the emotional involvement from aggression is not uncommon in our culture. After all, fighting in the physical or literal sense is not our commonest form of aggression. Many motives of others can be thwarted by aggressive activities on our part without our fighting. As the quality of aggression is attenuated so, too, is emotional arousal.

Determinants of aggressive tendencies. Sears and his associates (100) in the antecedent study were concerned with aggression as related to infantile experience. Aggressive behavior was investigated through nursery school teacher ratings and time-sampling observations in the already familiar fashion. Total ratings on aggression were obtained by summing ratings on such items as attacking, threatening or quarreling with other children, threatening the teacher, or destroying property of the other children.

They found no stable definitive relation between preschool aggressive behavior and infantile feeding frustration. There is enough evidence to suggest that if such a relationship exists it is between aggression and severity of toilet training. The more severe the toilet training the infants received, the more aggressive they were when they were a few years older.

The exception to the trends of this relationship was a minority of highly aggressive children who had experienced not average or severe toilet training, but very little frustration from this experience.

Sexual Tendencies

One of the most important of Freud's discoveries was the presence of sexual needs in infancy, despite the absence of genital maturity. Before Freud, sexual tendencies in infants were almost completely ignored. Freud, however, was so impressed with this fact that it contributed materially to his developing of the concept of the libido. Nevertheless, it is possible to consider sexual tendencies as present in infancy without use of the concept of the libido. Instead, sexual needs may be conceived as one among several basic organic drives that give rise to tendencies. The organic drives, on environmental interplay, speedily give rise to second order drives. If this modification be accepted, then the findings of psychology concerning learning may be seen to be compatible with many of the psychoanalytic contributions concerning sexual tendencies. This theme will be further developed in the last section of the next chapter which is devoted to a neo-Freudian interpretation of infancy.

Sexual behavior in the neonate and infant was described in Chapter 7. Sexual tendencies are subject to socialization pressure during infancy, but the effects of socialization become more apparent during early childhood. Consequently, further exposition is deferred until later chapters.

So far, we have been considering the socialization of primary drives and the development of secondary drives. There are other behavior tendencies, called exploratory, externally aroused behavior tendencies, which are less fully investigated and apparently do not develop as secondary drives through reinforcement.

Exploratory Externally Aroused Behavior Tendencies

Much of the infant's behavior is not concerned with satisfying primary and secondary drives. An infant seems intent on exploring his environment. When lying prone at a gathering of adults, he constantly raises his head to see what is going on; when crawling is achieved, he makes a wholehearted effort to reach the scene of any new activity. Is the well-fed baby happily cooing, kicking, and mouthing everything that comes his way not showing some sort of drive? Surely, it is not tension reduction that he seeks. He is showing the outgoing, exploring, activity-seeking, trying-out behavior that we call play. These behavior tendencies are insatiable; when one palls he turns to another play object. This becomes almost all-absorbing. Hunger or the need for elimination are often disregarded unless the infant is reminded by an adult. Of course, this cannot go on indefinitely—he suddenly screams from hunger pangs that have been building up unnoticed, or he has an "accident" and must be changed. He does not do these things because of a schedule of reinforcement—he does them because he *enjoys* them (*116*).

More systematic observational reports corroborating the presence of exploratory play tendencies are available. Gesell's normative studies (*41*) illustrate the appearance of behavior patterns at a given age. Many of them are typical of kinds of behavior under discussion. At one year of age an infant shows gross motor activity, playing with buttons attached to a garment, putting objects in and out of other objects, and reciprocal nursery games, such as "Where is baby?" At 18 months he climbs, moves furniture, plays with pull toys, teddy bears, dolls, pots and pans. At two years he feeds and toilets a doll or a teddy bear, takes them for a ride, plays with sand and water, filling and emptying dishes, and uses little cars and blocks. However, since these are isolated bits of behavior with no information provided about their origin, it cannot be said that they arise independent of more primary drives.

Stott (*112*) gives us more precise information. He kept a careful behavior diary of his infant son from birth to 18 months from which he eliminated items bearing a relation to either an organic or a social need. Those individual behaviors remaining, apparently unrelated to any organic or social need, formed the basis of the report. They were classified into five general categories—recognition (looking at the headboard, bending back head to do so); completion (fitting lid on kettle); control (standing in high chair and shaking until it nearly falls over); exploration (watching movement of adult's feet and hands); effecting change (studying hand movement). There seemed to be progressive effectiveness in the child's behavior as the child sought new ways of doing things. The observer could see no connection with either organic (primary) or social needs of these behaviors in his own infant. He could, of course, be mistaken. Nevertheless, in Russia, Federov (*31*) independently reached the same conclusions as Stott.

Piaget (*83*) gives an interpretation of play compatible with considering it a nonreinforced, externally aroused behavior tendency. Play is assimilation for the sake of assimilation, the incorporation of experience for the sake of that experience. Its most primitive beginning stages are seen in accommodation-free sucking movements, without presence of breast or bottle. If there be some question whether this is play or not, this is not the case with the next stage in which prior practice can be distinguished from the activities shown in carrying it on for its own sake. Illustrative is an infant who adopts the habit of throwing back his head to look at objects. At about two months of age he continues to do this "with ever-increasing enjoyment and ever-decreasing interest in the external results" (83, 91).

Piaget observed a seven-month-old infant who had learned to remove an obstacle in order to secure an object. When this kind of barrier continued to be put before him, the infant would push aside the cardboard and burst into laughter, completely forgetting the toy that was the original incentive for his learning. A still older infant was fond of pretending a piece of cloth was a pillow, or of "eating" paper, laughing aloud as she did so. Here symbolization has emerged as a play activity for the infant. Inadequate stimuli were treated as if they were adequate—as if they were something else.

In the diadic unit of mother and infant, one aspect of the relationship, the mother, has been emphasized. Now the focus shifts. The child is brought into the foreground, with the mother in the background. Infant social relationships from the perspective of *his* behavior and experience come to the fore. An "infant's-eye" view of this business of infancy is now to be stressed.

The development of self and social awareness

The nucleus of self appears to be that which is experienced as "I" or "me," as distinguished from everything else that is "not me." The newborn infant does not have this awareness of "I" and "not I." In addition, there is no awareness of the outside world and, therefore, no self-awareness by which to distinguish himself from that world. The whole world is wet or hungry or cold when he is wet, hungry, or cold. "I" and the "rest of the world" are intermingled.

The development of self in infancy is an area in which definitive, carefully controlled research is lacking. For example, after an extensive search of the literature, Wylie (122) stated there was no longitudinal data on which to base a description of the development of the self-concept in infancy. Only a variety of plausible, but speculative theoretical statements, and some scraps of evidence, probably accurate enough in themselves but not necessarily bearing a direct and unequivocal relation to the issue at hand, are available. Recourse will be made to the formulations of Freud and Piaget.

The psychoanalytic theory of the ego has already been discussed in

Chapter 5. It will be remembered that ego is broader than awareness of self since it also includes carrying on executive functions. At the moment, only awareness will be considered.

The infant at birth has no appreciation of the distinction between world and ego. Libidinal energy is directed upon himself. This state is referred to as primary narcissism, a term derived from the legend of Narcissus who fell in love with his reflection in a pool. The infant loves himself with supreme egoism because he is unaware of anyone or anything else. Sexual aims are autoerotic, that is, they are concerned with self-love.

The ego of the infant as a sense of self-awareness becomes differentiated when his needs are *not* met. If all of the infant's needs were to be gratified, he would continue to have no sense of ego as differentiated from the world. Anna Freud (34) offers an explanation in these terms. She maintains that the inner world of the infant at birth consists essentially of the contrasting feelings of pleasure and pain. Pain arises under the impact of bodily needs from within or irritations from without; pleasure comes when the needs are satisfied or the irritants removed. The contrasting nature of frustration and gratification leads to the beginning of the ego.

True, under the ministrations of the mother, the painful tendencies of the infant give way to relief. But his needs are not always met immediately. For example, when feeding is delayed, the inability to summon the breast or bottle immediately helps the infant to differentiate self from nonself. The mother's failure to meet his needs, the inevitable delays in ministering to his wants lead to his growing recognition of "I" and "not I." Awareness comes that for his needs to be met, to have his tensions reduced, something must be done by "mother." Thus, awareness of the mother's presence comes when she is not there! This leads to his losing the sense of omnipotence and the recognition of his dependence on others. He begins to realize that "others" must do something before his needs can be met.

There is social awareness, too, in the beginnings of ego development as indicated in discussing the "separation" of child and mother. The quality attributed to this other person is also produced in emerging social awareness. Taking feeding as central to this stage, what happens when the infant is fed? If the mother fondles him, is gentle in the process, helps him learn to suck, his first adjustment to what, as ego-awareness continues, is his first perception of another person is experienced as good. Consequently, he expects other people to be friendly as well. To use a term of Erikson (28), a psychoanalyst, a sense of trust is developed. But what if she is unfriendly and rough, forcing the bottle or breast? He does not "think" of her as an enemy; his mental processes are not yet developed to this extent. But he does react with fear, tension, and psychosomatic upsets, such as inability to suck, vomiting, and random bodily movements. The little world for him, which is the here and now of the mother-child interaction, is bad and hateful in the primitive beginnings of these terms.

Piaget makes no particular systematic use of the concept of self. His interpretation of problems relevant to it rests upon his conceptualization of the sensorimotor stage (9). The infant receives impressions and reacts to them, but there is not yet a "self between." There is only a shapeless absolute of self and environment intermingled without fixed boundaries. The infant's initial egocentrism is shown by his inability to distinguish the self from the world (33). In adapting to the external world, he thereby creates it. The Freudian and Piagetian views are not incompatible. In fact, they may be considered complementary.

It is evident that the task before the infant is to mark off the separate specific objects in his environment from himself. He is learning to specify the contours of his body, the sound of his voice, and to identify the various sensory kinesthetic processes from his own body. Simultaneously he also has the task of perceiving or learning to know other persons *as* persons. The mother's gentle voice, soothing touch, and warm body emerge from the fog of his impressions. Also emerging from this total matrix is a sense of the unity of his own person. Gradually, it is not pain but *my* pain, not hunger but *my* hunger, not hunger being fed but *mother feeding me.*

There are some scraps of evidence that help to understand the nature of infantile self-awareness. Using as his data several infants' responses to mirror-reflected images, Dixon (25) concluded that self-recognition appeared at about one year of age as shown in such behavior as alternately observing arm-finger movements and their reflection in the mirror.

A few behavioral indices related to emerging social awareness are available. Examination will show that some of the items concern the beginnings of the perception of other persons, others concern a recognition of the need for cooperation and communication, and still others concern the use of words that have self-reference. It has been observed that at about the age of four weeks responsiveness to social surroundings begins to appear (39). The infant reacts to social overtures by a reduction of bodily activity. For example, the infant ceases crying, at least for the moment, if held in someone's arms. At eight weeks his face shows signs of animation on seeing other persons and at 12 weeks he may vocalize his reply to their speech. Since the smile is one of the earliest socially instigated responses of the human infant, it has received considerable study (for example, *1, 16, 62, 96, 104, 110*). It seems fairly well established that a smile in response to the human voice or face first appears somewhere between the end of the first and the third months (*62, 104*).

By the beginning of the sixth month, Spitz and Wolf (*110*) found a smile on seeing the experimenter for the first time present in 98 per cent of their rather large sample.[4] A dramatic change was found by Spitz when these infants were observed again, this time in the last half of the first year. The indiscriminate smiling responses both to the mother and to a stranger give way to smiling sometimes at one person or another but not indiscriminately at everybody. One of the early signs of what is popularly called "self-consciousness" appears at about the end of the first half-year when an infant tries to hide himself when in the presence of strangers.

The smiling response is subject to reward and extinction just as are other social responses. If the infant's smile is rewarded by his being picked up, he is likelier to smile on subsequent occasions than the infant not so rewarded (*16*). The positive nature of social responsiveness in infancy is also noteworthy. For 16 infants, observers kept a weekly record for eight weeks (*90*) of positive responses—smiling, laughing, rolling, and reaching toward the adult—and of negative responses—frowning, crying, turning head away, and rolling and crawling away. Of a total of 527 social contacts only 65 instances were negative.

Murphy *et al.* (*78*) expresses the opinion that the self is based in part on experience the infant has in the use of proper names and when parents hold him responsible or reward him for his behavior. The attainment of the pronoun, "I," and related terms such as "me" and "you" are characteristic, according to Gesell (*41*), at about 24 months of age. In keeping with this, the sequence might be first "Jimmy does this," to, "me do this," and, then on perceiving self as doer, "I do this." In language, then, we find evidence of an emerging sense of self.

Another means whereby the self and social awareness emerge in the infant is found in the development of independent oppositional behavior (*69*). At age 18 to 24 months he is "into everything." He knows where things are kept and gets them out in what appears to some mothers an alarming profusion. He darts everywhere, and refuses to allow his arm to be held. If restrained, he often resists strenuously and vocally. A specific illustration from Levy is appropriate.

[4] The smile appears in rare cases as early as the twenty-fifth day. It may be that its appearance at this young age is due to visceral changes, which are known to produce a "smile."

A two-year-old tries to fill the sink with water. He struggles to turn the faucet. His efforts are persistent, exhausting, and fruitless. . . . The father silently turns the faucet. The two-year-old bursts into a loud scream. He runs out of the bathroom. He is angry and in tears. He refuses to be washed or bathed. For him, everything is spoiled. An obstacle was thrown in the path of progress towards his own goal: his own job, to be done by himself alone, without the slightest help, or suggestion, or interference (69, 114).[5]

Mothers can supply countless similar illustrations of behavior having this flavor of opposition which seemingly serves to sharpen the child's sense of being an individual person. These same ways of behaving show the pronounced influence of what earlier has been described as independence tendencies. His growing self-awareness leads to demands for independence.

Peer relationships

Social relationships to other infants lag behind development of relationships to adults. Prior to about four or five months active seeking of social contact with other infants can hardly be said to occur (19). As we know, at about this age, smiling at another infant or crying when an infant receives attention takes place. An investigation (74) of peer reactions of infants six to 25 months of age used the technique of "baby-parties."

Two infants of approximately the same age were placed together in a playpen, first, without play material, then, after a time, with hollow cubes introduced, followed by a drum and a drumstick for each, and, lastly, a ball was given them, preceded by showing them how to roll it between them. Each infant was paired with other infants at different observational periods and the reactions of each recorded. For each period, the findings are those for a typical infant at the designated age.

Six to eight months. One-third of the time the infant turns immediately to the surroundings, not to the partner or the play material. Nearly half the attempts of the partner to interact with him are ignored. Friendly contacts, when they occur, are limited to looking, smiling at, and grasping the partner. Games are few and short. Often they consist of unspecific manipulations of the same object without the partner receiving attention. Fights are equally impersonal, consisting of a blind attempt to get hold of the play material.

[5] From Levy (69). Copyright 1953 by Charles C Thomas, and published with permission.

Nine to thirteen months. Play material is responded to first. Since the partner often becomes an obstacle to getting it, fighting is at its maximum at these months. Conflicts now become personal; though it is not yet genuine hostility since nonpartner material (his own toys and clothing, hair, and so on) is still much preferred.

Fourteen to eighteen months. This is a transitional period wherein the infant shifts his attention from the play materials to his partner when his desire for playthings is satisfied. There is a pronounced decrease in fighting for material.

Nineteen to twenty-five months. The infant integrates his social interest in the partner with his interest in the playthings. Games show a considerable increase in frequency and length. The play becomes personal with much looking, smiling, and grasping, with a modification of his behavior in adjustment to that of his partner.

Disregarding the transitional 14 to 18 months' interval, the investigators concluded that the infant regarded the partner first as play material in itself (6 to 8 months), then as an obstacle to play material (9 to 13 months), and finally as a playmate (19 to 25 months). In other words, the infant has progressed from passivity to social contact, albeit crude, during the first two years of life.

The finding that infants of 19 months typically are more interested in their playmates than in the material suggests a primary social orientation at a very young age. Moreover, cooperation and competition in their crudest beginnings are apparent.

These findings indicate nothing about the factors responsible for the infant's social responsiveness; nor is there other research to which to turn for information. Presumably, the infant's first social relationships in the home, particularly with the mother, play an important part in determining his attitude and behavior in his relations with his peers. Behavioral generalization from the home setting would be expected.

We may lack understanding of their origin, but we do have evidence of individual differences in social reaction. Buhler (*19*), as a result of observation of infants' social settings, concluded that three patterns could be discerned—the socially blind, the socially dependent, and the socially independent. She describes them as follows:

> (a) The socially blind infant behaves in the presence of another child as if nobody were present; he looks at the other without any emotion, he takes toys, plays and moves without any regard for the other child; he does not pay any attention to the other's movements; he is neither impressed nor interested in the other's presence or activities. (b) The socially dependent, on the contrary, is deeply impressed by the other's presence and activities; he can either be inhibited or else be stimulated

by the other's presence. In the first case he will not move, will watch the other or copy him, will obey him, and sometimes even give signs of fear in front of him; in the second case, he will display in front of the other, will demonstrate objects and gestures, will try to rouse the other, and sometimes will even get enthusiastic and excited. In both cases all his movements are dependent on the presence of the other child; he observes the effect of his behavior on the other and carefully watches the other's reactions. (c) The third type is still different. The socially independent child is one who—though aware of the other's presence and responsive to his behavior—yet does not seem dependent on him, is neither intimidated nor inspired. He reacts to the other, wards him off when necessary, yet never becomes aggressive himself. He may or may not join the other in play, is not inconsiderate, but sometimes even consoles the other, encourages him, takes part in his activities; yet, with all that, he remains independent in his movements; for instance, he may suddenly turn away and do something for himself (19, 393–394).[6]

These types of social reactions in infants are congruent with the social development trends of the preceding study. Presumably, all infants are first socially blind. Even those who can still be so characterized, when other infants are more "dependent" or "independent," show change with increased age in the direction of greater outgoingness. Social dependence presumably is heavily influenced by the age of the other child. If the other child is older, dependence through dominance of the older is expected. By no means can these three characterizations be considered as hard and fast, unalterable by events. The three patterns are, nevertheless, suggestive of the emerging personality differences shown by infants in peer interaction.

Although there are social reactions to peers during infancy, it must be emphasized that social situations are almost completely confined to the family setting. Social interactions with adults far outnumber peer interactions. The "baby parties" after all were arranged by psychologists, not by the infants themselves!

Summary

In considering behavior tendencies in infancy, dependence tendencies have been examined. Dependence is found to be a secondary drive learned through social experiences. The helplessness of the infant demands his dependence on the mother. Dependence takes the form

---

[6] From Buhler (19). Copyright 1931 by the Clark University Press, and published with permission.

of both instrumental dependence and of emotional dependence (which includes considerable behavior ordinarily referred to as "affectionate"). Frustration is found to be related to dependency, although the literature is somewhat equivocal on this point. It is tentatively concluded that frustration arising from rejection during infancy leads to greater dependence on the part of children. Some evidence is offered that independent tendencies also appear during infancy.

Aggression also appears in infancy—hurting someone in order to gain some goal. During infancy aggression begins to take on the character of a secondary drive. Success of aggression reinforces that drive. Despite these findings, knowledge of specific determinants of aggressive tendencies in infancy is very meager.

Sexual tendencies, although present to some degree, are considered as assuming greater importance in the preschool period. Socialization pressures concerning sexual tendencies are not as great as they are later.

Although rigorous research evidence is as yet lacking, the presence of what has been called *exploratory externally*-aroused behavior tendencies have been demonstrated to exist. Play assumes particular importance in this connection when interpreted as assimilation for the sake of assimilation. Readiness, even eagerness, for experience seems to characterize the infant.

Shifting perspective from the mother to the child, the infant's behavior and experience in the development of self and social awareness was indicated. The emergence of the beginnings of a sense of self and of social awareness was presented as based on learning and maturation. A considerable variety of experiences is found to be responsible for the appearance of self and social awareness. These are: the objectification of objects, the perception of persons both as friendly and strange, the recognition of the need for cooperation and communication, the closeness yet separateness from the mother, the use of proper names and pronouns, the fact of being held responsible for actions, and the development of independence tendencies. The psychoanalytic position that awareness arises from the infant's experience of his needs not being met takes its place as one of the factors making for the emergence of the beginnings of a sense of self.

Peer relationships among infants were found to begin somewhere about six months of age progressing through stages until the end of infancy. By this time social responsiveness to peers can be integrated with interest in playing in a way resembling that exhibited in later life.

One of the most general conclusions to be drawn about the infant in his social setting is the all-pervasiveness of the influence of reinforcement or nonreinforcement upon making him the infant he is and the child and adult he is to become.

For Further Reading

Harlow (54) presents a fascinating study related to dependence tendencies that is valuable for the information it supplies on maternal attachment.   Sears and his associates (100) present an important study of dependency and aggression.   Anna Freud (34) offers a psychoanalytic interpretation on the development of self-awareness.

References

Follow Chapter 10.

10

Psychoanalytic Contentions

WHILE EXAMINING the infant in a social setting, the only psycho-analytic contentions touched on directly were those concerned with the emergence of the self. It now becomes necessary to consider psychoanalytic claims in more detail. First, the theory of psychosexual stages of orality and anality will be examined. This will be followed by a presentation of a typical case study, an examination of the research evidence for psychoanalytic contentions and, finally, a neo-Freudian interpretation which will attempt to reconcile Freudian and non-Freudian claims concerning infancy.

The oral stage

In psychoanalytic theory, the infant is seen as passing through the various stages of psychosexual development briefly reviewed in Chapter 5. Table 2 on pages 116–117 schematically presents these stages. Examination of the table will show that each stage is considered in terms of the areas of libidinal localization, the modes of pleasure finding, the object relations prevailing, the structural organization of the personality, and the mechanisms emerging during that particular stage.

In the first stage, libidinal localization centers in oral activities. Interest is focused on libidinal manifestations in the oral stage (mode of pleasure finding) and in what psychoanalysts call *object relations,* the relationship of the infant to other persons, especially the mother, who is the first object of every infant. Sucking gives libidinal pleasure.

Stimulation of the lips, mouth, tongue, and cheeks is exciting in and of itself. An illustration would be thumb sucking that stimulates the membrane of the mouth. If hunger alone were the motivation of thumb sucking, psychoanalysts insist, the infant would soon cease sucking since milk is not forthcoming. Sucking *after* a meal is a common observation among infants, as is going to sleep sucking a thumb. Sucking is pleasurable and thus is a manifestation of libido.

Phases

The first aim of autoerotic stimulation, the bringing about of pleasurable sensations from the mouth, is followed during this early oral phase by another aim, the desire to incorporate objects. The mother is not only viewed as food, but as Blum puts it, "the infant fantasies being united with his source of supply by swallowing or incorporating it, thus making the object a part of himself" (*13*, 38).[1] Fenichel (*32*) cites as evidence for this incorporative phase in later personality development, phenomena extending from fondness for animal crackers to the rites of communion, "becoming the same substance." "You're so cute I could eat you up," is an expression indicative of this same idea of incorporation.

Following this early oral phase, centering on sucking pleasure and on oral incorporation is the late oral phase, the "oral-sadistic" phase. This phase commences with the eruption of the infant's teeth. The sadistic aspect refers to the frustration engendered by the pain of their eruption against which the infant retaliates by biting. This biting is interpreted as a desire to injure or destroy, even to annihilate utterly the bitten object (the mother). In contrast to the relatively passive first phase, this late phase of the oral stage is aggressive.

Weaning results in hostility toward the mother. The infant is faced with his first major human problem—acceptance of frustration. Trouble is to be anticipated when weaning, either from breast or bottle, takes place before the infant is ready to relinquish this form of oral gratification. As a consequence of this frustration, a new relationship between infant and mother develops. This new relationship is termed ambivalence which signifies that two disparate feelings, one friendly and the other hostile, exist concurrently. The infant longs for incorporation of the mother, but now he also wishes to destroy her through biting. This is a new type of object relationship in which friendliness and hostility toward the mother exist side-by-side. Instead

[1] By permission from *Psychoanalytic Theories of Personality* by Blum. Copyright 1953. McGraw-Hill Book Company, Inc.

of having only a positive, friendly, loving feeling, the infant now has mixed feelings toward the mother. She is both "loved" and "hated" at the same time. The infant "wants" his mother, but also wishes that harm would come to her, even her destruction.

Weaning inevitably produces this effect, but too abrupt or too early weaning can intensify it. One of the important props of the infant's existence has been knocked out for reasons he cannot understand. The mother, as the agent of this frustration by her removal of the breast or bottle, has failed the infant. Both anxiety about the mother and hostility toward the mother are natural consequences. Digestive disturbances, refusal to eat, diarrhea, sucking of the thumb, and a host of other oral symptoms may appear.

The phenomena of the oral stage present problems to the infant that give rise to certain characteristic solutions. According to the degree of success in handling the problems of the oral stage, there is a relatively greater or lesser degree of fixation. Fixation refers to the prolongation of habits of pleasure seeking beyond the age for which they are appropriate. Fixation is an investment of libido at a level characteristic of a given developmental stage. In all of us, progress to the next psychosexual stage is never complete; characteristics of an earlier level still persist. In other words, some measure of fixation always takes place. The retention of oral characteristics (kissing, biting, and so on) in normal adult heterosexual behavior is illustrative. But to the extent that fixation has occurred, the individual is thereby weakened in meeting the problems of the next level, since some of the libidinal energy available, fixed in quantity, is now fixated at the earlier level. Freud (35) used the simile of advancing troops; the more occupation troops that must be left behind, the less the remaining army has as it marches on. Although a certain amount of fixation is inevitable, too great a degree is conducive to later personality difficulties.

The factors responsible for fixation at the oral (and other) stages have been developed by Fenichel (32). He categorizes these factors as: (1) experiencing excessive satisfaction so that the stage is given up with reluctance; (2) excessive frustrations leading to a demand for the withheld satisfaction; (3) alternation between excessive gratification and frustration; and (4) simultaneous oral satisfaction and reassurance for some anxiety. Illustrative of the latter category would be giving the infant a bottle of milk whenever he is frightened or otherwise disturbed.

Since undue frustration or too great indulgence can have a pernicious effect on personality, it is appropriate to comment on the optimal proportion of deprivation to indulgence. The optimal proportion would seem to be a large amount of indulgence combined with a small amount of frustration. If this optimal proportion is supplied, no more than the normal amount of fixation takes place.

Another way oral phenomena are manifest is through regression— the reactivation of behavioral patterns appropriate to an earlier stage of development after they have been given up. Faced with difficulties in later life, some individuals are predisposed to return to the behavior characteristic of earlier stages. A child of six may suck his thumb when he is frustrated; an adult may smoke excessively or eat compulsively when he is exposed to difficult situations; or, in a more general fashion, his social relations may show the problems of a particular earlier stage. He may be chronically homesick with a longing for the old and familiar. Regression characteristically occurs after the oral stage, as the illustrations attest. But it can occur within the confines of the oral stage itself. For example, an infant may regress from the late to the early oral phase.

An individual does not regress in all characteristics so that he behaves just like a child or that age level. Rather his behavior is focused on the type of libidinal gratification characteristic of the stage. But how he reacts will be attributable not only to his oral experiences but also to the complication and individually differential effects of the experiences in later stages. These experiences, moreover, may also be more generalized and complicated in nature than these specific introductory "indications" of oral regression might be taken to indicate.

Ego Formation

At birth, the infant does not have an ego. Out of the undifferentiated unconscious state of the id, consciousness of self begins to emerge. Libido originally in the service of id functions is diverted to ego functions. Before this, the infant cannot distinguish himself from others. He has, for example, no idea of the mother as an individual. The infant originally makes no distinction between the mother's breast and his own body. The process of "primary identification" is reflected in the infant's perception of the mother as part of himself. When the distinction is made and the mother is shifted to the "outside," this process carries with it part of the original "self-love," or narcissism, which is now applied to the mother. As the process continues, she gradually emerges as a person, and as a person he loves in his own fashion. Hence, libido is directed toward the mother. Other aspects of the emergence of awareness as a function of the ego have already been discussed in connection with the self on pages 240–241.

Mechanisms Emerging

Mechanisms—such as the ways the infant characteristically operates or behaves—already discussed are fixation and regression. Two other mechanisms emerging during the oral stage are introjection and projection.

In the later phase of the early oral stage, incorporation becomes important. Incorporation (introjection) and identification begin to develop at this stage. Projection appears as well. Their meanings and interrelationships have been well stated by Blum:

> The first judgment of the ego is said to be the distinction between edible and nonedible objects; the first acceptance is swallowing; the first rejection is spitting out. Introjection is a derivative of the former, projection of the latter. In the early stage of development of the ego, everything pleasurable is experienced as belonging to the ego (something to be swallowed), while everything painful is experienced as being nonego (something to be spat out).
>
> Originally, then, introjection or incorporation is an oral mechanism aimed at instinctual satisfaction. Later, when the infant no longer feels omnipotent, oral introjection of the powerful adult serves to regain the feeling. Still later, when incorporation is seen as destroying the independent existence of the outside person, the mechanism functions in a hostile manner as the executive of destructive impulses.
>
> At this point it might be well to attempt to clarify the terms "introjection," "incorporation," and "identification." Introjection and incorporation are generally used synonymously; some also employ identification in the same way. However, identification usually connotes a type of relationship to objects, in other words, a state rather than a process. Thus, oral introjection is said to be the executive of the "primary identification." By introjecting or incorporating, one achieves a state of identification. Primary identification refers to the first relationship to objects, whereas secondary identification is a later repetition of the earlier one.
>
> Projection starts as a primitive method of getting rid of pain, by attributing unpleasant stimuli to the outside world. It is a sort of reverse introjection—instead of the ego's being perceived as having the object's characteristics, the environment is perceived as having the ego's characteristics. In these early phases of development, the mechanism can function without difficulty. Later it requires a serious impairment of the sense of reality for it to play a major role (13, 46–47).[2]

The oral stage comes to a close some time after the end of the first year of life. But oral activities neither cease nor become unimportant; they continue as long as life. Some individuals bear a great impress

[2] By permission from *Psychoanalytic Theories of Personality*, by Blum. Copyright 1953. McGraw-Hill Book Company, Inc.

of the events of this stage all their lives. When this occurs the so-called oral character has emerged as a particular kind of personality.

The Oral Character

The essence of the concept of the oral character is that if unusual deprivation or gratification in infantile feeding behavior and experience occurs, a particular constellation of personality characteristics will be present in adulthood. An adult oral character will show undue oral fixations and tendencies to regression. Oral preoccupations, such as eating, drinking, smoking, and kissing are more important to him than to other individuals. Oral fixations are also expressed more symbolically in general attitudes of dependence or independence.

The infant frustrated or ungratified in oral drives is apt to become the adult dependent on others for his feeling of esteem. He wishes to be taken care of, but he does not actively seek this care. He hopes it will come his way without effort on his part. He is passively dependent. When emotionally upset, he eats to overcome the emotion. A pessimistic attitude may prevail. These feelings of dependency tend to persist throughout life, especially when the individual feels anxious and insecure. On the other hand, oral overindulgence in infancy, according to Fenichel (32), leads to the presence of adult feelings of optimism and self-assurance, even to a point beyond which this trait is desirable. Such a person may be so sure that everything is going to "turn out all right" that he feels no need to work toward his goals. This unperturbable optimism is often manifested in lofty ambitions accompanied by a sanguine expectation that the future will somehow take care of itself.

Frustrations arising during the second or late oral stage lead to a host of ambivalent adult attitudes: friendly-hostile, aggressive-submissive, and so on. For example, such a person may be aggressive and given to "biting" remarks, but have periods in which he tries to make amends by swinging in the opposite direction and becoming over-friendly and submissive.

The anal stage

Freud postulated that somewhere in the second year of life the anal region became the center with high libidinal satisfaction, value, and interest. This stage in our culture is bound up with toilet training. From about the age of a year-and-a-half (or before) to three years, the anal region receives a great deal of attention. Proper evacuation becomes a matter of much attention and considerable ceremony.

For a moment look at anality as the child might (63). The infant has no feeling of repulsion for excreta. He has created it; its odor, texture, and color are not inherently unpleasant. The infant senses that his mother seems to prize his excretion by the pleasure she shows when he has a movement and by her disappointment at his failure to do so. According to Freudian thinking, defecating is "perceived" by the infant as giving something to the parent. Defecating is the giving of a gift. But what happens when he makes the gift by having a movement? The mother flushes it down the toilet! This is just as confusing to the infant as it would be to a husband if his wife, on receiving a fur coat, proceeded to throw it down the incinerator. Illustrative of the concern the infant shows about this confusing behavior is his throwing toys in the toilet, only to retrieve them.

How rapidly and in what form adult disgust will develop depends on many circumstances. The infant's attitudes which begin to form at this time certainly owe much to his parents' particular attitudes and their strength.[3] In varying degrees all parents in our culture emphasize cleanliness. Attitudes toward cleanliness vary to be sure, but there is inevitably a conflict between the child's wishes and parental standards. In some homes, cleanliness has a moral aspect so that the dirty child is a bad child. In any case, a great deal of pressure is put upon the child in regard to toilet training.

Phases

Table 2 on pages 116–117 shows that, as in the oral stage, there are two phases—the expelling and retaining phases. Libidinal attachment is, in the early anal phase, centered on expelling and, in the late phase, on retaining of feces. Extending over both phases is a sadistic overlay—an emphasis on the use of anal behavior by the infant for hostile purposes. Hostility at this age is so common that psychoanalysts often refer to the "anal-sadistic," rather than merely to the anal stage.

[3] It might be well to interject the question of how adult attitudes toward matters of the anal stage affect our consideration of psychoanalytic theory. In much greater degree than do the phenomena of the oral stage, experiences of this stage undergo repression in the course of the person's development. In fact, in the adult, "disgust" predominates. This attitude inevitably colors our attitude toward the phenomena under discussion and practically invites a rejection of any theory which says our personality is, in part, determined by how eliminative functions are handled. This very human tendency, then, to reject that which we find repugnant is one which we can guard against only to a minor degree.

As Blum (13) states it, the aim of the early or expelling phase is the pleasure in the act of excretion. The sadistic element of this phase is derived from excreta being "viewed" by the infant as objects destroyed by elimination. Later, the child may use the expulsiveness as a means of defying the parents who wish to train him to be clean.

The aim of the later or retentive phase is the enjoyment of the intense stimulation of the mucous membrane which accompanies a full lower intestine. But there is also an appreciation by the infant of the high value placed by parents on excreta. The child may wish to keep, rather than give them. Again a sadistic element appears in that he can withhold excretion as a gesture against his parents. By withholding, he can reduce parents to distraction, or by choosing his own time and place of expulsion he can create annoyance, if not more. Thus the element of control now supplements that of destroying which appeared in the oral-expulsion stage.

Ego Formation

In the oral stage, the ego as self-awareness emerged in the manner depicted in the previous section. It will be remembered that id impulses of the newborn infant are directed by the so-called pleasure principle. The reality principle comes into use when the infant is confronted with frustrating experiences. Testing of reality, recognition of fantasy products as unreal, is demanded for normal adjustment. Guidance by the reality principle is shown in early infancy with the emergence of the ability to tolerate delay and to substitute future for immediate gratification. The infant not only becomes aware of changes in his environment but also begins to regulate his behavior in line with these changes. For example, an infant can resist grabbing an atrractive object for at least a short time. Here we have the beginnings of the ego as *executor*.

It is during the anal stage that the ego as executor shows major development. As the infant begins to control toilet activities (and other dawning motor skills), he manifests one of the requisites of ego as doer. This, as Blum (13) views it, depends on active mastery. During the oral stage, the infant is predominantly passive, inducing adults, particularly the mother, to do things for him. During the ages of one to three years, he becomes gradually less dependent on others. This is possible because he begins actively to manipulate his environment through (1) mastering motility in walking, talking, and keeping clean; and (2) growth in judgment. He can actively manipulate his environment when he can walk and control, albeit for short times, his bladder and bowel. Thus, he can begin to be independent.

In learning to talk, he introduces anticipation into his activities in that events can be planned in terms of words. The development of speech is important in ego development not only because of the increased ease and accuracy of communication with others, but also because it increases ease and flexibility in self-communication. Not only can the infant better handle the external world, he also can better handle himself. According to Freudian thinking, these advances in communication give rise to his belief in the magical power of naming. If one can name something, one can master it. In this connection, it is a common observation that children demand incessantly that objects be named for them. Illustrative of the magical power of words is the plea for reassurance that children find in the old saying, "Sticks and stones may break my bones, but names can never hurt me."

Thinking during the anal stage has another characteristic—extensive symbolism. Blum, in this connection, writes:

> Comprehension of the world originally comes from viewing objects as sources either of gratification or of threat, so that stimuli which provoke the same reactions are looked upon as identical. One illustration is the common symbolic equation of "departure" with "death." A less obvious tie is between "money" and "feces." Both represent possessions which are alike for everyone (not individualized) and thus are in danger of being lost as one's own. In other words, both are deindividualized possessions which are in constant danger of losing their ego quality (13, 65).[4]

Judgment, which in turn is partially dependent on speech, is a function technically already referred to as "reality" testing. The infant can explore the solution to a new situation by trying it out and seeing what the consequences are. The tentative, quickly withdrawn touching of the "kitty" by the child is an illustration. Another illustration, even earlier in time, would be the fixed alert stare of the infant who watches the "stranger" to see what he may do. If he remains quiet, he may be accepted, but if he moves too quickly or talks too loudly, the infant cries, shows fear, and attempts withdrawal. Reality testing as the child grows older emerges as a process in realistic thinking. A plan of action is formulated and then carried out. A hungry person thinks where he may find food and seeks it out in that place.

With the further development of the ego during the anal stage, the child also gradually comes to exercise another function of the ego as executor—the ability not just to postpone but actually to forego impulses. This is another defensive function of the ego. The ego gradu-

[4] By permission from *Psychoanalytic Theories of Personality*, by Blum. Copyright 1953. McGraw-Hill Book Company, Inc.

ally learns to ward off impulses that are dangerous and not to perform certain acts. But details of how this comes about must be postponed until discussion of the next or phallic stage of early childhood.

As the ego matures there is an increase in the ability to judge events and to anticipate the future. With this increase comes a more realistic perception of danger and a consequent anxiety. Although a prototype for anxiety existed before, as a consequence of the birth trauma, anxiety as such develops when the child can perceive a situation as threatening or dangerous. According to Freud, anxiety is a consequence of the danger of object loss. In this case, the object which might be lost is the mother, so we have a fear of loss of love developing in the infant. He learns that the environment in addition to offering satisfaction can also threaten. It has the power to produce pain. Anticipation of this pain gives rise to anxiety. If the child cannot cope with a situation he becomes anxious.

Mechanisms Emerging

The mechanisms that had emerged in the oral stage continue to operate with fixation, regression, introjection, and projection being operative. Although present in a very primitive form during the oral stage (13), a new mechanism, denial, emerges during the anal stage. Along with a gradually expanding sense of reality comes a contrary tendency, the denial of reality. Reaching full form in the second year and continuing in subsequent years, this is the process whereby a child (or an adult) can close his eyes, as it were, to an unpleasant truth and behaves as if it were not there. "If we close our eyes, it will go away," a not uncommon theme in cartoons, is illustrative.

Denial is an important facet of children's play. This denial of reality, this fantasy, is enthusiastically fostered by the child in his play. Toys, cops and robbers, the playing of the TV or movie hero of the moment, all breed this tendency at later ages. In infancy it is more primitive and simple but essentially the same. This tendency to use fantasy is abetted by an adult "conspiracy" to foster this mode of behavior. What child has not heard, "Oh it doesn't hurt," when, as a matter of fact, it does! However, this tendency of the adult to encourage denial wears thin or vanishes when the child fails to make the transition back to reality readily—on call, as it were.

All children, on occasion, show denial—for example, reluctance to come back from the wide open prairie or the high seas merely for the sake of eating lunch. Much more serious is the child who confuses reality with fantasy in such a fashion as to be unable occasionally to separate the two. Reality testing must, for normal adjustment to take place, exist side-by-side with the occasional mild use of denial of that reality in "play."

The Anal Character

Just as a child may bear a greater impress from the oral stage, so may the child who has developed disproportionate fixations and regressions from experiences of the anal stage develop an "anal character" in later life. As infants and children these individuals may have difficulty in learning to control the bowels. When this problem is finally overcome, certain anal character traits appear. In short, infantile toilet difficulties are replaced by adult character traits.

The three more prominent personality traits of the anal character are orderliness, parsimony, and obstinancy. Sometimes they are referred to as the three P's: pendantry, parsimony, and petulance. Orderliness in this context refers both to bodily cleanliness and to conscientiousness in the performance of petty duties. Parsimony refers to "tightness" about money and other matters even to the point of avarice. Obstinancy refers to unmovableness even to the point of defiance and irritability. Certain Scrooge-like characters in comic strips carry all three of these as prominent characteristics. A sadistic overlay of hostility or of desire to control other persons, or both, are also present in the anal character.

According to psychoanalytic theory, these characteristics are an extension of the child's compliance with his parents' wishes in regard to excretion. True, they may in this process become too compliant to their parents' wishes as extremes of these traits would suggest. Anal characters often show reaction formation, that is, the defensive transformation of a trait into its opposite. Thus, an undue interest in anal matters may be consciously paraded as a vociferous disgust with such matters. Orderliness of a compulsive character may reflect this defense mechanism. Sometimes there is a continuation of a childish desire to defy the parents in toilet training which shows itself as adult obstinancy. Parsimony as a characteristic is a more direct continuation of the habit of anal retentiveness itself.

A psychoanalytic case study

Psychoanalysis looks to the clinical study of individual patients for evidence to support the validity of its contentions. A more or less typical clinical report may exemplify the point. The case chosen for presentation deals with difficulties originating predominantly in the anal stage.

The boy described by Huschka was three-and-a-half and was seen in treatment sessions six times a week for two-and-a-half months. (The age of the child may cause some confusion. It was chosen because it illustrates how what happens in infancy may influence later development.) Psychoanalytically oriented play therapy was used. The play equipment included dolls, household furniture, trains, modeling clay, water, and at the window a Japanese dirt garden mentioned because it was incorporated into therapy. The boy was brought for treatment as a last resort because of a long history of constipation treated by diet, cathartics, and drugs. When seen, he was unable to have a bowel movement without an enema. Hereafter Huschka is quoted directly.

He was the older of two children, the younger being a girl of one-and-a-half years. . . . The mother, a petite, superficially gracious intellectual, was very tense; she obviously rejected the child and she was the type who quietly but relentlessly dominated those about her. In giving the history, the parents stated that the child had always been "regular" with respect to his bowel movements until the age of two-and-a-half years. At that time his nurse, who had cared for him since birth, and to whom he had been devoted, returned to her home in England. One week before she left he became constipated and he had remained so ever since. . . . In telling about the child's presenting symptom, the parents remarked incidentally that he also had a difficult personality. He was unhappy, petulant, irritable, and exceedingly stubborn, these characteristics being precipitated by the birth of his sister which occurred when he was two years old. As the father put it, "The little fellow sometimes acts as if he hates the whole world."

With regard to development, it was learned that in infancy there was difficulty with feeding. The child took the breast well but, because the supply of milk was inadequate, got only about three ounces at each feeding. Complementary feedings were therefore necessary. The mother said she disliked the nursing experience, the nurses making her feel inferior because she had so little milk. The child never seemed satisfied, and at three months he was taken off the breast altogether and fed by bottle. Although slow at emptying the bottle, he took it fairly well, and he seemed happier and gained weight. At five or six months there was a gradual addition of soft solids to the diet. This he did not like. The age at which the bottle was given up was not recalled.

Toilet training was effected by the nurse who cared for the child for the first two-and-a-half years of his life, and to whom he was devoted. She was an exceedingly neat, meticulous, strict woman. She began his toilet training when he was between three and four months old by holding him on a pot in her lap. The parents did not recall the length of time which it required, but it was "very short" and the nurse took pride in achieving quick toilet training. She was also fastidious about the child's general cleanliness, washing his hands many more times than was necessary. Obviously such training was coercive.

Clinical findings: The patient was a good-looking, blond-haired, blue-eyed, intelligent boy. The day he was seen for psychiatric examination he looked serious, unhappy, and harassed. Only once in the first session did he smile. A bit pale, he was fairly well nourished though not robust. He talked very little; usually he declined to respond to conversational leads, and when he did speak, his voice was low and conspicuously lacking in childhood enthusiasm. Negativism, an outstanding feature of his behavior, was demonstrated by his declining to have his wraps removed, refusing to come into the office and rebuffing all overtures to interest him in the toys. His need to control those about him was seen in the play with the truck when he ordered the physician about, also in the tea party play when he made her wait for her tea. Because of the child's refusal to enter the office, most of the treatment during the first few weeks had to be carried on either in the waiting room or in the hallway leading from there to the office. Significantly, on the day of his initial visit, the toy which he first began to play with was a truck with an automatic dumping device in the rear end, and throughout the entire treatment period this dump truck was one of the chief implements of his play. On leaving the office that day he asked if he might take the nursing bottle home, but on discovering the toy toilet, chose that instead and according to his mother, "He kept it in his hand all day."

The second day he suddenly picked up a piece of modeling clay and saying, "Want me to make something?" piled up a mass of clay, grunting and panting as he added blobs to it and pounded them into place. When he was asked what it was, he replied, "A castle." The castle, too, was a theme present throughout the treatment. He always guarded it and for some time he would not let the physician or any of the dolls come near it. In his play he crossly ordered the analyst about: "Make something," he shouted, or "Get up!" "Stay in that room." "Open the door" (in rear of truck). "Give me that dirt!" (from garden at window). As the treatment proceeded, hostility toward the analyst and toward each member of his household in turn became an outstanding feature of the play. Calling one of the dolls his sister and describing her as a "teeny, weeny baby," he said sweetly that she was "very nice," but simultaneously drowned her in a tub of water. In riding the dump truck he always backed into the office and he became anxious whenever the plasticine was about to pass through the hole in the rear, abruptly giving up his play and unloading it. Also he showed anxiety whenever his hands became slightly soiled, immediately having to wash them. After about two weeks of treatment, his mother telephoned that he was beginning to show "rage and temper" at home, screaming at his nurse and telling his mother to "Shut up!" He developed great interest in the messes which the new puppy made on the floor. At this time it was learned that his term for defecation was "making a dump." In the twentieth hour of treatment, when the child's hostility toward the physician was at its height, he expressed great hatred toward the doll whom he called "the mother," twisting off her head, crushing her and saying, "Bang! She's dead. She's all burned up. She's all dead now!" And he threw her across the room. His face during all this was vicious and there was clenching of fists and teeth. Shortly afterward he picked up the nursing bottle and threw it across the room, exactly duplicating the movements used in the earlier destruction of the mother. At this point in the treatment, friendliness toward the analyst began to appear from time to time, accompanied by verbalizations such as, "Would you like some presents?" Coincidently the child introduced play having to do with proffering gifts. A doll of plasticine, which he identified as his first nurse by a reference to her glasses—the nurse who had managed the toilet training—came in for a great deal of harsh treatment. "Crinkle her up! . . . Hit her with the gun." He pushed her across the room, then twisted off her head and broke her body in two. Suddenly he smiled sweetly and said, "She wears glasses and she's very funny," but quickly added, "Bang her on the ground. . . . Take that stone and bang her on the ground." He then began playing "the boy (doll) is sick," and decided to give him an enema. Holding "the enema thing," a colored crayon to the doll's anal region, he shouted in a vindictive tone, "Give him a lot! How much has he got now?" The father, represented by the Beccasine (amputation) doll, came in for destruction, too. In the fortieth hour the child tore him to pieces, saying, "He's a bad man." (What did he do that was bad?) "He slept with his mother last night. I'm going to spank him." He then spanked the doll and added, "And he hit his mother with his hand." This theme involving the father floated in and out of the treatment during the subsequent sessions. About two weeks later when the child again called the father "bad" and was again asked what the father did that was bad, he replied, "He gave his mother a kiss, he gave his mother a dump." A few days later, "He gave his kiss to his mother." (What else?) "He brought a birthday present to his mother." At that he pounded the father so viciously that he broke the neck of an unusually strong doll.

Coincident with all this release of anger at his family, the child's stubbornness gradually disappeared, he became amiable, and there was reduction of his uneasiness about dirt to the extent that the day following a particularly active session of aggression toward the physician, he spontaneously began playing in the mud from the Japanese garden. A little later (fifty-fifth hour), following play involving the inter-change of gifts which was stimulated by his sister's birthday party, he started taking the "castle" to pieces, and a few days later began smearing the sides of the dump truck with it. One day during this phase of treatment, on chancing to see a crib in the psychologist's examining room, he said, "I want to be a baby." In the baby-play period of regression that followed he passed flatus, gurgled and babbled in unintelligible monosyllables and he pawed the air with the poorly coordinated movements of an infant. Shortly afterward, when he began making mud pies, he let down completely with respect to his rigid cleanliness and enjoyed an ecstatic bout of smearing (60, 301–303).[5]

At this point treatment was terminated by the mother who felt that she could no longer defer hospitalization. Just before treatment at the hospital the boy had a normal bowel movement and after a complete intensive study was pronounced well.

The case was selected because of the classic picture it paints of a psychoanalytically interpreted and treated infantile neurosis in which a relationship is said to exist between coercive bowel training and the symptoms through which the child's neurosis expressed itself. Deprived in early infancy because of unsatisfactory breast feeding, the infant then met coercive bowel training at the hands of an excessively demanding nurse who started training during his third month. Frustrated again at the age of two-and-a-half by the permanent loss of this nurse, he showed the symptoms of persistent constipation on the basis of what was now an irritable stubborn negativism. Behind this stubbornness was marked hostility which, in the safety of the therapy sessions, found release in destructive aggression.

A hazard common in the clinical situation is the invariable selection of factors considered significant which are presented as evidence. The case history of this boy with anal difficulties may be used as an illustration. First, it is evident that Husckha did not report *everything* that went on in the approximately 65 hours of treatment. She had to select, and she undoubtedly did so on the basis of her theoretical preconceptions of what was significant. She looked for certain factors and perhaps ignored others. The clinical situation makes selection inevitable. The only safeguard against omissions of significant factors is the clinical experience of the investigator and the criticism of colleagues with whom he consults.

Evidence

From the comments in the previous chapter regarding the results on the relation of specific practices to general personality development, we would be prepared to take a skeptical view. Specific practice studies that do not support psychoanalytic contentions are not construed as evidence against psychoanalytic theory. A single factor, for example, that the child was (or was not) breast fed, cannot be interpreted meaningfully, except in the context of the enormous reaches of mother-child interactive behavior about which the single behavioral item tells us nothing. Only recently have infants themselves been studied in the light of controlled research methods.

Unfortunately, the research findings today most often are neither direct nor crucial tests of the validity of their theoretical position. Rather, they are tests of whether the facts on the basis of which the propositions have been advanced do or do not hold when checked by controlled research methods. It must also be noted that even if the facts do hold, it does not follow that their theoretical explanation is correct. Other assumptions may account for the facts equally well or even better.

The Oral Stage

The dominance of the oral zone is said to characterize the oral stage. Anyone even cursorily observing an infant during his first year will vouch for the importance of the mouth. But this does not give us a clear indication of oral dominance, a necessary prerequisite for oral libidinal theory to be correct.

One research study has attempted to do this. Lustman (72) stimulated 32 three-day-old babies both by massage and by air stream on the lips, the skin of the abdomen, the genitalia, and the anus. Response was measured by temperature increase in the stimulated area. Massage of the lips showed the greatest change in magnitude and air pressure in the same area was third in magnitude. The hyperresponsiveness of one infant was largely responsible for air pressure stimulation of the genitalia falling in second place. Dominance of the oral zone in early infancy is suggested. But variability is also suggested by the infant's sensitivity in the genital area. Oral primacy is relative, not absolute, and sensitivity in other areas is also present. In specific infants, sensitivity in another area may be even greater than mouth sensitivity.

It will be remembered that the psychoanalytic theory of the libido as manifested in the oral stage proposes that erotic pleasure arises from stimulation of the mucous membrane of the mouth. Sucking is the universal way this is expressed. If libidinal theory is correct, then sucking pleasure must be in large measure independent of sucking as related to hunger. Fenichel (32) contends that if erogenous stimulation does not occur, the infant would not suck his thumb since by so doing he produces no milk. This position follows from regarding the sexual drive (libido) as primary, hunger being regarded as merely one of the tissue needs of little importance to personality development.

Let us first consider some general observational findings. Obstetricians report finger sucking to be present before birth, as shown by a swollen thumb inserted in the mouth following the birth cry (40). Several observers (12, 53, 87) have reported sucking very shortly after birth. Gesell states that finger sucking is commonly evident in the first few weeks of life. He significantly adds that this is the case especially when the infant is hungry. Early appearance of sucking behavior indicates strength of this form of behavior.

In 1928 Levy (66), through a questionnaire, found from mothers that the frequency of thumb sucking in infancy was higher among those infants who took less time at breast or bottle. The finger suckers finished eating more quickly, because they were forced to by a time-limited feeding, because there was a very rapid flow of milk, or because they were fed by dropper. Those taking greater time turned out to be nonsuckers.

Levy (67) also found that when the sucking of puppies was interfered with, they engaged in nonnutritional sucking. Four puppies were taken from one litter and placed on bottle feeding. Amount of food was constant for all puppies. One pair sucked from nipples in which the holes were small, the "long-time feeders." The other pair was fed from nipples with large holes, the "short-time feeders." The latter tended to suck all kinds of objects between meals—towels, straws, their own, and each other's bodies. Levy argued that thumb sucking in human infants could be similarly explained because of the infant's inadequate opportunities to satiate his 'sucking impulse.' Levy's results were substantiated by independent studies.

Roberts (94) found that finger-sucking human infants during feeding actually sucked fewer minutes than those infants who were nonsuckers except at feeding. Yarrow's research (123) also supports this view. Using the carefully collected data of a longitudinal research program, he found that children having short feeding times developed severe thumb sucking.

These studies of Levy and the others lead easily, though not necessarily, as we shall see in a moment, to the conclusions that (1) the oral drive, expressed in sucking, is largely constitutional and the infant needs sucking satisfaction; and (2) the researches could be offered as support of the Freudian contention of the libidinal (drive) character of this oral behavior.

Probably no one would insist that sucking is completely independent of hunger. Freud himself postulated that there was an association. He considered sucking as related originally to one of the self-preservative functions (i.e., taking food) but later becoming independent of it. Nevertheless, many Freudians interpret nonnutritional sucking, occurring because of less nutritional sucking, as evidence that the sucking need is innate and as evidence for the libido concept. The question now arises whether this is so. The alternative position with which it may be contrasted is that sucking behavior is "a secondary drive established (or strengthened) through the almost universal rewarding of the sucking act by food getting" (98, 107).[6] Hence, the libido and the secondary drive interpretation are contrasted in terms of research findings.

[6] From Sears (98). Published 1950 by Annual Reviews, Inc., and used with permission.

A well-controlled study relating to the drive properties of oral activity and the reinforcements accompanying cup, breast, or bottle was performed by Davis, Sears, Miller, and Brodbeck (22). The investigators took the position that if sucking was an inherent biological drive, then cup babies, lacking opportunity to reduce their sucking drives during feeding, would show *more* nonnutritional sucking. On the other hand, if sucking were a secondary learned drive, cup-fed babies, having little opportunity to associate sucking with hunger reduction, would show *less* nonnutritional sucking. In their study, nonnutritional sucking strength was measured by length of time each infant sucked a nipple-covered finger.

At the end of ten days, infants who sucked at the breast developed a stronger sucking reflex than those who either sucked bottles or were fed by cup. This clearly supports the learning hypothesis. Cup feeding provided no reinforcement of the sucking response and bottle feeding, in view of the "open" type of nipples used, provided relatively little reinforcement. Breast feeding, on the other hand, provided repeated reinforcement. Thus the oral drive appears to be influenced by experience and the results suggest that spontaneous sucking activities may be a by-product of the almost universal method of feeding by letting the infant suck. Sucking acquires habit strength and thus becomes gratifying in its own right through primary reinforcement of hunger.

Another study of the effect of different amounts of rewarded practice in sucking was performed by Sears and Wise (101). If the oral drive is, in part at least, a product of the sucking act during food-taking, its reinforcement strength should vary with the number of opportunities for reinforcement. Thus, the longer a child feeds by sucking, the stronger his oral drive should be. Drawing on the private practice of a pediatrician, the investigators secured data on mothers and 80 normal children, aged two to seven, concerning child-rearing practices and the behavior of the children. The children were divided into three groups on the basis of information concerning the age of weaning. These groups were: (1) the early weaned (cup from birth, or weaned before two weeks); (2) the middle weaned (weaned between two weeks and three months); and (3) the late weaned (after four months). Thus, the groups differed in the amount of rewarded sucking experience, extending from the early weaned who had little rewarded sucking experience to the late weaned who had a great deal.

One measure of drive strength used was the number of frustration reactions to weaning (disliking meals, refusal to eat, irritability, and crying). Another measure of drive strength was the amount of thumb sucking. This was considered as a manifestation of oral drive strength on the basis of the reasons advanced earlier. It was hypothesized that if the strength of the oral drive increases with reinforcement, the more reinforcement, the stronger the drive will be, and the greater the frustration at weaning. The stronger the drive to suck, the more the child will be upset by weaning. The late-weaned children were found to have (1) the greatest number of frustration reactions to weaning; and (2) slightly greater incidence of thumb sucking. Thus the children whose sucking had been rewarded more frequently (the late weaned) were found to have the strongest oral drives. Put another way, the oral drive gets stronger with age, because sucking is rewarded.

The relationship between sucking and nourishment can be described in terms of instrumental acts and goal responses. As will be remembered, an instrumental act consistently leading to a goal response develops, in its own right, the properties of a goal response. Sucking is an instrumental act in infant feeding. Sucking, therefore, becomes a secondary goal response in infancy.

Sears, Maccoby, and Levin (99) in their "pattern" study of child rearing found evidence corroborating the finding that the later the weaning, the stronger the upset. About twice as many of their children showed "some upset when weaning was begun after eleven months of age as when it was begun under five months" (99, 86).[7] This group, it will be noted, was in general weaned later than those of the Sears and Wise study (whose "late" weaned were all weaned after only four months). This helps allay the suspicion arising from the criticism sometimes brought against the Sears and Wise study that the so-called late weaning at four months is really still early weaning.

Whiting and Child (119) also found relevant evidence in their cross-cultural comparisons among societies. Up until 13 to 18 months, age of onset of weaning increased as amount of emotional disturbance increased, but thereafter as age further increased emotional disturbance decreased. Weaning frustration increases with age and then decreases. But within the age range of the controversy over its libidinal character, weaning frustration increases with age.

The results obtained in the studies just presented must be discussed from two points of view: their relation to the results of Levy, Roberts, and the others and their implications for libido theory.

It must be emphasized that the Sears and Wise study in no way contradicts the results of Levy, Roberts, and the others. These other workers reported on puppies and babies *whose earliest feeding had been achieved by sucking.* In these instances when sucking during feeding

---

[7] From Sears, Maccoby, and Levin (99). Copyright 1957 by Row, Peterson, and published with permission.

was interfered with, nonnutritional sucking occurred. Sears and his colleagues reported, in part, on babies *who did not have sucking experiences at all.* For these babies who have not learned to suck, not sucking does not necessarily mean frustration.

The Sears studies show that it is possible to interpret sucking behavior in terms of a secondary goal response. If there is a sucking drive postulated, the data may be interpreted as indicating that this drive is increased by practice. The experiments discussed are not a direct test of libido theory. The Sears studies do not demonstrate that there is no primary oral drive or libido. Their results do, however, seem to weaken the necessity of postulating a libido to account for such behavior.

The more parsimonious explanation of nonnutritional sucking being a secondary learned drive makes libido theory less convincing. There is, of course, the possibility that, instead of a secondary drive, we are dealing with a habit or a conditioned response, but at any rate sucking is very definitely affected by learning (75). Sucking in nonnutritional settings does not seem innate, but learned.

Research studies on the oral character are relatively few in number. In general, they either do not support the psychoanalytic contention or are difficult to interpret because of ambiguities. The findings of Thurston and Mussen (115) do not support the psychoanalytic position. Using male college students as subjects, they collected information through their mothers about the presence or absence of breast feeding, the age of weaning, the duration of bottle feeding, and the strictness of the feeding schedule. The subjects themselves were given selected cards on the TAT. The TAT protocols thus secured were scored for various oral personality traits (dependency, pessimism, and so on). Tests of relationships between these traits and the criteria of gratification in infancy showed only chance relationships. Thus, no support was found for the concept of oral character structure. But it should be noted that the study did not take into account the interrelationships among, or the effects of, the various other stages of psychosexual development intervening between the subjects' experiences with these practices and the evaluation of their effects. Psychoanalysts might justifiably argue that the study is irrelevant.

Blum and Miller (14) studying third grade children found that the psychoanalytic traits attributed to the oral character did, in fact, cluster. Their measures of food intake, food interest, concern over giving, need for being liked, social isolation, and tolerance for boredom were intercorrelated above chance expectation. But other measures, theoretically expected to be correlated with the others, such as the children's need to be ingratiating, did not fall in this cluster. A partial agreement and partial disagreement with Freudian theory seems indicated by their results.

Goldman (51) has reported a factor analytic study based on self-ratings of adults. As subjects, she used 115 middle-class men and women—college students, personal friends, and neurotic patients in psychoanalytic treatment. She developed a variety of rating scales relevant to oral characteristics such as groups of items designed to measure optimism, pessimism, passivity, desire for the unobtainable, ambition, and dependence. The 19 scales she developed were standardized through various statistical tests of consistency. Reliability was checked and found to be adequate. Using the ratings of her subjects, she extracted two factors from the intercorrelations of ratings on these traits—pessimism-optimism and impatience-aggression-autonomy. She interpreted these two as factorial aspects of the oral character.

The major results of Goldman's studies (49, 50), which will now be explored, also favor accepting the validity of an oral character structure. She was interested in relating the characteristics of the oral "optimist" and of the oral "pessimist" to experiences of gratification or frustration in feeding in the oral stage. She did this by finding out the length of breast feeding of each of her subjects and relating it to the findings on the optimism-pessimism factor she had isolated in the previous phase of her study.

In this phase of the study with a group of adults, she found by correlation techniques how closely each of 100 subjects corresponded to the oral pessimist type. She also obtained from the mothers of these subjects information on the age at which they were weaned. Defining early weaned as those weaned at not later than four months, and late weaned as those weaned at nine months and more, she found significant differences between the two groups on oral pessimism scores. The correlation she found between early weaning and oral pessimism was .30. She also found that the early weaned tended to be located toward the oral pessimistic end of the scale, whereas the later weaned showed a tendency to develop oral optimistic characteristics.

There were certain ambiguities in her presentation that make her rather complex procedure difficult to follow and evaluate. It is not at all clear just how she separated her two extreme groups for factor analysis or whether she used the same subjects on the two phases of the study. This weakens the confidence we can place in her results. She herself concludes that there are factors other than duration of feeding involved in oral pessimism, as yet uninvestigated. This is told graphically by the relatively modest correlation of .30 she found, since this leaves 91 per cent of the variability unaccounted for. On the other hand, it will be remembered that the nature and extent of oral fixation according to Freudian theory depends not only on many other oral phenomena but on events in later stages as well. In the light of what we know about specific practice studies and that only information on weaning was used by her, any significantly positive correlation at all is somewhat surprising. Other neglected oral phenomena might supply the unaccounted-for 91 per cent of variance. We simply do not know.

Although the psychoanalytic theory of orality and oral character receives some support from the literature surveyed, it is not particularly impressive. Again the relation of specific practices to personality characteristics can, at the most, be said to receive only slight support. It is clear, however, that oral behavior is important in spite of the fact that sucking would appear to be a secondary learned drive.

The Anal Stage

It will be recalled that the psychoanalytic position calls for libidinal interests at this stage to be directed toward anal matters—particularly expelling and retaining feces. The task now before us is to examine the research evidence relevant to the psychoanalytic interpretation of the anal stage.

Unlike the oral stage, there is no direct research evidence, other than from clinical experience, indicating whether the pleasures of the anal stage are to be considered as subsumed under an "anal" primary drive or whether they might be considered as arising from learning. Direct evidence concerning the pleasures associated with anal elimination and retention seems difficult, if not impossible, to obtain. It is clear that infants are as interested in feces as they are in other objects or parts of the body.

Knowledge of anality is found in studies in which there has been interference with functioning in this area. For example, there is some evidence concerning the pernicious effects of coercive bowel training. Huschka (60, 61) made a study in child guidance clinics of the incidence of emotional disturbances as related to bowel and bladder training. Over half of the children had been started on bowel training "prematurely," or the training had been accomplished by coercive methods, such as the use of shaming, a rigid schedule, or unduly frequent placement on the toilet. Many of the children reacted immediately during or following training in that they showed a history of constipation, diarrhea, fear, negativism, excessive cleanliness, and guilt. In the individual histories of their later difficulties, she could trace a direct connection between events in toilet training and subsequent maladjustment. She concluded that coercive training is an important determinant of personality disturbance.

Methodologically, the study is weakened by the absence of a control group. True, the percentages are high, but without knowledge of comparable figures in normal children, it may be a noncausative purely incidental relationship. The results are suggestive in that they support the contention that severe practices in this area are followed by immediate temporary upset and (less certainly) by later problem behavior. Her findings, too, are in line with clinical experience which would predict that socialization in this area is accompanied by strong emotional reactions and sometimes by personality disturbances.

Amount of emotional upset created by toilet training was studied in the Sears "pattern" study (99). It was found that emotional disturbance of their normal child subjects was most prevalent (in about 45 per cent of the cases) if the age at beginning of training was 15 to 19 months. Training beginning both before and after these ages produced the least amount, with five to nine months' onset or after 20 months' onset of training conducive to the least number of children showing upset. Severity of training (scolding and punishing for deviation, frequent taking to toilet) by these mothers did not succeed in completing training any sooner, but it did produce emotional upset.

Over half of the most severely trained children showed some disturbance, whereas no more than one-sixth of the least severely trained showed disturbances. These findings, it must be remembered, are based on the mothers' opinions, not upon independent verification by outside sources. Hence, the results are not as conclusive as one would like.

It is clear that the results are not incompatible with general psychoanalytic theory, but the evidence does not demonstrate conclusively the correctness of the psychoanalytic position. The findings are also compatible with both learning theory and frustration theory.

A major group of research investigations on anal character represents attempts to find out whether the alleged characteristics of orderliness, parsimony, and obstinacy are actually interrelated. In these studies, no attempt is made to study the infancy or childhood of the subjects. Naturally, the studies tell us nothing about the *origin* of the triad of characteristics mentioned above, merely whether they are interrelated.

Sears (97) had the members of a college fraternity, who knew one another well, rate one another on the three characteristics of obstinancy, parsimony, and orderliness. He then calculated the intercorrelations of these ratings. They were all about .37, showing a positive interrelation of the three characteristics.

Using college students as subjects, Beloff (8) factor analyzed statements from a questionnaire on anal traits, both for self-statements and for impressions of peers. In both instances a single factor of anality was found. He compared a group of statements by graduate students about their anal traits with their bowel training histories obtained through interviews with their mothers and found no significant relationships between the two. However, the anal characteristics of the mothers, as determined by the questionnaire, were significantly related to the anal characteristics of their offspring. He concluded that the anal character forms a meaningful dimension, that it is not related to the toilet training experiences of his subjects, but that it is related to the anal characteristics of their mothers.

Barnes (4) performed a factor-analysis involving material selected as appropriate for the oral, anal, and phallic stages. The research is reported at this juncture because insofar as he found corroborative findings they apply at the anal stage. From the psychoanalytic literature, he first derived a number of trait adjectives, such as "stingy," associated with each of these stages. A large number of college students rated themselves on these trait adjectives. The trait scores thus derived were intercorrelated and a factor analysis was performed. He found an anal factor including meticulousness, orderliness, reliability, law abidance, and cleanliness. This factor is clearly in lines with psychoanalytic theory. Two of the remaining factors he found offered some, but less, support at the other two psychosexual stages.

Five other factors which he found, however, could not be explained by any Freudian hypothesis. The nonsupportive factors had clustering of tests which included in their composition some theoretically placed at the oral, anal, and phallic levels. For example, the factor of "externalized aggression," as he named it, was made up of "phallic" tests of aggression but also included sadism (anal), biting (oral), and several others from each of the three psychoanalytic levels. He concluded that the Freudian theory of levels of psychosexual development was not, as a whole, supported by his results.

Rapaport (89), in still another investigation, first developed a self-rating scale consisting of items relevant to experiences of the anal stage. Items were developed to measure obstinancy, orderliness, and parsimony. One type was multiple-choice items concerned with preferences, interests, and reactions to social situations. Representative were the items which asked about hobbies which were appealing, or interest in saving money. Responses showing interest in collecting were interpreted as showing anal interests, as was emphasis on the saving of, or the spending of, money.

The second type of item involved selecting from pairs of proverbs the one of the set which expressed the person's feelings. A typical item would be the choice between "A wise man turns chance into good fortune," and "A bird in the hand is worth two in the bush." In this instance, the one with the anal slant should be obvious.

The third type of item was similar to those used by Goldman and consisted of descriptions of habits on which the subjects were to rate themselves. Typical items included saving odds and ends, operating according to a system, and disinclination to lend money.

The items he constructed were submitted to three psychoanalytically-oriented psychologists with a request that they judge their applicability to the problem of anality. Items judged unsuitable by them were eliminated. The remaining items considered applicable were administered to college student subjects. An item analysis was then performed. Reliability was also checked and found satisfactory. The "purified" items were administered to a cross-validation group and intertrait correlation calculated. The results in terms of intertrait correlations involving orderliness, obstinancy, and parsimony yielded only one statistically significant correlation, instead of three, which would have been predicted in line with psychoanalytic theory.

So far this study resembles other intertrait studies, but Rapaport went beyond this. By means of TAT protocols he now investigated the extent of felt aggression, feeling of persecution, preoccupation with financial matters, and obsessive compulsive concerns with cleanliness and with control of the environment. In each instance, it was hypothesized that anal characters would tend to show to a greater extent the end of the continuum suggested by these terms than would nonanals. The "anal" person would be expected to show more aggression, more feelings of persecution, and so on, than would the nonanal person. Subjects were college students who were at either extreme on the anality scale previously developed.

To these subjects he administered the TAT and had judges score the protocols obtained against the criteria mentioned previously. Although the majority of obtained differences were in the predicted direction, none of them was statistically significant. So, again, we have a study showing some slight support for the psychoanalytic point of view, but not with sufficient decisiveness that psychoanalytic contentions were verified conclusively.

The study of Beller (6, 7) (page 232) is relevant to the question. He showed oral and anal behavior to be related to dependency and also found that the ratings for oral traits and anal traits were correlated .57 and .64 respectively for boys and girls. Children high (or low) in oral behaviors are also high (or low) in anal behaviors. Since the correlations are rather high, they tend to cast doubt on the distinction between a separate oral and anal character.

Another method of research attack on the problem of the anal character involves trying to relate the nature of the toilet training experiences received in infancy to later personality characteristics. In the course of a more extended study dealing with other issues, Wittenborn and his associates (120) secured information concerning the relation of aggressiveness in children to the severity of their toilet training. Severe toilet training (early placement on toilet, ridicule or hitting for soiling, disgust on part of mother for child's messes) was significantly correlated with the child's aggressiveness (anger with the mother or other children, calling names, having a temper tantrum, and doing spiteful things). At age five in one group the correlation was .36 and at age eight or nine in another group the correlation was .30. Sears and his associates (100), in the antecedent study, also found that severity of toilet training in boys had a positive relation to later aggression. This was not the case in the girls they studied.

A more extended study of the relation of toilet training to later characteristics was undertaken by Bernstein (10). Drawing on a sample of children attending a public well-baby clinic, he studied the relation between coercive toilet training and certain characteristics in later childhood. Information on 47 children, about five years of age at the time of the study, was obtained from the clinic records, play interviews, and observations which he carried out. Sixty-six per cent of these children were considered to have been coercively trained. The criteria of coercion used were training begun before six months of age, or training begun later which was accompanied by punishment if the child failed to comply. The noncoercively trained children were so classified if they were started in their toilet training after they were six months of age and they received no punishment for their mistakes.

A variety of measures was used to supply information about the children's behavior at the time of the study. Information on their tendency to collect stamps, coins, and so on (collecting) was obtained from the interview. They were observed on how much smearing of fingerpaints and cold cream occurred (smearing). Their willingness to leave the mother to go into the playroom for the interview was measured by the time consumed in getting them to do so (separation anxiety). Their willingness, or lack of it, to perform six tasks at the request of the investigator during the session was observed (negativism). Information on constipation, uncommunicativeness, and immaturity was also obtained. There was a statistically significant relationship between coercive toilet training on the one hand and separation anxiety, negativism, uncommunicativeness, and immaturity on the other. But no relationship was found between coercive training and collecting, constipation, or smearing. Again the results found sometimes favored the psychoanalytic contention, sometimes not.

Controlled investigation gives some support to psychoanalytic theories of the oral and anal stages. The results, however, are predominately negative. It may be, when negative results are found, that we are in the position of pursuing a delicate, finely spun theory with unsuitable and clumsy tools. Chasing butterflies with a meat-axe is an analogy. Whatever the reason, positive research evidence is scanty. If the orthodox psychoanalytic theories of orality and anality be accepted in their entirety, it must be on the basis of clinical evidence obtained in psychoanalytic hours, not on the basis of controlled research evidence.

A *neo-freudian interpretation*

An attempt to reconcile Freudian clinical insights with results from non-Freudian research sources is referred to as a *neo-Freudian interpretation*. A familiar instance is to be found in considering the emergence of a sense of self. The psychoanalytic contention of failure to meet needs was combined with other factors to account more completely for its emergence. A neo-Freudian interpretation implies rejection of some Freudian contentions and acceptance of others. Naturally, there is variation of acceptance and rejection from one interpretation to the next, resulting in differences of opinion among interpreters. Nonetheless, two points on which many neo-Freudian interpretations agree involve rejection of libido as a driving force and minimization of the paramount position given to the sexual motive.

Orality and anality meet the criteria of behavior tendencies, namely the presence of interrelated responses and response tendencies with roughly comparable drives and goals. But by the same token, orality and anality are just *two* among a variety of behavior tendencies rather than *the* drives of infancy.

Dependence-independence, aggression and externally aroused behavior tendencies have been presented as being of considerable importance in personality formation in infancy. Sexual aspects of behavior in infancy are narrower and less important, whereas other behavior tendencies are broader and more important than orthodox psychoanalytic thinking would admit. No special energy is postulated to account for oral and anal behavior, and the results of the various investigations reviewed earlier in which oral and anal behavior were interpreted as secondary learned drives are easily assimilated if this view is accepted. The position just sketched has the virtue of being more congruent with what we know to be operative from socialization and culture than is the concept of a blind primordial force called libido. To postulate libido as a special energy source is unnecessary and nonparsimonious. Instead, both constitutional and learning factors are considered to be effective in these and, perhaps, other unidentified behavior tendencies.

Acceptance of the concept of infantile sexuality in its all pervasive form is not required. The analogy to the flowering from a tulip bulb put so poetically by Josselyn as quoted in Chapter 5 is seen as a bit forced and broad. We can define a life instead of a flower in such a fashion, too, so that relationship between amoeba and man, which does exist, is there for all to see. But man and amoeba are discriminable, one from the other. Scientific progress is seldom served by subsuming discriminable variables under this same conceptual category. Infants are intensely emotional, and derive pleasure from sucking and elimination. But there are emotions and sucking and eliminatory pleasures separable from adult sexuality, even though personality being all of a piece will show relationship in adulthood between such behavior and adult sexually motivated behavior. Sensory pleasure and sexual pleasure are interwoven in adult life. In infancy, the sensual predominates.

None of the evidence discussed detracts from the Freudian insistence, now accepted quite generally, that much of an infant's interests are occupied with oral and anal matters. That which absorbs so much of his time and energy (as well as that of his parents) cannot be disregarded. Consider the number of repetitions of feeding and toilet experiences facing the infant. Conservatively estimating an average of from four to six feedings a day, he is fed nearly 4,000 times during the first two years of life. Soiling occurs, say, from six to ten times a day. In the first year alone somewhere around 2,000 changes of diapers take place. Repetition of the two problem situations over and over again is certainly present during infancy. It is plausible to infer that many habitual attitudes and behavior patterns will be acquired during these repetitions. The terms orality and anality are still considered appropriate for the ages under scrutiny. They are seen as important features of the total situation which the infant faces at this age.

Another neo-Freudian interpretation that has gained considerable acceptance emphasizes much more than Freud, the importance of social factors. Freud developed what he considered to be a picture of *innate* instinctual development. Most orthodox psychoanalytic statements concern behavior imbedded in developmental sequences with little emphasis on the socializing facets as separable from the maturational. It is, however, possible to relate the phenomena he observed more closely and coherently with the research findings described if modification is made leading to an emphasis on social factors.

In a social context the oral and anal stages function as critical periods. Child psychologists of many different theoretical persuasions, other than psychoanalytic, accept certain child situational relationships at a particular age as being of crucial importance. In the course of socialization, the infant typically faces certain problems. If the conflicts and difficulties of a period are surmounted, the child proceeds toward adequate adjustment. Failure to meet the demands of the period through unsatisfactory resolution of the conflicts will in varying degrees mar personality development and the sense of self.

The particular susceptible age at which socialization pressures in connection with a given tendency are applied form a critical period. It is the age limits in each tendency where its effects are most pronounced. Although critical periods are not generally considered to be a part of psychoanalytic thinking, the concept may be appropriately applied to what the psychoanalysts call the psychosexual stages. In brief, the present writer would consider that the phenomena of infancy occurring during the psychosexual stages may be interpreted as instances of critical periods.

The very concept of critical periods suggests that the significance of socialization pressures should vary with the age of the child to whom they are applied. The effects should vary in that critical periods vary with age, and socialization pressures are capable of being applied too early, optimally, or too late. Thus the psychoanalytic findings concerning psychosexual stages which stand research scrutiny may be subsumed under the rubric of critical periods. This introduces a flexibility that the psychosexual stage theory lacked. The psychoanalytic position called for certain fixed stages, and no others. In terms of critical periods, the ones psychoanalysts identify are found to be important. But there may be others that also deserve consideration, not included in their scope.

Oral Tendencies

The oral tendencies arise from their relations to the hunger drive. Many oral phenomena become in themselves secondary drives. Among the more important of these already discussed is sucking. Orality is important because the mouth provides a major means whereby the infant contacts the world. In the words of Thompson, a prominent neo-Freudian:

> The oral stage seems to be chiefly determined by biological development. The newborn infant is chiefly a mouth. The most developed part

of the cortex at birth is that which governs the oral zone.   We are justified in assuming that the infant contacts the world and comprehends it in the beginning primarily in terms of the mouth.   We, however, question whether the erotic satisfaction obtained is the determining factor. It seems more likely that he contacts the world by mouth because it is the most adequate organ.   Thus the oral stage is organically determined but not primarily because of its pleasure value (113, 35).[7]

Orality is a major determinant of the infant's reactions to other people.   If the situation is a pleasurable one, hunger tensions and secondary drives, such as sucking, become attached through identification with the mother figure.   Thus, emphasis may be placed upon the relation of mother and infant in which the latter uses the mouth as a means of contact, rather than orality as a drive.   The reality in which the infant is immersed even at the oral level is social in that the mother and her ministrations make it a social situation.   Milk may be nonsocial, but the agency bringing it to him is not.

Behavior-social learning theory may be used to account for the development of this relationship between mother and infant.   By responding to his needs, she is associated with tension-reduction experiences and thus acquires reward value.   But if her mothering is inadequate, either expressed through negative factors such as rejection or through dilution of the relationship as in an institution, then the infant will not have these pleasant tension-reduction experiences and the first reaction to other people will be frustrating.

A general, though perhaps implicit, hypothesis held by many neo-Freudian investigators and practitioners is that gratification in the infantile feeding aspects of the oral tendencies generalize to other situations. Thus, satisfaction and security in relations with the mother spread to other social situations.   One way this is expressed is what Erikson (28) refers to as a sense of trust—a sense that the world can be approached confidently and handled adequately.   Similarly, dissatisfaction and insecurity will also generalize.   The infant and child builds his attitudes toward the world from his experiences with his own little world.   How well his needs are met, how secure he feels will help to establish his later attitudes, not only towards himself, but also towards the world and toward other individuals.   Orality is one of the ways these attitudes are learned.

Anal Tendencies

The middle part of the second year of life is critical in that parents may credit the child with more ability than they should.   The child

[7] From Thompson (113).   Copyright 1950 by Clara Thompson, and published with permission.

walks and talks a bit, and seems to "understand" much of what is going on about him. Therefore, discipline is instituted by parents in the form of toilet training.

To make the matter specific, just what is toilet training? Certainly, it involves the child's learning to withhold expulsion of feces and urine until the "proper" time and place. Thus expulsion and retention appear as facets of the learning process. Aside from these essential similarities there are wide differences in how parents and children work out the problem. Some parents may emphasize regularity—the child should defecate at regular intervals. If he fails to have a movement during the day, the mother may worry or resort to enemas. With still other parents, the emphasis may be on cleanliness rather than schedules. The child should not wet or soil himself. No matter what pattern of emphasis may develop, there is little question that toilet training is an important experience in the life of children in our culture.

A plausible neo-Freudian interpretation would place the emphasis in the anal stage on the struggle with the parents, rather than the pleasure from expelling and retaining of feces. Emphasis is shifted from the erotic pleasure to the interpersonal situation. The infant does not originally want to develop the habits which are the goals for our methods of toilet training. His wishes are quite different from those of his parents. In fact, we have here a major source of conflict between the infant's needs and the parent's wishes. Unlike the case of the feeding situation, what he wants to do and what the parents want him to do are not the same. Toilet training is not a need and satisfies no drive in the infant of this age. This, however, does not mean that there are no anal interests on the part of the infant. They are there, but the emphasis can be placed on the relinquishment of something pleasurable to the demands of socialization.

Toilet training demands the substitution of voluntary control for involuntary or reflex action. This makes toilet training a function of learning. In learning terms there must be a "reversal of a strong innate connection between a cue and a response" (27, 137).[8] A full bowel originally produces automatic evacuation. This original sequence is broken by toilet training given the child. The automatic discharge must be held while a definite sequence of behavior gradually develops. The child must learn to call his mother and go through the usual steps of waiting until undressed and placed on the toilet. Then, and only then, may evacuation take place in a socially approved manner. He also learns loathing and disgust for these originally pleasurable objects.

[8] By permission from *Personality and Psychotherapy* by Dollard and Miller. Copyright 1950. McGraw-Hill Book Company, Inc.

He also learns, if he is to be conventional, to restrict verbal reference to the process of defecation to medical consultations and to humor.

If trained coercively (too early or punished severely), it would be predicted on the basis of learning principles that this would both generalize and produce personality disturbances in much the same way as rats faced with an insoluble problem. Huschka's results reported earlier are a case in point. Moreover, studies confirm the prediction that early imposition of training delays the acquisition of control (50). Enuretic problems were found to follow in normal boys who were slow maturing physiologically and who had been started on training too early to be followed by success.

The child, during this period, learns not only from his struggles for independence with the parent over toilet training but also from conflicts with the parents in other areas of his daily life. He must give up any sense of omnipotence and take his place as a dependent child, assuming the role of a satellite to a dominant parental figure (2). Exaggerated resistive behavior is a consequence. He is at an age where he can crawl and walk. He can get into prohibited areas, for example, the sidewalk or road. He can break precious objects and grasp dangerous ones. These, too, enter the picture as part of his "training" period. How he is encouraged or prohibited in these areas as well as in toilet training probably also influences his personality development.

The so-called temper tantrum as a reaction to a frustration, major or minor, is characteristic of this age and may readily be interpreted as the infant's attempt to maintain his integrity in the face of parental pressures. Stubbornly refusing to be trained is a quieter more prolonged manifestation of this same behavior mechanism.

If learning to conform to parental authority is accepted as crucial to the anal stage, the so-called anal characteristics, such as cleanliness and orderliness, can be seen as among the goals of socialization, or, as Kardiner puts it, "forms of acquiescence to cultural demands" (64, 44).[9] In our culture, these characteristics are highly prized virtues. In another culture, such as Pilaga, they would hardly apply and the "anal" stage may take quite a different course and have radically different outcomes.

If cultural factors are important and causative in the patterns of personality that emerge from this or other stages, then we are in a better position to understand the exceptions found in the research. For example, sometimes, the "anal character," in a classic pristine sense, may emerge from the vicissitudes of this period. But more often, other, perhaps as yet unrecognized, characteristics may be acquired precisely be-

[9] From Kardiner (64). Copyright 1939 by the Columbia University Press, and published with permission.

cause the anal stage involves more than the orthodox psychoanalytic position would postulate. Specific maternal practices and attitudes will enter the situation in such a fashion as to make it impossible methodologically to account for the effect of these other variables.

Anal matters generalize into the sexual area. The infant does not clearly differentiate between toilet training and sexual functioning and, if truth be told, neither does the mother (99). The same words are apt to be applied by the mother during sex and toilet training. It is plausible to believe that generalization of training of bladder and bowel will extend over sexual behavior as well. This may be one of the reasons not only for the relation of sex and anal matters but also for anxiety about sex and a belief that it is somehow, "dirty."

For Further Reading

Some basic references to psychoanalysis were given in connection with Chapter 5. Thompson (113) gives a representative neo-Freudian account.

References

1. Ambrose, J. A.   The development of the smiling response in early infancy. In B. M. Foss (Ed.), *Determinants of infant behavior.* New York: Wiley, 1961, 179–196.
2. Ausubel, D.   Negativism as a phase of ego development.   *Amer. J. Orthopsychiat.,* 1950, 20, 796–805.
3. Banham, Katherine M.   The development of affectionate behavior in infancy. *J. Genet. Psychol.,* 1950, 76, 283–289.
4. Barnes, C. A.   A statistical study of Freudian theory of levels of psychosexual development.   *Genet. Psychol. Monogr.,* 1952, 45, 105–175.
5. Behrens, Marjorie L.   Child rearing and the character structure of the mother. *Child Develpm.,* 1954, 25, 225–238.
6. Beller, E. K.   Dependence and independence in young children.   *J. Genet. Psychol.,* 1955, 87, 25–35.
7. Beller, E. K.   Dependency and autonomous achievement striving related to orality and anality in early childhood.   *Child Develpm.,* 1957, 28, 287–315.
8. Beloff, H.   The structure and origin of the anal character.   *Genet. Psychol. Monogr.,* 1957, 55, 141–172.
9. Berlyne, D. E.   Recent developments in Piaget's work.   *Brit. J. Educ. Psychol.,* 1957, 27, 1–12.
10. Bernstein, A.   Some relations between techniques of feeding and training during infancy and certain behavior in childhood.   *Genet. Psychol. Monogr.,* 1955, 51, 3–44.
11. Bishop, Barbara M.   Mother-child interaction and the social behavior of children.   *Psychol. Monogr.,* 1951, 65, No. 328.

12. Blanton, Margaret G. The behavior of the human infant during the first thirty days of life. *Psychol. Rev.,* 1917, 24, 456–483.
13. Blum, G. S. *Psychoanalytic theories of personality.* New York: McGraw-Hill, 1953.
14. Blum, G. S., and D. R. Miller. Exploring the psychoanalytic theory of the "oral character." *J. Pers.,* 1952, 20, 287–304.
15. Bowlby, J. *Maternal care and mental health.* Geneva: World Health Organization, 1951.
16. Brackbill, Yvonne. Extinction of the smiling response in infants as a function of reinforcement schedule. *Child Develpm.,* 1958, 29, 115–124.
17. Bridges, Katherine, M. B. Emotional development in early infancy. *Child Develpm.,* 1932, 3, 324–341.
18. Brody, Sylvia. *Patterns of mothering: maternal influences during infancy.* New York: International Universities Press, 1956.
19. Buhler, Charlotte. The social behavior of children. In C. Murchison (Ed.), *Handbook of child psychology.* (2nd ed., Rev.) Worcester: Clark University Press, 1931, 374–416.
20. Caldwell, Bettye M., *et al.* Mother-infant interaction in monomatric and polymatric families. *Amer. J. Orthopsychiat.,* 1963, 33, 653–664.
21. Coleman, Rose W., E. Kris, and Sally Provence. The study of variations of early parental attitudes: a preliminary report. *Psychoanal. Stud. Child.,* 1953, 8, 20–47.
22. Davis, H. V., R. R. Sears, H. C. Miller, and A. J. Brodbeck. Effects of cup, bottle and breast feeding on oral activities of new born infants. *Pediatrics,* 1948, 3, 549–558.
23. Dennis, W. Infant development under conditions of restricted practice and of minimum social stimulation. *Genet. Psychol. Monogr.,* 1941, 23, 143–189.
24. Dennis, W., and Marsena G. Dennis. Development under controlled environmental conditions. In W. Dennis (Ed.), *Readings in child psychology.* New York: Prentice-Hall, 1951, 104–131.
25. Dixon, J. C. Development of self recognition. *J. Genet. Psychol.,* 1957, 91, 251–256.
26. Dollard, J., L. W. Doob, *et al. Frustration and aggression.* New Haven: Yale University Press, 1939.
27. Dollard, J., and N. E. Miller. *Personality and psychotherapy.* New York: McGraw-Hill, 1950.
28. Erikson, E. *Childhood and society.* New York: Norton, 1950.
29. Escalona, Sibylle K. Approaches to a dynamic theory of development: round table, 1959:3.Discussion. *Amer. J. Orthopsychiat.,* 1950, 20, 157–160.
30. Escalona, Sibylle. Emotional development in the first year of life. In M. J. E. Senn (Ed.), *Problems of infancy and childhood: transactions of the sixth conference.* New York: Macy, 1953, 7–92.
31. Federov, V. K. Cited in Harriet L. Rheingold, and W. C. Stanley, Developmental psychology. *Annu. Rev. Psychol.,* 1963, 14, 1–28.
32. Fenichel, O. *The psychoanalytic theory of neuroses.* New York: Norton, 1945.
33. Flavell, J. H. *The developmental psychology of Jean Piaget.* Princeton: Van Nostrand, 1963.
34. Freud, Anna. Some remarks on infant observation. Psychoanal. Stud. Child, 1953, 8, 9–19.

35. Freud, S. A general introduction to psychoanalysis. Garden City: Garden City Publishing, 1943.

36. Fries, Margaret E., and P. J. Woolf. Some hypotheses on the role of the congenital activity type in personality development. Psychoanal. Stud. Child, 1953, 8, 48–62.

37. Gardner, D. B., G. R. Hawkes, and L. G. Burchinal. Noncontinuous mothering in infancy and development in later childhood. Child Develpm., 1961, 32, 225–234.

38. Gardner, D. B., D. Pease, and G. R. Hawkes. Responses of two-year-old children to controlled stress situations. J. Genet. Psychol., 1961, 98, 29–35.

39. Gesell, A., and Catherine S. Amatruda. Developmental diagnosis: normal and abnormal child development: clinical methods and pediatric applications (2nd Rev. ed.). New York: Hoeber, 1947.

40. Gesell, A., and Frances L. Ilg. Feeding behavior of infants: a pediatric approach to the mental hygiene of early life. Philadelphia: Lippincott, 1937.

41. Gesell, A., et al. The first five years of life: a guide to the study of the preschool child. New York: Harper, 1940.

42. Gewirtz, J. L. A learning analysis of the effects of affective privation in childhood. Acta Psycholgica, 1961, 19, 404–405.

43. Gewirtz, J. L. A learning analysis of the effects of normal stimulation privation and deprivation on the acquisition of social motivation and attachment. In B. M. Foss (Ed.), Determinants of infant behaviour. New York: Wiley, 1961, 213–299.

44. Goldfarb, W. Infant rearing and problem behavior. Amer. J. Orthopsychiat., 1943, 13, 249–265.

45. Goldfarb, W. The effects of early institutional care in adolescent personality. J. Exp. Educ., 1943, 12, 106–129.

46. Goldfarb, W. Psychological privation in infancy and subsequent adjustment. Amer. J. Orthopsychiat., 1945, 15, 247–255.

47. Goldfarb, W. Effects of psychological deprivation in infancy and subsequent stimulation. Amer. J. Psychiat., 1945, 102, 18–23.

48. Goldfarb, W. Variations in adolescent adjustment of institutionally-reared children. Amer. J. Orthopsychiat., 1947, 17, 449–457.

49. Goldman, Frieda. Breast feeding and character formation. J. Pers., 1948, 17, 83–103.

50. Goldman, Frieda. Breast feeding and character formation, II. J. Pers., 1950, 19, 189–196.

51. Goldman-Eissler, Frieda. The problem of "orality" and its origin in early childhood. J. Ment. Sci., 1951, 97, 765–782.

52. Gray, P. H. Theory and evidence of imprinting in human infants. J. Psychol., 1958, 46, 155–166.

53. Halverson, H. M. Mechanisms of early infant feeding. J. Genet. Psychol., 1944, 64, 185–223.

54. Harlow, H. F. The nature of love. Amer. Psychologist, 1958, 15, 675–685.

55. Harlow, H. F. Primary affectional patterns in primates, Amer. J. Orthopsychiat., 1960, 30, 676–684.

56. Heathers, G. Emotional dependence and independence in nursery school play. J. Genet. Psychol., 1955, 87, 37–57.

57. Hebb, D. O. The organizations of behavior: a neuropsychological theory. New York: Wiley, 1948.

58. Hess, E. H.   Imprinting: an effect of early experience, imprinting determines later social behavior in animals. *Science,* 1959, 130, 133–141.
59. Hess, E. H.   Two conditions limiting cultural age for imprinting. *J. Comp. Physiol. Psychol.,* 1959, 52, 515–518.
60. Huschka, Mabel.   The child's response to coercive bowel training. *Psychosom. Med.,* 1942, 4, 301–308.
61. Huschka, Mabel.   A study of training in voluntary control of urination in a group of problem children. *Psychosom. Med.,* 1943, 5, 254–265.
62. Jones, Mary C.   The development of early behavior patterns in young children. *J. Genet. Psychol.,* 1926, 33, 537–585.
63. Josselyn, Irene M.   *Psychosocial development of children.* New York: Family Service Association, 1948.
64. Kardiner, A.   *The individual and his society.* New York: Columbia University Press, 1939.
65. Kubie, L. S.   Margaret A. Ribble. The rights of infants: comments. *Psychoanal. Stud. Child,* 1945, 1, 415–416.
66. Levy, D. M.   Finger-sucking in and accessory movements in early infancy: an etiologic study. *Amer. J. Psychiat.,* 1928, 7, 881–918.
67. Levy, D. M.   Experiments in the sucking reflex and social behavior of dogs. *Amer. J. Orthopsychiat.,* 1934, 4, 203–224.
68. Levy, D. M.   *Maternal overprotection.* New York: Columbia University Press, 1943.
69. Levy, D. M.   The early development of independent and oppositional behavior. In R. R. Grinker (Ed.), *Mid-century psychiatry.* Springfield: Thomas, 1953, 113–121.
70. Lorenz, K. Z.   *King Solomon's ring: a new light on animal ways.* New York: Crowell, 1952.
71. Lorenz, K. Z.   Morphology and behavior patterns in closely allied species. In B. Schaffner (Ed.), *Group processes.* New York: Josiah Macy, 1955, 168–220.
72. Lustman, S. L.   Rudiments of the ego. *Psychoanal. Stud. Child,* 1956, 11, 89–98.
73. Macfarlane, Jean W., Lucile Allen, and Marjorie Honzik.   *A developmental study of the behavior problems of normal children between 21 months and 14 years.* Berkeley: University of California Press, 1955.
74. Maudry, Maria, and Maria Nekula.   Social relations between children of the same age during the first two years of life. *J. Genet. Psychol.,* 1931, 39, 393–398.
75. McKee, J. P., and Marjorie P. Honzik.   The sucking behavior of mammals: an illustration of the nature-nurture question. In L. Postman (Ed.), *Psychology in the making.* New York: Knopf, 1962, 585–661.
76. Mednick, S. A., and J. B. P. Shaffer.   Mother's retrospective reports in child-rearing research. *Amer. J. Orthopsychiat.,* 1963, 33, 457–461.
77. Miller, D. R., and M. Hutt.   Value interiorization and personality development. *J. Soc. Issues,* 1949, 5, 2–30.
78. Murphy, G., Lois B. Murphy, and T. M. Newcomb.   *Experimental social psychology.* New York: Harper, 1937.
79. Murphy, Lois B.   *The widening world of childhood: paths toward mastery.* New York: Basic, 1962.
80. Newton, N. R., and M. Newton.   Relationship of ability to breast feed and maternal attitudes toward breast feeding. *Pediatrics,* 1950, 5, 869–875.

81. O'Connor, N., and C. Franks. Childhood upbringing and other environmental factors. In H. J. Eysenck (Ed.), *Handbook of abnormal psychology: an experimental approach.* New York: Basic, 1961, 393–416.
82. Orlansky, H. Infant care and personality. *Psychol. Bull.,* 1949, 46, 1–48.
83. Piaget, J. *Play, dreams, and imitation in childhood.* New York: Norton, 1951.
84. Pinneau, S. R. A critique of the articles by Margaret Ribble. *Child Develpm.,* 1950, 21, 203–228.
85. Pinneau, S. R. The infantile disorders of hospitalism and anaclitic depression. *Psychol. Bull.,* 1955, 52, 429–452.
86. Porter, B. M. Measurement of parental acceptance of children. *J. Home Econ.,* 1954, 46, 176–182.
87. Pratt, K. C., A. K. Nelson, and K. H. Sun. The behavior of the newborn infant. *Ohio State Univ. Contrib. Psychol.,* 1930, No. 10.
88. Rabin, A. I. Behavior research in collective settlement in Israel: infants and children under conditions of "intermittent" mothering in the kibbutz. *Amer. J. Orthopsychiat.,* 1958, 28, 577–586.
89. Rapaport, G. M. A study of the psychoanalytic theory of the anal character. Unpublished doctoral dissertation, Northwestern University, 1955.
90. Rheingold, Harriet L. The modification of social responsiveness in institutional babies. *Monogr. Soc. Res. Child Develpm.,* 1956, 21, No.2.
91. Rheingold, Harriet L., and Nancy Bayley. Later effects of an experimental modification of mothering. *Child Develpm.,* 1959, 30, 363–372.
92. Rheingold, Harriet L. The measurement of maternal care. *Child Develpm.,* 1960, 31, 565–575.
93. Ribble, Margaret A. *The rights of infants.* New York: Columbia University Press, 1943.
94. Roberts, E. Thumb and finger sucking in relation to feeding in early infancy. *Amer. J. Dis. Child.,* 1944, 68, 7–8.
95. Ross, S. Sucking behavior in neonate dogs. *J. Abnorm. Soc. Psychol.,* 1951, 46, 142–149.
96. Salzen, E. A. Visual stimuli eliciting the smiling response in the human infant. *J. Genet. Psychol.,* 1963, 102, 51–54.
97. Sears, R. R. Experimental studies of projection: I. Attribution of traits. *J. Soc. Psychol.,* 1936, 7, 151–163.
98. Sears, R. R. Personality. *Annu. Rev. Psychol.,* 1950, 1, 105–118.
99. Sears, R. R., Eleanor E. Maccoby, and H. Levin. *Patterns of child rearing.* Evanston, Illinois: Row, Peterson, 1957.
100. Sears, R. R., J. W. M. Whiting, V. Nowlis, and Pauline S. Sears. Some child-rearing antecedents of aggression and dependency in young children. *Genet. Psychol. Monogr.,* 1953, 47, 135–236.
101. Sears, R. R., and G. W. Wise. Relation of cup feeding in infancy to thumb-sucking and the oral drive. *Amer. J. Orthopsychiat.,* 1950, 20, 123–138.
102. Sewell, W. H., and P. H. Mussen. The effect of feeding, weaning, and scheduling procedures on childhood adjustment and the formation of oral symptoms. *Child Develpm.,* 1952, 23, 185–191.
103. Sewell, W. H., P. H. Mussen, and C. W. Harris. Relationship among child training practices. *Amer. Sociol. Rev.,* 1955, 20, 137–148.
104. Shirley, Mary M. *The first two years: a study of twenty-five babies. Vol. I. Intellectual development.* Minneapolis: University of Minnesota Press, 1933.

105. Skeels, H. M. *et al.* A study of environmental stimulation: the orphanage preschool project, *Univ. Iowa Stud. Child Welf.,* 1938, 15, No. 4.
106. Spitz, R. A. Hospitalism. *Psychoanol. Stud. Child,* 1945, 1, 54–74.
107. Spitz, R. A. Hospitalism: a follow-up report. *Psychoanol. Stud. Child,* 1946, 2, 113–117.
108. Spitz, R. A. The importance of the mother-child relationship during the first year of life: a synopsis in five sketches. *Ment. Hlth Today,* 1948, 7, 7–13.
109. Spitz, R. A. The psychogenic diseases in infancy: an attempt at their etiologic classification. *Psychoanal. Stud. Child,* 1951, 6, 255–275.
110. Spitz, R. A., and K. M. Wolf. The smiling response: a contribution to the ontogenesis of social relations. *Genet. Psychol. Monogr.,* 1946, 34, 57–125.
111. Stone, L. J. A critique of studies of infant isolation. *Child Develpm.,* 1954, 25, 9–20.
112. Stott, D. H. An empirical approach to motivation based on the behavior of the young child. *J. Child. Psychol. Psychiat.,* 1961, 2, 97–117.
113. Thompson, Clara. *Psychoanalysis: evolution and development.* New York: Hermitage, 1950.
114. Thompson, W. R., and W. Heron. The effects of restricting early experience on the problem-solving capacity of dogs. *Canad. J. Psychol.,* 1954, 8, 17–31.
115. Thurston, J. R., and P. H. Mussen. Infant feeding gratification and adult personality, *J. Pers.,* 1951, 19, 449–458.
116. White, R. W. Motivation reconsidered: the concept of competence. *Psychol. Rev.,* 1959, 66, 297–333.
117. Whiting, J. W. M. *Becoming a Kwoma.* New Haven: Yale University Press, 1941.
118. Whiting, J. W. M. The frustration complex in Kwoma society. In C. Kluckhohn and H. A. Murray (Eds.), *Personality in nature, society and culture.* New York: Knopf, 1948, 137–145.
119. Whiting, J. W. M., and I. L. Child. *Child training and personality.* New Haven: Yale University Press, 1953.
120. Wittenborn, J. R., *et al.* A study of adoptive children. *Psychol. Monogr.,* 1956, 70, 1–115.
121. Wood-Gush, D. G. M. Comparative psychology and ethology. *Annu. Rev. Psychol.,* 1963, 14, 175–200.
122. Wylie, Ruth C. *The self concept: a critical survey of pertinent research literature.* Lincoln: University of Nebraska Press, 1961.
123. Yarrow, L. J. The relationship between nutritive sucking experiences in infancy and non-nutritive sucking in childhood. *J. Genet. Psychol.,* 1954, 84, 149–162.
124. Yarrow, L. J. Maternal deprivation: toward an empirical and conceptual reevaluation. *Psychol. Bull.,* 1961, 58, 459–490.
125. Zemlick, M. F., and R. I. Watson. Maternal attitudes of acceptance and rejection during and after pregnancy. *Amer. J. Orthopsychiat.,* 1953, 23, 570–584.

PART III

EARLY CHILDHOOD

11

Individual Development

THE PERIOD of early childhood starts at the age of three and lasts through the age of five. Psychological development in this period may be seen from examining the same processes considered in relation to infancy. Thus, let us take up in sequence physical growth, motor, emotional, cognitive, perceptual and conceptual, and language and intellectual development.

Physical growth

The years of early childhood continue the rapid physical growth in height and weight so obvious in infancy but at a somewhat slower pace (7). Different parts of the body, however, have different periods of rapid and slow growth so that the proportions are changing throughout childhood with the skeleton remaining more stable while fat deposits increase and diminish. There are anatomical changes conveniently classified (58) as changes in kind, as in prenatal life with the appearance of new types of cells; changes in number, as in the sheer quantity of cells, in organs, teeth, and bones; changes of position, as in that of the heart and the teeth which shift position at different ages; changes in size, shape, and composition, as in darkening in eye color or skin.

At five years of age the average child will have gained about nine inches in height from that of age two (74). A weight gain of about four or five pounds per year will also be found. Here again there is variability between the slow-growing and fast-growing child. At five

289

the average boy weighs 43 pounds and is 44 inches tall. The girl is slightly shorter and lighter. By five a child's stature is a fairly good indicator of his final mature height since the correlation between the height measures at five and at maturity has been found to be .70.

Sensorimotor development

During these years the child coordinates the motor skills he has established, and learns many new ones. The five-year-old, says Gesell (31), is poised and controlled, with an economy of movement and an adeptness with fingers and hands—a far cry from the clumsy, uncoordinated two-year-old. Indeed, by the age of three most of the traces of the clumsiness of the infantile patterns in motor behavior have disappeared.

Gesell and his associates (30) mention as characteristic of the three-year-old his ability to accelerate and decelerate in walking and running, to turn sharp corners, to go upstairs by alternating his feet, and to stand on one foot, even though only for short periods of time. From the child's perspective, being three years old is being at the age when he is ready to leave behind the infantile "kiddy car" with its primitive, shoving form of propulsion for the tricycle with its complicated means of movement. Jumping, climbing, and riding tricycles occupy a not unconsiderable portion of the preschool child's time. Such activities are derived essentially from the simpler ones of infancy, but carried out with considerably greater ease and efficiency. New skills also appear.

Learning and Maturation in Sensorimotor Skills

The influence of learning may be readily seen in such skills as talking, writing, and buttoning clothes. Maturational influences are not confined to infancy, but are also operative during the preschool period. Since several studies produce substantially similar results, only one illustrative study, that of Hicks (39), will be reviewed. Sixty children between two-and-one-half and six-and-one-half years of age were divided into two groups on the basis of their initial ability in throwing balls at a moving target. The experimental group practiced ten throws once a week for eight weeks. Thereafter, both groups were retested and found to have made gains. However, the experimental group was not significantly better in performance than was the control group who received no practice. It would appear that improvement in skill did not result from the specific practice in throwing balls, which the one group had, but resulted from maturation and autogenous learning.

Autogenous learning refers to the fact that children, whether or not they were actually throwing at a moving target, were, in the course of their daily living, practicing many of the coordinations of body, eye, arm, and hand which are utilized in the complex skill of hitting a moving target. As far as clarity of results is concerned, this complicating factor of autogenous learning appears to be an insuperable obstacle to a clear demonstration of maturational effects with children. Specific practice may be instituted by the experimenter or parent, but the child continues to live and learn (practice) in ways which probably affect the results obtained. Nevertheless, it is plausible to believe that maturation is still taking place.

Stages of Motor Development

A given motor skill may be considered as passing through stages beginning with nonachievement, or absence of skill, through various degrees of proficiency. Gutteridge (35), in connection with some research to be considered in a moment, developed a rating scale defining steps of motor development. Specific motor skills of a child may be evaluated against this scale. Table 10 is adapted from her work.

TABLE 10

DEGREES OF MOTOR SKILL *

Stage	Degree of Motor Skill
No attempt made	1. Withdraws or retreats when opportunity is given.
	2. Makes no approach nor attempt but does not withdraw.
Skill in process of formation	3. Attempts activity but seeks help or support.
	4. Tries even when not helped or supported, but is inadept.
	5. Is progressing but is still using unnecessary movements.
	6. Is practising basic movements.
	7. In process of refining movements.
Basic movements achieved	8. Movements coordinated.
	9. Easy performance with display of satisfaction.
	10. Evidence of accuracy, poise, and grace.
Skillful execution with variations in use	A. Tests skill by adding difficulties or taking chances.
	B. Combines activity with other skill or skills.
	C. Speeds, races, or competes with self or others.
	D. Uses skill in larger projects such as dramatic play.

* Adapted from Gutteridge (35). Copyright 1939 by the Archives of Psychology, and published with permission.

Four general stages of major motor development are indicated: the first stage in which no attempt is made to carry out the motor skill in question; the second stage in which the skill is the process of formation; the third stage in which the basic movements have been achieved; and the fourth stage in which there is skillful execution with variation in its use. Within each stage there are various degrees of skill. The use of initial letters beyond the first ten numbered degrees of skill indicates Gutteridge's recognition that beyond the point in the scale which indicates skilled performances, the child uses his skills in all sorts of variations of the activity executed, despite no further increase in proficiency. It is only in the first three stages that we have degrees of increase in skill in any strict sense. A rating of eight or better on her scale is considered as indicating the child is proficient in the particular motor skill. Although another investigator might use another way of formulating the stages and degrees of motor skill, her scale has enough generality to be of significance quite apart from the research in which it has been used. These four major stages and their related, more precisely defined degrees of motor skill are considered applicable to the motor skills of childhood in general.

Some changes in motor skills. Gutteridge (35) used ratings of these degrees of motor skill in an investigation of various activities of nearly 2,000 children, most of whom were four, five, and six years of age. The motor activities studied were climbing, jumping, sliding, tricycling, hopping, galloping, skipping, throwing, bouncing, and catching balls. Teachers, trained as raters, made the necessary observations in the natural settings of classroom and playground. No attempt at special training in these skills was given; the children's own "methods of attack" were studied. The degree of proficiency exhibited by the children at each age level was ascertained for each activity. Four of these activities exemplify her results.

Climbing was "proficient," as defined for the test, at the end of the third year in nearly 60 per cent of the children. By the end of the sixth year, 97 per cent were proficient. Considerable variability was found; a child or two in the sample was proficient before reaching two years of age, and three per cent of them were still not proficient even at the end of the sixth year. The children climbed on every conceivable piece of equipment whether it was designed for this purpose or not. Anything with height might become a challenge to climb. Most of them climbed as high as opportunity afforded. Some "stunting" occurred even at as young an age as two years.

Jumping was proficient in 40 per cent of the children by the age of three-and-a-half, whereas about 85 per cent were efficient by the age of six. There was a sharp rise in the percentage of proficiency from the youngest child to that of the four years, six-months-old children for whom the median rating was nine points. From this age on, there was relatively little increase in proficiency since for the oldest, six-year group, the median rating was only a little over nine. Variability was considerable at all ages. In the five-year group the range covered nine of the ten possible points, while even in the six-year group it still covered six points.

Tricycling was an accomplishment in which at three years of age, 63 per cent of the children were proficient, while by four years of age 100 per cent were proficient. Doing tricks on a tricycle was very evident as most mothers know; riding backwards, turning corners, and navigating narrow spaces were common.

Ball-throwing was a motor skill in which even some of the two- and three-year-old children showed proficiency. By the end of the sixth year, about 85 per cent were proficient. Range of achievement at all ages, even the oldest, extended from awkward to excellent.

These, then, are some representative findings on the development of some motor skills in preschool children in relation to chronological age. It is pertinent to consider comparative skill among the activities at a given age. In general, Gutteridge's study indicates that a fair proportion of children are proficient in some motor activities before the age of three years, ranging from 17 per cent in tricycling to 50 per cent in sliding. However, proficient use in the throwing and catching of balls and control of movements in such activities as hopping, skipping, and galloping do not appear before age four or five.

Sex differences and variations were found within the individual child. Boys are ahead of girls in climbing, jumping, sliding, skipping, and ball-throwing; girls are more proficient in tricycling, galloping, hopping, bouncing and catching balls. Variation within each child from one skill to another was also noticeable, although Gutteridge states there is some evidence of consistency of pattern. This consistency appears to be tendencies for each child to use certain kinds of motor movements to the relative exclusion of other kinds.

Interrelation among Motor Skills

Some workers would argue that there is a high and positive interrelation among motor skills. For example, Ames (2), as a consequence of studying manual and locomotor behavior in infants, stated that slow creeping means slow climbing and slow prehending. Bayley (6) found considerable evidence of substantial correlations among infant motor abilities. However, she suggested there was a possibility that motor functions at later ages were more discrete and independent than in infancy.

The evidence tends to bear out Bayley's suggestion that there is greater functional independence of motor abilities at the preschool ages than during infancy. A representative study is that of Hartman (38) who studied a variety of gross motor coordinations in about 60 boys and girls who were between four and six years of age. The motor tests she used were the hurdle jump, jump-and-reach, standing broad jump, baseball throw, and the thirty-five-yard dash. After establishing the proficiency of each child, she intercorrelated the achievement scores of the children. She found intercorrelations ranging between only 0.36 and 0.56.

Hartman concluded (correctly in the writer's opinion) that different motor abilities were being sampled rather than a general motor ability. A child who is high in one motor skill may not be high in another motor skill. A child may even be quite unskilled in one motor performance and still do quite well in others. Or, to put it in terms of specific skills, knowing a child's skill in throwing a baseball does not enable us to predict with any degree of certainty what he would do on the hurdle jump. We cannot speak of "motor ability"; rather there are motor abilities with a child excelling in one not necessarily excelling in another.

This point of view receives support from factor analytic studies. If motor ability were a unitary matter, then factor analysis should show the existence of a general motor factor. Instead, often several group factors emerge when this matter is studied in children. For example, using 250 children from the first three grades, aged six through ten as subjects, Carpenter (17) applied a battery of motor tests and then performed a factor analysis. She found three factors—a strength factor, a speed factor, and a factor of sensory-motor coordination that was associated with ball-handling. Disregarding this last more limited group factor, a speed factor and a strength factor were isolated. It would seem that at least two of the major components of motor ability are speed and strength. Strength measures seem to be interrelated and speed measures seem to be interrelated, but there appears to be much less relation between those for strength and those for speed.

Presumably other factors, perhaps not yet isolated, are operative in determining motor ability. At any rate, we would expect that more elusive possible determinants, such as interest or lack of interest, willingness or unwillingness to take a chance, intrepidity or timidity in the face of a challenging activity, and self-confidence or the lack of it, might influence proficiency in motor skills. However, the evidence concerning the influence of these determinants is either nonexistent or confusingly contradictory. Thus, little more is possible than to assume that these factors do influence motor skill. Speed and strength, at any rate, are factors in the motor skills of early childhood.

Emotional development

The emotions of young children continue to show the differentiated patterns already established in infancy. As in infancy, the two streams of emotion differentiated from excitement, the unpleasant, disruptive emotions such as anger and fear, and the pleasant, integrative emotions, will again provide a framework for discussion. Maturation continues to play a part. Nevertheless, the topics to be discussed, appearance of these emotions, developmental changes in expression, frequency, and duration, and the immediate causes for their appearance, all indicate the relatively great influence of learning during the childhood years.

Anger

The physiological responses in anger, such as change in heart rate and blood pressure and tenseness and crying, are not learned, but appear to be innately determined. The relationship, however, between these responses and what at one time in the history of the child were neutral (nonemotional) cues is a matter of learning. Stimuli which originally did not elicit the physiological responses now do so. The child learns to be angry about certain situations that previously did not arouse these responses.

In a now classic study, Goodenough (34) investigated anger in 50 children (most of whom were of preschool age) in such a definitive fashion that her results still merit detailed discussion. The mothers of these children kept daily records of the anger incidents that occurred, noting the time, the place, and the duration of the outburst, the immediate cause, and the kinds of behavior they exhibited. From records kept for periods extending from about one to four months, Goodenough collected over 1800 instances of anger outbursts.

Developmental changes in expressions of anger. Goodenough's first classification of the expressions of anger was more global and consisted of classification in terms of the direction the energy was expended—(1) undirected energy—anger not directed toward any end except that of an emotional outlet, such as in kicking randomly, holding the breath, and screaming; (2) motor or verbal resistance—anger expressed in opposing doing what was asked, such as verbal refusal or resisting being held; and (3) retaliation—anger expressed in motor or verbal attempts at revenge, such as biting the agent or giving him a verbal scolding.

As the children increased in age from about two to five, there was a steady decline in expression of anger in mere random discharge, no consistent trend in connection with expression through motor or verbal resistance, but an increase in expression through retaliating behavior. These age trends appear to verify common observations concerning undirected discharge of anger as characterizing younger, immature children and an increase in retaliative behavior with increasing age. Failure to separate motor from verbal resistance may have obscured the possibility that motor resistance decreases with age as verbal resistance increases. Thus, with increasing age expressions of anger are less random and more directed toward something or someone.

The second approach that Goodenough used took the form of study of the various specific acts associated with anger. Crying was the most frequently encountered form of vocal behavior up to about four years of age. Nevertheless, crying decreased fairly regularly with increase in age. Kicking decreased as well, but stamping increased slightly, whereas striking increased regularly, and throwing self on floor increased until age three and four and then decreased. Goodenough found that these were the major specific acts during anger. Contrary to popular opinion, jumping up and down, stiffening the body, making the body limp, refusing to budge, and glaring "defiantly" were some of the less common forms of expressing anger at these ages. Holding the breath also belongs in this less common category, since only four instances occurred in the 1,800 outbursts that she studied.

Developmental changes in frequency and duration of anger outbursts. Figure 10 presents Goodenough's findings on age and sex differences in the frequency of anger outbursts. Omitting the findings for children under one year of age because of the small number of cases (two children), rapid decrease is found in anger outbursts with increasing age from the initial high point at the age of one-and-a-half years. The sharp decline in anger with increase in age probably reflects the older child's increasing sensitivity to social demands and increasing ability to meet frustration by forms of behavior other than anger. A

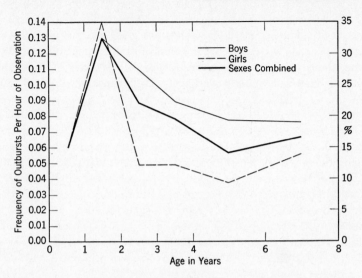

Figure 10. Frequency of anger outburst as related to age and sex. (Florence L. Goodenough, Anger in Young Children. Copyright 1931 by the University of Minnesota.)

consistent sex difference, with girls showing fewer anger outbursts, is also apparent. The results help us to understand the contention, often made, that boys are more difficult to raise than girls. It also represents a difference in the sex roles, with boys showing the expected greater amount of aggressiveness.

According to Goodenough's findings, the duration of specific anger outbursts underwent little change during the first eight years of life. In other words, there was no particular evidence of decrease or increase in duration as age increased. Fewer than one-third persisted for as long as five minutes.

Developmental changes in the immediate causes of anger. Goodenough found certain categories of immediate causes of anger to encompass adequately her findings—(1) *conflicts over routine physical habits,* such as objection to going to the toilet, to bed, to coming to meals, or to having the face washed; (2) *conflicts with authority,* such as the child's response to being refused permission to carry out some activity, to being forbidden some activity in progress, to being punished, and to having to take the logical consequences of his own act; and (3) *problems of social relationship,* such as being denied attention, inability to make desires understood, a blocking of desires to share in the activities of others, an unwillingness to share, or a desire for someone else's possession. In terms of the percentage of the total number of anger outbursts at all ages, those in connection with routine physical care made up over 20 per cent, conflicts with authority nearly 20 per cent, and problems of social relationship nearly 30 per cent. These three immediate causes of anger totaled nearly 70 per cent of all the incidents the mothers reported.

A few of Goodenough's subjects were under two years of age, making possible a comparative account involving later infancy as well as childhood. During the second year, she found the major source of anger to be conflict over establishment of routine physical habits. Almost equally prevalent was anger brought about by conflict with authority.

In children between the ages of three and four, social difficulties, particularly difficulties with playmates, reached their maximum, accounting for nearly 45 per cent of all outbursts. Conflicts with authority and over routine physical habits account for an additional 35 per cent. In children four years and older, social problems continue to be the largest single category. Conflict with authority accounts for 35 per cent of the anger outbursts.

Anger, even at these ages, may appear in other social settings than the home, particularly the nursery school. Landreth (49) found nearly 40 per cent of the anger outbursts related to conflicts with persons and about the same per cent related to personal care routines (where a parent was present in the situation). In the nursery school, on the other hand, about 75 per cent of all outbursts involved social conflicts with other children or with adults.

In another study, Ricketts (65) found similar results concerning the relative differences in the source of anger in nursery school and in the home. These two studies, as well as that of Goodenough, attest to the increased importance with age increase of social conflict as the immediate cause of anger in younger children.

General conditions for the appearance of anger. The nature of the immediate disturbing circumstances giving rise to anger has been examined. Let us turn now to the general conditions that cause anger. The activity that the child is engaged in at the moment affects his response to the immediate disturbing circumstance. In other words, it is not simply some stimulus to anger alone which we must consider, but also the activity and state of the child at the time the immediate cause for anger occurs. A hungry child playing desultorily is not angered by the call to lunch, but a child not so hungry and engrossed in his play as well may be angered by this same call.

Other factors, such as his general physical condition, may also enter.

For example, a hungry child who has a cold may react angrily to the call to lunch even if not particularly wrapped up in his playing.

Goodenough in her study found a variety of general conditions that lower the threshold for anger. Frequency of anger outbursts was positively related to: (1) *the time of day,* in the sense that more anger outbursts occurred at certain hours, namely, either just before mealtime or after eight in the evening when fatigue had set in; (2) *condition of temporary poor health,* such as the child having a cold or being constipated; and (3) *atypical social conditions,* such as the presence in the home of visitors. A comment by Goodenough in connection with these factors is relevant.

> It should be noted that the establishment of a relationship between any or all of these factors and the frequency or duration of anger outbursts does not always afford evidence as to the essential nature of the relationship. An increased number of outbursts may be due either to the increased irritability of the child himself, causing him to become disturbed over minor conditions that would ordinarily be ignored, or to external factors involving an increase in the irritating conditions to which the child is subjected. Variations in the frequency of anger may thus be brought about either by internal conditions resulting in differential responses to constant stimuli or by external conditions affecting the frequency and intensity of the annoyances to which the subject is exposed. Although the nature of the factor under consideration in many instances enables us to infer with a fair degree of certainty whether its major influence is external or internal, there are other cases in which either or both types of influence may be at work (*34,* 84–85).[1]

Individuality in anger. Individual differences in expressing anger must be noted. Anger in each child will differ in its direction, frequency, duration, and susceptibility to general conditions. Goodenough in her study of anger lists, among other specific forms, kicking, stamping, jumping up and down, throwing oneself on the floor, holding one's breath, pulling, struggling, pouting, frowning, throwing objects, grabbing, biting, striking, crying, and screaming. No child would be "talented" enough to display all these forms of becoming angry in one or in many settings. He would have his own particular repertoire with a definite preference for some and not for others. Moreover, with the passage of time, he would show his own unique changes in his repertoire of the acts used in expressing anger.

Anger and frustration-aggression. The most general conclusion to be drawn from the over-all results of the Goodenough study is that the commonest source of anger she found were situations which interfered

[1] Florence L. Goodenough, *Anger in Young Children.* Copyright 1931, University of Minnesota.

with the goal-seeking behavior of the children. In short, anger is produced by frustration which leads to aggression on the part of the children. On this point Sears said:

> The theoretical derivation of aggression suggests that its origin lies in the effectiveness of producing pain in others as a method of removing their interference with goal-directed behavior. For example, if the mother fails to provide the child with food when he is hungry or with attention when he is seeking affection, he may strike her or cry loudly enough to make her uncomfortable.
>
> In order to eliminate this pain or discomfort, she may then give the child food or offer it affection. This reward act not only reinforces the early, and perhaps more or less random, acts of injuring the mother, but it does two additional things. First, it establishes the act of hurting, as exemplified by the mother's expressions of dislike or pain, as a secondary drive. Increasingly thereafter, with continuing reinforcement, the child therefore secures pleasure from injuring other persons. Second, the immediate stimulus situation that accompanied the rewarding act becomes an effective stimulus for eliciting the acts he used at that time. In other words, the child who is rewarded for his injurious acts develops a secondary drive of aggression (i.e., to make a goal response of injuring others, the necessary environmental event being to see the expressions of pain), and he learns to repeat the act when he is frustrated.
>
> Goodenough also found, as have a number of other investigators, that not every aggressive or angry act was immediately preceded by a discernible frustration. This suggests that other stimulus aspects of the frustrating situation besides the fact of frustration itself, i.e., the mother, mealtime, cross talk between parents, are sufficiently often associated with frustration to become the instigators to aggression (68, 230–231).[2]

It is probably the path of caution to accept the possibility that there are multiple causes of anger. True, children may show anger when needs are frustrated, but the general conditions found by Goodenough to lower the threshold for anger, such as poor health, also appear to be operative as aspects of the dynamics of anger.

Fear

Fear in young children will be discussed in almost the same sequence as anger. As a means of centering discussion, the studies of fear by Jersild and Holmes (49) will serve in the same fashion as did Goodenough's study of anger. In their work there were two major phases, the observational and the experimental study. In the first study they had parents record on observation forms all situations in which their children displayed fear during a specified period. The nearly 140

[2] From Sears (68). Copyright 1953 by Henry Holt and Company, and published with permission.

children who were observed for fear incidents ranged in age from under one year to slightly over 12 years of age. The procedure in this study was much the same as Goodenough's. In the second or experimental study, other children, aged from two to six years, were invited to enter into situations, such as coming into a dark room, which were known to be effective in causing fear in at least some children of this age.

Developmental changes in expressions of fear. In Chapter 7, it was indicated that fear was found by Bridges to differentiate from the "distressed" pattern at about six months of age. As might be expected on the basis of our knowledge of the work of Bridges (*11*), fear in later infancy is expressed in a global fashion. Crying, along with general bodily distress, characterizes fear at this age.

As children become older, fear responses become increasingly specific. With increasing maturity fear becomes more often expressed in a withdrawing from the fearful situation. The preschool child runs away, avoids fear-provoking situations, or, when faced with such situations, uses verbal responses such as, "Take it away."

Developmental changes in frequency of fear. In the Jersild and Holmes parent-observation study they had mothers report any fears which they had noted in their children during a 21-day period of observation. After two years of age the number of fears sharply declined. For the group of two-year-olds, the average daily number of fears was about six, but for the next year group the average number of fears was only 3.7. For the four-to-five-year group only two fears per child were reported. Variability, however, at any one age level is so great that some children at all ages deviated considerably from the average.

Since their experimental study was based on the study of *selected* fears, there may have been an inclusion of fears to which children of certain ages were relatively more susceptible. Consequently, all we can say from examining Table 11 is that for the fears included in this study the two- and three-year-olds showed about an equal amount of fear, whereas the four- and five-year-olds showed a considerable decrease. The two studies show no particular discrepancies.

The decrease in frequency of fear needs to be related to developmental changes in the expression of fear. The diminution of overt signs of fear—the characteristic crying, trembling, shrinking away or retreating—does not necessarily mean that there is no longer as much fear as before in the life of the child. This decline may be a decline only in overt expression of emotion similar to that already noted in the case of anger. In our culture social pressures against displaying fear are

TABLE 11

PERCENTAGE OF CHILDREN AT YEARLY AGE LEVELS WHO SHOWED FEAR IN
RESPONSE TO THE VARIOUS EXPERIMENTAL FEAR SITUATIONS [*]

Age in Months

Situation	24–35 Percentage Showing Fear	36–47 Percentage Showing Fear	48–50 Percentage Showing Fear	60–71 Percentage Showing Fear
Being left alone	12.1	15.6	7.0	0
Falling boards	24.2	8.9	0	0
Dark room	46.9	51.1	35.7	0
Strange person	31.3	22.2	7.1	0
High boards	35.5	35.6	7.1	0
Loud sound	22.6	20.0	14.3	0
Snake	34.8	55.6	42.9	30.8
Large dog	61.9	42.9	42.9	0
Average	32.0	30.2	18.1	4.5

[*] Adapted from Jersild and Holmes (49). Copyright 1935 by Teachers College,
Columbia University, and published with permission.

operative. Moreover, many of the more symbolic fears characteristic
of the older child leaves him with nothing to "flee" from, since such
fears do not have as definite a locus as do the earlier, more specific
fears. Transitory feelings, a minor tremor soon concealed, a slight
trembling of the lip, clammy hands, and the like may for him be the
only expressions of fear displayed. These manifestations of fear are
easier to overlook than are the more frank, obvious, open ones shown
at a younger age. Fear is still shown; the overt manifestations produced have declined in frequency.

In the experimental study of Jersild and Holmes, intelligence and sex
differences were found to be related to the number of fears the children
expressed. There was a correlation of .53 between intelligence and
number of fears for the children in the 24 to 35 months' range. In
other words, the smarter the child was at this age, the greater the
instances of fear. This relation may be seen as to be expected if we
consider that fear may arise after appraising the dangerous qualities of
a situation. Some children, more advanced intellectually than the
others of the same age, were able to perceive danger where other
children did not. Since intelligence is at least partly a matter of
maturation, it suggests that maturation plays a role in children's fears.
A precocious child is afraid of situations that do not disturb other
children of the same age until they are older.

For the specific situations they studied, the correlation between fear and intelligence declined to almost zero by the age of five. By that age all of the children were able to perceive the fearsome aspects of these situations, so intelligence was no longer a factor. This may be true only for the specified situations. Other situations might be found where the relation between intelligence and number of fears again became a positive one.

In almost every situation of the Jersild and Holmes study the percentage of girls at a given age who showed fear was higher than the percentage of boys. This finding is in keeping with general observation that girls tend to show more fear than do boys.

Developmental changes in the immediate causes of fear. The immediate causes of fear in the experimental study have already been presented in Table 11. Those selected fears of being left alone, falling boards, a dark room, a strange person, the possibility of falling from high boards, a loud sound, a snake, and a large dog, with one exception, show a decrease with age. Only the fear of snakes was manifested by roughly the same percentage of children throughout all ages. No child between five and six years of age showed fear in these situations with this one exception.

The findings for fear situations in the observational study are reported in Table 12. Many fears show either a steady fall (noises and falling) or an irregular fall (animals, sudden rapid motion, and strange objects) with age. Except for fear of strange objects, no child older than five years of age showed fear in any of three situations just mentioned. Other fears (pain, the dark, harm, and being alone) show an increase with age.

Those fears that decline and those that increase with age form two roughly distinguishable groups. Fear of tangible immediate situations declines with age. This includes fear of noises, specific objects, falling and danger of falling, strange objects, and the like. Fears of a more symbolic kind, such as fear of imaginary creatures, of the dark, of being alone, and so on, increase with age.

In the experimental study only selected situations of tangible, immediate nature were used and again a decline with age was found. More symbolic situations are, by the nature of the situation, harder for an experimenter to arrange. Even the dark room situation they used does not qualify in this instance. They found that fear of the dark room declined with age, but in this instance it was a dark room with an adult not more than 18 feet away. His presence would be more reassuring to the older children. So, fear of the dark, which increases with age in the observational study, is not contradicted by their finding in the experimental study.

TABLE 12

SITUATIONS IN RESPONSE TO WHICH FEAR WAS SHOWN [*]

Situation in Response to which Fear Was Shown	Per Cent of Fears Occurring at Each Age					
Age in Months	0–11	12–23	24–35	36–47	48–59	60–97
Number of children	8	23	45	46	22	9
Number of fears	25	75	151	99	49	17
Animals (not including imaginary animals)	8	10.7	11.9	21.5	18.4	0
Sudden rapid motion, lights, flashes, shadows, reflections	8	5.3	11.3	6.1	4.1	0
Noises, events associated with noise, and noise plus motion	24	18.7	17.2	19.4	12.2	0
Falling, heights, danger of falling, sudden or gradual displacement	12	10.7	9.9	6.1	6.1	0
Pain, persons, objects, situations inflicting or associated with pain and tactual shock	8	16	6	7.1	6.1	29.4
Strange objects, situations, and persons	16	16	15.9	14.3	8.2	5.9
Harm, danger of bodily injury, falling	12	10.7	9.9	16.2	14.3	17.6
The dark and being alone in the dark	0	2.7	3.3	4.1	4.1	11.8
Being alone or abandoned by parents	0	4	2.6	4.1	4.1	5.9
Imaginary creatures	0	4	2.6	2	10.2	5.9

[*] Adapted from Jersild and Holmes (49). Copyright 1935 by Teachers College, Columbia University, and published with permission.

The fear of the infant and younger child is of the tangible events and situations in his immediate environment (47). As he grows older, his perceptual and intellectual prowess increases. The preschool child is afraid not only of more things but also of different things than the infant. As intelligence increases, he begins to recognize potential, real, and imaginary danger that he had not recognized before. Meanings, not before open to him, become part of his behavior repertoire.

As his symbolic linguistic and conceptual prowess increases, the nature of his fears changes, as shown in the increase in fears of imaginary creatures, the dark, and of being alone. By the same token, an increase in intelligence and in general knowledge renders him less susceptible to fears of tangible objects, noises, and falling. The fear of strangeness decreases in that not so many things are strange any more. The bell of the ice cream vendor may startle the infant, but is known for what it is by a five-year-old.

General conditions for the appearance of fear. Up to this point fear has been examined as if its expression were independent of any other aspects of the situation (with the exception of intelligence). This omission has painted too simplified a picture. Aspects of the situation other than the "fear" stimulus itself help to determine whether fear will or will not be shown. Consider for a moment the percentage changes with age found for fear of snakes. The fear of snakes rises substantially between three and four years of age from what it was before. Then this particular fear declines. At first (in infancy) there is no fear of snakes, then at the age of two or three a snake is perceived as a potentially dangerous, noxious stimulus which increases to a peak at three or four. With increasing experience the still older child recognizes that the snake is nondangerous *in the particular situation in which it is seen.* A similar explanation could be offered of the situation, "being alone," which shows a similar rise and fall. Both seeing a snake and being alone might, under other situational circumstances, bring about fear in these same children. The study of Arsenian (4) described on page 375 shows the fearsomeness of a strange situation when the child was alone. With the mother's reassuring presence the child was not afraid.

Since most fears are learned, it is plausible to believe that some fears that children show are acquired from the behavior of their parents. Hagman (36), on investigating this hypothesis, found a relationship between the fears of the mothers and those of their children. He interviewed the mothers of 70 preschool boys and girls about their own and their children's fears. There was a distinct tendency for the child to have the same fears as his mother, particularly fears concerning dogs, insects, and storms. Consider a specific example of what might be happening in the situations that give rise to these complementary fears. Suppose a child unexpectedly hears a barking dog. No matter what, he will be afraid for just a moment if the situation is new or strange. But if the mother handles the situation calmly, the fear passes rapidly. But suppose she, too, is frightened by dogs. His fear may persist thereafter.

In a summarization of the studies of fear with which he has been associated, Jersild (48) considers that there are three major ways in which fear is aroused in relation to the fear situation. In each instance he is considering how the child learns to be afraid. First, there is a specific relation in which persisting fears can be traced to the event itself. For example, a child is bitten by a dog and thereafter fears that dog. Second, the child may respond with fear not only to the specific stimulus, but also to aspects of the situation in which the fear took place. A child bitten by a dog not only fears the dog, but also is afraid to go into the neighborhood where he was bitten. Or he may be afraid, not only of the dog who bit him, but of other dogs as well. Third, the child may respond in an indirect and generalized way. Bitten by the dog, he has a bad dream that night, and, thereafter, is afraid to go into his bedroom in the dark. This formulation of the ways in which the child learns to be afraid appears to be both plausible and adequate.

Fear and Anxiety

Anxiety may be conceived as fear in which the source of the fear is vague or somehow obscured. In other words, the person, child or adult is not clearly aware of what he is being fearful. In this sense the source of the fear, although not the emotional state itself, may be said to be unconscious. Since awareness of the source is not present, it follows that the situation about which one is fearful is not directly and immediately present to consciousness (at least not in the form which generates the emotion). Hence, anxiety is anticipatory. The child is anxious about the coming visit to the dentist but fearful in the dentist's chair. It is this anticipatory element which Mowrer (60) stresses. He argues that anxiety is a learned response that enables individuals to face potentially harmful events in the advance of their occurrence. Sometimes, then, anxiety is adaptive in that the child is led to do something about the situation. One investigation (1) from which it was concluded that anxiety may be constructive was conducted by relating anxiety shown by preschool children to the quality of their play. Anxiety correlated *positively* with constructive play suggesting that mild anxiety facilitates learning.

Often, however, anxiety is debilitating, causing avoidance of the situation or fruitless anticipation of situations which are not really dangerous. In such instances, anxiety is even more generalized than it is in less pathological forms. Anxiety may pervade almost all aspects of life. Anxiety described as "free-floating" catches this latter aspect of the meaning of the term quite aptly. Anxiety is "in the air"; the fear is related to something or somebody which cannot be precisely specified and which is not yet being directly encountered. Since anxiety is of great significance for the social and psychopathological aspects of the development of the child, it will be considered again.

The Relation of Fear and Anger

Anger and fear are related in a variety of ways. Clinical observation often demonstrates that an apparently anxious or fearful child on closer examination will be found to be one in whom his anxiety is a mask for considerable anger and aggressiveness. Conversely, an apparently "cocky" (angry) child may be found essentially to be a very frightened child. Quite apart from such admixtures, sometimes an individual vacillates between fear and anger as when he faces a disagreeable situation first by attack but, on this failing, flees from it only to return to attack later. Or, on "being cornered," a child previously afraid may find himself angry and therefore attack.

This intimate relationship between fear and anger is useful in describing conflict in learning on the part of children. Dollard and Miller (26), for example, trace how fear becomes attached to anger cues. Anger on the part of the adult produces punishment, and hence the situation becomes one in which the fear of punishment may outweigh the anger. It is their contention that this often happens during the period of toilet training. Presumably, anger may become attached to fear cues as well, as in an instance where a child who is originally afraid of an older child finds his fear unnecessary and now finds himself angry.

The relative frequency of fear and anger in preschool children has been investigated by Felder (28). He found that anger outbursts were far more frequent than were displays of fear. It is plausible to believe that we live in a society in which we protect our children from fear situations while exposing them more to anger-provoking situations. Also it is probable that the higher incidence of observed anger is due to our relatively greater emphasis on a child concealing his fear while permitting him to express his anger more openly.

The physiological changes occurring in anger cannot clearly be differentiated from those of fear (15), but the overt behavior of these emotional patterns is dramatically different in direction. As Goodenough puts it, "Fear is emotional avoidance; anger is emotional attack" (34, 48–49). In general, fear behavior takes the form of avoidance or escape, whereas anger is characterized by approach-attack in motor or verbal aggression.

Affectively Pleasant Emotions

It will be remembered that Bridges (*11*) found that delight was the first of the affectively pleasant emotions to differentiate from excitement. This occurred somewhat before the third month. Before the infants reach 24 months of age, she also observed elation, affection, and joy. It is to these positive emotions that attention is now directed. Unfortunately, not very much research has been devoted to the study of emotional changes with growth in the affectively pleasant emotions. Perhaps this, in part, is because they have a less dramatic character than do anger and fear. Certainly, they are not marked by as severe or as extreme behavioral signs. Often their expressions are less spectacular, partaking more of the character of pleasant feelings than of the pronounced changes of fear and anger. Indeed, anything resembling the pronounced visceral changes accompanying the disruptive emotions is not generally apparent. The visceral changes, although present in the affectively pleasant emotions, are often of so mild a character that they go unnoticed.

Smiling and laughter are the major external behavior indices of the pleasant emotions. Since these indices are observable and quantifiable, research has tended to focus on them.

Brief reference has already been made to smiling and laughter in the account of infancy. That account, however, by no means exhausted the important relevant research literature. Consequently, one or two studies will be briefly described so as to make it possible to consider the commonalities among the causes of laughter and smiling. Leuba (*53*), studying laughter in his own two infants, found that at about six or seven months smiling and laughter appeared in response to mild, intermittent tickling. Before the end of the first year, the laughter and smiling had been conditioned to the sight of the moving fingers (preparatory to tickling). Washburn (*73*) observed the development of laughter and smiling of 15 infants from eight weeks to one year of age at monthly intervals. By means of a check list, facial responses to a standard set of stimuli were obtained at each monthly observation. Some of the "stimuli" she used were (1) smiling, "chirruping," and talking to infant; (2) peek-a-boo; (3) threatening head (lowering of head toward infant and saying "ah boo"); (4) hand clapping; (5) sudden reappearance from under table; and (6) tickling. All of the stimuli she used were effective in producing smiles at one or more of the monthly age levels. However, some were more effective in producing laughter than others. Laughter in one-half or more of the subjects was produced by peek-a-boo, the threatening head, and hand clapping. The study by Dennis and Dennis described on page 215 also attests to the importance of the adult's presence in producing smiles in infants.

The study of Justin (50) was specifically designed to test the various major theories of laughter: (1) surprise-defeated expectation; (2) superiority-degradation; (3) incongruity and contrast; (4) social smile as stimulus; (5) relief from strain; and (6) play. She devised test situations for each of these categories and then applied them all to nearly 100 children between the ages of three and six. She found that *some* children laughed in *all* of the situations.

Insofar as the situations she devised were tests of the theory on which each was presumably based, each theory accounted for some laughter. Some were more effective than others, but as she indicates, she may have been more adroit in preparing situations appropriate to one theoretical position than she was in another. At any rate, the most effective were the social smile and the surprise situations which produced laughing in more than 90 per cent of the children, whereas the least effective was the relief from strain situation, which, however, still produced laughter in about 50 per cent of the children. Quite apart from the groupings by theory, she noted that situations in which the children were active participants, instead of being spectators, were the most effective in producing laughter.

Three other relevant studies of laughter were based on the observation of younger children in the nursery school-kindergarten situation. No attempt was made in any of them to direct or change the situations from which they derived their findings. Instead, the observers unobtrusively, but systematically, observed the children with particular attention to laughter-provoking situations.

Both Brackett (10) and Ding and Jersild (25) found that laughter occurred most often in social situations—situations in which the children were interacting with one another. Brackett found that almost 85 per cent of the laughter of her groups occurred in social settings. Moreover, laughter in a given child was predominately found when laughter occurred in the other children who were present. Laughter was much less frequent when the children engaged in solitary play or parallel play (the latter being play in which both children use the same material, such as a sandbox, but do not apparently pay attention to or react with one another).

Ding and Jersild (25), in addition to noting the social setting of laughter, also collected considerable evidence that laughter occurred predominately in connection with physical activity on the part of the children. The children they studied laughed most often when they were engaged in active physical play. Laughter, then, seemed to be related to having a motor outlet.

Blatz and his associates (9) also studied laughter in the nursery school setting. They were particularly interested in laughter associated with performing certain activities—falling, using the swing, climbing on the jungle gym, going down the slide, and the like. They found that almost always the laughter occurred *after* the completion of an event, that is, after the child had reached the bottom of the slide, after he had jumped into the pool, after he had fallen, after a toy he had thrown actually landed in the water, and so on. They consider that their results indicated that laughter comes when a conflict of some sort has been resolved. That is, the activity the child was engaging in had reached a solution and the conflict about whether the desired result would happen was resolved by its completion. At the top of the slide, for example, there is a tiny element of danger. When a child arrives at the bottom unhurt, he laughs.

In summarizing the major findings it would seem that there is some research support for the following statements concerning smiling and laughter, and, consequently, concerning the affectively pleasant emotions of which these are the indices: The sheer presence of sensory stimulation, especially sudden stimuli, seems to be important in infants (Leuba, Washburn). As sources for the pleasurable emotions in both infants and preschool children, physical activity seems to be very prominent (Brackett, Ding and Jersild, Blatz, and probably Leuba and Washburn). The presence of others in the social situation, the parents in the case of the infant (Washburn, Dennis and Dennis) and other children in that of the preschool child (Justin, Brackett, Ding and Jersild), seems to be operative in producing pleasurable emotions. Another source seems to be the resolution of conflicts (Blatz). It seems that relief from strain (Justin) may be related to this same source. Other sources, such as surprise-defeated expectation, superiority-degradation, incongruity and contrast (Justin) may be operative as well.

The account of the sources of pleasurable emotions cannot be left without indicating that some of these same sources in other circumstances can produce other than the affectively pleasant emotions. Consider the production of laughter and smiling in infants by sudden stimuli. Just a few pages before it was indicated that sudden stimuli produce fear. In fact, this source of fear is a prominent one. It would appear that situational factors must be operative in which sudden stimuli under some circumstances produce fear and under others produce affectively pleasant emotions. What these situations may be cannot be specified with any degree of precision; however, it is plausible to consider that the foreground stimuli (such as the sudden ones just mentioned) are pleasant or unpleasant just as the general backgrounds for the stimulation are pleasant or unpleasant (a trusted adult versus a strange person). In any event, the situation helps to determine whether laughter and smiling do or do not appear.

Cognitive development

At the end of infancy, generally at about 18 months, the infant begins to make internal symbolic representations and to invent solutions rather than depend on trial and error (29). He is passing into the beginnings of what Piaget calls preoperational thought. Symbolic play with a stick as a sword or a tricycle as a horse illustrates this passage.

Piagetian Levels of Cognition

According to Piagetian theory (8), the child, two to four years of age, uses preconcepts or representations—that is, stimuli to represent other objects—that are midway between the concept of an object (this table) and that of a class (all-four-legged tables). For example, a child of this age was observed in a walk through the woods to say "snail" each time he sighted one, but questioning showed that he did not know whether he saw the same snail or a succession of different snails. In fact, this particular distinction meant nothing to him—they were all "snail." Or, to use another illustration, a person without clothes does not have the same name as the person clothed.

During the preschool years, the child is passing through a subperiod preparatory to that of concrete operations (29). His conceptual operations have not yet taken on stability and coherence which should occur from about ages seven to 11. This preceding subperiod of preparation includes three stages: beginnings of representational thought (2–4); simple representations (4–5½); and articulated representations (5½–7). This last stage creates a certain awkwardness since it extends beyond the age limits set for this chapter, but in the interests of achieving a greater unity of exposition, it, too, will be considered. Rather than labor over the subdivisions, it is possible to summarize them by saying that preconcepts are first used at two to four years; that simple, global representations appear by four years, and that thereafter the representations are more complex, having subparts and relations of one subpart to another.

The important issue is not these steps, but the shift in representation that takes place. The preschool child learns to manipulate representation, that is to use symbolic function in which *signifiers* (a word, an image) are differentiated from *significates* (a perceptually absent event). He becomes capable of internally evoking a signifier, a word or image that symbolizes a significate, a perceptually absent event, as well as being able to differentiate the two clearly. Although infants possess the ability to use cues, usage brought about by symbolic functioning differs in several ways. Infantile sensorimotor ability makes them capable of linking actions or perceptual states one by one; representation allows considering a broader sweep of events simultaneously. Second, sensorimotor ability allows action, whereas representation permits contemplation or reflection as well. Representation, moreover, permits cognition to go beyond the immediate present to include past and future, and enables persons to share with others through use of language the steps through which their thinking has gone.

If left at this point, the description of preoperational thought might give an impression of a much greater maturity than, in fact, the young child possesses. Although knowing the permanence of concrete objects, he has as yet no fully developed concepts of matter, weight, movement, number, or logic. He is approaching, but has not reached, operational thinking. His cognitions are preoperational as shown by a considerable variety of characteristics which help to bring out clearly the lack of maturity.

Egocentricism

The child is egocentric in his representations, just as he was egocentric in his sensorimotor actions. He cannot put himself in the perspective to another person. He has passed from initial egocentricity of the sensorimotor stage to logical and social egocentricity. Piaget illustrates this new level of egocentricity in the existence of the inability of a preschool-aged child to take the perspective of another person. A child in this age range was shown a model of three mountains and asked to select from a number of pictures of these mountains the one that showed the way it looked to the *doll* who was placed in the mountains. The child, instead of selecting from the perspective of the doll, selected the one showing how it appeared from his own vantage point. As the doll was shifted from one place in the mountains to another, he persisted in selecting the picture that showed his own view of the mountains. He did not understand that an observer sees the same mountains quite differently from various points of view. An everyday example of the same phenomenon is the difficulties children have with personal pronouns. To put it in doggerel, "I am I and you are you, and how can you be I and I be you?" The young child's own personal perspective is absolute, not relative.

Animism

The young child is also animistic—he tends to attribute life to inanimate objects, such as clouds. Although research investigations tend to use older children, the evidence will be examined here since Piaget considers it characteristic of early childhood.

Piaget (63) distinguishes four definite stages. As summarized by Russell (66), in the first stage, everything is alive (unless broken or damaged) for children between four and six years of age; in the second stage, everything is alive which moves for six- and seven-year-old children; in the third stage, everything that moves by itself is alive for eight- to ten-year-old children; in the fourth stage, life is reserved for animals and plants, or animals alone, by children aged eleven or older.

Nearly 800 children six to 15½ years of age were interviewed by Russell (67) concerning animism. Ninety-eight per cent of their answers could be classified into one or another of the stages of animistic thinking. Furthermore, examination of the classification by stages at each chronological and mental age showed that probably they passed through the series in the sequence suggested by Piaget. Although the fundamental validity of Piaget's classification was accepted by Russell, he could find no evidence that the age range for each stage was limited in the sharp fashion thought by Piaget to exist. Instead, each of the concept stages was found throughout the entire chronological and mental age range covered in the study.

The question of whether these results might merely be an artifact of the child's usage of the terms "living" and "dead" was also investigated by Russell (67). In other words, a child might be saying something is living because he is not familiar with the essential meaning of the term itself. Some of the children on whom he had information about animistic thinking from the previous study were now questioned whether the same objects used in the earlier study were capable of "knowing" and "feeling." Classification by Piaget's stages of "knowing" and "feeling" and then correlating them with the findings on animistic stages for the same children showed a substantial degree of relationship among animism, knowing, and feeling. This would seem to be rather convincing evidence that if confusion about the meaning of living did exist, it also extended to the most specific meanings of knowing and feeling. In general, it would appear that the children do know what "living" means when they give animistic answers.

Despite this impressive array of evidence, there are some studies whose findings are negative. Typical is the study of Huang and Lee (42). They asked children aged three-and-a-half to eight years of age not only whether the objects in question were living but also whether they had life, felt pain, were capable of wanting, and the like. They found only a slight tendency to attribute life to such objects as a tree, river, pencil, bicycle, and watch. The children did not attribute feeling pain, wanting, or the like to these objects to as great a degree as they said they were living. The term "living" was applied more loosely than "having life." Evaluation of these disparate results will be considered in a later chapter in the setting of a general critique of Piaget's conceptions.

Centering

The child also tends to "center," that is to attend to a single striking feature of the object of his reasoning, disregarding other features, and, thus, to distort his thinking. For example, on seeing two identical thin containers, he will agree that they both contain identical amounts of liquid. But when the contents of one is poured into a short, broad container, he will now deny that the remaining twin and the broad container contain equal amounts, arguing either way according to whether he "centered" on the "tall" or "broad" container, to wit, B contains more because it is broad or A contains more because it is tall.

Perceptual-conceptual development

The principle of differentiation is clearly operative in perceptual development among young children. A five-year-old is able to discriminate to some degree among the objects of a classroom, the blackboards, chairs, books, windows, and the rest, whereas the infant sees them as a conglomeration of color and shapes only beginning to be separated as recognizable objects. However, this is only a relative differentiation on the part of the young child. He may perceive a "big" book and a "little" book but not realize that the former is an atlas and the latter the teacher's record book, a discrimination an adult would be able to make at a glance.

A lack of differentiation sometimes extends to the point of fusing the data from the various sense modalities. Although by no means present in all young children, so-called *synesthesia* occurs when a specific stimulus arouses not only the corresponding sensation but also another sense-modality united with it (79). Color-tones and color-smells are illustrative: a three-year-old boy "smelled green" and a girl from her third to sixth year had to be often corrected in her expression of synesthesias since she persisted in referring to the "gold and silver striking of the hour" and "light- and dark-red whistling." This phenomenon tends to disappear with increasing age, suggesting that it is related to increasing differentiation.

Differentiation in perception is also shown by less subjective research procedures. As an example of increased discrimination with age, children of four to six were better able with increasing age to judge from photographs the age of adults pictured (51).

Recently, research on perception among children has emphasized those determinants that are motivational in character. It has been found that a child tends to perceive in line with his needs. For example, in one study (70) children were presented with a task involving two facial profile drawings, a reward being offered in association with one of them. Thereafter the two facial profiles were fitted together into a single, somewhat ambiguous figure. Presented to the children in this fashion, the component parts were not recognizable but the part that had been rewarded was said to be brighter, having darker contours, and "happier" as compared with the unrewarded part. To use another example, the "poor" child estimates the size of coins as larger than does the "rich" child (13). In a more carefully conducted follow-up study (18), it was found that "poor" children, even on the basis of memory alone, perceived coins as being larger than did more well-to-do children. This influence of need upon perception has been demonstrated again and again: perception is not immune from the influence of motivational factors even among young children.

Let us turn now to another aspect of the development process—concept formation. Under concept formation several characteristic attainments of early childhood may be subsumed. Unlike the infant, the young child is capable of using concepts that make him different from the infant he has been. Above all, concepts facilitate the ease and accuracy of thinking of children (and adults). By use of the categorizations called concepts, certain advantages accrue (14). Concepts (1) reduce the complexity of the environment; (2) they provide the means by which the objects of the environment are identified; (3) they reduce the necessity of relearning at each new encounter; (4) they help provide for direction, prediction, and planning of any activity; and (5) they permit ordering and relating classes of objects and events as in cause and effect. In short, conceptualizing makes reasoning possible.

Granting that the beginnings of conceptualization occur in infancy, what are some of the conceptual tasks the young child emerging from infancy has before him? He enters early childhood with very hazy conceptions of space, time, weight, number, form, color, and size. It is during early and later childhood that he makes his greatest strides in mastering these classes of concepts.

It is impracticable to discuss all of these major classes or aspects of concepts. Instead, discussions of space and time concepts will serve to illustrate conceptual development during early childhood. Some of the objective findings of Gesell and Ilg (31) on space conception receive attention first.

Even at one year of age there is enough appreciation of space dimensions to perform gestures for up and down and to play "peek-a-boo." By two years of age the child has in his vocabulary such expressions as "up high," "in," "out," and "go away." By the age of three he can tell what street he lives on, but usually not the number. At the age of five he is still very much literal and factual, although capable of taking simple routes through the immediate neighborhood. He is beginning to appreciate the significance of maps and even may make simple maps indicating the route he takes to school, and so on.

These facts, however, tell us nothing about how these conceptualizations came about. One plausible but as yet not thoroughly documented theory that helps in this regard was advanced by Piaget.

To Piaget, space is not immediately given but must be constructed through experience. Spatial representations are built up by the child's acting on the object in space (64). First there are the sensorimotor activities of the infant, but later internalized activities take over as more efficient and economical. In very broad outline, this is the theory he advances. Suppose we examine it in more detail.

As stated in Chapter 7, Piaget held that during the sensorimotor stage the infant constructed objects from his experiences. He learns that objects retain identity even when out of sight and that he, the infant, can influence objects by touching them. Space, then, is not independent of objects.

During the preschool years the child moves on to a level in which objects in space are apprehended as related to one another, independent of the perceiver (29). He is now free from the egocentric illusion and can take into account movements of objects when they go through positions in which he, himself, does not participate. To use as an illustration of Piaget's—Jacqueline had thrown a ball under a sofa. Instead of looking under the sofa, she realized it had passed under and beyond the sofa to another part of the room. Since the way the ball passed was blocked by furniture, she turned away from where the ball disappeared to go around the sofa to find the ball. She had followed a path different from the ball and had elaborated an independent, organized spatial concept through representation of the displacement of the ball; and by detour she found it again. This detour behavior showed her ability to apprehend space in which bodies other than her own had travelled.

In the preschool years this process of moving toward objectivity repeats itself, this time in terms of the preoperational stage. This again includes the child's egocentricity of a logical and social sort. The inability of a child of four or five to conceive that the mountain would look different from the other side is again illustrative.

Concepts of time are among the most abstract, more so than space, for example, in part because of the lack of obvious clues on which to build them. Nevertheless, some development of the conception of time takes place during infancy. Gesell and Ilg (31) find that the child of 18 months lives very much in the present. It is characteristic that he finds it difficult to wait and the only time word that is used is "now." Only the slightest indications of any sense of timing have yet appeared; for example, the sight of juice and crackers may bring him to the table. At two years of age although he still lives chiefly in the present, he has begun to use words denoting the future, as for example, "gonna" and "in a minute." He is also beginning to comprehend simple time sequences as implied in "have dollie after juice."

Ames (3), studying 18- to 48-month-old nursery school children, found that within those ages words indicating the present came first, then those for the future, and, lastly, those indicating the past. Parts of the day, morning and afternoon, were understood before the day of the week. By the age of three the child knows his own age, and most basic time words are now in his vocabulary. He can be persuaded to wait for things. Although he shows only pretense of telling time, the very fact that he does so shows a dawning conceptualization in this area. During these years he is still living very much in the here and now, as shown by the fact that even at five years it is very difficult for him to conceive of not being alive, of dying, or of anyone living before him. At this age he can name the days of the week and is interested in clocks and calendars, although by no means adroit in handling these time phenomena.

One study of conceiving clock time (71) with four-, five- and six-year-olds as subjects found a developmental progression to exist. The youngest children could relate time in descriptive terms to regular events in their preschool schedule; those somewhat older used imaginative but not unreasonable clock time, such as fifteen o'clock in the afternoon; still older children expressed reasonable but incorrect time; and the oldest conceived of the correct time.

Hours are learned first, then half-hours, and, finally, quarter-hours. Time first is conceived as a sequence in relation to activities, then as outstanding divisions of time, such as morning and afternoon, followed by an understanding of the days of the week, and thereafter calendar and clock time. This sequence seems to be the order of development. The young child seems to be moving from a concrete action level toward levels of greater and greater abstraction.

To Piaget, time, like space, is constructed progressively throughout the child's development and is intimately related to spatial experiences. Piaget considers the development of time conceptualization to go through a variety of steps (29). Although even the youngest infant, it is true, goes through a temporal series of activities, say in sucking or in turning toward a sound source, the presence of this sequence of perception does not guarantee that he has a perception of sequence. Rather, this conceptualization of a sequence begins somewhere toward the end of the first year of life.

Earlier stages involve vague perception of duration to the infant's actions; following learning of cause and effect sequences he becomes aware of before and after. He then advances to an object stage, best exemplified in the search for a hidden object, as when the infant seen by Piaget was able to persist in seeking an object behind a screen (page 176). Coping with displaced objects shows an ability to keep events in memory and, hence, increased conceptualization of time. Recall of remote past events follows, and awareness of time as a generalized phenomenon has begun. This sequence, we should warn, does not carry much beyond infancy; the stages for later ages have not been systematized in Piaget's theoretical formulation.

The development of other concepts in early childhood could also be traced, but enough has been said to illustrate the nature of age changes in conceptual development.

It now should be apparent that concepts are organized at various different levels of abstraction in which each higher level includes within it other, more specific ones. Thus, fruit is at a higher level of abstraction than apples, peaches, and pears. Welch (77) uses a hierarchical organization to sketch these levels.

There is, first, the concrete or object level of, for example, "this dog."

Beyond this concrete level there are varying degrees or levels of abstractness, each referred to as a hierarchy. This may be illustrated by considering the five levels of abstractness of the concept from the concrete level of "this dog." The first hierarchy level is that of "collie"; the second, "dog"; the third, "animal"; the fourth, "living substance"; and the fifth, "substance." These are levels of increasing abstractness on a logical basis. The logical order is based on the fact that the next higher hierarchy includes the lower and so on to the highest level. The first order, "collie" is included in the second, "dog," and this in turn in the third, "animal," and so on.

The developmental order, however, may be quite different from the logical. Indeed, this is what has been found. To quote Welch:

The child in learning a language may begin to use some of the words which are found at the second or third hierarchy level in the logical order. This does not necessarily imply that the child is using second or third hierarchy concepts, but rather that he is erroneously applying to concrete objects, a term used by the mature organism to designate classes at a higher level of abstractness. If the child has not grasped the fact that animals may be thought of as cats and as dogs, he will be using the class animal as a first hierarchy concept only. Unless he thinks of a class as including another class, he is not using a second hierarchy concept, and unless he thinks of a class which includes a class which in turn includes a class, he is not making use of a third hierarchy concept.

If dog is his first class concept, then dogs, cats, cows and horses, in fact, all four-legged animals will be regarded by him as members of this class, while as yet, he will be unable to divide this class into subclasses, such as the class of dogs, cats, etc. The child will have comparatively little difficulty in learning other *1st hierarchy* concepts such as cat. He may have greater difficulty, however, in learning that dogs and cats belong to the class of animals. The relationship between the class of animals and the classes of dogs and cats is what is known as a genus-species relationship. It appears to be quite simple, but it is really very complex. The child does not understand this relationship until he is aware of the fact that this thing over here is a dog and that other thing over there is a cat and that both are animals. To the underdeveloped mind this seems to be a paradox or even a contradiction. If the child in his confusion could verbalize he might complain by saying:

You call all of these things animals. That means they are the same. Then you turn around and call one a dog and another a cat. That means they are different. Why don't you make up your mind! Are they the same or are they different?

The answer is quite obvious! They are the same in some respects and that is why we think of them as a class of animals; still, they are different in other respects and that is why we think of them as dogs and cats. Things *can* be similar in some respects and different in others, but the task of considering their similarities one moment and their differences the next is much more difficult than considering the similarities without the differences. In other words, it is much simpler to think of things which are *either* dogs or cats under the circumstances, and never members of a more inclusive class, animals (77, 203–204).[3]

He goes on to indicate that there are two kinds of abstract concepts —(1) first-order, those representing classes as, for example, a chair; and (2) second-order, those showing characteristics divorced from any object, such as number or justice. The second kind of abstract concept is illustrated in the learning of arithmetic. Progressing from two apples and two apples equaling four apples to $2 + 2 = 4$, the child is also moving from the first to the second order of abstract concept (77).

To find out when children begin to grasp concepts, Welch (76) gathered data from about 80 children aged between 21 and 72 months. His procedure consisted of two parts. First the child was faced with objects consisting of a toy dog, a cow, a horse, a pig, a soldier and a nurse, a hat, coat and shoes, a chair and table, a carrot and a potato, an apple, a banana, and an orange. One at a time he was asked to group together two animals, the man and woman, two vegetables, and two pieces of fruit when given their species name (first order concepts).

The second part consisted of questions designed to show whether the child had knowledge of "games," "color," "food," "weather," and the like. An over-all maximum score of 21 for first-order concepts was possible. In Figure 11 the number of first-order abstract concepts at various ages is given. Knowledge of abstract concepts increases steadily from two to six years of age. There appears to be an evolution of concepts with gradual changes rather than a saltatory, discrete series of levels.

Welch found that at the age of 21 to 26 months a group of children manifested an average of little more than one first-order abstract concept. The trend of development with increasing age was linear with an average of about six concepts at age 34 to 39 months, an average of about 14 concepts at 53 to 58 months, and 20 concepts at 65 to 72 months. Second-order concepts made their first appearance in a few children at three years of age. By five years of age practically all knew at least one second-order concept, such as apples are fruit and potatoes are vegetables.

According to American research work, concept formation shows considerable similarity of conceptualization in young children with that of adults. In contrast, Piaget's position stresses the differences of

[3] From Welch (77). Copyright 1947 by The Journal Press and published with permission.

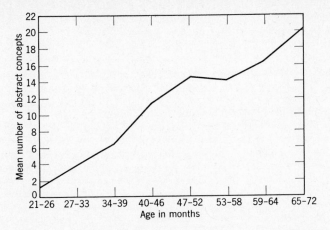

Figure 11. Number of abstract concepts at various ages. (After Welch (76). Copyright 1940 by the Journal Press and published with permission.)

conceptualization of children from that of adults. At the present stage of knowledge, the difference of emphasis cannot be resolved. Both points of view are in agreement that there are some differences in concept formation. We shall return to this topic with older children in a later chapter.

Language development

Chapter 7 indicated normative landmarks in language development during infancy but neither stressed the importance of learning nor said much about the various functions of language. Both topics are explored here along with normative findings about the growth of vocabulary and certain other language skills. We shall also pay attention to individual differences in language development.

Learning and Speech

That speech is learned is already evident from consideration of speech in infancy. When internal processes (the higher mental processes) are involved in the child's interactions with his environment, these processes are mediated by cue-producing responses. Language is most often involved in cue-producing responses. Hall and Lindzey in discussing behavior-social-learning theory summarize so well the position of Miller and Dollard (59) on cue production and language that they are quoted at length as follows:

One of the most important cue-producing responses is the labeling or naming of events and experiences. The individual may immediately increase the generalization or transfer between two or more cue situations by identifying them as having the same label, for example, by identifying two completely different situations as "threatening" the individual may greatly increase the likelihood that he will behave in the same manner in both situations; or he may build up a sharp discrimination between two similar situations by giving them different names, for instance, two individuals who are objectively very much alike may be labeled respectively as "friend" and "enemy" with the result that they will be responded to in a highly individual manner. Within any culture there will be critical generalizations and discriminations which are emphasized and thus made easier by the structure of the language. The often repeated examples of tribes where a given commodity, such as cattle or coconuts, is of great importance and where the language contains a tremendous number of differentiated labels for such objects illustrate this principle.

Not only may words serve to facilitate or inhibit generalization, they may also serve the important function of arousing drives. Further, words may be used to reward or reinforce. And, most important of all, they serve as time-binding mechanisms, permitting the individual to instigate or reinforce present behavior in terms of consequences which are located in the future but susceptible to verbal representation in the present. It is clearly the verbal intervention in the drive-cue-response-reinforcement sequence which makes human behavior so complex and difficult to understand and at the same time accounts for much of the difference between man and lower species (37, 438–439).[4]

Language as a product of learning can be seen as an important aspect of development. Without the learning of language much of our characteristically human prowess would be lost.

The preschool years show an enormous increase in the use of words. This is significant not only because of the ease and subtlety of communication, but also because it facilitates other learnings. Even in infancy the increased efficiency of subjects who use words was found in the study of Gellermann (page 180). A considerable number of studies (16, 24, 45, 62, 75) have shown that children learn to discriminate among stimuli presented to them if prior to the study itself they are given experience in naming the stimuli. In other words, possession of verbal facility allows ease of learning.

The study of Weir and Stevenson (75) is representative. They studied this problem with children of three, five, seven, and nine years

[4] From Hall and Lindzey (37). Copyright 1957 by John Wiley and Sons, and published with permission.

of age divided into two groups. Both groups gave a pushing response to register their choice of the "correct" picture of two common animals shown together. Before making the response the children in one group were instructed to say the name of the animal they thought fitted the correct picture. The children in the other group were exposed to the same pretraining procedure but nothing was said about giving a name to the stimulus. Both groups practiced to the same level of proficiency. They then faced a more complicated but similar task. Those who had been asked to verbalize in pretraining showed consistently better learning at every age studied.

The Functions of Language

This account of the study of language skills of preschool children will emphasize the careful, detailed research of Dorothea McCarthy in her "preschool study" (55) and the insightful but somewhat haphazardly collected data of Jean Piaget (63). McCarthy investigated several related aspects of language by obtaining 50 consecutive verbal responses from each of 140 children, 20 at each of seven age levels from a year-and-a-half to four years and six months. There were about an equal number of boys and girls with an average IQ of 109 that falls in the normal range.

In the main, Piaget relied on about 1,500 remarks made by two children, aged six-and-a-half, although supplemented by other findings from Swiss private schoolchildren between two and eleven years of age. By American standards his work is considered to be relatively unsystematic and "loose." Even his classification of the speech of his subjects bore within it contradiction from one part to another (56). Nevertheless, it was the work of Piaget (63) that focused contemporary attention on the functions of language as being both a means of communication with self and with others—the egocentric and socialized functions of language respectively. This distinction between egocentric and socialized speech has been generally accepted, despite disagreement over definition, relative proportion, and age at which they make their appearance.

As Piaget described it, egocentrism refers to the infant's isolation within himself. In an infant egocentrism is epitomized by his inability to distinguish the self from the world as expressed in the discussion of this problem in Chapter 7. In a preschool child it is shown in egocentric speech—in his talking without knowing to whom he is speaking or whether he is being listened to. Egocentric speech may be expressed in any one of three forms: (1) repetition, or talking for the sake of talking; (2) monologue, or talking to oneself as though thinking aloud; and (3) collective or dual monologue, or the other person serving both as stimulus and as recipient of the speech, although that person's point of view is not being considered.

Extending the concept of egocentrism beyond its manifestation in language, it means that an egocentric individual shows no consideration of the other person's point of view. This is in contrast with socialized speech in which the talker addresses the listener, considers his viewpoint, at least to some degree, and tries to communicate with him. Piaget seems to regard adult speech and thought as highly socialized and egocentrism as a characteristic of immaturity. In fact, for him the more egocentricity there is in speech and thought, the greater the degree of immaturity of the individual.

In studying egocentric speech in the manner mentioned earlier, Piaget found that the speech of children showed considerable egocentricity, but with a decrease in the proportion of egocentricity and an increase in sociocentric speech as age increased. He classed 38 per cent of the 1,500 remarks in the egocentric category with about 45 per cent classed as spontaneous social speech. (The remaining 17 per cent was made up of answers to remarks or questions and thus not spontaneous.) He found even higher percentages of egocentric speech for less intensively studied children ages three to five as well as lower percentages for children ages seven and eight. It is only at about the age of seven or eight that he considers true social maturity to appear simultaneous with the virtual disappearance of egocentric speech.

This work of Piaget has stimulated a considerable number of research studies both here and abroad. These investigators were motivated by a desire to explore more thoroughly and with larger samples of children these intriguing distinctions between egocentric and socialized speech. McCarthy (56), in summarizing these investigations, found that some studies which tried to follow Piaget's approach literally, or at least very closely, defined the meaning of egocentricity differently from Piaget. Usually the definitions of egocentricity adopted by the latter group of investigators were based on considering the sentence either egocentric or not egocentric on the basis of the grammatical subject. For example, when the sentence had the self as subject, it was considered to be egocentric in nature. Paradoxically, in studies using these other definitions of egocentricity, they found percentages that agreed rather closely with those Piaget found following his own definition. Others using his definition found much less egocentricity.

In her preschool study McCarthy (55), with due attention to reliability and objectivity, followed Piaget's meaning of egocentricity closely in classifying her samples. She found the percentage of egocentric speech to range only between 1.3 and 6.5 per cent for children aged one-and-a-half to four-and-a-half. The average for all ages was 3.6 per cent, a proportion considerably less than that held by Piaget.

Rather than explore other specific research findings concerning egocentric speech in children, an attempt will be made to offer a summary. It would appear that there is general agreement among investigators that a certain proportion of the young child's speech *is* egocentric. There is similar agreement that a decrease takes place in this proportion with increasing age. Turning now to the magnitude of this proportion, even if we accept as more valid those studies finding the highest percentages, they never reach 50 per cent.

Egocentrism in the speech of young children does exist, but it does not predominate. The present evidence indicates that the percentage of egocentric speech in children is less, perhaps considerably less, than reported by Piaget.

Egocentric speech, it should be indicated, does serve a useful function. By naming things to himself, the child is learning to communicate with *himself*. He is learning the names of objects and properties. His first active use of words—omitting the use of interjections, "bye-bye," "hi!" and so on—is learning to name people, acts, and things such as "mama," "doggie," "baby," "milk," "eat," and the like. He develops a great interest in names and is always demanding (in his own version, of course), "What's that?" Talking to himself does not mean he is not still learning. Is it any wonder, then, that he repeats words to himself? Naming seems to make an experience his very own. If he can name what he is doing to himself in egocentric fashion, he can use them better later for social communication. Despite this, egocentric speech is primarily an indication of immaturity.

The increase in socialized speech with increasing age is the complement of the decrease of egocentric speech. From the point of view of socialization of the child, it is interesting to explore the various forms that socialized speech may take. McCarthy in her preschool study (55) followed Piaget's classification of sociocentric speech with only minimal modifications. Consequently, giving her classification at this point serves two purposes—preparation for giving her findings and the presentation of Piaget's classification of socialized speech. The first major category of socialized speech was called (1) adapted information. Adapted information categorizes the child's speech when he "exchanges" his thought with others. Subcategories of adapted information include naming, remarks about the immediate situation, remarks associated with the situation, or irrelevant remarks. The other major categories were (2) criticism; (3) emotionally toned responses, including commands, requests, and threats; (4) questions; (5) answers; (6) social phrases such as "please" or "thank you"; and (7) dramatic imitations of adult conversation and imitations of animal sounds, and the like. These categories are considered to encompass socialized speech.

In McCarthy's speech samples, adapted information was by far the largest single category of socialized verbal responses. At most ages it made up as much as 40 to 60 per cent of the total verbal responses. There was a definite trend of an increase with age in adapted information. Questions, and especially answers, also showed an increase with age in her sample. On the other hand, emotionally toned responses showed a decrease. The other categories included few responses and no age trends could be noted.

The shift from egocentric to sociocentric speech with increasing age reflects the influence of socialization. It is plausible to believe that the change from egocentric to sociocentric speech partly stems from rewards for such speech from persons in the child's environment, whereas egocentric speech is simultaneously discouraged. The socially oriented verbalizations that the child learns bring with it rewards. Through sociocentric speech rather than egocentric speech he can manipulate his environment. Moreover, everyday observation would indicate that egocentric speech is actually discouraged as the child grows older and hence not rewarded.

As McCarthy (56) indicates, it is more than accidental that a marked degree of socialization occurs in the behavior of older preschool child. Language is becoming a more efficient means of communication and it plays a considerable role in the socialization taking place during the period. When the child can understand instructions, when he can ask and answer questions, when he can defend a course of action, when he can tell what he is doing, then he is in a position to profit expeditiously from the socialization efforts of those around him. Every parent knows how much more facility there is in controlling a child's behavior when his understanding of spoken language improves.

The views of the functions of language as egocentric and socialized by no means exhausts the ways its functions may be formulated. For example, a more eclectic view is offered by Lewis (54). He holds that language functions in three ways: (1) expressive of emotions; (2) representative of things and their being pointed out; and (3) evocative or social in that it arouses a response in the listener. Although his position appears plausible, relatively little research work bearing on it has been carried out. Mention, brief though it may be, will suffice to indicate that there are other ways of conceiving the functions of language. Egocentric and socialized functions of language are important, but not exclusive.

Growth of Vocabulary

The size of children's vocabularies grows extensively during the preschool years. The figures reported in a number of normative studies (56) on the average size of a child's vocabulary vary considerably for reasons not hard to isolate.

First, there is difficulty in getting agreement on what is meant by "knowing" a word. One investigator may ask only that a word be recognized in context, another that it be used in a sentence, and still another that it be defined. Although all of these methods have some claim to legitimacy as indices of the growth of vocabulary, they yield different size vocabularies. Second, quite apart from how it is to be measured, there is the ambiguity created by the various meanings a given word has; the same word is apt to have different meanings, as anyone consulting a dictionary knows. Differing standards toward the variety of meanings to be counted also result in differing estimates of the size of the vocabulary.

Fortunately, there seems to be agreement (56) that a study performed by Smith (69) is, to some extent more definitive than most of the other studies. Smith standardized a vocabulary test on children one to six years of age. She did so by selecting every twentieth word from a list developed by Thorndike containing the 10,000 words most frequently encountered in writing samples. The meanings of these words were elicited by Smith from her subjects by carefully probing for their meanings by using objects, pictures, and questions. Consequently, more than usual care was taken by her to find out whether the child did or did not know the word meanings. The total words correctly known by a child was multiplied by twenty, since every twentieth word from the list of 10,000 was used. This gave the child's oral vocabulary. As distinguished from McCarthy's procedure in her preschool study, yielding vocabulary of use, this study gave a vocabulary of recognition.

The vocabulary sizes Smith obtained for various ages are reported in Table 13. It will be seen that at first the vocabulary increases slowly and then more rapidly and then again more slowly. According to Smith's findings, the one-year-old has a vocabulary of three words, the two-year-old nearly 300, the four-year-old about 1,500, the five-year-old about 2,000, whereas the six-year-old has a vocabulary of about 2,500

TABLE 13

AVERAGE SIZE OF VOCABULARIES OF CHILDREN IN RELATION TO AGE *

Age			Number of	
Years	Months	N	Words	Gain
	8	13	0	
	10	17	1	1
1	0	52	3	2
1	3	19	19	16
1	6	14	22	3
1	9	14	118	96
2	0	25	272	154
2	6	14	446	174
3	0	20	896	450
3	6	26	1222	326
4	0	26	1540	318
4	6	32	1870	330
5	0	20	2072	202
5	6	27	2289	217
6	0	9	2562	273

* From Smith (69).   Copyright 1926 by the University of Iowa Press, and published with permission.

words.   A really pronounced increase occurs during the period from two years six months to three years of age when 450 new words become known.   Many authorities (for example, 56) believe that the most pronounced increase occurs *after* mastery of the motor skills of locomotion, especially walking.   When younger, the child is so busy mastering these motor skills that, until they have been achieved, less emphasis on learning new words occurs.   The relatively great increase at this particular age thus becomes plausible.

From a variety of lines of evidence (56), these findings seem to place the size of vocabulary at any given age a bit too low.   Most important is that Smith's selection of words came from a specific and, therefore, limited list of words.   No credit for knowing words not on the Thorndike list could possibly occur.   Moreover, a study by Templin (72), although not supplying total oral vocabulary scores for the preschool years, did so for older children, making possible a comparison with Smith's findings for later years.   Considerably larger vocabularies were found by Templin.   Since Templin was stricter in scoring than Smith the difference is most likely attributable to the fact that the Smith study appeared in 1926 and the Templin study in 1957.

During recent years it would appear that the average oral vocabulary of the young child has shown an increase. This superior loquacity of today's children, Templin (72) attributes to the superior communication media available to them, such as television and radio. Although probably reflecting growth trends quite accurately, Smith's findings tend to be low at each age.

Developmental Changes in Other Language Skills

Growth in clearness of articulation, in the integration of words into sentences, in the sheer length of sentences, and changes in the relative usage of the grammatical parts of speech take place during the pre-school period. Ability to give the sounds of their language correctly increases as children grow older. Wellman, Case, Mengert, and Bradbury (78) report that the correlation between age and clearness of articulation is 0.80. In their study the average two-year-old child was able to articulate correctly only about 32 per cent of the sounds he made. At age three the most marked increase was made to an average correct of 63 per cent. As age increased the percentage of correct articulation rose steadily; at age four it was 77 per cent; and at age five it was 88 per cent.

Growth in language skills with age is shown in changes in the integration of words into sentences. In this connection, Nice (61) outlines four major stages of sentence development. Stage one, the single word stage, begins at approximately the end of the first year and lasts from four to twelve months. The second is the early sentence stage. Only one or two words are used by infants, with a preponderance of nouns. Even if the infant uses but a single word, he still uses it to convey differences of meaning to others. This single word may function as a sentence, although not yet having its grammatical form. Mothers soon learn of single words functioning as whole sentences. Even the same word may, on different occasions, serve as several sentences. For example, the single word, mama, used with varying inflections and gestures means "mama look," "mama is here," and "mama come quickly." A small vocabulary, using one word at a time, may still go a long way. This stage lasts until about 28 months of age. The next stage, the short sentence stage (three to four words), is one in which nouns and verbs are used by the young child, but tenses, comparatives, and other inflections are not mastered. This stage lasts until approximately the fourth year. Beginning at this age, the last stage, the "complete" sentence stage, involves six to eight words and is also characterized by a fairly precise use of inflections.

Closely related to the integration of words into sentences is the sheer length of the verbal response which also increases with age. Templin (72) observed this in her study. She found that at three the average number of words per remark was 4.1, increasing to 5.4 at four, and 5.7 at five. However her findings showed significantly longer responses than the earlier McCarthy study of similar design. Again there is the implication that verbal skills have increased for present-day children as compared to those of the recent past. Changes in relative usage of the different grammatical parts of speech are related to age. In the McCarthy preschool study she found that nouns which constitute about 50 per cent of the speech of the eighteen-month-old children decrease to about 19 per cent in the 54-month-old sample. Verbs increase from 14 per cent to 25 per cent over the same age range. Although this is an increase, it is relatively slight as compared to that for adjectives and pronouns which almost double during the age range in question. Prepositions do not show up at all until about 24 months of age and connectives are hardly found until children are 30 months old.

These various developmental differences in the speech of children help to explain its particular so-called childish quality in the younger preschool child. This is most apparent in their usage of grammatical parts. Relative to adult speech the younger preschool child uses many nouns, a fair number of verbs, but very few pronouns and adjectives, and hardly any prepositions or connectives. Speech is direct and bald without the later nuances he learns with age. It is essentially disconnected and lacking in, what to adult ears is, rhythm and fluency. When to this differing grammatical usage is added three properties of relatively poor articulation, shorter sentences, and a small vocabulary, we have the speech of the younger preschool child. Over the years of this period profound changes take place, the nature of which have just been sketched. These changes take the five-year-old, on his leaving the preschool period, a great distance in the direction of adult speech. Certainly, the preschool years are the period of the greatest changes in speech development of the child. By the same token he advances in the degree of his socialization.

Individual, Group, and Sex Differences in Language Development

Children of five years of age differ considerably in their facility with oral language. Some are chatterboxes, talking from the moment they wake up in the morning until they fall asleep at night. Others are quiet, almost silent children, economical with words, speaking only when spoken to and often using a nod or a shake of the head where a flow of words would be forthcoming from another child. Some children speak with a variety of good and poor articulations, a sparse or rich vocabulary, and so on.

To put the matter in terms of the specific aspects of oral language, there are individual differences among children of the same age in size of vocabulary, clarity of articulation, ability to integrate words into sentences, length of verbal responses, and the relative usage of different grammatical parts of speech. In fact, from time to time we have drawn attention to these differences. Nevertheless, stress was placed on changes with age. Attention was focused on individual differences, but on differences in speech brought about by differences in age. In one sense, age was tacitly treated as the source of differences, although it is, of course, recognized that changes are a matter of maturation and learning concomitant with age, not age itself. It is only in this sense that age is a source of differences. Other sources of differences in speech skills during the preschool period are individual, group, and sex factors.

Individual differences among children in language skills reflect the importance of practice and reinforcement. Several lines of evidence may be mentioned. Studies (32, 33) of institutionalized children show vividly the importance of lack of reinforcement. Because of lack of contact with others, institutional children do not have as many reinforced speech responses as compared to the other children—those living in foster homes. The speech of the institutional children was found to be impoverished. There are other sources of evidence for the effect of lack of reinforcement. For example, twins and triplets are slower in learning speech than singletons (56). Presumably, they are not so highly motivated to learn language because many of their reciprocal social needs may be met by means other than verbal communication which results in less language reinforcement.

There are also situations that increase exposure to reinforcement of language responses. Increased vocabulary development is associated with vacation travel (27). In this instance, there would be exposure to the words for new objects and new processes seen. Thus "tractor" or "harvesting" may be learned from a visit to the farm. Upper (or upper middle) socio-economic circumstances (72) appear to increase vocabulary. Exposure to the material things that go with upper socio-economic circumstances, such as the magazines and the encyclopedia, help to broaden the language horizon (19, 20, 21, 22, 23). Only children are also more advanced in vocabulary than others. They tend to associate more with adults than do other children and are thus exposed to more opportunities for reinforcement of new language responses.

Sex differences in language skills have often demonstrated that girls show superiority over boys in nearly all aspects of speech development (56). One aspect of speech development, length of response, will illustrate. McCarthy (56) summarizes 14 major, carefully controlled studies of length of speech responses at preschool ages. Of the 64 comparisons, 43 favor the girls. However, the relatively recent and exhaustive study of Templin (72) casts considerable doubt on this contention since she found the sex differences in favor of the girls to be much less pronounced. It may be that recently social forces have been at work that tend to remove this source of difference.

Differences in intelligence is another potent factor related to differences in language ability. In fact, size of vocabulary as measured by the Stanford-Binet Intelligence Scales is generally considered to be the most important single test of intelligence among the scales. Indicative of the popularity of the vocabulary section is the common practice that when a relatively short intelligence measure is wanted, the vocabulary test is used alone. The correlation between the vocabulary test and the total Stanford-Binet Scales is about 0.70 or 0.80 (57), thus showing a remarkably high degree of relationship between the two.

To give an illustration from studies of language development, in the McCarthy preschool study approximately the same degrees of relationships to language indices were found for mental age as for chronological age. Mental age could be substituted for chronological age in stating any of the previous findings from this study with similar results. Here again with the recent Templin study (72) the correlations with IQ seemed to be somewhat lower. They average about .50 with the number of different words in 50 remarks through age 4.5, but drop to about .25 for age five onward, indicating a sharp break at the age where functions other than intelligence presumably becoming more operative.

What ever the degree of relationship, it must be emphasized, these findings do not indicate that intelligence "causes" language ability or language ability "causes" intelligence. We must be content with knowing that there is a relationship, without having precise knowledge of cause and effect.

Language and Hierarchization

A significant point concerning the acquisition of the names of things has been made by Brown (12). On the basis of the developmental principle of differentiation we would expect that vocabulary would build from relative lack of differentiation to increased differentiation. As a matter of fact, there is evidence that some of the child's vocabulary is learned this way—milk and water are acquired before liquid, apple and orange are learned before fruit, mother and father before parents, and the like.

Some concrete terms appear in the vocabulary before abstract or superordinate terms (69). But this is by no means always the case; the child also learns fish before perch or bass, car before Chevrolet or Ford, house before bungalow or mansion. However, this finding, seemingly contradicting developmental principles, need not be, as Brown points out, embarrassing. The child's vocabulary is being determined in part for both trends by the naming practices of adults. Sometimes they want children to know first the subordinate words, orange or father, before the superordinates, fruit or parents. Sometimes they want them to know the superordinate word first, fish or car, before the subordinates, perch or Chevrolet. Primarily the parent chooses the word that meets the child's and his own needs, and this is the commonest name at its usual level of utility.

Intellectual development

As in infancy, intelligence in early childhood may be considered both at a descriptive level of examining the content of an intelligence test and seeing how predictive it may be, and at a more systematic level of examining its nature through findings from factor analysis. Because of developments in language and conceptualization during early childhood, there arises the greater usefulness of verbal materials for the measurement of intelligence. This is reflected in the contents of the California Preschool Schedule, an intelligence test especially developed for use with children of this age. Although it includes items on block building, manual facility, and drawing, it also includes conceptual material such as spatial relations and size and number discriminations; also included are verbal items on language comprehension, language facility, and immediate recall of verbal materials (41). As can be seen from this listing, conceptual and verbal materials are not neglected.

It will also be noted that a relatively wider array of abilities has been included than in infant tests. As might be expected from greater weighting with verbal-conceptual materials and from wider sampling of abilities, intelligence tests administered during the preschool years are better predictors of later intelligence than are scores on tests administered in infancy (41).

As part of the Guidance Study of the University of California Institute of Child Welfare (described in Chapter 1), 250 children were given periodic intelligence tests beginning at the age of one year, nine months, and continuing for a 16 year period (*41*). The California Preschool Schedule was given to each child during early childhood, whereas the Stanford-Binet (described on pages 499–505) was administered during later childhood. The correlations they found between intelligence test scores in early and later childhood are given in Table 14.

They show an improvement in prediction over that found between measures first given during infancy and then later.

TABLE 14

CORRELATION BETWEEN INTELLIGENCE TEST SCORES IN
EARLY AND LATER CHILDHOOD *

Age	Correlation with S-B Age 8	Correlation with S-B Age 14
2	43	21
3	49	35
4	61	54

* Adapted from Honzik *et al.* (*41*). Copyright 1948 by the *Journal of Experimental Education*, and published with permission.

As children grew older their test scores became increasingly more related to scores obtained still later in childhood, and hence, increasingly more predictive. This continues a trend, mentioned in Chapter 7, for intelligence test prediction to become increasingly more accurate the older the child is when tested. Correlations of intelligence test scores of preschool-age children with those obtained in later childhood are relatively more predictive even over much longer periods of time. However, the correlations are not high enough to eliminate the possibility of large differences in the scores of individual children from test to retest. Individual children may still differ markedly from age to age in test scores, despite these substantial correlations.

Much inconsistency still remains. It may be attributed to a considerable number of causes such as different rates of growth in the various abilities included and differing adjustments to the test situation.

Turning to factor analytic studies in early childhood, we saw that the study of Hofstaetter (*40*), reported in Chapter 7, found a factor of sensorimotor alertness to account for the results of intelligence testing during infancy. Let us now review his results for early and late childhood. The sensorimotor factor continues to contribute somewhat to intelligence during the 20 months following infancy, but by 40 months of age this factor has practically disappeared. From 40 months onward, Factor III, called "manipulation of symbols," accounts for the correlations. It, along with Factor I, contributes to the period from the 20th to the 40th month, but the major factor in accounting for a child's intelligence between 20 and 40 months is Factor II called "persistence"—acting in line with an established set, rather than considering interfering stimuli.

To summarize, sensorimotor alertness accounts for intelligence during the first 20 months; persistence plus sensorimotor alertness and manipulation of symbols, the period between 20 and 40 months of age, and manipulation of symbols from 40 months onward increasingly account for intellectual processes. In the second decade of life, it is practically only Factor III that accounts for the intellectual processes.

A factor analysis (43) was performed using data from the Merrill-Palmer Scale obtained from superior children aged 36 to 42 months. Three factors, accounting for more than one-half the variance, were identified as not occurring in intelligence tests at later ages, thus confirming Hofstaetter's general conclusion. Moreover, one of these factors was identified as "persistence," confirming him in this particular finding. The other two factors were willingness to cooperate and fine motor coordination, reminiscent of Hofstaetter's finding concerning infants. It would appear then that preschool years, dominated by the persistence factor, and perhaps others, are something of a transitional period, bearing some sort of relation to the negativism commonly found at this age, and perhaps, to what Piaget referred to as egocentricity.

Major consideration of intelligence will be discussed in connection with older children. This will include analysis of the effect of preschool attendance on intelligence, a concern of importance to children of the age considered in the present chapter (pages 511–515).

Summary

Rapid physical growth characterizes the young child although the various parts of the body have different growth curves. In motor development he progresses from the clumsy two-year-old to the coordinated and graceful five-year-old.

Both learning and maturation contribute to this development. For a given motor skill, stages may be traced beginning at the level where no attempt is made, progressing through the stage in which skill is in the process of formation, to the point where the basic movements are achieved. Illustrative changes in these degrees of motor skill are given.

The isolation of a strength and of a speed factor has been achieved on studying the interrelation among motor skills.

Emotional patterns of anger and fear in early childhood show developmental changes in expression, frequency, causes, and general conditions for their appearance. Although fear and anger differ from each other in regard to all of these characteristics, they are related in a variety of ways, including their being simultaneously aroused. In contrast to anger and fear that are the disruptive emotions, the affectively pleasant emotions have received less systematic attention. Smiling and laughter are found to be their major external behavior indices. The sources that brought about their arousal were explored and a considerable variety of instigators unearthed.

Cognitive development as seen through the eyes of Piaget shows a growth toward symbolic representations expressed in stages preparatory to preoperational thought. The child manipulates representations but has not yet reached mature or full symbolic functioning. His concepts are not yet fully developed.

Perceptual-cognitive development was examined through an account of some modern research efforts, especially concerning concepts of space and time. Piaget's theoretical framework was again utilized but the research showed that his view, although not incompatible, was incomplete. The hierarchical development of concepts according to levels of abstraction as formulated and studied by Welch closed the discussion.

Language development was seen as a cognitive function dependent on learning processes. Its usefulness in problem solving was demonstrated through research findings.

Language development in early childhood brings out clearly that both egocentric and socialized functions are being served. Although there is disagreement on the proportion of the speech of the child serving each of these functions, there is general agreement that both functions are present and that a decrease in egocentric speech takes place with increasing age. Other functions of language were examined briefly. The growth of vocabulary size continues during these years. Other developments during this age period are changes in clearness of articulation, in the integration of words into sentences, in the length of sentences, and the relative use of the grammatical parts of speech. All are found to show greater maturity as the child grows older. Despite these similarities, there are individual, group, and sex differences in language development.

Intellectual development is only briefly considered since considerable attention is devoted to this facet of development in a later chapter.

Intelligence at a descriptive level through examination of a typical test for this age shows that verbal-conceptual materials are increasingly used for measurement. Tests of intellectual status are more predictive here than tests administered during infancy. Factor analysis shows a characteristic pattern of kinds of abilities utilized in intelligence functioning at this age.

For Further Reading

Exhaustive reviews of emotional and linguistic development appear in the *Manual of Child Psychology: Second Edition*, edited by Leonard Carmichael (New York: Wiley, 1954). These are the chapters by Arthur Jersild and Dorothea McCarthy. Many of Piaget's books have been translated. For a general review Flavell (29) is again recommended.

References

1. Amen, E. W., and N. Renison. A study of the relationship between play patterns and anxiety in young children. *Genet. Psychol. Monogr.*, 1954, 50, 3–41.
2. Ames, Louise B. The constancy of psycho-motor tempo in individual infants. *J. Genet. Psychol.*, 1940, 57, 445–450.
3. Ames, Louise B. The development of the sense of time in the young child. *J. Genet. Psychol.*, 1946, 68, 97–125.
4. Arsenian, Jean M. Young children in an insecure situation. *J. Abnorm. Soc. Psychol.*, 1943, 38, 235–249.
5. Baruch, Dorothy W. Doll play in preschool as an aid in understanding the child. *Ment. Hyg.*, 1940, 24, 566–577.
6. Bayley, Nancy. The development of motor abilities during the first three years. *Monogr. Soc. Res. Child Develpm.*, 1935, No. 1.
7. Bayley, Nancy. Development and maturation. In H. Helson (Ed.), *Theoretical foundations of psychology*. New York: Van Nostrand, 1951, 145–199.
8. Berlyne, D. E. Recent developments in Piaget's work. *Brit. J. Educ. Psychol.*, 1957, 27, 1–12.
9. Blatz, W. E., Kathleen D. Allen, and Dorothy A. Millichamp. A study of laughter in the nursery school child. *Univ. Toronto Stud. Child Develpm. Ser.*, 1936, No. 7.
10. Brackett, Catherine W. Laughing and crying of preschool children. *Child Develpm. Monogr.*, 1934, No. 14.
11. Bridges, Katherine, M. B. *Social and emotional development of the preschool child*. London: Kegan, Paul, 1931.
12. Brown, R. How shall a thing be called? *Psychol. Rev.*, 1958, 65, 14–21.
13. Bruner, J. S., and C. C. Goodman. Value and need as organizing factors in perception. *J. Abnorm. Soc. Psychol.*, 1947, 42, 33–44.
14. Bruner, J. S., et al. *A study of thinking*. New York: Wiley, 1956.
15. Cannon, W. B. *Bodily changes in pain, hunger, fear and rage*. New York: Appleton-Century-Crofts, 1929.

338   EARLY CHILDHOOD

16. Cantor, G. N. Effects of three types of pretraining on discrimination learning in preschool children. *J. Exp. Psychol.*, 1955, 49, 339–342.
17. Carpenter, Aileen. The differential measurement of speed in primary school children. *Child Develpm.*, 1941, 12, 1–7.
18. Carter, L. F., and K. Schooler. Value and need as organizing factors in perception. *Psychol. Rev.*, 1949, 56, 200–207.
19. Davis, Edith A. *The development of linguistic skill in twins, singletons with siblings and only children from age five to ten years.* Minneapolis: University of Minnesota Press, 1937.
20. Davis, Edith A. Mean sentence length compared with long and short sentences as a reliable measure of language development. *Child Develpm.*, 1937, 8, 69–79.
21. Davis, Edith A. The mental and linguistic superiority of only girls. *Child Develpm.*, 1937, 8, 139–143.
22. Day, Ella J. The development of language in twins: I. A comparison of twins and single children. *Child Develpm.*, 1932, 3, 179–199.
23. Day, Ella J. The development of language in twins: II. The development of twins; their resemblances and differences. *Child Develpm.*, 1932, 3, 298–316.
24. Dietze, D. The facilitating effect of words on discrimination and generalization. *J. Exp. Psychol.*, 1955, 50, 255–260.
25. Ding, Gladys F., and A. T. Jersild. A study of the laughing and smiling of preschool children. *J. Genet. Psychol.*, 1932, 40, 452–472.
26. Dollard, J., and N. E. Miller. Personality and psychotherapy: *an analysis in terms of learning, thinking, and culture.* New York: McGraw-Hill, 1950.
27. Drever, J. A study of children's vocabularies: I, II and III. *J. Exp. Ped.*, 1915–1916, 3, 34–43, 96–103, 182–188.
28. Felder, J. G. Some factors determining the nature and frequency of anger and fear outbreaks in preschool children. *J. Juv. Res.*, 1932, 16, 278–290.
29. Flavell, J. H. *The developmental psychology of Jean Piaget.* Princeton: Van Nostrand, 1963.
30. Gesell, A., et al. *The first five years of life: a guide to the study of the preschool child.* New York: Harper, 1940.
31. Gesell, A., and Frances L. Ilg. *Child development: an introduction to the study of human growth.* New York: Harper, 1940.
32. Goldfarb, W. Psychological privation in infancy and subsequent adjustment. *Amer. J. Orthopsychiat.*, 1945, 15, 247–255.
33. Goldfarb, W. The effects of early institutional care on adolescent personality. *J. Exp. Educ.*, 1943, 12, 106–129.
34. Goodenough, Florence L. Anger in young children. *Univer. Minn. Inst. Child Welf. Monogr. Ser.*, 1931, No. 9.
35. Gutteridge, Mary V. A study of motor achievements of young children. *Arch. Psychol., N.Y.*, 1939, No. 244.
36. Hagman, E. R. A study of fears of children of preschool age. *J. Exp. Educ.*, 1932, 1, 110–130.
37. Hall, C. S., and G. Lindzey. *Theories of personality.* New York: Wiley, 1957.
38. Hartman, Doris M. The hurdle jump as a measure of the motor proficiency of young children. *Child Develpm.*, 1943, 14, 201–211.
39. Hicks, J. A. The acquisition of motor skill in young children: a study of the effects of practice in throwing at a moving target. *Child Develpm.*, 1930, 1, 90–105.

40. Hofstaetter, P. R. The changing composition of "intelligence": a study in T-technique. *J. Genet. Psychol.*, 1954, 85, 159–164.
41. Honzik, Marjorie P., Jean W. Macfarlane, and Louise Allen. The stability of mental test performance between two and eighteen years. *J. Exp. Educ.*, 1948, 17, 309–324.
42. Huang, I., and H. W. Lee. Experimental analysis of child animism. *J. Genet. Psychol.*, 1945, 66, 69–74.
43. Hurst, J. G. A factor analysis of the Merrill-Palmer with reference to theory and test construction. *Educ. Psychol. Measmt.*, 1960, 20, 519–532.
44. Jaffa, Adele S. The California Preschool Mental Scale (form A). *Univer. Calif. Los Angeles Syllabus Ser.*, 1934, No. 251.
45. Jeffrey, W. E. The effects of verbal and non-verbal response in mediating an instrumental act. *J. Exp. Psychol.*, 1953, 45, 327–333.
46. Jersild, A. T. Emotional development. In L. Carmichael (Ed.), *Manual of child psychology* (2nd ed.). New York: Wiley, 1954, 833–917.
47. Jersild, A. T. Research in the development of children. *Teach. Coll. Rec.*, 1936, 38, 129–143.
48. Jersild, A. T. Studies of children's fears. In R. G. Barker *et al.*, (Eds.), *Child behavior and development: a course of representative studies*. New York: McGraw-Hill, 1943, 329–344.
49. Jersild, A. T., and Frances B. Holmes. Children's fears. *Child Develpm. Monogr.*, 1935, No. 20.
50. Justin, Florence. A genetic study of laughter provoking stimuli. *Child Develpm.*, 1932, 3, 114–136.
51. Kogan, N., J. W. Stephens, and F. C. Shelton. Age differences: a developmental study of discriminability and affective response. *J. Abnorm. Soc. Psychol.*, 1961, 62, 221–230.
52. Landreth, Catherine. Factors associated with crying in young children in the nursery school and the home. *Child Develpm.*, 1941, 12, 81–97.
53. Leuba, C. Tickling and laughter: two genetic studies. *J. Genet. Psychol.*, 1941, 58, 201–209.
54. Lewis, M. M. *Infant speech: a study of the beginning of language.* New York: Humanities Press, 1951.
55. McCarthy, Dorothea. The language development of the preschool child. *Inst. Child. Welf. Monogr. Ser., Univer. Minn.* 1930, No. 4.
56. McCarthy, Dorothea. Language development in children. In L. Carmichael (Ed.), *Manual of child psychology* (2nd ed.). New York: Wiley, 1954, 492–630.
57. McNemar, Q. *The revision of the Stanford-Binet Scale: an analysis of the standardization data.* New York: Houghton Mifflin, 1942.
58. Meredith, H. V. A descriptive concept of physical development. In D. R. Harris (Ed.), *The concept of development: an issue in the study of human behavior.* Minneapolis: University of Minnesota Press, 1957, 109–122.
59. Miller, N. E., and J. Dollard. *Social learning and imitation.* New Haven: Yale University Press, 1941.
60. Mowrer, O. H. A stimulus-response analysis of anxiety and its role as a reinforcing agent. *Psychol. Rev.*, 1939, 46, 553–565.
61. Nice, Margaret M. Length of sentences as a criterion of a child's progress in speech. *J. Educ. Psychol.* 1925, 16, 370–379.
62. Norcross, Kathryn J., and C. C. Spiker. The effects of type of stimulus pre-

training on discrimination performance in preschool children. *Child Develpm.*, 1957, 28, 79–84.

63. Piaget, J. *The language and thought of the child.* New York: Humanities Press, 1926.

64. Piaget, J., and Barbel Inhelder. *The child's conception of space.* London: Routledge & Kegan Paul, 1956.

65. Ricketts, A. F.   A study of the behavior of young children in anger.   *Univer. Iowa Stud. Child Welfare*, 1934, 9, No. 3, 159–171.

66. Russell, R. W.   Studies in animism: II. The development of animism.   *J. Genet. Psychol.*, 1940, 56, 353–366.

67. Russell, R. W.   Studies in animism: IV. An investigation of concepts allied to animism.   *J. Genet. Psychol.*, 1940, 57, 83–91.

68. Sears, R. R.   Personality development in the family.   In R. F. Winch and R. McGinnis (Eds.), *Marriage and the family.*   New York: Holt, 1953, 215–240.

69. Smith, Medorah E.   An investigation of the development of the sentence and the extent of the vocabulary in young children.   *Univer. Iowa Stud. Child Welfare*, 1926, 3, No. 5.

70. Solley, C. M., and R. Sommer.   Perceptual autism in children.   *J. Gen. Psychol.*, 1957, 56, 3–13.

71. Springer, Doris.   Development in young children of an understanding of time and the clock.   *J. Genet. Psychol.*, 1952, 80, 83–96.

72. Templin, Mildred C.   *Certain language skills in children.*   Minneapolis: University of Minnesota Press, 1957.

73. Washburn, Ruth W.   A study of smiling and laughing of infants in the first year of life.   *Genet. Psychol. Monogr.*, 1929, 6, 397–537.

74. Watson, E. H., and G. H. Lowrey.   *Growth and development of children.*   Chicago: Yearbook Publishers, 1958.

75. Weir, M. W., and H. W. Stevenson.   The effects of verbalization in children's learning as a function of chronological age.   *Child Develpm.*, 1959, 36, 173–178.

76. Welch, L.   The genetic development of the associational structures of abstract thinking.   *J. Genet. Psychol.*, 1940, 56, 175–206.

77. Welch, L.   A behaviorist explanation of concept formation.   *J. Genet. Psychol.*, 1947, 71, 201–222.

78. Wellmann, Beth L., Ida M. Case, Ida G. Mengert, and Dorothy Bradbury. Speech sounds of young children.   *Univer. Iowa Stud. Child Welfare*, 1931, 5, No. 2.

79. Werner, H.   *Comparative psychology of mental development.*   New York: Harper, 1940.

12

Parental Influences

GREAT STRIDES were made in psychosocial development from the neonatal period to the end of infancy. The infant's social behavior repertoire increased enormously. During infancy he encountered the problems of the oral and anal phases and worked out some solution to them. He learned social needs. He learned to be dependent, but also took the first steps toward independence. He learned, to some degree, to direct and control his aggression. He encountered sex in its primitive beginning. He began to recognize himself as a person and to appreciate the presence and effect of other persons. Above all, he developed a complex pattern of relationships with another human being, his mother. But at the end of infancy he was by no means a fully socialized human being.

Allport expressed this point very well when he wrote:

> Even at the age of two, the child is, when measured by standards applied to adults, an unsocialized horror. Picture, if you can, an adult who is extremely destructive of property, insistent and demanding that every desire be instantly gratified, helpless and almost totally dependent on others, unable to share his possessions, impatient, prone to tantrums, violent and uninhibited in the display of his feelings (2, 28).[1]

To put it in Freudian terms, the infant is still ruled primarily by the pleasure principle, although he is beginning to appreciate the reality principle with its demand for sacrificing present pleasure either for future gain or for avoidance of punishment.

To examine the psychosocial development that takes place between

[1] From Allport (2). Copyright 1955 by the Yale University Press, and published with permission.

the second birthday and the end of the fifth year, we shall follow in the next several chapters the same course of presentation used for infancy: parental influences on socialization, the behavior tendencies, peer relationships, and self and social awareness, and then the phallic stage, sex tendencies, the evidence for psychoanalytic contentions, and neo-Freudian summaries.

Specific maternal practices

There is no reason to believe that the "specific maternal practices" of early childhood will be any more predictive of children's behavior than they were in infancy. This scepticism is reinforced by the lack of relationship between specific maternal behaviors and the attitude mothers take toward their children, which was the finding of one research investigation (161).

A sample of middle-class mothers was observed in interaction with their children through a one-way mirror in a child development laboratory. The observational categories are identified in the first column of Table 15.

TABLE 15

FREQUENCY OF APPEARANCE OF CATEGORIZED MATERNAL BEHAVIORS *

Behavior Category	Number
Being un-cooperative	6
Contacting	6420
Criticizing	10
Directing	920
Giving permission	30
Giving praise or affection	42
Helping	84
Interfering	36
Interfering by structurizing	92
Lending cooperation	170
Observing attentively	4688
Playing interactively	202
Reassuring	41
Remaining out of contact	1285
Restricting	31
Structurizing	133
Teaching	210

* From Zunich (161). Copyright 1962 by The Journal Press, and published with permission.

This table shows that the most frequent maternal behaviors directed toward young children were contacting, directing, lending cooperation, observing attentively, playing interactively, remaining out of contact, teaching, and *structurizing*, the last having to do with a description of a situation in the fashion that makes the child's decision his own. Maternal-attitude measures were those scales related to attitudes toward children contained in the Parent Attitude Research Instrument (*133*). The correlations between maternal behaviors and attitudes showed little or no relationship. Actually, there were 12 statistically significant relationships, but this was from a pool of 272 comparisons. No weight can be placed on the relationships found since on the basis of a customary statistical level. About 14 significant relationships could be expected by chance alone. Within the limits of this study, there appears to be no relationship between specific maternal behaviors and maternal attitudes.

Since the study of specific practices indicates no relationships, it seems sensible to pass on to a consideration of maternal attitudes and home atmosphere as related to children's behaviors.

Parental attitudes and home atmospheres

Parental attitudes are already familiar; home atmospheres, a new concept, are phases of the familial situation that have been isolated for study, such as the democratic atmosphere of the home, or the presence of unharmonious family relationships. The home atmospheres appear to be somewhat more general in nature than attitudes. Although these two approaches are distinguished methodologically both have often been used in the same study. Hence, there will be no attempt to isolate the results in separate discussions. The neutral term, patterns, will be used to refer to them collectively.

Baldwin's Approach to Patterns

One of the most significant research programs concerning parent behavior came from the Fels Research Institute. The investigators utilized the *Fels Parent Behavior Rating Scales* as their major instrument. These carefully contrived rating scales were designed to measure 30 variables of parental attitudes, parental behavior, and home atmospheres. Each scale was concerned with something considered important for its psychological impact on the child. The scales range from such global, all inclusive judgments as "adjustment of the home" to such specific variables as "restrictiveness of regulations."

Baldwin, Kalhorn, and Breese (12) correlated the interrelationships among the 30 variables. The subjects they used were drawn from 124 homes, a major portion of the Institute's permanent cooperating population. The parents, in the main, were above average in intelligence, economic status, and education. A visitor observed both mother and child in the home and made the ratings on the scales. The intercorrelations of the ratings on each variable with every other variable were calculated and the table of intercorrelations studied. Three syndromes, or groups of homes, were isolated that accounted for the intercorrelations obtained. These syndromes, as identified in the left-hand portion of Figure 12, are democracy in the home, acceptance of the child, and indulgence. The variables that made up the syndromes and from which they derived their summarizing names are also included and listed in order of their importance to the cluster. (At the moment no attention need be paid to the individual ratings given in the diagram portion of the figure.)

Knowing that homes fall into these three syndromes does not tell into which category a specific home would fall. It would be too much to expect that the three categories describing homes in general would be suitable for classification of individual homes. In specific homes we would expect varying positions from high to low on each syndrome. Consequently, the investigators first subdivided each of the three syndromes into regions of "high," "low," and "middling," and then classified the homes in these terms. A given home might be placed in any one of the three subdivisions for each of the syndromes. This allows emergence of 27 combinations. Actually, a considerably smaller number of patterns accounted for all but a few of the homes. It was possible to classify the majority of the homes into three major patterns, rejectant, acceptant, and casual.

Rejectant patterns. The rejectant pattern characterized the homes of one-quarter of the parents. In terms of the categories of Figure 12 these were the parents who more or less consistently received ratings at the low or rejectant end of the variables in the acceptance syndrome. Basically, they were consistently hostile, unaffectionate, and disapproving. These attitudes were so pervasive as to prevent them from being genuinely solicitous or democratic in dealing with their children. Instead, they were autocratic toward them. Although having these attributes in common, rejectant parents did fall into two groups. One group was *nonchalant,* with a general atmosphere of unconcern; the

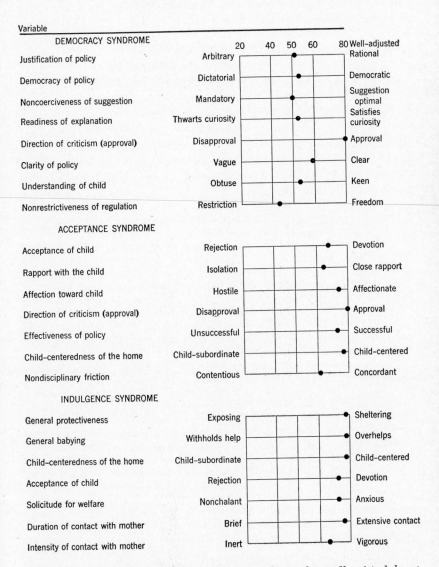

Variable

Figure 12. Syndromes of parent behavior and sample profile of indulgent behavior. (Adapted from Baldwin et al. (12). Copyright 1945 by the American Psychological Association and published with permission.)

other group was *dominant,* with hostility very prominent. General similarity of the rejectant pattern to instances described in earlier chapters makes further comment unnecessary.

Acceptant patterns. Acceptance characterized a little more than another quarter of homes of the parents. Although they had acceptance in common, there were three major groups: *indulgent, but not democratic; democratic, but not indulgent; and democratic-indulgent.* Figure 12 gives a sample profile of an acceptant, indulgent, but not democratic home. In this home the parents were especially prone to be very high in indulgence and acceptance items, but only about average for almost all the items in the democracy syndrome. A description of an acceptant, indulgent, but not democratic home, which could be the one given in the figure, follows:

Mrs. Harper is extreme in almost every variable of behavior making up the *indulgent* syndrome. Her attitudes and behavior toward Shirley Ann are obvious reflections of her smug, narrow set of values and her complete identification with the child. She is "living again" in her child, in the most literal sense of the phrase—setting her own adult standards for Shirley's behavior, interpreting Shirley's motives as identical with what her own would be, enjoying Shirley Ann as a new and more attractive version of her own self. Seeing Shirley Ann as a replica of herself, she freely gratifies any of her whims with which she can identify. . . . It is only when Shirley Ann's behavior violates Mrs. Harper's strict code of morals and proprieties that it meets uncompromising opposition.

A professional woman, married when she was thirty-three to a middle-aged salesman, Mrs. Harper has become a smug and proper middle-class mother. . . . Money, morals, and mores are her values. Shirley Ann was a much desired child, and her birth represented fulfillment to both parents. Being attractive and intelligent, Shirley is a social asset to the Harpers, and their appreciation of her unique qualities has led them to be two completely doting parents who make no effort to conceal or rationalize their adoration of the remarkable handiwork they have brought forth.

From Shirley Ann's birth, indulgence and child-centeredness have been the central features of the Harper household. When Shirley was two and a half months old, the home visitor reports: "Mr. and Mrs. Harper have apparently lost all objectivity in dealing with the child. Their treatment of her is a succession of lavish kisses, affectionate conversation, and considerable handling, almost mauling. Baby talk abounds, even when Shirley is not present. . . ."

Even in disciplinary situations Mrs. Harper finds it necessary to temper her severity with indulgent sympathy because, as she says, "punishment just about breaks Shirley's little heart. . . ."

Next only to the Harpers' rapture over the "bundle from heaven" they have produced comes their concern with molding this property into an utterly nice, utterly proper child. At three months Shirley was being broken of thumb sucking. . . . Muss and clutter are forbidden and from the very earliest age Shirley was subjected to intense restriction as to how many toys she could have out at one time and to rules about picking up one thing before going on to the next.   This imposition of adult standards of propriety, neatness, orderliness, reaches into the area of "free play" too, of course, since little of Shirley's life may be conducted according to her own initiative or taste.   Another visitor reports: "Mrs. H. remarked to me with some despair after she had fruitlessly tried to get Shirley to arrange the blankets on her doll in correct order (sheet, blanket, quilt, and spread), 'How old do they have to be before they learn to do things *right?*'"   The proprieties which Mrs. Harper attempts to dun into the child vary from good manners at the table, including saying grace, to a subservient respect for her elders; this old-fashioned, rigorous philosophy of the docile child who is to be seen but not heard conflicts continually, of course, with the rapt adulation of the parents. . . .

The combination of indulgence and insistence on social graces leads to an extremely restricting form of protectiveness.   Throughout infancy Shirley was kept in a condition of "surgical asepsis."   When she was three, for example, she had a special doll to take to bed that she couldn't play with at any other time because it was kept laundered, fresh, and supposedly germ free.   Her social life is similarly kept free from possible taint.   Very few outsiders are permitted more than the most casual relationship with Shirley, all being found "bad for her" in one way or another.   The paternal grandfather has all but been forbidden the house, for instance, because he persisted in "spoiling" Shirley Ann (laughed when she sucked her thumb, kept her from a nap to entertain her, etc.); children are uniformly not good enough to play with her—they are dirty, infectious, bad-mannered or contaminating in some other way. . . .

Though in reality Shirley is far from being a docile, conforming child, she stays well enough within the limits imposed by the parents to assure a safe margin of approval.   Disciplinary crises are rare, but small mischievous types of disobedience are common enough to warrant continual suggestions and nagging.   An interviewer summarizing a conversation with Mrs. Harper wrote: "The general impression of the home is that Shirley is the apple of the eye; she has a secure place, but is handled with old-fashioned strictness about routine and 'niceness,' is being brought up 'properly.'   I felt that Shirley was on to this and could manage her parents skillfully, crying, loving, being cute, good, independent, etc., within the well-defined discipline limits, and that she is far more dominating and sure of herself, more indulged and self-centered than her parents suspect.   I had the feeling that Shirley was well in command of the situation and was keeping her parents happy" (12, 37–39).[2]

The acceptant, indulgent, nondemocratic home bears considerable resemblance to the overprotective home described in connection with infancy. The acceptant home, democratic but not indulgent, would appear to be related to acceptance within normal limits as described in a chapter on psychosocial development in infancy. The finding by

[2] From Baldwin *et al.* (12). Copyright 1945 by the American Psychological Association, and published with permission.

Baldwin and his associates that these two belong in separate groups serves to strengthen the contention made earlier that acceptance and overprotection should be distinguished.

Although having the acceptant pattern in common, three subpatterns of democratic homes were found: (1) *pseudo-democratic*—the parents allow the child to participate in some decisions, but at the same time give no freedom concerning anything fundamental or important; (2) *scientifically democratic*—the parents, although fond of their children, tend not to show it, but conscientiously apply and even force democracy because they know it is "right"; (3) *warm democratic*—the child is treated warmly, accepted in his own right, and treated democratically. A description of an acceptant, warm democratic home follows:

The Rampion household represents a rather happy combination of those factors judged by the authors to be productive of a "good environment" for the child. The parents themselves are well-adjusted, vital, outgoing; they enjoy children as such and their own children as individuals. They show a healthy balance between the type of psychological detachment which allows them to appraise the child objectively and a warm emotionality that permits them to exhibit their devotion without embarrassment or artificiality. The child occupies his proportionate place in the household, is a full member of the family group, and is neither catered to nor ignored.

Mrs. Rampion herself is a healthy "farm-woman" type of person, sturdily built, stable, kindly, and good-humored. She was a professional woman before her marriage and possesses to a remarkable degree qualities of tolerance and patience. With a keen sense of humor she embellishes the most mundane situations, making life interesting and flavorful for her family. She is alert and interested in community life, contributes generously of her time and services for a variety of groups and causes. Liberal in her political philosophy, she is a genuinely democratic person in the home and in the community.

The maturity Mrs. Rampion exhibits in her personal life and in her general attitudes is also displayed, naturally enough, in her behavior toward the children. Respecting them as individuals, she makes a conscious and conscientious effort to maintain an emotional distance, a detachment giving objectivity to her appraisal of them. An incident which reveals her imperturbability in the area of sex behavior is equally illustrative of her ability in general to see the children's behavior in perspective. "There is some possibility that Leonard masturbates, although Mrs. R. does not know definitely. He likes to stick out his penis and run around the house. Bobby is disgusted with the performance, Carol and Bud think it funny. Leonard also likes to rub himself on a toy horse which the children play on. 'He's very sexy,' Mrs. R. remarked. She had no emotional reaction to it, seemed casual and straightforward about the situation. It is definitely not a problem in her mind."

Her philosophy of nonintervention is further illustrated by the following incident: "The three children were playing well together. Once Carol got too near a ladder the boys were balancing. Mrs. R. called out the window for Leonard to watch her. She remarked that she hated to do it, and only resorted to warnings when she could foresee serious injury." If anything, the parents are too loathe to intervene. In their determination to stay out of the children's disputes they sometimes allow an undue amount of social pressure to be exerted upon the unfortunate culprit who incurs the disapproval of his siblings.

The Rampions, more than any other family in the study, have explicit and formalized techniques for expressing their democratic philosophy of child care. Family council is traditional, with full and equal membership being accorded each child as soon as he can meet the requirement of repeating verbatim and explaining the motion before the group. The agenda may consist of matters ranging from the question of who shall wash and who shall wipe the dishes to the decision as to whether Mrs. R. should take a job offered her. The council convenes at the request of any member, and customarily handles the arbitration of all disputes. For example: "A situation has recently arisen in the Rampion family which is significant in that it shows the technique of settling difficulties among members of the family. While Bobby was combing his hair upstairs, Leonard 'dibbsed' on the wishbones from two chickens. Bobby was furious when he found what L. had done, said that it was unfair because one could never dibbs on more than his share, that he had never done it, etc. As a matter of fact, Bobby had done it more than any of the others. The two argued about it far into the night. Both Mr. and Mrs. R. kept out of the argument, hoping, however, that Leonard would stick to his guns and that Bobby's fallacy in argument would be brought out by him. The night of my visit Bob had called a family council to settle the question, said that he would abide by the council's decision. Mrs. R. said that she was not going to bring up the fact that Bobby was the prize dibbser unless the other children mentioned it first."

In spite of the formality of democratic government and in spite of the emotional distance which the Rampions maintain, the home atmosphere is not bleak or forbidding. The warm tone so evident in all the family's relationships characterized their attitudes toward one another. Without a great deal of fondling or other overt symbols of affection, the parents convey to the children their deep devotion.

It should be emphasized that the Rampion home is not "perfect" nor even optimum in its effect on the child—so far as we can, at present, evaluate the optimum. Mrs. Rampion faces the usual run of disciplinary crises, feeding problems, and general reversals that come to most mothers, although she handles such situations with more than average patience and understanding. In this democratic atmosphere Leonard is, at present, making an excellent social adjustment, although his development in the past has illustrated some of the difficulties peculiar to such a closely knit and satisfying family structure. On the one hand his home background has been so encompassing in its satisfactions that Leonard found the outside world, by comparison, somewhat dull and uninteresting. His social adjustment during the preschool years was marked by shyness and withdrawal. At the same time, Leonard has suffered from his failure to meet the high standards of the Rampion household. He has been the most irresponsible and lazy of the children and, as a consequence, has been subjected to tremendous pressures, not from the parents as much as from his siblings. As a result, he has suffered from rather severe feelings of inferiority which have only been alleviated by his quite remarkable popularity in school (12, 49–51).[2]

Casual patterns. The casual pattern of parent behavior included nearly 50 per cent of the homes in the sample. These homes could not be as neatly categorized as those in either the acceptant or the rejectant patterns. They were united only by being mild and casual, not being either acceptant or rejectant. Along with other lesser groupings, there were two which the investigators thought deserved particular mention—the *casual autocratic* and the *casual indulgent.*

In order to consider the casual autocratic home, it is helpful to refer to the rejectant pattern. Parents in the rejectant pattern were autocratic in a negative way because of their dislike for children. Autocracy in the parents in the casual pattern is a positive technique adopted either out of policy or out of expediency, without being accompanied by rejection. An autocrat cannot be warm, but he is not necessarily rejectant. Illustrative is the fact that "old-fashioned" discipline is autocratic as a policy. Some "more modern" parents try to be sympathetic, but when faced with crucial issues become autocratic as a matter of expediency. The other major casual pattern, the casually indulgent, includes parents who react as the mood moves them, generally in a mild and haphazard way.

Other findings. In a later study Baldwin and his associates (13) found somewhat different patterns. Democracy and indulgence were verified as important, but a new pattern emerged which was "warmth," a combination of what in the earlier study was primarily the acceptance syndrome with some of the characteristics earlier assigned to indulgence. Still another new major cluster they found was intellectuality (striving to hasten development, readiness to explain to the child, and an understanding of his abilities and needs). Without going into detail it is possible to summarize these later findings along with the earlier ones and state that the major patterns of parent behavior, so far as this research has now taken us, are warmth, democracy, intellectuality, and indulgence.

It is a common experience to hear from a mother that she "learned on her first child," which carries the implication that she corrected her mistakes when dealing with the second child. It is, therefore, of interest to see what Lasko (86) found in this connection. She studied a first and a second child of the same mother by administering the Fels Scales separately for the two children and then studying the varieties in the warmth and indulgence patterns between them. The first child's initial experiences were found to be much more child-centered (a warmth variable) than those of the second. At the youngest age it would appear that the first child experiences a somewhat more fervent relationship than the second child of the same family. There was also a tendency (though not statistically significant) for the mother to have been more solicitous toward the first child and to protect and to baby him more than the second child at the same age. However, for both first and second children child-centeredness declined markedly from age two until age five.

Maternal expression of certain kinds of needs has been found to be related in a consistent fashion to certain expressions of her behavior toward children. The relation between the verbally expressed needs of the mother and her overt behavior toward the child was examined by Crandall and Preston (41). The mothers' needs were evaluated through scores provided by *Edwards Personal Preference Schedule* both on the need to be aggressive and the need to nurture others. Overt maternal behavior was measured through some of the *Fels Behavior Rating Scales*. Those considered to represent affectional maternal behavior were those for affectionateness toward the child, rapport with the child, direction of criticism, and intensity of contact. Representing protective maternal behavior were the scales for protectiveness, solicitousness, babying, and child-centeredness of the home. These two clusters of maternal behavior scales, affectional and protective, were among those found earlier as broad major dimensions of parent behavior (see page 350).

It was found that verbally expressed maternal aggression correlated negatively with the amount of affection mothers displayed toward their children. In other words, women with high aggression scores showed toward their children less overt affection, less close rapport, more criticism than approval, and less intense contacts. Their expressed need to nurture others was positively associated with their protectiveness toward their children. Those mothers with a strong general need to nurture others expressed toward their children more protectiveness, more solicitude. They over-helped them and gave them homes that were child-centered.

Results of factor analysis. Another approach to the patterns of data obtained by Baldwin and his collaborators is through factor analysis of the Fels Behavior Rating Scales. For the 30 scales Roff (126) found seven factors: (1) concern for child, (2) democratic guidance, (3) permissiveness, (4) parent-child harmony, (5) sociability-adjustment of parent, (6) activeness of home, and (7) non-readiness of suggestion. Since there was substantial correlation among these factors, Lorr and Jenkins (93) used Roff's matrix to perform a so-called second-order factor analysis. This was an attempt to eliminate this correlation and to reduce further the number of factors. They reported three second-order factors which they labeled (x) dependency-encouraging, (y) democracy of child training, and (z) organizations and effectiveness of control in the home.

The largest correlations with the x factor among the original scales were child-centeredness, solicitousness for the child, protectiveness, intensity of contact, duration of contact, and acceptance of the child, that is devotion rather than rejection. Over-all, the x factor seemed to represent encouragement of the child's emotional dependence on the parents.

The second factor, y, is best described by the scales for democracy of policy, noncoerciveness of policy, nonrestrictiveness, nonreadiness of criticism, readiness of explanation, and clarity of policy. Clearly, democratic values in child training are being upheld in the y factor.

The third factor, z, is characterized by the scales for vigilance of enforcement, severity of penalties, attempts at accelerating, and coordination of the household. This z factor seems to be concerned with organization and effectiveness of control ranging from strict orderliness at one extreme to chaos at the other.

Parental patterns and the behavior of the children. In the illustrations presented in the previous section, some hints of the differential behavior of children faced with differing patterns of parental behavior can be discerned. Nevertheless, no systematic examination of the relation between patterns of parental behavior and the behavior of these children has been given. Baldwin and his associates (10, 12), however, have reported on the relation of the patterns of parental behavior to the behavior of the children in these homes. In gathering information, trained child specialists observed the children's behavior both in the preschool situation and in their homes and then rated them on a number of characteristics.

They meant their findings about children's behavior in connection with an earlier study (12) to be more illustrative than definitive. One group, children from the rejectant homes, was not systematically dealt with in their later research, and hence their earlier report will be drawn upon. The actively rejected children were found to be nonconformists and resistant to adults. Less actively rejected children showed somewhat milder forms of these same characteristics.   If one word could be used to describe these children from rejectant homes as a group, it would be aggressive (125).

Baldwin, in a more definitive study (10), investigated three clusters of home variables—democracy, warmth, and indulgence—as related to the behavior of children from homes with these characteristics.   The subjects were 56 nursery school children between the ages of three and five years.

The democratic parental pattern was found to be associated with that for warmth and hence the results of children from these homes are treated together.   These children were found to be socially outgoing in both friendly and hostile fashion, to be active participants in school activities, and to be generally assertive.   They were also socially successful and popular.   In more general terms they may be described as social and assertive.   The children from indulgent homes showed the opposite kind of personality characteristics.   They tended to be inactive, unaggressive, and socially unsuccessful.   In general, they may be described as unsocial and nonassertive.

Radke's Approach to Patterns

Another approach to the patterns of parent behavior and attitudes in relation to their children's behavior is that of Radke (125).   Her subjects, mothers and fathers of 43 preschool children, completed questionnaires and were interviewed concerning disciplinary practices and ways in which they carried on authority functions of the family.   The items in the questionnaire were grouped into scales which made it possible for the investigation to make judgments concerning (1) philosophy of authority, from autocratic to democratic; (2) parental restriction, from strict and firm to lax and easy-going; (3) severity of punishment, from severe to mild; and (4) parent-child rapport, from good to poor.

What are some of the characteristics of the children who come from homes characterized as autocratic, democratic, restrictive, or severely disciplined?   A summary answer to this question may be obtained from information Radke had collected about the children and the home.

Children from relatively autocratic homes compared with children from more democratic homes were found to rate as more unpopular with other children, as more given to fighting and quarreling, as more inconsiderate, as more emotionally unstable, as more daring and uninhibited, and as more insensitive to praise or blame.   Radke suggests in explaining these results that they come about from the shift of setting which such a child experiences.   A child coming from an autocratic home to the presumably less autocratic atmosphere of the school finds himself in the midst of contemporaries whose powers are not as strong as those of his parents. As a consequence, he assumes the behavior of his parents toward the other children, acting without sensitivity or consideration for others. Unpopularity and not getting along well with schoolmates are logical outcomes. In general, the patterns from the restrictive homes and those where severe discipline is used give the same picture as that from autocratic homes.

Children from more democratic homes were found to show an opposite constellation of behavior characteristics to those of the autocratically controlled children. Thus, they are more popular, nonquarrelsome, considerate, compliant, emotionally stable, sensitive to the opinions of others, and nonleaders (though not followers).

Sears' Approach to Patterns

A factor analysis of the ratings on the Sears, Maccoby, Levin child-rearing scales performed by Milton (*111*) isolated five major factors: (1) permissiveness-strictness; (2) general family adjustment; (3) warmth of mother-child relationship; (4) responsible child-training orientation; and (5) aggressiveness and punitiveness. In discussing the effects of child rearing on the children Sears and his colleagues chose to emphasize the mother's warmth and the effects of punishment and of permissiveness.

The other end of the warmth continuum, maternal coldness, associated in their research with the development of feeding problems and persistent bed-wetting, contributed to high aggression and was an important background condition for emotional upset during severe toilet training and for the slowing of conscience development. The second factor, punishment, and the third, permissiveness, were related primarily to the first factor of permissiveness-strictness and secondarily to the fifth factor, aggression and punitiveness. Since relation to the last factor may not be immediately apparent, it should be mentioned that the scales defining it were for use of high physical and severe punishment and low permissiveness for aggression toward parents as well as high demands and permissiveness for aggression toward other children.

Punishment was important—mothers punishing severely for toilet accidents or punishing dependency severely tended to have bed-wetting children in the first instance and dependent children in the second. The children who were punished severely for aggressiveness were apt to be more aggressive than those who were punished lightly.

Permissiveness, the third quality, had no discernible relation to dependent behavior. But permissiveness for aggression was an important source of continuing aggression and was associated with a low frequency of feeding problems. Permissiveness about sexual matters was less associated with a low frequency of enuresis.

A Comparison among the Patterns

The studies of Baldwin, Radke, and Sears, although derived by different methods, with different populations, and with varying scope of content and direction of interest, permit comparison of their major findings on parental factors. Their results, already reviewed, are summarized in Table 16. Another source in the search for patterns of attitudes is the factor analysis of the questions concerned with attitudes toward child rearing and the family presented by the Parent Attitude Research Instrument (PARI). Answers in one study came from 100 unmarried student nurses (132), in another study from 100 mothers, and in still another from a large heterogeneous sample of mothers (160). Their findings, also given in the table, need review.

TABLE 16

THE MAJOR DIMENSIONS OF PARENT ATTITUDES FOUND BY VARIOUS
INVESTIGATORS

Fels (Lorr and Jenkins)
Dependency encouraging
Democracy of child training
Organization and effectiveness of control

Radke
Autocratic-democratic
Parental restriction
Severity of punishment
Parent-child rapport

Pattern (Sears)
Strictness
General family adjustment
Warmth
Responsible orientation
Aggressiveness and punitiveness

PARI (Schaefer and Bell)
Interpersonal distance
Hostile rejection homemaking role
Excessive demand for striving

TABLE 16 (Continued)

Overpossessiveness
Hostile punitive control

PARI (Schaefer)
Approval of maternal control
Approval of expression of hostility
Approval of positive attitudes toward child-rearing

PARI (Zuckerman)
Authoritarian control
Hostility-rejection
Democratic attitudes

Originally Schaefer and Bell found five relatively independent factors: (1) suppressive and interpersonal distance—which has to do with a close to distant relationship, and seems to be related to warmth; (2) hostile rejection of homemaking role—adequately defined in itself; (3) excessive demand for striving—a need for conformity and achievement on the part of the child; (4) overpossessiveness—keeping the child indebted to the mother, and dependent and immature; (5) hostile primitive control—parental dominance and submission of the child. However, in a subsequent factor analysis (130) (132) using 100 multiparal women (mothers of more than one child) only three factors were found: (1) *approval of maternal control;* (2) *approval of expression of hostility;* and (3) *approval of positive attitudes toward child rearing.*

Schaefer tends to place greater emphasis on the results of this second factor analysis, not only because it was carried out with experienced mothers but also because it agrees with the results found by Zuckerman and his associates (160). These latter investigators obtained results on PARI from a large heterogeneous sample of mothers. Factor analysis revealed three factors: *authoritarian control* that has to do with authoritarian, suppressive, primitive, and restrictive kinds of attitudes; *hostility-rejection* that has to do both with hostility toward children and rejection of maternal role; and *democratic attitudes* which involve encouraging verbalization, equalitarianism, comradeship, and sharing. It might seem that this last factor is the opposite of the first factor, but this is not the case. Some mothers are actually high in both.

Clearly there are some similarities among the findings. Schaefer and Zuckerman and his associates substantially agree, despite differences in terminology. Moreover, a study of parental attitudes of fathers (119), heretofore not mentioned, found a high degree of agreement with the result of other investigators who had studied mothers.

The democratic theme with or without an autocratic component is apparent throughout all of the analyses. A continuum of attitudes toward punishment is prominent. Something that might be called love-hostility also seems present. Indeed, Schaefer and Bell (132) were so encouraged to find that their factors agreed with those obtained from other analyses that they thought a stable set of dimensions might be emerging. It is just as evident that there are differences and confusing discrepancies.

In order to supply a tentative integration, attention is directed to one final study by Schaefer (130, 131). The approach is said to be more molar than the molecular approach of Sears and his associates. (Presumably this same criticism could be expressed about all factor studies, including Schaefer's own earlier study.)

Using some of the data of the earlier studies, Schaefer applied a quite different method of analysis, the so-called *circumplex* model, which is said to have the advantage of isolating more molar social emotional interactions of mother and child. His practice of referring to the results as "dimensions," rather than as factors, will be followed here to signalize the shift in intent and in statistical method. He isolated two major dimensions, love versus hostility and autonomy versus control (130). Thereafter, he proceeded to an analysis of the literature (131) and finally arrived at a hypothetical circumplex model given in Figure 13.

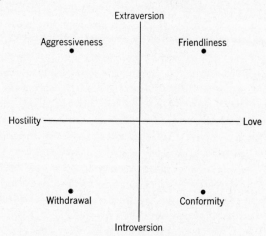

Figure 13. *A hypothetical circumplex model for maternal, social and emotional behavior. (From Schaefer (131). In C. Glidewell (Ed.), Parental attitudes and child behavior, 1961. Courtesy of Charles C Thomas, Publisher.*

The two reference dimensions of love-hostility and extraversion-introversion would show various combinations identified by the other terms in the figure. These are *friendliness,* involving out-going positive behavior; *uniformity,* involving compliant, controlled positive behavior; *withdrawal,* involving the hostile and fearful avoidance of interaction; and *aggressiveness,* involving hostile attack with little impulse control. Future research may or may not verify this model. Once it is emphasized that this is a *hypothetical* model, it has much to recommend it as a way of summarizing the parental patterns and home atmospheres brought to bear on the young child.

The socializing effect of the father

Though relatively less accessible for research study, the father has not been neglected as much as might first appear. In the Fels series of studies under Baldwin and the study of Radke, the socialization patterns that emerged bore the imprint of the father as well as the mother. *Parents,* not mothers alone, were their subject of study. Nevertheless, very little direct reference has been made to the father as such.

Radke's approach (*125*) made possible a comparison of the mothers' parental behavior and attitudes with those of the fathers'. On her four scales the responses of the mothers, when compared with those of the fathers, showed only a few relatively specific differences in connection with philosophy of authority, parental restriction, and severity of discipline. In the entire area of philosophy of authority, the only item showing differences was that the mothers more often explained to the children the reasons for the discipline they received than did the fathers. In the area of parental restriction, mothers were more lenient in allowing the child to have his own way. It was in the area of parent-child rapport that differences were more widespread. As compared with mothers, fathers showed less rapport with their children, fewer shared confidences, less amount of time devoted in answering questions, and less amount of affection shown their children. The father was less of a supervisor, less affectionate, and yielding.

It would appear not incompatible with Radke's findings that, as Kardiner (*81*) states, the father, although standing in the background, is often the final authority, even though executive power is exercised through the mother. Supporting evidence for this point is to be found in a section of the next chapter concerned with the child's perception of the situation. To anticipate, investigators have found that children perceive the father as the source of authority.

One direct and crucial way to study the socializing effect of the father is to examine homes in which the father is absent, and thus to see what effect this absence has upon the children. Both in early (*141*) and later childhood (*8*), boys from father-present homes demonstrated much more aggression than did those from father-absent homes. A girl's aggressive tendencies were not affected by the father's absence. These results are examined in more detail later in connection with the discussion of aggressive tendencies.

The father, it would seem, serves as a model, especially for the boy. This is brought out very clearly in discussion of identification and sex-typing in a later chapter. Serving as a model is one of the father's major functions. But it is not his only function. Besides being a father, he is a husband, an economic provider, a source of intellectual and social stimulation, an arbiter, and a friend. Not always does exercise of these functions involve the child directly. As a husband, his functional relations are primarily with his wife. Always, however, he is a member of a network of social relations. Affecting one part of that network ultimately affects all parts. So the child in this social complex is ultimately affected by all of the father's functions.

Material is emerging showing that when the father is examined in terms of his parental role rather than his general personality characteristics, significant relationships to his child's behavior are obtained (*19*). This work is in its infancy so no attempt is made to present more specific results. There is no doubt, that the father's role in the psychosocial development of young children has been underestimated.

Techniques of discipline

The problem of discipline has not yet been examined explicitly. The mother wants the child to continue certain forms of behavior and to stop others. She may use rewards or incentives and she may use threats, punishments, or distractions. The scales used by Baldwin and his associates include those concerned with the degree of restrictiveness of regulations, the direction of criticism, and the effectiveness of parental policies, which appear relevant to the problem. Similarly, three of Radke's four scales, authority, parental restriction, and severity of punishment, have a distinct disciplinary cast to them. Permissiveness-strictness was one of the factors found by Sears, Maccoby, and Levin. In the three studies, information about discipline in a rather general supervisory sense has already been examined. There is another more restrictive, specific, and technique-oriented aspect to discipline which needs examination.

Discipline is essential for the child. Without it the world is too disorganized to permit his adjustment to it. If there are no rules to the game of living, he cannot learn to play it. A paradoxical condition of social living is that for full development to occur, child and adult alike, one must give up some of one's freedom. Without limits by discipline a child cannot learn to deal with the demands set by the environment when they run counter to his own inclinations. A balance or a compromise must be set between his needs and the restrictions placed by the environment. Discipline is very much an instrument of the process of socialization in that through it the parent guides the child in the direction of what is socially acceptable in his culture.

From the point of view of the child, much of the discipline he receives is arbitrary. For reasons he often does not understand, he discovers he is expected to behave in certain ways and not in certain others. In fact, it is because of his failure to understand that the imposition of discipline takes place.

With this discussion as background, we are now in a position to turn to the empirical results concerning parental discipline and the young child. Radke's study (125) supplied information about the types of punishment used by the parents of preschool-age children. The kinds and percentage of homes reporting the kinds of punishments are shown in Figure 14. Spanking, isolating, rewards and praises, allowing conduct to bring about its consequences, verbal appeals, and depriving were the commonest kinds of punishment. Commenting on the influence these punishments may be presumed to have on the children's behavior, Radke states that most of the kinds of punishment "are aimed at undermining the power of the child or at restricting his freedom, either physical or psychological" (125, 49).[3] Spanking, isolating, and depriving are illustrative of undermining or restrictive tendencies. Allowing the child to suffer the natural consequences is also somewhat restrictive. Discipline as practiced by the parents in her sample thus seems to be predominantly restrictive.

Quite possibly these kinds of punishment tend to decrease the child's sense of security. Radke's results were stated without regard to changes in punishment practices as children grew older. The reports concerning punishment practice at time of preschool entrance were taken one-and-a-half to three years before the reports collected in connection with the research study data heretofore considered. Changes with ages are also reported in Figure 14. It is apparent that there was an increase in the amount of almost all kinds of punishment as the children became older.

[3] Marian J. Radke, *The Relation of Parental Authority to Children's Behavior and Attitudes.* Copyright 1946, University of Minnesota.

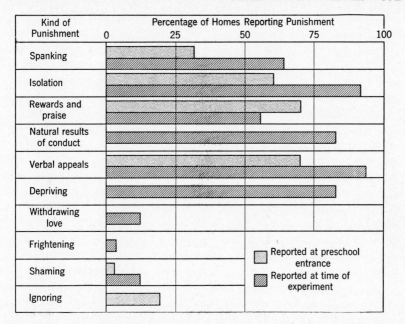

Figure 14. The kinds of punishment reported by parents of pre-school-age children. (Marion J. Radke, The Relation of Parental Authority to Children's Behavior and Attitudes. Copyright 1946, University of Minnesota.)

What did the children think of their parents' punishment practices and how effective did they appear to be in the light of their opinions? Information about what the children thought was collected in the course of Radke's interviews with them when she asked about what they disliked in their parents' behavior. Although about a quarter of the children had no criticism to offer of either father or mother, 50 per cent mentioned they disliked most being punished and having their parents interfere with play.

Even more relevant to the question of the efficacy of punishment was Radke's finding that only 14 per cent of the children stated that punishments made them penitent or resolve to do better. Evidently the punishments used did not serve the function of effective discipline. Probably, the predominance of restrictive punishments is one of the reasons for its inefficiency. A further clue to its ineffectiveness is contained in the significant finding that over 50 per cent of the mothers and fathers showed anger when disciplining the child. Moreover, over a third of the children reported their parents gave them no explanation of the reasons for the punishment.

It is perhaps reassuring to note that the great majority of the children felt that their parents were justified in their punishments and that children should do what their parents tell them. The fact remains that, although accepting parents as rightful authorities, the children did not believe that punishment motivated them toward better behavior.

Sears, Maccoby, and Levin (140) in seeking information in their "pattern" study about training used many categories similar to those of Radke (125). They made a distinction between positive and negative sanctions. Those techniques that provide a reward include praise, a symbolic reward, and tangible rewards. Both praise and reward serve as reinforcers of preceding behavior. About 60 per cent of their samples fairly often or frequently used tangible rewards. Only 12 per cent of the mothers claim they never used rewards. Almost 80 per cent used praise fairly often, moderately, or occasionally. No use of praise is claimed by one per cent of the mothers.

Negative sanctions provided punishment including physical punishment, deprivation of privileges, withdrawal of love, and isolation. The investigators used both spanking and slapping as indices of physical punishment. In their sample, about 80 per cent are included among those who spanked rarely and only occasionally and those who spanked fairly often, sometimes severely. Only one per cent report never using physical punishment. A little more than 70 per cent are included in the area extending from occasional use of deprivation of privileges and slight use of isolation to frequent use of deprivation and considerable use of isolation.

The extent of use of withdrawal of love deserves a more detailed statement. Three per cent are explicit in saying they never use it, 37 per cent make slight or moderate use, while ten per cent make considerable or much use of withdrawal of love as a technique of punishment. Its use was not ascertained in 50 per cent either due to the reluctance of the mothers to speak of it or because its manifestations could not be detected by the raters.

Sears and his associates concluded that parental punishment was a dismal failure. To quote: "Our evaluation of punishment is that *it is ineffectual over the long term as a technique for eliminating the kind of behavior toward which it is directed*" (140, 484).[4] Punishment just did not work. It did not eliminate the kinds of behavior for which the mothers used it. As they state, their generally negative conclusion does not mean that punishment might not have been successful in eliminating some specific act, or another, say, a specific aggressive act such as a

[4] From Sears, Maccoby, and Levin (140). Copyright 1957 by Row, Peterson, and published with permission.

boy picking on his sister. In the long run and extending over more general forms of behavior, however, punishment was not effective.

We cannot leave this topic of patterns of parent behavior with its emphasis on authority, restriction, punishment, and control without considering how children "controlled" parents. In interviews the children had been asked by Radke how they got their own way against their parents' requests. Table 17 summarizes the findings. Each figure in the table refers to the percentage of the boys or girls who used the method in question. Thus the first entry, "pays no attention," shows that 25 per cent of all the boys used this method with their mothers. This means that the remainder, or 75 per cent, did not. Each entry in the table represents the percentage of the total sample of boys or girls who used the particular method of control with their mother or their

TABLE 17

PERCENTAGE OF CHILDREN USING VARIOUS METHODS
OF CONTROLLING THEIR PARENTS *

Method	Used with Mother		Used with Father	
	Boys	Girls	Boys	Girls
Pay no attention	26	25	39	29
Cries, has tantrums	21	26	17	14
Refuses parent's request	50	26	41	19
Whines, begs, and so on	47	39	53	33

* Marian J. Radke, *The Relation of Parental Authority to Children's Behavior and Attitudes.* Copyright 1946, University of Minnesota.

father. Naturally, many used more than one technique which accounts for the fact that going down any one column will not give a total of 100 per cent. Whining, begging, and other verbal appeals, and plain refusal appear to have been most successful. Crying and having tantrums worked least well. Girls, it may be noted, "get away" with less than do boys. As Thompson (147) suggests, this table might be studied with some profit by children of this age!

Changes in parental behavior with age

Parental concern about toilet training, eating habits, sex training, and the host of other psychosocially oriented behaviors would be expected to change as the child grows older. In general, there would be expected to be less contact between parent and child and fewer restrictions on his behavior (9). Not only would parents expect different things in the way of appropriate behavior when their child was older, but also they would hold with different attitudes, or attitudes different in degree from those that prevailed when the child was younger.

Baldwin (9), using the Fels Parent Behavior Rating Scales, investigated differences in attitudes of parents toward three- and nine-year-old children. The results are stated in terms of the now familiar patterns. Parents of nine-year-old children were less warm, less indulgent, less intellectually stimulating, and more restrictive than parents of three-year-old children. He stresses that this is due, in part, to changes in cultural standards in handling children. Norms of socialization shift and parents are expected to change as the child grows older. For example, hostility toward a three-year-old is considered more reprehensible in our society than is similar behavior toward a nine-year-old. Presumably other factors are at work as well.

Summary

Parental influences on the young child have now been examined. Specific maternal practices were again found to be unrelated to patterns of child behavior. Their examination, however, gave some conception of some of the practices that mothers follow with young children.

Patterns of parental behavior expressed in attitudes and home atmospheres have been found with a certain degree of consistency in different studies using different subjects and procedures. These patterns may be related to characteristic behavior in the children exposed to these patterns. When the patterns of different studies are compared by factor analysis and other means of study, authoritarianism, love-hostility, and democracy seem to be recurrent themes. A final summary in terms of a circumplex model with the dimensions of love-hostility and extraversion-introversion is tentatively suggested.

Although the relationships that have been reported are not to be taken as evidence that long-term patterns of child behavior are inevitably and precisely associated with particular patterns of parent behavior, they do demonstrate that important relationships exist between the behavior of mothers and fathers and the behavior of their children.

Variations in home atmosphere and parental attitudes have been found to vary concomitantly with constellations of behavior in the child. It is tempting to conclude that direct causative relations have been found between parental behavior and consequent child behavior. Unfortunately, the picture is not so simple. There is undoubtedly an interaction effect and a reciprocal relation of child and parent behavior. Future research will help serve to untangle the skein of cause and effect.

Caution must be offered concerning interpretation of these congruities between paternal and child behavior. True, certain characteristic trends in child behavior were isolated for a given paternal pattern. But these characteristics, it must be emphasized, are of a general nature and do not hold for all children from homes with that paternal pattern. Children in any one home pattern may react in many different ways. Children from a rejectant pattern may react as described in the group trends or, as clinical studies demonstrate, they may become overdependent or withdraw into themselves or develop a precocious self-sufficiency, or react in several other ways. In dealing with group trends, as we are, individual exceptions inevitably are lost to view. A second limiting factor in the generality of the findings about parent and child behavior is the fact that the subjects investigated were what might be described generally as "middle-class" parents and children. Generalization of the findings to other socio-economic classes should only be done with considerable caution.

Turning to the socializing effect of the father, as compared with the mother, he is found to be less affectionate and yielding, and less in rapport with his children but apt to be the court of final appeal.

Techniques of training used by parents that stressed punishment were found to be ineffectual. Investigators found that changes in parental behavior with increasing age of the children consisted of older children receiving less contact and fewer restrictions in general; yet, parents applied more severe restrictions when situations arose which, in their judgment, required these restrictions.

For Further Reading

The book by R. R. Sears, Eleanor E. Maccoby, and H. Levin, *Patterns of Child Rearing* (Evanston, Ill.: Row, Peterson, 1957), is recommended. They give an account on what happens in the process of rearing the younger child in our contemporary culture. The interrelation which forms the various patterns is brought out in vivid detail. The somewhat different approach of A. L. Baldwin is brought out in the monograph he wrote in collaboration with Joan Kalhorn and Fay H. Breese called, *Patterns of Parent Behavior* (*Psychological Monographs*, 1945, 58, No. 268).

References

Follow Chapter 14.

13

Behavior Tendencies, Self, and Peer Relationships

I<small>N THE</small> young child, as in the infant, the expression of behavior tendencies is a factor of vital importance for psychosocial development. So too are further acquisition of self and social awareness and the broadening scope of peer relationships that are characteristic of this particular age. Because of their significance for development in early childhood all these facets are considered again in detail at this juncture, beginning with the behavior tendencies shown by the young child.

Behavior tendencies

In this chapter we shall expose to systematic examination three classes of behavior tendencies: dependence-independence, aggression, and achievement. Sex tendencies will be discussed in a subsequent chapter in the setting of psychoanalysis.

Dependence and Independence Tendencies

We begin this phase of our study with a presentation of evidence showing the extent to which dependence tendencies are separated from independence tendencies, together with a more detailed investigation into the meaning of these terms.

Relation of dependence and independence tendencies. During infancy dependence tendencies become firmly established. The same

366

cannot be said for strivings for independence. Moreover, it would be incorrect to assume without evidence that dependence and independence were merely opposite ends of the same continuum. For this reason changes in dependence occurring in infancy were described as moving from dependence to less dependence, rather than from dependence to independence. The ages three through five appear to be the critical period for optimal normal development of independence. Dependence was a necessary condition of infancy; independence is a task of the younger child.

Certainly, the diminishing dependence of the child as he grows older is a fact. It must be, in part at least, the result of positive development of more independent ways of responding to the same situations which, when younger, elicited dependent reactions. The preschool child appears to be motivated to perform independently, and a series of studies shows how real this independence behavior tendency is.

As components of independence behavior, Beller (20) suggested the following five: taking initiative, overcoming of obstacles, persistence, just wanting to do something, and wanting to do things by oneself. Using these as the components of independence, Beller constructed rating scales based on each component. Children about three to nearly six years of age were then rated on these scales by their nursery school teacher. Highly significant relations among the rating scales were found. The five indices of independence were found to "hang together" in that most of the children were consistent from one to another of these scales, thus demonstrating the reality of an independence drive so far as these components were concerned.

The second phase of his study was concerned with specific behavior components selected to furnish evidence of a general dependence drive. Rating scales were constructed for five components, namely, seeking help, physical contact, proximity, attention, and recognition. He used the same subjects, raters, and procedure as in the previous phase of the study. A highly significant degree of relationship among components was again found. Children differed consistently from one another in composite dependency scores. Thus, at least for these five components, there was evidence of a dependence drive.

Beller next performed the third phase of the study which is crucial to the issue of whether dependence and independence are separable. The correlation between independence and dependence, as he had measured them, was calculated for this group of children. If dependence and independence were merely opposite ends of the same continuum, a correlation approaching (but because of errors of measurement not reaching) a perfect negative correlation of -1.00 would be expected. The correlation he did find was a moderately negative -0.53. This relatively small correlation suggests that assuming dependence and independence to be merely bipolar ends of the same continuum is not indicated. Instead, they should be treated as separable, although related, tendencies. He confirmed his own results in a repetition of the study with different subjects (21).

Additional evidence of the validity of his dependence and independence measures was obtained by factor analysis of six samples consisting of one patient and two nonpatient groups, each separated into boys and girls (26). In each sample the items for the defining dependence or independence scale had high loadings with a common factor. This evidence seemed to show that each behavior tendency was a more or less unitary construct.

An additional bit of relevant evidence is to be found in Wittenborn's study reported in more detail on page 373. He found by cluster analysis of children's customary behaviors that dependence on adults was a separate cluster from taking an adult role (independence). In other words, there was no high (negative) correlation between children seeking dependent relations with adults and their desire to take on adult roles.

Still further support for considering dependence and independence as separate tendencies is to be found in a study by Heathers (65), reported in more detail on page 378. He found dependence and independence may be negatively, positively, or noncorrelated, depending on the specific independence and dependence measure considered.

With the samples used for the factor analyses, Beller (26) analyzed the sex differences in dependence and independence. Girls were more generally dependent than boys, but even more so on certain scales, especially in seeking more physical contact and nearness to adults. However, with independence no consistent pattern emerged, although if anything, the girls were more independent. This would be a finding hard to reconcile with the position that dependence and independence were only opposite ends of a continuum. Conceiving of them as such remove the seeming contradiction that girls, at the same time, may be more dependent and independent than boys.

Dependence and independence seem best conceived as separate components of child behavior. It is proper, therefore, to speak of the child while learning to depend on others as simultaneously learning to be independent. He shows both tendencies. He learns to help himself at the same time as he learns to depend on being helped. Independence responses and dependence responses both acquire habit strength when they are reinforced. This is another way of saying the determinants of dependence and independence tendencies must now be considered.

Determinants of dependence tendencies. During infancy and early childhood the child wants both to be dependent and to be independent. These incompatible behavior tendencies can involve the child in considerable conflict. Beller's measures of dependence and independence were constructed to permit investigation of the balance between the two (*24*). His measure of conflict was the degree of similarity between dependence and independence scores. Those children with a higher dependency conflict were more inhibited and inconsistent in their expressions of dependence. Inhibition and inconsistency were measured by placing the child in a situation where he and an adult were in a room with toys on the shelf within the reach of the adult, but not the child (*22*). The measure of inhibition was the inability of the child to ask for the toy outright. Moreover, such children showed more behavior problems, such as difficulties in toilet training, defiance, and compulsive behavior.

It is worth while to examine what forms dependence tendencies take at these ages. We already have clues from the work of Beller (*20*). He was found to define dependence in terms of seeking help, physical contact, proximity, attention, and recognition. Sears and his associates in their "pattern" study (*140*) found many indices of dependence in five-year-old children akin to those of Beller. The investigators questioned each of the mothers in their sample about how much attention their child seemed to want, how much and whether he ever followed her about hanging onto her skirt, and his reaction on her going out of the house leaving him with someone else. About 25 to 35 per cent of the children showed quite a bit or a great deal of attention-demanding and following about. Only about 15 per cent objected in any degree to her going out without him.

These aspects of dependency studies by Beller and Sears will be seen to have an obvious inspiration in the early pioneer work of Levy (*91*), who was concerned with overprotection as a determinant of dependency. He used the method of case sifting described in Chapter 2 to isolate 20 instances of pure maternal overprotection. Hundreds, if not thousands, of case records were examined by him in the process of finding this group. Maternal overprotection is distinguished from overprotection which masks as rejection in that the child is *wanted*. "Pure" maternal overprotection with which Levy was concerned refers to instances in which the child was, consciously at least, wanted by the mother.

Maternal overprotection is the unhealthy exaggerated manifestation of what within optimal limits has been called acceptance. Even when the child is past infancy, the mother "is always there," "treats the child like a baby," and "won't take any risks." To speak a bit more technically, by using Levy's terms there is apt to be (1) excessive contact; (2) infantilization; and (3) prevention of independent behavior.

Consider the following case history of a four-year-old boy:

> *Excessive contact:* There is still much fondling, sitting on mother's lap, constant kissing. Because she would not leave her children, the mother, until recently, rarely went out with her husband.
>
> *Prolongation of infantile care:* Mother still dresses him (until modified by treatment) at age 5.
>
> *Prevention of independent behavior:* The patient refuses to play with other children, preferring always to be where mother is (*91*, 35).[1]

The first two of these factors, excessive contact and infantilization, reinforce dependent behavior directly; the third factor, prevention of independent behavior, certainly does not reinforce independent behavior. But a fourth factor, excessive maternal control, seems crucial because its presence would appear essential if dependency is to appear. The group of 20 children whose histories showed excessive contact, prolongation of infantile care, and the prevention of independent behavior, sharply divides into two distinct groups based on differences in the kind of maternal control exercised. One subgroup was dominated by its parents and these children unequivocally showed dependent behavior.

The boy, whose case description was just given, had a very dominant mother. He did just as she told him and was considerate and solicitous of her. The dominant, overprotecting mothers were found to be very much intent in trimming their children to a desired shape. Their children showed docility, neatness, cleanliness, obedience, politeness, and diligence—but with all of these virtues were so timid and submissive as to be called sissies and fools by their playmates. Clearly, these children can be described as dependent. Overprotection combined with maternal dominance reinforces dependence. The other subgroup in which indulgence accompanied overprotection was found to lead to aggression and will be considered later in connection with aggressive tendencies.

In evaluating the determinants of dependency, it is appropriate to return to the study by Sears and his associates (*142*) of antecedents of aggression and dependence. They were concerned with the relation

---

[1] From Levy (*91*). Copyright 1943 by the Columbia University Press, and published with permission.

of frustration and dependence. In addition to infantile frustrations, considered earlier, they studied the relation of maternal punitiveness directed toward the preschool-aged subjects in relation to their dependence tendencies. They found a positive relation between the amount of punitiveness in the home and dependence tendencies in boys, but found the opposite relation in girls. By and large, the boys' dependency varied positively with the amount of punitiveness of the parents just as did their responses to other frustrations in infancy, but with the girls, dependency varied to some degree negatively with the amount of punitiveness of the parents.

In both boys and girls the distributions were slightly curvilinear, instead of being a straight line. Figure 15 illustrates this lack of linearity and also serves as a means of conveying Sears and his associates' interpretation of the different findings for boys and girls. To explain the different results of boys and girls, they make two assumptions. The first concerns the curvilinear relationship between amount of frustration of a drive and dependence tendencies. The second is that girls are more susceptible than boys to punishment by their mothers. The essence of their complicated argument is well-caught by Baldwin.

> The first assumption to be made is that the strength of drive that is formed from the combination of reinforcement and punishment depends upon the severity of the punishment Whereas a mild punishment or a threat of one may only strengthen the motive that is frustrated, a very severe punishment may inhibit behavior completely. The severity of punishment required to inhibit action may depend upon the strength of

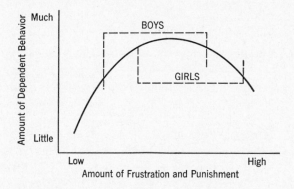

Figure 15. Hypothesized relation between frustration punishment and dependent behavior. (Adapted from Sears et al. (142). Copyright 1953 by The Journal Press, and published with permission.)

the motive. This hypothesis overlaps to some extent an earlier one we have discussed regarding the effect of tension level upon the directedness of behavior. Moderate tension permits directed adaptive behavior; very high levels result in restless undirected behavior. So the theory now hypothesized is that the combination of reinforcement and moderate frustration or punishment establishes a drive of maximum strength. Too much or too little frustration results in a weaker drive.

Now, a second assumption is that girls are more susceptible to punishment by their mothers than are boys. This in turn depends upon the assumption that girls are more identified with their mothers, whereas boys are more identified with their fathers. Thus, when a mother punishes her daughter, the punishment has greater psychological impact than when she punishes her son; it is more likely, therefore, to inhibit than to accentuate the motivation (11, 569).[2]

To support their argument Sears *et al.* (142) offer evidence that girls have higher identification with their mothers than do boys. Three of their pertinent findings are that girls (1) use the mother doll more often as the agent in doll play; (2) were rated higher by the mothers as emulating adult behavior; and (3) showed significantly higher dependence on their female teacher.

To return now to Baldwin's presentation he goes on to state:

> Putting these two assumptions together, let us suppose that the effect of frustration upon the strength of drive is represented by the curve in Figure ... [15]. Now, if punishment by the mother were more severe for girls than for boys, then the sample of girls in this study would fall toward the right-hand end of the curve. In this region of the curve, the more punishment, the less drive. The boys, on the other hand, are less affected by being punished, so they would fall along the left-hand end of the curve. Within this region, the more punishment, the more drive. This corresponds to the empirical finding (11, 569).[2]

Current frustration in relation to dependency seems thus to be accounted for. Amount of dependence behavior of preschool children is a curvilinear function of the amount of frustration and punishment of dependency-instigated behavior. Both lesser and greater amounts of frustration and punishment are associated with less occurrence of dependency, whereas the maximum occurrence of dependency is produced by moderate amounts of frustration and punishment. Girls identify more closely with their mothers than do boys and therefore a given degree of maternal frustration or punitiveness has a stronger effect on girls. This leads to a greater generalized inhibition in the severely punished girls than it does in boys and also to the fact that dependence is positively correlated with maternal punitiveness in boys and negatively correlated in girls.

[2] From Baldwin (11). Copyright 1955 by the Dryden Press, Inc., and published with permission.

The positive relation between current frustration and expression of dependence receives support from the research of Wittenborn and his associates (155). A cluster (intercorrelation of variable) approach was used in their study of adopted children. In an interview they asked 100 five-year-old children what they would do in certain familiar social situations. Responses from these children were correlated and certain clusters of positively related items emerged. These clusters they called: (1) dependence on adult; (2) aggression; (3) socialized compliance; (4) taking an adult role; (5) weakness-avoidance; and (6) constructive approach. The items indicative of dependence on an adult had in common that when asked what he would do, a child replied he would tell an adult; for example, he would tell an adult if a toy broke, if he hurt himself, if other children would not let him play with them, or if other children called him names.

Interviews with the adoptive mothers provided information on the conditions of child rearing in the adoptive home (155). Again using a cluster approach, they found the clusters of conditions of child rearing to include one concerned with rejection of the child. One of the higher degrees of relationship they found was that between rejection of the children and the children's expressions of dependency. The correlation, although not high in absolute terms (+0.30), was statistically significant. Since rejection is presumably frustrating, supporting evidence is thus found for the contention that dependency and frustration are related. In this study, data from boys and girls were not treated separately, so sex differences, if they were present, were not isolated.

In a later study, the "pattern" study, Sears and his associates (140) gave some of the nuances of the relationship between dependence and maternal behavior without contradicting the findings so far offered. In their study, the findings on boys and girls were treated as a single group. Opinions about the causes of dependence expressed by the mothers are worth attention. One theory they advanced had to do with the original production of dependency. Some mothers expressed the opinion that fondling and cuddling would produce overdependence during the period in which these practices were followed. Little support for this view was found by Sears and his associates when the group data were analyzed.

Another source of dependency the mothers suggested was that the amount of their child's dependent behavior was related to insecurity and that, therefore, they should give the child more affection and security. This view was, in general, supported by the findings of Sears and his associates. Rejection of the child, withdrawal of love used as a disciplinary technique, and severity of punishment for aggression toward the parents were each positively related to child dependency.

The *total* amount of physical punishment was *not* related to the child's being dependent. Only the more specific punishment for aggressiveness toward parents was so related. Sears *et al.* suspected the reason for the greater potency of the latter form of punishment was that aggression toward the parent is an action threatening the bond between them. "If you don't love me, I don't love you." This will cause the child to seek reassurance through an effort toward increased dependence that his parents really do love him.

The other points of view expressed by the mothers were concerned with the handling of dependence once it had developed. Some mothers took the position that if dependency were punished sufficiently, it would be reduced. Sears and his associates found no evidence whatsoever that punishment for dependency helped to eliminate it. Instead, punishment only made the children more dependent. Other mothers expressed the opinion that rewarding dependence, such as dropping what she was doing and going to the child's aid, or generally being permissive, would increase dependence. This again did not work out in actual practice. Rewarding dependence was not related to dependence in the child.

The investigators summarize their findings on dependence as follows:

> Mothers who repeatedly demonstrate their affection for children are providing many supports for whatever actions the children have performed in order to obtain such demonstrations. These actions often involve following the mother around, touching her, smiling at her and talking, and keeping some kind of contact with her. These are the actions, of course, that we have labeled dependency. Once the child has developed these habitual ways of acting—and all children develop some—he may be expected to use them as devices for reassuring himself that his mother does love him. That is to say, if she shows signs of rejection, if she uses withdrawal of love to discipline him, and if she is punitive toward his aggression, he may be expected to double his efforts to secure her affection. This will simply increase the frequency and persistence of the acts we have defined as dependent, and hence the mother will describe more of them.
>
> The influence of affectionate demonstrativeness, if we may suggest a theoretical point, is an influence on the *learning* of dependent behavior. The effect of withdrawal of love, punishment of dependency and aggression, and other behaviors that threaten the child's security, is an effect on performance or *action*. Therefore, the actual amount of dependency observed and reported by a mother is a product of both factors. It follows that the most dependent children should be those whose mothers express openly their affection for the child but repeatedly threaten the affectional bond by withholding love as a means of discipline and by being punitive toward his displays of parent-directed aggression.
>
> These relationships are exactly what we have found, but just which

way the cause-and-effect arrows point is impossible to say. We are skeptical that there is any single direction of cause-and-effect relations in the child-rearing process. True, the mother's personality comes first, chronologically, and she starts the sequence of interactive behavior that culminates in the child's personality. But once a child starts to be over-dependent—or is *perceived* as being so by his mother—he becomes a stimulus to the mother and influences her behavior toward him. Perhaps, within the present group of mothers, over-dependency of their children increased the mothers' rejective feelings, made them more angry and hence more punitive for aggression. The whole relationship could be circular. An enormous amount of painstaking research will be required to untangle these phenomena (*140*, 174–175).[3]

To sum up the determinants of dependence in preschool children it would appear that domination with overprotection (*91*), the kind and amount of frustration and punishment experience (*140*), and rejection (*155, 159*) are the major causes. Both dominance with overprotection and rejection are probably frustrating and involve punishment. Hence, emphasis may be placed on the kind and amount of frustration and punishment experience as the major determinant of dependence tendencies in early childhood. Frustration in current parent-child relationships is related to strong dependence tendencies, although differentially for girls as contrasted with boys. Differences in reaction of boys and girls to frustration are attributable to differential identifications with their mothers.

The influence of situational factors on dependence tendencies. Consideration has been given to factors determining dependence as they apply throughout this age period. No attention has been given to situational factors which may modify the degree of dependence tendencies. Manifestations of dependence may be affected by the immediate situation so that the child's more or less consistent degree of dependence is changed temporarily (and perhaps permanently).

One of the factors causing temporary fluctuation is situational insecurity which increases dependence on the mother. In childhood, strangeness evokes fear and is considered to be one of the conditions of insecurity in childhood. In Arsenian's research on this problem (5), the insecure situation was a room strange to the children but containing many toys. The investigator observed through a one-way screen the influence of the mother's presence or absence on the one- to three-year-old child's reaction to this strange room. She hypothesized that security was a function of the mother's presence. She systematically varied the presence or absence of the mother with the child.

[3] From Sears, Maccoby, and Lewin (*140*). Copyright 1957 by Row, Peterson, and published with permission.

Some of the children were accompanied by their mothers, some were not. Children left alone in the room for the first few sessions spent most of their time crying as well as showing agitated nonadaptive movements such as hanging around the door, and the like. When children were accompanied by their mothers from the first, they played with the toys in the strange room with little evidence of insecurity. Her presence made it possible for the child to react adaptively to the new situation. Security was felt by the child because of his dependence on the mother. The situation of being left alone temporarily increased his dependence tendencies. The absence of the mother created a stress situation for the child which increased dependency.

Another approach to stress was used by Beller (23, 24). He took the position that since the parental figure had reduced painful stimulation during the child's infancy, her presence and attention was synonomous with relief in his later (preschool) years. Actual or even anticipated deprivation would produce a heightened level of dependence. In his study, Beller not only confirmed the hypotheses that dependent behavior would be higher in a dependency stress situation than in a nonstress situation, but also found that the higher a child's initial dependence, the greater would be his increase in the stress situation.

Using a sample of some of the children described earlier, Beller compared the children on the number of times they would look at an adult or at an adult-child interaction in free play in which the adult was relatively less available to any one child (dependency stress situation) with the number of times they would do so in organized work and play where the adult was readily available (nonstress situation). His measures were based on direct observation of the child's eye movements in looking at adults or at adult-child interactions during ten two-minute time samples in the two situations.

Initial dependence correlated significantly with the amount of increased looking at adults and of adult-child interactions in the dependency stress situations. This finding was verified in the setting of eight psychotherapy sessions for each of 16 children. The dependency stress situation used in this study was the occurrence of "separation experiences," that is, the therapist's canceling, postponing, or being late to a session. The nonstress sessions lacked these experiences. The number of requests for help coming from the child was the measure of dependence. Again, initial dependence scores correlated significantly with the magnitude of increase of dependency responses in the stress situation.

Deprivation of adult social contact can heighten a child's dependence (60). Frustration of dependency needs through withdrawal of friendly, rewarding, encouraging, affectionate behavior from an adult (non-nurturance) has an effect on a child's behavior. The investigator compared two groups of preschool aged children matched on dependency rating scales of the type used by Beller. In one group each child was given ten minutes of consistently nurturant attention (smiling at, talking to, and so on) by a female experimenter; in the second group each child had five minutes of nurturant behavior and then five minutes in which the investigator withdrew from interaction with the child (nurturance withdrawal) on the excuse of being "busy." Thereafter the children were given two cognitive learning tasks.

The groups learned with differential efficiency. The girls, both from the high and low dependence subgroup with withdrawal-nurturance experience, and the high dependent boys with that experience were the more efficient learners. Nurturance-withdrawal supplies greater motivation for learning than does consistent nurturance. These results seem to support the clinical finding reported for infancy that there is a significant relationship between frustration and inconsistent gratification, on the one hand, and increased dependency in children, on the other. Moreover, the findings are consistent with those of Beller in that again it was found that dependency behavior was higher in a dependency stress situation than in a nonstress situation.

Changes in dependence tendencies with increasing age. The mothers' attitudes toward dependence are important in connection with age changes. Parental attitudes about the desirability of dependency are subject to change with time. Mothers expect the infant to be completely dependent, but also expect that he will become gradually less dependent as he grows older. The mother, as the principal agent of socialization during infancy, fosters dependence in some degree and manner, but at least in later infancy also introduces training with the aim of decreasing dependence. The infant is expected under his own direction to learn to feed himself, to keep himself clean, and in general to adapt to certain rules of the game of living in the family. The goal of socialization is first to foster complete dependence and then to bring about less and less dependence.

It is probable, though not backed by specific definitive research, that during younger childhood emotional dependence takes a different course from instrumental dependence. The mother wishes to lessen instrumental dependence. But with emotional dependence her goal is not so much to lessen dependence as it is to bring about in her child culturally approved and suitable "mature" expressions of emotional dependence.

Consider the two-year-old and his manifestations of affection. He is most direct and open, hugging, kissing, and clinging, and tugging at his mother's dress. But adults believe there is something "infantile" about such behavior. Their goal of socialization, whether they are conscious of it or not, is to bring about a fondness for the mother, a pleasure in her company, and not this embarrassing, demanding, passionate attachment. Above all, the child's incessant demands for proofs of affection must somehow be curtailed. Modification of emotional dependence rather than elimination is the goal. In addition to modification of emotional dependence on her, the mother teaches her child to seek affection and attention from other adults and from his peers. If she fails or does not try, then the "mama's boy" of Levy (91), who is a social isolate, is one vivid consequence.

Changes with age in dependence tendencies during these years have been investigated empirically. Sears and his associates (140), in their "pattern" study, found that physical clinging decreased during early childhood, but that more verbal forms of seeking attention from the mother were still quite strong at the age of five.

In another relevant study (144), seven categories of dependent behavior—seeking information, help, recognition, praise, affection, reward, and permission—were summed together. Dependency scores were contrasted with seven categories of helpful behavior—giving help, reassurance, permission, praise, affection, reward, and information. Observations during 1,300 two-minute periods were collected for 30 boys and 35 girls in a university nursery school and kindergarten. For purposes of analysis of age trends, there were four groups, 38–46, 47–55, 56–63, and 64–75 months. As age increased, dependent contacts with adults decreased in frequency and proportion whereas helpful contacts with both adults and children increased significantly.

Heathers (65) systematically studied changes with age in dependence (and independence) tendencies of two different groups. One was composed of 20 two-year-old children, the other of 20 four- and five-year-old children. Teachers in a nursery school observed the behavior of the children in both groups toward their teachers and toward other children during play, recording their findings on a variety of relevant variables. Included were four emotional dependence categories. For dependence tendencies directed toward both children and adults, the categories were clinging to and seeking affection, and seeking attention and approval. Two hypotheses concerning the relation of age to the development of emotional dependence were investigated. The first hypothesis was that during the early years of childhood emotional dependence on adults declined relative to emotional dependence on children. The second hypothesis was that emotional dependence as expressed in seeking reassurance and affection tended to decline with age relative to its expression through seeking attention and approval.

By comparing the behavior of the younger and the older groups, Heathers found concerning the first hypothesis a marked significant decline in teacher dependence in both clinging-affection seeking and in attention-approval seeking. He found clinging-affection seeking in relation to children showed no significant decline with age, but that attention-approval seeking by children showed a reliable increase. As Heathers hypothesized, there was a shift of dependent behavior away from the teacher. The hypothesis that concerned seeking reassurance and affection as declining relative to seeking attention and approval was also supported though not in as clear-cut fashion. The subjects showed no change with age in clinging-affection seeking toward adults, but a definite decrease toward other children. In general, there was a declining teacher-dependence and a declining clinging or affection seeking from them. ". . . in the process of socialization, emotional dependence tends to shift away from a passive, 'infantile' dependence toward a more active and assertive dependence on one's peers" (65, 56).[4] Thus, changes in dependence tendencies with increasing age have been established.

Determinants of independence tendencies. As dependence declines and independence increases the child at each point in time must strike a balance. He must learn and relearn the areas and manner in which he is expected to be independent and dependent. A ratio of dependence versus independence must be struck. Otherwise, overdependence of the sort described earlier or too great independence may result.

This age of three through five seems to be the period that is critical for the development of optimal balance. Research definition of this assertion still is necessary. Consequently, this statement is not to be considered as anything more than plausible. At least, problems of independence-dependence balance appear important to the behavior of the young child.

Resistant behavior towards adults when encountered in a setting of proffered assistance may be interpreted as an instance of the young child testing his capacities for independence. Social resistance expressed in saying, "No!", or "Don't" is a way the socially maladroit children have of dealing with attempts of others to direct their behavior. Sometimes their resistance is an essential feature of healthy growth.

[4] From Heathers (65). Copyright 1955 by The Journal Press, and published with permission.

It has been observed that resistant behavior, or negativism, reaches a high frequency when the child is about two or three years of age. Ausubel (6) offers the interpretation that this is due to the frustration suffered by the child when his parents slow down their nurturance and begin to make demands for independent behavior. This phenomenon he called "ego devaluation."

Frustrations result from learning independence. As Dollard and his associates put it:

> Under normal circumstances each child may also be said to decrease steadily its dependence on its parents. It must learn to walk where it has formerly been carried; and being carried is, of course, a *response* in this situation. It learns not to be picked up when it has experienced some small disaster. It must give up much of the cuddling, holding, and petting which is the prerogative of the smallest darling. Childish approximations of table manners and etiquette must be altered in favor of the customs preferred by adults. The child must learn to wait for its food, to keep its face clean, to submit to having its hair combed, to eat in the regular stages designated by our table techniques. At some time or another all of these lengthened sequences involve frustrations and elicit protest from the child (45, 64–65).[5]

Whiting and Child (152) in their cross-cultural study investigated what they called severity of socialization arising from dependence and independence training, and socialization anxiety. None of the societies they studied seriously tried to begin independence training before the age of two and the median age of serious efforts was about three and a half years. The American group began somewhat earlier at about two-and-a-half years. Severity of independence training in the American group received a rating at the median. Two aspects of severity of independence training were isolated—freedom to act on his own initiative without adult surveillance and responsibility for taking on the adult role. As compared with other societies, ratings emphasizing the former were on the severe side in the American group, the latter on the mild side. The measure of severity of socialization involves the behavior of parents. But from another point of view, and one more fundamental to Whiting and Child's intent in connection with this particular problem, it is also an index of socialization anxiety aroused in the child.

Consider the four aspects used in arriving at a judgment of severity of socialization or socialization-anxiety—brevity, severity of punishment, frequency of punishment, and signs of emotional disturbance in the child. Each of these is potentially an arouser of anxiety in the child; the briefer the transition, the stronger is the anxiety, the more severe the punishment, the greater is the subsequent anxiety, the more

[5] From Dollard *et al.* (45). Copyright 1939 by the Yale University Press, and published with permission.

frequent the punishment, the greater is the anxiety developed, and the more signs of disturbance, the greater is the anxiety.

In dealing with indices of anxiety in children of different cultures, the investigators related the indices to indices of adult anxiety. The adult anxiety index in these cultures derived from the explanation of illness as being either loss of soul or spirit possession. Whiting and Child considered such explanations as being projective of anxiety about dependence. When the soul leaves the body, it communes with ancestral spirits. They interpreted this as a metaphorical dependence on parent-figures. Spirit possession also shows a metaphorical dependence, but its parentlike character is not so clear. Nevertheless, both loss of soul or spirit possession as explanations of illness were positively related to severity of socialization stemming from dependence. Societies with these explanations were more severe; societies without these explanations were more lenient in socialization resulting from dependence. The adult anxieties ascribable to dependence phenomena were found to be related to the anxieties in their children.

Training for and encouragement of independence increase independence. Striving for independence takes place in areas where moderate difficulties still exist for the child. If the activity in question has been thoroughly mastered, neither parent nor child sees in it anything of a challenge to striving for independence. Thus, a child strives for independence in areas where his ability is still marginal. In this sense, strivings for independence are reflected as an aspect of level of aspiration, that is, the level toward which a person is striving.

Fales (47) studied nursery school children in the course of their activity of putting on and taking off their wraps. The percentage of refusal of help was taken as an index of "rudimentary aspiration." Next, one group of children was trained in taking off its wraps. Afterward, it was compared with another group not so trained. The group receiving the training increased considerably in its percentage of refusal as compared to the control group. In another related study by Fales (47), a group of children was praised (encouraged) in connection with its endeavors whereas another group was not. The praised group increased considerably in independence.

It would appear that both training and praise increase independence. Both these incentives are probably important in accounting for the learning of independence. Increase in independence tendencies with age probably reflects the effect of both incentives. Conversely, if the parent and other adults engaged in socialization give no training or actually discourage independence tendencies, a less independent child may be expected.

Some research studies ostensibly concerned with motivation to achieve may in our present perspective be considered as studies of independence. These are the studies where *independent* accomplishment is stressed. Independence is the goal; achievement is a means of accomplishment. This was the case in the Fales study and will be also for the Winterbottom study (*154*) of the older children reported in Child (*38*), to be presented in Chapter 16. This is not meant to imply that all achievement is independence-oriented; achievement may be neutral in this respect or even dependence-oriented.

In one of his later articles, Beller (*21*) concluded that his particular measures of independence were equally characteristic of so-called autonomous striving to achieve, or the *mastery motive*. Still later (*26*), he spoke of it as an *aspect* of independence and described it as a disposition toward unaided, effortful striving, but *not* as a measure of need for achievement. Since the writer is in agreement with Beller that independence, or autonomous striving to achieve, is a separable behavior tendency from need for achievement, consideration of the latter is deferred until later in the chapter.

Changes in independence tendencies with increasing age. Independence, as differentiated from lessened dependence, was also investigated by Heathers (*65*). His measures of emotional independence included those meant to be measures of self-reliance as evidenced in nondistractibility, namely, the extent to which children: (1) ignored stimuli from teacher; (2) ignored stimuli from a child; and (3) played alone. He also included measures of self-assertion or dominance in social interaction with other children as other criteria of independence, namely, the extent to which they: (1) organized another child's play (telling him what to do or showing him how); (2) interfered with another child's play; and (3) resisted another child's interference or aggression. Of all of these measures only ignoring stimuli from teacher and organizing another child's play showed an increase with age. Some support, although meager, is thereby given to the hypothesis that independence increases with age.

Behavior maturity has been found to increase with age. Through ratings Joel (*78*) studied what he called the behavior maturity in nursery school age children. He found that certain items he used showed progressive changes from two- to five-and-a-half years of age. Some of Joel's differentiating items between his younger and older subjects were those concerned with going to the toilet without help or reminder; removing wraps without help or reminder; facing difficulties without appeal to adults or fussing; being absorbed in an activity; self-sufficiency in play; showing initiative; playing constructively with others; being able to see another child's viewpoint; and initiating group play. All of these behavioral changes with age may be interpreted as changes in increased independence tendencies. From both studies it would appear that in the younger child independence increases with age.

Aggressive Tendencies

Aggression is widely prevalent in young children. Many of the phenomena of their anger, as discussed in the previous chapter, can be seen to have had an aggressive component. Young children direct aggression against the persons in their environment, including their parents. Every one of the 379 mothers studied by Sears, Maccoby, and Levin (140) had to deal with aggressive episodes, and 95 per cent reported experiences of having strong aggression directed against them by their children.

A preliminary view of the meaning of overt aggressiveness is given in the scales developed by Beller (26). These had to do with threatening others, derogating others, destroying materials or possessions of others, attacking adults physically, and attacking children physically. Not only do such scales seem plausible as constituents of aggression but also Beller's factor analysis of them showed they possessed a strong commonality. Thus, they supply evidence that aggression is a unitary construct.

From the point of view of socialization, it should be apparent that our society encourages aggression in certain forms. Under some circumstances we expect the individual to be aggressive and "to defend his rights," although the reverse also holds—there are occasions in which parents punish aggression. Most parents will not tolerate physical aggression directed against themselves, whereas they permit it on occasion in aggression against peers.

As Child (38) indicates, the strength of tendencies to be aggressive is only one aspect of aggressiveness in relation to socialization. The other aspect is the nature of control or inhibition of tendencies to be aggressive. All societies and individuals have ways of controlling the expression of aggression. Without such controls on in-group aggression, life in a society could not long endure.

In various ways aggressive behavior draws punishment. Punishment for aggression means the extent to which the child is pained or thwarted because he acted in an aggressive manner. Of course, any punishment is a kind of frustration, but for the sake of clarity it may be distinguished from other frustrations. Punishment for aggressiveness during infancy seems hardly likely. Quite probably the child learns during early childhood that aggressive behavior brings punishment. What happens when this occurs needs scrutiny.

Determinants of overt aggressive tendencies. The constitutional determinants of aggressiveness are very evident, though definitive research has not isolated their exact effect. Consider how at the age of four height, weight, strength, and sheer activity may be crucial in determining the winner (and the loser) in preschool "bopping" contests. Consider further how the reinforcement or failure of reinforcement affects aggressive tendencies. These characteristics are, at least in considerable measure, attributable to a constitutional factor. But they are by no means simple, direct determinants. Other factors soon overlay the constitutional sources of difference, creating a pattern in which the latter are totally overshadowed. We need to look elsewhere to examine the determinants of aggression.

Boys are characteristically more aggressive than girls. This is perhaps the single, most thoroughly documented finding on childhood aggression (35). The most important determinant of this sex difference appears to be sex roles to be discussed in connection with psychoanalysis. At least in part, this difference comes about because we reward boys more for being aggressive than we do girls. Quite possibly, constitutional differences accentuate the greater aggressiveness of the male. This, is course, does not mean the girls are not subjected to rewards for aggression. They are, but to a lesser degree.

Research studies show that a permissive attitude toward aggression increases aggression. In effect, this attitude means that the child receives rewards for being aggressive. This determinant of aggression will become self-evident as we consider the research on aggression.

From knowledge of the socialization process of aggression in infancy, we would also expect the experience of the young child also to contain instances in which frustration would serve to breed aggression. In accordance with learning theory, a child will express aggressive responses to the extent that his past history includes reinforcement or failure of reinforcement for such responses.

Let us evaluate the proposition that frustration leads to aggression. Before examining new evidence, it should be pointed out that the principle already has received support. Earlier discussion attests to its operation during infancy. The findings of Baldwin and his associates (11), that the rejecting home pattern breeds aggressive children, are suggestive of the same conclusion, since rejection is a form of frustration. But we cannot be content with the bald statement that frustration leads to aggression. We must explore the qualifications and interrelations that accompany this general statement. In each of the following studies it is not so much this general proposition that needs elucidation as it is the further complications and nuances of frustration-aggression relationships which the investigations show.

As in dependence tendencies, we may begin with the evidence from the historic research of Levy (91). His was the pioneer study which demonstrated something about the determinants of aggression in pre-school children. It will be remembered that Levy found two patterns of maternal overprotection. One of these, that associated with dominance, was found to be related to dependence in children. The other pattern of overprotection was associated with indulgence. The parents falling in this latter pattern showed prolongation of infantile ways in their children and prevention of independence, as well as indulgence. These parents gave the children their own way. Their children uniformly showed overactivity, obstructive behavior, fighting, and disobedience. In short, under this regime the children were aggressive.

Maternal-child interaction as studied by Merrill (110) becomes relevant. Through a one-way screen she observed each mother in interaction with her child. The first session served to develop behavior categories relevant to the mother's behavior toward her child. Divided into two groups, one group of mothers was told that its children had not shown their full capabilities; the other was treated in the same way as in the first session. The mildly criticized mothers tended to assume more direct control of their children's behavior in directing, interfering, and criticizing. Merrill found that the frequency of maternal restricting and controlling of behavior was positively correlated to indices of frustration in the children during these sessions, namely, their irritable or complaining behavior. Or to put it another way, at one extreme were the more controlled children who manifested considerable irritability and complaints; at the other extreme were the less controlled children who showed less irritability and complaints. The study demonstrates not only that frustration breeds aggression in the form of irritability, but also that there are individual differences in the extent to which children are exposed to frustrating reinforcements of aggressive behavior.

Another finding emerges from this study. Generalization of aggressive tendencies to other situations is shown by the finding that the children who were more restricted by their mothers were more complaining when they played in other sessions with an unfamiliar young woman rather than with the mother. This woman had been deliberately trained to be equally neutral toward all children so that her behavior would be as constant and as similar as possible toward them. The children who were more aggressive with their mothers continued to be more aggressive than other children in the presence of this neutral young woman.   Habits of aggressiveness established with the mother tended to carry over into this new situation.   Moreover, in a second session when each child was more familiar with the woman, the child's behavior became even more similar to that he had shown toward his mother.   Evidently, experiences with the mother established habits that carried over into other situations.   The young woman by a process of stimulus generalization elicited similar degrees of aggressive behavior.

A study investigating aggression in relation to punishment was the Sears's antecedent study (142).   The group investigated the severity of punishment meted out to their subjects for the expression of aggression (punitiveness).   They collected their data by further interviewing the 40 mothers of preschool-aged children used in other phases of the study.   Assignment of a high rating on punitiveness meant that a mother used severe forms of punishment and consistently and vigorously attempted to suppress the child's aggressive activity in the home.   They also secured information on the overt social aggression exhibited by the children in preschool.

For the boys, the correlation between punitiveness and aggression was 0.56.   In other words, the more punitive the mothers, the more aggressive the boys were in preschool.   For girls, however, the correlation was slightly negative although both low and high punishment were associated with low aggression.   In girls, moderate maternal punitiveness is related to higher aggression, whereas low or high punitiveness leads to lower aggressive behavior.   These differential results for boys and girls were precisely the kinds of relationships they had found in the dependency phase of their study—a positive correlation between punitiveness and amount of dependency in boys and a slightly negative correlation in girls.   It is possible to use again the same arguments to account for their results with aggression.   (Pages 371–372 give a full account of the argument.)

A similar interpretation may be made by assuming that there exists greater identification of the girl with the mother and consequently, a stronger effect from a given degree of maternal punitiveness; this in turn leads to a greater generalized inhibition of aggression in severely punished girls than it does in boys.   Since the girls have taken over (identified with) their mothers' values, they are more self-punitive than are the boys when their mothers reprimand them.   Hence, girls actually suffer more severe frustrations than do boys from given amounts of maternal punitiveness.   "Severely" punished boys presumably were not punished hard enough for this to happen and, in their case, the more punishment the more aggressive tendencies they showed.

A considerable number of studies have been concerned with age changes in aggression. When comparing study with study the results appear contradictory—one finds an increase, another no change, and the third a decrease in aggression (35). What seems to have happened is that various *kinds* of aggression have been studied. Either pooling several kinds of aggression or terming one special kind "aggression" obscures developmental change with age. If we study temper tantrums, then there is a decrease with age; if we study retaliation and counteraggression, then there is an increase with age; if we combine them in a single measure, perhaps there is no change with age.

It would seem that Goodenough's pioneer study (53) of many years ago gives the best possible summarization. Over the pre-school years her subjects showed a decrease in random discharge and an increase in retaliatory behavior. The latter is aggression under a more circumscribed name. This form of behavior with intent to injure seems more in keeping with what is meant by aggression than does blind striking out. Thus, it may be concluded that within the age limits under consideration aggression increases with age, provided Goodenough's measures are accepted as representative. Her information on parental methods of control is also relevant. She found that with increasing age, use of physical punishment (such as spanking), coaxing, and ignoring diminished and shifted to use of scolding, threatening, and isolation. For these and other methods of control, some mothers were successful, whereas others failed.

Fantasy aggression. The studies of aggressiveness in preschool children reported so far have used indices of behavioral aggression exhibited in day-to-day situations at home or in preschool, or in specially contrived settings as in the Merrill study. Other studies have been performed which are dependent on indices of covert or fantasy aggression expressed in play.

Much of the research in this area was done by Robert Sears and his colleagues. They used the standardized doll play equipment described in Chapter 2. At each session instances of aggressive behavior shown by a particular child were noted by trained observers.

The greater aggressiveness of the boy is again the single, most thoroughly documented finding here (90). This is a definitive finding in all studies of doll play aggression reported here, with the exception of that of Hollenberg and Sperry (69). Moreover, there are only two or three studies out of about 20 more not considered here which did not obtain this finding. The burden of explanation would seem to fall on the few exceptions (90). Greater fantasy aggression in boys than in girls, such that sex becomes a determinant of this behavior, seems well established.

Increase in aggression in the second as compared to the first doll play session with the same experimenter present has been found in several studies (69, 88, 134). The children, nevertheless, maintain about their same relative rank position (134). The increase in aggression has been interpreted as resulting from the child's discovery that the usual restraints against aggression do not apply to doll play. By the second session permissiveness to be aggressive, tacitly given by the experimenter, is interpreted by the children as actual encouragement to be aggressive. Consequently, permissiveness to be aggressive is still another determinant of fantasy aggression.

In one study (89) the usual increase in fantasy aggression was not found when a strange young woman was introduced in the second session. There was a decrease in aggressiveness. In another group in the same study the mother was present at the second session, but not at the first. For this situation each of the children became more aggressive at the second session. A plausible interpretation of these differences is available. Fantasy aggression is very similar to ordinary fanciful play and make-believe fighting in the home from which the children probably had not been restrained. In the doll play situation with the mother present, the children probably interpreted her presence as permitting aggression. On the other hand, it is not unlikely they had also been taught that such behavior is not permissible in front of a stranger. Hence, their aggressiveness decreased in the presence of the strange woman. Both the increase and the decrease of aggression seemed to depend on whether the mother or a strange woman were present.

The relation between overt and fantasy aggression. The relation between overt and covert (fantasy) aggression needs clarification. Let it be stated at the outset that fantasy aggression expressed through play does not have a high, linear correlation with independently derived indices of aggression obtained from interview or observation. This has been found by Korner (84) and Sears (136), to name but two investigators. Correlations in the neighborhood of only 0.13 to 0.21 are found. This lack of appreciable direct relationship, then, is a fact and one not to be ignored. The inference, however, is not to be drawn that overt and fantasy aggression are unrelated. Both are forms of behavior; both tell us something about the child. Since a simple linear relation does not hold, investigators have tried to find out if there are more intricate ways of relating the two kinds of expressions of aggression.

Let us start with the assumption that some, but only some, of the fantasy aggression reenacts aggression a child would actually display in home or school. Let us make certain other assumptions. Some fantasy expression reflects aggression directed toward himself, as when he reenacts some punishment that actually did happen to him. Some of his fantasy aggression represents aggression he feels he would like to indulge in but cannot, as when he stuffs the father doll down the toilet. Moreover, conditions will be present which *inhibit* expressions of fantasy aggression. Although he would like to express them, for some reason he cannot. The most obvious source of inhibition is punishment by the parents for aggression. Their punishment does not necessarily eliminate aggression; it may merely inhibit him in his expression of it in play. Thus, fantasy aggression expressed in play may have several different meanings and implications. These assumptions are subject to empirical investigation.

Sears (*136*) has related fantasy aggression and overt aggression in preschool on the basis of the following expectations. Child punishment serves to frustrate a child and hence to increase his aggression. More severe punishment at home would tend to inhibit aggression there because of fear of punishment, but increase aggression elsewhere. This was the finding of Hollenberg and Sperry (*69*) in a study reported later, namely, that punishment of aggression decreases aggression in the situation in which it occurs and increases it in dissimilar situations. This term, "dissimilar," suggests "less similar" which in turn suggests that a *gradient* of similarity may be involved extending from most to least similar. Another more technical way to express it is to speak of a gradient of stimulus generalization (see page 101).

Two response tendencies instigated by the parents have now been established: aggression and fear of punishment for aggression. They operate in opposite directions. Sometimes, if punishment is mild, aggression wins out. Their relative influence will depend not only on the strength of the opposing tendencies, but also on the similarities of the home situation to a new situation. It will be agreed that the school with its parent surrogate, the teacher, is similar in many respects to the home. The child may make the same response in school as he does in the home because of stimulus generalization. On the dimension of similarity, doll play lies further out on the gradient, that is, it is less similar than the school setting. If anxiety created by inhibition and punishment generalizes less extensively than aggression, then the inhibition of severe punishment would be expected to affect behavior toward the preschool teacher; aggressive doll play is not inhibited, instead it is increased because of the increased frustration created by the punishment.

This was neatly demonstrated by Sears (137) among preschool children, divided into three groups based on estimates of the amount of punishment of aggression in the home. The first group came from homes low in punitiveness, the second from homes moderately punitive, and the third from homes highly punitive. The moderately punished group showed the most aggression in school. The low and high punished group were found to be approximately the same in mean frequency of aggression. Both were reliably lower in aggression than the moderately punished group. This corresponds to the expectancy outlined earlier.

The same children were placed in the doll play situation. In their doll play, the children from highly punitive homes showed more aggression than either of the other two groups. Thus, the more severely punished group was highest in fantasy aggression but inhibited in overt aggression. Fear of punishment did not show enough generalizations to reach the doll play situation, so aggressive tendencies, inhibited in the preschool situation, were permitted to appear.

To return to the issue of the relation of fantasy and overt aggression, the group in which a linear correlation of only 0.13 was found between the two forms of aggression was now found to show an intelligible high interrelationship when the additional factor of the mothers' punitiveness was taken into consideration.

Determinants of fantasy aggression. It is now possible to consider the determinants of fantasy aggression when studied independent of overt aggression. A phase of the study of Hollenberg and Sperry (69) demonstrated that frustration leads to fantasy aggressiveness, but they went beyond this simple relationship. From interviews they derived a measure of home frustration based on the number and kinds of restrictive rules, forcing of the child, and the like. The mothers interviewed were divided into high and low frustration groups on this basis. Thirty children from these homes were observed in highly permissive play sessions and their aggressive responses were measured. They found that the children highly frustrated in the home tended to be more aggressive in doll play. The differences between the high and low frustration groups, however, although in the predicted direction, were not statistically significant. In general, frustration does lead to fantasy aggression, but it is evident that other factors are at work which also must be considered.

The fact that Hollenberg and Sperry obtained a suggestive, but not statistically significant, trend shows that we must look beyond a simple statement that the greater the degree of frustration is the greater the degree of fantasy aggression. The blurred, nonconclusive differentiation they obtained was removed when another factor, the severity of punishment for aggression the mothers inflicted on their children, was taken into consideration. A measure of punishment for aggression based on an interview-rating of frequency, intensity, and duration of spanking, threatening, isolating, denying privileges, and derogating the child was also available. Instead of dividing the children into two groups, low and high frustration, they now subdivided the original two groups each into a low and a high punishment group. Thus a given child might be, to use initials, low P—low F, low P—high F, high P—low F, or high P—high F.

When this was done, the difference among the groups, blurred when frustration alone was considered, became more definitive and clear-cut. It would be expected that the high P—high F group would be the most aggressive in doll play and the low P—low F group would be the least aggressive, with mixed groups of low and high P and F in the middle. This was the case in their study. High frustration *and* high punishment led to the greatest doll play aggression, while low frustration and low punishment led to the least aggression.

They also investigated the effect of punishment with another group of preschool children. This time they hypothesized that the young child *inhibits* his fantasy aggression in situations where fear and anxiety have been associated with punishment-producing responses. At first glance this appears contradictory to their former findings that punishment produces aggression. The crux of the matter is the situation in which aggression is expressed. They had previously measured fantasy aggression in a situation *different* from that in which punishment had been inflicted. They now studied both punishment and aggression in the *same* setting.

About 25 preschool-aged children were observed in four consecutive doll play sessions. The control group was treated permissively throughout all four sessions. The experimental group was given the first, third, and fourth sessions under conditions of permissiveness identical with those accorded the control group. However, during their *second* play session the experimental group was punished by verbal disapproval every time they made aggressive responses. That is, if the child kicked the baby doll he was asked if he did not know that nice boys should not do such things.

Turning to the results, in the control group aggressive responses increased steadily from session to session. Under conditions of permissiveness an increase in aggressiveness through the sessions would be expected rather than maintenance of the same amount from session to session. On the first session, the experimental group behaved as the control group did, but during the second session when verbally punished, there was not the increase in aggression that characterized the control group. In the third session (after the punishment session), aggressive responses decreased. In short, punishment of aggression decreased the frequency and intensity of aggression in the situation in which the punishment occurred. Presumably, this finding in doll play would apply in the home situation as well. If aggressive responses are punished in the home, the child will learn to inhibit aggression in that setting. Neither in doll play nor in the home does this mean that his aggressiveness is no longer present. He merely does not show his aggressiveness because of his fear of punishment.

The parallel argument for both dependency and overt aggression concerning the greater susceptibility of girls to maternal punishment as compared to boys was advanced by Sears and associates to help explain the curvilinear results they had obtained. They had not demonstrated this in the study in question; they had merely advanced it to help explain the results. But their point about identification raises the question of its importance in relation to aggression.

Levin and Sears (88) investigated identification as a determinant of fantasy aggression. They advanced various hypotheses having to do with identification, arguing that fantasy aggression was in part a function of the child's identification with aggressive role models. Several measures other than those for aggressiveness were necessary to test their hypotheses.

First, they found the degree of identification of the children with their parents through questioning about how the child acts when he has done something naughty; for example, "What does he do when he is naughty?" "Does he tell you about it?" "What do you do if he denies something you are fairly sure he has done?" They proposed that identification could be estimated from the stage of development of internalized control the child had reached. An example they give of high control (superego) for this age was a child whose mother recounted that when he did act naughty he held out for a while, but after a short time came to her and, without prodding, admitted he had done something naughty. Second, the severity of punishment for aggression toward parents was assessed. Third, which particular parent usually punished the child was ascertained from interviews. Two sessions of doll play with 126 boys and 115 girls of five years of age were carried out to provide information on the amount of aggressiveness displayed, through recording the frequency with which it appeared in the play session.

In view of the complexity of their design it is worth while to summarize information Levin and Sears acquired about these children and their parents. On the one hand, they knew the degree of identification the child exhibited along with related findings and, on the other, they knew the frequency of doll play aggression he or she showed. To test their hypotheses they had merely to relate these two sets of data, treating the data for the boys and girls separately.

Their results supported the hypotheses they had advanced. Boys who were highly identified with the father and had the cue for male aggressiveness by being usually punished by their fathers showed the highest frequency of doll (or fantasy) aggression. The boy's identification with an aggressive male model is then a determinant in the frequency of fantasy aggression. For girls, identification was related to high aggression only when it was associated with the mothers' being the agent of severe punishment. In other words, when the girls, as well as the boys, were identified with an aggressive model, then identification was related to high aggression.

The influence of situational factors upon fantasy aggression. Situational factors affect expressions of aggression. These factors vary from the transitory, almost momentary incident, to the longer maintained situation. The previous discussion of determinants included references to various situations that modify aggression. Those situations with which we are now concerned differ only in degree. By and large, they are less common than those dealt with earlier which are of the sort that all, or almost all, children must face. Situational factors now to be considered are more transitory and relatively more unusual.

An illustration of increased frustration due to a transitory factor is shown in a study by Bach (7). The more frustrated group had a preschool nap of one to two hours, the less frustrated group had one of only 10 to 20 minutes. Using the standardized play technique already described, he found that the group forced to take a longer nap showed significantly more aggressive themes in their play than the children who had had less frustration. Play fantasies of an aggressive sort appeared significantly more often in the more frustrated group.

Situational factors related to the expression of fantasy aggression include the situation in which actual training is given. Keister (83) studied training as a means of reducing frustration in children between three and six years of age. Placing her subjects in the mildly frustrating situation of having to solve a difficult puzzle, she recorded their manipulatory and verbal behavior. The children showed crying, sulking, and destructive behavior as a consequence of the situation. She then proceeded to eliminate many of these negative reactions to failure by building up their self-confidence through a series of successes with other tasks of graduated difficulty. After training, they tried longer and manifested more interest in solving a comparably difficult problem. Failure of a control group to show similar gains demonstrated that the success of the trained group was not simply a function of increased age at the time of the training phase of the study or of longer preschool attendance, but of the training situation as well.

The presence or absence of the father in the home as related to aggressive tendencies is another situational factor having a possible effect on aggression. If, as later discussion shows, the father is the identification model for the boy and if aggressiveness is a masculine quality, then we would expect the boy to be influenced in his aggressive tendencies by the presence or absence of the father. During the Second World War, this situation was neither so uncommon nor in any sense suggestive that other factors might be making children from these homes different or atypical. Two major studies were performed. One by Sears and his associates (141) involved preschool-age children; the other by Bach (8) concerned school-age children. Both investigators used substantially similar procedures, with data being collected through doll play procedure.

Sears et al. (141) studied doll play aggression, as expressed in the fantasy of the play situation, with 63 preschool-aged children whose fathers were absent from the home and 63 comparable children whose fathers were at home. The father's absence had little observable effect on the amount of aggression shown by the girls. Boys from father-present homes demonstrated much more aggression in general than did boys from father-absent homes. As to direction of aggression, these same boys showed more self-aggression, that is, aggression toward the boy doll with whom they presumably identified themselves, and also greater aggression toward the father than the boys from father-absent homes. These results are compatible with the interpretations that the father serves both as a model for the boy and as a source of frustration for him.

It is reasonable to assume that the adult male is more aggressive than the adult female. Hence, the father in serving as a model is a more aggressive model than is the mother. Boys from father-absent homes lacked this model and hence were less aggressive. Moreover, the father's aggressiveness would operate as a frustration to the son. This view can be held on the basis of the results just mentioned. In addition, even more specific evidence is at hand. When the father is absent, equal aggression toward both parent dolls is shown; when he is present, more aggression is shown toward the father doll. Greater self-aggression (aggression toward the boy doll) when the father is present in the home suggests that the father's control is more rigid than the mother's.

Bach (8) studied the father fantasies of a smaller group of father-separated children and of a control group, both six to ten years of age. The fathers in the doll play of the father-absent children were portrayed as affectionate and agreeable, whereas the fathers of the father-present children were portrayed as more aggressive in the sense used in the Sears's study. As far as sex differences were concerned, the fantasies of the father-absent girls and boys were both very similar to those produced by the *girls* in the father-present families. This suggests that father-separated boys of from six to ten years of age under the increased influence of the mother were becoming somewhat feminine in their outlook.

Although only speculative, it might be well to mention that father-absent homes probably resemble those in which the father, though present, is such a cipher as to be psychologically absent and consequently to wield only a negligible effect on the child's socialization. Matriarchal homes have been known to produce feminized sons.

On the basis of research described earlier, it has been established: (1) frustration often leads to aggression, presumably because it has been rewarded, that is, found effective in removing interference; (2) punishment of aggression may produce inhibition of subsequent aggression responses in the setting in which they are punished; (3) permissiveness with regard to aggression may lead to subsequent aggressive responses. When these findings are applied in the setting of a particular situation, the following hypotheses emerge. (1) The extent to which children are likely to manifest aggression in a given situation is partially dependent on the amount of frustration in that situation. (2) Similarly, it is partially dependent on the amount of punishment of or permissiveness for aggression.

Studies have corroborated these hypotheses. One by Yarrow (159) is particularly clear-cut and definitive. Sixty preschool children from lower- and upper-middle class families equally split as to sex were divided into three groups. In the first session all were allowed to play freely. Immediately before the second session, the so-called, failure group was given a task beyond its abilities—building a difficult Tinker-Toy windmill—which resulted in failure and frustration. The so-called satiation group was given pegboards and encouraged to place the pegs in the board for 20 minutes preceding the play session. The control group received neither frustration nor satiation experiences before the second doll play session.

As would be expected from the permissive character of the first session, all three groups on the second session displayed more aggression than they had in the first session. The permissive atmosphere weakened inhibition against expression of aggression and consequently it increased. The influence of situational frustration and satiation was nevertheless apparent. The frustrated group and the satiated group showed significantly greater increase in aggression than the control group. Thus, both predicted hypotheses were verified—that amount of aggression in a given situation is dependent both on the amount of frustration and the amount of permissiveness for aggression in that situation.

The prevalence of aggressive models in delinquent subcultures and the opportunity for identifications with them to develop has helped to explain delinquency. It is not surprising that the influence of aggressive models has been extensively investigated in recent years (17).

Bandura and Walters (17) in summarizing their own and other studies indicate that the increase in the number or intensity of aggressive responses involves two rather different effects. There is the *modeling* effect in which the child reproduces the novel response of the model, and there is the *disinhibiting* effect in which observation of the model results in weakening the inhibition of those aggressive responses already in the repertoire of the child.

A representative study (14) involving the presence of adult models is described on page 443 in a discussion of identification. An investigation demonstrating the generalization of imitative aggressive responses to a setting in which the model was absent was performed by Bandura, Ross, and Ross (16).

Twenty-four nursery school boys and girls were so situated as to observe adult models, either of the same or opposite sex, behave aggressively toward an inflated five-foot clown doll. These adults punched it, tossed it up and down, and hit it with a mallet, along with making verbally aggressive remarks. In the first minute of the session in which the child observed him, the adult had busied himself with a Tinker-Toy assembly. Another 24 children were placed in a non-aggressive condition in which the adult model spent the entire period with the Tinker-Toy, ignoring the clown doll. A control group of the same size had no exposure to the models at all.

Thereafter, in another room each child in the three groups was first exposed to a situation conducive to arousing some degree of aggression.

This arousal experience was necessary in order to make sure that the children entered the test for delayed imitation somewhat predisposed to aggressive activities. This condition was produced by each child's being shown attractive toys (fire engine, doll set), allowed to play a sufficient time to get involved, and then told that these were the very best toys, and that it had been decided to reserve them for the other children.

The test series followed immediately in another adjacent room. This room contained a variety of toys, some nonaggressive in character (tea set, crayons, cars, and the like) while others were conducive of aggressive responses (three-foot clown doll, mallet, dart gun). Each subject spent 20 minutes alone in the room, his behavior being noted through a one-way mirror. Measures rated included imitation of physical and verbal aggression, imitative nonaggressive verbal responses (remarks made earlier by the adult model, such as "he sure is tough"), and nonimitative physical and verbal aggression, including use of the guns. The subjects previously exposed to the aggressive models reproduced a great amount of aggression, differing significantly in this respect from the nonaggressive and control groups. Subjects who had observed the nonaggressive model were less aggressive than the control subjects. Boys showed more aggression than girls, following exposure to the male model.

It would seem that observation of cues for aggression from the behavior of models is effective in eliciting the same forms of responses in nursery school children. Subjects not so exposed only rarely performed in this fashion. That aggressive behavior was disinhibited by the communication of permissiveness increased the probability of aggressiveness. That the subjects expressed their aggression in ways clearly modeled on the novel patterns of the adult offers evidence of learning by imitation of the model.

The relation of aggressive and dependence tendencies. The kind and amount of frustration and punishment experiences are major determinants of both dependence and aggression. Since dependence and aggressive tendencies are both related to frustration, it is plausible to infer that they would be correlated with each other. This raises the question that, if this be the case, are we justified in speaking of them as separate tendencies? Sears and his associates (*142*) in their study of the antecedents of dependency and aggression did, as a matter of fact, find a high correlation between frequency of aggressive and dependent behavior. That is, if a given child were given to considerable (or little) aggressive behavior he tended to show considerable (or little) dependent behavior. Fortunately, there was also available a measure of activity level—an amount of physical movement and frequency and persistency of social interaction. Both aggression and dependence are highly correlated with level of activity. When the effect of activity level was statistically removed or held constant, the relationship between dependency and aggression was considerably reduced, suggesting that the two tendencies are sufficiently different so that they vary independently. Hence, we are justified in speaking of aggressive tendencies as distinct from dependence-independence tendencies.

Despite distinctiveness, the two forms of behavior tendencies may show relationship. Indeed, by a slight recasting of some of Beller's results (24) we would see that one form of that relationship has already been discussed. It will be remembered that Beller established that in a "dependency stress situation" there was heightened dependence as compared to that shown in a nonstress situation. This "stress" is a *frustration* of dependency, and frustration is said to incite aggression. In this instance we can say that deprivation and frustration of dependence lead to a *heightening* of dependency with no sign of aggression.

How is this reconcilable with the general frustration-aggression hypothesis? Beller (25) postulated that when frustration consisted of an interference with reaching a dependency goal, the result would be an *inhibition* rather than an increase of aggression. Moreover, Beller found that the higher the initial dependency, the more it would increase in the stress situation. This leads to the supplementary hypothesis that dependency frustration would be more inhibiting in high dependent children than in low dependent children.

The subjects were 24 children, three to six years of age, from an urban area nursery and clinic. Dependent strivings were measured by the already familiar five rating scales and, in the experimental situation, by the child's seeking of physical closeness to the experimenter. The effect of dependency frustration on dependent responses was measured by the change in the child's closeness to the adult from one experimental setting to another. In other words, this was the measure sensitive to situational change.

The usual ratings of dependence were of the child's general level; once established, they gave the high and low dependent group. Aggression measures were based on a mildly destructive response involving knocking down obstacles which blocked the path to the toys. The toys were behind apertures and could only be reached by knocking over a tower of pans. The child was told a touch would be enough but that this was the only way to secure the toys (25). Two experimental sequences were used. The crucial difference was whether the experimenter did or did not help the child get toys from shelves out of the child's reach. By not helping the child, dependency frustration was introduced. The effects of frustration were measured separately for high and low dependent groups, that is, children above and below the median of the dependency ratings. The two hypotheses were supported by the results. To quote Beller:

> Dependency frustration led to an initial increase of dependent responses and simultaneously to an initial inhibition of aggressive responses in both high and low dependent children. However, in the low dependent group, this effect of dependency frustration soon dissipated, and aggression became the dominant response. By contrast, in the high dependent group, this initial effect of frustration was sustained for a longer period of time. Dependent responses remained dominant, and aggressive responses inhibited (25, 14–15).[6]

Achievement Motivation

In our society a child is expected to learn to value certain accomplishments. To be considered normal he must compete to meet certain standards of excellence (106). A child receives positive reinforcement for the competencies he demonstrates. What these competencies may be varies from home to home. The child is led by his family, and later by the other agents of his socialization to cherish "success," to want what he does not have, to be able to do what he cannot do. Inculcated with these tendencies by these agents the child develops achievement striving—trying to do well.

A systematic, maintained investigation of achievement development in younger children has been conducted at the Fels Research Institute under the direction of V. J. Crandall (41, 42, 43, 44). He and his associates suggest (42) three criteria on which to distinguish achievement behavior from other behavior tendencies—(a) inferred goal of the behavior, (b) unique characteristic of behavior involved, (c) nature of the situations in which the behavior occurred. The goal is the attainment of approval, either self or other; the unique characteristic is competence of performance; and the nature of the situation is one in which some standard of excellence might be applied. In the research efforts achievement motivation was conceived as being exhibited in several areas—intellectual, physical, artistic-creative, and mechanical—but neglecting social skills achievement.

Determinants. One of their investigations (43) involved the relationship between achievement and dependence behavior. Thirty nurs-

---

[6] From Beller and Haeberle (25). Published with permission.

ery school-age children and their mothers were studied; the children were observed in free play for achievement efforts and help-emotional-and-approval-seeking from adults and, at home, in interaction with their mothers on the same variables. The mothers were observed for their reactions to their children and rated on the degree to which they rewarded the four forms of behavior. The results showed that high achieving children were less dependent on adults for both help and emotional support. Maternal reactions to children's dependence over-tures, as such, were not predictive of the children's achievement behav-ior, but *direct* maternal rewards of achievement efforts were. (They did *not* study maternal reactions to the children's independence efforts as a predictor of achievement development.) The children rewarded for achievement striving in the home displayed stronger strivings out-side the home, thus establishing maternal reward as one of the determinants of achievement striving. Consistency of the child's achievement standards in home and nursery school was also found in that there was a moderate but significant correlation of the behaviors in the two settings.

In another study (44), discussed in more detail on page 541, younger, unlike older, children preferred to return to a successfully completed task rather than one about which they were told they had not suc-ceeded. This motivation for task mastery had not yet appeared in younger children.

A promising beginning of systematic investigation of achievement behavior has been made. Research continues.

The development of self and social awareness

We now turn, as we did for infancy, to the issue of self and social awareness—the inner feeling of individuality and the perception of other social beings. As was the case in infancy, we are plagued by a lack of carefully controlled research findings created by the methodo-logical problems that arise when this segment of early childhood ex-perience is examined.

The Self

It might appear that since we are concerned with self-awareness we would use this very awareness of self as the method of investigation. If we want to know what a child thinks about himself, it appears that all we should do is simply to ask him. This, however, is a method doomed to failure. The history of the psychology of introspection shows this clearly. Moreover, psychoanalytic investigation has established that there are distortion and deception created by the defensive stratagems of the personality. It is for this reason that introspection failed as a technique of psychological investigation (66). True, by such procedures we may get some crude approximations of what children think they think about themselves, but little more.

The vague, yet expansive, boundaries of the self in the young child further complicate the matter. Already familiar from the work of Piaget is the inability of the young child to take the position of the other person, or, to use Piaget's terminology, to show reciprocity. Confusion over "me," simultaneously representing both the child himself and someone else speaking of himself, is illustrative of the child's inability to see the mountain scene model in any but his own perspective. Everything known by the child, moon and stars included, is for his express benefit, showing his vast egocentricity.

Localization of the self. One introspective study cannot be eliminated not only because of its general interest, but also because it demonstrates some of the confusion attendant upon use of the method. This is the study by Horowitz (72) on the spatial localization of the self. He asked young children and college students, in terms appropriate to their ages, where the "self" was located. An overwhelming variety of localizations emerged, especially in the replies of the children. The vividness and definiteness of this localization of the self are shown in an illustration taken from the account of Horowitz.

> Conversation yielded that the child's name was Lena; Lena was three years old (accuracy unchecked). Lena localized herself in the body, at first. As we continued exploring, in order to check the consistency of the response, Lena appeared in her lower right jaw. She was not in the hand, arm, or leg, nor in the eye, head, nor other (left) jaw. Lena seemed fixed in her lower right jaw. The definiteness of this localization may be indicated by her petulant response when we touched her right cheekbone and asked, "Is this Lena?" *"What is the matter with you? I told you three times this* (pointing to lower right jaw) *is me"* (72, 383).[7]

The child just mentioned "was" in the right jaw, another in the abdomen, another in the head, and so on. Most adults tended to locate the "self" in the head, brains, face, and eyes, but a few placed it in other parts of the body. Even the locus of the self gives little consistent agreement among children and adults.

[7] From Horowitz (72). Copyright 1935 by The Journal Press, and published with permission.

Memory and the self. In considering the self, one important difference between the infant and the younger child must be noted. The infant has a very poor memory. The idea of self is partly as a unifying generalization of the continuity of one's personal memories (66). It is necessary for the memory capacity to be better developed for this generalization to take place. During infancy this memory capacity gradually increases. It is probable, however, that this factor of memory as a contributor to self emerges in major importance only during early childhood. Through continuous memories of one's past, a child (and an adult) is led to have a sense of personal identity. He is a person who has done this and that and the other. These are seen as personal and very much a part of oneself.

Self-evaluation in the self-concept. From the discussion of psychoanalytic concepts in the next chapter, it will be seen that it is also in early childhood that self-criticism develops. Self-evaluation or self-criticism is considered by Hilgard (66) as a necessary feature in understanding self-organization. Self-evaluation is shown through guilt feelings. The presence of guilt feelings indicates that the individual considers himself an active agent responsible for what he does. If he fails to do that which he considers worthy and right, he develops self-reproof in the form of guilt.

On the other side of the coin is the effort of the self to protect against criticism in order to reduce guilt. In trying to keep a good opinion of ourselves we are capable of self-delusion. We try to make our motives acceptable to ourselves. Self-respect (even if we cannot always give it) is important to children and adults. Again the protective function, the mechanisms of defense to use psychoanalytic terminology, comes to the fore. The individual strives but does not always succeed in keeping a sense of self-worth. He values his opinion of himself and goes to great lengths to protect his favorable view of himself.

The self itself is a value. We expect desirable things from ourselves and expect to behave in ways that are admirable. We are ever ready to defend our evaluation of our self. We become aggressive or show other defensive maneuvers when something threatens our self-evaluation. Indeed, the psychoanalytic conception of defense mechanisms is expressly defense of the ego. If something does not fit these values or we fall short of our view of ourselves, we are apt to explain by saying, "I was not myself." We have self-esteem to the degree to which we have self-confidence or satisfaction with our behavior. In short, we value ourselves to some degree. True, there are varying degrees of self-acceptance. Sometimes we do not value ourselves very highly. We may on occasion dislike or even hate ourselves, and we may even be among those who take so jaundiced a view of ourselves that this disparaging view prevails. By and large, however, our self is something we hold dear.

Parental attitudes contribute to the child's self-evaluation. For example, in earlier discussion considerable emphasis was placed on parental rejection. From the child's point of view, rejection is something he experiences. He feels unwanted, despised, unattractive, or somehow found lacking. Fortunately, he also comes in contact with other parental attitudes and atmospheres. The prevalence of positive fostering attitudes helps to establish in children self-evaluations which are of a more healthful nature than the one chosen for illustration. Whatever their outcome, parental attitudes are experienced by the child and affect his self-evaluation.

Children's standards of behavior. Values and the self are also related through finding out what values of good and bad the child holds. The younger child's pattern of values of what is good and what is bad throws light on the self as he sees it. Knowledge of his values helps to understand how socialization works through the standards he internalizes as part of himself. The boy or girl is continuously admonished to be "good," and not to be "bad."

Radke (*125*) asked her preschool children what is a "good" and what is a "bad" or "naughty" boy (girl). Each child was urged to continue until four answers were given to both of the questions. Table 18 shows the summarization of her results when she had grouped their answers into categories.

Both goodness and badness at the preschool age appear to have a paucity of moral content. Doing "nice, kind things," and "saying bad words, is cross, isn't nice," are the most moral of the categories respectively in the table. Most of the values these children express may be called utilitarian and practical. A child is good or bad to the extent that he fits in with the family routine, takes care of himself, and avoids arousing maternal displeasure. The father's influence as an authority is strikingly absent.

Boys and girls show certain differences. In terms of the more prominent percentages of both good and bad behavior, girls stress helping, obeying the mother and avoiding being disobedient to her, self-help, doing nice, kind things, playing nicely, and avoiding violence. Boys emphasize helping mother, doing nice, kind things, and avoiding violence. These findings express their ideal concepts of a good boy and a good girl. A "good" girl or a "good" boy is one who seeks certain

TABLE 18

CHILDREN'S STANDARDS OF BAD AND GOOD BEHAVIOR *

| | Percentage of Responses | | |
Bad Behavior	Girls	Boys	Both
Doesn't do what mother asks	28	7	18
Doesn't do what other people tell him	0	14	6.5
Does overt acts of violence (that is, spits, scratches, snatches, hits, breaks windows, throws mud, and so on)	47	55	51
Cries, says bad words, is cross, isn't nice	12.5	17	15
Makes mother sad	0	7	3
Miscellaneous and doesn't know	12.5	0	6.5
Good Behavior			
Helps mother (specific items such as dusts, washes, cleans, and performs other household tasks)	20	40	29
Takes care of own routine (that is, dresses self, goes to toilet, picks up toys, cleans up his mess, and so on)	13	6	10
Plays (that is, plays gently with dolls, colors, and so on)	28	6	18
Does nice, kind things (that is, does good things, does things for people and so on)	13	30	21
Obeys mother (that is, does what mother says, and so on)	8	6	7
Doesn't destroy or break things (that is, doesn't break records, and so on)	3	3	3
Stays out of mother's way (that is, doesn't bother mother, and so on)	3	6	4
Miscellaneous and doesn't know	12	3	8

* Marian J. Radke, *The Relation of Parental Authority to Children's Behavior and Attitudes.* Copyright 1946, by University of Minnesota.

kinds of behavior and avoids other kinds. This does not mean that each individual child sees his responses as his own self-concept—that *he* or *she* exhibits these seekings and avoidances. In his or her own estimation he or she may, in varying degrees, fall short of these ideals.

Origin of the self-concept. There emerges in the child a concept of himself—an awareness of what he thinks he is like. It is his conception of who and what he is. From where comes this self-concept? Stagner (*143*) has given us a thoughtful analysis of the answer to this question. He considers that the sources of the self-concept (self-image) include the child's (1) real characteristics; (2) descriptions by adults; (3)

comparisons with others; and (4) inner pressures. Each will be considered in turn.

(1) "Real" characteristics refer to the objective characteristics of the child—his physique, his manner, his intelligence, his emotionality. (2) Perhaps almost as important are the characteristics which he knows have been attributed to him by adults—his assimilation of what they think of him. To some extent the self is created by what Sullivan (146) called "reflected appraisals." What a child's self-appraisal is, in part, is what others think and feel about him. Both gross overevaluation or derogation can create harmful effects expressed through his self-image. If "everyone" regards a child as clumsy or naughty or what you will, it should come as no surprise that the child believes them and acts to some degree in a way to correspond to their view. More often than not, however, a child's self-concept is less of a consistent pattern than these illustrations imply. After all, the way he is viewed differs from person to person even in a short space of time. He may be seen as mother's "darling," to the neighbor boy as a "sissy," and to his big sister, a "pest,"—all in the same hour. How he assimilates these pressures and makes his own is contingent not only upon this factor of attribution of traits but also upon the other sources of the self and the effect of past experience. (3) Comparison of the self with others enters through comparison with members of the groups in which the child finds himself. A bright child with even brighter older siblings will think of himself (as will others in the family) as less smart than if he were closer to them in intellectual ability. A child, actually average in height, may perceive himself as rather large if all of his classmates and playmates happen to be short. A child's self-concept is based partly on comparison with other persons. (4) Inner pressure as a determinant of the self-concept acts through the aspirations or ambitions the child holds. A girl with operatic ambitions may distort her inner evaluation to fit more in line with these ambitions. A boy who conceives himself as an athlete may be under self-pressure to try to fit this conception. These inner pressures may, of course, be reinforced by outer pressures from adults and others who hold similar expectancies for them. Inner pressures also act through interpretation of the situation. The view the boy holds may or may not correspond to the situation as others view it. A child may feel that a parent favors a brother or sister or is unduly harsh toward him when from the parent's point of view such is not the case. But the child's inner pressures will influence him whether they reflect reality or not. The influence of the sex roles on the origin of the self-concept will be taken up in the next chapter.

Social Perception

In early childhood social awareness may be viewed as the problem of social perception. Emphasis will be placed on the child's perception of parental roles. In brief, the issue at hand is what do children think about parental practices and about their parents as parents.

Perception of discipline. Differences between parents' reports of home situations and children's perceptions are very apparent. Earlier, Radke's report (125) of the kinds of punishment employed by parents was analyzed. The children perceived the punishment quite differently from the parents, and, in general, might be said to have considered the punishment received as ineffective.

Using a sample of preschool children, Neill (118) as reported by Hawkes (64) found considerable difference between what the parents reported the situation to be in their household concerning punishment and their children's perceptions of the same issue in the same home. Fifty per cent of her children named corporal punishment as what they expected from their parents; parents reported using corporal punishment only as a last resort. Only about 10 per cent of the children seemed aware that their parents expected them to take the consequences of their acts; about 70 per cent of the parents said they used this practice. Twenty-five per cent of the children agreed that their parents might put them to bed forcefully; 50 per cent of the parents said that, if necessary, they would do this. Even from these brief illustrations it is possible to sense the vast difference between parental practices and the ways in which these children perceived the same situations.

It is significant in this connection that Hansen as reported by Anderson (3) has found that whereas parents emphasized disciplinary and management controls, their children tended to see these parents primarily as sources of frustration. As Brown (32) suggests, it may be the way the child perceives the parent, not his attitude as objectively given, that determines the child's personality adjustment.

That the perception, not the real situation, is crucial is rendered at least plausible by Itkin's findings (75) with a sample of about 400 college students. He had a variety of attitude scales completed both by the students and by their parents. Through these scales he had information about the attitudes of these students toward their parents and information about how their parents supervised these students. From examination of the pattern of intercorrelations the scales provided, Itkin reached the conclusion that if children had a favorable attitude toward their parents, they tended to approve of the supervision they received irrespective of whether the parents were dominating or submissive in their attitudes; conversely, if they had negative attitudes toward the parents, they tended to judge parental supervision as dominating regardless of what their parents' attitudes might be.

Perception of parental roles. The children's perception of parental roles was investigated by Finch (49). Subjects were children between three and seven years of age drawn from 20 professional families. Among other techniques, a set of photographs was used, each of which showed both a father and a mother following some child care routine. From each picture the child told a story, at the conclusion of which the boy or girl was asked whether the mother or the father should carry out the task shown in the particular picture. Responses were categorized as mother, father, or both. It was found that, instead of either parent alone, the children spoke more frequently of both mother and father as performing 10 of the 13 roles—bedtime, baths, meals, prayer, companionship, affection, discipline, teaching, illness, and protection. Almost unanimously the father was seen as economic provider and the mother as housekeeper and contributor to the children.

Before knowing the children's replies, the mothers had been asked what they expected them to reply. Some roles which the mothers expected the children to consider to be those of the mother—bathtime, meals, and care during illness—were roles for which the children chose both father and mother. In response to the direct question, "What is daddy?" about 75 per cent of the children replied in terms of his being an economic provider. To a similar question about the mother, 50 per cent fell in the category of household duties and 25 per cent in that of caring for children. It would seem that the child sees the roles of the father in the home both as more numerous and as more important than general opinion might lead us to expect.

The egocentricity of the young child shows itself in his relative inability to recognize how others feel in a specific situation. A clear-cut study (34) compared one group of children, age three to five, and another of five to six-and-a-half in their empathic ability, that is, the ability to infer the feelings of others. Empathic responses were contrasted with egocentric responses or those in which the child imputed his own feelings to pictured figures.

Four crucial and four noncrucial pictures were used, one set for boys, another for girls. Crucial pictures showed (1) a birthday scene complete with cake and presents, (2) the same scene with the addition of a boy (girl) with a *frown* on his face, (3) a doctor with a long needle standing behind an empty chair, (4) the same scene with the addition of a boy (girl) with a *smile*, sitting on the chair. The noncrucial pictures showed a boy catching a fish, a girl pushing a doll carriage, and the like. The children in the two groups were told there was a boy (girl) in the picture, and asked, "How does he (she) feel?" An egocentric response would be scored if the child described the frowning boy at the birthday party as happy and the smiling boy in the dentist's chair as unhappy. The results found appear in Table 19.

TABLE 19

NUMBER OF EMPATHIC RESPONSES TO INCONGRUOUS PICTURES

		Number of empathic responses		
Groups	N	0	1	2
Younger (under 5 yr)	17	8	8	1
Older (over 5 yr)	22	2	7	13

The number of empathic responses in which they correctly judged the feelings of the children was significantly lower in the younger children than in the older subjects. The older children recognized that the children were not experiencing the same feelings that they themselves would have felt in the situation; the younger children, with few exceptions, failed to do this and attributed to the pictured child what their own feeling would have been.

Peer relationships

The young child interacts not only with his parents and other adults but also with his peers. His relationship to other children depends in part on the influence parental attitudes have had on him. Sometimes this influence is very direct and overt. This can be illustrated from the attitudes expressed by Mrs. Harper toward Shirley Ann (13). It will be remembered that, although indulgent, Mrs. Harper insisted that most children were not good enough for her darling. By her very actions in this connection she directed Shirley's acquaintance with other children into certain channels. Instances of direct and deliberate channeling of the child's social interactions are certainly common.

The effect of other parental influence may not be directly planned in that a specific result is expected. This is presumably the case with the young children studied by Baldwin and his associates (12, 13). It will be remembered that they found children from rejectant homes tended to be aggressive, children from democratic homes to be socially out-going and popular, and children from indulgent homes to be inactive and socially unsuccessful. Children from each home pattern had characteristic ways of reacting in social settings, including social settings with their peers.

Social Participation

Social participation with a child's peers increases in versatility and complexity between the second and fifth years. These increases with age are shown by the more cooperative nature of their participation. Parten (*121, 122*) studied the size of the groups in which children played and the nature of their play activity by a technique of time sampling.

Playing in groups of two occurred 30 per cent of the time for the children two- to two-and-a-half years of age, whereas groups of five only nine per cent of the time. For children aged four- to four-and-a-half the picture had changed considerably, since groups of five had increased to 24 per cent. Thus, the size of the play group increased with age during the preschool years. Parten also classified the play behavior of the children into the following categories: (1) *unoccupied;* (2) *solitary* (independent play); (3) *onlooker;* (4) *parallel activity* (playing alongside, but not with other children); (5) *associative activity* (common activity with borrowing, lending, and turns taken); and (6) *cooperative* (working toward some common goal; different roles by various members that supplement one another).

The youngest children tended to engage either in solitary or in parallel play. The older children tended to engage in associative or cooperative play to a much greater extent than the younger children. To bring together the results of the classification of their behavior, each category was given an arbitrary weight for cooperativeness with the highest category, *cooperative* play itself, considered the most cooperative and given the highest weight, and *unoccupied* considered the least cooperative and given the lowest weight. The weighted social participation score correlated with age of the children was found to be 0.61. As age increased the preschool child engaged more in associative and cooperative play and less in idleness, solitary play, and serving as an onlooker. Parallel play was the only category that did not change materially over the years. It is evident that with increasing age social participation increased.

Another way of summarizing these findings would be to put the results in the familiar framework of socialization theory. We already know that the two-year-old tends to be egocentric, and that during the preschool period, socialized responses increase. In social behavior, in the peer group, too, during the preschool period, there is a transition from egocentricity to increased socialization in the sense of increased cooperation.

Social Acceptance

We turn now to a child's social acceptancy by his peers. What is meant may be illustrated from the terminology used in the research studies on this topic. Investigators of social acceptance have referred to reputation, popularity, social success, social status, and prestige values. The common question is what makes a person socially acceptable or not socially acceptable to his peer group.

One of the tools used to study social acceptability and other forms of group interactions has been called sociometric tests by their originator, Moreno (112). Sociometric tests have in common the fact that they may be used to elicit positive or negative or mutual responses about members of a group by other members of that group (92). They may be used to select or exclude companions for any group, actual or potential, of which the child might become a member. These positive or negative responses are shaped by a particular investigator to suit his needs. The test of social acceptability is concrete. Not mere liking in general, but the liking for someone in a particular setting or particular activity is found to be most conducive to precise results—a seat mate, a playmate, fellow TV watcher, a party guest, or what you will.

The work of Marshall and McCandless (100, 101, 104, 105) has been outstanding.[8] Their picture sociometric technique was an attempt to overcome some of the difficulties plaguing earlier studies. All of the pictures for a particular group of subjects were fastened to a white background cardboard. After finding and pointing to their own pictures, each child pointed or named the others on the card. Then came the sociometric choices. The child was asked, "Whom do you like to play with outdoors?" until three preferred playmates were selected. The same procedure was followed for the three he would prefer to play with inside, and for three children with whom he would like to listen to stories. Either three or four separate sociometric sessions were held about ten days apart for three different groups. A child's socio-

---

[8] Earlier research studies of sociometric testing of pre-school children have been reviewed by Marshall (99) who demonstrated that they presented no satisfactory evidence that the data obtained predicted social acceptance. The early literature is therefore not considered.

metric score was the sum of weighted (first choice, five points, and so on) choices of the child as a playmate by all subjects for all sessions.

Teachers' judgments of best friends were also acquired. Three to five teachers for each group listed for each child choices of their four best friends in order of closeness. The two measures, children's sociometric choices and pooled teachers' judgments, correlated significantly, demonstrating that sociometric choice was a useful device for studying friendships among preschool children.

In addition, social behavior in a free play situation was observed (100) in a series of two minute observation in order to give a score on social interaction. This score was based on ratings of associative play of the sort used by Parten—friendly approach, hostility, such as interfering or snubbing, and conversation—and the best friend was identified by finding the child with whom the most associative play and friendly approaches were carried on.

Social acceptance and social participation (101, 105) was related to dependence on adults and sex differences. Dependency on adults was measured by observing the social interactions with adults in the free play situation. A negative relationship with sociometric choice was obtained. The higher the dependency on adults, the lower the social acceptance, and *vice versa*. Dependency on adults is accompanied by both low social status and participation.

In terms of sex differences as found in a later study with a different population (103) being dependent on adults interferes no more with girls' social acceptance than it does with that of boys—a reversal of a cultural stereotype and "common sense." Girls initiated fewer conflicts than boys but engaged in as many.

Concerning sex differences in general (102), girls had higher sociometric scores than boys, but no other sex difference could be demonstrated through teacher judgments of social acceptance, observed social acceptance, or degree of interaction with peers. By using three consecutive testings over time as a measure of progress of acquaintance, no consistent sex difference in sociometric scores emerged.

A consistency of behavior and lack of sex differences, perhaps more than is usually judged to exist, has been found. It would seem that social acceptance and social participation in preschool children are stable dimensions of their behavior.

Leadership

Closely related to social participation and acceptance is leadership. We cannot lead others without participating in social settings; thus it is not surprising that Parten (*121*) found a correlation of 0.97 between amount of social participation and degree of leadership.

Using the same preschool subjects as before, she classified the child's role in the groups under these general headings: follower (F); neither leading nor following but following own inclinations (N); both directing some children and following some others (B); reciprocally directing with another child (R); and directing the group as a whole (D). A composite leadership score based on minus to plus scores extending from F to D was calculated for each child; it was then correlated with social participation scores with the result mentioned.

Turning to the extent to which each kind of behavior was shown, the following of one's own independent inclinations was by far the more frequently indulged in by this group. All but three of the children, at some time or another, were followers, although more than half only in a very small number of instances. Incidentally, even the greatest followers were sometimes directors, which suggests that the idea, sometimes advanced, that some individuals are born followers is fallacious. The reciprocal leaders tended to be older than children who did not follow this role. The children who were definite leaders were found to be of two types—the diplomat and the bully. The former were subtle and rendered suggestions; the latter employed sheer bossiness in their directive role.

Friendships

Friendship, that is preference for the company of certain children and not others, can be observed in the youngest preschool child. One factor, of course, that makes for friendship is propinquity—the sheer physical proximity or availability of someone to be a friend. Children may live near one another, or attend the same school, and thus be drawn together. This factor has little in the way of dynamic significance. Generally, it serves merely as a background factor—a necessary, but not a sufficient cause. This is demonstrated, once it is realized that in most instances an individual, child or adult, has a choice among at least several more or less equally available potential friends. The factors that make for choice beyond mere availability need to be considered.

A study by Challman (37) of friendship in preschool children was dictated by the consideration that it was plausible to assume that similarity in some fashion or another is conducive to the formation of friendships. He selected for investigation likeness of sex, chronological age, mental age, intelligence quotient, height, and attractiveness of personality. He obtained measures of each of these characteristics for boys and girls whose average age was about three-and-a-half. They were observed in the nursery school setting, and the number of times each child was with every other child was used as the measure of the strength of friendship. The outstanding finding was that even the youngest of these children discriminated in their friendships very decidedly on the basis of sex. Only one boy and one girl showed a more marked tendency to form friendships with children of the opposite sex. All of the rest of the children tended to form friendships within their own sex. This is also characteristic of peer-age children. In the study of Tuddenham (148), his subjects chose children of their own sex almost without exception. As we shall later see in discussing latency phenomena, sex segregation is characteristic of this age.

To return to the study of Challman, none of the other factors, with the possible exception of chronological age, seemed to have any influence on friendships. Since the range of chronological age was not particularly great as there were few cases at the extremes, the study was not especially suitable for investigating the effect of age.

This narrowness of age range was remedied in another nursery school study, that by Green (55). Using the number of contacts as her measure of friendship, she found that it increased with age. From age two to three this is due to an increase in the number of friends; from age three to five this is due to the depth of friendship measured by playing more often with specific children rather than due to an increase in the total number of friends. These relationships in friendships may be interpreted in terms of behavior-social learning theory. As Mussen and Conger state:

> This shift in friendship patterns may be viewed as a consequence of the child's learning in these new interpersonal situations. In his first experiences outside the home, the child may interact with many different children. Some of these early relationships do not bring rewards and may even bring punishment. With time, the child learns that relationships with certain children are more likely to be gratifying than others. Hence he forms closer attachments to these children (115, 276–277).[9]

A careful study of Marshall and McCandless (100) that related social interaction, social acceptance, and spontaneous play to the child's sociometric scores and teachers' judgment of social acceptance was conducted. It was found that both the children's sociometric scores and the teachers' judgments of friends were stable over the 10-to-30-day intervals. However, despite some stability of friendships that these

[9] From Mussen and Conger (115). Copyright 1956 by Harper and Brothers, and published with permission.

findings demonstrated, it was sufficiently modest in degree to suggest that friendships changed with time. In other words, choice of friends, although somewhat stable, did change even within the short time span studied. This agrees with general experience that young children's friendships do fluctuate considerably.

Conflict and Aggression

It has already been indicated that personality reactions to home situations, especially to parental attitudes, carry over into social behavior. Aggression is no exception. For example, in the Sears antecedent study (142), it was found that for boys the more maternal punitiveness there was, the more aggressive the boys were in preschool. With girls, however, those with aggressive (punitive) mothers were less aggressive. Despite the sex differences, aggressive behaviors show the effect of maternal behavior in expressing aggression in social settings.

Aggression is intimately related to conflict. A child faced with a conflict often tries to overcome the resistance of his peers by sheer forceful aggression. If he wants a toy, he tries to pull it away from the child who has it. In turn, that child holding the toy is apt to respond by counteraggression.

Increased social participation inevitably brings in its wake the chance of conflict between children. It will be remembered that Landreth (85) found that 75 per cent of the situations causing crying in the nursery school were conflicts with other children. Preschool children are still quite socially maladroit. They can blunder in and out of conflict with astonishing ease. We are again reminded of the tendency to "want what they want when they want it," noted as exemplifying the grip the pleasure principle has upon younger children. Preschool children continue to show the tendency noted earlier to find the other child an obstacle to doing what comes naturally and to manipulate him as he would inanimate objects. He is very much wrapped up in his own concerns.

Jersild and Markey (77) found that about two-thirds of the conflicts of preschool children were aggressive acts against another child's possessions, the space he occupied, or his play activities, whereas only one-third of the conflicts were brought on by aggression against the child himself. In other words, snatching toys, intruding on the space he was occupying, or blocking what the other child was doing were more common as causes of conflict than were direct attacks on the other child. Sometimes, the child bringing on the conflict wanted the toy, or as it were, needed the space the other child was occupying and just came charging in. When the attack was directed upon the person of the other child, it appeared unprovoked from the observer's viewpoint in that there was no detectable behavior on the part of the child who was attacked which could be considered provocative of aggression.

Jersild and Markey found these results through observations of nursery school children aged about two to four in free-play situations. On the average, a conflict occurred every five minutes of their observation time. In a more recent study this finding was substantiated (162). A conflict occurred among boys every five minutes and among girls every seven or eight minutes. To return to the Jersild and Markey study individual children varied enormously in the number of conflicts in which they engaged. One child engaged in 141 conflicts, another in 17 conflicts during the same period of time. The number of conflicts also varied among the three nursery school settings in which information was collected. In one group the average number of conflicts was 34, whereas in another group for a comparable period of observation the number of conflicts was 81. Apparently, conflicts vary according to the setting.

A follow-up study by Jersild and Markey a year later showed that proneness to conflict was a fairly stable personality characteristic. Frequency of conflict was measured for some of the children in each of the various groups, and rank-order correlations ranging between 0.80 and 1.00 were found between the frequency of conflict behavior shown by children on two occasions a year apart. As compared to their behavior of a year before, a considerable increase in aggressiveness was observed. Whereas the average number of aggressions in nursery school per unit of observation had been six, a year later they averaged 17.

The peer group serves to modify the aggressive behavior of children. Fite (50) observed children in free play on the playground and in staged play settings which were designed to draw the child out in respect to his attitudes toward aggression. She shows that children admonished not to fight by their parents will, when in a play group where there is a considerable amount of fighting, show a conflict, but eventually the need to stand up for one's rights forces them to deviate from parental rules. The tendency for other children to regard aggressive behavior more leniently than their parents tended to relax the standards of some children. It would seem that the disinhibiting effect observed in behavior of children toward adult models also operated when other children served as models.

In a discussion of the systematic importance of aggression we are apt to lose sight of the fact that the young child shows other responses as well. A reassuring study (149) closes the discussion. The investigators compared affectional and aggressive behavior and demonstrated that at three-, four-, and five-years of age the children were more affectionate than aggressive in their relations with other children. Although concerned here with peer relationships, it should be mentioned that the same results held for relations to adults. At all ages the children were more verbally than physically affectionate, with little difference in frequency of physical and verbal aggression. Aggression tended to increase with age, and boys were more aggressive than girls.

Sympathy

It is during the preschool years that children become capable of what we would call sympathetic behavior (114). A child of this age often will help other children in distress—try to help satisfy their physical and social needs, protect them, defend them, and help remove the cause of their distress. This is what is meant by sympathy. It comes about from a slow process of growth, since, in large measure, the ability to sympathize is dependent on the child's ability to perceive what is happening.

For example, one cannot sympathize with a child who is humiliated unless one knows what it is like to be humiliated and can recognize in him the signs that he is feeling humiliated. Murphy (114) found that two- and three-year-old children might recognize the sight of the flow of blood as an occasion for sympathy, but not black and blue marks or swellings. Even when recognizing a distress situation, children of this age were more apt to stand about, with or without signs of anxiety, rather than doing anything actively. The ability to perceive subtle situations that will arouse sympathy increases as the child grows older. This results in a wider range of situations that become signals that distress is present. It is not surprising that older preschool children show more sympathetic responses than younger in the forms of activities of comfort, help, and defense.

Lois Murphy studied the manifestations of sympathy in groups of preschool children in the settings of playgrounds. Murphy supplemented this study by interviewing the parents as well as through a variety of experimental situations arranged so as to elicit sympathy.

Factors other than age seemed to influence the amount of sympathy, according to her findings. One especially prominent, positive relationship was the somewhat surprising one that sympathy and aggressiveness were related to each other. The more aggressive the child, the more often he tended to be sympathetic. Items from her rating forms show this association. They included association between a tendency to join in an attack on children and to defend children attacked by others; an attempt to comfort other children and push or pull other children; and to help children out of painful situations and pummel those who fell accidentally.

A definite relation for sympathetic and aggressive behavior to be positively related to each other seems established. Jersild and Markey (77), in their study of conflict behavior, found the same relation between frequency of sympathy and of aggressiveness. Perhaps, sheer gregariousness helps to explain this apparently paradoxical relationship. The aggressive-sympathetic child was "in" on most social situations, including both those in which aggression might be elicited and in those in which sympathy might be forthcoming. The less aggressive and less sympathetic child, not being so psychologically close to the social settings, behaved as he did because of his detachment.

Intelligence, too, seems to be related to sympathetic behavior. In one group, Murphy found a correlation of about 0.50 between amount of sympathetic behavior and mental age. However, the relatively modest magnitude of correlation implies that there is still plenty of opportunity to feel that high intelligence does not necessarily insure sympathy. In maladjusted children we would not expect such correlations, as cases cited by Murphy herself illustrated; nor would this relationship necessarily hold as the child grows older. It may be that the less intelligent child she studied had not as yet attained the capacity for recognizing the situation as one in which sympathy would be appropriate as much as his more intelligent peer. With increasing age, this relationship presumably would be sharply reduced or even disappear.

Murphy also utilized experimental situations in studying sympathetic behavior, such as leaving a child at the side of a playpen in which a two-year-old infant was confined. Toys for the infant, such as a doll and a ball, were *outside* the playpen. The child's reaction to the situation was studied. If at the end of 30 seconds he had done nothing to help the younger child, he was asked what he thought the infant wanted and was otherwise encouraged to interact with the infant. Other situations designed to elicit sympathy were arranged as well. The children responded to them very differently—from complete inhibition to wholehearted sympathy. It was possible to find characteristic patterns concerning sympathy among the children. Of 18 children tested, seven were consistently sympathetic in their behavior, five consistently unsympathetic, and six showed no consistency.

Cooperation and Competition

The nature and interrelation of cooperation and competition are enormously complicated and in many ways still not understood. Here we can refer to only a small percentage of available information. In our society, cooperation and competition are both considered as praiseworthy, and yet these tendencies may and do come in conflict. We play for the team, but we play for ourselves as well, both in childhood and adulthood.

Very young infants may hardly be said to compete. At the age of six to eight months at the baby parties of Maudry and Nekula, infants did not, since their "fighting" over equipment was impersonal. Between nine and 13 months, we may argue that since their conflicts became personal, there was competition over play equipment. The beginnings of cooperation seemed to occur later with the adjustment of one infant's behavior to that of the other, first occurring between 19 and 25 months. Their study, however, was not designed to measure cooperation and competition, specifically or definitely and, hence, must be considered as merely suggestive of the beginnings of these forms of social behavior.

Competition becomes more evident in the preschool period (87, 56). Leuba used a peg board situation with which preschool children played either singly or in pairs. The number of pegs placed properly in these two settings was compared. Two-year-olds were little affected by the presence of other children. Three- and four-year-olds, while competitive, were so distracted that they did more poorly when working in pairs than singly. Five-year-olds were not only competitive, but also definitely increased their output. In the second study the investigator encouraged a child to use building blocks competitively in building something bigger and (later) prettier than his companion. Using several criteria of rivalry, she found no competitive responses for children aged two to three, 43 per cent for children aged three to four, 69 per cent for children aged four to five, 75 per cent for children aged five to six, and 86 per cent for children aged six to seven. At age two to three there was no competition, but in subsequent years there was a steady increase in amount of it. Young children are not particularly competitive, but in our culture at least, children become progressively more competitive as age increases. Presumably, this reflects the child's assimilation of the competitive value of our society.

For competition to have an opportunity to appear, the task at which children are competing must be within the purview of the child concerned. Perhaps making something "bigger" or "prettier" was conceptually beyond the two-year-old child and consequently he did not compete. If it had been a task that he understood or was capable of doing, he, too, might have competed. Hence the finding that Maudry and Nekula's infants did compete, whereas Greenberg's two-year-olds did not, may be reconciled. A similar explanation may hold for Leuba's peg board study. At any rate, competition seems established in children in our culture at a relatively early age.

Aggression is not as closely related to competitive behavior as at first might be imagined. We might conceive of competition as simply a particular form of aggression. If this be the case, there should be a substantial correlation. However, it is possible that competitive behavior, or desire to excel, may develop independently of behavior with the aim of injury to another. McKee and Leader (107) investigated this comparison in 112 three- and four-year-old children, divided equally into groups on the basis of sex, age, and lower and higher socio-economic status. Each child was faced—first alone, and then later with a child matched in sex, age, and socio-economic status—with a table on which construction bricks were placed with which he was to play. Later analysis of the behavior was in terms of behavior in which the intent seemed to be to excel (competition) and behavior in which the intent seemed to be to injure (aggression). The relationship between competition and aggression was expressed in a correlation coefficient of only 0.22. In view of the small size of the correlation, competition and aggression can be conceived as independent patterns of behavior— highly competitive children are not necessarily highly aggressive.

When the contrasting socio-economic groups were compared, the results verified the hypothesis held by McKee and Leader that competitive behavior was more intense among children from lower socio-economic groups. The explanation for this finding may lie in the fact that those deprived of status are likely to seek it more vigorously than those not so deprived. Or it is also possible that lower status youngsters have already learned the advantage of competing for material benefits which for them, in any event, are in limited supply. In the same study both boys and older children were more competitive than girls and younger children.

Unfortunately, there are few comparably precise studies of preschool children in cooperative situations. In a somewhat general and less precise way, all studies of social participation in which there is harmony are studies of cooperation.

There is no question, then, that cooperation is possible at the preschool age. Wolfle and Wolfle (157) established that cooperative behavior was dependent on communication skills. They did this by pairing children and pairing monkeys in an identical situation in which the pair could obtain a reward only if they cooperated. Child (or monkey) A must give his aid if child (or monkey) B is to obtain food from a cup. A, in this instance, must pull a string to bring the cup containing the food within range of B. The roles of A and B were reversed in the second phase of the study. The monkeys gave no cooperation to one another. The younger preschool children co-operated only slightly. The older preschool children readily secured the cooperation of their companions.

There is some evidence that younger children are more cooperative (and friendly) than competitive (and hostile). Mengert (109) observed paired children in a playroom. Their overtly friendly responses outnumbered the overtly unfriendly ones by a ratio of over four to one. The greater amount of friendliness than aggressiveness, a finding from a variety of studies, points in the same direction. Sympathy, for example, frequently involves cooperation, so Murphy's results on sympathy in preschool children become relevant. Social participation itself may be predicated on cooperation as was the case in Parten's studies. To give a fresh illustration, Wright (158) found that when a newcomer was introduced into a group of children, they tended to be friendly toward him rather than hostile. The newcomer was given toys more frequently than they were given to already-established members of the group.

Summary

Behavior tendencies in early childhood were first considered in terms of dependence and independence tendencies. Evidence was introduced to show that dependence and independence should be considered as distinguishable, although related behavior tendencies. The kind and amount of frustration and punishment are the major determinants, so far established, for dependence tendencies in early childhood.

It was found that girls are more dependent than boys, a difference attributable to differential maternal identifications. Manifestations of dependency were shown to be influenced by situational factors, such as the presence or absence of the mother in a situation strange to the child, or other forms of stress situations leading to an increase in dependency. Instrumental dependence was found to decrease with age.

Turning to independence tendencies, they are shown to be related to dependence socialization anxiety, to training for and encouragement in independence, and to independent accomplishment. Some support is found for the hypothesis that independence increases with age. The young child wants to be both independent and dependent, conflict arises, but, in general, dependence decreases and independence increases.

Aggressive tendencies in preschool children are shown to be related to permissiveness toward aggression, to frustration, and to punishment. Boys are characteristically more aggressive than girls. Aggression as expressed in random discharge decreases with age, but retaliatory behavior, more in keeping with the meaning of aggression, increases with age. Fantasy aggression is greater in boys than in girls. Changes in aggression from successive investigative sessions have been found which take different forms, according to what particular adult is present.

Overt and fantasy aggression do not have a high linear correlation, but they are found to be much more interrelated when the additional factor of maternal punitiveness is taken into consideration. Frustration, as such, leads to fantasy aggression, but the relationship becomes considerably greater with severity of punishment for expression of aggression. High frustration when accompanied by high punishment leads to the greatest fantasy aggression; low frustration and low punishment lead to the least fantasy aggression. Identification is also found to be a determinant of fantasy aggression. Boys highly identified with their fathers show the highest frequency of fantasy aggression. For girls, identification is related to aggression only when it is associated with their mothers being the agents of their punishment. The effect of temporary situational factors was also explored. It was found that when they led to increased frustration this in turn led to increased fantasy aggression. The influence of aggressive models in increasing aggressive behavior has been established. Aggression and dependence, although both related to frustration, are separate behavior tendencies. Achievement motivation, the desire to do well, was found to be related to maternal rewards for achievement efforts.

Shifting perspective to the child, the development of self-awareness was first considered. The self rests, in part, on memory continuity and is expressed in the self-evaluation of the self-concept. Knowing what is held to be good and bad throws light on the self as the child sees it. Consistent ideal concepts of "good" boys and "good" girls emerge. As for the sources of the child's self-concept, attention is given to his "real" characteristics, his reflected appraisals of others, his comparisons of self with others, and his inner pressures.

Discussion of social perception centered on the child's perception of parental roles. He sees his parents as the sources of frustration, with the father being the greater source of authority and the mother being the greater source of affection. The young child is still relatively weak in his ability to recognize how others feel in a specific situation as shown by his lack of empathy.

During early childhood peer relationships expressed in social participation increase in versatility and complexity, moving from solitary or parallel play toward associative or cooperative play. What determines social participation, social acceptance, leadership, friendships, conflict and aggression, sympathy and cooperation, and conflict were explored.

For Further Reading

No general reference can be given for this chapter. Instead, several sources, each touching upon an aspect of the chapter, will be suggested. Bandura and Walters (17, 18) on aggression and social learning are recommended as is Buss (35) on aggression. Sears (139) gives a closely reasoned account of his views on dependency motivation.

References

Follow Chapter 14.

14

Psychoanalytic Contentions

To ROUND out the discussion of developments in early childhood, we come now to the matter of psychoanalytic views. These deal with the nature of the phallic stage, including the evolution of the Oedipus complex, the formation of the superego, and the interrelation among ego, superego, id, and environment. After we explore this theoretical setting, we shall delve into sexual tendencies that take the form of sexual curiosity, masturbation, awareness of genital differences, prohibitions, and sex-role training. The latter portions of the chapter place special emphasis on identification and the superego, on castration anxiety, and on the Oedipus complex. Owing to space limitations evidence concerning the functioning of ego defense mechanisms must be foregone. Its evaluation has appeared in other places such as (67, 135). Fortunately, the psychoanalytic hypotheses on the phallic stage neither stand nor fall on this evidence.

The phallic stage

At about the end of the third year the focus of libidinal energy shifts from the anal to the genital zone and continues to predominate until about the age of six. To put it another way, libidinal localization is displaced to the genital zone, and new modes of pleasure finding become prominent. This does not mean that genital interests and activities have been absent before this stage—erections occur, and masturbation and sex play are not unknown before this age—but that erotic

423

pleasure is now centered on the genital organs, instead of the other erogenous zones. To distinguish it from the genital stage of adolescence, this earlier aspect which cannot come to fruition in reproduction is called the phallic stage.

Occurrence of the shift of libidinal localization is made possible by the new degree of maturation of the sexual organs which occurs at this age. The sexual organs become richer in sensations than they have been before. Interest in them is greater; masturbation increases; a greater desire for physical contact takes place, especially with members of the opposite sex; and exhibitionistic tendencies appear. Sexual fantasies as well as these behavioral manifestations are found. The young child places a high value on the sex organs, in the case of the boy on the penis and in the case of the girl on the clitoris. This high valuation, as much as the pleasure obtained, marks the phallic stage.

One consequence of the phallic stage is that the boy and the girl learn identifications appropriate to their own sex. In normal development the boy becomes more masculine and the girl more feminine during this stage. As a consequence it is no longer possible to use "he" generically for both boys and girls. From now on the sexes must be distinguished.

Phallic Development and the Oedipus Complex in Boys

The mother as love object is already established for the boy. With awakening phallic sex interest, it is considered inevitable that the attitudes the boy holds toward the mother will be sexual, despite their fumbling, childish expression. His sexual emphases are that of an adult although he has no grasp of their implication, nor is he capable of adult practices. Thereafter, as Munroe puts it:

> Sooner or later, the mother rebuffs behavior in her son that is dimly recognized as "sexual." The social taboo begins operating in a variety of ways. It is especially important that the little boy observes that the father enjoys privileges with the mother from which he is excluded. It may be that the privilege of creeping into mother's bed is revoked when father is home. The child may have witnessed the primal scene (that is, his parents in intercourse) or have suddenly remembered such scenes witnessed at a time when he was too young to "understand" them even in the confused way typical for infancy. Freud suggests that phylogenetic memories of the primal horde in which father and sons were in open competition of sexual possession of the women (mother and sisters) may also be a factor in the attitude of the little boy toward the father (113, 200).[1]

---

[1] From Munroe (113). Copyright 1955 by The Dryden Press, Inc., and published with permission.

The tensions which this situation creates between father and son are interpreted in terms of what is called the Oedipus complex. Oedipus, of Greek legend and drama, is the central character of the tragedy in which Oedipus murders his father and marries his mother. In symbolic terms, Freud said, this is the drama the boy must play. Every boy is fated to have death wishes toward the father (to kill the father in fantasy) and to desire to "marry" his mother. This is an inevitable step in the course of libidinal growth.[2]

On this matter, society is at its firmest in forbidding such desires being put into practice. Mother-son incest is unthinkable in our culture and, indeed, may be so in all other cultures. The social taboo, then, is massive and uncompromising. In a sense, every boy at this stage of development is at war with society (as expressed at the family level) as well as a rival of his father. If this were not enough to create an intolerable impasse, there is the fact that he is dependent on his father and under his authority. Small wonder he develops anxiety and fears loss of love of both his parents as a consequence of the Oedipus situation. But in addition to the anxiety engendered by this fear of loss of love there is a more specific anxiety. It will be remembered that the penis is overvalued. Consequently, this gives rise to what is known as castration anxiety.

Castration anxiety refers to anxiety about implied or actual injury to the genital organs, especially the penis. Some parents actually do threaten harm to the penis to stop masturbation. The anatomical lack in the girl, once the boy notices such differences, can reinforce the idea that castration does take place. Even without this specific threat (which was probably more common in Freud's time than it is now) other factors are operative. Hartmann, Kris, and Loewenstein put it as follows:

> While in many cases the child in our civilization is no longer being threatened with castration, the intensity of the veiled aggression of the adult against the child may still produce the same effect. One might say that there always is "castration" in the air. Adults who restrict the little boy act according to patterns rooted in their own upbringing. However, symbolic or distant from actual castration their threats might be, they are likely to be interpreted by the little boy in terms of his own experiences (59, 21–22).[3]

[2] To the statement that introspectively one cannot remember these stirring times in his own childhood, Freud would reply that the psychoneurotic manages to get along by repression of his Oedipus complex, whereas the normal person who has worked it through has amnesia for these early longings and incidents.

[3] From Hartmann et al. (59). Copyright 1947 by the International Universities Press, and published with permission.

In the boy, castration anxiety, along with the other anxieties of the situation, is so great that he gives up his desires for the mother. Repression both of sexual desires for the mother and of the hostility toward the father takes place. Repression, discussed in more detail earlier, refers to the excluding from consciousness some unacceptable impulse. With the sexual and hostile impulses now unrecognized for what they are, as the result of repression, a new relationship with the mother and the father becomes possible. With the resolution of the Oedipus complex, object choices are replaced by identification, that is, sexual attractions are replaced by wanting to be like someone. The state of affairs now existing permits an identification to be made by the boy with his father. His dangerous erotic feelings or object choices for the mother are converted into harmless, tender affection. Identification with the father results in desexualization of his wishes toward the mother (58).

Thus the Oedipus situation is "smashed," but residuals remain because repression results not in eradication of the impulses but merely in their not being consciously experienced.

Phallic Development and the Oedipus Complex in Girls

The problem of the Oedipus complex is more complicated in the girl than in the boy. The boy, after all, maintains a positive relation with his pre-Oedipal object, the mother. The girl, however, must switch affections from the original love object, the mother, to the father and also learn to "hate" the mother.

Along with an awakening interest in her own sex organ is an interest in the sex organs of others and the discovery of anatomical differences. As expressed elsewhere:

> . . . the castration anxiety of the boy is impossible for her since the lack that this implies is already a fact. This lack she notices, and "penis envy" develops. She has fantasies that this castration has happened as a punishment, and she wishes to regain it through the father. This drives her into the Oedipus situation in which the loss may be repaired again in fantasy by having a child through the father. She "loves" the father, and therefore "hates" the mother, her rival, whom she also blames for her castration. As a means of solving this problem, the girl learns to identify with the mother. The already existing ambivalence toward the mother aids in this displacement to the father. In this way the girl is prepared for the Oedipus shift, the events driving her into it, rather than destroying it, as was the case with the boy. As a consequence of the way it was formed there is less drive for the girl to overcome it as abruptly as does the boy and, as a matter of fact, the Oedipal situation remains in effect

with the girl for longer periods and is continued more or less indefinitely (*151*, 452).[4]

Formation of the Superego

The formation of the superego is a direct consequence of the Oedipus situation in both boys and girls. During the phallic stage, parental views continue to be respected and these include identifications with their prohibitions. The boy and the girl incorporate their parents' views concerning these matters as their own partly on the basis of these positive factors. The child's parents' views become internalized. As Blum states:

> The frustrations of the Oedipus complex are said to cause a regression from more differentiated types of object relationships to introjection and orality, and the sexual longing for an object is replaced by an asexual alteration within the ego. The introjected parents do not fuse with the rest of the ego because of the feeling of distance between parents and child. Instead they combine with the previously existing parental introjects or superego forerunners to form a precipitate within the ego. These later identifications differ from the forerunners in the following way: the child, in order to escape conflicts revolving about love, hate, guilt, and anxiety, does not identify with the parents as they are, but with the idealized parents. He purifies their conduct in his mind, and the identification proceeds as if they were consistently true to the principles they explicitly profess or aspire to observe. According to Freud, the child identifies with the superego of the parents. Idealization was present earlier in terms of attributing magical powers to parents, but now for the first time the idealization concerns moral behavior (*28*, 97).[5]

The superego has now come into being. On the basis of its origin it is now easier to see how it has a "drive" quality and why it is so irrational and punitive.

The superego, in one of its aspects, functions as the conscience. However, it is broader since, in part, it functions unconsciously. Its unconscious aspects arise because it was incorporated by the child without awareness on his part during those early years that are the phallic stage. Anxiety was already operative before the appearance of the superego. Now that the superego is present, anxiety becomes expressed in guilt, that is, the superego is the internalized agency which punishes the child by making him feel guilty when he violates the social sanctions of his culture. No longer is external danger alone

[4] From Watson (*151*). Copyright © 1963 by Robert I. Watson. Published by J. B. Lippincott Company.

[5] By permission from *Psychoanalytic Theories of Personality* by Blum. Copyright 1953, McGraw-Hill Book Company, Inc.

conducive to anxiety. An inner representation of that danger, the superego, takes over some anxiety and expresses itself in the child's experience and behavior as guilt.

There is also another more positive aspect to the superego—the ego-ideal. The ego-ideal is the child's conception of what his parents consider to be morally good. The child assimilates his parents' standards of what is good and virtuous. Internalization of parental approval and reward allows him to control his behavior in line with their wishes. Instead of relying upon parental approval, he now secures self-approval and pride through the superego's functioning.

To speak more generally concerning the functioning of the superego, moral demands, ideals, and the like are expressed through it. The superego serves the purpose of controlling those sexual (and aggressive) impulses that, if permitted uncontrolled expression, would endanger social stability. The inner restraints imposed by the superego permit man to live in society—but at a price.

The Phallic Character

Castration anxiety and penis envy produce the particular characteristics which typify the phallic character. In later childhood and adulthood, the boy showing disproportionate effects of the phallic stage in the form of castration anxiety gives an impression of being a reckless, strutting daredevil who behaves in an aggressive, firm, self-assured fashion. Overevaluation of the penis and confusion of it with the whole body produce intense vanity, exhibitionism, and sensitiveness. In keeping with expectation of assault the phallic character is prone to attack first. Professional wrestlers, "beach" athletes, weight lifters, and motorcyclists at least fit the stereotype of the picture, even though all such individuals are not phallic characters. A similar process takes place in the girl who is motivated by strong penis envy. She tries to assume a masculine role and strives for superiority over men.

Basically, the phallic character, male or female, is dependent and narcissistic, unable to form mature relationships, and contemptuous of the opposite sex. Sexual conquests are attempts to demonstrate masculinity or femininity, not based on real feeling for their partners.

Sexual tendencies

There is a general impression that there is an increase in the scope and frequency of sexual behavior in early childhood over that in infancy. Definitive controlled research on this question of frequency and scope is lacking. We must be content with general descriptions.

Sexual Curiosity

Isaacs (74) observed 30 English children (mostly boys) in the setting of a nursery school. Her observations covered a period of three years. She reports her findings in an anecdotal fashion as the quotations below about sexual curiosity exemplify.

> When the children were playing a family game with the puppy as baby, Duncan said: "Undress him." Priscilla: "Yes." Duncan: "and then we can see his bim-bom." There was great laughter and excitement among the children and all repeated, "see his bim-bom." Priscilla undid the rug in which he was wrapped and called others to look: "Come on, come on, look underneath." The puppy stood on its hind legs near Priscilla. Duncan: "Oh, he tried to get to your what-d'ye-call-it." . . .
> Jane and Conrad went with Mrs. I. to the ethnological museum today. When looking at a human figure made of bamboo, Conrad pointed out the prominent penis, giggling, and saying, "What is that funny thing, sticking out? We know, don't we?" They whispered and giggled about it (74, 141–142).[6]

In addition to sexual curiosity, exhibitionism (exposing genitals) and voyeurism (looking at others' genitals) were frequently observed by Isaacs. The sheer wealth of her observations support the contention that sexual activities are common in preschool children. Her unsystematic method of selection makes this the only conclusion which can be safely drawn from her data. Her results are not capable of yielding quantitative comparison among ages or between the sexes.

In another study Hattendorf (62) interviewed a large number of mothers about the nature of the sex questions their children asked them. Despite the distortion and unreliability brought about by the retrospective nature of the mothers' recall, her results are of some value. For over 800 children from two to five years of age the most frequent questions these children asked their mothers centered on the origin of babies and the coming of another baby. The next most frequent question concerned physical sex differences. Sexual curiosity during preschool ages seems to be established.

Masturbation and Related Activities

Although reported in infancy it is not surprising that studies mentioning male masturbation have centered in early childhood as the earliest

[6] From Isaacs (74). Copyright 1933 by Harcourt, Brace and Company, Inc., and published with permission.

age for sufficient frequency to occur to make possible reliable observations. Many studies depend on retrospective report of mothers or of the subjects themselves. This introduces the factors of forgetting, of repression, lack of opportunity of observation, and of dissimulation which presumably would mean that whatever the findings were concerning frequency, there would be an understatement. Moreover, some studies finding very small percentages of conscious recall may be based on the reporting of the presence of *habitual* rather than occasional activity. This is the explanation that Sears (135) offers of Willoughby's 1937 summary of the literature (153) in which only five per cent of men and 18 per cent of women could recall having masturbated before the age of ten.

Later somewhat more adequately controlled studies show higher percentages. About 60 per cent of the mothers interviewed by Sears and his associates (140) in their "pattern" study reported they had observed masturbation in their children who by then were five or six years of age. Sex play with other children was reported by over half of the mothers. Most mothers were not permissive toward these activities. On the other hand, quite a few were moderately permissive, not making an issue of it although discouraging these practices. Huschka (73) in presenting data on 300 problem children reported about the same percentage of masturbation. These mothers of the problem children dealt with the problem much more destructively than the mothers in the Sears study. In fact, about two-thirds on detecting masturbation used direct threats predominantly of a physical sort and specifically threats of genital injury.

Awareness of Genital Differences

Most of the available research on awareness of genital differences concern older children. However, Freud had held that discovery of genital differences during the phallic stage had considerable consequence for the child's development. For this reason we discuss the subject here.

A young child can readily identify himself as a boy or a girl. This does not necessarily mean awareness of genital differences on the child's part. Often children stress, as we shall see, differences in dress or hair arrangement even when aware of genital differences. In fact, the situation recalls the old story of the little boy asked about the sex of a baby he had seen in the process of being bathed who replied, "I don't know, it's so hard to tell with the clothes off."

Conn and Kanner (40) interviewed 200 children, mostly between five and seven, concerning sex awareness in the setting of doll play. The children spoke about sexual matters, not in relation to themselves, but for boy dolls, girl dolls, father dolls, and mother dolls, making the situation a projective one. A doll with a dress was introduced to lead up to questions on how to tell boys and girls apart. "Modesty" was investigated through using a toy bathroom with a doll on the toilet.

In their sample, 140 gave in the first session "certain" awareness of genital differences. To be sure, other differences were mentioned, with those in clothing, tonsorial distinctions, and urination posture being prominent. Differences were stated in childish terminology and not less than 61 different names for the genital organs were given. Awareness of sex differences at these ages seems established.

A better controlled study of awareness of genital differences was performed by Katcher (82). Conn and Kanner's subjects were children referred to a psychiatric clinic and hence may have been a rather atypical population. Katcher used as subjects over 200 normal children of higher and lower socio-economic status in preschool or school settings. Their task was to identify the sex of the drawings of figures of clothed and nude children and adults. Excluding hair, the outline of the figures used was a compromise between male and female. The same outline was used in all pictures; adult nude figures were cut off at the waist. Systematically varied cues from which they could make identification were added to the outline figure—hair, clothes, breasts, and external genitals. These figures were presented in pairs in random fashion for the children to make a choice as to sex.

The errors they made were analyzed by age and socio-economic differences. In general, except for breast cues, errors decreased with age. No significant socio-economic difference was found. The most readily identified sex-differentiating characteristic was clothing, followed in order by hair, genitals, and breasts.

Genital errors produced several findings of interest. No subject older than eight years made a single error in identifying genitals. Older children were more accurate than younger ones. Girls throughout tended to be superior to boys in identification of both male and female genitals. For ages four and five, by which the phallic stage is said to be in operation, there were still over 50 per cent of the children making mistakes on genital cues. Breasts, presumably theoretically less traumatic in their import than the genitals, nevertheless showed more errors.

Interpreting the over-all results of awareness of genital differences in terms of Freudian thinking is not impossible. However, there is nothing crucial to contraindicate a learning or experience interpretation, quite apart from Freudian thinking. Except in terms of specific details, with some favoring one view, some the other, there is little in the evidence itself on which to base a choice between the alternative hypotheses. Katcher (82) himself considered his results favored the experience hypotheses.

Discovery of genital differences, postulated by Freud to account for much of the subsequent development in the phallic stage, has not been submitted to crucial controlled research. The available evidence does, however, suggest that factors other than discovery of sex differences, such as socialization pressures, also contribute and that undue emphasis has been placed on what is but one of the factors responsible for increased sex differentiation during early childhood. Increased general maturity and learning experiences of the preschool child over that of the infant may help to account for the results. There is nothing in these researches to show that it is the specific discovery of genital differences which makes for this increase in sex differentiation.

Awareness of genital differences apparently is complete by the end of the fifth year. However, this is only an aspect of a broader and more vague differentiation between the sexes. It seems plausible to accept the conclusion of a review of the literature (31) that by the fifth year most children make a clear differentiation between the sexes.

Prohibitions

Our culture is still hostile toward expression of childhood sexuality. Indeed we are more severe in restrictions on sex behavior in children than many, if not most, other societies (51, 152). Restrictive efforts by parents have three objectives: to avoid or minimize chances of their stimulation, to avoid opportunity for erotic play with other children, and to inhibit sexual impulses toward family members (140). To use only one facet of restriction, the typical parent is still misinformed about the "pernicious" effects of masturbation (76). He does not hesitate to use forceful measures, including threats and coercion, to stamp it out. Since the customs of our group require that self-stimulation be prohibited, the parents must find ways to discourage the child's discovery of his capacity for this particular form of self-enjoyment. All of this means that sexual expression of children is a problem of socialization.

From the child's point of view parental efforts along these lines are restrictions which must be learned. He experiences pleasure in touching his genitals and is affectionate toward his parents and his peers. He must learn when to inhibit, to redirect his impulses, or to hide them from view.

If we can generalize from the findings of the Sears "pattern" study, parents in general wish children to inhibit sexual tendencies (*140*). What they try to do is to prevent sex activity from starting at all. Even labels for sexual activities are not always provided—either no words are used, or befitting the occasion vague terms of reference, such as "it," "down there," or "not nice," for some aspect of sexual behavior; or private family names or baby terms are used. Unlike feeding and toilet procedures where there are socially approved outlets, no redirection is given for sexual tendencies. No substitutes are offered. Prohibition is stressed. To be sure, arranging conditions to prevent stimulation, such as separate sleeping rooms, separate bathing hours, and closed doors, are used. The practices show that much sex training is expressed through training in modesty.

Distraction is also practiced, moving the child's hand or finding something else for him to do. But prohibition—saying "No!" in a multitude of forms—is perhaps the principal agent. None of these parental practices offers the child other substitute outlets—they are all restrictive in intent. Punishment may lead to elimination of masturbation, but other effects may follow. Small wonder, then, that seeds of maladjustment in many children can be planted within this area.

It is important to note that observed sex behavior in children is not always evidence that sexual needs are present. Plant (*123*), on the basis of his clinical experience, indicates that many children in engaging in sex experiences are motivated, not by sex tendencies, but by other factors. There may be a desire to break taboos, including sexual ones, a desire to be "grown up," a desire to be sought after and to gain prestige, a facet of general curiosity, and the like. Thus, various other needs may be expressed through "sexual" behavior that are not motivated by sexual tendencies, but by other socialization tendencies.

Sex-role Training

Prohibitions are focused on the prevention of sexual activity in the narrower sense. But there is another facet to this problem of socialization—sex-role training, in order to carry on *nonsexual* activities appropriate to sex. Sex-role training (sex typing) is imitative or modeling behavior, most often done as a matter of course because the boy or the girl is reinforced selectively by adults.

Sexual differentiation in the individual requires consideration of the intense and prevalent sex-role training which socialization introduces. In our society, the infant is distinguished as to sex at birth by the blue or pink blankets used. From then on sex roles are relentlessly drilled in. Confining one's self to girls, it may take the form of more "fussing" with them, telling them how pretty they are as babies, presenting toilet training as a sex differentiated activity, selecting dolls and carriages for them as young children, and throughout, using appropriate verbal appellation such as, "That's a good girl," or encouraging identification by suggestion to them that they be "just like mommy." It is not surprising that by early childhood distinguishable sex differences are to be found.

Not only are sex differences to be found, they are also of the kind our society expects to find in boys and girls. The data of a study by Hattwick (63) may be used for this purpose. She studied sex differences in several hundred nursery school children aged two- to four-and-a-half and made ratings on 60 observable behavior characteristics. Statistically significant differences were found between boys and girls on 27 of these items. Eleven of the items showed greater occurrence in boys. These were attacking others, breaking toys, grabbing toys, being hard to reason with, ignoring requests, laughing and jumping around excessively, rushing into danger, handling sex organs, leaving tasks incomplete, tenseness at rest, and wasting time at routines. Girls showed greater occurrence on 16 characteristics. These were avoiding risk, avoiding play with others, bossing, criticizing others, crying easily, fearing strange places, fearing high places, jealousy, misrepresenting facts, refusing food, shrinking from notice, staying near adults, sucking thumb, twisting hair, telling fanciful stories, and seeking praise. These, then, are established differences in behavior characteristics between younger boys and girls.

Her findings do not demonstrate whether these sex-linked behavioral differences are expected in our culture to be characteristic of boys and girls. Social expectations were investigated by the writer (150). The 27 terms used for types of behavior which Hattwick found for differentiating between preschool age boys and girls were arranged on a report form in alphabetical order; then 59 boys and 138 girls in a college undergraduate child psychology class were asked to check whether boys or girls at this age would show more often each particular behavior item. No discussion of this topic had yet occurred in class or in text.

Their opinions concerning what to expect in sexual differences agreed with the empirical results found by Hattwick. For boys, 10 of the 11 observed sex differences were expected by both male and female raters either in statistically significant degree or at least with differences in the expected direction. The only exception was the expectation rating by both males and females of laughing, squealing, and jumping around excessively as more characteristic of girls than of boys. For girls, 13 of the 16 observed sex differences showed statistically significant agreement or differences in the expected direction by both male and female raters.

Hattwick's and the writer's results both fit the notion that the girl both is and is expected to be timid and more passive; the boy both is and is expected to be aggressively forceful in our culture. Expectancy and actuality concerning sex differences seem to agree.

The role of the parent in creating sex differences in roles of the child has been demonstrated in the studies of Sears and his associates (141) and Bach (8) discussed earlier in connection with the role of the father. The father was hypothesized as supplying for the boy the primary patterns and rewards for masculine traits such as aggression. If absent, the child would lack him as a model and be less masculine. He does not serve as the model of sex appropriate behavior for girls and consequently it was hypothesized that his absence would have little influence on them, which was found to be the case. In general, with the qualifications and nuances mentioned in the earlier discussion, boys from father-absent homes manifested less aggression, whereas girls were not affected.

In the "pattern" study of Sears and his associates (140), intentional sex typing was investigated. A variety of questions was asked the mothers, the answers to which threw light on this issue. Using the questions about boys as illustrative, the investigators asked about how important the mother thought it for the boy to be a real boy, to play or not play with dolls; about differences in ways boys and girls ought to behave, and how boys should treat little girls. It was possible to reduce their findings to a single scale on sex-role differentiation. Only about 5 per cent believed little or no sex-role differentiation existed at this age, but only about 4 per cent were at the other extreme of always stressing it. Most mothers did put some weight upon sex-role differentiation.

It was also possible to take up all of the training practices followed by the mothers and compare the ratings of the mothers of boys to those of the mothers of girls. Girls were more warmly treated in infancy, were more often disciplined by their mothers, were more often subjected to withdrawal of love, and praised for their conduct. Boys received more physical punishment. It was in the area of aggression where the greatest distinction was made. Boys were allowed more opportunities for aggression, although not permitted to fight with brothers and sisters. It was evident that, to many mothers, being "boylike" implied being aggressive. No particular differences were found in connection with toilet training and, most surprising perhaps, no differences in sex training in the narrow sense. Evidently this latter source of differentiation does not start as early as the preschool age.

Identification and the superego

Identification and the superego as intertwined processes have many aspects and nuances. Crucial to their meaning are: (1) the internalization of the parent's code of values; (2) feeling of guilt when this code is violated; (3) self-satisfaction when the code is followed. These three aspects came about because there is an emotional tie with the parent in such manner that his or her behavior is taken on, and made the child's own. In short, the parent's behavior is "internalized." When this has occurred, the child no longer needs to depend on his parents' rewards and punishments as guides for his conduct; he is able to reward or punish himself. When identification has developed, the child behaves without their urging in ways they have instilled in him. He has learned self-control, he feels guilty when violating his parents' standards, and he feels pleasure when he is able to resist temptation and follow the dictates of the conscience (the ego-ideal). Now the conscience or superego is operative.

Although this account may appear to be reasonably clear, a host of other meanings and nuances of meaning begin to appear when we begin to inquire more carefully what is meant. The confusion is so great that one psychoanalyst (129) suggested that the term, identification, be scrapped entirely. Since this solution shows no sign of taking place, it is necessary to try to unravel the various aspects of the problem. There are other closely related activities which, although they may contribute to the results obtained by identification, must be differentiated from it.

Relation of Identification to Other Processes

Identification is closely related to, and sometimes has been confused with, sex-role training, sex-role preferences, and sex-role adoption. Along with identification, these processes will be referred to as sex-related activities.

Sex-role training was heretofore discussed without appeal to identification. It was shown to be a particular form of socialization, obviously wider in scope than merely parental teachings, in which pressures were exerted on the child for appropriate sex-related behavior. It did not seem to require for its explanation anything more than the usual principles of learning. It may be that evidence presented later will show that identification, as a special additional concept, also helps to account for sex-role training.

Sex-role preferences have been distinguished from identification. Sears (as reported by Brown, 29) seems to have been the first to make this distinction. Sex-role preference, he pointed out, refers to sex-linked behavior a boy or a girl perceives as the preferred or more desirable behavior to follow. Hence, the child imitates the behavior perceived as desirable. Identification requires that there be an actual incorporation from the roles of the adult with whom the child identifies, not just role preference. Identification refers to sex-linked behavior that an individual introjects and makes his own. The two processes of identification and sex-role are interrelated. In many cases an individual identifies with a given sex model as well as preferring sex-roles appropriate to that model—he identifies with what he prefers and prefers that with which he identifies. But sex-role preference does not demonstrate identification.

With this distinction in mind Brown delineated three sex-role patterns: " . . . (a) Identification with and preference for the sex role of one's own sex, e.g., a girl may identify with and prefer the feminine role; (b) Identification with the sex-role of one's own sex but preference for the sex role of the opposite sex, e.g., a girl may identify with the feminine role but prefer the masculine role; (c) Identification with the sex role of the opposite sex but preference for the sex role of one's own sex, e.g., a girl may identify with the masculine role but prefer the feminine role. Of the two processes, identification appears to be primary, while preference is more or less secondary, relative to sex-role behavior. In normal development the two form a single integrative process" (31, 237).[7]

A child may have appropriate sex-role identification and yet be poorly identified with the same sex parent (96). Conversely, a child may be well identified with the same sex parent and yet poorly identified with the appropriate sex role. This last would come about when the parent himself was poorly identified with his appropriate sex role. It is apparent that, just as is the case with identification and sex-role training, identification and sex-role preference are closely if not inextricably related, and yet must be distinguished if there is to be any reality to the concept of identification.

In addition, sex-role adoption, masquerading as sex-role preferences, may occur. Sex-role adoption takes place when the particular activi-

[7] From Brown (31). Copyright 1958 by the American Psychological Association, and published with permission.

ties, often associated with a particular sex-role, are liked not for their own sake, but carried out for the sake of expediency (95). For example, behavior characteristic of one sex, say women wearing trousers at work, or men becoming beauty operators, can occur without either sex-role preferences or identification being involved.

Evidence Concerning Sex-role Preferences

A systematic examination of the evidence concerning sex-role preferences in children is called for, both for its own sake, and to clarify further how it may be distinguished from identification. Brown (29) quantified a scale for the measurement of sex-role preference. It consisted of picture cards showing various objects, figures, and activities commonly associated with masculine or feminine roles.

Some of the cards showed single items such as a necklace, a tractor, a doll, or a purse. Other cards bore paired items such as trousers and shirt with a dress, and cosmetic articles with shaving articles. The last section of the scale was a picture of a girl, a girlish boy (boy dressed as a girl), a boyish girl (girl dressed as a boy), and a boy. A child-figure, undetermined as to sex, called "It," was used by each child who made choices from the cards for It. For the single item cards, each child subject picked eight liked best by It. For each pair and for the four-child figures, one was selected as preferred. Range of the total weighted scores on the sex-role cards was from zero, an exclusively feminine score, to 84, an exclusively masculine score. Seventy-eight male and 68 female middle-class children aged five and six were used as subjects. Their mean scores respectively were 66 and 38. This resulted in a large and statistically significant difference, indicating definite sex-role patterns in young children.

A follow-up study, using essentially the same technique (61), showed that four-year-old boys were more masculine and four-year-old girls more feminine than were three-year-olds. Lest the results seem to imply an invariable progression of increased femininity with increase in age, it should be indicated that Brown (30) found that after the age of four a change toward *masculinity* took place in girls continuing up to the age of ten.

To return to Brown's first study, further analysis showed that a number of children (twice as many girls as boys) indicated a mixed preference pattern. Some even showed a strong opposite sex-role pattern. Boys showed significantly greater preference for the masculine role than girls showed for the feminine role. The sex-role ambiguity of girls may express her minority status in a culture where the male role has the dominant status. Among the sex-typed toy objects, 70 per cent of all choices of boys were masculine, only 49 per cent of the choices of girls were feminine. On choosing between wanting to be a boy or a girl or a mixture, only one boy in ten expressed desire for the female role, whereas one girl in three expressed a preference for the male role. In general, there was evidence that the masculine role had greater value and prestige.

Lynn (95) has suggested that girls may be more femininely oriented in early childhood because of identification with their mothers, but that exposure to a masculine-oriented world tends to break down this identification and make their sex-role preferences more masculine. In our culture there is also a relatively greater freedom of girls to adopt male roles in dress and play than there is for boys to adopt feminine ones (30). To be more specific, there is by no means as much concern about the "tomboy" as there is about the "sissy," and their grown-up counterparts.

Sex-role preferences seem to be shifting with the passage of time. In the late fifties Rosenberg and Sutton-Smith (128) studied the games played and liked by boys and girls, and compared their findings with a similar investigation carried on in the twenties. The results showed that the girls they studied disclosed greater preference for boys' games than their counterparts of the twenties; but the boys studied demonstrated no particular preference changes over those expressed in the twenties. The hypothesis of increased masculinity of feminine sex-role preferences seems to be supported; the sex-role preferences of boys is still definitely nonfeminine whereas that of girls is more masculine. In keeping with higher valuation of masculine tendencies are the findings of mixed sex-role preferences in girls. It seems well established that a higher percentage of girls show a preference for male roles than the reverse, thus having less firmly fixed sex-role preferences. The results of Brown (29) in his study with sex-role preferences supports this contention.

According to psychoanalytic theory, the girl is expected to have more difficulties in assuming her feminine role than the boy has in assuming his masculine role. Certainly, the evidence on sex-role preferences is in agreement that girls prefer a role with more infusion of the masculine elements than do boys. This, however, is not evidence there is any struggle on the part of girls. The girl may not have difficulty about assuming her feminine role "where it counts," and still have mixed sex-role preferences.

It should be obvious from earlier discussion that sex-role preferences are affected by sex-role training. Preferences, then, are partly a product of training. In a few children sex-role training may be accepted with reluctance, and in fewer still, it may be actively resisted. Their varying degrees of acceptance show different degrees of sex-role preference in reaction to this training.

Sex roles are decidedly a matter of socialization to fit in with the expectations of a particular culture. This fact is shown by consideration of how sex roles vary from culture to culture. All sorts of diametrically opposed behavior is expected of males and females in different cultures. An illustration is chosen for presentation which runs counter to some degree at least to the expected trend in our culture. This group, studied by Mead (*108*), are the Tchambuli of New Guinea. The group, Mead significantly remarks, was the only one of all those in which she has worked where little girls of 10 or 11 were more alert, bolder, and enterprising than little boys. In adulthood, unadorned Tchambuli women with shaven heads are the managers and providers; they fish and go to market. Activity is expected of her —if childbirth is hard, Tchambuli say, "The mother has not gathered enough firewood." The men, decorated with strings of ornaments and bedorned with real or false curls, spend their time practicing dance steps, carving, and painting. They are the artists managed by the strong practical women. They are gossips and easily show hurt feelings in a skittish sort of a way. This culture shows almost a complete reversal of what might be considered a caricature of the roles of men and women in our society. But even in this particular society the male is pursuing the ideal of his society, which happens to be furtherance of the arts, and women are carrying on more pedestrian humdrum tasks. In this as in most societies masculine traits are more prized.

In our culture "masculine" tendencies are prized which are quite different from those held as prominent by the Tchambuli. Horney (*71*) specifically relates so-called penis envy to cultural conditions arising from this prizing of masculine traits. Instead of feminine envy being rooted in a biological difference and in experiences of early childhood, she attributes it to an envy of the qualities the male has. These qualities such as strength, independence, and relative right to choose sexual partners are at the root of women's envy. This point of view bears strong resemblance to Adler's (*1*) "masculine protest" wherein women react against inferiority feelings by assumption of masculine roles.

Results on sex-role preferences are consistent with a theory of identification of Freudian thinking, but are also consistent with cultural theory in which the male is seen to have a preferred status. It is the path of caution to refer to the phenomena just considered as evidence of sex-role preference while admitting they may involve still another closely related process of identification.

Learning and Identification

The influence of learning has been very evident in the account of sex-related activities. Sex-role *training* is synonymous with sex typing, clearly implying its learned character. Sex-role adoption and sex-role preferences are also learned. Identification, too, shares in this dependence on learning. However, it is a more complicated process than these other sex-related activities. Some psychologists are content to say that identification is a learned drive to be like another individual of the same sex. If so, these other processes would seem to explain the evidence adequately, and there is no need for conceptualizing an additional process of identification. Other psychologists cannot accept this interpretation.

Indeed, identification will be found to involve learning. With this comment there is little disagreement. However, it is much more difficult to disentangle identificatory learning from other sex-related activities. There is also the disputed claim that all the phenomena of identification can be explained by learning. For these reasons explicit attention to learning in relation to identification seems to be required.

Views of learning pertinent to sex-related activities have been expressed by Kagan, Bandura and Huston, Hill, and others. Their accounts warrant examination since they seem to supplement one another.

Kagan (79) distinguishes among imitation learning, prohibition learning, and identification. In imitation learning a child copies or carries out matched dependent behavior by initiating and practicing certain responses which emulate models. Praise and affection strengthen the child's tendency to imitate. Prohibition learning, that is, adopting and practicing the prohibitions of parents, may be seen as a major motivation for children developing acquisition anxiety over anticipated loss of love.

To Kagan, identification learning occurs when a child makes part of his behavior repertoire those behaviors of a model which cause him to react to events experienced by the model as if they had happened to him. Perceived similarity may result, in which case some of the characteristics of the model are seen as similar to those of the child. Each time the identifying child perceives or is told he is similar to the parent, reinforcement of identification occurs.

The motivation for a given characteristic may arise from any or all three processes. As Kagan puts it: "Thus, 'eating neatly,' 'getting good grades,' or 'being nonaggressive' could be motivated by the desire for praise as in imitation learning, by anxiety over loss of love as in prohibition learning, or by the desire to create perceptual similarity between the S and M as in identification" (79, 301).[8] Similarity of a child's characteristics to a parent may arise from one or another of these forms of learning. In keeping with this analysis, the question of perceived similarity seems to be the crucial characteristic as we shall see when research on identification is evaluated.

Hill (68) contends that identification should be interpreted in terms of already established principles of learning. He relates the behaviors and processes subsumed under it to three kinds of reinforcement—"primary," secondary, and vicarious. He considers "primary" reinforcement, as heralded by the quotation marks, to include not only the commonly understood physiological reinforcers, but also other positive reinforcers, such as attention and praise, and the negative reinforcers of criticism and rejection. These nonphysiological reinforcers are, themselves, at least partly learned and in this sense secondary, but in a way irrelevant to the points he wished to make. Many so-called instances of identification, he argues, are really primary reinforcement. Direct reinforcement of imitative behavior and conformity to verbal instructions takes place as does the formation of a generalized tendency to imitate others. Consequently much identification may be attributed to primary reinforcement.

Secondary reinforcements arising from unessential aspects of parental nurturant and caretaker behavior are also important sources of learning to identify. The gestures, words, and facial expressions that accompany the nurturant behaviors of the primary reinforcers of feeding can become secondary reinforcers. By stimulus generalization there should be some reward, although less so, when the child performs these actions himself.

Vicarious reinforcement, not previously discussed, and not at a level of equal importance with primary and secondary reinforcement nevertheless does occur under certain circumstances, according to Hill, and can contribute to so-called identification. Vicarious reinforcement involves learning arising from the reinforcers others receive, such as, a generalization of reinforcing effects from others to oneself. If one person is reinforced, then an observer might find it rewarding to imitate the first person even though he, the second person, never has

[8] From Kagan (79). Copyright 1958 by the American Psychological Association, and published with permission.

been rewarded for this particular behavior. A person who observes and then uses techniques of solving a problem others have been seen to use successfully has learned through vicarious reinforcement.

The presence of all three forms of reinforcement creates a complex situation. This situation is nevertheless realistic since the reinforcement of different and conflicting behavior may occur and the conflict must be explained.

To illustrate what he means, Hill points out that a child may have a nurturant mother whose mannerisms become secondarily reinforcing and at the same time, may have a domineering father, perceived as successful in mastering the environment, so that vicarious reinforcement would operate. Secondary reinforcement from the mother and vicarious reinforcement from the father would then both be functioning. Now suppose that the nurturant mother's and the dominating father's behaviors were such that they were different or even opposite. Conflict in the child would result because of the clash of the reinforcers to which he is being exposed. Any situation in which there is a discrepancy between what the child is told to do, what he sees others doing, and what he is rewarded for doing is the setting for a potential conflict situation; attention must be given to the kinds of reinforcement he is receiving.

It would seem that an important supplement to Kagan's and Hill's analyses of learning and identification is provided by appeal to incidental learning. This becomes pertinent when it is remembered that Freud contended that much identification was an *unconscious* introjection of parental edicts. A more parsimonious psychological interpretation would infer that this were an instance of incidental learning. Incidental learning is learning without intent to learn and, therefore, without awareness that learning is taking place—and without the fact of learning being verbalized by the child. "Secondary reinforcement," as Hill uses the term, emphasizes the role of reinforcement in this process of incidental learning, but without mention of this particular point.

Incidental learning has been established by Bandura and Huston (*14*) in a situation similar to that used in investigating identification. This imitation, they contended, is facilitated if a warm nurturant relationship with the child is arranged. They formulated a study to answer the question whether children, while learning to select one of ten boxes to get a toy reward, would also learn to imitate certain of the experimenter's behaviors irrelevant to the performance of the task.

In the first phase of the study each of a group of nursery school subjects were played with by an adult who was later to serve as a model. The adult sat close to the child, responded to his bids for attention and help, and did everything to make their interaction a warm and rewarding one (nurturant session). In the same playroom with each member of another group, this adult merely told them to play with the toys and then busied herself with paper work (non-nurturant session). Thereafter, each child learned the box problem mentioned earlier, after observing the adult model perform. In the course of making the selection the model-to-be performed certain *irrelevant* activities, such as saying "here I go," marching slowly toward the box, knocking a rubber doll off the top of the box, replacing the doll after opening it, and the like. The learning of which box to select was of no particular interest. What was being investigated was whether the children would reproduce the irrelevant behavior of the model.

They did so beyond chance expectation. Moreover, those in the nurturant interaction group patterned their behavior on that of the model to a greater extent than those in the group treated coldly and indifferently. They not only learned to imitate an adult model, but those who received nurturance also did so to a greater extent than those who did not. The nurtured group was more imitative of the model than the non-nurtured group. A warm rewarding relationship with a model—in this case an experimenter, but analogously a parent— fosters imitation of that person's irrelevant behavior. Incidental learning, as such, and greater incidental learning after a nurturant relationship with an adult model, is thus demonstrated.

There have been still other attempts at interpreting identification phenomena in more familiar learning terms which do not require detailed comment. Modeling, imitation, and noninstrumental learning have been stressed as relevant by several investigators (16, 18, 79, 97).

Transmission of aggression through imitation of aggressive models, as demonstrated by Bandura and his associates (16), has already been discussed in the previous chapter. Children exposed to aggressive models showed more aggressive behavior in the later testing situation than did children who did not undergo this experience.

Suppose an observer were present at this testing session who had no knowledge of the children's exposure to aggressive models, and he were asked to rate the subjects on the degree of their identification as expressed by their aggressive behavior. According to theory, aggressive boys would be masculine, showing more masculine identification; aggressive girls would be showing a failure to identify with their mothers while identifying with their fathers instead. The boys who were most aggressive, of course, were mostly to be found among those who were exposed to an aggressive model. They would be rated as most identified with their fathers, whereas the girls who were from the same exposure group would be rated as aggressive and, therefore, suspected of not having made appropriate identification with the mothers but having to depend on identification with their fathers. This, of course, is pure fantasy, but it does help to show how imitation may be confused with identification.

It will be remembered that the development of self-control was mentioned as an aspect of identification in Freud's interpretation. Acquisition of self-control through learning has been neatly demonstrated (15) in a study of modeling. Children played a bowling game with either an adult or peer model. The scores they could make ranged from 5 to 30 but were actually due, not to their skill, but to secret control by the experimenter. A plentiful supply of candy was available from which they understood they could help themselves, that is, take as much as they wanted, after each game.

In one experimental undertaking, the model, who played the game first, set a high standard, rewarding himself with candy and self-praise at the end of the trial if he made a score of 20 or more—a relatively high level of performance; if he scored less than 20, he took no candy and berated himself. In another experimental test, the standard the model set for himself was 10, a relatively low level of performance. After exposure to their respective models, children played the games, in the course of which they received a wide range of controlled scores. The trials on which they took the candy reward and voiced self-approval were noted.

The children followed closely the behavior of their particular model. Those exposed to the model with high standards adopted a high criterion for self-reinforcement; those exposed to a model with low standards rewarded themselves generously. Adult models were more influential in standard-setting than were the models of their own age. Members of a control group with no exposure to models tended to reward themselves for minimal performance. Self-administered rewards came about from imitation. Self-control had been acquired on observation of a model, and in the absence of punishment.

Evidence on Identification

A variety of studies has been made in which the investigator assumed that he was studying identification. His use of the term will be accepted and criticism offered only after analysis of the results obtained.

That boys tend to identify with their fathers and girls with their mothers has been substantiated by Blum (27). A subsidiary finding was that identification is less clear-cut in females. The Blacky test used needs some description. The test consists of a series of cartoons mounted on cards which tell of the adventures of Blacky, a young dog. The frontispiece to the series introduces the characters—Blacky, Mama, Papa, and a sibling, Tippy, unspecified as to age and sex. When the test is given to boys, Blacky is described as "son" and when given to girls as "daughter." The cartoons in the series were designed to study stages of psychosexual development. Cartoon VII reproduced as Figure 16 is relevant to the present problem of identification. Spontaneous stories told to this cartoon, illustrating strong and not strong identification, are given by Blum as follows:

Strong:
Now listen you, you little pooch, when I bark, you jump, do you get that? Blacky feels very superior to this little dog. He is making believe that he's the boss, or maybe pretending to be his father talking to him in a superior tone.
Not Strong:
Blacky has found something peculiar. It looks like a dog, but it doesn't move or bark at her. She's a little afraid of it at first, but later she realizes

Figure 16. A Blacky Card. (Copyright 1950 by The Psychological Corporation, and reproduced with permission.)

she's bigger and the toy can do her no harm—so she settles down to enjoy it (27, 32).[9]

After seeing the cartoon, about 100 male and 100 female college students responded to the following questions:

(1) Who talks like that to Blacky—Mamma or Pappa or Tippy? . . .
(3) Whom is Blacky imitating here—Mama or Papa or Tippy?
(4) Whom would Blacky rather pattern himself after—Mama or Papa or Tippy?
(5) Blacky's disposition, actually, is most like the disposition of which one—Mama or Papa or Tippy? (27, 78).[9]

On all four questions 119 young adult males significantly more often responded "Papa," and 90 young adult females replied, "Mama." Blum thus verified that identification normally occurs with the parent of the same sex.

Identification was less clear-cut in females as compared to males. As mentioned before, males tended to say "Papa" and the females, "Mama" to the question, "Whom would Blacky rather pattern himself (herself) after?" However, the males were significantly more decisive in that a greater percentage of males chose "Papa" than females chose "Mama." Moreover, to another question for the same cartoon, "Whom is Blacky most likely to obey—Mama or Papa or Tippy?" *both* males and females say "Papa" significantly more often than "Mama." Females seem less sure with which parent they seek to identify and the father is the one most likely to be obeyed—as Blum indicates, this latter is a relevant point in that the decisive frustrating agent is a crucial influence in developing identification.

England (46), too, has found evidence that boys tend to identify with their fathers and girls with their mothers. As material, he used one drawing of two "stick" figures, resembling those that might be made from match sticks, one seated on a bench by the figure of a man and the other beside the figure of a woman. Another drawing showed the stick figures walking down the street hand in hand, one with "mother" and the other with "father." The task was to identify the stick figures as boys or girls. He also used a drawing which was to be completed. The drawing already showed a woman seated on a bench with a tree immediately on her left. In this instance, the task was to draw a boy and a girl sitting with the mother. The arrangement of the drawing forced the child to place either the boy or the girl closer to the mother.

The three tasks were given to the 134 boys and girls aged five to

[9] From Blum (27). Copyright 1949 by The Journal Press, and published with permission.

fourteen. In each instance, scoring for identification was made by assuming that a boy or girl placed the boy or girl figure beside the parental figure with whom he or she identified. In general, girls associated with the mother and boys with the father according to the selection of both boys and girls. For example, 72 per cent of the children drew a girl beside the mother with the boy on the other side of the girl. The girls were found to be more pronounced in the parental identifications, with only four per cent saying the boy should be closer to the mother and only eight per cent saying the girl should be closer to the father. Since no age differences were found, results were given without age breakdown.

It will be remembered that Kagan distinguished among imitation, prohibition, and identification learning. He made the latter depend on perceived similarity of child to parent. Research evidence concerning such similarity is available.

Gray and Klaus (54) in a study of identification of college men and women with their mothers and fathers used the Allport-Vernon-Lindzey Study of Values as their measure of perceived similarity. The Study of Values is a measure of the relative strength of six values or motives in the personality. Filling out this measure based on the classification of values as theoretical, economic, aesthetic, social, political, and religious gives information about how strongly the individual holds certain values as his own. For example, a person with a high "political" score values power for its own sake.

The investigators chose the instrument as one which it could be assumed tapped aspects of personality in which parental influences would be of major importance. Each student filled it out (1) for himself; (2) as his mother would; and (3) as his father would. It was also actually answered by his father and mother. When scored and the various scores interrelated, the investigators were dealing with both actual similarities between child and parent and similarities with his parent as perceived by the child.

Without going into their statistical findings it is possible to summarize the results. They found considerable evidence for the following statements: (1) *both boys and girls were more like their same-sex parents in areas of major interest than their opposite-sex parents;* (2) *both boys and girls tend to perceive themselves as more like their same-sex parents than their opposite-sex parents;* (3) *girls were more like and perceived themselves as more like their mothers than did boys their fathers.* These findings, as they point out, are compatible both with psychoanalytic and general social learning theory.

Cava and Raush (36) have studied the relation between identification and father-son relationship which also hinged on perception of the father, although not of perception of *similarity to* the father. They gave the Blacky pictures in an investigation of the perception that 37 adolescent boys had of their fathers. Several Blacky pictures were selected which were theoretically related to identification, for example, Figure 16 and another card concerned with castration anxiety. Scores were calculated for each picture used. The subjects were then classified as weak (less conflict) or strong (more conflict) for each Blacky picture and for a total combined identification score. To serve as a measure of the similarities the boys perceived between themselves and their fathers, they filled out the Strong Vocational Interest Blank twice, once to describe themselves and then as they thought their fathers would fill it out.

The Strong Vocational Interest Blank is a standardized measure of interests and preferences. Its items are responded to in terms of likes and dislikes. The score on perceived similarities on this measure was derived from the number of times the subject showed agreement between his own responses and those he attributed to his father. This gave them an operational measure of identification. Although "perceived" similarities are not actual similarities between fathers and sons, they are nevertheless of some significance.

The question the investigators raised had to do with whether those boys who showed conflict on identification matters also perceived their fathers as less like themselves than the other boys who showed less conflict. The differences they obtained were all in the direction to be expected on the basis of the foregoing hypothesis. Those for Castration Anxiety and Total Identification were statistically significant. The boys showing statistically significantly more conflict over castration anxiety perceived their fathers as less like themselves. This is in line with psychoanalytic theory in that boys with more conflicts about castration anxiety would be expected to have made less "identification" with their fathers.

Mussen and Distler (*116*) gave the *IT Scale for Children* to a group of 38 five-year-old boys and found the ten highest and the ten lowest in scores. The boys in these extreme groups were considered as having developed high and low male role identification respectively. Each boy was then placed in a doll-play situation so formed by use of a story-telling game with which the doll play was interwoven that measures of his perception of his parents and his degree of masculine identification could be ascertained. For example, while playing with the mother, father, and child doll, he was told in one story-telling situation that the boy (doll) wants a toy which he cannot reach, that mother and father are both busy in the living room, and that he goes in and asks for help. What happens? The stories were so constructed that in his solution either nurturant or punitive behavior from either mother or father could eventuate. His feelings about his parents' treatment toward him could be derived from what he replied. In short did he get nurturant or punitive treatment from either mother or father?

The sex typing, high or low, was not related to perception of mothers, thus supporting the studies of Levin and Sears (88) and the Sears' "pattern" study (140). The boys' interaction with the father did show relation with strong or weak male role identification. It was found that boys strongly identified with the male role had a perception of the father as a powerful source of both reward and punishment, not merely one or the other. The boys with weak identifications with the male role did not have this perception.

The investigators consider that their results are most consistent with the so-called role theory of identification. Role theory holds that the child is likely to assimilate the role of an individual with whom he has intensive interactions, especially if that individual is powerful. Dispensing of both rewards and punishments makes the adult a more powerful person than merely reward alone or punishment alone would not have done. A rival theory would be the developmental theory which postulates that identification is dependent on a rewarding, nurturant interaction only. Since the investigators found that the boys identified with punitive, threatening fathers, as well as nurturant ones, the results are inconsistent with this position. It would seem that a high level of masculine identification does not depend on a specific type of father-son relationship since both nurturant and punitive father perceptions were found associated with this level.

The mothers of the kindergarten boys in the high and low masculine groups, who were subjects of the study just reported (117), were interviewed and their replies rated on a series of scales. These scales included those concerned with father-son relationships such as father's standard of obedience, frequency with which father spanks; mother-son relationship; family climate, such as strictness about bed time; sex-role differentiation; and conscience development, such as spontaneous telling of deviations and admission of deviations when asked.

Obtaining significant difference between high and low masculinity groups led the investigators to conclude that: (1) the nature of the father-son relationships is more related to sex-typing than is that pertaining to mother-son relationships; (2) mothers reported that fathers of the highly masculine boys had stronger affection for their sons than did the fathers of boys low in masculinity; (3) fathers of the high masculine boys play a greater role than do those of low masculinity in their son's upbringing (more caretaking and greater responsibility for child-rearing practices); (4) highly masculine boys experience a more permissive, less punitive, easy going, familial climate and more love-oriented techniques than do the less masculine boys; and (5) boys high in masculinity tend also to be high in conscience development.

It will be remembered that in the Sears, Maccoby, and Levin "pattern" study (140) they appealed to identification (pages 371–372) in interpreting their results. They had linked the behavior observed from doll preferences with "identification." However, this interpretation has been questioned. Choice of dolls, says Lynn (95), is a measure of sex-role preference, not identification. This disagreement over the nature of process involved cannot be resolved at the present time. Whether Sears and his associates were measuring sex-role preference or identification, they had defined what they were measuring by their measurement technique and the results would require no particular change even if we were to accept Lynn's opinion. Moreover, it should be emphasized that it was not through doll preference study alone that Sears and his associates arrived at their contentions concerning higher identification in girls; they also used ratings of emulation of adult behavior and higher dependence on female teachers. A personal preference for interpretation in terms of identification has already been expressed through the very manner in which their results were reported, but this is a point on which there can be disagreement.

Evidence on Conscience Development

The development of conscience (superego) is an integral aspect of the processes being considered. Sears, Maccoby, and Levin in their "pattern" study (140) reasoned that a high index of conscience development would also imply a high index of identification. Conscience they defined as inner control with resistance to temptation when there is a genuine acceptance of parental standards, with deviation from self-instruction making the child feel guilty and ashamed.

Sears and his associates give a vivid illustration. It concerns a bright, lively seventeen-month-old girl on a visit with her mother and father to a friend's home. She explored the living room avidly. One of the floor lamps especially fascinated her. Twice her eager grip on it brought about a teetering and swaying and twice her father said clearly and distinctly, "Martha, don't touch!" To quote hereafter:

> After the second interruption, Martha began a general exploration of the room again. Now she went a little slower, and several times glanced

at her father. As she came closer to the lamp, however, she stopped looking his way and her movements were all oriented toward the lamp. Deliberately she stepped toward it, came within a couple of feet of it, and lifted her arm partly, a little jerkily, and then said sharply, commandingly, *"Don't touch!"*

There was an instant of struggling silence. Then she turned and stumbled across the room, flopped down on the floor, and started laughing excitedly. Her father, laughing with her, and obviously adoring, reached out and hugged and snuggled her for several minutes (*140*, 365–366).[10]

They go on to indicate that it was not simple fear of her father. She did not look at him furtively, did not whimper, did not oscillate on her decision. She clearly looked to herself for guidance, not her father. She had accepted her father's standards as her own.

This incident gave no opportunity to observe the conscience operating in the face of a temptation when no one was present, nor of guilt feelings when the temptation was not overcome. These two characteristics—control in face of temptation when no one is present and guilt—are the characteristics Sears and his associates allege to be those by which conscience control may be recognized. In their "pattern" study (*140*) they found a gradual growth in behavior which showed these characteristics. The three-year-old is trustworthy but only to a point, the four-year-old somewhat more, and the five-year-old still more. Even when five or six, the children's age at the time of the study, 13 per cent of the mothers reported no evidence of the development of conscience, that is, the child still hides and denies his infractions and does not seem unhappy when naughty.

Sears and his associates, then, stress three intertwined aspects of a unitary process in the conscience—resistance to temptation, self-instruction, and guilt. Maternal interview data on these matters were rated collectively yielding a conscience measure, ranging from weak to strong, which was then related to their other findings.

It was found that the more often withdrawal of love was used as a technique of discipline, the stricter the conscience of the child. There is an important qualification to this generalization—to be effective, withdrawal of love as a method of control had to come after the mother had been heretofore warm and loving. Withdrawal of love from a child already treated coldly created a situation where there was nothing to lose.

Actually, steady rejection and coldness on the mother's part seem to

[10] From Sears, Maccoby, and Levin (*140*). Copyright 1957 by Row, Peterson, and published with permission.

be associated with less complete conscience development in the child. Already relatively warm mothers who then made their love contingent upon the child's good behavior were creating a situation where the child risked her love if he did not behave as she wished. Habitual use of love-oriented techniques, such as praise, and then withdrawing it as a means of control were found to be associated with high conscience development, especially in boys. Moreover, boys with accepting fathers were more likely to develop strong consciences than boys who were rejected by their fathers. Conscience, then, is a consequence of an identification based on fear of loss of love.

It will be remembered that Sears and his associates in the "pattern" study found punishment to be of no avail in changing the behavior of children. Consequently, learning through punishment is not appealed to; rather, the reward of love or withdrawal of love, the absence of this reward, is considered as dynamic.

Objecting to their acceptance of the three criteria—resistance to temptation, self-instruction, and guilt—as forming a unit, Hill (68) interpreted their results in terms of his analysis of the learning processes. Resistance to temptation, he pointed out, is avoidance learning. Self-instruction, he went on, is characteristically human and is indulged in when confronted by a difficult situation of any sort. Moreover, self-instruction may be an imitative act learned in connection with any of the forms of reinforcement discussed earlier. Guilt is more complex, but, as yet, has not been satisfactorily isolated from other behaviors. At any rate, Hill could argue that conscience did not appear to be unitary—at least not until more empirical research has been conducted.

In an as yet incompletely reported study,[11] Sears and his associates (4) bring together the results of several part studies into an integrated whole to demonstrate the development of conscience in children. Their subjects were three- to five-year-old children.

First, they wished to find out whether a child's dependence at least influences, if not determines, the level of his identification. Dependency was measured by leaving the mother and her child in a room alone while observing them through a one-way mirror. The mother had been asked to complete a long, complicated questionnaire which required considerable concentration on her part. The focus of interest

---

[11] What is available at the time of writing is a study guide (4) accompanying a film reporting results on individual children depicted in the film. The analyses of the results, it may be presumed, had proceeded far enough that the investigators were reasonably certain that analysis of group data would reflect the same findings.

was the manner in which the child and she interacted while she was busy with the questionnaire. Results may be illustrated in terms of the contrasting behavior of two boys.

The first boy interrupted the mother and continued on several occasions to ask for her attention. However, this took but a few minutes. Thereafter, he accepted the fact that she was busy and turned to some toys on the other side of the room. The second boy (the one to be followed through the various phases of the study) could not accept her preoccupation and tried throughout the session to get her attention, finally reaching almost the level of a tantrum because she would not pay attention to him. These two children, although treated with equal gentleness in this setting, clearly differed in their degree of dependency.

In an interview of the mothers, it was found, as was suspected from their behavior under observation, that although they handled their son's dependency in similar ways, the father of the first boy was warm and outgoing, whereas the father of the second boy was withdrawn and anxious in his dealings with his son. Similar results presumably were obtained with other subjects of the study. Withdrawn, anxious fathers have sons who show immature dependence on their mothers. This establishment of a relation between increased dependence on the mother when the father was withdrawn and anxious was the first step in the study.

The next phase of the study was to obtain information about identification by finding out which parent was taken as a model. The children were told stories in which the child protagonist does something he is not supposed to do. After the stage was set, the child was asked to finish the story. The completions offered could be scored as mild (feminine) or aggressive (masculine). A typical girl finished it mildly. But, so too, did the boy, whose father was anxious and withdrawn. It was inferred therefore that he was not able to use his father as a model, identifying with his mother instead. Withdrawn, anxious fathers do not serve as models for their sons, so that perforce the boys identify with their mothers.

The ability of these children to resist temptation, to admit misconduct, and to attempt to impose their own standards of conduct on other children was next investigated. This situation called, "Quoting the Rule," involved placing the child in a room filled with toys, but also containing a bowl of candy prominently displayed, which the child had been told not to eat. No matter what their behavior (playing, taking candy, and so on) after a specified time a younger child entered the room, who had been told before she came in that she might take some candy.

Consider the behavior of three different children in this situation. The first, a girl, came into the room, amused herself with the toys, and showed no sign of yielding to the temptation to take candy. When the younger child entered and went directly to the candy, the girl tried to stop her by distraction and interesting her in the toys. The girl's behavior is considered to show a great deal of self-control and to be adult-like. On interviewing the mother it was found that both she and the father had stressed high standards of conduct for their daughter. Now for another child—this time a boy. He, too, resisted temptation and also tried to deter the younger child from taking the candy. However, his means of doing this took the form of threats of physical punishment. This aggressive behavior was found to be characteristic of boys who identify with their fathers. The child we are following, when faced with this particular situation, helped himself to the candy immediately and, although at first he tried to prevent the younger boy from taking the candy, he soon gave up his efforts. This boy, seen before not to be identified with the appropriate parent, was considered to show a low level of conscience development. Conscience development, it would seem, is a measure of identification.

In the last part of the study, each child was brought into a room filled with interesting toys. In the corner was a live hamster in a cage. The experimenter showed the child the hamster and explained he must leave the room for a while and that the child should stand watch alongside the hamster to see that it did not escape. From the child's position by the cage he is too far away from the toys to more than glance at them.

Three children who reacted quite differently will serve as illustrations. What happened to the first child will also serve to explain further the procedure. The first boy watched the hamster for fifteen minutes, then succumbed to the toys. When he went over to them, an observer, who had been watching through a one-way screen, dropped the caged hamster through a trap door and closed it again, leaving an empty cage. The boy, after playing a while, returned to the cage, and discovered the hamster missing. He looked for it with an expression of concern and when the experimenter returned, confessed that he had left the cage and played with the toys. Both then looked for the hamster, which the boy and the experimenter, with a second hamster in his pocket, proceeded to find. This boy is considered as showing a high level of conscience, resisting temptation, as he did, for fifteen minutes, showing concern for the hamster's disappearance and confessing readily. A second subject, a girl stood guard for half an hour, but instead of going to the toys, rushed out to the psychologist to say she was so tempted she could not stand it any longer. The third child, the one we are following, left the hamster almost immediately and played with the toys. On finding the hamster missing, he became almost paralyzed with guilt and fear, but would not confess any wrongdoing.

To summarize in terms of the boy showing dependence on the mother, who did not identify with his father but with her—he was found to show a low level of conscience development by not resisting temptation, by disclosing extreme guilt about his wrongdoing, and being unable to confess his wrongdoing. This particular pattern illustrates one way in which these processes of identification and conscience development interrelate.

Sears and his associates would be among the first to admit that their evidence on this complicated process is still incomplete. Indeed the study as reported only followed through the various steps for one kind of development of identification and superego—that exemplified by the third child. In other evidence, they stress the influence of the technique of withdrawal of love as making for a stricter conscience (not brought out in this study at all). There will also be other courses of development established, as yet not unearthed. The study did have the virtue of moving through separate stages to show something, not only of the part processes, but also of the total sweep of the intertwined processes.

An explicit neo-Freudian summarization concerning identification and the superego, apart from what has already been said, is unnecessary. An implicit neo-Freudian interpretation in terms of utilization of other processes, specifically those of learning as formulated in nonpsychoanalytic psychology, has been appealed to throughout. Other processes of learning seem to go a long way toward explaining identification, yet a hard core of meaning for identification seems to remain. Identification, as an explanatory construct, is not rejected.

It would seem that identification is established in some form at least by the time the child is five and that some of its consequences have been isolated. Nothing incompatible with a social learning theory interpretation seems to have been encountered, but, by the same token, incontrovertible evidence against the psychoanalytic interpretation has not been found. The process of identification has been divorced from the Oedipus complex in the present context. Instead of identification being considered a consequence of the Oedipal situation, it has been interpreted as arising both during and after the age at which the Oedipus drama is supposed to take place.

Castration Anxiety

The discovery of genital differences and consequent castration fears and penis envy has been employed in Freudian literature. In research, castration anxiety sometimes is not investigated directly, instead, the researcher reasons that if castration anxiety did exist, there would be general emotional disturbances apparent when children discovered sex differences. Even if such disturbances were universally and unequivocally shown to be present, this would not demonstrate the existence of castration anxiety in itself. It would demonstrate that the necessary concomitant for castration anxiety to be present, that is, emotional disturbance, actually did occur.

Huschka's data (73) on masturbation threats directed at problem children, although interpreted by her as evidence of castration anxiety, may be more parsimoniously interpreted as demonstrating emotional disturbance on the part of children who were threatened about masturbation. In other words, problem children are emotional about masturbation, but this does not prove they are disturbed because of castration anxiety. Nevertheless, the presence or absence of emotional concomitants of discoveries of sex differences are of interest.

Conn and Kanner (40) found that even among children referred to a psychiatric clinic most of them accepted genital differences with tranquility. From an aggregate of 200, only ten boys and eleven girls thought of differences between the organs of the two sexes in terms of absence through loss. Conn (39) using play techniques found that 17 out of 50 children were disturbed by the discovery of sex differences but that the majority were not. It may be that the relative absence of castration thoughts which the investigators discovered indicates merely that they failed to gain rapport with their subjects or that their research methods failed to get through defenses to deeper levels and consequently that their results were of too superficial a nature to be of great significance. Despite this possibility, lacking other more definitive evidence, it would appear that disturbances over discovery of sex differences (and consequently, castration anxieties) are not universal or inevitable in our culture.

Friedman (52) made an investigation of the castration complex on the assumption that its content was unconscious and most appropriately studied through use of projective materials. The subjects came from a middle-class, white, Protestant background, randomly selected from a school population. His was a cross-sectional, developmental study in that his subjects were 50 five-, six-, seven-, eight-, fifteen-, and sixteen-year-old boys and an equal number of girls. The particular ages were chosen because psychoanalytic theory calls for a heightened castration anxiety to be present at age five or six (or even a little younger), a diminution at seven or eight during latency, and for a resurgence of castration anxiety at fifteen or sixteen.

For testing castration anxiety, he developed three incomplete fables involving animals or a child in which something happened to a project-ing organ. The subjects were to complete the fables. They were so arranged that they invited the subjects to do so by either cutting-off or not cutting-off the projection. Is the response of cutting-off or not cutting-off a sign of anxiety? A good case could be made for either. He solved the problem by finding separately the average reaction times of those subjects who cut off and those who did not cut off the projec-tion. Those who ended fables by *not* removing the projection took longer or "blocked" in their reaction times. He assumed that people who "block" are more anxious; he further assumed that the greater anxiety in the face of the castration stimulus existed in the group who did not remove the projection.

Psychoanalytic theory would call for the youngest (Oedipal) and the oldest (pubertal) age groups to be more disturbed by castration anxiety and therefore to end the fables by removing the projecting organ signifi-cantly less often than would be the case with the middle (latency) age groups. The members of the "Oedipal-pubertal" group failed to cut off the projection significantly less often than did those in the "latency" group, thus supporting the psychoanalytic concept. When responses for boys and girls were analyzed separately, the results for the boys supported the psychoanalytic hypothesis at both Oedipal and pubertal ages, but for girls the hypothesis was confirmed only between the latency and the pubertal ages but not between the Oedipal and latency ages.

A Neo-Freudian interpretation. Castration anxiety receives little support from studies of acknowledged conscious disturbances of chil-dren when they become aware of sex differences. This evidence may be objected to as being superficial and irrelevant, since the child may not be consciously aware of his "anxiety." The study by Friedman in which projective materials were used is not subject to these criticisms. He finds results compatible with psychoanalytic theory. Thus, support from one study can be mustered for the reality of castration anxiety, but obviously much more work will be necessary before it can be decided if the psychoanalytic interpretation of castration anxiety is a valid one.

Little more need be said about castration anxiety. It may well exist in varying degrees in some children. But its role may be divorced from the impetus for the Oedipus situation and seen as one rather infrequent difficulty some children face. No particular importance need be given it.

The Oedipus Complex

It is very difficult to evaluate a problem so broad as that of the Oedipus complex. Anthropological evidence gives us the nearest approach to a global test. Through such evidence we can see whether the Oedipus complex seems to take the same general form in all cultures.

Many anthropologists would argue that the Oedipus complex does not exist in some cultures. After a study of the anthropological evidence, Honigmann (70), for example, concluded that hostility toward the father and rivalry for the affection of the mother (essential characteristics of the Oedipus complex) existed in some, but not all, societies.

One important study is that of Malinowski (98) who investigated the Trobriand Islanders. Family organization in this group is quite different from our own. Fatherhood among the Trobrianders is a purely social relationship. The father plays with his children, is affectionate, and watches and cares for them, but he has no authority and never issues orders or forces obedience. Authority and discipline are vested in the mother's oldest brother who, it is agreed among the Trobrianders, is the model for the child to follow. He, not the father, is the source of pride and social ambition, wealth, and social status which comes to the boy. On his death he leaves his worldly possessions to the boy.

In this culture, the most important taboo, or restriction on social interaction, is that concerning brother-sister relationships. Brothers and sisters are separated at an early age and are never permitted to be socially intimate. According to Trobrianders it is common knowledge that a brother or a sister shows not the "slightest interest" in the love affairs of the other. The sister is a mysterious being forever hidden from the boy. When questioned about brother-sister incest, Trobrianders are emotionally disturbed. In general, this and other evidence indicates that the forbidden sex attraction is more apt to exist between brother and sister than between mother and son. Mild amusement, rather than disturbance, characterizes their discussion of mother-son incest.

As Malinowski indicates, the complex of sex attraction and repulsion appears to be quite different from that in our own society. Hostility is directed against the uncle, not against the father, despite the fact that Freudian theory says that it is sexual relations between father and mother which are at the root of the son's hostility. It is this and other anthropological evidence that argues against the universality of the Oedipus complex.

There has been considerable criticism of Malinowski's findings from the orthodox psychoanalysts (for example, 127) on this matter. They rest their charge on the anthropologist's lack of competence to detect subtle manifestations of Oedipal functioning. If this criticism is accepted, it means that there is still a possibility that the Oedipus complex does exist in the Trobrianders (and in the other groups) in a form analogous to our own. Nevertheless, it is probable that this complex does vary. The classic form which the Oedipus complex is supposed to take does not appear to be universal.

Other evidence is available. There are those nonanthropological research studies that must be referred to in connection with Oedipus complex. First, there is a phase of the study of Blum (27) using the Blacky pictures. He investigated a hypothesis derived from psychoanalytic theory that girls would show greater vestiges of pre-Oedipal attachments after passing through the Oedipal situation than boys. In this connection it must be remembered that his subjects were all young adults who had thus passed through the Oedipal stage. One of the cartoons of the Blacky series (Cartoon IV) was designed to tap "Oedipal intensity." It depicts Blacky wearing an "unhappy" expression, lurking in the bushes and watching Mama and Papa close together and "holding paws," with the usual cartoon device of love, a series of small hearts hovering over their heads.

For this cartoon two questions and their respective answers are relevant to the question of sex differences in the extent of pre-Oedipal attachments.

> Which of the following makes Blacky most unhappy?
> (1) Papa keeping Mama all to himself (Mama keeping Papa all to herself).
> (2) The idea that Mama and Papa seem to be ignoring him (her) on purpose.
> (3) He (she) is ashamed watching them make love out in the open.
> Which would make a happier picture?
> (1) Mama left on the outside watching Blacky together with Papa.
> (2) Papa left on the outside watching Blacky together with Mama (27, 42).[9]

For the first question, the first alternative answer is conceived to be the Oedipal alternative, the second, the pre-Oedipal alternative, that is, that which would be the interpretation of the situation if pre-Oedipal object relationships were strongest. Significantly more males than females select the Oedipal alternative and significantly more females than males select the pre-Oedipal alternative. In connection with the second question, significantly more females than males answered that Blacky would prefer to be with the same sex parent, thus indicating a greater pre-Oedipal attachment. Blum concluded that psychoanalytic theory and the results from his test were in agreement concerning the greater retention of pre-Oedipal components in girls than in boys.

Friedman (52), using the children studied in connection with castration anxiety, investigated the Oedipus complex. Specially designed projective fables and picture cards were given the children who told stories about them. These stories were then submitted to thematic analysis with special attention to the attitudes expressed toward parental figures. Friedman found positive attitudes toward the cross-sex parent and negative attitudes towards the same sex parent. Moreover, the adolescent girls' fantasies retained a more Oedipal character than did those of the boys, which is in line with psychoanalytic theory.

A neo-Freudian Interpretation. There is, then, some research support for the Oedipus complex, but again this support is from findings neither incompatible with theory nor crucial to it. In our own society something resembling the Oedipus complex, if not identical with it, probably does exist. Many clinical workers, including nonpsycho-analysts (for example, 145), agree that many instances of emotional disorders stem from excessive attachment to opposite-sex parents and excessive hostility to same-sex parents. Moreover, the preschool child is still profoundly dependent on his mother and gives her affection. In fact, this is one of the basic themes stressed earlier in the chapter. But it does not follow that this interpersonal situation is only a disguised version of the Oedipus situation.

Acceptance of the reality of these clinical findings does not demonstrate that the Oedipus drama follows the lines laid down for it in psychoanalytic theory. Controlled research evidence has not been found which shows that the Oedipus situation works through the steps ascribed to it, nor does research show that all boys and girls follow the particular patterns ascribed to its course. From what we know about socialization it would not be surprising that overdependence can be confused with so-called Oedipal attachment.

Intensification and prominence of sexual interplay in the family have been repeatedly observed with children in the clinical setting. This is an observation of many workers, whether psychoanalytically oriented or not. It is also a common finding that parents are responsible for many of the personality disturbances in their children. It may be that an intensification of sexuality in the situation is primarily an expression of the *parents'* sexual needs which they work out through the child.

A not uncommon neo-Freudian interpretation of the Oedipus complex is in terms of a child's struggle to free himself from the authority of the parents. It is an attempt to emerge from dependency. Sexual factors may be present, but they are not the cause of the struggle with the father. In effect, this places the Oedipus struggle in a framework of an aspect of socialization. This position is obviously compatible with the earlier discussion of dependence-independence tendencies.

Behavior-social learning theory throws an interesting light on the so-called Oedipus drama. In the family structure in our culture the father is probably the major source of punishment of the child. It would be plausible in learning theory terms that the child would react with hostility to punishment at his hands. But adherents of Freudian theory would reply that this hostility is attributable to sexual relations between the parents. Here the findings of Malinowski about the Trobrianders become pertinent. Despite sexual relations between the parents hostility of the child was directed against the mother's brother. In Trobriand culture, it is he, not the father, who is the disciplinarian. It is also in this culture that he is the target of hostility. Thus, behavior-social learning theory accounts for the hostility in relation to punishment in both our own and in Trobriand culture.

Perhaps more than in any other psychoanalytic hypothesis, the Oedipus complex appears to be due to socialization factors in the child's experience rather than being a universal phenomenon (135). This may be one reason that many psychoanalytic workers, even though more or less orthodox concerning other issues, are apt to take a broader view of the Oedipus complex than prevails in the direct Freudian conception. Innateness, inevitability, and strict pattern of development of the Oedipus situation are not insisted upon. Fenichel (48), for example, speaks of the complex as a product of family influences. Whether this is a neo-Freudian interpretation or not, it is one to which this writer can subscribe.

Summary

As was the case in infancy, the reality of sexual behavior in early childhood has been amply proved. But its existence does not prove that the *interpretation* that psychoanalysts make of this behavior is correct. The behavior does exist, this much the evidence shows, but alternative nonpsychoanalytic interpretations of its significance have been made.

Sex-role training, sex-role preference, sex-role adoption, and emotional dependence can be understood without appeal to an identificatory process. Moreover, the results of these other processes may well affect the course of events so as to produce the same relation to parents as does identification itself. In fact, in many instances the evidence to be considered does concern these other related processes.

Sex typing and sex-role preferences are clearly matters of learning and the usual principles of learning seem satisfactorily to explain their development. With identification there would not be this consensus of agreement. Most psychoanalysts and some psychologists would argue that it was a unique process, not explicable in learning terms. Other psychologists take the position that all or almost all of the heterogeneous phenomena with which it is associated is amenable to explanation by application and extension of principles of learning.

Is identification a special process distinct from other processes? The answer must be equivocal. Certainly considerable progress has been made in isolating it from closely related, but distinguishable phenomena. It is plausible to think that still further inroads into the global concept of identification will be made until these part processes account for all of the phenomena of so-called identification. And yet, this is clearly not the case at present. Identification still seems a necessary and important construct around which to integrate significant findings concerning child behavior. Elucidation of identification in terms of learning principles will still be necessary and the construct may well survive as a means of signalizing the complex of part processes involved. In any case whether called identification or not, its reality has been demonstrated. The psychoanalytic interpretation of identification has not been demonstrated; interpretation in terms of an intertwined constellation of learning processes seems to be indicated.

The Oedipal situation may be the result of excessive emotional dependence, an already familiar concept. Oversolicitude from the mother may make the son overdependent, causing him to see the father who interferes with this situation as an interloper to be resented and resisted. Overattachment to the mother and hatred of the father are then present without the Oedipal drama being played out. A struggle for independence or an acceptance of continued dependence may occur thereafter.

For Further Reading

The specific research studies of Blum (27) on psychosexual development, Brown (30) on sex-role preferences, and Lynn (96) on sex-role and parental identification are recommended. The theoretical papers of Hill (68) and Kagan (79) are outstanding. In his account of Summerhill, a school where a permissive, psychoanalytic and child-centered spirit is carried to its logical extreme, A. S. Neill, its guiding spirit, states his point of view vividly and with conviction, (*Summerhill: A radical approach to child rearing*. New York: Hart, 1960).

References

1. Adler, A. *Understanding human nature*. New York: Greenberg, 1927.
2. Allport, G. W. *Becoming: basic considerations for a psychology of personality*. New Haven: Yale University Press, 1955.
3. Anderson, J. E. Parents' attitudes on child behavior: a report of three studies. *Child Develpm.*, 1946, 17, 91–97.
4. Anon. *The conscience of a child: a study guide: A 30 minute film on current research in developmental psychology*. New York: National Educational Television, 1963.
5. Arsenian, Jean M. Young children in an insecure situation. *J. Abnorm. Soc. Psychol.*, 1943, 38, 235–249.
6. Ausubel, D. Negativism as a phase of ego development. *Amer. J. Orthopsychiat.*, 1950, 20, 796–805.
7. Bach, G. R. Young children's play fantasies. *Psychol. Monogr.*, 1945, 59, No. 272.
8. Bach, G. R. Father-fantasies and father-typing in father-separated children. *Child Develpm.*, 1946, 17, 63–80.
9. Baldwin, A. L. Differences in parent behavior toward three- and nine-year-old children. *J. Pers.*, 1946, 15, 143–165.
10. Baldwin, A. L. The effect of home environment on nursery school behavior. *Child Develpm.*, 1949, 20, 49–62.
11. Baldwin, A. L. *Behavior and development in childhood*. New York: Dryden, 1955.
12. Baldwin, A. L., Joan Kalhorn, and Fay H. Breese. Patterns of parent behavior. *Psychol. Monogr.*, 1945, 58, No. 268.
13. Baldwin, A. L., Joan Kalhorn, and Fay H. Breese. The appraisal of parent behavior. *Psychol. Monogr.*, 1949, 63, No. 299.
14. Bandura, A., and Aletha C. Huston. Identification as a process of incidental learning. *J. Abnorm. Soc. Psychol.*, 1961, 63, 311–318.
15. Bandura, A., and Carol J. Kupus. The transmission of patterns of self-reinforcement through modeling. *J. Abnorm. Soc. Psychol.*, in press.
16. Bandura, A., Dorothea Ross, and Sheila A. Ross. Transmission of aggression through imitation of aggressive models. *J. Abnorm. Soc. Psychol.*, 1961, 63, 575–582.
17. Bandura, A., and R. H. Walters. Aggression. *Yearbk. Nat. Soc. Stud. Educ.*, 1963, 62, Pt. 1, 384–415.

18. Bandura, A., and R. H. Walters. *Social learning and personality development.*
New York: Holt, Rinehart, Winston, 1963.
19. Becker, W. C. The relationship of factors in parental ratings of self and
each other to the behavior of kindergarten children as rated by mothers,
fathers, and teachers. *J. Consult. Psychol.,* 1960, 24, 507–527.
20. Beller, E. K. Dependency and independence in young children. *J. Genet.
Psychol.,* 1955, 87, 25–35.
21. Beller, E. K. Dependency and autonomous achievement striving related to
orality and anality in early childhood. *Child Develpm.,* 1957, 28, 287–315.
22. Beller, E. K. Dependency, socialization and emotional disturbance in early
childhood. Paper presented at Symposium on Dependency in Personality
Development at the Annual Meeting of the American Psychological Association, 1957.
23. Beller, E. K. A study of dependency and perceptual orientation. *Amer.
Psychologist,* 1958, 13, 347. (Abstract).
24. Beller, E. K. Exploratory studies of dependency. *Trans. N.Y. Acad. Sci.,*
1959, 21, 414–426.
25. Beller, E. K., and Ann Haeberle. Dependency and the frustration-aggression
hypothesis. Paper presented at the Annual Meeting of the American Psychological Association.
26. Beller, E. K., and J. leB. Turner. Dependency and aggression: sex differences
in "normal" and "emotionally disturbed" preschool children. Paper presented
at the Annual Meeting of the American Psychological Association, 1962.
27. Blum, G. S. A study of the psychoanalytic theory of psychosexual development. *Genet. Psychol. Monogr.,* 1949, 39, 3–99.
28. Blum, G. S. *Psychoanalytic theories of personality.* New York: McGraw-
Hill, 1953.
29. Brown, D. G. Sex-role preference in young children. *Psychol. Monogr.,* 1956,
70, No. 421.
30. Brown, D. G. Masculinity-femininity development in children. *J. Consult.
Psychol.,* 1957, 21, 197–202.
31. Brown, D. G. Sex role development in a changing culture. *Psychol. Bull.,*
1958, 55, 232–242.
32. Brown, F. An experimental study of parental attitudes and their effect upon
child adjustment. *Amer. J. Orthopsychiat.,* 1942, 12, 224–229.
33. Burchinal, L. G. Mother's and father's differences in parental acceptance of
children for controlled comparisons based on parental and family characteristics. *J. Genet. Psychol.,* 1958, 92, 103–110.
34. Burns, N., and Lorna Cavey. Age differences in empathic ability among
children. *Canad. J. Psychol.,* 1957, 11, 227–230.
35. Buss, A. H. *The Psychology of aggression.* New York: Wiley, 1961.
36. Cava, Esther L., and H. L. Raush. Identification and the adolescent boy's
perception of his father. *J. Abnorm. Soc. Psychol.,* 1952, 47, 855–856.
37. Challman, R. C. Factors influencing friendships among preschool children.
Child Develpm., 1932, 3, 146–158.
38. Child, I. L. Socialization. In G. Lindzey (Ed.), *Handbook of social psychology.* Vol. 2. Cambridge: Addison-Wesley, 1954, 655–692.
39. Conn, J. Children's reactions to the discovery of genital differences. *Amer.
J. Orthopsychiat.,* 1940, 10, 747–754.
40. Conn, J. H., and L. Kanner. Children's awareness of sex differences. *J.
Child Psychiat.,* 1947, 1, 3–57.

41. Crandall, V. J. and Anne Preston.   Verbally expressed needs and overt maternal behaviors. *Child Develpm.*, 1961, 32, 261–270.

42. Crandall, V. J., W. Katkovsky, and Anne Preston.   A conceptual formulation of some research on children's achievement development. *Child Develpm.*, 1960, 31, 787–797.

43. Crandall, V. J., Anne Preston, and Alice Rabson.   Maternal reactions and the development of independence and achievement in young children. *Child Develpm.*, 1960, 31, 243–251.

44. Crandall, V. J., and Alice Rabson.   Children's repetition choices in an intellectual achievement situation following success and failure. *J. Genet. Psychol.*, 1960, 97, 161–168.

45. Dollard, J., L. W. Doob, N. E. Miller, O. H. Mowrer, and R. R. Sears.   *Frustration and aggression.* New Haven: Yale University Press, 1939.

46. England, A. O.   Cultural milieu and parental identification. *Nerv. Child,* 1947, 6, 301–305.

47. Fales, E.   Genesis of level of aspiration in children from one and one-half to three years of age.   Reported in Lewin, K. *et al.* Level of aspiration.   In J. Mc. V. Hunt (Ed.), *Personality and the behavior disorders.* Vol. 1.   New York: Ronald, 1944, 333–378.

48. Fenichel, O.   *The psychoanalytic theory of neuroses.* New York: Norton, 1945.

49. Finch, Helen M.   Young children's concepts of parent roles. *J. Home Econ.*, 1955, 47, 99–103.

50. Fite, Mary D.   Aggressive behavior in young children and children's attitudes towards aggression. *Genet. Psychol. Monogr.*, 1940, 22, 151–319.

51. Ford, C. S., and F. A. Beach.   *Patterns of sexual behavior.* New York: Harper, 1951.

52. Friedman, S. M.   An empirical study of the castration and Oedipus complexes. *Genet. Psychol. Monogr.*, 1952, 46, 61–130.

53. Goodenough, Florence L.   Anger in young children. *Univer. Minn. Inst. Child Welf. Monogr. Ser.*, 1931, No. 9.

54. Gray, Susan W., and R. Klaus.   The assessment of parental identification. *Genet. Psychol. Monogr.*, 1956, 54, 87–114.

55. Green, Elise H.   Friendships and quarrels among preschool children. *Child Develpm.*, 1933, 4, 237–252.

56. Greenberg, Pearl J.   Competition in children: an experimental study. *Amer. J. Psychol.*, 1932, 44, 221–248.

57. Hartley, Ruth E.   A developmental view of female sex-role definition and identification.   Paper read at Meeting of the Society for Research on Child Development, April 1963.

58. Hartmann, H., and R. M. Loewenstein.   Notes on the superego. *Psychoanal. Stud. Child,* 1962, 18, 42–81.

59. Hartmann, H., E. Kris, and R. M. Loewenstein.   Comments on the formation of psychic structure. *Psychoanal. Stud. Child,* 1947, 2, 11–38.

60. Hartup, W. W.   Nurturance and nurturance withdrawal in relation to the dependency behavior of preschool children. *Child Develpm.*, 1958, 29, 191–201.

61. Hartup, W. W., and Elsie A. Zook.   Sex and role preference in three- and four-year-old children. *J. Consult. Psychol.*, 1960, 24, 420–426.

62. Hattendorf, Katherine W.   A study of the questions of young children con-

cerning sex: a phase of an experimental approach to parent education. *J. Soc. Psychol.*, 1932, 3, 37–65.

63. Hattwick, LaBerta A. Sex differences in behavior of nursery school children. *Child Develpm.*, 1937, 8, 323–355.

64. Hawkes, G. R. The child in the family. *Marriage and Fam. Liv.*, 1957, 19, 46–51.

65. Heathers, G. Emotional dependence and independence in nursery school play. *J. Genet. Psychol.*, 1955, 87, 37–57.

66. Hilgard, E. R. Human motives and the concept of self. *Amer. Psychologist*, 1949, 4, 374–382.

67. Hilgard, E. R. Experimental approaches to psychoanalysis. In E. Pumpian-Mindlin (Ed.), *Psychoanalysis as science*. Stanford, Calif., Stanford University Press, 1952, 3–45.

68. Hill, W. F. Learning theory and the acquisition of values. *Psychol. Rev.*, 1960, 67, 317–331.

69. Hollenberg, Eleanor, and Margaret Sperry. Some antecedents of aggression and effects of frustration in doll play. *Personality*, 1951, 1, 32–43.

70. Honigmann, J. J. *Culture and personality*. New York: Harper, 1954.

71. Horney, Karen. *New ways in psychoanalysis*. New York: Norton, 1939.

72. Horowitz, E. L. Spatial localization of the self. *J. Soc. Psychol.*, 1935, 6, 379–387.

73. Huschka, Mabel. The incidence and character of masturbation threats in a group of problem children. In S. S. Tomkins (Ed.), *Contemporary Psychopathology*. Cambridge: Harvard University Press, 1944, 49–62.

74. Isaacs, Susan. *Social development in young children: a study of beginnings*. New York: Harcourt, Brace, 1933.

75. Itkin, W. Relationships between attitudes toward parents and parents' attitudes toward children. *J. Genet. Psychol.*, 1955, 86, 339–352.

76. Jaques, E. H. Miscomprehensions of parents concerning child health and behavior. *Amer. J. Orthopsychiat.*, 1942, 12, 202–213.

77. Jersild, A. T., and Frances V. Markey. Conflicts between preschool children. *Child Develpm. Monogr.*, 1935, No. 21.

78. Joel, W. "Behavior maturity" of children of nursery school age. *Child Develpm.*, 1936, 7, 189–199.

79. Kagan, J. The concept of identification. *Psychol. Rev.*, 1958, 65, 296–305.

80. Kagan, J., and H. A. Moss. *Birth to maturity: a study in psychological development*. New York: Wiley, 1962.

81. Kardiner, A. *The individual and his society*. New York: Columbia University Press, 1939.

82. Katcher, A. The discrimination of sex differences by young children. *J. Genet. Psychol.*, 1955, 87, 131–143.

83. Keister, Mary E. The behavior of young children in failure: an experimental attempt to discover and to modify undesirable responses of preschool children to failure. *Univ. Iowa Stud. Child Welf.*, 1937, 14, 29–82.

84. Korner, Anneliese F. Relationship between overt and covert hostility— economy and dynamics. *Personality*, 1951, 1, 20–31.

85. Landreth, Catherine. Factors associated with crying in young children in the nursery school and in the home. *Child Develpm.*, 1941, 12, 82–97.

86. Lasko, Joan K. Parent-child relationships: report from the Fels Research Institute. *Amer. J. Orthopsychiat.*, 1952, 22, 300–304.

87. Leuba, C.   An experimental study of rivalry in young children.   *J. Comp. Psychol.,* 1933, 16, 367–378.

88. Levin, H., and R. R. Sears.   Identification with parents as a determinant of doll play aggression.   *Child Develpm.,* 1956, 27, 135–153.

89. Levin, H., and Valerie F. Turgeon.   The influence of the mother's presence on children's doll-play aggression.   *J. Abnorm. Soc. Psychol.,* 1957, 55, 304–308.

90. Levin, H., and Elinor Wardwell.   The research uses of doll play.   *Psychol. Bull.,* 1962, 59, 27–56.

91. Levy, D. M.   *Maternal overprotection.*   New York: Columbia University Press, 1943.

92. Lindzey, G., and E. F. Borgatta.   Sociometric measurement.   In G. Lindzey (Ed.), *Handbook of social psychology.*   Cambridge: Addison-Wesley, 1954, 405–448.

93. Lorr, M., and R. L. Jenkins.   Three factors in parent behavior.   *J. Consult. Psychol.,* 1953, 17, 306–308.

94. Lynn, D. B.   Father absence and personality development of children in Norwegian sailor families.   Paper presented at Midwestern Psychological Association, 1957.

95. Lynn, D. B.   A note on sex differences in the development of masculine and feminine identification.   *Psychol. Rev.,* 1959, 66, 126–135.

96. Lynn, D. B.   Sex-role and parental identification.   *Child Develpm.,* 1962, 33, 555–564.

97. Maccoby, Eleanor E.   Role taking in childhood and its consequences for social learning.   *Child Develpm.,* 1959, 30, 239–252.

98. Malinowski, B.   *Sex and repression in savage society.*   New York: Harcourt, Brace, 1927.

99. Marshall, Helen R.   An evaluation of sociometric-social behavior research with preschool children.   *Child Develpm.,* 1957, 28, 131–137.

100. Marshall, Helen R., and B. R. McCandless.   A study in prediction of social behavior of preschool children.   *Child Develpm.,* 1957, 28, 149–159.

101. Marshall, Helen R., and B. R. McCandless.   Relationships between dependence on adults and social acceptance by peers.   *Child Develpm.,* 1957, 28, 413–419.

102. McCandless, B. R., Carolyn Balsbaugh, and Hannah L. Bennett.   Preschool-age socialization and maternal control techniques.   *Amer. Psychologist,* 1958, 13, 320.   (Abstract).

103. McCandless, B. R., Caroyln B. Bilous, and Hannah L. Bennett.   Peer popularity and dependence on adults in preschool-age socialization.   *Child Develpm.,* 1961, 32, 511–518.

104. McCandless, B. R., and Helen R. Marshall.   A picture sociometric technique for preschool children and its relation to teacher judgments of friendship.   *Child Develpm.,* 1957, 28, 139–147.

105. McCandless, B. R., and Helen R. Marshall.   Sex differences in social acceptance and participation of preschool children.   *Child Develpm.,* 1957, 28, 421–425.

106. McClelland, D., J. W. Atkinson, R. Clark, and E. L. Lowell.   *The achievement motive.*   New York: Appleton-Century-Crofts, 1953.

107. McKee, J., and Florence B. Leader.   The relationship of socio-economic status and aggression to the competitive behavior of preschool children.   *Child Develpm.,* 1955, 26, 135–142.

108. Mead, Margaret. *Male and female.* New York: Morrow, 1949.

109. Mengert, Ida G. A preliminary study of the reactions of two-year-old children to each other when paired in a semi-controlled situation. *J. Genet. Psychol.,* 1931, 39, 393–398.

110. Merrill, Barbara A. Measurement of mother-child interaction. *J. Abnorm. Soc. Psychol.,* 1946, 41, 37–49.

111. Milton, G. A. A factor analytic study of child-rearing behaviors. *Child Develpm.,* 1958, 29, 381–392.

112. Moreno, J. L. *Who shall survive? A new approach to the problem of human interrelations.* Washington, D. C.: Nervous and Mental Diseases Publishing Co., 1934.

113. Munroe, Ruth L. *Schools of psychoanalytic thought: an exposition, critique, and attempt at integration.* New York: Dryden, 1955.

114. Murphy, Lois B. *Social behavior and child personality.* New York: Columbia University Press, 1937.

115. Mussen, P. H., and J. J. Conger. *Child development and personality.* New York: Harper, 1956.

116. Mussen, P. H., and L. Distler. Masculinity, identification, and father-son relationship. *J. Abnorm. Soc. Psychol.,* 1959, 59, 350–356.

117. Mussen, P. H., and L. Distler. Child-rearing antecedents of masculine-identification in kindergarten boys. *Child Develpm.,* 1960, 31, 89–100.

118. Neill, B. M. Perception by preschool children of parental roles in selected home situations. Unpublished M.S. thesis. Ames, Iowa: Iowa State College. 1946.

119. Nichols, R. C. A factor analysis of parental attitudes of fathers. *Child Develpm.,* 1962, 33, 791–802.

120. Parten, Mildred B. Social participation among preschool children. *J. Abnorm. Soc. Psychol.,* 1932–33, 27, 243–269.

121. Parten, Mildred B. Leadership among preschool children. *J. Abnorm. Soc. Psychol.,* 1932–33, 27, 430–440.

122. Parten, Mildred B. Social play among preschool children. *J. Abnorm. Soc. Psychol.,* 1933, 28, 136–147.

123. Plant, J. S. *The envelope.* New York: Commonwealth Fund, 1950.

124. Pope, B. Socio-economic contrasts in children's peer culture prestige values. *Genet. Psychol. Monogr.,* 1953, 48, 157–220.

125. Radke, Marian J. The relation of parental authority to children's behavior and attitudes. *Univ. Minn. Inst. Child Welf. Monogr.,* 1946, No. 22.

126. Roff, M. A factorial study of the Fels Parent Behavior Scales. *Child Develpm.,* 1949, 20, 29–45.

127. Roheim, G. Psychoanalysis of primitive cultural types. *Internat. J. Psychoanal.,* 1932, 13, 2–224.

128. Rosenberg, B. G., and B. Sutton-Smith. A revised conception of masculine-feminine differences in play activities. *J. Genet. Psychol.,* 1960, 96, 165–170.

129. Sanford, N. The dynamics of identification. *Psychol. Rev.,* 1955, 62, 106–118.

130. Schaefer, E. S. Organization of maternal behavior and attitudes within a two-dimensional space—an application of Guttman's Radex theory. *Amer. Psychologist,* 1957, 12, 40. (Abstract).

131. Schaefer, E. S. Converging conceptual models for maternal behavior and for child behavior. In C. Glidewell (Ed.), *Parental attitudes and child behavior.* Springfield, Ill: Thomas, 1961, 124–146.

132. Schaefer, E. S., and R. Q. Bell. Patterns of attitudes toward child rearing and the family. *J. Abnorm. Soc. Psychol.*, 1957, 54, 391–395.

133. Schaefer, E. S., and R. Q. Bell. Development of a parental attitude research instrument. *Child Develpm.*, 1958, 29, 339–362.

134. Sears, Pauline S. Doll play aggression in normal young children: influence of sex, age, sibling status, father's absence. *Psychol. Monogr.*, 1951, 65, No. 323.

135. Sears, R. R. *Survey of objective studies of psychoanalytic concepts.* New York: Social Science Research Council, 1947.

136. Sears, R. R. Relation of fantasy aggression to interpersonal aggression. *Child Develpm.*, 1950, 21, 5–6.

137. Sears, R. R. A theoretical framework for personality and social behavior. *Amer. Psychologist*, 1951, 6, 476–483.

138. Sears, R. R. The growth of conscience. In I. Iscoe, and A. W. Stevenson (Eds.), *Personality development in children.* Austin: University of Texas Press, 1960, 92–111.

139. Sears, R. R. Dependency motivation. In M. R. Jones (Ed.), *Nebraska symposium in motivation.* Lincoln: University of Nebraska Press, 1963, 25–64.

140. Sears, R. R., Eleanor E. Maccoby, and H. Levin. *Patterns of child rearing.* Evanston: Row, Peterson, 1957.

141. Sears, R. R., Margaret H. Pintler, and Pauline S. Sears. Effect of father separation on preschool children's doll play aggression. *Child Develpm.*, 1946, 17, 219–243.

142. Sears, R. R., J. W. M. Whiting, V. Nowlis, and Pauline S. Sears. Some child-rearing antecedents of aggression and dependency in young children. *Genet. Psychol. Monogr.*, 1953, 47, 135–236.

143. Stagner, R. *Psychology of personality* (2nd ed.). New York: McGraw-Hill, 1948.

144. Stith, Marjorie, and Ruth Conner. Dependency and helpfulness in young children. *Child Develpm.*, 1962, 33, 15–20.

145. Strecker, E. A. *Their mother's sons.* Philadelphia: Lippincott, 1946.

146. Sullivan, H. S. *Conceptions of modern psychiatry.* Washington, D. C.: William Allison White Psychiatric Foundation, 1947.

147. Thompson, G. G. *Child psychology: growth trends in psychological adjustment.* Boston: Houghton Mifflin, 1952.

148. Tuddenham, R. D. Studies in reputations: I. Sex and grade differences in school children's evaluation of their peers. II. The diagnosis of social adjustment. *Psychol. Monogr.*, 1952, 66, No. 333.

149. Walters, J., Doris Pearce, and Lucille Dahms. Affectional and aggressive behavior of preschool children. *Child Develpm.*, 1957, 28, 15–27.

150. Watson, R. I. Unpublished data, 1956.

151. Watson, R. I. *The great psychologists: from Aristotle to Freud.* Philadelphia: Lippincott, 1963.

152. Whiting, J. W. M., and I. L. Child. *Child training and personality: a cross-cultural study.* New Haven: Yale University Press, 1953.

153. Willoughby, R. R. Sexuality in the second decade. *Monogr. Soc. Res. Child Develpm.*, 1937, 2, No. 10.

154. Winterbottom, Marian R. The relation of childhood training in independence to achievement motivation. Unpublished doctoral dissertation. University of Michigan, 1953.

155. Wittenborn, J. R., *et al.* A study of adoptive children: I. Interviews as a source of scores for children and their homes. *Psychol. Monogr.*, 1956, 70, No. 408.

156. Wittenborn, J. R., *et al.* A study of adoptive children: III. Relationship between some aspects of development and some aspects of environment for adoptive children. *Psychol. Monogr.*, 1956, 70, No. 410.

157. Wolfle, D. L., and Helen M. Wolfle. The development of cooperative behavior in monkeys and young children. *J. Genet. Psychol.*, 1939, 55, 137–175.

158. Wright, Beatrice A. Altruism in children and the perceived conduct of others. *J. Abnorm. Soc. Psychol.*, 1942, 37, 218–233.

159. Yarrow, L. J. The effect of antecedent frustration on projective play. *Psychol. Monogr.*, 1948, 62, No. 293.

160. Zuckerman, M., B. B. Ribback, I. Monashkin, and J. A. Norton. Normative data and factor analysis on the Parental Attitude Research Instrument. *J. Consult. Psychol.*, 1958, 22, 165–171.

161. Zunich, M. Relationship between maternal behavior and attitudes toward children. *J. Genet. Psychol.*, 1962, 100, 155–165.

PART **IV**

LATER CHILDHOOD

15

Individual Development

L ATER CHILDHOOD spans the years from six to twelve. During this
period of later childhood great changes take place. The developments in psychological functioning are profound. Physical growth has
important consequences. Sensorimotor development approaches adult
standards. Emotional expressions and the situations eliciting them
take on a new direction and subtlety. Cognitive, language, perceptual
and intellectual processes not only continue to develop but also acquire
characteristics closer to those of adults than were shown by infants and
younger children. As a beginning to a perusal of the psychological
aspects of later childhood, this chapter explores these various facets of
individual development.

Physical growth

From six to twelve growth proceeds steadily but at a somewhat
decelerated rate as compared to early childhood. By the age of twelve
the average height is about five feet and the weight between 95 and
100 pounds (91). Changes in build are relatively slight.

Children mature physically at different rates. Consequently they
reach physical maturity at different ages (4). Some girls reach their
adult height at the age of 13, some boys do not do so until they are 22
or 23. Maturity is reached about two years earlier among girls than
boys, but in both variability of about four or five years is still within
the normal limits.

Although consideration is to be directed toward children from six to twelve (not those who have already reached maturity), variability of this sort is already operative. If anything, it is greater at about twelve than later. Before reaching puberty, a child is apt to have a spurt of very rapid growth, which the usual growth curves hide because of the differences in the particular age at which it occurs in each child (7). Differences in physical maturity in a large sample of children will extend as widely as that to be found at any age. This period starting at ten, eleven, or twelve lasts about two years, thereafter slowing down (78). At this age the girls tend to be about a year advanced physically, although the boys in the early adolescent years will make up this difference and soon be heavier and taller. Moreover, children are growing taller and have been reaching biologic maturity at an earlier age over the last 100 years (11). This increases the likelihood that children of today and of the future will develop interests of a social and emotional nature at earlier ages than did their parents.

The psychological consequences of differences in degree of physical maturity have been investigated quite extensively (46, 47, 53). In general the method has been to compare early and late maturing boys or girls of the same chronological age on a variety of personal and social characteristics. Differences found were then related to differences as mature adults. Boys who matured earlier showed greater self confidence, more matter of factness, and more maturity in social situations. Late maturing boys were expressive, talkative, eager, and attention-getting (47). When they reached the age of 33, the physical differences had almost disappeared as had many of the personality differences, but the differences remaining were still in the directions indicated by the original study (46). The scanty research carried on with girls permits no conclusion (53).

Sensorimotor development

During the school-age period children refine and extend their sensorimotor skills. During the earlier years of the period girls delight in such games as jacks and hopscotch which call for precise use of the musculature. Boys become interested in such sports as baseball and basketball which likewise call for greater refinement of eye-hand-muscle coordination. Bicycling and roller skating occupy both boys and girls. They naturally are not equally adept in fine-muscle coordinated activities, as any child of six will tell you when asked about his writing skills in keeping his "e's" from looking like "i's." Nevertheless, there is increasing skill with the smaller muscles, such as those of the hand. In fact, it often is said that this is the age to begin learning to play a musical instrument or to type if these skills are to become highly developed.

Most children keenly enjoy motor activities. They delight in constantly being on the go. "Spectators" among them are still very much in the minority. Although considerable advance in motor abilities has taken place during the infancy and preschool years, the psychological significance of motor development takes on even more importance in this period of later childhood. Much of its psychological significance rests on the fact that children have reached the age when they become aware of what others think of them, including their status in motor skills.

A high premium is placed on motor skills by older children. No adult with any contact whatsoever with children at play can fail to have noted either some child's outright rejection from a play group or his being grudgingly last chosen in making up a team because of his lack of strength, speed, or coordination. Having observed this situation we cannot but be convinced that such discrimination may contain the possibility of some psychological consequences. Those children fortunate enough to be adept in motor abilities are not only more acceptable to their playmates, but because of these skills are also more apt to be chosen as leaders. This choice may be made not only in tasks where their motor skills are important, but also may generalize to leadership functions essentially independent of motor skills, such as being elected as a class officer.

Age Trends

It will be remembered from the discussion in Chapter 11 that Carpenter (8) found two motor ability factors of general significance—strength and speed. These two factors will form the basis for discussion of age trends in motor development during later childhood.

Speed of response shows a regular increase with age. A study by Goodenough (22) is relevant in this connection. She had children from age three-and-a-half through eleven-and-a-half respond to a test whereby each made a voluntary movement on hearing a sound. At three-and-a-half years of age they took about five-tenths of a second to respond; at four-and-a-half years of age about four-tenths of a second. This increase in speed continued steadily, until at age eleven-and-a-half the children were responding in two-tenths of a second. This and other evidence indicate an increase in speed with age during these years.

There is a similar increase in strength with age according to a summarization by Metheny (59). Up until the age of puberty boys are superior to girls at most strength tests. In both boys and girls there is found to be a general positive relationship between the indices of strength and height and weight and health status. Thus among measures of motor development there is a tendency for the stronger to be taller, faster, and healthier than the weaker child. These relationships are closely related to similar relations between physical and mental ability.

The Relation of Physical and Mental Ability

The interrelationship between mental and physical measures in infancy was discussed previously. It will be remembered that there was found to be a relatively high degree of relationship. By the later childhood age this relationship had decreased considerably. There was however, still some degree of relationship.

In general, there is found to be a low, but positive correlation between physical and mental ability. Even physical measures such as height or weight have been found to conform to the same general rule (68). In other words, there is a *slight* tendency for the taller individual to be smarter than the shorter. But the relation is such that a number of exceptions to it are found. This does not mean that the relationship is so negligible in children that it can be dismissed, merely that relationships based on it must be interpreted with extreme caution.

Abernethy (1) studied physical and mental growth in nearly 200 boys and 200 girls. The Stanford-Binet Scales provided the measure of mental ability and a large battery of physical growth measures provided the indices of physical ability. Both kinds of measures were administered at regular intervals over an eleven-year period. Comparable measures were also given college men and women in order to provide measures to serve as a terminal standard of development. Low positive correlations between the physical and mental measures were found. In the case of height and mental ability, the average correlation was 0.26 for boys and 0.22 for girls over the age range of two to eight years. There was a general trend for the correlations to decrease after 14 or 15 years of age, eventuating in negligible correlations in the adult group. This general "togetherness" of physical and mental measures in childhood has been supported by a number of studies, for example, (64, 78). Enough information has been reported here to show that there is a slight positive relationship during later childhood which tends to decrease as the child grows older.

Learning and Sensorimotor Skills

Speed of sensorimotor performance has been studied at different ages and with various tasks. The specificity of task learning seems to be less with younger than with older children. One study (30) involved about 70 ten-year-old and 70 15-year-old boys. One task they studied was simple in nature—throwing a celluloid ball downward into a basket and then grasping a suspended tennis ball. The stimulus was a sound; no stimulus discrimination or choice was involved. The other tasks, although essentially similar, were more complicated—one involved a discrimination between two stimuli; the other required a choice to be made between which of two activities to carry out according to the particular stimulus on a given trial. In initial performance on all three tasks, the younger boys were slower; but they learned a greater amount by practice. Correlations of the amount of learning among the tasks were greater for the younger boys. This suggests that relative specificity of motor learning increases between ages ten and fifteen. It would seem that the ten-year-old's final skill depends more on ability to learn. In the older boys individual differences in initial skill served more to determine final skill.

Emotional development

As was the case with early childhood, emotional development in later childhood will be centered in a discussion of anger, fear, anxiety, and the affectively pleasant emotions.

Anger

A systematic study of anger of the scope of the Goodenough (21) study (described in Chapter 11) concerning older children has not appeared. However, it will be remembered that the age range of her subjects extended to over seven years, thus overlapping the ages now under consideration. It will also be recalled that certain age trends seemed to be operative. Some of her major findings were that (1) the immediate causes of anger shifted with increase in age and that the older children showed an increase of problems of social relationships; and (2) developmental changes in expression of anger showed less and less random behavior and more and more aggressive behavior directed toward something or someone.

The continuing prominence of social relationships as causes for anger was studied by Hicks and Hayes (31). In a group of older children and adolescents, 11 to 16 years of age, they found that the social situations most apt to evoke anger were being teased, being lied to, being treated unfairly, being imposed on by brothers and sisters, and other people being bossy or sarcastic. These causes of anger relate to people and the characteristics of people. Even more specifically it was the child's peers who often made him angry.

These "causes" of anger in older children can also be seen, from the perspective of the source of anger, as instances of angry behavior on the part of his peers. Although the investigators did not study the way these children directed their anger, but only what made them angry, it is not difficult to see that the instigators of the anger (often other children) were also expressing anger themselves. If this interpretation be accepted, it means that this study also throws light on how the older child expresses anger. As the child grows older, he learns to show deviousness in his expression of anger. Children become more roundabout in their aggressiveness, finding that through sneers, sarcasm, and so on they are able to stir up anger in older children. Just as in adults, a whisper may take the place of a blow, a joke the place of name calling.

A derivative of anger, annoyance, becomes more prominent in later childhood. Annoyance is an emasculated form of anger and frequently expresses more aptly the general kind of emotional response given during these years than does anger itself. In addition, the older child may be observed to express his anger in sulkiness, quarreling, fussiness, and being generally disagreeable.

Fear

Fear is still very much present in the life of children of this age range. The results of a study by England (15) bring this out dramatically. He asked about 100 seventh- and eighth-grade children of an average age of 11.8 years to make drawings of the most important events of their lives. Nothing in the instructions called for drawings depicting fear. Nevertheless, 88 of the resulting 290 drawings were identifiable as those of fear experiences. Since they were asked for drawings of their most important experiences, the relatively high number of drawings in which fear was the central element is impressive of their awareness of fear situations. Moreover, Pratt (72), in a carefully conducted study of the fears of children living in rural areas, found that children from grades five through eight reported both more fears and more different fears than children from the four earlier grades.

The study of fear by Jersild, described in connection with pre-school-aged children, was extended by him and his associates to school-aged children as well (42, 43). As might be anticipated from the growing subtlety of anger expression in children of this age, fear in its direct open sense was not the only form that was investigated. In fact, in one of the two major studies (42) in which they used a questionnaire check list, they were directly concerned with whether each of the children they studied "often," "sometimes," or "never" *worried* about their specified situations. Their particular choice of terminology, worry, aptly expresses the shift away from overt naked fear that takes place during childhood in the direction of more complex derivatives from it. In this study over 1,000 fifth- and sixth-grade children were presented with 25 one-sentence descriptions of situations and asked to express the degree to which they would worry about each one.

Apprehensions about commonplace occurrences in their own environmental situations were prominent among their worries. For example, more than four-fifths admitted that they sometimes worried about failing a test, more than two-thirds worried about the possibility of having a poor report card, and about two-fifths sometimes or often worried about being hit by rough children. In a sense, these were practical worries about realistic situations. However, many were pointless.

Almost one-fifth worried *often* about being left back in school and many hundred more *sometimes* worried about this. Analysis of promotion practices showed that less than one per cent were not going to be promoted. Fear of being attacked by animals was mentioned in an interview by 18 per cent of the children studied, yet less than two per cent of this sample had been attacked by animals. Even what appear on the surface to be realistic fears are found to contain a large amount of fantasy.

An interview study by Jersild, Markey, and Jersild (43) of 400 children aged five to twelve years bears out the contention that many fears of children of these ages are unrealistic. About 20 per cent of all fears of the children involved fear of imaginary creatures, of the dark, and of being alone. Another 10 per cent dealt with robbers and other criminal characters. Remote dangers, such as fear of wolves or tigers, also loomed large. In general, fears of a mundane sort were relatively low in frequency as compared to those fears of an anticipatory or imaginary sort. Such fears, then, are irrational in the sense that they often occur either when there is no danger or when it is very remote.

This raises the question of whether fear is useful in adjusting to daily problems. It is evident that often it is not. Many fears are restricting and fruitless wastes of energy.

A large proportion of the fears shown in childhood persists into the adult years. This was a finding of Jersild and Holmes (40) through the study of the recall by adults of childhood fears. Over 40 per cent of the fears they had had as children persisted in their later years. To be sure, they may have forgotten the nature of some of their childhood fears and thus failed to report them while reporting proportionately more of those that persisted into adulthood.

Those that showed the greatest persistence were fear of animals, of bodily harm through such dangers as fire, illness, or drowning, of the supernatural, of the dark, and of being alone. These fears are presumably kept alive by circumstances in the adult's life that make them in some way indices of present insecurities and conflicts. Their persistence, however, from childhood is still an impressive indication of the importance of the emotional experiences in these earlier years.

Anxiety

Anxiety is so pervasive a part of the child's life that it will be discussed later as it relates to activities in connection with self, school, and peers. Nevertheless, as an aspect of emotion it deserves consideration for its own sake.

A widely used self-report device is the Test Anxiety Scale for Children (TASC) developed by Sarason and his associates (76). It consists of 30 items concerned with manifestations of anxiety in their affective, physiological, and motor forms, and placed in a setting of test or test-like situations. Illustrative items include worrying about being promoted and worrying a lot before taking a test. The researchers also developed a so-called General Anxiety Scale for Children (GASC) with items about being afraid of snakes or worrying about becoming sick. These researches demonstrated that anxious children have more difficulty with various kinds of psychological tests than do nonanxious children (76). Moreover, they found that anxiety adversely affected learning since low anxious subjects performed better than high anxious subjects on a verbal learning task (90).

Another popular self-report of behavior and attitudes is the Children's Form of the Manifest Anxiety Scale (CMAS) (9). This 42-item questionnaire concerns physiological and psychological concomitants of generalized anxiety, worriment on such matters as blushing or angering easily, and having sweaty palms. Originally standardized for use in the fourth, fifth, and sixth grades, it has also been found to be useful with third-grade children (34, 35).

Unlike findings with TASC where anxiety adversely affected learning in general, Sarason and his associates obtained a differential effect related to the difficulty of the task involved as measured by CMAS. On complex and difficult tasks anxious children performed less well than nonanxious children but anxiety seemed to facilitate simple learning (10, 66). In the first of these studies, 37 fifth-grade children learned a particular combination of push-button pressing when faced with a particular combination of lights. Five combinations of varying difficulty as established in another sample of children were used as the learning task. Divided into high anxious and low anxious on the CMAS, the subjects were run through the series and their relative errors noted on the two easiest and two most difficult tasks. The high-anxious children were superior on the easy tasks; the low-anxious children on the difficult tasks. The consequences of level of anxiety varied with the circumstances.

Lest these results be generalized too broadly, it is well to caution that a study of the relation between CMAS scores and the concept of anxiety as used in a clinical setting yielded no significant relation. Children referred to a clinic, as compared to a large school population, did not differ on CMAS scores and psychologists' or teachers' ratings of anxiety did not relate to CMAS scores (76). Evidently the CMAS measures something different from the clinical concept of anxiety. However, this does not mean that measures of personality adjustment may not correlate significantly with ratings of anxiety of the sort being considered. As a matter of fact correlations in the neighborhood of .30 to .50 have been found (39, 50).

Affectively Pleasant Emotions

Relatively little research has been conducted on the affectively pleasant emotions in the school-aged child. Joy producing experiences have been studied somewhat indirectly through finding out what children consider their happiest experiences to be. Again it is the work of Jersild (41) to which we turn. In collaboration with Tasch, he made a study of children's interests which included inquiring into what they considered to be one of the happiest days in their lives. Table 20 presents the results in terms of the major categories into which their responses to this inquiry could be placed for various age groups.

TABLE 20

FREQUENCY OF RESPONSES IN VARIOUS CATEGORIES WHEN CHILDREN
DESCRIBED "ONE OF THE HAPPIEST DAYS OF MY LIFE" *

(The values represent percentage of children giving
one or more responses in each category.)

	Grades 1–3 Ages 6–9		Grades 4–6 Ages 9–12		Grades 7–9 Ages 12–15		Grades 10–12 Ages 15–18	
Number	Boys 363	Girls 331	Boys 309	Girls 343	Boys 282	Girls 290	Boys 159	Girls 171
Receiving or having or otherwise enjoying material things, gifts, toys, money, living quarters	8.7	8.1	10.4	7.2	10.1	4.5	5.6	3.1
Holidays, festive occasions, birthdays, Christmas, etc.	39.1	40.5	32.4	38.9	6.3	10.1	0.6	6.5
Sports, games, hiking, hunting, bicycling, etc.	10.2	6.4	9.1	5.5	12.4	5.8	13.0	7.3
Going to miscellaneous places of recreation, going to camps, traveling, going to resorts, to parks	9.6	9.0	10.1	11.4	9.7	13.9	30.2	6.9
Self-improvement, success in school, educational opportunity, evidence of vocational competence, getting a job	2.4	2.3	2.9	1.9	4.8	4.1	13.6	15.9
Happenings connected with school, including last day, end of school, going to a certain school	3.6	3.4	5.4	4.3	14.0	11.1	7.0	5.4
Relationship with people (explicitly described), companionship, being with certain friends, return home of relatives, etc.	7.7	15.9	8.0	15.8	10.5	22.0	8.7	19.9

TABLE 20 (Continued)

Residing in, moving to a certain city or community	1.3	1.0	0.8	2.9	0.9	2.9	1.4	5.0
Benefits befalling others, or mankind in general, including end of war	0.6	0.8	3.2	2.8	2.2	2.6	7.9	9.7

* Adapted from Jersild and Tasch (41). Copyright 1949 by Teachers College, Columbia University, and published with permission.

Younger children tended to stress a holiday or a birthday or other occasions when they received special attention and gifts more than was the case with older children. Children of all ages were apt to mention visiting friends, the return home of relatives, and the like. Girls much more than boys described joyful events as involving social relationships. The oldest-age boys had a sudden upsurge of interest in literally going places, such as parks and recreational centers and in traveling. Older children placed more emphasis on the pleasures of self-discovery and self-realization, opportunities for self-improvement, and for vocational preparation. Benefits for individuals other than themselves were mentioned more often by them than they were by younger children.

Many of the results of the Jersild and Tasch study were indirectly verified by still another study by Jersild and his associates (43). This was a study involving interviewing 400 five-to-twelve-year-old children about their wishes, dreams, fears, dislikes, and pleasant and unpleasant happenings. The youngest child's wishes, likes, and dislikes were more specific and the older child's more inclusive and social. Girls, again, were more concerned with social relations than were boys.

With increase in age the importance of social relationships and the opportunities for self-realization loom large. The period of later childhood, in terms of the affectively pleasant emotions, is the period of self- and social discovery.

Cognitive development

As formulated by Piaget, after the age of seven the child enters the period of *concrete* operations, and when he reaches the age between 11 and 15 he begins to use *formal* operations (38). Both levels will be examined here. This will be followed by an exposition of the research findings for the development of physical causality, and then by a critique of the Piagetian levels.

Piagetian Levels of Cognition

The period of preparation for the level of concrete operations that takes place between the ages of five and seven was discussed in Chapter 11 since its characteristics seemed to have more affinity with those levels occurring during early childhood.

Before considering these levels it is necessary to examine more precisely what Piaget meant by an operation. An operation is a cognitive act which is part of some pattern of acts. It may be seen in adding, subtracting, or in placing an object in a class, a quantity, time, or space. Any of these tasks requires a prior classification. We cannot classify without having some knowledge of what we are classifying; to add to or to subtract from a classification requires a classificatory system. It is more than learning to pick up all yellow counters from a varicolored pile; the child has acquired the ability to think of yellow objects as a group. He has recognized the class "yellow objects."

Concrete operations take on stability and coherence between the age of seven and eleven through the formation of cognitive structures (16). Consider the problem of differently shaped containers that lead the broad container and the tall, thin container hold the same amount (38). By about seven, however, he recognizes that the amount remains constant regardless of the shape of the container. His first crude preschool-aged child to "center" and not to understand that the short, approximation "that one is taller, but this one is broader," is an attempt to explain that the height of the one compensates for the width of the other. At a still older age he might say that when poured from one to the other it would be similar. In so doing he has recognized that the change in quantity is invariant despite change of state. This and similar instances, when submitted to more precise scrutiny by other investigators (51), verified Piaget's contentions, although with greater age variation from child to child than his account would suggest.

In another instance of a concrete operation used by Piaget (16), the child is first shown two balls of clay equal in size. He is asked to flatten one ball into a pancake and, then, asked about the amount in each ball. Most five- or six-year-olds believe that necessarily a change in form produces a change in amount. (Either the pancake is larger because it is more spread out or the ball is larger because it is higher.) When older, the child acknowledges that they have the same amount of clay "because the pancake is thinner, but wider." But this level of cognitive development is still preoperational.

A critical process in finally arriving at "conservation" is awareness of reversibility. This is shown when a child acknowledges that he can make the pancake into a ball again. He now understands that the process is reversible, that quantity is "conserved," in Piaget's usage of the term. Conservation, to Piaget (38), refers to a particular factor—weight, volume, and the like—remaining invariant despite changes of state. Conservation of matter becomes common at about eight to ten years of age. In short, the child at this age becomes aware that the volume of matter is constant in spite of change in shape. This attribute of the object, not merely the object as a whole, is now invariant. Similarly, there will be understanding of conservation of weight at a later age, and that of volume still later.

Now that operations have been described it is necessary to refer to the manner in which they may be said to be *concrete*. At this stage the child uses operations but only for the manipulation of *objects* that is, concretely. For example, eight- and ten-year-olds have no trouble arranging a series of dolls or sticks according to height but fail to solve a similar problem put verbally: "Edith is taller than Susan; Edith is shorter than Lily; who is the tallest of the three?" For this principle to be comprehended, progress to the stage of *formal* operations is necessary.

Somewhere between the ages of 11 and 15 the child begins to use formal operations. They are as operational as those at the concrete level of cognition but in a different way. Concrete operations are first-degree operations; formal operations are second degree and use first-degree operations, treating them not as realities but as conditions in representational thought. As types of action they may be verbal when proportions are manipulated or they may be physical when objects are manipulated.

In one experiment five vessels containing colorless liquids are provided; liquids A,B,C when mixed, turn pink, D removes the color, and E has no effect. These properties can be discovered only by systematically examining mixtures of every possible pair, every trio, and so on, in turn. It is characteristic, Piaget found, for children of this age to hit on two-by-two or three-by-three combinations as the way to solve the problem.

In another experiment the subject's task is to place two vertical rings of different diameters between a candle and a screen in such manner that their shadows will coincide. The child finally discovers that the problem is solved when the ratio between the distances of the two rings from the candle is the same as the ratio between their diameters. This demands understanding of proportionality.

Another characteristic of formal operations is reversibility, or the ability to "undo," that is, to return to a starting point and begin again. A graphic illustration of reversibility in action is the child, faced with the problem of finding a balancing weight, placing one on the scale, finding it to be too heavy, taking it off, and beginning to search for a lighter one.

The young child uses formal operations (logical rules), not consciously, to be sure, since ordinarily he has not been trained in logic. Nevertheless, the application of logic becomes part of his cognitive abilities. He may not be able to formulate the rule, if A is greater than B, and B is greater than C, then A is greater than C, but he can apply it, and moreover, apply it to situations with which he is unfamiliar.

Or to put it another way, he can consider hypotheses that may or may not be true and follow the form of argument while disregarding the concrete content (38). This ability to be guided by the form of argument, ignoring content, gives meaning to the name, formal operations. This ability to utilize difficult logical operations in different situations is the very essence of logical thinking (38).

The deductive procedures of science, as well as a host of other new intellectual procedures, become open to the child capable of formal operations. Some of these are formidable when placed in technical terminology, as, for example, the calculus of propositions which has to do with such matters as, if proposition "r" is true, then proposition "s" must be true. The rules are by no means beyond his own day-to-day use, although he does not formulate them as would the logician or mathematician.

The period of formal operations, then, is the years between 11 and 15. Although refinement, adroitness, and scope do take place thereafter, they do so with structures of the formal sort that the adult employs when thinking logically and abstractly. This final reorganization involving new structures allows the individual to deal with reality and also with the world of pure possibility, that of abstract propositional statements.

Physical Causality

It is appropriate to turn from Piaget's general theory of levels of development to consider a more specific aspect of his views. The emergence of conceptions of physical causality is chosen for detailed exposition (69). It was his work on physical causality which stimulated widespread interest in the manner in which children developed these conceptions. In studying physical causality various phenomena of nature were mentioned or demonstrated by Piaget and children were asked to explain them. Thus he would ask, "What makes the clouds move?" After the child had responded he would further question him until satisfied he had understood the child's conception. From work along these lines he arrived at a classification of 17 types of causal thinking. Five of these types moving from relatively great to less egocentricity as we move from one type to another are defined by Deutsche as follows:

> *Phenomenistic Causality.*—Two facts given together in perception, such that no relation subsists between them except that of contiguity in time and space. Pebble sinks to bottom of water because it is white. No concept of relations. . . .
> *Animistic Causality.*—An internal biological tendency that is both alive and conscious. Clouds move because they are alive. . . .
> *Dynamic Causality.*—Animism gone, but still sees in objects forces that are capable of explaining their activity and movements. . . .
> *Mechanical Causality.*—Explanation by contact and transference of movement. No internal force at all. Wind pushes the clouds. Pedals make bicycle go. . . .
> *Explanation by Logical Deduction.*—Explanation by the principle of sufficient reason. Water flows into the second of the connected tubes because water can go equally well in both directions. Uses concepts of density, specific weight, etc. (13, 51–52).[1]

The first three are definitely precausal (and egocentric), whereas mechanical causality may be considered as transitional, with explanation by logical definition belonging in the category of formal operations. According to Piaget these (and the remaining 12 levels) are discrete in that children's thinking proceeds during the course of development from one level to the next higher level with relatively little overlap. In terms of the levels, a child would be phenomenistic in his thinking rather than animistic, then animistic, and so on, until logical deduction developed. A child, say at the level of dynamic causality, would when at that level be incapable of logical deduction.

This view of conceptualization as a series of discrete levels is in sharp contrast with another prevailing view in which the position is taken that thinking emerges gradually. They would argue that younger children were capable of logical thought—that the youngest child's thought, though limited by sheer inexperience, is not qualitatively different from adult thought. Representative of this point of view is the study of Deutsche (13).

She performed one of the better controlled studies of children's thinking which tested Piaget's contentions. Several hundred children

---

[1] Jean M. Deutsche, *The Development of Children's Concepts of Causal Relations.* Copyright 1937, University of Minnesota.

aged between eight and sixteen were tested both through their reactions to demonstrations of physical phenomena and the completion
of a questionnaire. The demonstrations included placing a jar over a
lighted candle and asking why the candle went out; dropping blocks
and asking what made the noise; adding to beakers containing blue and
yellow solutions some colorless acid which changed the colors, respectively, to yellow and red and asking why a colorless substance changed
the colors; and playing different keys on a musical instrument and asking why different sounds were heard. The questionnaire included
items about what makes the wind blow, what makes a rainbow after
rain, what makes airplanes stay in the air, what makes boats float, what
makes shadows, and what causes thunder. For both demonstration and
questionnaire items, the children wrote their answers and were not
further questioned.

Classification into one or another of Piaget's classifications was made
by three independent observers. Table 21 shows the percentage by age
of the five types previously defined. Since the remaining dozen types
made up only about 10 per cent of the total, for the sake of economy of
presentation they may be disregarded.

TABLE 21

PERCENTAGE OF ANSWERS FALLING IN SEVERAL OF
PIAGET'S CLASSIFICATIONS *

Type of Causality	Age, Years								All Ages
	8	9	10	11	12	13	14	15–16	
Phenomenistic	37.3	32.5	29.5	22.4	16.1	11.9	12.4	10.3	20.8
Animistic	0.6	0.2	0.6	0.3	0.3	0.2	0.0	0.0	0.3
Dynamic	8.3	5.8	6.3	6.2	7.1	6.7	2.9	5.7	6.3
Mechanical	32.5	33.2	37.4	40.5	41.1	41.0	39.5	42.9	38.9
Logical	10.7	11.8	14.1	19.8	28.1	32.0	35.6	31.6	23.4

* Jean M. Deutsche, *The Development of Children's Concepts of Causal Relations.* Copyright 1937, University of Minnesota.

It can be seen from the table that only four of the types of causal
thinking advanced by Piaget were found in large enough frequencies
to permit study of age trends. Phenomenistic causality declined with
age and mechanical causality and logical deduction increased with age,
whereas dynamic causality showed no age trend. It might be said the
findings on the first three supported Piaget's contentions so far as the
direction of expected age trends are concerned. However, discreteness
of levels of thinking age by age was emphatically not found. Each

type of thinking was found to extend over the entire age range studied, suggesting that causality does not develop in saltatory stages. Deutsche found many more logical explanations of physical causality than we would expect from Piaget's account. Children even as young as eight carry on logical thinking. Moreover, children as old as fifteen or sixteen continue to use phenomenistic, dynamic, and mechanical types of causal explanation. A variety of other studies, for example, those reviewed by Huang (37), supports conclusions similar to those of Deutsche.

Factors other than sheer age affect children's concepts of personality. Nass (62) investigated the effect of personality, experience, and the form of wording of the questions asked on Piaget's types of thinking. The effect of personality was investigated by contrasting the responses of normal and withdrawn eight- to ten-year-old children, matched as to school attendance, age, sex, and intelligence test scores. The withdrawn children were selected from those referred to a child guidance clinic for this problem. The hypothesis was advanced that withdrawn children would be hampered in developing an objective point of view in Piaget's terms. In other words, they would be expected to function at a less mature level than normal children. This hypothesis was verified in that the withdrawn children displayed significantly more nonnaturalistic responses to a series of questions, akin to those used by Piaget and Deutsche. Thus, they functioned at a less mature level than normal children.

The effect of experience was investigated in subgroups of the normal and withdrawn matched groups by comparing their responses to items dealing with phenomena with which they were likely to have had direct experience—for example, radiators getting hot or a clock ticking—as contrasted with items dealing with phenomena with which the children could not have experienced the causal process directly—for example, thunder or the stars shining. The more remote phenomena with which the children had no direct experience produced more nonnaturalistic responses. The effect of the wording of the questions was studied through similar subgroups, the members of one of which were asked "Why" as in "Why does a car move?" The members of the other subgroup were asked "How" as in "How does a car move?" It was hypothesized that the first form of question would be more suggestive of dynamic or animistic forces than would the second form. Significant differences in the expected direction were obtained. Thus, personality, experience, and the form of the question were all found to affect the degree of naturalistic and nonnaturalistic explanations of physical causality in the thinking of children.

Using some of the Piagetian problems, Mogar (61) studied causal reasoning about natural phenomena in children aged five through twelve. In some respects the results support Piaget's contention. However, one almost incidental finding is very important. To a greater degree than the control children, the experimental subjects were exposed to repeated observation of demonstrations of the phenomena about which they were questioned. At the end of the study, they were much more capable than the control subjects of working out solutions at an earlier age than the developmental levels called for. In other words, special tutelage brought about advance over the expected levels. If children are *taught* to think in terms of formal operations, they can do so. Piaget, using few subjects, did not include any who happened to have these experiences from their daily living and therefore underestimated this capacity.

A Critique of Piagetian Levels of Development

This critique is also appropriate to Piaget's contentions about earlier developmental levels, as given in Chapters 7 and 11. There is no question that Piaget paid little attention to sampling or even to securing more than a handful of subjects. Moreover, data he did obtain lack precision and often are such that the manner in which he secured his evidence cannot be repeated by another investigator.

In some psychological circles, Piaget is dismissed because his own research rightly is not considered as sufficient evidence. The dismissal on this basis is essentially short-sighted and incorrect. The scanty data he has presented can be taken to illustrate, not to prove. It is his ideas which are stimulating, not his evidence. For evidence we turn to the work of other men who have tested his formulations.

Some of the differences between Piaget's findings together with the studies that support him and those of other investigators whose findings are in disagreement are to be found in the dissimilar methods they used. Piaget used a clinical method of adroitly questioning the children he interviewed. The method had the advantage of allowing him to trace down the particular meaning the child was giving to a word. Children, as Piaget's own work so ably shows, are in the process of developing sharpness and clarity in their use of words. There certainly is an advantage of this approach over using a group-written test where there is no follow-up of what the child meant by his answers. In a group test, the response obtained for each object or demonstration is equivalent only to the unfollowed-up first response in the interview procedure.

The group method, too, has advantages. It more readily permits a larger sampling of subjects and the application of a series of controls.

Although not intrinsic to the group testing method, the use of independent observers to measure reliability is a distinct advantage. These differences in procedure between Piaget and the American research investigators undoubtedly go far in accounting for the disparities in the results obtained.

Piaget's sharp contrast between childish and adult thinking probably is an overevaluation of verbal expression as a measure of thinking and an exaggeration of the logical nature of adult thought. Just as children's thinking is not so different from adult thinking because the child is more adult than pictured by Piaget, so, too, is the adult more childish. Children's thinking cannot be as sharply distinguished from adult modes of thought as Piaget would have it. There is confusion of fantasy with reality, as the psychoanalysts as well as followers of Piaget argue, but there is not a qualitative difference between the thinking of children and that of adults. Reality limits the child despite his creation of make-believe situations; fantasy enlivens and yet distorts the thinking of adults. A child's thinking does not differ fundamentally from an adult's by differing in kind, but rather in degree.

It is important to note that Piaget did not claim the entire absence of one form of thinking and then the full-blown appearance of another, with no residue of the earlier stage. For example, socialized speech in early childhood is recognized and accepted by Piaget. He claimed only that egocentric speech clearly predominated. Nevertheless, much more than others, he argued for relatively abrupt shifts in thinking on the part of the children at different ages. Many indications, besides the studies reported here, show that the cognitive stages of Piaget are not sharply separated, neither with quite different responses emerging at each level nor with the disappearance of those of the previous stage.

It would seem as if the weight of evidence (37) is against the saltatory shifting from one stage of conceptualization to the next. The almost universal finding of research studies other than Piaget's own is that, instead of there being leaps from one kind of thinking to another, there is a gradual orderly change in the child's conceptualization (no matter how defined). This forces disagreement in emphasis with Piaget on this point. For example, most studies, whether of physical causality or of the narrower problem of animism, find that the categorizations of thinking they used, whatever form they may take, extend over the age range of the subjects studied. Trends of change in stages of conceptualization are found to be sure, but they are progressive and not of an "all or none" variety.

Presumably, an important factor in the age placement of levels is the influence of training on the operations concerned. Differences among children, with those trained showing formal operations at a younger age than children without this training, have been established. The ramification of the problem of training deserves more careful investigation than it so far has received.

Perceptual development

Perceptual development in later childhood falls into the setting of time and space perception.

Time and Space Perception

Piaget (71) prefers to refer to time concepts rather than to time perception since he considers appreciation of time to involve not only perceptual data but also logical organization of these data. This position makes time an aspect of his general theory of cognitive development. The preoperative stage between the ages of two and seven had allowed the child to execute on the plane of thought the equivalent of the still earlier sensorimotor stage.

Up to about the age of seven the child shows a close relationship between his constructs of time and speed. Dolls are moved across a table surface at different speeds, B more rapidly than A, but stopped simultaneously. When a child is asked when they stopped, he refuses to say they stopped at the same time. This is not a perceptive error: he acknowledges when B stops; A no longer moves but he refuses to say they stopped at the same time. He may say B stopped before A because the former is "ahead" of the latter (in the spatial sense) or he may say that A stopped before B in the sense it is spatially closer. In either case he does not understand that they stopped "at the same time," because the notion "same time" is meaningless when two objects move at different speeds.

Only gradually does the conservation of relationships of *speed* come about at around seven or eight years of age. Then, and only then, is he ready, says Piaget, to conceive of the construct of time at the concrete level. Time constructs at the formal level have not been specifically worked out. It is safe to say that they partake of the general conceptualization characteristic of that level. Many of Piaget's contentions have been verified experimentally but with more variation over wider age range than would be expected (52).

Fraisse (18) makes a distinction between time perception and time estimation. He arrived at this differentiation by a study of long and short time intervals with time perception applying only to short intervals, that is, one second. He tested children aged six, eight, and ten for their ability to reproduce time intervals of .5, 1, 5, and 20 seconds, both filled with some activity and unfilled. He found only slight age differences for the short intervals. The major age difference was with the two longest intervals which were grossly underestimated by the youngest subjects, who also showed extraordinarily large variability for the longest interval. After eight the longer time intervals showed negligible time differences. Younger children are deficient primarily in time estimation, not time perception.

In summarizing the research on time perception for older children, Flickinger and Rehage (17) concluded that the concept of past *versus* present was reached at about eight; full understanding of our system of time measurement at about eleven; understanding of time-zone lines at about 13; and natural grasp of time words and dates at about 16.

Space representation, not perception, is stressed by Piaget (16) in order to emphasize that space is not immediately given in experience as something merely to be perceived. Organizations of actions performed in space, first through motor and later through internalized actions, give rise to operational systems. The topological projective or Euclidean geometric concepts that emerge later in childhood defy brief summarization.

Spatial relations are related to or coordinated with the child's own body (60). The child understands the elements of a spatial pattern with reference to his own body as right or left, high or low, and the rest. A factor analysis revealed that boys tended to exceed girls in spatial ability. This may possibly be due to the greater participation in construction activities during play.

Language development

Language is an integral aspect of cognitive development, essential as it is for perceptual-cognitive and intellectual growth. It even is to be discerned as effective in emotional development. Without the acquisition of words and some knowledge of syntactical construction, these cognitive processes would be stunted and chaotic. Without language as a means of communication, social interaction would be nearly impossible. Discussion of language is intertwined with all of these aspects of child development. Linguistic skills must, nevertheless, be examined for their own sake.

Developmental Changes in Language Skills

Growth in oral and written expression in a representative sampling of

320 children aged nine through 15 years of age has been studied by Harrell (29). After seeing a short movie, each child told a story that was tape-recorded. After another similar movie, each wrote a story about it. With the clause as the unit of measurement, the investigators studied the length of the stories by age, sex, and oral or written means of composition. The oral stories were longer than the written ones, and both increased in length with age, although repetitions and corrections decreased with age. Girls wrote longer stories than boys. It is significant that by the oldest age, fifteen years, there was no indication that a mature level had been reached. Considerably increase in skill was still to be expected in the years thereafter.

Some of the complexities of language acquisition of the child should be illustrated. Consider the problem of acquisition of word meanings. An adult might use a dictionary, but this is not characteristic of the child who does not acquire meanings in this fashion. Ingeniously, Werner and Kaplan (95) made use of 12 nonsense words, such as CORPLUM, placed in various contexts to see how children, eight through thirteen, would acquire their meanings. For each artificial word there were six sentences in which it was used, such as "a CORPLUM may be used for support;" "a wet CORPLUM doesn't burn;" and "you can make a CORPLUM smooth with sandpaper." After reading a sentence, one to a card, the child was asked what the word meant, and how and why the meaning he gave the word fitted into the sentence. With the first sentence card still in view, he then proceeded to the second and subsequent sentence cards, each time giving his interpretation of its meaning and how that meaning could be applied to that given to the preceding sentence. In this example CORPLUM meant wood. The major aim, however, was not correctness itself. Rather, the *process* of signification was the main concern.

It was found that one major category included those instances in which children did not clearly differentiate the word from the sentence as a whole. They so confused the word and its sentence context, that instead of learning a circumscribed meaning, the word meant to them the entire context in which it appeared. Thus in the sentence, "People talk about the BURDICKS of others and don't like to talk about their own," one child explained BURDICK meant, "talk about others and don't talk about themselves." Later, the same child when given the sentence, "People with BURDICKS are often unhappy," she said, "People talk about others and don't talk about themselves—they are often unhappy." It is not recorded whether she eventually found that BURDICK meant "faults."

The other major category involved instances in which children differentiated the word from the sentence, but did so in a variety of ways, most often giving too inclusive a meaning to the nonsense word. In the instance when the meaning should have been "collect" with one child it became successively, "collect ribbons," "collect autographs," and "collect information." In each instance what was collected would fit the context; to wit, people collect information quickly when there is an accident, but actually the "ribbons," "the autographs," and the "information" were entirely extraneous. "Collect" was all that was necessary. These so-called sentence-word fusions decreased most sharply at about 11 years of age, hardly to appear thereafter. Those in which there was no fusion of word meaning and context, although decreasing, were maintained through the oldest age studied. A shift in level of verbal abstraction seemed to be taking place at about the 11-year level.

The path of language acquisition is not the simple, straightforward one that adults might imagine. The child must move through difficult and devious paths of blind-alley irrelevancies to find the relevant strand of appropriate meaning.

Intellectual development

Brief reference has already been made in Chapters 7 and 11 to intellectual development during infancy and early childhood. This involved consideration of the kinds of intelligent behavior observed at these particular ages, the nature of the underlying processes that seemed to account for this behavior, and the prowess of tests given at these ages for prediction of later intellectual status. Here we undertake a more detailed examination of intelligence in later childhood.

The Nature of Intelligence

Intelligence becomes evident through the observing, the conceptualizing, and the thinking the child carries on. If observation, conceptualization, and thought are efficient, broad, and involve higher levels of difficulty, we speak of the individual as bright; if they are the opposite, we speak of the individual as stupid. It is only for convenience that we break down this continuum into discrete areas. Instead of there being a dichotomy of the bright and the stupid, there is a continuum from the highest degree of brightness to the lowest degree of stupidity.

Intelligence involves all of the cognitive processes, but with emphasis on the efficiency, scope, and level of difficulty of function which is expressed.   Concepts, for example, are *used* by a child in intellectual activity—with efficiency, breadth, and hierarchical level of capabilities helping to decide what we call the intelligence of the child in question.

As Woodworth (97) contends, intelligence is one of those nouns that should be considered a verb.   A child is intelligent insofar as he acts intelligently, stupid insofar as he acts stupidly.   Intelligence is always expressed in some behavior, reinforcing the necessity of considering it essentially a verb, since the emphasis is upon the behavior.   Intelligence is not an entity, but a construct about ways of behavior inferred and measured indirectly.   We infer from certain behaviors that are now learned that the individual will behave in this fashion.

Since the functioning of intelligence calls for a solution to a problem, there is an implication that the situation in which it functions is a new one in some particulars.   Habit carries us through many activities.   But before we have a habitual way of behaving, we must at some time have met what is now habitual as a new situation.   Then intellectual application took place.   Intelligence, then, is expressed in the application of the higher mental processes to accomplishing a task, particularly new tasks.

Intellectual development is related to learning.   From the infant's first explorations of his little world to the new conception of the universe by the physicist, there is a steady background of learning.   One learns more and faster because of more efficient intellectual functioning.   We measure intelligence on the basis of things we have learned; for example, vocabulary, common knowledge, and school attainment.   Intellectual development and learning are inextricably intertwined—intellectual development results in gaining knowledge.   This is a result of learning.

Intelligence is related not only to the cognitive functions and to learning, it also is embedded in all aspects of the personality.   Consequently, emotional life influences intellectual functioning.   For example, as Rapaport (73) indicated, knowledge is a threat to some people.   In them the natural endowment will become inhibited and refractory to acquisition of new knowledge, or, to put it in our earlier terms, refractory to observing, conceptualizing, and thinking.   Children may be affectively rather than intellectually stupid.

Intelligence is a unified intergrated way of behaving and in this sense is a function of the total personality.   An individual uses it to adapt to his changing environment.   Intelligence takes its place as one of the interrelated aspects of the psychological processes of the child.   Consequently, intelligence is discussed not only for its own sake as an integrated way of behaving but also because it again allows stressing the interdependence of personality factors which contribute to the development of the child.

There is considerable general agreement for the assertions about intelligence made up to this point. Consideration of the more precise composition of intelligence and its changes, or lack of them, during development from infancy to adulthood reveals disagreements. Spearman (84) held that there was a general factor, or *g*, influencing all intelligent behavior while there were many special factors, or *s*. Some *s* factors were heavily dependent upon *g*, for example, number ability, and others were relatively independent of *g*, for example, musical or motor ability. He stressed abstract ability, particularly that involved in arriving at relations, as in answering the question, "Sun is to earth as earth is to what?"

Thurstone (87), who studied the problem of intelligence for many years, disagreed with Spearman on the composition of intelligence. In contrast to *g* and *s* factors, Thurstone's position was that intelligence was made up of group factors, more or less mutually exclusive one from the other. In other words, numerical ability, or *N*, one of these multiple factors, is relatively unrelated to other mental abilities. He agreed with Spearman on the abstract nature of intelligence but disagreed on how it was distributed; instead of a general factor intelligence, he conceived of it as having multiple factors. Both Spearman and Thurstone tended to stress the fixed character of intelligence from infancy to adulthood.

Piaget (16) disagreed with this point. In his theory of cognitive development, intelligence is the adaptive aspect of cognition; its function remains invariant while the structures do not. They change in the manner analyzed in the earlier section on cognitive development.

The Stanford-Binet Intelligence Scale

The third revision of the Stanford-Binet Intelligence Scale (86) is one of the most widely used intelligence tests both in research and in clinical practice. It retains the characteristics of the original Binet scales described in Chapter 1—use of age standards, mental age, and IQ. Many of the research studies to be discussed used this particular scale. In its earlier revisions it dominated the field of intelligence testing and many of the developments and conceptualizations about intelligence arose from its use. For these reasons a rather detailed account is given. Terman and Merrill stress that, in general, the scale measures adaptability to new problems. They avoid giving more explicit meaning to the nature of intelligence, preferring to let the scale speak for itself, leaving to others the explication of this particular problem. Their position removes them from the controversy concerning the more precise meaning of intelligence. The reconciliation of continuity of development with Piagetian discontinuity was already considered in Chapter 7. The Stanford-Binet Scale increases by month and year but measures the products, not the operations, used by children in arriving at their answers. Steady increase in score with age is not incompatible with use of different operations at different ages.

Description. The scale contains 120 tests, six at each of the 20 age levels. The age levels start at the second year, jump to two years six months, and proceed at six-month intervals until the five-year level is reached. Yearly levels are supplied from age five until age fourteen which is followed by an average adult level and three superior adult levels. The tests are designed to be administered to one child at a time. The examiner selects the first test level, usually at or slightly below the child's actual age; testing continues through the levels until a specified number of test failures have occurred.

On the first examination of the material for these numerous tests a sense of bewilderment is apt to appear. Mazes, bead stringing, giving similarities to various words, arithmetic problems, memory span for digits, finding verbal absurdities in a sentence read to them, defining words, showing apparent opposites may be reconciled, and so on appear as items, but it would be grossly inaccurate to infer that they have been mingled together with no particular rhyme or reason. As consideration of each item composing the test is impracticable here, we shall examine only one of the classifications of the items. The classification chosen was based on a factor analysis of the standardization data collected by Terman and Merrill for the 1937 revision.

Jones (45) analyzed factorially the data for the 13-year-old standardization group consisting of 100 girls and 100 boys, selecting their performance on the items related to age levels 12, 13, and 14. Once the factors were derived, they were interpreted by him as much as possible in terms of underlying processes rather than in terms of the superficial content of the interrelated items. Each of the nine factors he found will be reported in two forms: (1) the general, more inclusive term that was applied; and (2) the precise more specific meaning given it by Jones.

The first is a Verbal factor more precisely defined as *"the process of supplying previously learned linguistic responses, primarily word meanings"* (45, 133).[2] The second is also a Verbal factor, *"the ability to manipulate words in a manner such that an appropriate meaningful relationship is imposed"* (45, 134).[2] The third factor likewise is a

---

[2] From Jones (45). Copyright 1954 by The Journal Press, and published with permission.

Verbal factor, *"the verbalization of gross ideas as contrasted with the definition or manipulation of words which serve as elements of these ideas"* (45, 134).[2] The fourth factor is a Memory factor, *"the ability to reproduce, immediately after presentation, a sequence of disconnected elements"* (45, 135).[2] The fifth factor is also a Memory factor, *"an ability for verbatim recall of meaningful verbal material"* (45, 136).[2] The sixth factor is a Space factor, *"visualization of movement within a particular configuration"* (45, 137).[2] The seventh factor is a Reasoning factor, not found capable of more specific statement by Jones. The eighth factor is a Closure factor, *"the ability to fuse a perceptual field into a single percept"* (45, 140).[2] The ninth and last factor is a Carefulness factor, *"the ability to carefully and precisely perceive the details of a spatial configuration"* (45, 142).[2]

The definition of these factors in two forms, general and precise, makes possible the relation of the general factors to previous studies of the factor composition of intelligence tests. The general factors, Verbal, Memory, and the like, are all ones that have been found in many other studies, although not necessarily in the form the more precise detailed description gives. The predominance of Verbal factors should be noted, since their predominance shows it is in this region that the Stanford-Binet is most heavily weighted. The classification arrived at by factor analysis helps us to grasp what is meant by intelligence when we say that the Stanford-Binet measures intelligence.

Standardization. Using a representative sample of about 4,500 children and adolescents, Terman and Merrill standardized the test. The object of the standardization was to construct scales so that average Intelligence Quotients (IQ's) of 100 were found at each of the age levels covered in the test. Keeping this goal in mind, they tried out in preliminary fashion a much larger variety of tests and items than was ultimately used. Only tests that met certain standards were included in the scale.

A child now taking the test could be compared with the results from this standardization sample. If he behaved on the test like an average child of his particular chronological age group, he would receive an IQ of 100; if he showed a performance inferior to that of his standardization peers, he would earn an IQ lower than 100; if he exceeded his peers, he would receive an IQ higher than 100. Thus, an IQ of 100 or 70 or 90 or 110 or 130 each has the same meaning at different age levels. How the quotient is actually derived will be mentioned in a moment.

Mental age. Each test successfully completed earns for the subject a certain number of months of mental age credits, with the maximum possible for any one year being twelve. Some tests, with easier and harder items spread over several age levels, can gain credit for the subject at more than one age level, depending on the percentage of children in the standardization sample who passed a definite number of items. A test which requires the detection of verbal absurdities is credited not only at age level nine if three of the items are answered correctly, but also at age 12 if all four of the items are answered correctly.

The average performance of subjects of the standardization group of a given chronological age provided the standard for mental age scores; the average child ten years old would have an MA of ten years. Passing all the tests up to and including the tenth year and failing all tests beyond this point give that child a mental age of ten years. Generally, success and failure are not so sharply separated; a few easier tests are failed and a few harder tests passed so that it would be more typical for a mental age of ten years to be based on failing, say, five tests below that age and succeeding on five above that age. The same mental age is obtained since each test counts equally for two months of mental age. Other children might similarly earn mental ages of five years six months, eight years three months, 15 years 11 months, and so on.

Derivation and distribution of the IQ. The mental age gives an absolute measure of intelligence, irrespective of the age of the child concerned. In contrast, the IQ gives an index of relative brightness or dullness in comparison with children of similar chronological age. A child might have a mental age of eight years but be six years of age. Another child also might have a mental age of eight but be ten years of age. The formula for calculating the index is MA/CA $\times$ 100 = IQ. In other words, the chronological age of the child translated into months is derived, and this chronological age value is divided into the total of the mental age month credits accumulated on the Stanford-Binet. Multiplying by 100 merely clears the obtained value of the decimal point, nothing more. Three examples below illustrate this calculation.

	John	Bill	Ed
Chronological Age (months)	37	65	96
Mental Age (months)	37	57	126
	$37 \div 37 = 1.00$	$57 \div 65 = 0.81$	$126 \div 96 = 1.31$

Clearing of the decimal points gives IQ's respectively of 100, 81, and 131.

The question now arises as to the meaning of these IQ's. Of course, to a person who uses the results of the Stanford-Binet testing in his daily work, such as a remedial teacher or school psychologist, the IQ itself numerically expressed has a direct meaning, especially when this value is supplemented with other information about the child. Thus, knowing that an IQ is 67, 89, 103, 120, or 157 is, in itself, meaningful quite apart from any other interpretation. Most of us, however, would find it impossible to give each of these IQ's a precise meaning. We could refer to John, Bill, and Ed as "average," "less than average," and considerably "above average" in IQ. But these are terms which do not necessarily have commonly understood meanings. What we need is some generally agreed-upon classification. One is presented in Table 22.

TABLE 22

DISTRIBUTION OF REVISED STANFORD-BINET IQ'S OF THE
TERMAN-MERRILL STANDARDIZATION SAMPLE *

IQ	N	Per Cent	Classification
160–169	1	0.03	Very superior
150–159	6	0.2	
140–149	32	1.1	
130–139	89	3.1	Superior
120–129	239	8.2	
110–119	524	18.1	High average
100–109	685	23.5	Normal or average
90–99	667	23.0	
80–89	422	14.5	Low average
70–79	164	5.6	Borderline defective
60–69	57	2.0	Mentally defective
50–59	12	0.4	
40–49	6	0.2	
30–39	1	0.03	

* From Merrill (58). Copyright 1938 by American Psychological Association, and published with permission.

Table 22 gives for various IQ levels, grouped by 10 point intervals, the number of cases in the 1937 standardization sample, the per cent of cases of the total sample falling in this group, and the verbal classification for each group suggested by Merrill (58). Inspection of the table will reveal that the total distribution of scores is approximately normal (bell-shaped). If the distribution of scores in the table were graphed, there would be a high point of IQ in the normal or average classification and on both sides IQ's would decrease symmetrically in such fashion as to give the impression of a bell shape. This is hardly surprising since the test was constructed by selection and rejection of items so that the scores would show this so-called normal distribution.

It will be noted that many of the children had IQ's in the so-called high average, average, and low average range. In fact, IQ's 80 to 120, those in the three groups, include 79 per cent of the cases. From this high point there is a gradual falling-off in number of cases. Between the "average" groups and the two extremes were borderline groups called "superior," with 11 per cent, and "borderline defective," with almost 6 per cent. At the extremes, the "very superior" make up a little over 1 per cent of the sample, while about 2.5 per cent were classified as "mentally defective."

This distribution gives us information on the distribution of brightness in the population. Although this distribution was derived from the testing of children, it also is applicable to adults and thus tells us something about the distribution of brightness in the population in general.

Through the information the IQ reveals, we are in a position to compare one individual to another despite differences in age as we did for the three boys a little earlier. If one child is seven and another 13, their IQ's give us indices of relative brightness. We are also in a position to compare an individual to the age group to which he belongs. The IQ permits comparison of a given individual to the norms and placement at a particular point on the curve of intelligence. Thus, we can compare a six-year-old to the general run of six-year-olds through the norms on the test. We are also in a position to compare one group of children to another. For example, we can compare one group of children initially matched to another group thereafter given an enriched accelerated school program and see if the IQ's are different on completion of the training.

This description was introduced in order to explain the derivation and meaning of IQ. Actually in the latest revision of the Stanford-Binet (86) statistical improvements have been introduced in order to remove unequal variability or spread of scores at different ages. These so-called deviation IQ's give a more precise IQ but make the foregoing method of finding it obsolete in practice. Instead, using a table and starting with the chronological age, we find the appropriate mental age and read off the IQ. The old method, however, renders intelligible what is being done despite the fact that the IQ is now found in a different way than dividing months of mental age credit earned by the chronological age of the child.

Constancy of the IQ. As an aspect of intelligence in relation to age, one of the most significant problems is the so-called constancy of the

IQ. The average IQ for each age is, by definition, 100. Tests using the IQ method of interpreting their results are designed to have this outcome. Moreover, they are designed to have the same distribution of IQ's for each age if an IQ of 80, 90, 110, or 120 is to have the same meanings at all ages. Only to the extent that the test constructors are successful in this regard do the IQ's have a constant meaning.

In order for a test of intelligence (or a test of anything else for that matter) to be useful, it must be reliable or stable—it must yield reasonably similar scores on repeated testings. Under ordinary conditions with an adequately reliable instrument, we would expect the average IQ to remain fairly constant provided there were no conditions working on the group to bring about a change. The IQ of an individual child will be less constant than that of a group. The child's environment is more often apt to be relatively constant, but there may be factors which affect it. This, then, becomes the problem of whether, under general circumstances, a given child's IQ remains constant or stable from age to age. We would expect a slight margin of fluctuation since no psychological measuring device yet developed is perfect in its precision. Fluctuations of IQ of both group and individual occur.

Factors intrinsic to the test material affect variability. For example, the test material used at one age may be related little or not at all to that used even on the same test at a different age. This may bring about variability. There may be differences in administrative procedure from age to age. There may be practice effects from repeated administration. There may be shifts in attitude toward taking tests by the children which might affect scores. Negativism, more common at certain ages than at others, might result in a lowered score. These complicating factors are sources of error.

For the investigator it is essential to know about them and to control or allow for them; otherwise he might confuse them with true changes in intelligence. Even if these factors were controlled adequately, we would expect a change of a few IQ points in an individual without assuming it represented a genuine change in functioning intelligence. Under ordinary conditions with an adequate and reliable instrument and with the child's environment remaining fairly constant, we expect some degree of constancy of the IQ. Whether the IQ is or is not constant is a matter of research investigation to be considered in the next section.

Constancy of Intellectual Development

In examining this topic we are viewing the question of the constancy of the IQ and other measures of intellectual development such as MA or even test scores as it relates to growth constancies and changes, not, as in the previous section, with its relation to sources of error of the test instrument or elsewhere. We are now concerned with the nature and extent of constancy of intellectual development over the years as it works out in a sample of children when a stable instrument has been achieved and other sources of error are relatively well controlled.

It will be recalled that tests given in infancy were relatively weak in predicting future intelligence test scores. It will also be remembered that tests given in the preschool years were somewhat more predictive in this respect. In connection with those years, the study by Honzik, Macfarlane, and Allen (36) was described in Chapter 11. It will be remembered that in their study they periodically administered intelligence tests to a group of children for a period of 16 years. Consequently, their findings can now be utilized for information about school-age children. Table 23 presents the correlations between intelli-

TABLE 23

CORRELATION BETWEEN INTELLIGENCE TEST SCORES IN
EARLY AND LATER CHILDHOOD *

Age	Correlation with Stanford-Binet, Age 14
2	0.21
3	0.35
4	0.54
6	0.67
8	0.85
9	0.87
10	0.87
12	0.92

* Adapted from Honzik et al. (36). Copyright 1948 by the Journal of Experimental Education, and published with permission.

gence test scores obtained at age 14 with those at earlier ages. The trend toward increased degree of relationship as the children become older is very apparent. The relationship becomes relatively stable at the older ages. Along with increasing age the interval between the first and second testings also shortens, which may also serve to raise the correlation. As they indicate, predictions are better over short periods and become increasingly predictive after the preschool years. Moreover, as other data show (not reported in the table), tests given during this period are relatively good predictors of intellectual status in early adulthood at age 18. For example, tests given at eight years of age or later tend to correlate about 0.72 with those obtained at age 18.

Another source of possible changes in test scores are contained in the data. As age increases, the constant age, to which it is compared, decreases. It may be that the increases in correlation are a function only of the decreases in interval and that if the age comparison was held to some constant length, another interpretation would have to be made.

Their results at a constant three-year interval are reported in Table 24. Each entry is based on the lapse of three years—ages two and five,

TABLE 24

RETEST CORRELATIONS AT THREE-YEAR INTERVALS *

Ages Compared	Correlation
2 × 5	0.32
3 × 6	0.57
4 × 7	0.59
5 × 8	0.70
7 × 10	0.78
9 × 12(13)	0.85

* From Honzik et al. (36). Copyright 1948 by the *Journal of Experimental Education,* and published with permission.

three and six, and so on, up to nine and twelve. The correlations again show a progressive increase with age, showing that the increases reported earlier were not due merely to shorter intervals.

Many other studies find substantially similar results (44). It would appear that there is considerable variability during infancy and that gradually the relationship becomes more stable so that by the age of six or thereabouts there is a relatively high correlation from year to year and over still longer periods. For groups, constancy of intellectual development within certain limits seems established.

It is also possible to examine constancy of intellectual development of individual children through consideration of changes in IQ. In the Honzik study (36) the extent of changes in IQ for the age period six to 18 years was analyzed. The IQ's of almost 60 per cent changed 15 or more points, the IQ's of a third of the group changed 20 or more points, and nine per cent changed 30 or more points. In 15 per cent of the group, the IQ changed less than 10 points over these same years. Using statistical techniques, the nature of which need not concern us, Honzik and her associates demonstrate that a prediction based on a single test administration at age six would be wrong by as much as 20 IQ points in one child out of three by the time he reached the age of 18 years. Variability of this magnitude should make us cautious concerning putting too much faith in the constancy of the IQ's of individual children.   Nothing has been said about the reasons for this variability except the sources of error considered earlier.   Variation that can be attributed to other psychological factors will be considered later.

The Curve of Intellectual Growth

The median performance of large samples of children will show a steady improvement in intelligence test scores with increasing chronological age.   Moreover, there is agreement that intelligence increases to some age beyond childhood before leveling-off.   This increase and an ultimate leveling-off are found in all research investigations on this point.   But the shape of the curve of increase and the age wherein the leveling-off takes place are a matter of disagreement.

There are various ways of presenting the curve of intellectual growth. Although there is not complete agreement on this point, conceiving it to resemble a logarithmic function has much to recommend it (such as, 4).   This form is claimed by Gesell (19) and others to represent the growth of intelligence.   This is a curve that is negatively accelerated; that is, it shows a rapid rise at first and then a slower rise thereafter. This curve implies that intellectual growth takes place at the younger ages very rapidly and then, as age increases, more and more slowly. Intellectual growth is assumed to increase until about 20 years of age where it levels off.   It is important to note that this form of curve is inferred from performance on tests that sample a variety of intellectual abilities.   By summation into one curve the unity of intellectual factors is tacitly accepted.   It may be that there are actually various curves with different rates of growth for different abilities.

Development Changes in the Organization of Intelligence

The relative failure of infancy tests of intelligence to predict what intelligence will be at preschool and school ages suggests the possibility that "intelligence," despite its considerable degree of unity, has a somewhat different composition at different ages.   In other words, although we may speak of intelligence, thus implying some sort of unity, it may be that it is a series of closely related developing functions.   If evidence can be cited about differences in intelligence, other than amount, at different ages, it may be more correct to speak of intellectual processes rather than of intelligence in the singular in this context.   It will be remembered that this was the position taken by Piaget.   Also the discussion of the organization of intelligence at the preschool age indicated an emerging factor concerned with manipulation of symbols.

Hofstaetter's analysis (33) of Bayley's data (3) showed that this factor accounts in considerable measure for the intellectual processes of the older child.

It might be thought at first that these findings on a changing organization of intellectual processes are contradicted by those that Jones found from his factor analysis of Stanford-Binet scores and the other evidence reported in the earlier section devoted to these scales. Jones (45), however, used the data of only one year's standardization group, the 13-year-old group. In the perspective of the age sweep now being considered, his results are an analysis of what was referred to as manipulation of symbols in the Hofstaetter study. His results also serve to remind us that not all intellectual processes in these later years of childhood are symbol manipulation alone, as a re-examination of the description of his factors will show.

The Space factor, the Closure factor, and the Carefulness factor that Jones found do not seem to involve manipulation of symbols, at least to the extent that the Verbal factors do. The Verbal factors, the Memory factors, and the Reasoning factors do seem to involve manipulation of symbols directly and avowedly. Jones's study, then, is in a sense a corroboration of that of Hofstaetter's, but also a corrective to the idea that intelligence in these years is only a matter of manipulation of symbols. Hofstaetter himself accepts the fact that limitations in the data made Factor III, or manipulation of symbols, appear to be of a unitary nature. This implies that he would not be surprised to see it broken down into other factors, some closely related to manipulation of symbols and some not so closely related. This factor represents what most tests of intelligence are designed to measure. Manipulation of symbols is still a convenient summary of the third phase of the development of the intellectual processes.

The probability of changes in the organization of intellectual processes with growth seems established. As Bayley (5) has expressed it, there is no reason to continue to think of intelligence as an "integrated" or "simple" entity growing "by steady accretions." Rather, there are "developing functions" which form a hierarchy with the more complex resting upon maturation of simpler functions.

There is considerable evidence (2) that with increase in age there is a trend toward increasing differentiation of the abilities making up intelligence. As the child grows older a more general ability in children becomes a group of relatively independent abilities in adults.

It may well be that a general factor is more important at younger ages and specialized factors at later ages. To typify these specialized factors of a later age, Thurstone's findings should be presented using tests he developed. Thurstone (87) summarized those he considered most important and mutually exclusive. The eight factors are (1) verbal comprehension; (2) word fluency; (3) numerical ability; (4) spatial (ability to analyze objects in space); (5) memory; (6) induction (discovering principles or rules); (7) deduction (applying principles or rules); and (8) flexibility and speed of closure (facility in sizing up a problem and moving from less to more promising problem solutions). The intimate relation of these factors to the earlier discussions of perception, language, and conceptualization is apparent.

It would seem that the views of the nature of the intelligence expressed by Spearman with emphasis on a general factor, by Thurstone with emphasis on multiple factors, and by Piaget with emphasis on its changing composition are not incompatible. Each fastened on an important aspect, but intelligence broadly conceived, embraces all three. There are general and specialized factors and changes in composition with age.

Factors Influencing the Growth of Intelligence

Factors that impede or accelerate the growth of intelligence need examination. Those to be considered are the effects of heredity, schooling, socio-economic status, and personality and emotion.

The effect of heredity. Children are born with differing potentialities for intellectual development. Just as individuals are not born with other aspects of their physique and person equal one to the other, so too intellectual functioning has a biological substratum. There is no doubt also that all degrees of intellectual ability exist in children whose environment is neither bad enough to retard development nor so superior as to accelerate development. The very existence of mental retardation, in spite of a stimulating environment, and the presence of the genius in spite of a barren environment stand witness to this undeniable fact. Individual differences due to constitutional factors cannot be denied.

There is a natural endowment unfolding maturationally which sets the limits of the adequacy of intellectual functioning. The maturation process is hindered or helped by the wealth or poverty of stimulation in the environment during the early years. This effect of stimulation produces differential learning. Hence, we are here concerned with the relative influence of various kinds of learning on the process of the maturation of intelligence. The influence of environmental alterations must be examined against the background of this genetic substratum.

The effect of schooling. The problem of social deprivation from the influence of institutionalization has already been examined in an earlier chapter. In contrast, the present problem is concerned with attempts to improve intellectual status of relatively nondeprived children.

The study of the effect of schooling on intellectual growth has produced considerable controversy. Some responsible investigators have interpreted their results as demonstrating that IQ changes are a function of some form of enrichment in schooling; other equally responsible investigators and critics have denied this. Consequently, the effects of schooling on intellectual development will be examined in greater detail than would have been the case if the results of research pointed in one general direction and the task was simply to choose illustrative representative findings with which to convey to the reader the present status of the problem.

It was child psychologists at the University of Iowa Child Welfare Station who championed the view that there was a positive effect on intellectual development from certain schooling or other enriching experiences. Their thesis is that intelligence is not static; it is a phenomenon of development showing growth changes due to learning experiences. They claimed that it was possible to increase permanently the intellectual level of young children by providing stimulating environments. Their studies of children exposed to preschool training (94), mentally retarded children exposed to enrichment through contact with older, brighter (but still mentally retarded) girls (80), and children placed in superior foster homes (81) are illustrative of their varied efforts. In general, they found a tendency for the IQ to increase in the special "enriched" environment.

The preschool offers unique opportunities for the study of the effect of a particular environment. Unlike grade school that nearly everyone attends, it is possible to find two groups that may reasonably be matched, one attending preschool, the other not. This advantage in a particular age group accounts for its popularity in research along these lines. However, the studies involving presumably matched groups of preschool attenders and nonattenders have been so severely criticized as being inadequately matched that the data chosen for discussion concern a group of preschool children tested on several occasions. This means that instead of having a separate control group, the children served as their own controls by being tested more than once.

In a summarization of the effects of preschool attendance upon IQ, Wellmann (92) presents data on children who were tested and retested in the fall and spring for one or more years. The dates of the tests were so arranged that the intervals between fall and spring and spring and fall were comparable. This is important because the interval between fall and spring is the preschool interval, whereas the interval between spring and fall (the summer vacation period) is the nonpreschool interval (although it does contain some weeks of preschool attendance since the school year is longer than six months). The problem, then, is a comparison of IQ's of children after attending preschool to their IQ's after a period of nonattendance at preschool. If their special environment made no difference, their IQ's should not differ appreciably between those obtained after a period of preschool or after a period without this preschool. The data for 67 children, who attended preschool three consecutive years, will be reported as a basis for exposition and discussion.

Table 25 presents the IQ's obtained in fall and spring over the three

TABLE 25

IQ CHANGES OVER A THREE-YEAR PERIOD OF PRESCHOOL ATTENDANCE *

Item	Year	Fall	Spring	Change
IQ, points	First	116.6	124.3	+7.7
C.A., months	First	31.7	37.7	6.0
IQ, points	Second	123.7	128.0	+4.3
C.A., months	Second	45.2	51.0	5.8
IQ, points	Third	125.4	127.1	+1.7
C.A., months	Third	58.1	63.9	5.8

* From Wellmann (92). Copyright 1940 by the National Society for the Study of Education, and published with permission.

years. It shows that during the first year of preschool attendance the children gained 7.7 IQ points, then over the summer lost 0.6 points (found by subtracting the IQ obtained in the fall of the second year from the IQ at the end or spring of the first year); during the second year gained 4.3 points and over the second summer lost 2.6; and over the third year gained 1.7 points. The over-all gain from the first fall to the third spring was 10.5 points. The hypothesis of the enriching effect of the preschool seems to be borne out. After attendance, the children gained IQ; after nonattendance, they lost, although not as much as they had previously gained. Moreover, this alternative process continued over three years.

A more detailed summary involving many more children might have been presented (93), although not involving as many intervals of attendance and nonattendance. Substantially similar results were obtained. Factors examined as possibly accounting for the results were the revision of the test used, testing conditions, bias of examiners, and certain measured parental characteristics. These did not appear to explain the differences found during times of attendance and non-attendance.

It is manifestly impossible to review here the plethora of critical articles which came forth shortly after the various reports appeared, alleging a positive effect on IQ from stimulating environment. We shall utilize only one critic's comments, that of McHugh (54), who summarized the criticisms of McNemar (55, 56) and Goodenough (23, 24, 25, 27) among others. He writes as follows:

> These writers have criticised the Iowa studies in the following major respects: (1) Failure to present the mental development of the same individual from age to age, and presentation of average I.Q. of rapidly diminishing or changing groups, thus ignoring selective factors operating. (2) No consideration given influence of hereditary factors in accounting for individual differences from group to group. (3) Changing tests without keeping separate records of children given one or the other. (4) Vagueness in reporting the selection of groups under consideration. (5) Errors in tabulation. (6) Failure to make mention of rapport factors which might have operated to depress the initial I.Q. (7) Use of incorrect or inadequate methods to determine statistical significance of obtained differences. (8) No account taken of tendency of re-test measurements to show regression towards the mean of the population with the result that artifactual changes have been attributed to the effect of the environment. (9) Frequent positive conclusions without foundation in facts reported in the studies. (10) The acceptance of the hypothesis "That intelligence tests given to infants and young children have the same predictive value for later mental development as those given after school age." (11) Overlooking the possibility of systematic error in testing as a result of the examiner's knowledge of previous test results for individual children and for the group (54, 3–4).[3]

In the opinion of the writer most of these criticisms do not apply to the particular data reported here. These criticisms were often well founded and applicable to one or another study that emanated from the University of Iowa during these years. It is the previous evidence of Wellmann that concerns us at the moment. Using the same numbers as McHugh's criticisms, we may argue that: (1) They did use the same individuals from age to age. (2) The same group was used, thus ruling out hereditary factors. (3) The tests for all children at a given age were the same. (4) There is a certain vagueness in reporting the nature of the group, thereby weakening the strength of the evidence somewhat. (5) There is no evidence of errors of tabulation for this group. (6) It is difficult to see why, if rapport accounted for the re-

---

[3] From McHugh (54). Copyright 1943 by The American Psychological Association, and published with permission.

sults, there would be this alternation of greater or less gain coincident with attendance and nonattendance. (7) They do not report statistical tests but calculations would show them to be significant. (8) Regression toward the mean does not apply in these reversible shifts. (9) Conclusion seems to stem from the findings. (10) Infant tests were not included. (11) There may have been systematic error based on the knowledge of previous test results, but this is a possibility in the great majority of studies.

Some studies, other than those performed at the Iowa Child Welfare Station, support the general findings of the increase in IQ under a supposedly enriching environment; others do not, for example, Olson and Hughes (*64*), Page (*65*), and Schott (*77*). In the Olson and Hughes study, in which they found nursery school children from privileged backgrounds did not significantly differ in their intellectual growth from a matched sample of nonnursery school children, they offer an explanation that shows that their results do not necessarily contradict the Iowa studies. They suggest that the home background of the children they studied was already of such a nature that the nursery school could add little to it. There is the suggestion in the Iowa data that the children of highest initial IQ were least affected by their nursery school experience. Their suggestion that the "enrichment," which in this instance failed to enrich their subject's backgrounds, is in keeping with the Iowa position.

Still other "non-Iowa" studies not directly concerned with the preschool situation seem to show the positive effect of a stimulating environment which might be mentioned at this point. These include studies of children who have migrated. Klineberg (*49*) in an intensive investigation of Negro intelligence, found that the longer the children lived in New York City, the higher was the IQ. Since the subjects had come originally from the South, it seemed that the improved educational opportunities in New York City helped to account for this higher IQ. The alternative explanation that some factor was causing less and less intelligent children to migrate year-by-year can be rejected as implausible.

In general, there is today comparatively calm acceptance of the finding that preschool attendance may bring about some increased ability in intellectual functioning. Originally, exaggerated claims of too sweeping a nature were offered. For example, there is no conclusive, commonly accepted evidence that mentally retarded individuals can be brought to normal functioning by any amount of enriched environmental experience, although this seemed to be the position taken by some of the Iowa investigations.

After a cautious and conservative review of the literature for an authoritative handbook, Jones states, "It is quite reasonable to expect some IQ gains among children released from a static and unstimulating environment, whether this release is provided by a nursery school, a foster home, or other environmental change" (*44*, 682).[4] With this, the writer is in agreement. After all, the claims of gain that are accepted as valid need not be of more than relatively modest proportions. It is contended here that the preschool environment does stimulate intellectual growth as shown in a rise in IQ which represents a true gain and that it is not a chance accompaniment of the testing or of the procedure followed. The findings of the effect of preschool training are in line with behavior-social learning theory. The children exposed to preschool have had thereby more learning opportunities and have profited from them.

The effect of socio-economic status. It has been found that groups of children of higher socio-economic status have a higher level of intelligence than do those of less favored socio-economic status. The higher (or lower) the socio-economic class of the groups, the higher (or lower) their average IQ's on the Stanford-Binet or similar verbal tests (*20, 28, 44*). For example, children from professional homes make higher average scores on verbal intelligence tests than children from homes of unskilled laborers. This has been found so often in a variety of investigations that there seems little doubt that such a relationship exists (*63*).

However, these differences between higher and lower socio-economic groups may be due to nonintellectual factors. Some of these factors serving to depress intelligence test scores among lower socio-economic groups could be greater resistance to taking tests (*44*), the effect of nutritional deficiencies (*67*), differential attitudes toward education (*32*), and suspicion, lack of rapport, and the like. Although any or all of these factors seem reasonable, there is no definitive research to establish the answer conclusively.

An interpretation in terms of differential reinforcement of verbal learning is plausible. Homes of higher socio-economic status probably offer greater opportunities for verbalization than do homes of lower socio-economic status. To put it in a bald fashion, children of higher socio-economic status tend to be taught words; children of lower status tend to be taught things. This, of course, is an overstatement since both groups are exposed to words and things, but in a relative sense the

[4] From Jones (*44*). Copyright 1954 by John Wiley and Sons, and published with permission.

statement seems to have validity. This contention is reinforced by the obvious finding that social-class differences are more pronounced with verbal than with performance materials.

In homes of higher socio-economic status, problems of socialization are handled through words. Consequently, the environment furnished by them is heavily weighted with verbal experiences which the children learn, and in turn they become proficient verbalizers.

This fact, however, has led to an even more serious criticism of most verbal intelligence tests. The question is whether a cultural bias in the direction of differential weighting with items more familiar to the middle- and upper-class children has not created this difference, instead of there being a true difference in intelligence. Perhaps, it is merely that many tests are inappropriate for children of lower status. All investigators of intellectual functioning admit that learning enters intelligence testing, but some claim the material used for this purpose is selected in such a way as to be equally available to all. But this contention has been challenged. In other words, there may be a cultural bias included in the material selected for the intelligence tests.

Many of the items in intelligence tests are apt to be more familiar to middle- and upper-class children than to those of lower status. For example, Davis (12) compares two items from one of the tests he used in studying high and low socio-economic groups. On the first item 78 per cent of the higher group answered correctly, but only 28 per cent of the lower socio-economic group were able to do so. This item required the child to be familiar with the term, "sonata." On the second, the percentage getting it correct was practically identical in the two groups. This item had to do with a "cutting tool."

Davis contends that the first item was more likely to be much more available to the children of the higher status, but the second was subject matter common to all socio-economic groups. He proceeded to amass considerable evidence concerning items which showed socio-economic differentials on a variety of conventional measures of achievement and intelligence. The major research stimulated by the position that there is a cultural bias in much present-day intelligence testing (14) has been subjected to serious criticism (89); thus no conclusion can be reached at this point about the reality of these demonstrated differences in intelligence in different socio-economic groups.

Those objecting to the cultural bias of tests would say this is another source of error in the sense this term was used earlier. Just as a change in score due to practice or to negativism is a source of error, so, too, is the cultural bias of certain or all items of a test a source of error. Those who contend it is not would retort that the usual culture-bound tests, after all, do reflect efficiency of adjustment to the culture for which they are designed.

For example, suppose we are using a test of intelligence (with, it is hoped, other necessary measures of information) to select children who are to go on to higher education. We can understand why children from certain subcultures do not do as well on the conventional intelligence test as they might do under other circumstances when culture-bound items are eliminated. But understanding the reason does not mean these cultural-bound hurdles can be disregarded merely because they are related to culture, provided, as evidence now shows, these conventional intelligence tests do predict academic success in the higher grades. The only satisfactory rebuttal would be for the critics of the conventional tests to produce test materials not only "culture free" but also equally as predictive as the present instruments. As yet, this does not seem to have been done.

The superiority in intelligence-test performance of upper- and middle-class children to that of lower-class children is attributed by some investigators to differences in environmental circumstances rather than to hereditary factors. At present, there is no unequivocal way to decide between these competing contentions. In some measure, certainly both are operative. We can do little to control genetic constitution; we can and should devote attention to finding the most effective environmental variables. The evidence offered in connection with preschool experience would seemingly favor environmental opportunity. Although their social status remained the same, Klineberg's Negro children who moved to neighborhoods with greater educational opportunities improved in intelligence test scores and continued to do so the longer they remained in these neighborhoods.

The effect of personality and emotional factors. At the Fels Research Institute (83) the longitudinal program included testing intelligence at periodic intervals. For a sample of 140 children the researchers had available IQ's from age three through age twelve. It was observed that over the years many of these children showed progressive changes in IQ; some showing a relatively steady increase (up to 40 IQ points) while others showed a similar decrease. It was decided to investigate the relation of these increases and decreases to personality and emotional factors in these children. The 35 children showing the greatest increase in IQ between ages of six and ten and the 35 children with the greatest decreases were isolated into groups and the two groups compared on a variety of measures that might be relevant to their increases or decreases.

The hypothesis investigated was that motivation is a means of increasing or decreasing intelligence test performance. From inspection of case records and without knowledge of IQ gains or losses, ratings were made on a variety of relevant scales. It was found that an accelerated IQ was associated with high independence, aggressiveness, self-initiation, problem solving, anticipation, competitiveness, and scholastic competitiveness. Moreover, the ratings on these scales were highly interrelated, suggesting a common dimension of personality which the investigators choose to call achievement motivation. A high need for achievement seems to be related to accelerated mental growth.

A still further study (48) was done, utilizing the TAT and the Rorschach Ink Blots. The TAT was scored for need for achievement from themes having to do with competition, as well as for themes of curiosity about nature, and for themes of passivity; the Rorschach was scored for aggressive responses on the assumption that aggressive competition was a socially acceptable form of aggressive behavior. The children who showed IQ increases had significantly more achievement imagery based on competition, more themes of curiosity, and fewer themes of passivity than those children showing IQ decreases. Only for boys having an increase in IQ was there a significant greater aggressive imagery on the Rorschach. It seems that high need achievement, curiosity about nature, and nonpassivity are correlated with gain in IQ because they are among those factors that facilitate acquisition of the skills measured by intelligence tests. The investigators caution that other factors are at work in making for IQ increase.

In dealing with individuals (82) they cite cases of some interest. Debilitating anxiety may account for lowered scores. For example, a boy moved from foster home to foster home, was found to have a high anxiety level, until finally he was adopted and had for the first time a stable, secure, human relationship. Thereafter, his intelligence test scores rose. Motivation making for a rise in IQ may be seen in the case of another boy to whom the test situation was a challenging problem to be surmounted for the assurance it gave him; in the same way, his competitive behavior in school, his satisfaction from mastery of school subjects, and his absorption in books, with little dependence on human relationships illustrate similar motivation.

Twice as many girls as boys showed decreases in IQ. Examination of the experiences of many of these girls showed that they had experienced what is called a flight into femininity. Now in their latency period, these girls were approaching the age when they would assume the adult feminine role. Although women's perceptions of their role differ, a considerable proportion find that competition and achievement are of importance only in being more feminine and charming, whereas school attainment (and the taking of intelligence tests) is of little emotional comfort or significance. In the investigators' opinion, a majority of the girls in the descending group could be thus accounted for.

It is a well-established clinical practice to consider the IQ and other means of summarizing intelligence as reflecting accurately the level of ability of the individual to function *at a particular time*. It is recognized that there may be circumstances operating that tend to create a discrepancy between *functioning* and *potential* intelligence. This is especially noticed with emotionally disturbed individuals. It is also operative in normal children faced with especially trying circumstances. This is the case with the Fels boy moved from foster home to foster home whose IQ rose on his being placed in a home where he could develop a secure relationship (pages 519–521).

It is plausible to believe that under certain circumstances, especially those in which the individual is made to feel that he has to function independently, anxiety will adversely affect intelligence. Such, at least, is the conclusion of Sarason and his associates (76) in reviewing the literature. One study (75) showed that test anxiety, as differentiated from more general anxiety, was related significantly and negatively to intellectual performance in high-school students, more so for girls than for boys. General measures of anxiety showed lesser degree, or no relationship to intellectual performance. The intellectual measure selected was that used to provide a measure of ability to get into college—a potent source for arousal of anxiety.

The effect of environmental factors on an individual child. Using the wealth of longitudinal data provided by the Berkeley Growth Study, Bayley (7) concluded that the pattern of intellectual growth in each child was unique. When we examine the child's history, it is often possible to find the reasons for deviation from a constant development of intelligence. Richards (74) studied the course of development of such a boy with emphasis on the relation of intelligence test performance at different ages to the child's life situation during the same period. In other words, there were two streams of data, test scores and a history of the individual's current adjustment at the time of each testing.

Figure 17 shows the child's Stanford-Binet performance at various ages. The mean IQ for all the testings was 124, with individual IQ's fluctuating between 117 and 140. There are four trends in the curve he obtained for IQ's between the ages of three and ten, first a rise of 11 IQ points from age three to four, then a drop of 13 points from five

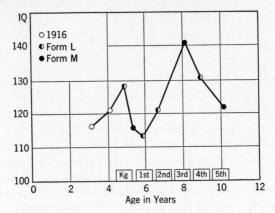

Figure 17. Changes in IQ in an individual child. (From Richards (74). Copyright 1951 by the Society for Research in Child Development, and published with permission.)

to six, a rise again of 25 points from six to eight years, and finally a drop of 18 points from eight to ten years. Space cannot be given to describe all the environmental data geared to these ages which Richards collected. Instead, concentration will be on the rise of 25 points, occurring between six and eight years of age.

The boy, called Bobby James, was studied at the Fels Research Institute, and the already familiar Fels Parent Behavior Scales were used several times throughout the years. Projective test results, including those from the Rorschach and TAT were available. Some pertinent comments about Bobby follow:

Bobby's father was a college graduate with an IQ of 127, and was a business man in moderately good circumstances. His mother had had some college training and had done some secretarial work before marriage. During his first five years, Bobby seemingly led a normal life, perhaps with a greater than usual attachment to the mother although he was also close to the father. The father played with and read to the boy quite frequently. During the period from when he was five to when he was six (immediately preceding the rise in IQ), his father, in addition to active business during the day, started a company which took most of his evenings. Bobby saw less of him but they continued to be congenial.

We now come to the period of age from six to eight when the IQ rose 25 points. In the middle of the second grade he was switched from a teacher who was a stern disciplinarian to one considerably more sympathetic. He continued with her throughout the remaining year and a half of the six to eight period. His father, about the same time, gave up his night work and started spending considerable time with Bobby. Tense and nervous while holding the two jobs, the father now "became a new man," thoughtful and easier to live with. The Fels Parent Behavior

Scales applied to their home during this time showed that the home, always "well-adjusted" and "democratic," now accentuated these characteristics. It was during this period his IQ was 140. Thereafter in the later phase, the home was more severe with less devotion, affection, and sheltering of Bobby.

In the last phase from eight to ten (showing a drop in IQ of 18 points) Bobby's "understanding" teacher gradually became "tired and inactive," culminating in the necessity of having a tumor removed. Bobby, himself, had been promoted to the fourth grade where he had a severe teacher.

In summarizing this history Richards comments on the following points: (1) the situation fluctuated with the rise and fall in IQ; (2) the role of the father fluctuated with the rise and fall in IQ; and (3) in the period where the highest IQ was obtained, the child-centeredness of the home was at its highest.

This instance of a single boy is, of course, only illustrative of a not uncommon finding that shifts in the IQ can be related to shifting environmental circumstances. The evidence shows plausible reasons for the shifts in intelligence, but, as Richards himself clearly indicates, no generalization to other children is possible on the basis of a single case.

Honzik et al. (36), whose study has been referred to several times, found similar correspondences between shifts in circumstances and shifts in IQ. But there are also instances of failure to find related environmental circumstances coincident with shifts in IQ. Honzik and her associates themselves found a considerable proportion of children whose scores remained constant, despite disturbing circumstances. Goodenough and Maurer (26), in a carefully conducted study involving repeated retests, found some individual cases who exhibited IQ changes as great as 20 to 50 points in an eight or nine year span. Yet, careful examination revealed no associated environmental circumstances that could account for such extensive shifts. The extreme shifts just discussed are exceptional, not typical. In the vast majority of children consistency, not inconsistency, of intellectual development is the rule. Emphatically, acceptance of the thesis that personal factors may affect intelligence does not mean that all children faced with unusual variations in their environment react with changed IQ's.

Summary

Physical growth in later childhood proceeds at a somewhat slower pace than it did in earlier years. Individual differences in degree of physical maturity become especially prominent, partly created by a characteristic spurt in growth that occurs sometime during these years but at different ages in different children. Late maturing and early maturing boys of the same age show differential personality traits but by the time they reach adulthood these differences tend to disappear. The results with girls are inconclusive.

During later childhood motor skills continue to develop showing both increases in speed and strength and greater refinement and adeptness. Mental and physical growth are found to have a positive, though relatively slight, relationship. There is some evidence that there is greater specificity of motor learning abilities at age 15 as compared to age ten.

The evidence concerning emotional development in later childhood attests to the importance of social relationship, especially those with one's peers, as instigators to emotions. Greater subtlety in sources of instigation and less overt and bald expressions of emotion are found with the increase in age of the child. During these years anxiety has been demonstrated to have a differential effect on learning according to the complexity of the task.

Cognitive development is visualized by Piaget in terms of the levels of concrete and formal operations. This last level brings the child to a point where there will only be changes in degree, not in level in the years thereafter. Piaget's views on physical causality are examined through characteristic research studies. On the basis of this evidence, and that reported in earlier chapters, a critique is offered emphasizing the finding of a lack of sharp separation of these postulated levels. Levels fail to disappear at an age by which it is supposed they have ceased to operate and rudiments of levels appear before they are expected.

Examination of changes in language skills, in the form of oral and written expression and the acquisition of word meanings, bring out both their complexity and steady growth. Time and space perceptions further illustrate the complexity of the development of cognition in the older child.

Intellectual development receives the greatest attention. Turning first to the nature of intelligence, it is indicated that it is closely related to the understanding, the observing, conceptualizing, and thinking that the child carries on. Intelligence involves the cognitive processes with emphasis on efficiency, scope, and level of difficulty of function that the child exhibits. Moreover, it is an interdependent aspect of personality.

Contrasting views of the nature of intelligence were examined. A general factor theory with specialized factors, and a group factor theory without a general factor were found to disagree on this point, but to agree on the relatively fixed character of intelligence. A third position stressed that the structure of intelligence changed with age. The three positions are not considered as incompatible.

In the sections pertaining to the *Stanford-Binet Intelligence Scale*, a description of the scale and the way it was standardized, the method and meaning of deriving mental age and IQ, and the distribution of the latter in the population were all presented; and the significance of the so-called constancy of the IQ as an aspect of the test instrument was considered.

Intellectual growth over the years of childhood and beyond was discussed in terms of the evidence for this constancy as it relates to growth constancies and changes. Through childhood the curve of intellectual development shows a steady increase with increasing age. That curve, although the evidence is not unequivocal, is conceived as logarithmic in shape.

With growth there are changes in the organization of intellectual processes. The organization of intelligence shows evidence of general and specialized factors and of change in its composition with age.

Factors either impeding or accelerating intellectual growth were examined. The effect of heredity cannot be denied. It results in differing potentialities for intellectual development. Environmental alterations were observed against the background of this genetic substratum. Attendance at preschool produced some increase in intellectual functioning. Socioeconomic status results were found to be equivocal. In emotional and personal factors, both accelerating and inhibiting factors affecting intellectual growth could be discerned. These inhibitions and accelerations were further illustrated by a case study.

For Further Reading

The article by Nancy Bayley, "On the Growth of Intelligence" (5), is a masterly summary of this topic. The lengthy chapter, "The Environment and Mental Development," by Harold E. Jones in *The Manual of Child Psychology*, 2nd Edition (New York: Wiley, 1954), edited by L. Carmichael, is a thorough, painstaking, and conservative review of the topic suggested by the title. Erika Fromm and Lenore D. Hartmann in their *Intelligence: A Dynamic Approach* (New York: Doubleday, 1955) give a stimulating account of how intelligence functions as an aspect of the total personality.

References

1. Abernethy, E. M. Relationships between mental and physical growth. *Monogr. Soc. Res. Child Develpm.*, 1936, 1, No. 7.

2. Avakian, Sonia A. An investigation of trait relationships among six-year-old children. *Genet. Psychol. Monog.*, 1961, 63, 339–394.
3. Bayley, Nancy. Consistency and variability in the growth of intelligence from birth to eighteen years. *J. Genet. Psychol.*, 1949, 75, 165–196.
4. Bayley, Nancy. Development and maturation. In H. Helson (Ed.), *Theoretical foundations of psychology.* New York: Van Nostrand, 1951, 145–199.
5. Bayley, Nancy. On the growth of intelligence. *Amer. Psychologist*, 1955, 10, 805–818.
6. Bayley, Nancy. Growth curves of height and weight by age for boys and girls, scales according to physical maturity. *J. Pediatr.*, 1956, 48, 187–194.
7. Bayley, Nancy. Individual patterns of development. *Child Develpm.*, 1956, 27, 47–75.
8. Carpenter, Aileen. The differential measurement of speed in primary school children. *Child Develpm.*, 1941, 12, 1–7.
9. Castaneda, A., B. R. McCandless, and D. S. Palermo. The Children's Form of the Manifest Anxiety Scale. *Child Develpm.*, 1956, 27, 317–326.
10. Castaneda, A., D. S. Palermo, and B. R. McCandless. Complex learning and performance as a function of anxiety in children and task difficulty. *Child Develpm.*, 1956, 27, 328–332.
11. Cone, Jr., T. E. Secular acceleration of height and biologic maturation in children during the past century. *J. Pediatr.*, 1961, 59, 736–740.
12. Davis, A. *Social class influences upon learning.* Cambridge, Mass.: Harvard University Press, 1948.
13. Deutsche, Jean M. The development of children's concepts of causal relations. *Univ. Minn. Child Welf. Monogr.*, 1937, No. 13.
14. Eels, K., A. Davis, R. J. Havighurst, N. E. Herrick, and R. Tyler. *Intelligence and cultural differences: a study of cultural learning and problem-solving.* Chicago: University of Chicago Press, 1951.
15. England, A. O. Non-structured approach to the study of children's fears. *J. Clin. Psychol.*, 1946, 2, 364–368.
16. Flavell, J. H. *The developmental psychology of Jean Piaget.* Princeton: Van Nostrand, 1963.
17. Flickinger, Alice, and K. J. Rehage. Building time and place concepts. In *Improving the reading of world history.* National Council for Social Studies, Twentieth Yearbook, 1949, 107–116.
18. Fraisse, P. Étude comparée de la perception et de l'estimation de la durée chez les enfants et les adultes. *Enfance*, 1948, 1, 199–211.
19. Gesell, A. *Infancy and human growth.* New York: Macmillan, 1928.
20. Goodenough, Florence L. The relation of the intelligence of preschool children to the occupation of their fathers. *Amer. J. Psychol.*, 1928, 40, 284–294.
21. Goodenough, Florence L. *Anger in young children.* Minneapolis, Minn.: University of Minnesota Press, 1931.
22. Goodenough, Florence L. The development of the reactive process from early childhood to maturity. *J. Exp. Psychol.*, 1935, 18, 431–450.
23. Goodenough, Florence L. Look to the evidence: a critique of recent experiments on raising the IQ. *Educ. Meth.*, 1939, 19, 73–79.
24. Goodenough, Florence L. Can we influence mental growth: a critique of recent experiments. *Educ. Rec.*, 1940, 21, suppl. 13, 120–143.
25. Goodenough, Florence L. New evidence on environmental influence on intelligence. *Yearb. Nat. Soc. Stud. Educ.*, 1940, 39 (I), 307–365.

26. Goodenough, Florence L., and Katherine M. Maurer. The mental growth of children from two to fourteen years: a study of the predictive value of the Minnesota Preschool Scales. *Univ. Minn. Child Welf. Monogr. Ser.*, 1942, No. 19.

27. Goodenough, Florence L., and Katherine M. Maurer. The relative potency of the nursery school and the statistical laboratory in boosting the IQ. *J. Educ. Psychol.*, 1940, 31, 541–549.

28. Haggerty, M. E., and H. B. Nash. Mental capacity of children and paternal occupation. *J. Educ. Psychol.*, 1924, 15, 559–573.

29. Harrell, L. E. A comparison of the development of oral and written languages in school-age children. *Monogr. Soc. Res. Child Develpm.*, 1957, 22, No. 3.

30. Henery, F. M., and G. A. Nelson. Age differences and inter-relationships between skills and learning in gross motor performance of ten- and fifteen-year-old boys. *Res. Quart. Ass. Hlth. Phys. Educ.*, 1956, 27, 162–175.

31. Hicks, J. A., and M. Hayes. Study of the characteristics of 250 junior high school children. *Child Develpm.*, 1938, 9, 219–242.

32. Hieronymus, A. N. A study of social class motivation: relationships between anxiety for education and certain socio-economic and intellectual variables. *J. Educ. Psychol.*, 1951, 42, 193–205.

33. Hofstaetter, P. R. The changing composition of "intelligence": a study in T-technique. *J. Genet. Psychol.*, 1954, 85, 159–164.

34. Holloway, H. D. Reliability of the Children's Manifest Anxiety Scale at the rural third grade level. *J. Educ. Psychol.*, 1959, 49, 193–196.

35. Holloway, H. D. Normative data on the Children's Manifest Anxiety Scale at the rural third grade level. *Child Develpm.*, 1961, 32, 129–134.

36. Honzik, Marjorie P., Jean W. Macfarlane, and Louise Allen. The stability of mental test performance between two and eighteen years. *J. Exp. Educ.*, 1948, 17, 309–324.

37. Huang, I. Children's conception of physical causality: a critical summary. *J. Genet. Psychol.*, 1943, 63, 71–121.

38. Inhelder, Barbel, and J. Piaget. *The growth of logical thinking: from childhood to adolescence.* New York: Basic Books, 1958.

39. Iscoe, I., and Irene Cochran. Some correlates of manifest anxiety in children. *J. Consult. Psychol.*, 1960, 24, 97.

40. Jersild, A. T., and Frances B. Holmes. Children's fears. *Child Develpm. Monogr.*, 1935, No. 20.

41. Jersild, A. T., and Ruth J. Tasch. *Children's interests and what they suggest for education.* New York: Teachers College, Columbia University, 1949.

42. Jersild, A. T., B. Golman, and J. J. Loftus. A comparative study of the worries of children in two school situations. *J. Exp. Educ.*, 1941, 9, 323–326.

43. Jersild, A. T., Frances V. Markey, and Catherine L. Jersild. Children's fears, dreams, wishes, daydreams, likes, dislikes, pleasant and unpleasant memories. *Child Develpm. Monogr.*, 1933, No. 12.

44. Jones, H. E. The environment and mental development. In L. Carmichael (Ed.), *Manual of child psychology* (2nd ed.). New York: Wiley, 1954, 631–696.

45. Jones, L. V. Primary mental abilities in the Stanford-Binet, age 13. *J. Genet. Psychol.*, 1954, 84, 125–147.

46. Jones, Mary C. The later careers of boys who were early—or late—maturing. *Child Develpm.*, 1957, 28, 113–128.

47. Jones, Mary C., and Nancy Bayley. Physical maturing among boys as related to behavior. *J. Educ. Psychol.*, 1950, 41, 129–148.

48. Kagan, J., L. W. Sontag, C. T. Baker, and Virginia L. Nelson. Personality and I.Q. changes. *J. Abnorm. Soc. Psychol.*, 1958, 56, 261–266.

49. Klineberg, O. *Negro intelligence and selective migration.* New York: Columbia University Press, 1935.

50. L'Abate, L. Personality correlates of manifest anxiety in children. *J. Consult. Psychol.*, 1960, 24, 342–348.

51. Lovell, K. A follow-up study of Inhelder and Piaget's "The Growth of Logical Thinking." *Brit. J. Psychol.*, 1961, 52, 153–193.

52. Lovell, K., and A. Slater. The growth of the concept of time: a comparative study. *J. Child. Psychol. Psychiat.*, 1960, 1, 179–190.

53. McCandless, B. R. Rate of development, body build and personality. In C. Shagass, and B. Passamanick (Eds.), *Child development and child psychiatry.* Washington, D. C.: American Psychiatric Association, 1960, 42–57.

54. McHugh, G. Changes in IQ at the public school kindergarten level. *Psychol. Monogr.*, 1943, 55, No. 250.

55. McNemar, Q. A critical examination of the University of Iowa studies of environmental influences upon the IQ. *Psychol. Bull.*, 1940, 37, 63–92.

56. McNemar, Q. More on the Iowa studies. *J. Psychol.*, 1940, 10, 237–240.

57. McNemar, Q. *The revision of the Stanford-Binet Scale: an analysis of the standardization data.* Boston: Houghton Mifflin, 1942.

58. Merrill, Maud A. The significance of IQ's on the Revised Stanford-Binet Scales. *J. Educ. Psychol.*, 1938, 29, 641–651.

59. Metheny, E. Breathing capacity and grip strength of preschool children. *Univ. Iowa Stud. Child Welf.*, 1941, 18, No. 2.

60. Michael, W. B., W. S. Zimmerman, and J. P. Guilford. An investigation of the nature of the spatial-relations and visualization factors in two school samples. *Educ. Psychol. Measmt*, 1951, 11, 561–577.

61. Mogar, M. Children's causal reasoning about natural phenomena. *Child Develpm.*, 1960, 31, 59–65.

62. Nass, M. L. The effects of three variables on children's concepts of physical causality. *J. Abnorm. Soc. Psychol.*, 1956, 53, 191–196.

63. Neff, W. S. Socioeconomic status and intelligence: a critical survey. *Psychol. Bull.*, 1938, 35, 727–757.

64. Olson, W. C., and R. O. Hughes. Growth of the child as a whole. In R. G. Barker *et al.* (Eds.), *Child behavior and development.* New York: McGraw-Hill, 1943, 199–208.

65. Page, J. D. The effect of nursery school attendance upon subsequent IQ. *J. Psychol.*, 1940, 10, 221–230.

66. Palermo, D. S., A. Castaneda, and B. R. McCandless. The relationship of anxiety in children to performance in a complex learning task. *Child Develpm.*, 1956, 27, 333–338.

67. Pasamanick, B. A comparative study of the behavorial development of Negro infants. *J. Genet. Psychol.*, 1946, 69, 3–44.

68. Paterson, D. G. *Physique and intellect.* New York: Century, 1930.

69. Piaget, J. *The child's conception of physical causality.* New York: Harcourt, Brace, 1930.

70. Piaget, J. *Psychology of intelligence.* Paterson: Littlefield, Adams, 1950.

71. Piaget, J. The development of time concepts in the child. In P. H. Hoch,

and J. Zubin (Eds.), *Psychopathology of childhood.* New York: Grune & Stratton, 1955, 34–44.

72. Pratt, K. C.   A study of "fears" of rural children.   *J. Genet. Psychol.,* 1945, 67, 179–194.

73. Rapaport, D. with collaboration of R. Schafer and M. Gill.   Manual of diagnostic psychological testing: 1. Diagnostic testing of intelligence and concept formation.   *Publ. Josiah Macy, Jr., Found. Rev. Ser.,* 1944, 2, No. 2.

74. Richards, T. W.   Mental test performance as a reflection of the child's current life situation: a methodological study.   *Child Develpm.,* 1951, 22, 221–233.

75. Sarason, I. G.   Test anxiety and intellectual performance.   *J. Abnorm. Soc. Psychol.,* 1963, 66, 73–75.

76. Sarason, S. B. *et al.*   *Anxiety in elementary school children: a report of research.*   New York: Wiley, 1960.

77. Schott, E. L.   IQ changes in foster home children.   *J. Appl. Psychol.,* 1937, 21, 107–112.

78. Shuttleworth, F. K.   The physical and mental growth of girls and boys age six to nineteen in relation to age at maximum growth.   *Monogr. Soc. Res. Child Develpm.,* 1939, 4, No. 3.

79. Shuttleworth, F. K.   The adolescent period: a graphic atlas.   *Monogr. Soc. Res. Child Develpm.,* 1949, No. 14.

80. Skeels, H. M., and H. M. Dye.   A study of the effects of differential stimulation in mentally retarded children.   *Proc. Amer. Assoc. Ment. Def.,* 1939, 44, 114–136.

81. Skodak, Marie, and H. M. Skeels.   A final follow-up study of one hundred adopted children.   *J. Genet. Psychol.,* 1949, 75, 85–125.

82. Sontag, L. W., C. T. Baker, and Virginia Nelson.   Personality as a determinant of performance.   *Amer. J. Orthopsychiat.,* 1955, 25, 555–562.

83. Sontag, L. W., C. T. Baker, and Virginia L. Nelson.   Mental growth and personality development: a longitudinal study.   *Monogr. Soc. Res. Child Develpm.,* 1958, 23, No. 2.

84. Spearman, C. E.   *The abilities of man.*   New York: Macmillan, 1927.

85. Terman, L. M., and Maud A. Merrill.   *Measuring intelligence: a guide to the administration of the new revised Stanford-Binet test of intelligence.*   Boston: Houghton Mifflin, 1937.

86. Terman, L. M., and Maud A. Merrill.   *Stanford-Binet Intelligence Scale: Manual for the third revision, Form L-M.*   Boston: Houghton Mifflin, 1960.

87. Thurstone, L. L.   Theories of intelligence.   *Sci. Monthly,* 1946, 62, 101–112.

88. Thurstone, L. L., and L. Ackerson.   The mental growth curve for the Binet tests.   *J. Educ. Psychol.,* 1929, 20, 569–583.

89. Tyler, F. T.   Comments on the correlational analysis reported in *Intelligence and Cultural Differences.*   *J. Educ. Psychol.,* 1953, 44, 288–295.

90. Waite, R. R., S. B. Sarason, J. J. Lighthall, and K. S. Davidson.   A study of anxiety and learning in children.   *J. Abnorm. Soc. Psychol.,* 1958, 57, 267–270.

91. Watson, E. H., and G. H. Lowrey.   *Growth and development of children.*   Chicago: Year Book Publishers, 1954.

92. Wellmann, Beth L.   Iowa studies on the effects of schooling.   *Yearb. Nat. Soc. Stud. Educ.,* 1940, 39 (II), 377–399.

93. Wellmann, Beth L.   IQ changes of preschool and nonpreschool groups during

the preschool years: a summary of the literature. *J. Psychol.*, 1945, 20, 347–368.

94. Wellmann, Beth L., and E. L. Pegram, Binet IQ changes of orphanage preschool children: a reanalysis. *J. Genet. Psychol.*, 1944, 65, 239–263.

95. Werner, H., and Edith Kaplan. Development of word meaning through verbal context: an experimental study. *J. Psychol.*, 1950, 29, 251–257.

96. Wirt, R. D., and W. F. Broen. The relation of the Children's Manifest Anxiety Scale to the concept of anxiety as used in the clinic. *J. Consult. Psychol.*, 1956, 20, 482.

97. Woodworth, R. S. *Psychology* (4th ed.). New York: Holt, 1940.

16

Parental Influences, Behavior Tendencies, and the Self

In the older child the same factors enter into psychosocial develop-ment as in the infant and the younger child. For this reason we shall examine this phase of later childhood through the same categories employed in earlier parts of this book. In this chapter we shall consider the effects of parental influences, behavior tendencies, and the self and social perception. Because of the importance of the older child's interaction with his peers and his experiences in a school setting, these subjects are deferred until the next chapter which is devoted to them exclusively.

Parental influences

The widening social scene to which the older child is exposed renders parental influence less crucial than it is with younger children. Nevertheless, as expressed in attitudes and patterns, it requires some attention. The first matter to be considered is consistency of maternal attitudes. This will be followed by some representative findings on parental attitudes and family patterns.

Consistency of Maternal Attitudes

Consistency of maternal attitudes poses the problem of whether mothers behave differently toward older children from the way they behaved toward them when they were younger. As might be expected, both similarities and differences have been found.

In studying this problem, Schaefer and Bayley (*110*) utilized the longitudinal Berkeley Growth Study sample. Observational data had been collected in the research center during the child's first three years. Interview data in the child's home were obtained when he was between nine and fourteen. The framework for the analysis was the circumplex model and procedure described in Chapter 12. It will be recalled that this resulted in the isolation of the two maternal dimensions, love *vs.* hostility (amount of affection displayed) and autonomy *vs.* control (degree of restrictiveness). The data for love *vs.* hostility in infancy correlated .68 with that at preadolescence. This represents a considerable degree of consistency of affection. Those mothers who were relatively more affectionate toward their infants were also more affectionate toward them as preadolescents, whereas those who were initially less affectionate, tended to remain less affectionate.

When the many experiences of the intervening years which would blur the relationship are taken into consideration, a remarkable degree of consistency of attitude emerges. Other factors, however, might account for differences. For example, different measures were used: in the earlier period, infant observation and later, parental interview. Moreover, there were different settings: earlier, the research center and later, the child's home. The substantial correlation in affection might have been even higher had not these procedural differences occurred.

These factors are actually mentioned for another reason. The second major finding of the Schaefer and Bayley analysis was an insignificant correlation between restrictiveness, or autonomy *vs.* control, at the two age levels. This correlation coefficient may reflect a true lack of relationship between maternal attitudes of restrictiveness at the two ages or it may be that these differences affected restrictiveness more than affection. The investigators chose to accept the former alternative.

They concluded that there were greater changes over time in autonomy *vs.* control than in love *vs.* hostility. On one dimension, love *vs.* hostility, the mothers were consistent; on the other dimension, autonomy *vs.* control, they were inconsistent. It is plausible to believe that maternal restrictiveness would change over time. The amount of restrictiveness a young child needs, say at three, is more or less constant one child to the next; that required by a fourteen-year-old varies according to his individual degree of maturity. Some preadolescents would need almost as much supervision and restriction as they did when much younger; others would not. Maternal affection, on the other hand, is less likely to change with time.

Unequivocal choice between these alternative explanations is impossible from the data available. The writer is inclined to accept tentatively the interpretation that as the children became older there was maternal consistency in affection and inconsistency, or possibly flexibility, in restrictiveness. In the same mother, some attitudes are consistent, others are flexible or inconsistent as the child grows older.

Parental Attitudes and Family Patterns

The familiar family pattern approach to the study of parent-child relationship was followed by Peck (*101*). Thirty-four children, equally divided as to boys and girls, were tested and retested over the years from 10 to 18. The measures included the Rorschach, a sentence completion test, self-ratings, sociometric ratings, and intelligence tests. Interview data and teacher ratings of the children were also available. These various measures were intercorrelated and factor analyzed, and trait clusters, or dimensions, were found. The most significant dimensions of child personality structure obtained were *ego strength* (emotional maturity, altruistic concern, personality integration, rationality of behavior, accuracy of self- and social perception); *superego strength* (behavior guiding conscience); *friendliness* (absence of observable hostility); and *hostility-guilt* (guilt about inner impulses, inner feelings of hostility toward mother, and lack of acceptance of father).

Without knowledge of these results, an independent research team studied the parents of the 34 children with emphasis on family interactions. Data of ten family variables eventuated. These variables were also intercorrelated and factor analyzed. Five of the dimensions of family interaction found were *consistency* (regularity, consistency of control, and family participation in common); *democracy* (child sharing in decisions); *mutual trust and approval* (good mother-father relation, parental trust of child, child's willingness to share confidences, parental approval); and *severity-leniency* (severity of parental control). The next step was the logical one of studying the interrelations of the dimensions of personality structure of the children with those of family interaction.

High ego strength in children was positively related to a family life high both in consistency and trust. High superego strength, not unrelated to ego strength itself ($r = .48$), insofar as it was a separate measure, was more related to high familial consistency than to high trust. Friendliness in children was most influenced by both high familial trust and high democracy. Lack of hostility-guilt was most related to high democracy and trust, and a lack of severity. Peck interprets the reverse, or the hostility-guilt end of this last dimension, as being the setting for a hostile, but unresolved dependent Oedipal complex. A nondemocratic (severely autocratic) untrusting and severe family serves to generate this complex in children.

The general climate of the home, the emotional relationships and disciplinary patterns of the family, then, seem to be related to the older child's personality characteristics. As with the infant and the younger child, the precise etiological sequence—family patterns influencing the child or the children at least helping to create the family pattern—is difficult to specify. Certainly what these children experienced in living with their parents is related to the personality characteristics they exhibit. With somewhat less assurance we can say that the child's personality reflects family influences to a greater degree than the family reflects the influence of his personality.

Studies directed not to the over-all relationship of the family and the personality of the older child, but to more specific problems have been conducted. Those that follow concern the relationship between (a) maternal contentment-discontentment, on the one hand, and the child's intellectual and emotional freedom and anxiety control, on the other; (b) maternal and child anxiety; and (c) attitudes of parents and the forms of emotional disturbance in their children. In the last mentioned relationship the extremely significant role of the father is again made evident.

Altman (3), in the course of a more extensive investigation, related the contentment-discontentment of mothers of boys and girls aged eight to ten to their children's characteristics and found a positive relationship. The measures for each of the mothers were based on a rating by a psychiatrist of the happiness of the mother's own childhood and her satisfaction with her marriage and her husband. Ten mothers at each extreme on these dimensions were selected for further study. The Rorschach Ink Blot Examination was given to the children and measures were derived from it for intellectual freedom (originality, adaptability, and vigor); emotional freedom (spontaneity and stability); and anxiety control (freedom from conflict and tension, high frustration tolerance, and freedom from guilt). Statistically significant differences were found in the characteristics of the children of the mothers of the two extreme groups. The children of the "contented" mothers were found to show significantly greater intellectual and emotional freedom and better anxiety control.

The hypothesis that degree of anxiety in children might be related to the degree of anxiety in their parents has been investigated by Adams and Sarason (1). Four anxiety scales, including the Test Anxiety Scale, were administered to male and female high school students and to their mothers and fathers. For girls and their mothers there was a consistent positive correlation obtained on all four scales. For the boys' scores inconsistent and lower relationships were found. Their scores were related more to their mothers' than to their fathers'. Very little relation was found between their scores and those of their fathers. It would seem that to some extent anxiety is acquired through home experiences, and that mothers play a more influential role in this respect than fathers, and that they influence their daughters more than their sons.

The attitudes of mothers and fathers and the particular form of maladjustment of disturbed children has been extensively investigated by a team of research workers led by Becker and Peterson (*15, 102, 103*). They also considered a subsidiary problem, the exploration of differences in child behavior and parental attitude relationships when younger and older children within the age range were compared. One sample (*102*) was between five and six, and the other between six and twelve years of age (*15, 103*). A guiding hypothesis throughout the series of studies was that the influence of the father was at least as intimately related as that of the mother to the occurrence and form of maladjustive tendencies in the child.

The investigators drew subjects from a clinic for children whose patients had been referred to it because of one or another form of behavior problems and from schools to obtain a normal, nonclinic population. For the mothers and fathers of the younger children, an adaptation of the familiar interview used in the Sears "pattern" study was conducted. A checklist of the children's problems was completed by teachers and by parents. Factor analysis of the responses to the problem check list showed the first two factors to be concerned with (*a*) conduct problems (disruptiveness, boisterousness, fighting, temper tantrums) and (*b*) personality problems (inferiority feelings, lack of confidence, anxiety, shyness, and social withdrawal). In a larger sense, the problems of both categories concern both personality and conduct, but the distinction between those children who act out their difficulties (conduct problems), and those children who withdraw within themselves (personality problems) is a useful and widely accepted one in clinical work with children. The research verification of this distinction is an incidental finding of some value.

The attitudes of fathers were even more intimately related to maladjustive tendencies in their children than were those of the mothers. Out of 65 possible relations calculated for each parent, 14 were statistically significant for the fathers and only eight for the mothers. The major finding was that harshness and cold aggressiveness in the fathers related to *both* forms of maladjustment. The investigators concluded that the younger child needed paternal love and kindness to prevent or, at least, to ameliorate both conduct and personality problems. No significant differentiating characteristic of the parents could be related to the distinction between conduct and personality problem categories into which their children had been placed.

In contrast, when older children were treated with considerable firmness, there was a reduction in the prevalence of conduct disorders. Parents of problem and nonproblem children were again compared, but this time they were the bases of personality inventory scores and interviews. The children were again placed in either the conduct or the personality problem group.

As compared with the parents of the normal children, the parents of the clinic patients were typically maladjusted. The maladjustments took different forms in the parents of conduct problem children and those of personality problem children. Over-restrictive controlling and thwarting fathers had children who were excessively shy and timid (personality problems). Again the father's role seemed to be more important than the mother's. Conduct problem children in general had arbitrary, emotionally unpredictable parents. Their mothers were active, tense, driving individuals over-ready to give advice. The fathers of conduct problem children tended to withdraw from the family situation when it became hectic and to leave the enforcement of regulations to the mothers. This may easily create a spiraling situation: the frustrated mother becomes more tense and demanding; the father still more frustrated by the mother, withdraws still more; and the cycle repeats always with the child in the middle.

A comparison (80) of parents of 40 children referred for psychiatric help with a carefully matched sample of parents of normal children corroborates these findings of Becker, Peterson, and their collaborators. The parental measure used was the Minnesota Multiphasic Personality Inventory. The fathers of disturbed children were more preoccupied with bodily complaints and disease, gloomier in outlook, less mature and more impulsive, and more depressed and anxious than the fathers of the normal children. The mothers were also less mature and more impulsive, depressed and anxious, while at the same time they were less honest and more inclined to act out their aggressive impulses than the mothers of normal children.

Over-all, it would appear that disturbed mothers and fathers tend to have more disturbed children than "normal" fathers and mothers and that there are characteristic distinguishable parental patterns for children with conduct problems as differentiated from those with personality problems. The role of the father is seen to gain importance, especially with relatively older children in the age range.

Behavior tendencies

As before, we shall concentrate on three classes of behavior tendencies—dependence-independence, aggression, and achievement motivation. Sexual tendencies, once more, will be perused in a psychoanalytic setting two chapters hence.

Dependence and Independence Tendencies

The widening scope of psychosocial relationships in older childhood has repercussions in dependent-independent behaviors. Parental influences have a lessening importance and teacher and peer influences an increasing importance, as we shall see in the next chapter. At the moment this will be reflected by a relatively short discussion of dependence-independence in relation to parental influences, which in turn indicates the relative paucity of studies concerning children of this age.

The theme of maternal nurturance within normal limits, as compared to excessive nurturance (overprotection), again appears. So does the long-term relation of dependence in childhood to that expressed in adulthood. Characteristic of the shift in emphasis to behavior outside the home is the examination of a new problem, that of maternal attitudes fostering or not fostering child independence in school achievement.

In a study of maternal influences, Finney (41) investigated maternal attitudes as related to children's dependence-independence. The subjects were 31 boys referred to a child guidance clinic and their mothers. The boys were between five and 16, nearly two-thirds being 13 or over. Behavior problems, as the term was used a little earlier, predominated in reasons for referral to the clinic. Ratings were made on the children by clinic personnel and by teachers. Independent observers made ratings of the mothers. Also obtained were therapists' evaluations, ratings from standardized interviews, and scores on the Minnesota Multiphasic Inventory. Correlation of maternal behaviors and child characteristics was the statistical technique used to test the hypotheses.

Before presenting the correlates of child dependency with maternal attitudes, it is necessary to consider a problem created by the correlation found between the two maternal variables of nurturance and overprotection. It will be remembered that this was a problem encountered in Chapter 8 when considering maternal-infant relationships. In the Zemlick-Watson study it was concluded (page 206) that those mothers who appeared most solicitous (nurturant) were really oversolicitous or over-protecting. With older children nurturance and overprotection might again be expected to show a considerable degree of correlation. Such, indeed, proved to be the case. Maternal nurturance and over-protectiveness correlated .78 in Finney's sample of mothers. The problem of interpretation which this interrelationship creates arises from the fact that nurturance and overprotection are predicted to have different, even opposed, effects in the characteristics of the children. If something were not done about this, the effect of either would mask the effect of the other, perhaps serving to cancel any relationship at all. We must eliminate or hold nurturance constant in considering over-protection, and, conversely, eliminate overprotection in considering nurturance.

This process of holding one variable constant while investigating another is done by the statistical procedure known as partial correlation. When overprotection is held constant (its effect eliminated), the more nurturant mothers have been shown to have less dependent children. When nurturance is held constant, overprotective mothers are found to have more dependent children. This is in keeping with results obtained with younger children and shows that even with older children it is possible to demonstrate a relationship between degree of maternal nurturance and characteristic dependence-independence in their children.

As with maternal attitudes earlier in the chapter, stability of child behavior through time is of interest. In this instance it concerns stability of dependency behavior. Using Fels Research Institute data collected on children when they were between three and six, six and nine, and again between 20 and 29, Kagan and Moss (71) studied the amount and kind of dependence they exhibited at these three age periods. While one psychologist examined the information in the files on dependence when the subjects were children, another interviewed each one about the extent of his dependence in adulthood. Without knowledge of each other's findings, each psychologist rated 54 subjects on various aspects of passive and dependent behavior.

Correlations of dependency measures at age three with those at six and at six with those at ten were fairly high for girls, but somewhat lower for boys. General dependence at the younger of the two ages correlated .61 and .63 respectively with emotional dependence and instrumental dependence in girls when they were older, but only .37 and .38 in boys. Correlations for both sexes and both ages with the dependence behavior they showed as adults were, generally speaking, positive. This showed that there was some consistency between being more dependent or less dependent and status in this respect as adults. Even more important were two specific findings: (*a*) The dependence ratings for ages six to ten were much more related to adult dependency status than were those for ages three to six. (*b*) For girls aged six to ten there were many more significant correlations (60 per cent) with adult dependency status than there were for boys (9 per cent). In other words, consistency of dependency between childhood and adulthood was much greater for girls than for boys.

The relatively greater amount of dependency responses in girls has been noted on several occasions. The new finding, greater relationship of adult to past dependency in girls, fits that pattern. Greater positive relationships for girls as compared to boys are probably to be accounted for by the fact that young girls are less punished for passive and dependent behavior as children, and, that as adults, they are still encouraged to be more passive. For example, dependent women in this sample consulted their family about purchases, had strong needs to keep a close tie with their family, and lived as closely as possible to them. To put the same point another way, there is an expectancy of a shift away from dependence in boys when they become men. This is reflected in the lower correlations obtained. Individual case analysis showed that a greater proportion of men than women shifted from high dependency in childhood to relative independence as adults, which supports this interpretation.

This study is of considerable importance. To be able to collect information about six- to ten-year-old children and from it predict adult patterns of dependence with reasonable precision is something of a scientific triumph.

Since the child has now reached school age, it is natural enough that parental attitudes toward independence training in relation to achievement in school should be studied. It is plausible to believe that variation in school achievement might reflect parental attitudes and practices. The specific theme of one study (27) was the relationship of differing maternal attitudes toward independence training and the school accomplishments of first-grade children who had experienced these differing maternal attitudes. Standardized tests measured the achievement of the children; maternal attitudes toward independence were measured by the mothers' answers to questions having to do with the ages they expected children to perform activities, such as trying hard things for themselves, making their own friends, being able to stay at home during the day alone, making decisions about purchases for themselves, and doing well in competition with other children. Mothers who favored earlier, as opposed to later, independence training had children who made less adequate reading and arithmetic progress relative to their ability than children of mothers who favored later independence training.

This result may serve as a needed corrective for what is perhaps an overeagerness on the part of mothers to foster independence in their children in our present-day culture. At the first-grade level and at least in this one study, mothers who fostered early independence had children who did less well academically than those who favored later independence training. This is but one study and a lot hinges on what is "early" and what is "late" independence training. It seems as if some of these mothers started too early. Another sample of mothers, not quite so eager about these matters, as well as relatively slower mothers, might have yielded results in which those working for "later" independence would have children who did less well academically. This, of course, is nothing more than speculation. At any rate, further research is indicated.

Aggressive Tendencies

Continuity has been demonstrated between the aggressive behavior of five-year-old children as related to early socialization experiences and their characteristic behavior when twelve (*111*). This was done in a follow-up by Sears of his "pattern" study. Of the original population of 379 five-year-old children, 160, now twelve years of age, were still in the schools from which they had originally been drawn. These children each filled out several self-administering scales concerned with aggressive attitudes. Their classmates, totaling 377, also completed these forms. As compared to boys, aged twelve, girls showed significantly higher scores on *aggression anxiety* (fear and dislike of aggression, such as being uncomfortable when seeing two friends argue) and *prosocial aggression* (aggression used in socially approved ways, as advocating punishing of someone who has clearly broken a rule). The boys, as compared to girls, exhibited higher scores on *antisocial aggression* (socially unacceptable forms of aggression, as settling an argument by a fight).

Current antisocial aggression was found to be related to high permissiveness and low punishment from their mothers seven years before. As related to high permissiveness antisocial aggression repeats the findings at age five; as related to low punishment it is the reverse of what it was at the earlier age. At the early age punishment seemed to produce aggression; at the later age punishment tended to have an inhibiting effect not present when the children were younger. Punishment, in this instance, did seem to work.

Current prosocial aggression and aggressive anxiety were also related to earlier high maternal permissiveness as before. This time, however, they were found to be associated with high punishment, quite the opposite of the relation to antisocial aggression. High permissiveness and high punishment promote prosocial aggression and aggression anxiety; high permissiveness and low punishment incite antisocial aggression.

Sex differences appeared to such an extent in the antecedents of the degree of anxiety over aggressiveness that different dynamics must be attributed to boys and girls. Severity of parental punitiveness for aggression during early childhood correlated significantly with aggression anxiety in older girls but not in older boys. It seems as if the boys' aggression anxiety arises when socialization is experienced in a love-oriented atmosphere; here there are dictates against aggression. In short, there is conformity. In girls, on the other hand, anxiety is induced by conflict. A forced conformity seems to occur, despite girls being less aggressive than boys either overtly or in fantasy (see page 384). In girls incipient aggressive tendencies are nipped in the bud and anxiety develops. Under most circumstances, aggression in girls is not acceptable in their sex-role training. In her sex role she is not supposed to show aggressiveness, does not do so, and becomes anxious.

Finney (41), in his research on material influence described in connection with dependency, also obtained information about maternal-child characteristics as related to aggressiveness. Particularly interesting is his finding on so-called *covert hostility*. This is not direct, overt aggression, but resentment expressed in bitterness, in sulking, and in easily hurt feelings. Hostile mothers, rigid mothers, and those lacking in nurturance, he found to have covertly hostile children. Covert hostility, Finney believes, is a fruitful concept needing more attention than it has so far received.

Achievement Motivation

The need to achieve in older children is closely related to independence training received from their mothers. This relationship was clearly demonstrated by Winterbottom (130) in the following manner. She studied the role of the mother in supplying her boy with learning experiences that would develop independence and a desire for mastery, and then related these measures of independence training to measures of the boy's own needs for achievement. Her subjects were 29 eight- to ten-year-old boys and their mothers in a small, middle-class community. The mothers were questioned concerning the number of demands they made for independent accomplishment in their children, the age at which they wanted these accomplishments to be evident, the number of restrictions they placed on independent activity on the part of their children, and the age at which they wanted the restrictions to be learned. To anticipate one aspect of her results, analysis of the items showed that the crucial discriminating ones concerning independence development centered on the child being able to "do" for himself, as in selecting clothes and choosing friends. She also collected teachers' ratings of indices of need achievement expressed by the children.

To measure need for achievement, she asked each boy to tell stories after giving them brief verbal descriptions, such as "A mother and her son. They look worried." One set of four stories was given under so-called relaxed conditions in which every effort was made to put the boy at his ease. Another set of four stories was given under so-called achievement orientation; just preceding the story telling, the boy was told that he was to take a puzzle test (a form board) which would show how smart he was, and that his results would be compared with those of the others in his class. After the puzzle he told stories to the second set of verbal descriptions. The stories for both sets were scored for achievement-related imagery. Stories under achievement orientation were significantly greater in the amount of achievement imagery. Winterbottom considered this to demonstrate that the achievement orientation did, in fact, increase achievement imagery. Consequently, the method used actually measured the need for achievement.

Two groups of children were isolated, one high and the other low in need for achievement. It was found that boys with high need for achievement were given earlier training for independence by their mothers, earlier (but fewer) restrictions on independent activity, and earlier demands for learning these restrictions. Early independence training by mothers clearly engendered stronger achievement motivation in their children. The high need achievers, as evaluated by their teachers, rated as trying harder, taking more pleasure in success, being more independent, and being more popular than low need achievers.

At first glance some contradiction might appear between Winterbottom's results and the findings of Crandall, Preston, and Rabson on younger children given on page 399. These investigators showed that high achieving children were less dependent on adults, but they did not study maternal reactions to the children's independence efforts; rather, they studied maternal reactions to dependence overtures from their children. No contradiction is therefore involved between their study and Winterbottom's, but again the treating of independence and dependence as separate tendencies seems justified.

Moreover, Winterbottom's results seem at variance with those of

Chance (27) on age of independence training. However, Chance measured actual achievement, not motivation to achieve, so that the two studies concerned different problems. It would seem that both ability to achieve and need to achieve are affected by age of independence training but in a different way. This is an intriguing difference, warranting further research, but there is no contradiction between the results of the two studies.

A rather specific aspect of achievement motivation is task mastery, a desire to complete tasks, even though failure occurred in previous attempts. Younger children have not yet developed to the point at which they manifest a desire for such mastery (p. 400). In a study by Crandall and Rabson (29), an older group of 29 six-, seven- and eight-year-olds was given the same tasks as the younger children. These consisted of two wire picture puzzles of equal difficulty. Each child was allowed to complete one puzzle, but on the second he was made to fail by being told his time was up; actually this was decided not by the time he had used, but by the fact he had five of the seven pieces of the puzzle in place. After working on both puzzles he was told that he could work again on the one of the two puzzles and that he was to choose which one. The investigators also collected ratings in free-play settings concerning such behaviors as the amount of help sought from adults and from peers, the amount of approval sought from adults and from peers, and the children's readiness to withdraw from threatening situations.

It was found that the older children preferred to repeat the previously failed puzzle, as contrasted with the younger children who preferred to repeat the successfully completed one. When the results of a study of the same problem by Rosenzweig (109), who used still older children, were related to theirs, Crandall and Rabson concluded that task mastery appeared to develop gradually with age, at least through preadolescence.

A sex difference, not evident at the younger ages, was clearly present by the early grade school age. Boys were found to prefer doing the previously failed puzzle more often than were the girls. Moreover, by this same age, boys were found to be less dependent on peers and adults for help and approval and less ready to withdraw from threatening situations than were girls. It will be noted that this phase of achievement motivation shows relationship to independence-dependence striving.

These results are congruent with those of Winterbottom. She found that independence training of boys was initiated earlier and emphasized more than for girls. Girls, both studies found, seem to show more passivity and open dependence than boys and, to return to the issue under discussion, less desire for task mastery.

Parental attitudes toward 40 boys of high and of low need for achievement were assessed in the home setting (108). These boys performed several achievement tasks while their parents observed them and commented on their performance. The investigators noted parental behavior and verbalization as their sons carried out their tasks.

In contrast to parents of sons showing low need for achievement, parents of boys with high need for achievement held higher aspirations and expectations for their sons' performances. They gave more approbation when performances were good and more readily criticized incompetent efforts. They tended to allow their sons latitude in choice of tasks to perform, but once the boys had decided, they held them to high performance in these tasks. Parents with boys showing high need for achievement, then, showed high aspiration and allowed freedom of choice, but once a task was selected, maintained high performance expectations.

The stability and validity of achievement fantasy in the same children at different ages has been studied through the parents and children associated with the Fels Research Institute (70). Achievement fantasy was measured by the TAT at approximately ages nine, 11 and 14. As age increased, the achievement themes increased for both boys and girls. Moreover, a fair degree of stability of achievement fantasy was also found. Amount of achievement fantasy themes on the first testing was significantly associated with that on the second and third testings. In other words, the children showed some tendency to retain their relative position in the group on amount of achievement fantasy despite its general increase over the age period studied.

Degree of maternal concern with achievement during the first three years of the child's life had been rated on the home visits by the staff. It was found that girls, whose mothers showed greater concern, had higher achievement fantasy scores six years later. Moreover, mothers with greater concern for their daughters' achievement actually had girls showing significant IQ *gains* from tests given on the semiannual testing during the years in question. For boys no correlation was found between degree of maternal concern at age three and later achievement fantasy, or IQ gain. Both among girls and boys there was a generally positive (although nonlinear) relation between the amount of achievement fantasy and the gain in IQ. In other words, boys and girls who showed increased achievement strivings at age 14, as compared to that shown at eight or nine years of age, tended to reveal a greater increase in IQ than children not showing this increase in striving. It would seem as if "trying" does make a difference. This conclusion urgently needs an independent research check, but in the meantime it stands as an established finding about children.

The researchers also found some indications that when the education of the same-sex parent was relatively greater, there was an increase in their children's achievement fantasy. It is plausible to believe a more highly educated parent would be more concerned with achievement and would communicate this concern to his child. Over-all it would seem that achievement fantasy serves as an index of the children's tendency to seek achievement goals.

Need for achievement expressed between the ages of six and ten has proven to be highly predictive of similar adult tendencies (92). As children, the subjects, had been evaluated for achievement behavior (tendency to persist with challenging tasks, and degree of involvement in tasks to which a standard of excellence was applicable). An investigator who had no knowledge of the results obtained in childhood interviewed and rated 71 Fels subjects again when they were between 20 and 30 years of age. Two areas on which he made evaluations were achievement behavior (attempts to master tasks for which self-satisfaction rather than social recognition was the goal) and concern for intellectual competence (value placed on intelligence, knowledge, and academic achievement regardless of whether goal is inner standards or social recognition). Ratings on achievement behavior at six to ten correlated with similar ratings in adulthood, .46 for males and .38 for females. Ratings on achievement behavior at six to ten correlated with concern for intellectual competence, .69 for males and .49 for females. Relationships at younger ages (first three years and ages three to six) were either unrelated or much less closely related to adult behavior. To translate chronological age into the corresponding school years, the measures taken during the first five years of schooling proved prognostic of adult mastery.

Overall, the Fels investigators (114) consider the period between the ages of six and ten to be crucial for the development of motivation to master intellectual tasks. If the child's experiences during these years are self-reassuring and give him freedom from too strong dependence on his parents, this desire develops. Since it proves to be highly correlated with achievement behavior in adulthood, it makes for an effective, problem solving, successfully competitive adult.

The development of self and social awareness

Each child in his own way as he moves through infancy and childhood reaches some sort of understanding of himself and of other persons. He acquires knowledge about and attitudes toward himself and others. Certainly, the older child has increased self-awareness, often expressed in self-consciousness. Entering school exposes each child to the always sharp, often critical, and sometimes unfriendly eyes of his classmates. Every foible, every weakness is open to them, and their comments range from such direct appellations as "fatso," "skinny," "dopey," and "four-eyes" to more individual and subtle, but equally critical, comments. A sharpening of the sense of self could hardly fail to develop under this regime.

Consideration of the self will center on self-esteem (self-acceptance), the ego-ideal (ideal self), and an issue closely related to the self, empathy (ability to take the other person's role). Despite the essential privateness of the child's self-concept, it is at least partially revealed in his behavior. It is only because of this that it is possible to suppose that poor or good self-concepts would have correlations in good or poor adjustment and that empathy might be measurable.

Social perception takes many forms. Chosen for exposition are perception of parents and of peers.

Self-esteem, the Ego-ideal, and Empathy

The importance for self-esteem of the influence of the group is put forcefully by White:

> . . . it is fair to say that the crucial arena for self-esteem is the arena of one's age-mates. At home there is an age hierarchy. Even the siblings are bigger or smaller, so that differences of competence are expected. The home, moreover, continues to be the source of love and provision of basic wants, even when the child ventures forth to playground and school. At home he must be *love-worthy:* this may include being competent, but it is heavily weighted on the side of being good, obedient, and affectionate. On the playground the values are different: he must be *respect-worthy,* able to command respect because he shows competence and handles himself with ease. It is a sharp strain for many children when they pass from the atmosphere of a child-centered home into the competitive realities of even a friendly play group. They must now show what they have in the way of physical prowess, courage, manipulative skill, outgoing friendliness, all in direct comparison with other children of their age. The penalities for failure are humiliation, ridicule, rejection from the group (128, 144–145).[1]

A relation has been found between children's self-concepts and the degree of anxiety they are prepared to admit (79). Approximately 300

[1] Robert W. White, *The Abnormal Personality.* Copyright 1948, The Ronald Press Company.

fourth-, fifth-, and sixth-graders served as subjects in this particular study. The self-concept scale each child completed consisted of trait-descriptive adjectives, such as happy, clean, popular, and courteous, prefaced by the phrase "I am . . . ." and followed by a five-point rating scale which ranged from "not at all" to "all of the time." The children were to choose the rating point that they thought best described them. Scores were given from one to five corresponding to these points on the scale so that the higher sums of scores indicated self-approbation, and the lower sum scores indicated self-disparagement. The already familiar Children's Manifest Anxiety Scale was the measure of anxiety.

The self-concepts correlated significantly with anxiety in all three grades and for boys and girls separately. In other words, more self-disparaging individuals were more anxious. Self-disparagement, the investigator indicates, would seem to be an antecedent for generalized anxiety. Although not commented on, it would appear that the reverse relation might hold as well, more anxious children might become more self-disparaging. At any rate, a relation between self-concepts of children and their degree of anxiety seems to exist.

An impetus is given to favorable self-concepts by accelerated physical maturity. In a comparison of physically accelerated boys and girls with those who were late in maturing, the latter consistently showed less favorable self-concepts in their responses to TAT pictures (67, 98). It seems that slower physical development exposed the child to an environment that had an adverse effect on his conception of his own personality development whereas more rapid physical development led to an environment that enhanced the self-concept.

The self-concepts of children who achieve more academically than might be expected from their intelligence (overachievers) have been compared with those who achieve less than that expected (underachievers). In Walsh's (127) study two such carefully matched groups of elementary school pupils were compared. He found that underachievers showed distinctly more signs of inhibition, insecurity, and defensiveness.

In still another study (91), this time involving high school boys, the underachievers and overachievers differed little in self-described emotional and school adjustment but considerably more underachievers described themselves as restless, undependable, and as belonging to cliques which showed negative attitudes toward school and opposition to authority. The investigators interpreted their findings as supporting a view that underachievers' behavior was "asocialized," that is, a mild form of delinquency which takes its major locus from the groups with which these particular children associate, the peer clique groups.

The question of the relationship between self-acceptance, a person's characteristic evaluation of himself, and social acceptability, the way others see him, is one in which the evidence is conflicting. Sometimes a positive relation is obtained (such as, 136) sometimes no relationship is found (such as, 87). A study by Reese (107) involving an adequate number of subjects, about 400, in a wide range of the fourth-, sixth-, and eighth-grades, as well as methodological and statistical sophistication and more than one means of measurement helped to clear up some of the discrepancies in earlier studies.

Without going into all of his methods, some of his results are presented as summarizing the current knowledge of the problem. A self-concept scale allows the child to describe himself in terms of relevant descriptive traits; a sociometric scale each child fills in, allows calculation of the mean of the ratings given each same-sexed classmate. Within each grade the same-sex subjects were divided into three groups, each consisting of a third of that class, on the bases of their self-concept scores. This yielded the highest, middle, and lowest third on self-concepts. Sociometric status in terms of acceptance by others was then calculated.

Reese found a relationship between the way a child perceives himself and the way he is accepted, but not a linear one. Instead, the relationship he obtained was curvilinear. If we turn to Figure 15, page 371, and substitute degrees of peer acceptance for amounts of frustration on the vertical dimension, and substitute degree of self-acceptance, ranging from low to high, for low to high amounts of frustration and punishment on the horizontal dimension, we have a curve corresponding to these findings. Moderate amount of self-acceptance would then be the high point of peer acceptance, high self-acceptance next, and low self-acceptance the lowest in peer acceptance. In other words, those with moderate self-concepts were most accepted by others, those with high self-concepts were next most accepted by others, while those with low self-concepts were least accepted by others.

The development of the ideal self or ego-ideal was studied by a group of investigators (62) who asked several hundred children to write a brief essay on the topic, "The person I would like to be like." They were given instructions to describe a person whether he be real or imaginary or a combination of several people. Most of the subjects ranged in age from eight to 18 and included both boys and girls. Several subgroups were used from widely scattered geographical regions and from varying levels of socio-economic status. The essays were first read by the investigators in order to arrive at categories of classification. Most of the essays fell into the categories of finding the ideal self in (1) parents; (2) glamorous adults (movie stars, athletes, and so on); (3) attractive and visible young adults (those within the range of observation of the child in question such as scout leaders, young uncles, and aunts, and so on); and (4) composite or imaginary characters (abstractions of a number of people).

The investigators studied age trends in these categorizations. The children from age 6 to about 8 tended more often to choose parents as ego-ideals. Older children move on to choose either a glamorous person or a young adult. Sometimes, from about age eight to 16 a glamorous person was chosen. Other children chose the young adult when eight or ten and either continued choices falling in this category through adolescence, or shifted their choice after this age to the more abstract ego-ideal or a composite imaginary person.

Thus, a developmental trend concerning the ideal self was found. In the youngest years studied, it was still an identification with the parental figures; however, after about ten years the parents played a declining role; moving on to a stage of romanticism or glamour, the ideal self finally culminated in late adolescence as a composite of desirable characteristics either symbolized by young adults known to them or by purely imaginary figures. It should be noted that the choices of children, at first fanciful, become more realistic and more conforming to the norms of socialization.

Empathic ability, it will be remembered, is the ability to predict the feelings and actions of others. Studies use the method of comparing a child's estimate of another child's attitudes with the actual attitudes as reported by this other child. Empathy, then, is sensitivity to the attitudes of others.

With younger children (see page 407) empathic ability increased with age. For children of the age under discussion, a similar increase in empathic ability with age (or at least with grade) has been demonstrated by Dymond and her associates (39). As a first step, cards, similar to those in the TAT, but adapted to the children's ages, were given to small groups of second- and sixth-graders with mean ages, respectively, of about seven and 11. After being told a simple story that accompanied each picture, each child was asked a standard series of questions about the thoughts and feelings of the characters in the story. Potential for empathy was measured by the ease (lack of prodding or of the necessity for asking specific questions) with which the child could voice opinions about a pictured individual's thoughts and feelings, that is, what is he thinking and feeling. The mean score in "empathy" was significantly higher in the sixth than in the second grade. These results demonstrated that older children, as compared to younger, could express themselves more easily about others' thoughts and feelings. This potential for empathy had no objective reference as to correctness in their expressions. This was studied in the second phase of the study.

A second measure, the social insight test, was given. After judging sociometrically whom in the class he would like to sit with, invite home to a party, and so on, each child judged the extent to which he was liked or disliked by each other member of the class. As a consequence, there was a measure of how the child thought he was liked and another of how he was actually liked. The empathy score was based on the degree of correspondence between the two. The children whose measures indicated agreement between how much they thought they were liked and how much they were actually liked showed high empathy. The children who showed a discrepancy showed low empathy. There was a clear difference that indicated greater empathy on the part of the sixth-graders than the second graders.

Within a grade, the sociometric and empathy scores correlated 0.26 for the second and 0.50 for the sixth grade. If every child expects himself to be well-liked, only actually popular children can get a high score on empathy or insight. Hence the relation is about as high in the sixth grade as we might expect. The correlation is so low for the second graders it appears that they show relatively little relation between sociometric or popularity status and empathy or social insight. It will be found from the discussion in the section on friendships that Dymond and her associates (39) observed that second-graders were choosing friends on the basis of external qualities, such as money and a nice home. Certainly, these are not qualities which emphasize understanding or empathy, so it is hardly surprising that those who were most popular were not high in empathy at this age grade level. But, by the sixth grade, children become more aware and better able to assess the feelings of others accurately, as shown by the increased correlation at that age.

In a somewhat similar study, Ausubel and his associates (12) used larger groups of subjects and separated the data for boys and girls for a more detailed analysis. They used a sociometric technique to determine the perceptions of one's own status and compared them with the perceptions held by others (the mean of the ratings given the subject by his classmates). The correlations were higher than those obtained by Dymond and were equally good for boys and girls. There was some increase with age as well.

An extensive carefully controlled study by deJung and Gardner (68), based on several hundred subjects from the fifth through the twelfth grade, confirmed these findings concerning increase in empathy, or accuracy of self-role perception with grade. They found reason to object to the reference to these increases being due to sheer age increase. Within each single grade, where there is a three-year age span, they found no significant correlations with age. Instead of age, they argue that what accounts for increase in empathic ability is (a) sheer experience in a social group, that is, the greater number of contacts within a social group or similar groups, the greater is the accuracy of self-role perception; and (b) greater ability to abstract from social experience the important normative experiences.

The lack of correlation within the restricted range of a single grade serves as a needed corrective to the idea that somehow it is age alone that makes for this ability. There is little question that age merely allows experiences to happen and is itself nothing more than index of experience. On the other hand, we may hazard a rejoinder that failure to find a correlation within a restricted range of three years does not mean it could not be found with a wider age span, provided one always keeps in mind that it is not age *per se* that is important, but the experiences to which a child is exposed.

Another facet of the self-social perception problem is the question of a relationship between perceived similarity and the valuation given another person. Davitz (35) found that the highest sociometric choices tended to be perceived as more similar to the self than the lowest sociometric choices, indeed, more similar to self than they actually were. He did this in a summer camp with a small group of boys and girls of an average age of about 10. They had been together 11 days when the study was conducted. Rankings gave sociometric choices, whereas social perception was measured by an activity inventory, with items consisting of two activities, such as dodge ball and ping pong; the subject was required to make choices between the pairs.

Each child filled out this measure (1) for his own preferences; (2) for his highest sociometric choice; and (3) for his lowest sociometric choice. Perceived similarity was the degree of correspondence between his own responses and his prediction of the responses of the other child, both high or low sociometric choice arrived at by counting the agreements between them. Actual similarity was the degree of correspondence between the child's responses and those predicted for him. As mentioned, Davitz found that the highest sociometric choices were perceived as those more like oneself than the lowest choices. In fact, these highest choices were perceived as more similar to oneself than they actually were.

This may be interpreted as a tendency to wish to be similar to valued persons—in this case one's peers. One way this is expressed is in the usual pattern of identification, of trying to make oneself like others. Here we have another way of being similar—trying to make the other person like oneself. This is what seems to have been happening in this study. It stands witness to the importance of the peer group.

Social Perception

The older child's perceptions of his parents are important. One way of expressing the problem is to ask which parent is seen as the source of authority and which is seen as the source of affection? Through interviews Kagan (69) obtained answers to questions from 217 children about who would be on their side in an argument (friendliness), who would punish them (punitiveness), and who was boss (dominance). The majority of both boys and girls perceived their mothers as friendlier, less punitive, and less dominant than their fathers.

Gardner (46) studied the perception of the father and of the mother through reports of about 400 boys and girls. She used a questionnaire approach which asked which parent was easier to get along with, who would punish them, and who was the bigger boss. The correspondence to friendliness, punitiveness, and dominance of mothers and fathers as studied by Kagan is apparent. Mothers were perceived as friendlier, less dominant, and about equally punitive. The studies, then, are in essential agreement about friendliness and dominance. Only in connection with punitiveness is there some difference in results.

This discrepancy about punitiveness is easily accounted for when age differences are taken into consideration. The children studied by Kagan ranged from six to ten years of age. The older children of about nine or ten in his sample, both boys and girls, tended to view the same-sex parent as more punitive and dominant than did the younger children. The differential handling of boys and girls as they begin to assume more definitive sex roles is suggested to account for this finding. The children Gardner studied were almost all 10 through 13, thus extending Kagan's age group. Kagan found that as age increased within his sample, punitiveness of the same sex parent increased. In Gardner's group, this had increased to such an extent that the parents were equally punitive. Thus, there is no discrepancy between the results of the two studies. The answer to the question with which these studies were introduced, which qualities are parents perceived as having, appears to be that the father is seen as the source of authority and the mother the source of affection; however, as age increases the same-sex parent assumes more and more a punitive role.

Children's attitudes toward their parents show changes with age. In a study of 3,000 children, about equally divided as to sex, ranging in grade from the third to the twelfth, Harris and Tseng (53) had them reply to sentence completion items with the stems, "My father ———" and "My mother ———." The completions were classified as showing positive, negative, or neutral attitudes toward the particular parent. Illustrative would be "My father is mean" (negative), "My mother is a teacher" (neutral), and "My father is the best in the world" (positive).

Younger boys in grade three were more favorable to their mothers and slightly less so to their fathers. Boys' attitudes toward both parents became steadily less favorable up to the fifth grade where attitudes more or less leveled off with a shift toward slightly greater favorable attitudes in the late high school years.

Lest this gives an incorrect impression, it should be indicated that for these boys even at the point of least favorable attitudes toward the mother, it never went as low as 50 per cent and toward the father never as low as 35 per cent. Girls showed about the same pattern, except, in general, they were throughout somewhat more favorable toward both mothers and fathers. Starting at grade seven, they showed a rather dramatic increase in favorable attitudes toward fathers, but never to the same level as toward their mothers. Through the years of the study the small proportion of boys showing negative attitudes toward mothers or fathers decreased steadily, whereas the small proportion of girls showing negative attitudes increased steadily.

Children are still very much under parental authority. But this authority can be expressed differently and with different outcomes in the perceptions of the children. Basically, authority means restricting and checking behavior. Although having this essential effect, the motivations for wielding authority may stem from different sources on the part of the parents. Exercising authority may arise from restrictive motivation on the part of the parent for authority's sake itself, or it may come from rational motivation on his part for the sake of the child's welfare. Further, either of these motivations may be expressed *concretely* by parents, having reference to restrictions concerning particular objects or events, or either may be expressed *abstractly* in terms of more general relations in which a principle is advanced rather than some sort of dictate laid down.

With these principles to guide him, Pikas (105) studied several hundred Swedish children by using a variety of specially constructed projective and nonprojective tests. He established that children's perception of parental rational motivation in an abstract form was correlated positively with the children's age and intelligence. In other words, the older and smarter the child, the more ready he was to accept rational, abstractly stated authority. Authoritarian motivations, especially when stated concretely, were negatively correlated with age and intelligence. The older and smarter the child, the more he rejected these ways of expressing authority. It would seem that as children get older, use of rationally imposed, abstractly stated authority is more acceptable and the smarter they are, the sooner this should be instigated.

These findings may well be related to those of Harris and his associates (52) who showed that responsibility in children is fostered when they perceive their parents as taking a constructive orientation toward them. Constructive, rational, parental motivation seems to be the most healthful way in which the still necessary authority over children may be expressed if children's perceptions are to be a criterion.

Summary

Analysis has shown that maternal attitudes exhibit both consistency and flexibility. Maternal attitudes toward infants when compared with those held as the same children reach preadolescence show that amount of affection displayed is consistent, whereas degree of restrictiveness is flexibly changed because of changed circumstances. As with other summary statements of this nature, there must be some parental-child relationships where they do not hold.

Family patterns, that is, the general climates of the home, are found to be related to the older child's personality characteristics. More specifically, familial consistency, trust, and democracy were found to be related to the children's high ego and superego strength as well as to friendliness. A nondemocratic, untrusting, severe family climate seems to be related to children's hostility and guilt.

Other findings about parental influences seem fairly well established; happy contented mothers, as contrasted to unhappy, discontented mothers, have children showing greater intellectual and emotional freedom; anxious parents tend to have anxious children; disturbed mothers and fathers tend to have children who are disturbed. Especially in older children, within the age range under consideration, a differential relation has been found between the particular characteristics of the parents and the kinds of disorders, namely behavior problems and personality problems, in their offspring. The role of the father as a dynamic agent in these patterns is shown to be important, perhaps even more important that that of the mother so far as boys are concerned.

Dependence in children and overprotection in mothers again were found to be related, whereas nurturance held within normal limits was related to less dependence in children. Dependence in six- to ten-year-old girls was relatively similar to that found when these same girls were studied as adults. Boys of the same age tended to shift toward lessened dependence when they were adults.

A continuity between the socialization experiences of young children and their aggressive behavior at age twelve has been demonstrated. Particularly notable is the differential effect of parental punitiveness in early childhood as correlated with anxiety about being aggressive. For girls, these measures correlated significantly; for boys, they did not. In older girls, anxiety seems to be conflict induced, that is, there is a conflict between the sex-role training not to be aggressive and feelings that are aggressive in nature. Girls do not show aggressiveness; instead, anxiety appears.

The needs for achievement in older children are epitomized by the findings that boys who later proved to have had a high need for achievement were given earlier independence training by their mothers, that older children sought task mastery whereas younger children did not, and that achievement fantasy might serve as an index of children's tendency to seek achievement goals. Emphasis can be placed on the years between six and ten as the critical period for the development of need to master intellectual tasks.

Self-acceptance has been found to be related to a variety of factors. Self-disparaging children seem to be more anxious. Less favorable self-concepts are held by children with slower physical development. The acceptance by peers is not linearally related to self-concepts. Children with moderately high, but not the highest, self-concepts are most accepted whereas those with low self-concepts are least accepted by their peers.

The influence of the peer group is shown by the fact that there is a stable (although not pronounced) relationship between the way a child perceives himself and, in turn, the way his peers perceive him. Self-acceptance and the acceptance on his part of his peers are both positively related to popularity. The ideal self of younger children is relatively fanciful, but, as they grow older, their conceptions of the ideal self become more realistic. This change in views on the ideal self demonstrates vividly the influence of socialization pressures.

Particularly noteworthy are the increase in empathy with age-grade, the changes in children's attitudes toward parents with increased age, and the different ways they perceive parental authority with greater acceptance of rational, abstract parental discipline.

For Further Reading

Much more than others L. Joseph Stone and Joseph Church in their book, *Childhood and Adolescence* (New York: Random House, 1957), have captured a child's-eye view of these years. Based on their intimate acquaintance with children rather more than on accounts of research findings, the book gives a realistic, but empathetic view of the struggle of growing-up.

References

Follow Chapter 18.

of this problem, Martin and Stendl[
which the peer group influences th[
the peer group provides (1) rewar[
(3) support. A peer-age child see[
that which he may model himself u[
adult can serve. He cannot model [
in seeking social acceptability—the[
own adult fashion through cocktails[
est novel (or through beer, pinoch[
These forms of behavior are not ye[
dren must serve as models.

To be accepted by the group is a r[
of the group in order to be accepted[
he develops new needs—he acquires[
a means to an end, approval of the a[
an end in itself. Thus, the peer gr[
also provide an identity of and for t[
son Bob, but Bob. As Martin and [
cessive identities provided by the g[
Scout, and so on up through the [
through sheer numbers in presenting[
have what others have because "all [

Although all of these positive, grou[
must also remember that groups and [
structure a measure of exclusiveness[
model club with a membership witho[
even in loosely knit groups, such as t[
there still will be "outsiders" (100).[
(listless, lacking in vitality, below nor[
the socially uninterested; and the soc[
lious, boastful, and arrogant). Negati[
will also be very evident in the discus[

Peer groups in their purer form sh[
groups at home, at school, or as impos[
individuals of the same age centered [
term concern. They are loosely orga[
tion rapidly (40). What the child le[
made his own uncritically and without[
if he behaves like all the others withou[
is "in" or "out."

This conformity, a tendency to ad[
others, can lead to acceptance of view[

17

Peer and School Relationships

PSYCHOSOCIAL DEVELOPMENT of the child between six and twelve may
be referred to as the peer-group age, the school age, or the latency
period. Reference to peer-group age signalizes the importance of these
years for the child learning to live with his age mates. School age
signifies that the range under consideration starts at the beginning of
compulsory school attendance and continues on through the grammar
school grades. The latency period serves to stress, from the psychoanalytic standpoint, the relative quiescence in sexual strivings between
the twin storms of the Oedipus situation and of adolescence. Each of
these three ways of considering the child will be useful provided we
do not lose sight of the fact that all apply to the same individual. It is
only for the sake of clarity that we separate these three aspects of the
older child's life. Here we consider the first two, deferring discussion
of the latency period until the next chapter.

Children of this age leave home, literally and figuratively, to a much
greater degree than younger children. As illustrated in Figure 18,
Wright (133) studied the average number of hours per day spent by
the children and adults in the family and in community settings in a
midwestern town. As shown in the figure, infants and preschoolers
spent, on the average, about one hour a day outside the home. An
increase to six or seven hours outside the home occurs in the age period
now under consideration (referred to as young-middle and old-middle
childhood in the figure). During these hours away from home the children were in school and at play. Most of this time they spent in the
company of their age mates.

Figure 18.
spent in fan
tings. (Fro
right 1956
search in C
published wi

The peer group

Many of the socialization s
groups. How a child will rea
exposed to in the group, but a
characteristics. His experienc
the effect of maternal attitude
negated.

How does the peer group hel

(20) children were shown a single black line which was to serve as standard, along with three other black lines of differing lengths. Their task was to state which of the three lines was equal in length to the standard. When alone, most children judged correctly. These same children when judging in a group made errors. Why? The child who erred did not know that the five children, who gave their judgments aloud before his turn came, were confederates of the experimenter who had been told to report the wrong answer. When his turn did come, this child tended to go along with the group and made an inaccurate judgment. Younger children (ages seven to ten) were more influenced in this regard than older children (ages ten to 13).

In a second experiment with different children, the teacher was the accomplice, giving her judgment first. Again the children were influenced, but not as much as they had been by the group of peers, and again, younger children were relatively more influenced. Peers seem to be even more important than the teacher in influencing judgment. The task itself was rather trivial. This, however, is not crucial. The results suggest the strong possibility that group pressures would sway the child when more important matters were at stake.

The shift from the family to the larger social setting, which this chapter represents, does require a change in perspective concerning independence and aggressive tendencies. Heretofore, these tendencies have been examined as they originated in the family and as they were expressed in this and other social settings. These "other" social situations, such as the preschool, up to this point were treated merely as settings for the appearance of family-instigated tendencies. They were not considered as they modified or further elaborated these tendencies. Instead of considering independence and aggression in and for themselves as separate topics, they are now seen as imbedded in these social settings.

The peer group, moreover, gives the child a chance to develop certain social qualities. These qualities—social acceptance, friendship, cooperation, and their polar opposites—will receive attention presently.

Independence and Aggressive Tendencies

During later childhood, the problem of achieving some independence from the family becomes prominent, even though it is customary to focus attention on adolescence as being the prime critical period. The seeking and finding of independence as an autonomous individual are continuous processes. It does not begin with later childhood, but before; it does not end with the close of this period, but continues through adolescence and into adulthood.

Independence as a tendency is expressed, so far as the peer group is concerned, as the continuing struggle to be more independent of parents. In this connection we are reminded of the chart presented in the beginning of the chapter concerning the amount of time spent in the family and in community settings. A dramatic increase in time spent in the community occurs after preschool age. This is clear evidence that at least a certain form of independence from the home takes place. Most children not only leave home physically for more hours, they also leave emotionally to some extent.

If a child is to be successful with his peers, he must have some degree of independence. This may be illustrated in circumstances in which parental control is so strong that the child is forced to rebel. Not coming directly home after school is often an expression of too heavy an insistence on being precisely on time. Hounded about being a minute late can drive a child to being an hour late. Of course, rebellion of even greater proportion and a more pervasive form may occur.

The investigation of aggressive tendencies can be related in a variety of ways to the peer group within which they take place. One study (88) concerned the interrelationships among patterns of aggressive behavior with other facets of social behavior as observed in a summer camp for emotionally disturbed and delinquent boys, ranging in age from seven to 15. For each cabin there was a high counselor-child ratio of eight boys to six counselors. The latter supplied the observational ratings, working morning, afternoon, or evening shifts in teams of three. The three counselors completed collective Behavior Check Sheets after each shift with their eight boys. With three shifts per day and 45 days, it would appear that the combined ratings on any one child's behavior pattern could be based on as many as 135 collective ratings. An adequate number of 59 subjects and a lengthy 45-day period of observation made the study especially noteworthy.

The rated behaviors involved swearing, sulking, fighting, fighting to protect self or others, competing without aggression, following others into trouble, seeking leadership, and friendliness with others. In addition to these child initiated behaviors, the responses of other children to each child were rated in terms of the latter's being accepted and rejected or being made the scapegoat. On the bases of their ratings on all behavior categories and peer reactions the boys were divided into thirds—high, medium, and low. This made it possible to relate the behavior categories, one to another, and these categories in turn to the peer reactions. To these results a statistical technique was applied in order to find out what relations were significantly greater than chance.

The children who fought frequently, often needing no justification, were also the ones who fought to protect others. This reminds one of

Lois Murphy's findings, reported in Chapter 13, that aggressive younger children were also sympathic children due to their sheer amount of activity. Lest the altruistic note be too strong here, it is rather clear the boys in the present study championed others not so much for their sake, as they did to get in the fight for its own sake.

One very notable correlate with high fighting was what might be expected, namely swearing and calling names. Another was less expected, namely, that children who fought a great deal were neither the best nor the worst in staying within the rules in organized competition. Indeed, those who fought the least were those who were unable to handle competition without hostility. As to the characteristics that did not distinguish the boys clearly, subjects addicted to fighting were not particularly friendly with their peers nor did they seek visible positions of leadership. Perhaps, as the investigators comment, the camp sample represented delinquent children who were leadership failures.

The interaction of these personal behaviors with the acceptance, rejection, or scapegoating of peers showed interesting relationships. Those who were rejected most were made the butt of severe and continued persecution in the form of scapegoating. There was no philosophy of live and let live which would be compatible with rejection as such. It follows, as they found, that scapegoated boys had little opportunity for leadership. The converse seems to occur for those accepted— they were rarely scapegoated and were freer to seek and attain leadership.

This study suggests clearly that aggression is not a unitary phenomenon, captured by one global estimate; instead, it appears in a pattern reflected in a child's interaction with his peers. Aggressive tendencies have been shown to be instigated in the peer group by characteristic relationships within that group.

Direct training within the peer group may bring about increased aggressiveness. This has already been implied in the studies of modeling and positive reinforcement reported on pages 396 and 443. A specific study of aggression training was made by Davitz (34) in the setting of peer interaction of 40 children aged seven to nine. He hypothesized that a child's response to frustration would be affected by his previous experiences in situations similar to that in which frustration was encountered. More specifically, he studied the differing effects of aggressive training and of constructive training on later responses to frustration.

In order to carry this out properly, several steps were necessary: (a) Free play for ten groups of children in the experimental playroom. (b) Five groups received ten-minute aggressive training sessions, involving playing games designed to incite aggression, such as one in which each tried to break everyone else's ping pong ball while protecting his own, and another in which each tried to secure everyone else's "scalp" (a piece of cloth tied around the arm) while protecting his own. During the games, aggressive behavior was praised and encouraged, and individual stars were awarded for winning. Five other training groups received constructive training sessions, involving drawing murals and completing jig-saw puzzles as a group. Throughout aggression was discouraged and cooperation praised and encouraged. (c) A frustration session for each group, aggressive and constructive alike, followed. The children were told they were to see movies just outside the playroom, five reels of film were brought out, the first was shown, and at the start of the second reel they were given candy, but at the climactic point of this reel, without explanation the experimenter stopped the film and took back what candy remained. (d) They were then led back into the playroom and told they could play with anything they wished.

Unknown to the children, their behavior in the earlier prefrustration period had been photographed and now in the postfrustration session was photographed again. Their behavior in the film was reduced to behavioral descriptions which were given to judges who had no knowledge whether a given behavior protocol was from pre- or postfrustration play. Judges were asked to rank the protocols in order of aggressiveness (20 out of 80 protocols showed no aggression at all). Now the data was divided into pre- and postfrustration behavior, and for each subject it was recorded whether there was a gain or a loss in rank.

The constructively trained subjects showed six gains, 11 losses, and three ties. The aggressively trained subjects showed 14 gains, five losses, and one tie. These differences were shown not to be due to chance alone. Constructively trained subjects when faced thereafter by a frustrating situation nevertheless behaved more constructively. Aggressively trained subjects faced with the same frustrating situation behaved more aggressively. Previous training, it was concluded, is a significant determiner of a child's postfrustration reaction to a frustrating situation. It is not merely the frustrating situation that determines the child's behavior. Stimulus conditions are not the only determinants of how one reacts to a frustrating situation; previous experience in the peer group must also be taken into account.

Social Acceptance

It has already been suggested that one of the major functions of the peer group is to supply a means by which the child may find social acceptability. The task is now to examine what are the correlates of social acceptability. Sociometric status, popularity, and leadership are treated as more specific aspects of social acceptance in what follows.

Constancy of social acceptability with increase in age during the peer-group ages has been established. Bonney (22) used the sociometric technique to differentiate socially acceptable from socially unacceptable children in the second through the fifth grades in three schools. The bases of choice of acceptability varied from grade to grade, but in each there were from five to six bases of choice, including with whom to have their pictures taken, partner for a party, and to whom to give Christmas presents. The children were also asked the names of their best friends. A composite score was derived for each child. Bonney used a semilongitudinal approach, with most of the subjects tested in successive grades (although there was pupil population turnover). Consequently, correlation between general social acceptance at successive age levels was possible, giving him a measure of social acceptance constancy.

Between the sociometric measure of the second and third grades the correlation was 0.84; between the third and fourth and fourth and fifth grade it was, respectively, 0.77 and 0.67. A high degree of constancy in degree of social acceptability is exhibited from grade to grade. To emphasize this point, the magnitude of the correlations in social acceptability was approximately as large as that between intelligence test scores for the same grades (0.75 to 0.86). In other words, social acceptability is almost as constant as intelligence.

This constancy of social acceptability was checked by a study of children who transferred from one school to another where, naturally, they were unknown. Although the group was small, in every instance their social acceptance scores at the end of the year in the new school gave them very much the same degree of social acceptability they had had in their previous schools. This constancy of social acceptability has also been found by other investigators. For example, Criswell (30) found that both first and second choices in elementary school children remained stable over a six-week period. Nearly 70 per cent of the first choices did not change over this period.

In spite of constancy of social acceptability, the peer-group members shift in their evaluation of desirable and undesirable personality characteristics over the years of this period. In other words, personality characteristics responsible for social acceptability change as the children grow older. This may be illustrated from data of the longitudinal study reported by Macfarlane (82) using a "Guess Who" technique. This involves short sketches of children about whom the subjects are to guess who is being described as in "Guess who it is that is always bossing other children?"

In the first grade "quiet" was given the highest mark by the children for what makes a real boy. By the third grade being "quiet" had almost dropped out of the pattern. If a given boy had maintained stability in the personality characteristic from the first grade to the third grade by remaining "quiet," he would thereby suffer change in reputational status as a "real boy." (Whether this bothered him or not is a different matter, dependent on whether he wanted this form of prestige.)

These findings were extended with a larger sample by Tuddenham (125) using the same "Guess Who" technique. Popularity in first-grade girls was associated with "acting like a little lady," "being quiet," and "not being bossy or quarrelsome." In the fifth grade "acting like a little lady" had little to do with social acceptability. By this age characteristics such as good looks, being a good sport, friendliness, and tidiness were most highly correlated with social acceptability. The evidence seems clear that the children evaluate other children's social acceptability somewhat differently at different age levels in the light of standards and values characteristic of that age level.

At first, it may appear that there is a contradiction between the constancy of social acceptability found by Bonney, and the shifts in characteristics making for social acceptability found by Macfarlane and Tuddenham. This is not the case. Bonney dealt with *constancy of individual acceptability status;* Macfarlane and Tuddenham with *shifts in characteristics making for social acceptability.* So there is no contradiction between their results. Characteristics may shift in the socially acceptable child so that he maintains his acceptability, but through different characteristics.

Social adaptability, whether deliberate or not, seems to be characteristic of the socially acceptable. The child maintains his acceptability while changing his characteristics.

In peer-aged children popularity is also associated with the traits that are characteristic of sex typing. Popular boys are regarded by their peers as athletic, daring, friendly, and leaders; popular girls are regarded by their peers as docile and unassertive (124). High prestige is related to conforming to sex typing.

Social acceptability varies at different socio-economic levels. In studying this matter Pope (106) used one group from the lower-lower class and another from the upper-middle and lower-upper class. The children came from different schools in different areas of a large city. Both groups averaged 12 years in age, but it was impossible to avoid an IQ discrepancy of 104 for the upper group as compared to 96 for the lower group. A variation of the "Guess Who" type of test yielded a reputational score for each child. The nature of the items may be inferred from the description of results that follow. Each of the 25 traits on which information was obtained was intercorrelated for the upper and lower groups, separately for boys and girls. Cluster analysis (a modification of factor analysis) was then performed. Inspection revealed clusters of traits which were interrelated, yielding characteristic patterns of social behavior.

Among lower group boys three major patterns could be discerned. The members in the first pattern, in which only a few boys fell, were the leaders who had the homage of the other boys and the companionship of the girls. They were aggressive, belligerent, and domineering. The second pattern for lower group boys was the one involving most of the boys who were happy, sociable, able to enjoy a good joke, and considerably less aggressive than their leaders. The third pattern, the sissy, was the one the rest could not tolerate. This pattern included the studious and classroom conforming boys as well as what other groups would call "sissy."

Among boys of high socio-economic status, the group leader, although active and skilled in competitive games, was not expected to be aggressive; in fact, being bossy and given to fighting would tend to make him unpopular. Somewhat more numerous were instances of the pattern of the friendly, personable, good-looking boy who was accepted by both boys and girls. Instances of another pattern would be described as the classroom intellectual. He is not actively rejected; in fact, he enjoys a certain respect. The sissy, in the narrower sense, belongs to still another pattern. However, he is no more acceptable than he was among low socio-economic boys. Along with the bossy, the unkempt, and the fighter, he is not accepted.

Among the girls of the lower socio-economic group, the type widely accepted is "the little lady" who is likeable, friendly, good, tidy, and a good student. She is, however, not likely to be a leader nor does she associate with boys. Another pattern which enjoys considerable prestige, but is less frequently encountered, is the somewhat rowdy, talkative, attention-getting, aggressive girl. She, rather than the little lady, associates with boys in the lower group.

High socio-economic girls instead of having two contrasting patterns of prestige, as did the lower group girls, have but one, that of the "little lady" pattern, but with certain differences. Although good-looking, friendly, and tidy, this girl is more vivacious than her low socio-economic counterpart and she is the one most likely to go out with boys. The tomboy has no place in the group, since any form of aggressiveness or bossiness is rejected. From these results it is apparent that there are distinct differences in the value systems in the two peer cultures. In other words, the members of the groups face different socialization pressures as shown by their differing criteria of what makes for acceptance. But in both, the peer group plays a direct role in personality formation.

For the moment, we are neglecting a systematic discussion of sex-linked characteristics as making for social acceptability. In later discussion of the latency period, it will be found that the characteristics conforming to cultural stereotypes—athletic skill and aggressiveness in boys, and docility and unassertiveness in girls—are definitely associated with social acceptability. Such generalizations as this, however, do not hold in all subcultures. For example, the tomboy of lower socio-economic status does not conform to this statement. Even here, however, there is an illustration of sex-related expectancy. Popularity with peers is related to conforming with expected patterns of sex-related characteristics.

Characteristics related to social acceptance by peers received thorough study from Davis (32). He drew a representative sample of boys from all eighth-grade classes of an entire city. Social acceptance was established by rating scales in which each boy rated every other boy in his homeroom on a variety of traits. These trait ratings were related to a variety of other indices.

The most popular boys proved to be better readers, more intelligent, better adjusted, and to have more favorable attitudes toward school. It is, of course, quite conceivable that intelligence is the common denominator running throughout these characteristics. No relationship was found between sociometric status and age, socio-economic class and academic over- or underachievement. Although these results held for a sample drawn from a whole city, this particular pattern of social acceptance would not hold for all socio-economic levels. Rather, it would appear that Davis' population most resembles the higher socio-economic group of Pope.

The correlates of social power or influence among second- and fifth-grades was found (135) to differ between boys and girls. Boys acquired influence through general intimidation; girls through decorous behavior and special social skills. Both intelligence and physical attractiveness were assists in the acquisition of power for boys and girls. The manner in which they used this power was dependent on individual personality characteristics. Just as an illustration, boys of lower intelligence tended to be frankly coercive and at the same time, inconsistent.

Davids and Parenti (*31*) found evidence that popular children, as determined by sociometric choice, tended to be relatively well-adjusted emotionally and to possess greater amounts of socially desirable personality traits (such as less anxiety, less resentment, optimism, and trust, as judged by professional personnel). The results have to be spoken of in relative terms since one of the samples studied was from a home for disturbed children. In this home population, the "disliked" group showed poorer adjustment than the "ignored" group.

Role playing skill is positively associated with sociometric status (*93*). Popular children are described as low in frustration, clear in expression, assured, and unhesitant. Twenty-six preadolescent Negro boys and girls from the sixth grade were subjects. Information to study this problem was supplied by a combination of sociometric selection by fellow students and judgments by adults who watched these children play "spur of the moment" roles. Each child played different scenes extemporaneously, in which they were assigned roles: (*a*) a friend who is sad, talking to an adult about not being invited to a party, (*b*) a playmate who is angry at another boy, and (*c*) a mischievous student sent to the principal's office for misconduct. Their role-playing ability seemed to be a social skill which contributed to their popularity with their classmates. Those children who were most skillful were also the most popular with their peers.

Friendships

Among older children a variety of factors seem to help to decide which particular peers will be chosen as friends. One phase of this problem is reserved for discussion in Chapter 18, that is, friendships decided along sex lines.

Peer-aged children as they become older show greater stability in their choice of friends according to Horrocks, Buker, and Thompson (*36, 63, 64, 122*). The data were collected simply. They asked about 350 suburban children from five through ten years of age and 900 rural and 900 urban children from 11 to 18 years of age to write down the names of their three best friends. Two weeks later the same request was made of them. The investigators worked out an index of constancy of friendship, extending from identity of names and order on the two lists, on the one hand, to no similarity between the two lists, on the other. They also presented data on whether the first choice of best friend on the two occasions remained the same.

Both methods of analysis showed essentially similar results. As age increased, stability of friendships increased from years five through 18.

For example, among urban children only about 40 per cent of the 11-year-old girls chose the same best friend two weeks later, but by age 15 the stability of choices over the same length of time had increased to over 60 per cent. Similar figures for the same ages in urban boys were 50 per cent and 60 per cent. These trends toward greater stability continued to the oldest age studied, that of the 18-year-old. The more fluctuating friendships of the younger child steadily gave way to relatively more permanent friendships of the mature person.

It will be remembered that Challman (26) found among preschool children that he could not establish very much relationship among similarities in the characteristics of friends. In the school-age child, personal characteristics do play a significant role in the formation of friendships. Furfey (44) found that 62 pairs of boy chums most resembled one another on social maturity, and somewhat resembled one another in chronological age, height, weight, and intelligence. In general, nonintellectual factors were more crucial than intelligence in the maintenance of friendship ties.

These results, incidentally, offered no support to the contention sometimes heard that "opposites" attract. Rather, friends tended to resemble one another. Whether this is because they were alike before the friendship or they influenced one another in the direction of greater similarity is a question where definitive research seems to be lacking. Presumably friends reinforce one another in their characteristics. In other words, friends may be more alike because they influence one another in that direction. Or it may be that the dominant one in a pair is the one who is imitated by the least dominant member.

In the course of a more detailed study, Dymond and her associates (39) examined the differences in friendship qualities chosen by second- and sixth-graders. Drawing on a list of descriptive phrases to characterize their friends, second-graders stressed externals, such as a nice home, being good-looking, and having lots of spending money. The sixth-graders, on the other hand, shifted to an emphasis on personality characteristics such as friendliness, cheerfulness, tidiness, and cleanliness. As they indicate, these changes in characteristics emphasized show an increase in socialization through the internalization of middle-class norms.

The causes of disruptions of friendships have also been investigated (10). After finding the three best friends of a group of 400 sixth-grade children, they checked on changes two weeks later. Sixty per cent changed in their choice of at least one of these friends. The major reasons for changing friends, in decreasing order of importance, were lack of recent contact, a quarrel, incompatibility, judgment that they were now conceited or bossy, disloyal or underhanded, bullying or quarrelsome, or dishonest or untruthful. Sheer physical unavailability in lack of recent contact was thus a major factor.

The second major factor, embracing all the rest of the reasons mentioned, is fluctuation in the child's social needs. In order for a friendship to endure, it must be mutually satisfying. Quarreling, incompatibility, and the like means that it is not, and the friendship is broken. If one or the other of the pair of friends gets nothing from it, or finds it frustrating, that friendship is headed toward dissolution.

As might be expected, children generally tend to choose friends to a greater extent among those living farther and farther away as they progress through the twelve grades of school (126). The older the child, the more socially mobile he becomes, and distance becomes less and less an important factor in influencing his choice of friends.

Cooperation and Competition

The peer group provides opportunities for both cooperation and competition. Children may work together toward a common goal and, hence, cooperate, or they may vie with one another and, hence, compete. Often, of course, both cooperation and competition simultaneously are present. In a basketball game a boy cooperates with his teammates in trying to beat his opponents, hence, he is cooperating with his own team and competing with the other one. But even among those with whom he cooperates, he is also competing in that he tries to be a better player than his teammates. In classrooms the same confusing admixture occurs. Teachers ask that children cooperate and then place only a few in the best reading group, or hang only selected paintings on the wall. This is not meant as a criticism for behaving one way or the other—both cooperation and competition seem necessary to us. However, this does make it difficult to appraise their relative influence, since the same behavior may be motivated by either cooperation or competition.

The study of Maller (84) is outstanding. He compared cooperation and competition in various groups of children, aged from eight to 17, from different schools, and different socio-economic levels. The task was simple one-place addition. Various forms of cooperation and competition were arranged. For example, competition was measured in an individual speed contest; from this result a list showing their ranks was to be posted. In addition, prizes for those scoring highest were offered. Cooperation was measured by staging a contest between classrooms.

Efficiency of work under competition was significantly and consistently higher than work under cooperation. When offered the choice between working for themselves or working for the group, the children selected the group in only 26 per cent of the choices. However, in one subsidiary experiment—a contest between boys and girls—the choice to work for the sex group among boys was higher than the choices to work for themselves. Nevertheless, in the over-all results, girls were more cooperative, choosing more often than boys to work for the group (though still predominantly in favor of competition).

It would appear that competition for the self improved performance over cooperation for the group. Moreover, with only one exception, competition was chosen by the children over cooperation. But as Doob (38) suggests, certain qualifications seem indicated. There is the fact that there were quite different rewards in the two situations. In competition both the prestige and prize were acquired. In cooperation there was no prize, and the given child could feel rewarded only if he belonged to a victorious group and he, himself, was strongly attached to the group. Classrooms of children are not necessarily conducive to *esprit de corps*.

Moreover, competition was organized in a particular situation. Certain competitive versus cooperative aspects of many other situations were absent. Interaction among children was minimal. For example, competition often meant that one tried to prevent competitors from reaching a goal, and cooperation required constructive assistance of one another rather than merely contributing to a common goal. Any or all of these factors may contribute to different results concerning the relative influence of cooperation and competition. Hence, although Maller's study indicates competition was favored over cooperation which may even be typical of many situations, it does not prove that competition is always favored over cooperation.

Members of groups working together for the good of the group actually increased their liking for one another (104). On the other hand, groups where one competed with another did not necessarily decrease their liking. In competing groups decrease in liking seemed to occur only when one or two members of the group got a disproportionate proportion of the rewards. If the individual rewards were fairly evenly distributed, then the effect might be similar to that holding in cooperating groups.

These results were obtained by dividing 40 fourth-grade children into eight groups of five, with four high and four low "cohesive" groups. The groups had been derived by presenting a sociometric questionnaire. This was then used to divide groups so that some were groups in which the members liked one another and others were groups in which they did not.

The questionnaire was again administered at the end of the study to see what changes were brought about by cooperation or competition. In cooperating groups members shared equally in the rewards; in the competitive groups they received them only according to their contributions to correctness. A form of the game "Twenty Questions" used for identifying animals was the task. Two high cohesive groups worked under cooperative conditions; two under competitive conditions. Low cohesive groups were similarly composed. The increase in cohesiveness even under competition, unless rewards were disproportionately distributed, was encouraging evidence of the ability of children to get along with one another.

The school age

There is no question of the importance of the influence of the peer group on the child. But there is the equally uncontrovertible fact that social behavior takes place under the watchful eye of adults, other than parents, who constantly impose on the child their own standards of socialization.

Wright (133), who studied the amount of time spent by children in community settings, also investigated who were the leaders in these settings. Almost all leaders were adults—in only eight per cent of community settings had children assumed leadership. In effect, this means that adults were almost always on hand to look after the children. Every Boy Scout troop has its scoutmaster. To be sure, in other communities, especially in the large cities and in lower socio-economic groups, children are much more "on the loose." Too little supervision can have a pernicious effect, but it also is possible that these findings imply that too much supervision is being given these children.

Teachers, recreation leaders, ministers, rabbis, priests, and the like are intent upon teaching the child forms of behavior which they consider proper. They wish to bring about an increase in cooperation, a diminution of conflict, and the other social values of our society. In what follows, teachers in school settings and their effect upon school-age children will be made central.

Socialization and the Teacher

The school, expressed through teacher practices, reflects educational philosophy and practices. The amount of time a child spends in school attests to its importance. To state it in terms of the shortest minimum range, from six to 16 years of age a child spends from four to six hours a day, five days a week in the classroom. Extracurricular activities and homework add to this already imposing total.

The school's task has broadened enormously within the years of this century (131). At the turn of the century, the schools were dedicated to imparting certain knowledge and skills. Today, the doctrine of the "whole" child motivates concern over personal, social, economic, political, and health development, and the imparting of knowledge and skills is a "minimal program."

Havighurst puts this issue in terms of developmental tasks:

In some societies the school goes far beyond this minimal program. The middle-class part of American society uses the school for a wider variety of purposes than any other society. Since American boys and girls are thrown together in the school by age-groups, the school becomes a place where they may learn the tasks of social development, and American educators consider the teaching of these tasks an important part of the school's responsibility. Also the American school is expected to help out other training institutions of society—the family, church, industry, youth-serving organizations—in the teaching of such diverse tasks as learning physical skills, selecting and preparing for an occupation, preparation for marriage, and learning a scale of values.

There is no developmental task of children or adolescents which the school can completely ignore, for the reason that the tasks are so closely interrelated that difficulty in one task, which may show in the school, is often tied up with difficulty in another task for which the school has little direct responsibility. For instance, failure in academic work may be due to failure in some other developmental task (59, 25-26).[1]

This becomes relevant when it is indicated that teachers not only share this view, but are also actively engaged in carrying it out in the classroom. How the teacher serves as an agent of socialization as reflected by a sample of certain relevant research results concerns us here.

The teacher chooses certain activities in preference to others. She sets up certain standards and not others; thus, she is giving direction to the group. She, of course, makes her choices on the basis of her conception of what children are like, how they should behave, and what they should learn; also involved is her own system of values—most often that of the middleclass (58). The desirability of correct speech, politeness, cleanliness, neatness, and respect for property and thrift are imparted along with more academic information.

The teachers proceed to socialize the child, using much the same methods as does the mother. She sets up standards of conduct to which the child is expected to conform. In addition to teaching subject mat-

---

[1] From Havighurst (59). Copyright 1953 by Longmans, Green and Co., and published with permission.

ter, the teacher performs a variety of socializing practices. For example, she helps individual children in the school group by a variety of consciously recognized devices—creating situations in which it would be possible to see a previously objectionable child in a new role, getting a child previously ignored to contribute a talent which the other children have not recognized, helping a child to accept her as a person by accepting him as a person of worth, hoping these will lead to peer acceptance.

The teacher uses rewards and punishments in her socialization efforts (25). Not only are these used at the formal level epitomized by the "gold star" or "staying after school," but also in a variety of more subtle and much broader ways (85). In the setting of behavior-social learning theory any behavior that serves as reinforcement may work toward socialization. A nod, a frown, a smile are means of reinforcing certain forms of behavior while attempting to extinguish others. Martin and Stendler offer the following illustration concerning Miss A, a third grade teacher:

> Miss A's class is writing a letter to Tony who is ill at home. Miss A walks up and down the aisles supervising the children's work. She stops at Pete's desk and picks up his paper.
> "Boys and girls," she says to get the attention of the group. "May I have your attention? That means you too, Matilda. This is Pete's paper. I want you to notice how carefully Pete has followed my directions. See? He has left margins at both sides and has written the heading exactly right. See how neat and clean his paper is, too?"
> Miss A returns Pete's paper with a beam of approval and goes on. She stops at Raymond's desk. Raymond does not fare so well. "Boys and girls." Again the heads go up. "Look at Raymond's paper. Raymond needs some help. See the smudges and spots on his paper? What can we tell Raymond to help him improve?"
> "He should wash his hands before he starts and not erase," say the children.
> The teacher returns the paper to Raymond with a look of disapproval. "It will have to be done over, Raymond, and that's wasting paper, you know."
> Some of the children finish their letters and must wait for all to finish. Several sit and do nothing. Miss A comments to the class.
> "I like the way some people are finding jobs to do when they finish. I saw two children studying spelling and one boy doing his workbook. That's using time wisely, isn't it, boys and girls? You'll have five more minutes to finish and I expect all of you to be done, if you haven't been dawdling" (85, 415).[2]

Quite apart from its contribution to academic skills, the material the

[2] From Martin and Stendler (85). Copyright 1953 by Harcourt, Brace and Company, and published with permission.

teacher selects in her teaching also influences the socialization process —the examples she uses with approval or disapproval, the events she talks about, and the textbooks she uses. Textbooks supply material for the development of academic skills and certainly none bear the title *Socialization: Grade 3.* Nevertheless, they also influence socialization.

Child, Potter, and Levine (28) analyzed the contents of a considerable number of third-grade readers according to motivational categories applied to the characters in the stories. The theoretical position they took was that of behavior-social learning theory; reinforcements and punishments expressed in the stories in 30 general third-grade readers were analyzed on the assumption that rewarded behavior would tend to increase the likelihood of similar future behavior, whereas punishment would tend to decrease similar future behavior. There was unequivocal evidence that certain motives were encouraged and others discouraged. Seeking help, information, or friendship were rewarded, but being aggressive or independent was punished. In general, the investigators concluded that the stories were of a sort that would encourage adjustment to our society. They went on to indicate, however, that the accounts tended to be unreasonably optimistic (good behavior is always rewarded and children are rarely asked to adjust to failure of any sort) and failed to encourage independent behavior. However, we cannot blame the textbooks. They can do no more than reflect society, not lead it.

Individual differences in personality among teachers are almost as great as those to be found among their pupils. The only reason for even as much restriction as this remark implies is that their predominately middle-class background, their specific choice of teaching as a profession, some degree of similarity of education, the predominance of women in the profession, and other related factors presumably allow at least somewhat less variability than would be found in their pupils. Nevertheless, there is still a tremendously wide range of personality variation.

The teacher's personality presumably has an effect on the children in her class. Some aspects of this are considered in more specific ways presently. A more general problem is the issue of teachers who show personality maladjustments. A considerable body of opinion has developed which would allege that if a teacher's personal adjustment was poor, her pupils also would show signs of maladjustment. Gladstone (48) made an analysis of the available data and reached the conclusion that there was no necessary relationship between maladjustment in the teacher and maladjustment in her pupils. It would seem that both adjusted and maladjusted teachers could bring about pernicious effects on their pupils. More important than any fuzzy concept such as general adjustment appears to be her empathy with, and acceptance of, children. These qualities are not confined to "adjusted" teachers only. Indeed, some teachers with emotional difficulties may be especially sensitive to particular kinds of problems in their students. Others, of course, release their pent-up aggression on their pupils. Neither the presence nor absence of maladjustment, *per se*, but the expression of the maladjustment should be the criterion of fitness to teach.

The criteria by which teachers evaluate the nature of children's behavior problems have been a topic of major interest since the appearance in 1928 of Wickman's widely quoted study (129). Wickman acquired ratings of mental hygiene specialists and teachers on the relative seriousness of various specified child behavior symptoms. The specialists and the teachers rated the relative seriousness of the same behavior item quite differently. The results were interpreted as showing that teachers rated as more serious those symptoms associated with noisier, more rebellious, disobedient, outgoing behavior which threatened the orderliness of the classroom, whereas the specialists rated as more serious the less threatening symptoms associated with withdrawal, anxiety, and sensitivity, while attaching little importance to almost all of those stressed by teachers.

It is evident that teachers were defining seriousness in terms of a moralistic point of view, with stress on aggressiveness against persons and property. Many of the problems the teachers placed as most serious were, in one way or another, challenges to their authority in the classroom. Evidently, seriousness was equated with seriousness as a threat to the smooth-running functioning of the classroom. Moreover, before we become too critical of the attitude expressed by the teachers it is well to remember the mental hygienist had a different frame of reference, being much more concerned with behavior which had an ominous implication for the child's future emotional and personal development. The withdrawing type of symptom, unsocialness, as well as depression, suspicion, fearfulness, and sensitiveness have been demonstrated to be most difficult to overcome in treatment and sometimes to be the precursors of a more serious form of maladjustment.

The results seemed to reflect discredit on the acumen of the teachers, or so it was widely interpreted. Actually, the Wickman study had many serious defects (16, 17) which render the results much less conclusive than they were interpreted to be. It should be noted that if the teacher is to do her job of communicating skills and values, this can be done only in an orderly environment. The aggressive child disrupts the class, the withdrawing child at least does not do this.

In a wealth of studies that followed the pioneer study of Wickman, teachers tended to be found to minimize the seriousness of withdrawal and other nonsocial form of behavior as compared to the clinicians. In this regard, however, they have recently been inclining more toward the attitude of the clinicians (16).

Pupil's Evaluations of Teachers and of School

Since teachers are the visible symbols of school, it is not too far-fetched to include, in the presentation to follow, information we have about attitudes of children toward school in general and teachers in particular.

There is no question that entrance into school is a stirring experience, whether favorably received or not. To quote Murphy and his associates on this point:

> Entrance into the conventional first grade marks a sharp break in the actual structure of the child's experience. For the first time in the case of many children, they are expected to conform to a group pattern imposed by an adult who is in charge of too many children to be constantly aware of each child as an individual. Flash cards are flashed at the group all at once. Stories are told and everybody must listen whether he will or no. Drawing paper and crayons are meted out whether you happen to feel like drawing at that moment or not. One child who found this shift quite beyond endurance remarked after his first day in school, "It's awful; all you do is mind all day long." And another day he added, "It really is awful. All you do it sit and sit and sit" (96, 652).[3]

This new pattern of conformity expected of the child is often softened by a somewhat less rigorous atmosphere in the modern school, but the teacher, no matter how progressive, cannot be aware of all the children at once. Group, not individual, methods must be used. Many children find entrance to school to be a pleasurable experience, while others do not. Children come to school with different expectancies. Some view it suspiciously, are reluctant, and prepared to dislike it and all that it stands for.

The school is a source of frustrations as well as satisfactions. The child must conform or suffer the consequences. If his experiences are too painful, if he is unable to satisfy at least some of his needs, he will reject the school and do everything he can to fight off its influences, awaiting only the day he is of age to leave. In the meantime, he struggles against the teachers, and the children who are acceptant of the school become his natural enemy.

[3] From Murphy, Murphy, and Newcomb (96). Copyright 1937 by Harper and Brothers, and published with permission.

Schoolchildren view the teacher as having the greatest influence in the areas of social values (132). This finding came about from an investigation into what activities children thought would gain them approval from their teachers and what activities would bring disapproval. Stated in positive terms, honesty, courtesy, and respect for others were, generally speaking, the most important behavior values gaining social approval in the classroom in the opinion of a large number of pupils of both sexes in grades six through twelve.

A child's feelings about himself are at least partially related to his parents' attitudes. The child, accepted by his parents and motivated to learn what they have to teach, will generalize this situation to the teacher in school (11). The child may see the teacher as a mother substitute and, if he receives the same acceptance from her that he does at home, will readily accept her teachings. He will be confident and eager to learn. If he is not so motivated, learning in school becomes less attractive and less necessary.

Although it might be hazardous to generalize the results for all sorts of schools in all areas, an investigation of the liking for school as expressed by New York City schoolchildren seems fairly representative. Spontaneous opinions were obtained from over 600 school children in grades six and seven (118). An effort to obtain a representative sample was made by gathering responses in three schools, one each in a superior, middling, and poor neighborhood. To make for naturalness of response the question was devised for these children to write down what they would reply to a friend who asked, "Did they like school?" They were to give their answer as they might speak it, with no attention to grammar.

The replies were classified into three categories—liking, disliking, and mixed feeling concerning school. About 50 per cent of the boys and 70 per cent of the girls liked school, whereas about 25 per cent of the boys and 10 per cent of the girls disliked school with the rest showing mixed feelings.

The reasons given for liking school centered on getting an education, helping to get a job, liking teachers and classmates, and having fun. Reasons for disliking school stressed work being too hard or the teachers being unfair. It would seem that these children were not very critical but they did show that the teacher loomed large as a source of liking or disliking school.

One of the sources of difference in attitudes toward school is social class. The resultant attitudes are a function of the teacher, the pupil, and his parents. As a broad generalization later to be qualified, upper- and middle-class children are favorably disposed, whereas lower-class children in varying degrees are not favorably disposed toward school. In reviewing a series of studies on the subject of social class (58), it was found that the social environment was essentially middle-class in its values. It follows that holding these values meant that the teachers reinforced the attitudes and habits taught in middle-class homes.

Metropolitan lower-class children may see the middle-class teacher as one more representative of authority. And yet there is another segment of the lower class, perhaps more often from rural or less urban areas, which looks up to the teacher as a model to be followed, and which holds middle-class values and aspires to the teaching profession as a means of moving up in the social scale. In a study of student teachers in Texas, 44 per cent were found to be so motivated (86).

Middle- and upper-class parents often display a marked interest and favorable attitude toward scholastic success. They may reward scholastic success by tangible steps, such as presents and trips. The child sees the effect of education on the success of friends of the family and relatives and neighbors who have gone into activities for which education has prepared them. So the prospect of future rewards reinforces pressures from the family.

Lower-lower class parents view education with suspicion and distrust, very often actively rejecting its values. The lower-class peer group reinforces these negative attitudes toward education. As Davis (33) indicates, the child from the slum is taught by his gang to view education as a trap, not to be taken in by the teacher, and to appreciate the disgraceful nature of doing homework. If by some mistake he were to get good grades, this must be concealed at all costs. Lower-class children find contradictions between what they have been taught at home and what they are taught in school. These weaken tendencies of liking school and the teacher in most pupils in this group, while strengthening it in others. Some may turn to school for what the family cannot teach them, but a greater number reject school.

In upper-lower class groups parental interest is somewhat greater although not to the extent that it is in the upper- or middle-class groups (60, 61). They see it as a means of vocational preparation perhaps, but do not believe in education *per se*.

In a sample of middle-class children, Stendler and Young (116) found that starting school gave them feelings of being "grown-up" and important. After three months they still liked school very much. After three months in school, their mothers were asked whether their children liked school more, the same, or less than when they started. They found 47 per cent liked it more, 48 the same, and only five per cent liked it less.

Stendler (*115*) found through interviewing first-grade mothers that almost 100 per cent of upper- and upper-middle class parents sent their children to preschool, whereas only 14 per cent of lower-lower class parents did so. She showed that economic circumstances alone could not be the cause of the difference. Similarly, parental expectations for schooling go down as one descends the social ladder. More upper- and upper-middle class mothers prepared their children for first grade by teaching at home the alphabet and the beginnings of reading and writing than did the other groups. Higher standards were expected in the higher groups. That these attitudes communicate themselves to the children there can be no doubt. Milner (*89*) administered measures of reading readiness, and found that children from middle-class families were better prepared for reading than children from lower-class families. These differences, it is obvious, temper the respective attitudes of children toward school and teachers.

One important study (*19*) of differences of attitudes in various social classes took advantage of the nature of the British school system to correct the influence of differences in intelligence which might have been reflected in the previous results on liking and disliking of school. At the age of eleven as the result of a rigorous examination selected young working-class children were transferred from their neighborhood school into already functioning middle-class schools with middle-class attitudes. The question was whether differences in attitude toward education could be observed between the pupils from middle-class and those from working-class homes now in the same grammar schools.

The children from the latter were far from typical by the fact of their selection, but this way of studying the matter did neatly control for intelligence and ability, since they were all in the school by virtue of the competitive examination. Various techniques, such as multiple-choice questions, checklists, and sentence completion, were used to collect information on (*a*) educational aspirations, (*b*) relative importance attached to work and play, and (*c*) interest in reading and classical music. In all three categories, middle-class boys were higher in percentage of positive attitudes toward education, although the differences were by no means all statistically significant. Among issues on which the two classes showed significant difference was the greater percentage of middle-class boys who, if free to do so, would like to stay in school until 16. Greater interests on their part in getting books from libraries, in classical music, and in similar interests were expressed.

In this connection it is relevant to observe that Wylie (*134*) found that children of lower socio-economic levels made more modest estimates of their ability than did children of higher socio-economic status.

About 150 white junior high school children made estimates, not of how they actually were doing in school, but of what they thought they could do if they tried their best. They made this estimate by (*a*) stating whether they thought their level of ability to do school work was in the top or bottom half of the class, and (*b*) whether, assuming they had financial support and parental approval, they had the ability to go to college.

Actual IQ's and a classification of socio-economic status based on the father's occupation supplied the other relevant information. Both higher and lower socio-economic status children were grouped by IQ at ten point intervals from 65 to 145, and the percentage at each interval who said they were in the top half in ability to do school work and in ability for college work was calculated. Consistently, those in the upper socio-economic group gave themselves higher self-evaluations; a greater proportion than actually merited it placed themselves both in the upper half of the class and as having ability for college work.

To draw an illustration chosen from those who objectively did not belong in the upper half, among children at IQ 85 about 20 per cent of the lower socio-economic youngsters thought they were in the upper half in ability, whereas nearly 60 per cent of the "upper" children thought so. At IQ 95, 80 per cent of the "higher" and 60 per cent of the "lower" children estimated they had ability for college work. It was only at IQ 115 that more than 80 per cent of the "lower" children conceded they had this ability. Children with IQ above 125 in both groups practically unanimously saw themselves as having these abilities but they were a miniscule proportion of the total group. Self-favorability bias, it would seem, is associated with higher socio-economic status.

There are, of course, other sources of differences of evaluation of school and teachers. Sources of differences extending over the gamut of psychological characteristics by which we distinguish one child from another may affect attitudes toward school. Social factors will also be important. For example, the nature of the child's reception by the peer group in school will undoubtedly influence his attitudes. Similarly, his self-concept, as already determined by experiences prior to school, will bring him to school receptive either to a favorable or an unfavorable attitude. It will be remembered from the account in Chapter 13 that Merrill-Bishop found that when children were placed with a "neutral" stranger, if their mothers were restrictive and, hence, produced aggression in their children, they behaved aggressively toward the strange woman. This was in contrast to the nonaggressive children who continued their nonaggressive behavior. Behavior toward the mother consistently generalized to other adults. Presumably, this includes behavior toward the teacher.

Attitudes at home in their interplay with school behavior are maintained as the school years go on. Hartshorne, May, and Shuttleworth (57), in the course of an extensive study of moral character, had occasion to administer a series of tests of honesty to pupils in grades five through eight. They used two summary measures that are relevant here—(a) a combined honesty measure; and (b) an integration score which had to do with the stability of these measures, that is, the degree to which one was stable or consistent in honesty from test situation to test situation in the classroom. These measures were obtained in two school populations. Population Y was located in a small town with a fairly stable population; population Z came from the underprivileged, slum section of a large city.

Population Y was the more favored in intelligence, emotional stability, and cultural and economic background. In the pupils drawn from that population, the correlations of age with honesty and with integration although low were significant. In other words, the pupils tended to become both more honest and more integrated in classroom behavior as they grew older. Children in population Z showed the opposite tendency with correlations with increasing age being negative. As they grew older these children became more dishonest and more inconsistent. In the first group, presumably pressure from home, neighborhood, and school worked together; in the second group, the three probably were at odds with one another.

Relevant to the school age are many other important issues. Two are chosen for exposition. These are the qualities of teachers which pupils like and their views of the teachers' dispensing of approval and disapproval. Jersild (65) asked children in grades one through twelve what were the characteristics of the teacher they liked best. They reported (1) human qualities, such as being kind, sympathetic, and considerate; (2) disciplinary qualities, such as being fair, consistent, and not scolding; and (3) performance as a teacher, through being helpful and interesting. Attractive physical appearance, grooming and voice, unimportant for the youngest group, was mentioned as a quality by children from the fourth grade onward. The youngest group in the first three grades stressed participation in activities, such as joining in games. Adults were asked to recall the teachers they had liked best, and substantially the same pattern was found, except for more stress on the human qualities. It would appear that most of the children and adults were probably of middle-class status.

From the pupil's point of view, teachers distribute approval and disapproval in a consistent, but unfair manner. A "Guess Who" technique was used by deGroat and Thompson (36) to find those pupils to whom the teacher gave approval and disapproval. The nominations were consistent in showing that a few children received most of the teacher's approval, and another small group the burden of disapproval. Moreover, a recheck, five weeks later, showed a correlation of 0.80 in the two inquiries into teacher approval and disapproval. The pupils receiving the greatest teacher approval were the most intelligent, showed the highest academic achievement, and had the best personality adjustment as measured by a personality questionnaire. Whether the approval or disapproval the teacher gives is actually assimilated, Martin and Stendler (85) indicate, is dependent on the relationship between the teacher and the pupil. If there is acceptance of the teacher by the pupil, if the learning situation is a rewarding one, then he learns from her. If it is not a rewarding one, he does not. It is not only what the teacher teaches that is important, but also what the pupil finds rewarding enough to learn. Learning, in this instance, takes place in an interaction between teacher and pupil.

Pupil-Teacher Interaction

The already familiar study of conflict in preschool children by Jersild and Markey (66) will be used to introduce the question of pupil-teacher interaction. Teachers injected themselves into about one-third of the children's conflicts. In many instances, the teacher did so before the children had ceased their struggles. Less frequently, but still fairly often, she stepped in *after* the children had ceased their conflict, either to renew the issue in an effort to bring about a compromise solution or to reverse the decision the children had reached. Often this took the form of giving the advantage to the child who had lost, thus depriving the victor of what he had gained. In about 70 per cent of the occasions in which she stepped in, the teacher decided definitely in favor of one child or the other. Almost always, the decision was against the child who had been the aggressor. It is significant to add that she often interfered in situations so mild that they could not be construed as either dangerous or one-sided for the children concerned. It is quite possible that, in these instances, the children would have been better off if left to their own devices.

The teacher, irrespective of the severity of the problem, tended to use the same bland methods. Since mild and severe problems were handled alike, this made it difficult for the child to distinguish between what was a grave trespass upon the person or rights of others and something that was relatively innocuous in nature. Consequently, Jersild and Markey urged the practice of differential severity on the part of the teachers.

In some school groups a substantial relation has been found between the extent of fighting and quarreling with one's peers and aggressive, resistant acts directed by the children toward the teacher. This was also a finding of Jersild and Markey. However, they found this relation to vary from group to group. In their three groups the correlations between frequency of conflicts with other children and frequency of conflicts with teachers were 0.47, 0.08, and 0.73. Over-all, for the three groups combined, the correlation was 0.28. In the second group in which the correlation was lowest, there were certain distinguishing characteristics. In this group the children were the oldest, they had the least conflicts among themselves, and teachers interfered the most when conflicts between children occurred. These findings, although not definitive, would tend to indicate that these factors may be important in influencing the nature of pupil-teacher interaction. We do know that the attitude of the teacher affects this interaction. The particular situation effects the patterns of aggression and related behavior.

This question of the effect of the particular situation on the patterns of aggression was investigated by Thompson (*121*). He equated two groups of four-year-old children for IQ, socio-economic status, and ratings by teachers on general personality characteristics. With one, a nursery school group, the teachers, although understanding and interested, were somewhat aloof and allowed the children to plan their own activities to a considerable extent. In the other group, the teachers were much more cooperative, maintained a great deal of personal contact, and to a much greater degree helped to guide their activities. The teachers shared equal time in both groups and the equipment used was identical, thus controlling the effect of these factors. After eight months of this experience, the children in the more highly guided group were found to be more ascendant, more constructive when faced with possible failure, and higher in social participation and in leadership. They were also less destructive. Teacher guidance, when it has certain goals, can bring about these goals by the kind of behavior adopted. Positive gains in social maturity seem indicated when the teachers adopt certain attitudes.

Also illustrative of the effect of teacher attitudes in interaction with pupils is an experiment by Trager and Yarrow (*123*). In this study substantial changes in attitude and behavior were found in one group of first- and second-grade children which did not appear in another.

With 14 sessions in each, two contrasting procedures were followed. In one group the adult leader accepted status differences and worked toward creating an atmosphere of intergroup understanding. Comparable groups of control children had comparable sessions without the intercultural content. Changes were measured through projective devices both before and after the sessions and through systematic observations during the sessions. They indicated changes in the children's responses in the direction of the atmospheres established by the leaders.

In the investigation of teacher behavior, a guiding theme of a considerable number of investigators has been that teachers' behavior in working with children may be related to a contrast between a dominating or authoritarian attitude, on the one hand, and a socially integrated or democratic one, on the other. These investigators related these contrasting attitudes to the behavior shown by the children, stressing the greater growth value, greater productivity, cooperation, and engagement in integrative-democratic procedures.

A series of studies was conducted by Anderson and his associates (4, 5, 6, 7, 8, 9). Dominating behavior was said to be shown by teachers who used force, commands, threats, bribes, shaming, and insistence upon conformity in dealing with their pupils. They also resist differences or change, thus being rigid or inflexible (4). In integrative behavior, in contrast, they are alleged to be yielding to other persons, finding common purposes with them and, consequently, to be spontaneous and flexible. Anderson and his colleagues (6) proceeded to study the relationship of teachers' dominating or socially integrated behavior to their pupils' behavior. They hypothesized that (1) integrative behavior in one person tended to increase similar behavior in others; and (2) dominative behavior, likewise, tended to bring about dominative behavior in others.

In collaboration with Anderson, Brewer (8), using an observational technique, made records of dominative and integrative behavior in two second-grade rooms in the same elementary school. Assignment to one room or the other had been by lot, minimizing the possibility of systematic differences between the children in the two rooms. The teacher in one room had been found to be consistently more integrative; the other to be consistently more dominative. The comparison of the behavior of the children under these contrasting teachers formed the basis of reporting the results of their study. The children with the more integrative teacher showed considerably more spontaneity in offering suggestions, in expressing appreciation, in making social contributions, and in telling of their own experiences, upon invitation by the teacher. The children under the more dominative teacher not only showed less of the behavior just described, but they also were more distractible and wasteful of time and nonconforming to teacher domination.

The investigators considered that their hypotheses were verified— integrative behavior and dominative behavior in the teachers induced corresponding behavior in their pupils. However, differences between the teachers were not significant for *spontaneous* offering of suggestions and in telling of their experiences. Since the "integrative" teacher was selected as being responsive, the fact that they proved she was responsive is hardly surprising.

Reed (9), in following up Brewer's two teachers with new classes a year later, found that they and their new pupils repeated their contrasting performances of the year before. Meanwhile, the pupils Brewer had studied had moved on to new teachers in the third grade. With their new teachers the children's behavior showed practically a zero correlation with their behavior a year before, attesting to the great (and fortunate) flexibility of children. Their behavior in the classroom seemed highly dependent on the behavior of their teachers. If presented with integrative behavior by their teacher, children respond with similar behavior; if they meet dominative behavior from their teachers, they become distractible and resistant. These results are interpretable in terms of behavior-social learning theory.

As Mussen and Conger (97) indicate these results are quite congruent with the requirement of a reinforcement theory of learning. The integrative teacher, unlike the dominative one, teaches in such fashion that she makes socially constructive responses rewarding so that the child is motivated to perform these responses. By the same token, she less often frustrates the child. The dominative teacher more frequently frustrates the children in her class, and aggressive and hostile behavior eventuates. Although she may inhibit overt behavior of this kind by her domination and threats of punishment, she is not instilling the positive desire for cooperation that comes from the behavior of the integrative teacher.

These studies are open to certain criticisms as Sechrest (112)[4] shows. It has already been noted that the effects were transitory; when the children were promoted and taught by new teachers little or no relationship could be found to their behavior the year before. What had

---

[4] The studies of Lewin, Lippitt, and White (76, 77, 78) are so frequently cited in connection with the present topic that a justification for their omission must be offered. Unfortunately, they are open not only to variations of these criticisms, but also to others even more serious (112). Hence, they are not reported here.

been demonstrated was limited to the situation in which the children were observed. Moreover, the results concerned average children; there may well have been some children who profited more from the regime that stultified the majority. Since no achievement measures were involved, we simply do not know what effect the differing leadership had on accomplishment as such.

Summary

The interrelated problems of peer and school relationships of the older child have been reviewed.

In the peer group, the older child is able to find himself in relation to the social group and to obtain independence from parental restrictions as well. He tends to conform to the group standard even when it is wrong.

Social acceptability, friendships, and cooperation and competition are used for illustrative purposes. During the peer-group age, as age increases constancy of social acceptability goes hand in hand with shifts in characteristics making for this social acceptability. What makes for social acceptability is found to vary at different socio-economic levels. Peer-group friendships are found to rest on propinquity and similarities in nonintellectual factors rather more than in intellectual ones. Greater stability of friendships with increasing age is found. Reflecting society's stand, cooperation and competition are found to exist side-by-side in children. Both cooperation and competition were clearly manifest in the preschool years and may well have had their beginnings in infancy. Competition is more intense in lower socio-economic groups than it is in other groups. Whether competition or cooperation is stronger in children in general is, in a sense, a pointless question. Relative strength of competition or cooperation when either or both are possible depends on the situation and the child.

The school-age child has the teacher as the prime agent of socialization. Consequently her role is central. The teacher brings pressures to bear on the child through her reflection of the school's philosophy and through her reflection of her own background. To further these socialization aims she helps children, uses rewards and punishments, and selects material for teaching purposes.

Pupils react variously to these pressures from teachers and other adults. Nevertheless, social-class differences are found—upper- and middle-class children are more favorably disposed toward school and lower-class children are less favorably disposed.

The school is seen by the child not only as a source of rewards but also of frustrations as well. He is influenced in his attitudes toward school by parental pressures, by the social class from which he comes, and by his reception from the peer group.

Pupil-teacher interaction depends in large measure on the methods the teacher uses. Research findings in this area are confused or limited. Results of research presented are illustrative, not definitive.

For Further Reading

No general, definitive references can be given for the topics and the age range considered in this chapter. It can only be suggested that cited research reports be examined.

References

Follow Chapter 18.

18

Psychoanalytic Contentions

FROM A psychoanalytic standpoint many aspects of later childhood merit attention. First of all it is the latency period and the genital stage. In connection with these at least some mention of adult personality structure is required. Then, too, the sex behavior tendencies of later childhood have been set aside for consideration until now because of their obvious relevance to psychoanalytic views. These tendencies will be examined in a setting of peer relationships and attendant problems. In addition, drawing on these findings, we shall endeavor to reconcile and integrate a neo-Freudian interpretation of latency with psychoanalytic theory. Finally, this chapter will attempt to summarize the writer's position by presenting a more general evaluation of psychoanalytic theory as it relates to the psychology of the child.

The latency period

According to psychoanalytic theory the latency period, starting at about six years and lasting until prepuberty at about ten, is different from the psychosexual stages because no new area of libidinal localization develops during this interval. (Reference to Table 2 on page 117 will give an outline of this period and the succeeding genital stage.) Originally, it was thought that sexual impulses remained latent, accounting for the name the period bears. It is now recognized that during the years of latency there is no true recession of sex impulses. Sexual interests are quiescent and to some extent dormant but by no means nonexistent. Repression and a renunciation of erotic behavior mask the sexual activities of latency.

During the latency period there appears to be a consolidation of already existing ego, superego, and id relationships. The strengthened ego and superego make latency possible. A slackening of pace occurs, changes take place slowly, following the patterns already laid down. There is a significant extension of object relations on the child's part to his peers, especially to children of his own sex. The libidinal desires for parental love "are replaced by sublimated expressions of affection— tenderness, devotion, and respect" (21, 129).[1] There is a reaching out toward others, a desire for companionship of peers, schoolmates, and neighbors. As a result, the parents are seen more objectively and less blindly. The child may even be more influenced by the opinions of his peers than of his parents. The child is developing standards which he accepts as his own (superego development) and developing mental and physical skills which serve the purpose of adaptation (ego development).

Among those already established mechanisms, sublimation and reaction formations are prominent. Thus, the child redirects his libidinal desires by sublimated affection for his parents. He also uses reaction formations to hold in check forbidden impulses. For example, curiosity about sexuality may now be sublimated in an interest in how things work and how things were in other times and places. There is thus a realistic orientation to the child's interests.

The genital stage

In psychoanalytic theory the genital stage is subdivided into the prepubertal and pubertal phases. The first phase, beginning at about age ten, is preparatory to physical sexual maturity. There is considered to be a sharp increase in libidinal energy. Libido is again directed toward the love objects of childhood. Oedipal fantasies reappear. Anna Freud describes the changes from latency to prepuberty vividly:

> Aggressive impulses are intensified to the point of complete unruliness, hunger becomes voracity and the naughtiness of the latency period turns into the criminal behavior of adolescence. Oral and anal interests, long submerged, come to the surface again. Habits of cleanliness, laboriously acquired during the latency period, give place to pleasure in dirt and disorder, and instead of modesty and sympathy we find ex-

[1] By permission from *Psychoanalytic Theories of Personality* by Blum. Copyright 1953. McGraw-Hill Book Company, Inc.

hibitionistic tendencies, brutality and cruelty to animals. The reaction-formations, which seemed to be firmly established in the structure of the ego, threaten to fall to pieces. At the same time, old tendencies which had disappeared come into consciousness. The Oedipus wishes are fulfilled in the form of fantasies and day-dreams, in which they have undergone but little distortion; in boys ideas of castration and in girl penis-envy once more become the centre of interest. There are very few new elements in the invading forces. Their onslaught merely brings once more to the surface the familiar content of the early infantile sexuality of little children (42, 159).[2]

In short, there is a reactivation of earlier modes of pleasure finding. There is also a general disruption of the balance among the structural aspects of personality. The truce between the ego and the id, prevailing in the latency stage, is now torn asunder. When id impulses predominate, lapses into pregenital gratifications take place and aggressive, even criminal, behavior may result as has been described in the quotation from Anna Freud.

When the ego dominates, there is an increase in anxiety, and neurotic symptoms may appear. Ego defenses of all sorts are called into play and new ones, such as asceticism and intellectualization, appear. Asceticism may be expressed through a distrust of enjoyment, avoiding company of other individuals of his own age, cold showers, getting up early, and so on. Asceticism as a defense is an attempt by the ego to keep the id in bonds by use of general prohibition. Intellectualization is the defensive use of abstract, lofty (but empty) discussions and thoughts on love and marriage, philosophy, religion, and so on. In intellectualization, in contrast to asceticism, there is an attempt by the ego to make id impulses conscious by cloaking them in these abstractions and thus to control them.

With the arrival of bodily sexual maturity in the second or puberty phase itself, there tends to be a dropping away of the "sloppiness" of the prepubertal phase. Greater refinement, even fussiness, may appear in general behavior and dress. Sexual interests are again extended beyond the family; nonparental object relations appear. Not only is there this positive force pulling him away from home but there is also the necessity of overcoming the prepubertal Oedipal fantasies. There is uneasiness over displays of affection received from the parents. The adolescent typically behaves almost like a stranger with members of his family.

In many cases, strong friendships with people of his own age and "crushes" on older persons appear. The latter are, of course, substi-

[2] From Freud (42). Copyright 1946 by the International Universities Press, and published with permission.

tutes for the parents. In this reaching out toward others there is a whole-hearted (but narcissistic) absorption in the subject of the child's affection. Nevertheless, these affairs are of short duration and, once over, are rather quickly forgotten as far as his conscious life is concerned. The *form* of the relation is, however, preserved in the inevitable next episode. The disruption of the prepubertal structural organization of personality gives way during the pubertal phase to a reorganization which normally leads to the genital character of adulthood.

Adult personality structure

The psychoanalytic theory of normal adult personality structure is a description of types of personality arising from differential childhood experiences. Major kinds of personality structures, or "character structures" in psychoanalytic terminology, are attributed to events characteristic of each of the psychosexual stages. In effect, there is a carry-over (or reversal) of certain characteristics in adult life, the origins of which are to be found predominantly in the experiences of a particular psychosexual stage.

In earlier chapters the oral, anal, and phallic characters were identified. The genital character still needs description.

The Genital Character

The genital character is, in a sense, an ideal, imperfectly achieved even by those considered to deserve being referred to in this fashion. The mature or genital personality is the culmination of the sequence of psychosexual stages of development. Adequate heterosexual adjustment is the *sine qua non* of the genital character. Full, nonneurotic satisfaction through genital orgasm in heterosexual relations is a pragmatic test. Sublimation is extensively used. Emotions, instead of being reacted to by the use of ego defense, are thus used constructively by the ego. To be sure, such a person shows the effects of the previous psychosexual stages but in proportion and form conducive to an effective and happy life. Pregenital impulses are in the main sublimated, though vestiges still appear in the love-making preceding the sexual act.

It must be emphasized that the various forms of adult personality structure fall within the normal range. Character structures of those suffering from personality disturbances cannot be presented. Of necessity, the descriptions paint an extreme picture of each kind of character structure. Most individuals do not stay at these extremes, but instead vary in degrees and proportions. There is enough preponderance of one to enable placement in a given category.

Sex behavior tendencies

Sex behavior tendencies will be examined as they appear in the extent and nature of sex behavior, in peer relations between the sexes, in general socialization pressures, and in sex-role training, identification, and the superego.

Extent and Nature of Sex Behavior

Some socially approved forms of behavior indicate interests in sex. Much of the teasing and tussling going on among boys and girls is a crude form of amorous play. Under the ritualized content of games, such as Post Office, there is a sexual undercurrent. By and large, however, this sexual behavior is not of a self-evident or obvious sort.

The child's interest in sex may not be as submerged as parents and other adults think. Awareness of their disapproval may result in his keeping his thoughts and actions to himself. Through informal observation in the setting of a progressive school, Alpert (2) was led to the conclusion that as children progressed through the grades, sexual curiosity, instead of being latent, merely became disguised and less outspoken.

There is a considerable amount of socially hidden sex behavior occurring in children of these ages, as Kinsey and his associates (73) show in their studies. This behavior may take the form of tentative heterosexual exploration, but such behavior may include deviations from heterosexual behavior. Kinsey et al. show that among boys from ages five to ten the incidence of all sexual play increased from 10 per cent to over 35 per cent, with both heterosexual and homosexual incidents in evidence. For many of the children, activities of this sort were limited to a single experience. Some had much more extensive experience, since a third of the males continued sexual play of heterosexual or homosexual sort for five years or more. They conclude that this play did not extend further because of cultural restraints.

Peer Relations between the Sexes

Characteristically, among infants and younger children boys associated with boys and girls with girls. This sex cleavage, however, was casual and unplanned so far as the children were concerned. This pattern continues during the years under consideration. Indeed, Moreno (90) found in a public school that after the third grade, in choosing with whom one wants to sit in the classroom or to sit near, the percentage of boys choosing girls or girls choosing boys in no grade through the eighth exceeded five per cent and most often was only about two per cent.

The mutual avoidance of contact between members of the opposite sex is perhaps the most obvious indicator of what Freud called latency. Preference for own-sex peers over that of the opposite sex is very evident at this age. The older child is now more self-conscious and aware of what is going on; he now aids and abets his parents and other adults in sex-typing. Sometimes it seems that each sex seems "oblivious" of the other, but there are various indications that this is not the case.

What are the attitudes of boys and girls toward one another? A partial answer is given by Harris and Tseng (53). In the same study in which they investigated attitudes toward mothers and fathers, they also asked about peers, expressed in the sentence completion stems of "Most boys . . . ," and "Most girls . . . ." Again the completions were scored as positive, negative, or neutral. This made possible a comparison, over grades three to twelve, of the attitudes of boys both toward other boys and toward girls, and similar comparisons for girls. Boys and girls are most favorable to their same-sex peers as compared with opposite-sex peers at every grade. Girls expressed more negative attitudes toward girls as they grew older. The "antipathy" of boys and girls is more a matter of girls' lessening their unfavorable attitudes beginning at about the seventh grade; boys maintain about the same percentage of unfavorable attitudes through all the grades studied.

These findings concerned attitudes of girls toward boys and boys toward girls; it supplied no information about the personality qualities each attributes to the other. This was studied by Smith (113). He asked 100 boys and 100 girls from ages eight to 15 to vote whether boys or girls possessed to a greater degree each of 19 desirable and 14 undesirable traits. The questions were in the form "Who are . . . kinder to animals (bossy, selfish, honest, generous, good sports) . . . boys or girls?"

In graphic form, with increase in age the boy's curve shows that the proportion favoring their own sex for more possession of desirable traits and less possession of undesirable traits is steadily upward; for girls the curve is steadily downward. Each sex thought better of its own than of the other sex, but by age 14 girls think almost as well of boys as they do of themselves. There are, of course, exceptions, such as being bright in school or kind to animals, in which both boys and girls are overwhelmingly of the opinion that girls excel. Nevertheless, the results show that, for the traits included, boys and girls both have a progressively higher opinion of boys and a progressively lower opinion of girls.

Tuddenham (125) using the "Guess Who" technique in the first, third, and fifth grades shows that social acceptability as seen by the boys and girls studied conforms to the expected picture of sex differences. He says of his results:

> The picture of the typical boy and girl as conceived by children even in the primary grades seems to be almost a photostat of the common identification by adults in our society of aggressiveness, restlessness, and daring with masculinity, and of amiability, docility, and timidity with femininity (125, 19).[3]

This point of view had repercussions for the popularity of children displaying these characteristics (124). Girls who were quarrelsome and noisy were unpopular; the absence of these characteristics was rewarded by peer acceptance. These very same characteristics had little to do with the prestige of boys. Aggressiveness and loudness, if not making for popularity, did not interfere with it. Withdrawn girls of ten or eleven were less popular than socially outgoing girls. The evidence in general suggests that attitudes of sex-appropriate behavior are formed rather firmly while still in childhood.

There are characteristic patterns of social relationships among boys and girls during the latency period. This was clearly brought forth by Campbell (24) in her account of an observational study made in the setting of recreational clubs, whose memberships were made up of the "alumni" of a large, well-known nursery school. The groups they formed, the relationships between boy and girl groups they established, the kinds of relationships (or lack of it) between individual boys and girls were all largely a matter of choice on the part of the children. Her summaries for boys and girls, respectively, follow:

A. Social-Sex Development of the Boy

1. Youngest Stage (Ages 5–8)

A boy at this stage will play with a group otherwise made up entirely of girls, because he is not yet conscious of sex differences, nor is he embarrassed to be found in such a group . He does not object to having adults of either sex show physical affection for him. He is not yet modest as to posture, gesture, clothing, etc. He does not differentiate games according to sex. He shows no protective habits toward women and girls. When in a game not involving physical skill, he is not inclined

---

[3] From Tuddenham (125). Copyright 1952 by the American Psychological Association, and published with permission.

to choose his own sex over the other. He fights physically with girls. He is not yet self-conscious or embarrassed by physical contact with girls. He is careless of his personal appearance. Work is work to him, and he does not regard any one kind of work as suitable to boys and another as suitable to girls. The concept of "sissy" is still to be discovered. He is not concerned with girls as attractive creatures. On the whole, he prefers women to girls; at least, women who play with him. He is in a creative period in handicrafts and keeps very busy, and is not tempted to leave his work to play with girls, as he will be later.

2. Middle Period (Ages 9–14)

At this stage the boy is found playing pursuit games with girls, such as informal tag games indoors. So much attention he will pay to girls, but in general he shows no interest in what they are doing and even in games not involving physical skill he prefers boys on his "side." When allowed to choose, he always sits next to boys rather than girls. He will not join in a game in which he is the only boy, but must have other boys with him when he plays with girls. Toward the end of the period he becomes sufficiently conscious of sex so that he does not wish to touch girls or show them any attention except under socially approved conditions, such as in games or dancing. If he finds himself in a group of girls, he leaves quickly. Still later in this period he begins a teasing derogatory kind of talk about his friends who have girls, with the intention of "fussing" the boy in question. He is extremely self-conscious and modest about the physical aspects of sex and would not for the world undress or go to the toilet before girls or even women, except where the relationship is parental. . . .

B. Social-Sex Development of the Girl

1. Youngest Stage (Ages 5–8)

The girl of these ages is perfectly willing to play in groups composed entirely of boys. In choosing sides in games not involving physical skill she has no particular preference for one sex over the other. She is not yet modest about physical matters, will sit in any posture without embarrassment, show her underclothes, and go to the toilet where boys are. She is not embarrassed in a group of boys, as she will be later. She pays no attention if a boy touches her. She likes to have either men or women show physical affection for her. She is careless about her personal appearance, even when with boys. It has never occured to her that tasks should be allotted on sex lines.

2. Middle Period (Ages 8½–12½)

In this period the girl shows no interest in what boys are doing merely because they are boys. She will not stay long in a group of boys if she is the only girl. In choosing sides she is likely to choose girls unless it is a game involving physical skill, when she may choose a boy in the interests of victory. She prefers men to boys. She sits next to girls if given a choice. She will not participate in an activity unless other girls are included. She will invite men to sit next to her, but never boys. She begins to be sufficiently conscious of sex so that she will not deliberately touch boys except under conventional circumstances, as in games or dancing. She classifies games according to sex—boys play this, girls play that.

Later she enters the "whispering period" with her girl contemporaries. She is shyer with a group of boys than with a single boy. If she dances, she prefers to dance with other girls. She would not admit that a certain boy is attractive to her, though she begins to take a covert interest. By this time she is modest about exposing her body and underclothing before boys—probably more so than she will ever be again. She is sufficiently conscious of the sex attraction of clothes to admire the clothing of women and her girl friends. She begins frankly to enjoy dancing (24, 523–526).[4]

Her results give a vivid picture of the patterns of social relationships of the latency-aged child. However, patterns of social interaction among boys and girls may vary greatly with socio-economic status and other variables. It is evident that the groups Campbell described are those composed of middle-class children. Patterns in other classes probably differ in some measure.

Although involving adolescent boys and therefore somewhat older than the age range of later childhood, a study of Bene (18) neatly illustrates the influence of cultural factors on heterosexual interests. This study, conducted in England, involved a comparison of the suppression of heterosexual interests among 300 middle-class and working-class grammar-school boys. They anonymously completed a variety of multiple-choice, open-end, and sentence-completion items. Some of these items were relevant to the present problem. One inquired of the boy whether he often took a girl to the movies. Another concerned whether he would pick as a friend a boy who had no girlfriend. Still another asked whether he disagreed with the statement that boys of his age would like to be in love. A final example inquired whether he condemned boys of his age who went out with girls.

It was hypothesized that working-class boys would "suppress" heterosexual interests less than middle-class boys, that is, show more interest in relations with girls. All but one of eleven relevant items were significant in the predicted direction. Working-class boys showed less suppression in that in each instance they disclosed more approval of heterosexual interests. This was a matter of a comparison of the same item for the two class samples. The absolute values agreeing or disagreeing with the item showed a close parallel between working- and middle-class boys.

For example, the highest percentage for an item was 89 and 78 per cent, respectively, of middle- and working-class boys who did not often go to the movies with a girl. The lowest percentage, only 14 and six

[4] From Campbell (24). Copyright 1939 by The Journal Press, and published with permission.

per cent, respectively, believed it was actually wrong to go out with girls. The other items, falling between the extremes—such as 40 and 26 per cent, respectively, saying that they would pick as a friend a boy who had no girlfriend—showed a similar parallelism. Their choices were similar, but always the working-class boys were more enthusiastic about relations with the opposite sex. The investigator concluded that both middle- and lower-class boys had an interest in the other sex so long as this interest could remain theoretical. The boys are apt to say at one and the same time they would like to be in love, but they do not want to be around girls! This mixture of childish and mature attitudes exists in both classes, but middle-class boys suppress their heterosexual interests more than working-class boys.

Thus, we can see the various ramifications of peer relationships between the sexes. In considering the more general socialization pressures and then the more specific processes involved in acquiring sex-roles, identification, and conscience, we shall find a tentative explanation of the observed attractions and repulsions that characterize these relationships.

General Socialization Pressures

Cultural pressures from adults for differentiated behavior of boys and girls continue during the years of later childhood. This occurs in cultures other than our own. In a cross-cultural study akin to those by Whiting and Child described in Chapter 4, Barry, Bacon, and Child (14) searched reports of primitive societies for evidence of differential treatment of the sexes. In terms of indulgence in infancy, the judges agreed in finding no evidence of sex differences. But in childhood there was considerable evidence that among these societies there was a widespread pattern of pressure on girls for greater nurturance (helpfulness), obedience, and responsibility; and greater pressure on boys for self-reliance and achievement strivings.

Differences in school achievement in which girls excel boys (119) may be related to cultural expectations. Girls are expected to be more interested in writing, reading, and arithmetic, whereas boys are expected to be more aggressive toward teachers and not interested in school subjects. Of course, there are large and varied exceptions, but no one can deny that scholarship is occasionally confused in the peer group with being a "sissy," as witness the lower-class group studied by Pope (106).

Even textbooks may be used for sex-socialization purposes. The texts analyzed by Child and his associates (28) referred to in connection with the school-aged child, portrayed females as sociable, kind, timid, easily frightened, unambitious, and uncreative. Heroes are invariably boys or men; females have unimportant roles. Girls satisfy their needs by passive dependence or by rivalry with overtones of rather emotional immaturity; nor is there a realistic appraisal of natural relationships between the sexes. Presumably what is read by children is still another source of differential socialization of the sexes—with most of the advantages going to the male.

Sex differences in recreational interests presumably reflect differential social pressures. In a masterly survey of sex differences in general, Terman and Tyler (119) included discussion of differences among boys and girls in recreational interests. Although these interests are subject to superficial changes based on momentary fads, the findings, most of which were collected some years ago, are still of concern. Terman and his associates had developed a masculinity index based on the pursuit of various activities by boys and by girls of elementary-school age. The masculine activities, more or less in order of descending masculinity, were using tools, shooting, playing with kites and marbles, wrestling, boxing, football, baseball, fishing, garden work, basketball, swimming, rowing, hunting, racing, coasting, hiking, riding, playing checkers, chess, and billiards. A line of neutrality occurred at this point and included such activities as Red Rover, follow the leader, croquet, volley ball, dominoes, snap, and cards. As for the characteristically feminine activities from least to most feminine they were Jackstraws, post office, fox and hounds, tennis, authors, tag, hide and seek, solving puzzles, jackstones, skating, drop the handkerchief, ring around the rosy, London Bridge, farmer in the dell, cat and mouse, jumping rope, guessing games, charades, dancing, sewing, playing store, knitting, playing school, cooking, playing house, hopscotch, dressing-up, and dolls. The most immediately obvious feature of this list is the predominance of strenuous activities at the masculine end of the listing.

Lehman and Witty (75) found similar results and, in addition, found that boys more often engaged in competitive and more highly organized games than did girls. Games become more and more clearly sex-linked as age increases until the ages of about eight-and-a-half to ten-and-a-half, the period during which the social separation among boys and girls is at its greatest.

In a recent and detailed examination (45) of both American and Finnish children in the fourth and fifth grades, a rather complex picture of sex differences in reading preferences was found. Both national groups and both sexes preferred fiction over fairy tales, informational, biographical, animal, or religious stories. Irrespective of story categories, tales of travel, pursuit, and escape were favored. It would seem as if they found some support to the already clinically favored view that latency-age children like "change of milieu."

Second choice among the story categories did reveal clear sex differences. Girls chose fairy stories; boys chose informational stories. Moreover, within the stories there were characteristic sex differences. The girls' favorite stories tended to have leading characters of the same age as the subjects; the boys' favorite stories tended to have adults or at least older characters. A considerable variety of other differences within the stories was also found. Latency-age sex differences in reading interests seem to take certain characteristic forms.

Sex Roles, Identification, and the Superego

In the older child sex-role preferences continue although showing certain specifiable variations. Sex-role preference over the age range five-and-a-half to eleven-and-a-half was investigated by Brown (23). He used the familiar *It Scales for Children* with 300 boys and 300 girls enrolled in the kindergarten through the fifth grade of an elementary school. He found: (a) Girls of all ages were significantly more variable in their sex-role preferences than boys. (b) Boys showed much stronger preference for the masculine role than girls did for the feminine role. Indeed, girls at the kindergarten level showed equal preference for masculine and feminine roles and an even strong preference for the masculine role from the first through the fourth grades. Only in the fifth grade did girls show a stronger preference for the feminine role.

These results are consistent in general with those findings reported for younger children in Chapter 14. It should be emphasized that Brown's results have been stated in terms of averages. Some girls at all ages preferred the feminine role. Nor do his results imply that the girls' identifications may not be feminine. Girls, after all, are more encouraged than boys to engage in activities typical of the opposite sex.

Taking on of adult roles by children is considered by Maccoby (81) to be an aspect of identification. Role taking is a class of behavior which the child learns from his interactions with his parents, such as the behaviors they perform toward him when carrying out their adult role. They establish rules, apply discipline, scold him, give him medicine, and the like. Whereas the child himself seldom performs these activities overtly for reasons that should be obvious, they do occasionally appear in his play and it is likely that he performs them in fantasy. All children presumably practice some of the adult-role behavior that characterizes their parents. There should be differences from child to child in the amount learned. It is plausible to expect that in social interaction with their peers some children will employ the same kinds of behavior the parents used toward them in similar situations.

The problem for which Maccoby set herself to discover was what conditions resulted in the child's taking on adult-role behavior. The specific task she selected was the child's tendency to enforce rules when another child deviated from them. Material about the children from the "pattern" study and the follow-up data when they were in the sixth grade utilized by Sears in his study of aggression (page 538) were studied. The 160 sixth-grade children still available from the original preschool sample were given a so-called role-taking questionnaire. Among the scales included was the rule enforcement scale, which contained such items as that of asking whether he would say nothing or tell a boy to pick up the pieces if he saw him break a bottle on the sidewalk while both were walking to school. Scores on this scale supplied information about the amount of rule enforcing the children showed. Antecedents of rule enforcement were sought in the information obtained six years earlier about the parents' behavior toward their children.

Boys high in rule enforcing had parents who had been restrictive (nonpermissive) about their children's impulsive behaviors in the earlier years. Hence, the parents were fairly strict rule enforcers themselves. If the boy was relatively dependent, and if the parents were relatively warm during early childhood, the son's present rule enforcing tendencies became even more closely matched to earlier parental behavior toward him.

Rule-enforcing girls tended to have relatively punitive parents and the match became significantly greater when the child was more, rather than less, dependent on the parents. It would seem that boys and girls, although showing different forms of interrelationships, had both acquired during early childhood some adult-like behavior tendencies manifested in connection with role-taking about rule enforcing.

Remarkable stability has been demonstrated in sex-role related behavior. By extending the data already available at the Fels Research Institute, Kagan and Moss (72) had material on the same individuals from infancy through adulthood. Their findings became so extensive as to require a tightly written, full-length book. So striking were certain findings that two of the five major topics around which their summary is organized concern matters relevant to the present issue: (a) that an intimate relation exists between behavior change or stability of behavior and the traditional standards for sex-role characteristics; and (b) that sex-role identification is a major governor of behavior.

To show how they reached these conclusions, it will be necessary to examine their procedure and subjects. This can be briefer than usual since it is already familiar from the account on pages 536–537 where dependence was the topic. Moreover, the 36 boys and 35 girls who formed the sample were presumably included among those reported in studies of younger children, such as the Baldwin study mentioned in Chapter 12. At any rate, observations through such devices as the Fels Parent Behavior Rating Scales were used to collect the material for the younger ages. As adults between 19 and 29 years of age, an investigator, without knowledge of the earlier findings in the files, interviewed them for five hours and administered a test battery.

In presenting their results emphasis will be placed on those obtained at age six to ten as compared to adult behavior. Figure 19 presents a summary of some of the correlations of child behavior and the phenotypically similar adult behaviors. "Phenotypically similar" refers to the fact that adult behavior may on the surface appear to be different from child behavior, but that an underlying similarity still exists.

Inspection of the figure will show that at the left are two relations—passivity-withdrawal and dependence-dependence family—in which the correlation is relatively higher in females than in males. The next two relations—behavior disorganization-anger arousal and heterosexuality-sexuality behavior—show the reverse, that is, higher correlations for males than for females. Male dependence between six and ten is uncorrelated with dependence on the family as an adult but in females these two phenotypically similar behaviors at the two ages correlate positively at .30. This finding is one among the various correlations that led to the earlier conclusion that a greater proportion of men than women shifted from high dependence in childhood to relative independence as adults. It is now seen as exemplifying differential sex-typing. Passivity in childhood and withdrawal in adulthood show the same trend, again reflecting the influence of differential cultural pressures. Passivity and dependency are both subject to consistent cultural disapproval in men but not in women. The differential correlations obtained on both relations presumably reflect the rewards and punishments the children received, which differentially reinforced these tendencies in boys as compared to girls.

Behavior disorganization (anger and tantrums) in childhood and anger arousal (aggressive behavior) in adulthood, and heterosexuality in childhood and sexual behavior in adulthood, the next two relations in Figure 19, show substantial correlations in males, but relatively little in females. Anger and tantrum behaviors in boys were better predictors of adult aggressive behavior than similar behaviors in girls. This finding is the same as that found in the follow-up of the "pattern"

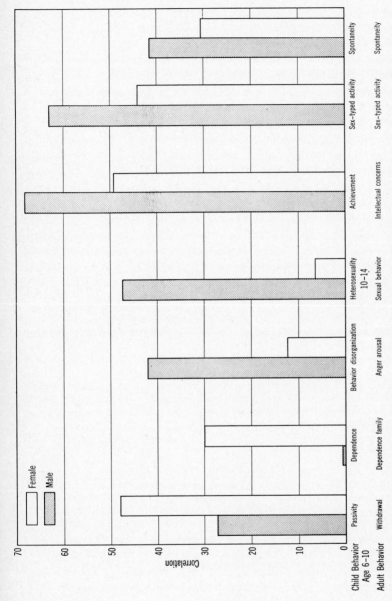

Figure 19. Summary of relations between selected child behaviors (6 to 10 years of age) and phenotypically similar adult behaviors. (From Kagan and Moss (72). Copyright 1962 by John Wiley and Sons, and published with permission.)

study by Sears (*111*) when discussing aggressive tendencies in the previous chapter. Greater antisocial aggression of boys as compared to girls was found.

This continuity of aggressiveness in males from childhood to adulthood and discontinuity in females is reasonably explained by the realization that aggressive behavior is a much more accepted component of traditional masculine behavior than of the traditional feminine one. The boy is not punished for aggression as often or as extensively as the girl; her role model is a less overtly aggressive one. As we saw earlier from the Sears' study, this does not prevent the girl from developing anxiety about aggression, but she does not show open expression of aggression. This inhibits such overt behavior, whereas boys, with more freedom in this respect, can and do continue to express aggressive behavior.

The remaining three relations, appearing in the right in the figure, although showing higher correlations in males, also show substantial correlations in females. They involve achievement as a child and intellectual concerns as an adult, and sex-related activities and spontaneity at both ages. These relations are also explained by Kagan and Moss on the basis of differential and similar cultural pressures. They write:

> A low threshold for anger, direct aggressive retaliation, and frequent sexual behavior, on the other hand, are disproportionately punished in females, whereas males are given greater license in these areas. The data revealed that childhood rage reactions and frequent dating during preadolescence predicted adult aggressive and sexual predispositions, respectively, for men but not for women. . . .
> Intellectual mastery and adoption of appropriate sex-typed interests are positively sanctioned for both sexes, and both of these behaviors showed a high degree of continuity for males and females from the early school years through adulthood (72, 268).[5]

They go on to summarize:

> The preceding discussion places the construct of sex-role identification in a central position in directing the selective adoption and maintenance of several behavior domains. The expression of aggression, competitiveness, passivity, dependency, or sexuality is determined, in part, by the individual's assessment of the congruence of the behavior with traditional sex-role standards. For many individuals are motivated to behave in a way that is congruent with a hypothetical ego ideal or idealized model that embodies the essential qualities of masculinity or femininity (72, 271).[5]

The significance of these results at this even more general level, as Kagan and Moss see them, is worthy of examination. Sex-role identifi-

---

[5] From Kagan and Moss (72). Copyright 1962 by John Wiley and Sons and published with permission.

cation is a governor of behaviors in that the goal state toward which they strive and the incentives for these behaviors are in the cognitive system of the individual. It would seem that these children evaluated their behavior against an internalized standard and behaved not merely as called for by an external situation but weighed against this internalization. Each person has an idealized cognitive picture of himself against which he checks his behavior. This model, they believe, is ranged along a dimension of highly masculine to highly feminine and is a prime determinant of an adult's behavior.

The Finney (41) study referred to earlier collected information concerning conscience development. The maternal ratings of firmness, or lack thereof, proved to be relevant. The 39 items rated involved such matters as the mother not having the heart to be firm. Over-all, the items centered on lack of firmness in setting limits. Conscience in the child was evaluated through ratings by teachers and clinic personnel on such matters as cheating at school work or games (negatively scored) and giving instruction to other children concerning what is the right thing to do. Lack of firmness was related to less conscience development. Mothers who were not firm had children who showed less conscience development ($r = .38$).

Resistance to temptation and guilt (readiness to admit transgression and voluntary confession), it will be remembered from Chapter 14, was considered by Sears as integral aspects of conscience development. Another follow-up of the "pattern" study neatly demonstrated that the socialization training concerning these matters received by five- and six-year-old children was highly resistant to extinction (50). Seventy boys and an equal number of girls served as subjects. Those boys who admitted transgression and those girls who made voluntary confession at age five or six were found to be resistant to temptation at eleven or twelve.

The temptation situation was a "ray-gun shooting gallery." Sharpshooter badges were the prizes varying according to the scores made. With no apparent chance of detection, each child could record higher scores than they made or take extra shots. The extra scores they gave themselves furnished a measure of resistance to temptation. The antecedent variables related to this measure of resistance to temptation were those studied by Sears years earlier.

In addition to resistance to temptation being associated with guilt in the form of admission of transgression and of voluntary confession in boys and girls, respectively, other predictions of association at the two different ages were verified. In boys, being held to high parental standards of neatness and obedience during preschool age, turned out to be associated with resistance to temptation at the older age. Among girls, strong sex training and pressures for weaning and bowel training were associated with resistance to temptation when older.

Resistance to temptation as a measurable consequence of conscience development is thus shown to be related to child-rearing antecedents of conscience and guilt. Subjects who experienced guilt at five or six years of age resisted temptation at eleven or twelve. Stability of behavior over the years in this regard seems to have been demonstrated.

A neo-freudian interpretation of latency

According to psychoanalytic theory, the latency period follows the highly sexually charged phallic stage. The Oedipus situation was supposed to have resulted in repression of sexual interests. Latency is supposed to be a period of relative quiescence with a reduction of sexual interests, and, consequently, of considerably less dynamic interest than the psychosexual stages, so far as the effects of events occurring during this period are concerned. They are of less significance for the formation of personality than are the earlier stages or the later stage of adolescence. Consequently, there has been a relative neglect of these years by orthodox psychoanalytic workers. Relatively few articles have appeared concerned with latency or its effects. The neglect can be made specific by citing the fact that Munroe (94), in an authoritative account of psychoanalytic schools of thought, devotes less than two pages to the latency period out of the 330 which she devoted to Freud. According to the index, no other direct reference to latency is made anywhere in the volume.

Whether the repressions of the Oedipus situation are responsible for events in the latency period is a disputed question. In Chapter 14 evidence was offered which tended to cast doubt on the omnipresence of the Oedipus situation. In keeping with that earlier discussion, emphasis would then be placed on social pressures preventing too open manifestations of sexual interests during the school years. Certainly, sex interests and sex play are not given up during the latency period.

The psychoanalytic description of the latency period is not too inaccurate a description of the public sex behavior of latency-aged children in our culture. But as we have seen from previous discussion, everything is not quite as serene and asexual as it appears. An active sex life may be still very much present.

The latency period is not a universal phenomenon. Malinowski (83), in his study of the Trobriand Islanders referred to in Chapter 14, has given us an instance of a society in which genital sexuality continues during the so-called latency period. There were no moral sanctions and no adult authority against sexual behavior. Sexual behavior gradually became more direct and "adult" as the child grew older with no break in the continuity. Consequently, it was individual temperament which decided a child's behavior in this sphere. There was no evidence of latency. Other primitive societies show similar attitudes. In the Mohave, Devereux (37) attributes the absence of latency to the tolerant attitudes of adults toward sexuality in the child.

Cultural determinants of the presence or absence of the latency period seem evident. In our culture, emphasis is on a suppression of the specifically sexual aspects of masculine and feminine behavior during the phase of childhood. As Devereux (37) indicates, it is the presence, not the absence, of the latency period which needs explanation. Its appearance seems to be due to socialization pressure present in major segments of our society.

Sullivan (117) emphasizes cooperation and competition as part of normal development in what he calls the juvenile period. This comes about because the child has now reached the age where he can view his peers with some objectivity and thus is able to develop these tools of social living. It is an age when children try out their abilities and gain or fail to acquire self-confidence and self-reliance.

With Thompson (120) the writer is in agreement that, in addition to disapproval of sexual interests, there is a widening of the social horizon during this age period. The child's school and play interests absorb him in the world of his contemporaries. With this widening, sexual interests may assume less importance simply because his scope of interest has widened.

Perhaps, Freud himself was coming to a more culturally oriented interpretation in his later years. In an autobiographical study (43) originally published in 1935, he comments that, although latency is a maturational phenomenon, it can lead to a complete interruption of sexual behavior only in a culture which has suppression as a part of its way of life. It can perhaps be argued that no culture can succeed in carrying through this suppression completely. At any rate, Hartmann, Kris, and Loewenstein (56), after quoting Freud on the matter above, proceed to discuss a variety of psychoanalytic topics in cultural perspective. It is significant that they at least consider themselves as working within an orthodox psychoanalytic framework.

Latency, insofar as it occurs, would appear to be learned, as the evidence adduced earlier suggests. This conclusion is reinforced by evidence from endocrinology. No shift in endocrine balance has been observed during these years (99). Instead, the concentration of hormonal substances (androgens and estrogens) shows a progressive rise throughout childhood to a peak at puberty. There is no qualitative change from the phallic age to the latency period to adolescence—only this progressive rise.

We have attempted throughout this chapter to show what is happening to children during these years. In general, the years appear important for the formation of social relationships. In their formation, events of infancy and early childhood have contributed their share, but events happening during latency itself, too, have their effect. Orthodox psychoanalytic formulation for these years in the concept of the latency period seems to minimize unduly this important age period.

As the older child progresses through the latency period, sex tendencies are found to be more related to the ones shown by the peers of the child than was the case when he was younger. Characteristic patterns of social relationships of boys and girls at various ages have been sketched in order to show changes with age in relation to their social groups. Sex behavior and interest are not as submerged during the so-called latency period as conventional opinion would have it.

Differential reinforcement by parents, teachers, and other adults goes a long way toward accounting for the findings concerning general socialization pressure on older childhood. It is encouraging to find that psychological research has made a beginning in explaining how the phenomena of sex-role identification and the superego come about. In the main, this was accomplished by showing how maternal training experienced by the child left its mark upon him, not only at the time, but when he was older. This was not a simple linear relation of childhood characteristics continuing into later life in direct childish form, but an instance of their being put away, with phenotypically similar characterizations appearing in later life.

General evaluation of orthodox psychoanalytic formulations

Psychoanalytic hypotheses are in crying need of systematic research verification. Lack of research personnel and skills and attitudes, the demand for treatment, and the position that clinical findings do not require research verification help to account for this paucity of research. Research is deterred because of the general nonoperational terms in which findings are stated and the amorphousness of the theory that makes coming to grips with it very difficult. The sheer complexity and subtlety of this theory are both a challenge and a deterrent. Often research done on some small segment can be cogently criticized by the psychoanalysts either as not paying sufficient attention to, or as not showing adequate understanding of, other related aspects of psychoanalytic theory. Often, research critical of the position can be dismissed as irrelevant or immaterial by those sufficiently acquainted with psychoanalysis as a theory and as a clinical approach. The fact remains that frequently psychoanalytic propositions are stated in a manner incapable of proof or disproof.

Freud's influence on child psychology involves a paradox. More than any other man his work has made us recognize the importance of the influence of family members on the child's development. And, yet, in his own theoretical framework, its influence is given a subordinate, almost incidental place. A serious neglect chargeable against orthodox psychoanalysis is its neglect of the influence of learning on development. This is expressed not only in neglect of learning in its narrow sense, but also learning as expressed in socialization and culture. The constitutional factor has been emphasized over environmental ones. Even the external events considered, such as castration anxiety, are supposed to produce relatively fixed and inevitable results.

Many of the phenomena of childhood have been illumined by psychoanalytic hypotheses. Many of the forms of behavior and experience in childhood are compatible with their views without, however, excluding the possibility of other interpretations. Very little in the way of crucial research has appeared which would prove unequivocally that psychoanalytic views are valid and opposing views are invalid. The relative neglect of the influence of learning is the most serious charge that can be made against orthodox psychoanalytic contentions.

Freud himself saw the individual in relation to others, but the relation seemed to be a matter of using these others to satisfy instinctual needs —other individuals as a means to an end. Social factors were not given causal strength in themselves; they reflected instinctual attractions and repulsions.

Within psychoanalysis itself, there are current developments that may make for greater rapproachment between it and the rest of psychology. It is a current development whose scope and function are not entirely clear. It was mentioned briefly in Chapter 5 where passing reference was made to the fact that ego development involves not only instinctual drives and outer reality, but also an energy of its own. In short, an autonomy of the ego is being postulated with the implication that some human activities are not inexorably bound to the precise pattern of development.

Moreover, how the ego functions in areas other than conflict has become increasingly important in psychoanalysis. The ego has an autonomy of its own, that is, an independence of the influence of id. This means that the ego is not merely a product of the conflict between instinctual drives and reality but develops through maturation and learning (55). In addition, derived motivations develop their own semi-autonomy; the surgeon is interested in surgery for its own sake, not merely as an outlet for his sadistic impulses; the stamp collector carries on his activities for their own sake, not merely to work out his anal impulses (47). These conceptualizations imply that the energy employed is not sexual, but is more neutralized. Motivational factors alone do not determine behavior, other factors do, so that the experiences of the individual enter more dynamically into the causal sequence.

Sometimes this new position seems to extend so far that there is a rejection of libido theory even within orthodox psychoanalysis. However, this rejection of libido theory does not imply that relatively primitive drives have been dethroned from a position of importance (47). Here the contribution of psychoanalytic thinking still stands firm.

What has Freud contributed to our knowledge? The writer knows of no more comprehensive and discriminating summing-up than that offered by Gardner Murphy in discussing the impact of Freud on psychology. What he has to say he says for child psychology as well.

> . . . first, the specifications of drive; second, the conception that life tendencies are deeper, more primordial then the phenomenon of consciousness, which is at best an elaboration or screening technique which can in no way obliterate or weaken the basic drive modulations; third, as James Harvey Robinson said, the discovery that, "as children, we are at our most impressionable age"; fourth, the conception that the ego is a derivative rather than a primary expression of life; and fifth, most general of all propositions, that all psychological activity is motivated, driven, guided, directed by life tensions seeking resolution. It is in this latter sense that psychoanalysis is a consistently dynamic psychology. It begins with force and ends with the dissipation of force through a tension-reducing process always to be followed by fresh tension accumulations and further discharges. Every idle fancy, every quick calculation, every odd remark, every whim and every great decision alike, spring basically from the tensions of the tissues within us (95, 664).[6]

He goes on to say that child psychology has so far only been influenced by psychoanalysis in a relatively limited way. What has been presented in this and some previous chapters is an attempt to show the relevance of psychoanalysis to child psychology.

[6] From Murphy (95). Copyright 1956 by the American Psychological Association, and published with permission.

Whatever the eventual outcome of psychoanalytic formulations of personality development, they have had and will continue to have a profound effect on thinking, studying, and working with children. To what extent they will be assimilated into child psychology as a science is a solution of the future, not of the present. But that they will be assimilated in the course of their modification is certain.

For Further Reading

The volume edited by Levitt, *Readings in Psychoanalytic Psychology* (New York: Appleton-Century-Crofts, 1959) contains many papers relevant to the issues discussed. J. Kagan and H. A. Moss in their research report *Birth to Maturity* (72) give a wealth of material relevant to the problems of this chapter which could only be sampled. The paper by M. Gill (47) very adequately summarizes the present status of orthodox psychoanalytic theory.

References

1. Adams, Elsie B., and I. G. Sarason. Relations between anxiety in children and their parents. *Child Develpm.*, 1963, 34, 237–246.
2. Alpert, Augusta. The latency period. *Amer. J. Orthopsychiat.*, 1941, 9, 126–132.
3. Altman, Charlotte. Relationships between maternal attitudes and child personality structure. *Amer. J. Orthopsychiat.*, 1958, 28, 160–169.
4. Anderson, H. H. Domination and integration in the social behavior of young children in an experimental play situation. *Genet. Psychol. Monogr.*, 1937, 19, 341–408.
5. Anderson, H. H. Domination and social integration in the behavior of kindergarten children and teachers. *Genet. Psychol. Monogr.*, 1939, 21, 287–385.
6. Anderson, H. H., and Gladys L. Anderson. Social development. In L. Carmichael (Ed.), *Manual of child psychology* (2nd ed.). New York: Wiley, 1954.
7. Anderson, H. H., and H. M. Brewer. Dominative and socially integrative behavior of kindergarten teachers. *Appl. Psychol. Monogr.*, 1945, No. 6.
8. Anderson, H. H., and J. E. Brewer. Effects of teachers' dominative and integrative contacts on children's classroom behavior. *Appl. Psychol. Monogr.*, 1946, No. 8.
9. Anderson, H. H., J. E. Brewer, and Mary F. Reed. Studies of teachers' classroom personalities: III. Follow-up studies of the effects of dominative and integrative contacts on children's behavior. *Appl. Psychol. Monogr.*, 1946, No. 11.
10. Austin, M. C., and G. G. Thompson. Children's friendships: a study of the bases on which children select and reject their best friends. *J. Educ. Psychol.*, 1948, 39, 101–116.
11. Ausubel, D. P. Ego development and the learning process. *Child Develpm.*, 1949, 20, 173–190.

12. Ausubel, D. P., H. M. Schiff, and E. B. Gasser. A preliminary study of developmental trends in sociempathy: accuracy of perception of own and others' sociometric status. *Child Develpm.*, 1952, 23, 111–128.

13. Bandura, A., and Carol J. Kupers. Transmission of patterns of self-reinforcement through modeling. *J. Abnorm. Soc. Psychol.*, 1964, 1969, 1–9.

14. Barry III, H., Margaret K. Bacon, and I. L. Child. A cross-cultural survey of some sex differences in socialization. *J. Abnorm. Soc. Psychol.*, 1957, 55, 327–332.

15. Becker, W. C., D. R. Peterson, L. A. Hellmer, D. J. Shoemaker, and H. C. Quay. Factors in parental behavior in children. *J. Consult. Psychol.*, 1959, 23, 107–118.

16. Beilin, H. Teachers' and clinicians' attitudes toward the behavior problems of children: a reappraisal. *Child Develpm.*, 1959, 30, 9–26.

17. Beilin, H., and Emmy Werner. Sex differences among teachers in the use of the criteria of adjustment. *J. Educ. Psychol.*, 1957, 48, 426–436.

18. Bene, Eva. Suppression of heterosexual interest and of aggression by middle class and working class grammar school boys. *Brit. J. Educ. Psychol.*, 1958, 28, 226–231.

19. Bene, Eva. Some differences between middle class and working class grammar school boys in their attitudes toward education. *Brit. J. Sociol.*, 1959, 10, 148–152.

20. Berenda, R. W. *The influence of the group on the judgments of children.* New York: Kings Crown Press, 1950.

21. Blum, G. S. *Psychoanalytic theories of personality.* New York: McGraw-Hill, 1953.

22. Bonney, M. E. The constancy of sociometric scores and their relationship to teacher judgments of social success, to personality self-ratings. *Sociometry*, 1943, 6, 409–424.

23. Brown, D. G. Masculinity-femininity development in children. *J. Consult. Psychol.*, 1957, 21, 197–202.

24. Campbell, Elise H. The social-sex development of children. *Genet. Psychol. Monogr.*, 1939, 21, 461–552.

25. Campbell, Nellie M. The elementary school teacher's treatment of classroom behavior problems. *Teach. Coll. Contr. Educ.*, 1935, No. 668.

26. Challman, R. C. Factors influencing friendships among preschool children. *Child Develpm.*, 1932, 3, 146–158.

27. Chance, June E. Independence training and first graders' achievement. *J. Consult. Psychol.*, 1951, 25, 149–154.

28. Child, I. L., E. M. Potter, and Estelle M. Levine. Children's textbooks and personality development; an exploration in the social psychology of education. *Psychol. Monogr.*, 1946, 60, No. 279.

29. Crandall, V., and Alice Rabson. Children's repetition choices in intellectual achievement situations following success and failure. *J. Genet. Psychol.*, 1960, 97, 161–168.

30. Criswell, Joan H. Social structure revealed in a sociometric retest. *Sociometry*, 1939, 2, 69–73.

31. Davids, A., and Anita N. Parenti. Personality, social choice, and adults perception of these factors in groups of disturbed and normal children. *Sociometry*, 1958, 12, 212–224.

32. Davis, J. A. Correlates of sociometric status among peers. *J. Educ. Res.*, 1957, 50, 561–569.

33. Davis, W. A. *Social class influences upon learning.* Cambridge: Harvard University Press, 1948.
34. Davitz, J. R. The effects of previous training on postfrustration behavior. *J. Abnorm. Soc. Psychol.,* 1952, 47, 309–315.
35. Davitz, J. R. Social perception and sociometric choice of children. *J. Abnorm. Soc. Psychol.,* 1955, 50, 173–176.
36. deGroat, A. F., and G. G. Thompson. A study of the distribution of teacher approval and disapproval among sixth grade children. *J. Exp. Educ.,* 1949, 18, 57–75.
37. Devereux, G. The primal scene and juvenile heterosexuality in Mohave society. In G. B. Wilbur and W. Muensterberger (Eds.), *Psychoanalysis and culture.* New York: International Universities Press, 1951, 90–107.
38. Doob, L. W. *Social psychology.* New York: Holt, 1952.
39. Dymond, Rosalind F., Anne S. Hughes, and Virginia L. Raabe. Measurable changes in empathy with age. *J. Consult. Psychol.,* 1952, 16, 202–206.
40. Elkin, F. *The child and society: the process of socialization.* New York: Random House, 1960.
41. Finney, J. C. Some maternal influences in children's personality and character. *Genet. Psychol. Monogr.,* 1961, 63, 199–278.
42. Freud, Anna. *The ego and the mechanism of defense.* New York: International Universities Press, 1946.
43. Freud, S. *An autobiographical study.* London: Hogarth, 1936.
44. Furfey, P. H. Some factors influencing the selection of boys' "chums." *J. Appl. Psychol.,* 1927, 11, 47–51.
45. Gaier, E. L., and Mary J. Collier. The latency-stage story preferences of American and Finnish children. *Child Develpm.,* 1960, 31, 431–451.
46. Gardner, L. Pearl. An analysis of children's attitudes toward fathers. *J. Genet. Psychol.,* 1947, 70, 3–28.
47. Gill, M. The present state of psychoanalytic theory. *J. Abnorm. Soc. Psychol.,* 1959, 58, 1–8.
48. Gladstone, R. D. Do maladjusted teachers cause maladjustment? A rereview. *J. Except. Child.,* 1948, 15, 65–70.
49. Gray, Susan W. Masculinity-femininity in relation to anxiety and social acceptance. *Child Develpm.,* 1957, 28, 203–214.
50. Grinder, R. E. Parental childrearing practices, conscience, and resistance to temptation of sixth-grade children. *Child Develpm.,* 1962, 33, 803–820.
51. Gump, P. V., and J. S. Kounin. Milieu influences in children's concepts of misconduct. *Child Develpm.,* 1961, 32,·711–720.
52. Harris, D. B., K. E. Clark, A. M. Rose, and F. Valasek. The relationship of children's home duties to an attitude of responsibility. *Child Develpm.,* 1954, 25, 103–109.
53. Harris, D. B., and S. C. Tseng. Children's attitudes toward peers and parents as revealed by sentence completion. *Child Develpm.,* 1957, 28, 401–411.
54. Hartmann, H. *Ego psychology and the problem of adaptation.* (Trans. by D. Rapaport) New York: International Universities Press, 1958.
55. Hartmann, H., E. Kris, and R. M. Loewenstein. Comments of the formation of psychic structure. *Psychoanal. Stud. Child,* 1947, 2, 11–38.
56. Hartmann, H., E. Kris, and R. M. Loewenstein. Some psychoanalytic comments on "culture and personality." In G. B. Wilbur and W. Muensterberger (Eds.), *Psychoanalysis and culture.* New York: International Universities Press, 1951, 3–31.

57. Hartshorne, H., M. A. May, and F. K. Shuttleworth. *Studies in the organization of character.* New York: Macmillan, 1930.
58. Havighurst, R. J. Child development in relation to community social structure. *Child Develpm.,* 1946, 17, 85–90.
59. Havighurst, R. J. *Human development and education.* New York: Longmans, Green, 1953.
60. Havighurst, R. J., and Fay H. Breese. Relation between ability and social status in a midwestern community: III. Primary mental abilities. *J. Educ. Psychol.,* 1947, 38, 241–247.
61. Havighurst, R. J., and L. L. Janke. Relation between ability and social status in a midwestern community. I. Ten-year-old children. *J. Educ. Psychol.,* 1944, 35, 357–368.
62. Havighurst, R. J., Myra Z. Robinson, and Mildred J. Dorr. The development of the ideal self in childhood and adolescence. *J. Educ. Res.,* 1946, 40, 241–257.
63. Horrocks, J. E., and Mae E. Buker. A study of the friendship fluctuations of preadolescents. *J. Genet. Psychol.,* 1951, 78, 131–144.
64. Horrocks, J. E., and G. G. Thompson. A study of the friendship fluctuations of rural boys and girls. *J. Genet. Psychol.,* 1946, 69, 189–198.
65. Jersild, A. T. Characteristics of teachers who are "liked best" and "disliked most." *J. Exp. Educ.,* 1940, 9, 139–151.
66. Jersild, A. T., and Frances V. Markey. Conflicts between preschool children. *Child Develpm. Monogr.,* 1935, No. 21.
67. Jones, Mary C., and P. H. Mussen. Self-conceptions, motivations, and interpersonal attitudes of early- and late-maturing girls. *Child Develpm.,* 1958, 29, 491–502.
68. deJung, J. E., and E. F. Gardner. The accuracy of self-role perception: a developmental study. *J. Exper. Educ.,* 1962, 31, 27–41.
69. Kagan, J. The child's perception of the parent. *J. Abnorm. Soc. Psychol.,* 1956, 53, 257–258.
70. Kagan, J., and H. A. Moss. Stability and validity of achievement fantasy. *J. Abnorm. Soc. Psychol.,* 1959, 58, 357–364.
71. Kagan, J., and H. A. Moss. The stability of passive and dependent behavior from childhood through adulthood. *Child Develpm.,* 1960, 31, 577–591.
72. Kagan, J., and H. A. Moss. *Birth to maturity: a study in psychological development.* New York: Wiley, 1962.
73. Kinsey, A. C., W. B. Pomeroy, and C. E. Martin. *Sexual behavior in the human male.* Philadelphia: Saunders, 1948.
74. Leeds, C. H. A scale for measuring teacher-pupil rapport. *Psychol. Monogr.,* 1950, 64, No. 6.
75. Lehman, H. C., and P. A. Witty. *The psychology of play activities.* New York: A. S. Barnes, 1927.
76. Lewin, K., R. Lippitt, and R. K. White. Patterns of aggressive behavior in experimentally created "social climates." *J. Soc. Psychol.,* 1939, 10, 271–299.
77. Lippitt, R. An experimental study of the effect of democratic and authoritarian group atmospheres. *Univ. Iowa Stud. Child Welf.,* 1940, 16, No. 3.
78. Lippitt, R., and R. K. White. The "social climate" of children's groups. In R. G. Barker, J. S. Kounin and H. F. Wright (Eds.), *Child behavior and development.* New York: McGraw-Hill, 1943, 485–508.

79. Lipsitt, L. P. A self-concept scale for children and its relationship to the children's form of the Manifest Anxiety Scale. *Child Develpm.*, 1958, 29, 463–472.

80. Liverant, S. MMPI differences between parents of disturbed and non-disturbed children. *J. Consult. Psychol.*, 1959, 23, 256–260.

81. Maccoby, Eleanor. The taking of adult roles in middle childhood. *J. Abnorm. Soc. Psychol.*, 1961, 63, 493–503.

82. Macfarlane, Jean W. Study of personality development. In R. G. Barker, J. S. Kounin and H. F. Wright (Eds.), *Child behavior and development.* New York: McGraw-Hill, 1943, 307–328.

83. Malinowski, B. Prenuptial intercourse between the sexes in the Trobriand Islands, N. W. Melanesia. *Psycholanal. Rev.*, 1927, 14, 26–36.

84. Maller, J. B. Cooperation and competition: an experimental study of motivation. *Teach. Coll. Cont. Educ.*, 1929, No. 384.

85. Martin, W. E., and Celia B. Stendler. *Child development: the process of growing up in society.* New York: Harcourt, Brace, 1953.

86. McGuire, C., and G. D. White. Social origins of teachers—in Texas. In L. J. Stiles (Ed.), *The teacher's role in American society.* New York: Harper, 1957.

87. McIntyre, C. J. Acceptance by others and its relation to acceptance of self and others. *J. Abnorm. Soc. Psychol.*, 1952, 47, 624–625.

88. McNeil, E. B. Patterns of aggression. *J. Child. Psychol. Psychiat.*, 1962, 3, 65–77.

89. Milner, Esther. A study of the relationship between reading readiness in grade one school children and patterns of parent-child interaction. *Child Develpm.*, 1951, 22, 95–112.

90. Moreno, J. L. Changes in sex groupings of school children. In G. E. Swanson, T. M. Newcomb, E. L. Hartley, *et al.*, (Ed's.), *Readings in social psychology.* (Rev. ed.) New York: Holt, 1959, 266–271.

91. Morrow, W. R., and R. C. Wilson. The self-reported personal and social adjustment of bright high-achieving and under-achieving high school boys. *J. Child Psychol. Psychiat.*, 1961, 2, 203–209.

92. Moss, H. A., and J. Kagan. Stability of achievement and recognition seeking behaviors from early childhood through adulthood. *J. Abnorm. Soc. Psychol.*, 1961, 62, 504–513.

93. Mouton, Jane S., R. L. Bell, Jr., and R. R. Blake. Role playing skill and sociometric peer status. *Group Psychother.*, 1956, 9, 7–17.

94. Munroe, Ruth L. *Schools of psychoanalytic thought: an exposition, critique, an attempt at integration.* New York: Dryden, 1955.

95. Murphy, G. The current impact of Freud upon psychology. *Amer. Psychologist,* 1956, 12, 663–672.

96. Murphy, G., Lois B. Murphy, and T. M. Newcomb. *Experimental social psychology: an interpretation of research upon the socialization of the individual* (Rev. ed.). New York: Harper, 1937.

97. Mussen, P. H., and J. J. Conger. *Child development and personality.* New York: Harper, 1956.

98. Mussen, P. H., and Mary C. Jones. Self-conceptions, motivations, and interpersonal attitudes of late—and early—maturing boys. *Child Develpm.*, 1957, 28, 242–256.

99. Neustadt, R., and A. Myerson. Quantitative sex hormone studies in homo-

sexuality, childhood and various neuropsychiatric disturbances. *Amer. J. Psychiat.*, 1940, 97, 542–551.

100. Northway, M. L. Outsiders: a study of the personality patterns of children least acceptable to their age mates. *Sociometry*, 1944, 7, 10–25.

101. Peck, R. F. Family patterns correlated with adolescent personality structure. *J. Abnorm. Soc. Psychol.*, 1958, 57, 347–350.

102. Peterson, D. R., W. C. Becker, D. J. Shoemaker, Zelda Luria, and L. A. Hellmer. Child behavior development problems and parental attitudes. *Child Develpm.*, 1961, 32, 151–162.

103. Peterson, D. R., W. C. Becker, L. A. Hellmer, D. J. Shoemaker, and H. C. Quay. Parental attitudes and child adjustment. *Child Develpm.*, 1959, 30, 119–130.

104. Phillips, B. N., and L. A. D'Amico. Effects of cooperation and competition on the cohesiveness of small face-to-face groups. *J. Educ. Psychol.*, 1956, 47, 65–70.

105. Pikas, A. Children's attitudes toward rational versus inhibiting parental authority. *J. Abnorm. Soc. Psychol.*, 1961, 62, 315–321.

106. Pope, B. Socio-economic contrasts in children's peer culture prestige values. *Genet. Psychol. Monogr.*, 1953, 48, 157–220.

107. Reese, H. W. Relationships between self-acceptance and sociometric choices. *J. Abnorm. Soc. Psychol.*, 1961, 62, 472–474.

108. Rosen, R. C., and R. G. D'Andrade. The psychosocial origins of achievement motivation. *Sociometry*, 1959, 22, 185–218.

109. Rosenzweig, S. Further comparative data on repetition choice after success and failure as related to frustration tolerance. *J. Genet. Psychol.*, 1945, 66, 75–81.

110. Schaefer, E. S., and Nancy Bayley. Consistency of maternal behavior from infancy to preadolescence. *J. Abnorm. Soc. Psychol.*, 1960, 61, 1–6.

111. Sears, R. R. Relation of early socialization experiences to aggression in middle childhood. *J. Abnorm. Soc. Psychol.*, 1961, 63, 466–492.

112. Sechrest, L. Studies of classroom atmosphere. *Psychol. in Schs.*, 1964, 1, 103–118.

113. Smith, S. Age and sex differences in children's opinion concerning sex differences. *J. Genet. Psychol.*, 1939, 54, 17–25.

114. Sontag, L. W., and J. Kagan. The emergence of intellectual achievement motives. *Amer. J. Orthopsychiat.*, 1963, 33, 532–535.

115. Stendler, Celia B. Social class differences in parental attitude toward school at Grade I level. *Child Develpm.*, 1951, 22, 37–46.

116. Stendler, Celia B., and N. Young. The impact of beginning first grade upon socialization as reported by mothers. *Child Develpm.*, 1950, 21, 241–260.

117. Sullivan, H. S. *Conceptions of modern psychiatry.* Washington: William Alanson White Psychiatric Foundation, 1947.

118. Tenenbaum, S. Uncontrolled expressions of children's attitudes toward school. *Elem. Sch. J.*, 1940, 40, 670–678.

119. Terman, L. M., and Leona E. Tyler. Psychological sex differences. In L. Carmichael (Ed.), *Manual of child psychology* (2nd ed.). New York: Wiley, 1954, 1064–1114.

120. Thompson, Clara. *Psychoanalysis: evolution and development.* New York: Hermitage, 1950.

121. Thompson, G. G. The social and emotional development of preschool chil-

dren under two types of educational programs. *Psychol. Monogr.*, 1944, 56, No. 258.

122. Thompson, G. G., and J. E. Horrocks. A study of the friendship fluctuations of urban boys and girls. *J. Genet. Psychol.*, 1947, 70, 53–63.

123. Trager, Helen G., and Marian R. Yarrow. *They learn what they live: prejudice in young children.* New York: Harper, 1952.

124. Tuddenham, R. D. Studies in reputation: III. Correlates of popularity among elementary school children. *J. Educ. Psychol.*, 1951, 42, 257–276.

125. Tuddenham, R. D. Studies in reputation: I. Sex and grade differences in school children's evaluation of their peers. II. The diagnosis of social adjustment. *Psychol. Monogr.*, 1952, No. 333.

126. deVault, M. V. Classroom sociometric mutual pairs and residential proximity. *J. Educ. Res.*, 1957, 50, 605–610.

127. Walsh, Ann M. *Self-concepts of bright boys with learning difficulties.* New York: Bureau of Publications, Teachers College, Columbia University, 1956.

128. White, R. W. *The abnormal personality: a textbook.* New York: Ronald, 1948.

129. Wickman, E. K. *Children's behavior and teacher's attitudes.* New York: Commonwealth Fund, 1928.

130. Winterbottom, Marian R. The relation of need for achievement to learning experiences in independence and mastery. In J. W. Atkinson (Ed.), *Motives in fantasy, action, and society.* Princeton, N. J.: Van Nostrand, 1958, 453–478.

131. Witmer, Helen L., and Ruth Kotinsky (Eds.). *Personality in the making: the fact-finding report of the Midcentury White House conference on children and youth.* New York: Harper, 1952.

132. Witryol, S. L. Age trends in children's evaluation of teacher-approved and teacher-disapproved behavior. *Genet. Psychol. Monogr.*, 1950, 41, 271–326.

133. Wright, A. F. Psychological development in Midwest. *Child Develpm.*, 1956, 27, 265–286.

134. Wylie, Ruth C. Children's estimates of their schoolwork ability, as a function of sex, race and socioeconomic level. *J. Pers.*, 1963, 31, 203–224.

135. Zander, A., and E. Van Egmond. Relationship of intelligence and social power to the interpersonal behavior of children. *J. Educ. Psychol.*, 1958, 49, 257–268.

136. Zelen, S. L. The relationship of peer acceptance, acceptance of others and self-acceptance. *Proc. Iowa Acad. Sci.*, 1954, 61, 446–449.

Index of Names

Index of Subjects

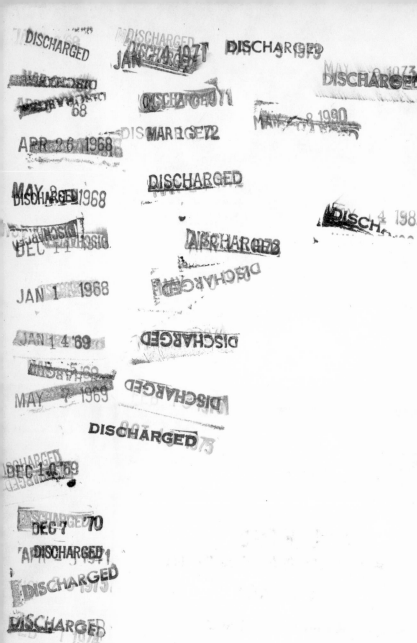